Race, Crime, and Justice

Race, Crime, and Justice

A Reader

Edited by
Shaun L. Gabbidon
Helen Taylor Greene

Routledge
New York and London

Published in 2005 by
Routledge
270 Madison Avenue
New York, NY 10016
www.routledge-ny.com

Published in Great Britain by
Routledge
2 Park Square
Milton Park, Abingdon
Oxon OX14 4RN U.K.
www.routledge.co.uk

Routledge is an imprint of the Taylor & Francis Group.

Printed in the United States of America on acid-free paper.

10 9 8 7 6 5 4 3 2 1

Library of Congress Cataloging-in-Publication Data
Race, crime, and justice : a reader / [edited by] Shaun L. Gabbidon, Helen Taylor Greene.
p. cm.
Includes bibliographical references and index.
ISBN 0-415-94706-5 (hardback : alk. paper) — ISBN 0-415-94707-3 (pbk. : alk. paper)
1. Crime and race—United States. 2. Discrimination in criminal justice administration—United States. I. Gabbidon, Shaun L., 1967– II. Greene, Helen Taylor, 1949–
HV6197.U5R334 2004
364.973'089—dc22

2004016598

DEDICATION

For Ian. The supportive big brother others wish for,
but I am fortunate to have. I love you, Bro!
S.L.G.

For my father, the late William E. Taylor, Sr., who persevered in spite of racism and other insurmountable odds for the benefit of his children.
H.T.G.

Contents

Acknowledgments

The authors would like to thank Ilene Kalish, former senior editor at Routledge, for supporting the project from the proposal stage. Former editorial assistant, Salwa Jabado, was also helpful in the beginning stages of the publication process. After Ilene's departure from Routledge, we thank Mary MacInnes and Mike Bickerstaff for taking over and ensuing that the project moved along. Amanda Rice, Amy Rodriguez, and Lynn Goeller, are also acknowledged for their contribution to the completion of the project.

At Penn State, Professor Gabbidon thanks Dr. Steven A. Peterson, Director of School of Public Affairs, for continuing to support his scholarly efforts. He also thanks two of his graduate assistants, Nancy McGee and Patricia Patrick, for organizing and securing most of the permissions. Dr. James Stewart, Senior Faculty Mentor at Penn State, is also acknowledged for providing funds for Dr. Gabbidon's graduate assistant during the summer 2004.

Dr. Taylor Greene thanks her former colleagues in the Department of Sociology and Criminal Justice at Old Dominion University and Dean Don Anthony Woods and colleagues in the Barbara Jordan-Mickey Leland School of Public Affairs at Texas Southern University for support and assistance in the completion of this project. Dr. Taylor Greene extends a special thanks to Dr. Gabbidon for his conceptualization of this project and admirable zeal.

Preface

Even though we titled our book *Race, Crime, and Justice*, we are aware that, while there are slight biological differences among groups, in general, race is simply a way of classifying groups (principally based on color). Furthermore, while the focus of this edited book is on race and crime, over time this topic has become a proxy for studies of racial minorities and street crime; a topic which has a long and controversial history. As has been noted over the past decade or so, while much has changed in the administration of criminal justice, at varying levels, race continues to matter (Mann 1993; Tonry 1995; Russell 1998; Walker, Spohn, and De Lone 2004). Since at least the late 1800s, scholars have sought to explain why racial minorities have been overrepresented in arrest and prison statistics. Prominent among these explanations was the notion of biological inferiority. At the time, although other minorities were present in our country, the focus of these explanations was on the recently emancipated black population. A cadre of scholars at predominantly black colleges in the South was involved in refuting these biological explanations by pointing to the role of social, political, and economic conditions. Early on, however, very few authors devoted entire books to the subject. One early exception was an edited volume by W. E. B. Du Bois, which was a compilation of conference papers from his annual studies on African American issues published by Atlanta University Press (Du Bois 1904). Except for this pioneering volume, most scholars were resigned to publishing an article here or there on the topic (see, for examples, Work 1913; Sellin 1928).

Unlike contemporary texts, authors of early criminology textbooks usually devoted a chapter to the topic of race and crime (Gabbidon and Taylor Greene 2001). Following Du Bois's early volume on the subject, other works began to appear which devoted significant attention to the topic (Du Bois and Dill 1914; Sellin 1938; von Hentig 1942; Bonger 1943; Myrdal 1944). Books devoted to race and crime began to appear in the 1960s and early 1970s (Wolfgang 1964; Wolfgang and Cohen 1970; Reasons 1972; Gary and Brown 1976; Owens and Bell 1977). The 1980s saw an increase in the number of volumes published on the subject (McNeely and Pope 1981; Georges-Abeyie 1984; Hawkins 1986; Flowers 1988; Myers and Sims 1988). By the 1990s, and into the twenty-first century, race and crime had become firmly entrenched within criminology and criminal justice programs, with more universities looking for faculty with specialties in race and crime (del Carmen and Polk, 2001). Furthermore, because more criminology and criminal justice programs offer courses on race and crime (Gabbidon and Preston 2003), edited volumes continue to appear with more frequency (Lynch and Patterson 1991, 1996; Hendricks and Byers 1994, 2000; Sulton 1994; Hawkins 1995 2003; Mann and Zatz 1998, 2002; Markowitz and Jones-Brown 2000; del Carmen and Bing 2000; Milanovanovic and

Russell 2001; Gabbidon, Greene, and Young 2002; Tarver, Walker, and Wallace 2002; Free 2003). However, such courses remain on the periphery of the discipline.

While this brief review is not comprehensive, it does show that, over time, the subject matter has garnered increasing attention from criminologists. Part of this attention is likely attributable to the increased focus on Latinos, Asians, and Native Americans. Our edited volume is an attempt to build on the race and crime literature from the past by presenting some older and newer representative publications. While we began the project hoping to put together a definitive reader on the subject, the exorbitant copyright expenses precluded us from including the more than forty chapters we had in our initial proposal. Nonetheless, we have included twenty-four important chapters under six distinct sections. Each section begins with a brief overview which provides some context for the chapters that follow. The book opens with a section that includes reprints of four chapters highlighting early perspectives on crime in the African American, Asian, and Native American communities. A final chapter in the section looks at what some might term the earliest form of hate crime: the lynching of blacks by whites.

Section II provides four reprints of chapters that are related to the disproportionality thesis, which was essentially related to the discrimination thesis (DT) versus no discrimination thesis (NDT) which was heavily debated during the 1980s and 1990s. The four chapters in Section III examine race, crime, and gender, a neglected area of the race and crime discourse. These chapters provide insights into several topics including historical explanations, female involvement in more serious crimes, and domestic violence. Section IV looks at race, crime, and communities, a central area of focus among race and crime researchers. The opening chapter provides an ecological approach to understanding the importance of communities. The following chapters focus on the hotly debated topic of racial profiling. Section V focuses on race and violent crime. Specifically, the chapters in this section seek to explain the acute level of violence in African American and Latino communities. A chapter on domestic violence in Asian American communities also shows the attitudes toward such violence in communities where, because of the model minority label, violence is often overlooked. The final section looks at race and punishment. The first chapter provides an interesting context for understanding the role of prisons. Each of the remaining chapters explores the interaction of race and sentencing in America.

References

Bing, R. and del Carmen, A. eds. 2000. *Perspectives: Race and crime.* Madison, WI: CourseWise Publishing.

Bonger, W. 1943/1969. *Race and crime.* Montclair, NJ: Patterson Smith.

del Carmen, A. and Polk, O. E. 2001. "Faculty employment in criminology and criminal justice: Trends and patterns." *Journal of Criminal Justice Education* 12: 1–17.

Du Bois, W. E. B. ed. 1904. *Some notes on Negro crime, particularly in Georgia.* Atlanta, GA: Atlanta University Press.

——— and Dill, A. eds. 1914. *Morals and manners among Negro Americans.* Atlanta, GA: Atlanta University Press.

Flowers, R. B. 1988. *Minorities and criminality.* Westport, CT: Greenwood Press.

Free, M. ed. 2003. *Racial issues in criminal justice: The case of African Americans.* CT: Praeger.

Gabbidon, S. L., Taylor-Greene, H., and Young, V. D. eds. 2002. *African American classics in criminology and criminal justice.* Thousand Oaks, CA: Sage.

——— and Preston, P. 2003. "Teaching race and crime: Perspectives from the classroom." *Journal of Ethnicity in Criminal Justice* 1: 109–124.

——— and Taylor-Greene, H. 2001. "The presence of African American scholarship in early American criminology textbooks (1918–1960)." *Journal of Criminal Justice Education* 12: 301-310.

Gary, L. and Brown, L. eds. 1976. *Crime and its impact on the Black community.* Washington, DC: Howard University Institute for Urban Affairs and Research.

Georges-Abeyie, D. ed. 1984. *The criminal justice system and Blacks.* New York: Clark Boardman.

Hawkins, D. 2003. *Violent crime: Assessing race and ethnic differences.* Cambridge: Cambridge University Press.

——— ed. 1995. *Ethnicity, race, and crime.* Albany: State University of New York Press.

——— ed. 1986. *Homicides among Black Americans.* Lanham, MD: University Press of America.

Hendricks, J. E. and Byers, B. eds. 1994. *Multicultural perspectives in criminal justice and criminology.* Springfield, IL: Charles C Thomas.

——— and ——— eds. 2000. *Multicultural perspectives in criminal justice and criminology*, 2nd ed. Springfield, IL: Charles C Thomas.

Joseph, J. and Taylor, D. 2003. *With justice for all: Minorities and women in criminal justice.* Upper Saddle River, NJ: Prentice-Hall.

Lynch, M. and Patterson, E. B. eds. 1991. *Race and criminal justice.* Albany, NY: Harrow and Heston.

———. (1996) *Justice with prejudice.* Albany, NY: Harrow and Heston.

Mann, C. R. 1993. *Unequal justice: A question of color.* Bloomington: Indiana University Press.

——— and Zatz, M. eds. 2002. *Images of color, images of crime* (2nd ed.). Los Angeles: Roxbury.

———. 1998. *Images of color, images of crime.* Los Angeles: Roxbury.

Markowitz, M. and Brown-Jones, D. eds. 2000. *The system in Black and White.* New York: Praeger.

McNeely, R. L. and Pope, C. eds. 1981. *Race, crime, and criminal justice.* Beverly Hills: Sage.

Milanovanovic, D. and Russell, K. eds. 2001. *Petit apartheid in the U.S. criminal justice system.* Durham, NC: Carolina Academic Press.

Myers, S. L. and Simms, M. eds. 1988. *The economics of race and crime.* New Brunswick, NJ: Transaction Books.

Myrdal, G. 1944. *An American dilemma: The Negro problem and modern democracy.* New York: Harper & Brothers.

Owens, C. and Bell, J. eds. 1977. *Blacks and criminal justice.* Lexington, MA: Lexington Books.

Reasons, S. and Kuykendall, J. eds. 1972. *Race, crime, and justice.* Pacific Palisades, CA: Goodyear.

Reasons, C., Conley, D., and Debro, J. eds. 2002. *Race, class, gender, and justice in the U.S.* Boston: Allyn & Bacon.

Russell, K. K. 1998. *The color of crime.* New York: New York University Press.

Sellin, T. 1928. "The Negro criminal: A statistical note." *Annals of the American Academy of Political and Social Sciences* 140: 52–64.

——— 1938. *Culture and conflict in crime.* New York: Social Science Research Council.

Sulton, A. T. ed. 1994. *African-American perspectives on: Crime causation, criminal justice administration, and crime prevention.* Englewood, CO: Sulton Books.

Tarver, M. Walker, S., and Wallace, H. 2002. *Multicultural issues in the criminal justice system.* Boston: Allyn & Bacon.

Tonry, M. 1995. *Malign neglect.* New York: Oxford University Press.

von Hentig, H. 1942. *The criminality of colored women.* University of Colorado Study Series, 1(3): 231–260.

Wolfgang, M. 1964. *Crime and race: Conceptions and misconceptions.* New York: Institute of Human Relations Press.

——— and Cohen, B. 1964. *Crime and race: Conceptions and misconceptions.* New York: Institute of Human Relations Press.

Woodson, R. L. eds. 1977. *Black perspectives on crime and the criminal justice system.* Boston: G.K. Hall & Co.

Work, M. N. 1913. "Negro criminality in the south." *Annals of the American Academy of Political and Social Sciences* 49: 74–80.

Race and Crime: Early Writings

Early scholarship on race and crime is presented in the following articles. Much of the earliest race and crime literature was rooted in the marriage between white supremacy and the subsequent rise of biological determinism. By the late 1800s, Lombrosian criminal theory had an increasing following. Followers of this doctrine often pointed to the connections between physical characteristics and crime, which, at times, were further linked to people of color. Describing the characteristics of the typical criminal, Rowlands (1897) wrote:

> The criminal is further to be recognized by his tastes and occupation; he is fond of alcohol, cards, and sexual vices; he dislikes regular work, and is sentimental, religious, or superstitious; he is given to write poetry on the walls of his cells or on the kitchen utensils; he is both stupid and cunning; he is frequently tattooed, and generally justifies his misdeeds on high moral principle. And, finally, the typical criminal would have "projecting ears, thick hair, and thin beard, projecting frontal eminences, enormous jaws, a square and projecting chin, large cheek bones, and frequent gesticulation," and would in type resemble the Mongolian or sometimes the Negroid." (245)

Such a connection was devastating for both Blacks and Asians. During slavery Blacks were seen as inferior, and following emancipation, because of continuing notions of inferiority, race and crime became indelibly linked. In the first chapter by preeminent intellectual W. E. B. Du Bois, he discusses the nature of the convict-lease system and reveals the "evils" of a justice system where both the state and private landowners profited on the labor of recently emancipated Blacks. Contrary to the prevailing biological perspective, Du Bois's analysis provides a sociological explanation for why Blacks were prominently represented in the criminal justice system.

Because of the dislike of their culture and increasing economic competition, Asians, particularly in the West, were attacked and brutalized by whites. The Chinese Exclusion Act of 1882 (later extended until the 1940s), which banned the immigration of Chinese to the United States, served as an extension of the negative attitudes of whites toward Asians (Mann 1993). While overall there was little crime in Asian communities, connecting crime to color was a continuing strategy used to derogate Asians. The second chapter by Hayner, like the one by Du Bois, also points to sociological reasons for explaining crime among Asians. Written in the first half of the twentieth century, Hayner reviews the varying levels of crime among the various Asian groups. Thus, at a time when most people clumped all Asians into one category (Oriental), Hayner seeks to explain the differences in offending patterns among Asian Americans.

Native Americans continue to be one of the least studied groups in criminology and criminal justice (Lester 2003; Russell 2004). However, in chapter 3, Hayner provides an early look at an analysis of crime in Native American communities. His analysis shows the devastating impact of what he refers to as the "Americanization" of tribal communities. Whereas long-standing customs dictated how Native Americans lived their lives, the exposure to American values and customs impacted their behavior. Most notably, the introduction of alcohol led to an epidemic of alcohol-related crimes, which proved devastating for the maintenance of centuries-old traditions.

The final chapter in the section is by Oliver Cox who reviews the dynamics of lynching, which he defines as "an act of homicidal aggression committed by one people against another through mob action for the purpose of suppressing either some tendency in the latter to rise from an accommodated position of subordination or for subjugating them further to some lower social status" (576). While the practice had its origins in the early 1800s, following the Civil War, whites began in earnest to institutionalize the practice when there was the belief that blacks had either violated the law or had breached some informal racial etiquette (i.e., talking back to a white person, competing for jobs with whites, etc.). Playing on the worst fears of whites, the myth that blacks were frequently raping white women was perpetuated to "legitimize" lynching in the eyes of the white ruling class. Cox's analysis provides a framework for understanding the cyclical nature of the event. Pointing to the economic and political dimensions of the act, he shows how the event was typically instigated, the progression leading up to the actual killing of the "suspected" black criminal, and the return to "normalcy" following the event.

REFERENCES

Cox, O. C. 1945. Lynching and the status quo. *Journal of Negro Education* 14: 576–88.

Lester, D. 2003. Native Americans and the criminal justice system. In *With justice for all: Minorities and women in criminal justice*, eds., J. Joseph and D. Taylor, 149–60. Upper Saddle River, NJ: Prentice Hall.

Mann, C. R. 1993. *Unequal justice: A question of color.* Bloomington: Indiana University Press.

Rowlands, E. B. 1897. Instinctive criminality and social conditions. *Law Quarterly Review* 13: 59–69. Reprinted in D. M. Horton, ed., *Pioneering perspectives in criminology: The literature of 19th century criminological positivism*, 239–50. Incline Village, NV: Copperhouse Publishing.

Russell, K. K. 2004. *Underground codes: Race, crime, and related fires.* New York: New York University Press.

1
The Spawn of Slavery
The Convict-Lease System in the South

W. E. B. Du Bois

A modified form of slavery survives wherever prison labor is sold to private persons for their pecuniary profit.

—Wines

Two systems of controlling human labor which still flourish in the South are the direct children of slavery, and to all intents and purposes are slavery itself. These are the crop-lien system and the convict-lease system. The crop-lien system is an arrangement of chattel mortgages so fixed that the housing, labor, kind of agriculture and, to some extent, the personal liberty of the free black laborer is put into the hands of the landowner and merchant. It is absentee landlordism and the "company-store" systems united and carried out to the furthest possible degree. The convict-lease system is the slavery in private hands of persons convicted of crimes and misdemeanors in the courts. The object of the present paper is to study the rise and development of the convict-lease system, and the efforts to modify and abolish it.

Before the Civil War the system of punishment for criminals was practically the same as in the North. Except in a few cities, however, crime was less prevalent than in the North, and the system of slavery naturally modified the situation. The slaves could become criminals in the eyes of the law only in exceptional cases. The punishment and trial of nearly all ordinary misdemeanors and crimes lay in the hands of the masters. Consequently, so far as the state was concerned, there was no crime of any consequence among Negroes. The system of criminal jurisprudence had to do, therefore with whites almost exclusively, and as is usual in a land of scattered population and aristocratic tendencies, the law was lenient in theory and lax in execution.

On the other hand, the private well ordering and control of slaves called for careful cooperation among masters. The fear of insurrection was ever before the South, and the ominous uprising of Cato, Gabriel, Vesey, Turner, and Toussaint made this fear an ever-present nightmare. The result was a system of rural police, mounted and on duty chiefly at night, whose work it was to stop the nocturnal wandering and meeting of slaves. It was usually an effective organization, which terrorized the slaves, and to which all white men belonged, and were liable to active detailed duty at regular intervals.

Upon this system war and emancipation struck like a thunderbolt. Law and order among the whites, already loosely enforced, became still weaker through the inevitable influence of conflict and social revolution. The freedman was especially in an anomalous situation. The power of the slave police supplemented and depended upon that of the private masters. When the masters' power was broken the patrol was easily transmuted into a lawless and illegal mob known to history as the Ku Klux Klan. Then came the first, and probably the most disastrous, of that succession of political expedients by which the South sought to evade the consequences of emancipation. It will always be a nice question of ethics as to how far a conquered people can be expected to submit to the dictates of a victorious foe. Certainly the world must to a degree sympathize with resistance under such circumstances. The mistake of the South, however, was to adopt a kind of resistance which in the long run weakened her moral fiber, destroyed respect for law and order, and enabled gradually her worst elements to secure an unfortunate ascendancy. The South believed in slave labor, and was thoroughly convinced that free Negroes would not work steadily or effectively. The whites were determined after the war, therefore, to restore slavery in everything but in name. Elaborate and ingenious apprentice and vagrancy laws were passed, designed to make the freedmen and their children work for their former masters at practically no wages. Some justification for these laws was found in the inevitable tendency of many of the ex-slaves to loaf when the fear of the lash was taken away. The new laws, however, went far beyond such justification, totally ignoring that large class of freedmen eager to work and earn property of their own, stopping all competition between employers, and confiscating the labor and liberty of children. In fact, the new laws of this period recognized the Emancipation Proclamation and the Thirteenth Amendment simply as abolishing the slave trade.

The interference of Congress in the plans for reconstruction stopped the full carrying out of these schemes, and the Freedmen's Bureau consolidated and sought to develop the various plans for employing and guiding the freedmen already adopted in different places under the protection of the Union army. This government guardianship established a free wage system of labor by the help of the army, the striving of the best of the blacks, and the cooperation of some of the whites. In the matter of adjusting legal relationships, however, the Bureau failed. It had, to be sure, Bureau courts, with one representative of the ex-master, one of the freedman, and one of the Bureau itself, but they never gained the confidence of the community. As the regular state courts gradually regained power, it was necessary for them to fix by their decisions the new status of the freedmen. It was perhaps as natural as it was unfortunate that amid this chaos the courts sought to do by judicial decisions what the legislatures had formerly sought to do by specific law—namely, reduce the freedmen to serfdom. As a result, the small peccadilloes of a careless, untrained class were made the excuse for severe sentences. The courts and jails became filled with the careless and ignorant, with those who sought to emphasize their new-found freedom, and too often with innocent victims of oppression. The testimony of a Negro counted for little or nothing in court, while the accusation of white witnesses was usually decisive. The result of this was a sudden large increase in the apparent criminal population of the Southern states—an increase so large that there was no way for the state to house it or watch it even had the state wished to. And the state did not wish to. Throughout the South laws were immediately passed authorizing public officials to lease the labor of convicts to the highest bidder. The lessee then took charge of the convicts—worked them as he wished under the nominal control of the state. Thus a new slavery and slave-trade was established.

The Evil Influences

The abuses of this system have often been dwelt upon. It had the worst aspects of slavery without any of its redeeming features. The innocent, the guilty, and the depraved were herded together, children and adults, men and women, given into the complete control of practically irresponsible men, whose sole object was to make the most money possible. The innocent were made bad, the bad worse; women were outraged and children tainted; whipping and torture were in vogue, and the death rate from cruelty, exposure, and overwork rose to large percentages. The actual bosses over such leased prisoners were usually selected from the lowest classes of whites, and the camps were often far from settlements or public roads. The prisoners often had scarcely any clothing, they were fed on a scanty diet of corn bread and fat meat, and worked twelve or more hours a day. After work each must do his own cooking. There was insufficient shelter; in one Georgia camp, as late as 1895, sixty-one men slept in one room, seventeen by nineteen feet, and seven feet high. Sanitary conditions were wretched, there was little or no medical attendance, and almost no care of the sick. Women were mingled indiscriminately with the men, both in working and sleeping, and dressed often in men's clothes. A young girl at Camp Hardmont, Georgia, in 1895, was repeatedly outraged by several of her guards, and finally died in childbirth while in camp.

Such facts illustrate the system at its worst—as it used to exist in nearly every Southern state, and as it still exists in parts of Georgia, Mississippi, Louisiana, and other states. It is difficult to say whether the effect of such a system is worse on the whites or on the Negroes. So far as the whites are concerned, the convict-lease system lowered the respect for courts, increased lawlessness, and put the states into the clutches of penitentiary "rings." The courts were brought into politics, judgeships became elective for shorter and shorter terms, and there grew up a public sentiment which would not consent to considering the desert of a criminal apart from his color. If the criminal were white, public opinion refused to permit him to enter the chain gang save in the most extreme cases. The result is that even today it is very difficult to enforce the laws in the South against whites, and red-handed criminals go scot-free. On the other hand, so customary had it become to convict any Negro upon a mere accusation, that public opinion was loathe to allow a fair trial to black suspects, and was too often tempted to take the law into their own hands. Finally the state became a dealer in crime, profited by it so as to derive a new annual income for her prisoners. The lessees of the convicts made large profits also. Under such circumstances, it was almost impossible to remove the clutches of this vicious system from the state. Even as late as 1890 the Southern states were the only section of the Union where the income from prisons and reformatories exceeded the expense.[1] Moreover, these figures do not include the county gangs where the lease system is today most prevalent and the net income largest.

The effect of the convict-lease system on the Negroes was deplorable. First it linked crime and slavery indissolubly in their minds as simply forms of the white man's oppression. Punishment, consequently, lost the most effective of its deterrent effects, and the criminal gained pity instead of disdain. The Negroes lost faith in the integrity of courts and the fairness of juries. Worse than all, the chain gangs became schools of crime which hastened the appearance of the confirmed Negro criminal upon the scene. That some crime and vagrancy should follow emancipation was inevitable. A nation cannot systematically degrade labor without in some degree debauching the laborer. But there can be no doubt but that the indiscriminate careless and unjust method by which Southern courts dealt with the freedmen after the war increased crime and vagabondage to an enormous extent. There are no reliable statistics to which one can safely appeal to measure exactly the growth of crime among the emancipated slaves. About seventy per cent of all prisoners in the South are black; this, however, is in part explained by the fact that accused Negroes are still easily convicted and get long sentences, while whites still continue to escape the penalty of many crimes even among themselves. And yet allowing for all this, there can be no reasonable doubt but that there has arisen in the South since the war a class of black criminals, loafers, and ne'er-do-wells who are a menace to their fellows, both black and white.

The appearance of the real Negro criminal stirred the South deeply. The whites, despite their long use of the criminal court for putting Negroes to work, were used to little more than petty thieving and loafing on their part, and not to crimes of boldness, violence, or cunning. When, after periods of stress or financial depression, as in 1892, such crimes increased in frequency, the wrath of a people

Table 1.1 Income and Expense of State Prisons and Reformatories, 1890

	Earnings	Expense	Profit
New England	$299,735	$1,204,029	—
Middle States	71,252	1,850,452	—
Border States	597,898	962,422	—
Southern States[2]	938,406	890,452	$47,974
Central States	624,161	1,971,795	—
Western States	378,036	1,572,316	—

unschooled in the modern methods of dealing with crime broke all bounds and reached strange depths of barbaric vengeance and torture. Such acts, instead of drawing the best opinion of these states and of the nation toward a consideration of Negro crime and criminals, discouraged and alienated the best classes of Negroes, horrified the civilized world, and made the best white Southerners ashamed of their land.

What Has Been Done

Nevertheless, in the midst of all this a leaven of better things had been working and the bad effects of the epidemic of lynching quickened it. The great difficulty to be overcome in the South was the false theory of work and of punishment of wrong-doers inherited from slavery. The inevitable result of a slave system is for a master class to consider that the slave exists for his benefit alone—that the slave has no rights which the master is bound to respect. Inevitably this idea persisted after emancipation. The black workman existed for the comfort and profit of white people, and the interests of white people were the only ones to be seriously considered. Consequently, for a lessee to work convicts for his profit was a most natural thing. Then, too, these convicts were to be punished, and the slave theory of punishment was pain and intimidation. Given these ideas, and the convict-lease system was inevitable. But other ideas were also prevalent in the South; there were in slave times plantations where the well-being of the slaves was considered, and where punishment meant the correction of the fault rather than brute discomfort. After the chaos of war and reconstruction passed, there came from the better conscience of the South a growing demand for reform in the treatment of crime. The worst horrors of the convict-lease system were attacked persistently in nearly every Southern state. Back in the eighties George W. Cable, a Southern man, published a strong attack on the system. The following decade Governor Atkinson, of Georgia, instituted a searching investigation, which startled the state by its revelation of existing conditions. Still more recently Florida, Arkansas, and other states have had reports and agitation for reform. The result has been marked improvement in conditions during the last decade. This is shown in part by the statistics of 1895; in that year the prisons and reformatories of the far South cost the states $204,483 more than they earned, while before this they had nearly always yielded an income. This is still the smallest expenditure of any section, and looks strangely small beside New England's $1,190,564. At the same time, a movement in the right direction is clear. The laws are being framed more and more so as to prevent the placing of convicts altogether in private control. They are not, to be sure, always enforced, Georgia having several hundreds of convicts so controlled in 1895 despite the law. In nearly all the Gulf states the convict-lease system still has a strong hold, still debauches public sentiment and breeds criminals.

The next step after the lease system was to keep the prisoners under state control, or, at least, regular state inspection, but to lease their labor to contractors, or to employ it in some remunerative labor for the state. It is this stage that the South is slowly reaching today so far as the criminals are concerned who are dealt with directly by the states. Those whom the state still unfortunately leaves in the hands of county officials are usually leased to irresponsible parties. Without doubt, work, and work worth the doing—i.e., profitable work—is best for prisoners. Yet there lurks in this system a dangerous temptation. The correct theory is that the work is for the benefit of the criminal—for his correction, if possible. At the same time, his work should not be allowed to come into unfair competition with that of honest laborers, and it should never be an object of traffic for pure financial gain. Whenever the profit derived from the work becomes the object of employing prisoners, then evil must result. In the South today it is natural that in the slow turning from the totally indefensible private lease system, some of its wrong ideas should persist. Prominent among these persisting ideas is this: that the most successful dealing with criminals is that which costs the state least in actual outlay. This idea still dominates most of the Southern states. Georgia spent $2.38 per capita on her 2,938 prisoners in 1890, while Massachusetts spent $62.96 per capita on her 5,227 prisoners. Moreover, by selling the labor of her prisoners to the highest bidders, Georgia not only got all her money back, but made a total clear profit of $6.12 on each prisoner. Massachusetts spent about $100,000 more than was returned to her by prisoners' labor. Now it is extremely difficult, under such circumstances, to prove to a state that Georgia is making a worse business investment than Massachusetts. It will take another generation to prove to the South that an apparently profitable traffic in crime is very dangerous business for a state; that prevention of crime and the reformation of criminals is the one legitimate object of all dealing with depraved natures, and that apparent profit arising from other methods is in the end worse than dead loss. Bad public schools and profit from crime explain much of the Southern social problem. Georgia, Florida, and Louisiana, as late as 1895, were spending annually only $20,799 on their state prisoners, and receiving $80,493 from the hire of their labor.

Moreover, in the desire to make the labor of criminals pay, little heed is taken of the competition of convict and free laborers, unless the free laborers are white and have a vote. Black laborers are continually displaced in such industries as brick-making, mining, road-building, grading, quarrying, and the like, by convicts hired at $3, or thereabouts, a month.

The second mischievous idea that survives from slavery and the convict-lease system is the lack of all intelligent discrimination in dealing with prisoners. The most conspicuous and fatal example of this is the indiscriminate herding of juvenile and adult criminals. It need hardly be said that such methods manufacture criminals more quickly than all other methods can reform them. In 1890, of all the Southern states, only Texas, Tennessee, Kentucky, Maryland, and West Virginia made any state appropriations for juvenile reformatories. In 1895 Delaware was added to these, but Kentucky was missing. We have, therefore:

	1890	**1895**
New England	$632,634	$854,581
Border States	233,020	174,781
Southern States	10,498	33,910

And this in face of the fact that the South had in 1890 over four thousand prisoners under twenty years of age. In some of the Southern states—notably, Virginia—there are private associations for juvenile reform, acting in cooperation with the state. These have, in some cases, recently received state aid, I believe. In other states, like Georgia, there is permissive legislation for the establishment of local reformatories. Little has resulted as yet from this legislation, but it is promising.

I have sought in this paper to trace roughly the attitude of the South toward crime. There is in that attitude much to condemn, but also something to praise. The tendencies are today certainly in the right direction, but there is a long battle to be fought with prejudice and inertia before the South will realize that a black criminal is a human being, to be punished firmly but humanely, with the sole object of making him a safe member of society, and that a white criminal at large is a menace and a danger. The greatest difficulty today in the way of reform is this race question. The movement for juvenile reformatories in Georgia would have succeeded some years ago, in all probability, had not the argument been used: it is chiefly for the benefit of Negroes. Until the public opinion of the ruling masses of the South can see that the prevention of crime among Negroes is just as necessary, just as profitable, for the whites themselves, as prevention among whites, all true betterment in courts and prisons will be hindered. Above all, we must remember that crime is not normal; that the appearance of crime among Southern Negroes is a symptom of wrong social conditions—of a stress of life greater than a large part of the community can bear. The Negro is not naturally criminal; he is usually patient and law-abiding. If slavery, the convict-lease system, the traffic in criminal labor, the lack of juvenile reformatories, together with the unfortunate discrimination and prejudice in other walks of life, have led to that sort of social protest and revolt which we call crime, then we must look for remedy in the same reform of these wrong social conditions, and not in intimidation, savagery, or the legalized slavery of men.

Notes

1. *Bulletin No. 8*, Library of State of New York. All figures in this chapter are from this source.
2. South Carolina, Georgia, Alabama, Mississippi, Louisiana, Texas, and Arkansas.

2

Social Factors in Oriental Crime

Norman S. Hayner

The Pacific Coast of North America is especially well suited for a study of the distinctive crime patterns of variant racial groups. Murder for purely economic reasons is supported by Eskimo mores. Chinese violate the Narcotic Drug Act. Mexicans are frequently arrested for carrying weapons—a regular practice in many rural communities of their homeland. Indians commit sex offenses that are supported by Indian custom but are defined as rape by the white man. Unique traditions, widely differing community influences, and contrasting family situations are important in the explanation of distinctive patterns.

The Siskiyou Mountains on the southern boundary of Oregon divide the Pacific Coast into two main districts. To the south stretch the productive valleys of California; to the north, the evergreen-forest belt of Oregon, Washington, and British Columbia, commonly known as the Pacific Northwest. The total population of this northern zone is about the same as that of Chicago. In the most recent official counts the Chinese of this area numbered 31,409; the Japanese, exactly 45,000; and the Filipinos, whose immigration has been limited to Oregon and Washington, 4,546.

The extent of criminality among Orientals in America seems to vary inversely with the extent to which they are incorporated in closely integrated family and community groups. In those places where a large proportion of the population is included in groups of this kind, the rate of delinquency is low. Orientals living in aggregations of homeless men, on the other hand, with no stable nucleus of family life, tend to present more problems of maladjustment. Data on Japanese, Chinese, and Filipino offenders in the Pacific Northwest show the importance of both family and community factors.

None of these Oriental groups presents a problem when compared with whites, but they do show interesting variations in the extent of criminality when compared with one another. A study of 1,944 Japanese, Chinese, and Filipino male arrests in Seattle for the five-year period 1928–32 shows that when these arrests are compared with the estimated number of Oriental males fifteen years of age and over, the average annual rate is 5.7 percent. The rate for white males of the same age is 11.1 percent. When considered separately the Japanese men have a rate of 2.6 percent, the Chinese of 9.6, and the Filipino of 11.8.

This typically low rate of criminality for the Japanese in America[1] is especially noteworthy for juvenile offenders. Average rates of boy delinquency in Seattle for two successive three-year periods from 1929 to 1934 show the Bailey Gatzert School District, in which about 80 percent of the boys are Japanese and about 10 percent are Chinese, third from the lowest in a list of seventy. This achievement is more remarkable when it is realized that the Bailey Gatzert district is located in a deteriorated section of Seattle—a section that shows the highest concentration of homicides, houses of prostitution, unidentified suicides, and cheap lodging houses in the city. Of the seven hundred and ten boys sent to the Parental School from Seattle during the period from 1919 to 1930 only three were Japanese. An average rate would have given the Japanese six times this number. Case studies of the three Japanese delinquents reveal the significant fact that in no instance did the boy come into vital contact with the racial colony.[2]

Studies in Vancouver, B.C., show results similar to those in Seattle. During the last nine years an average of 51 percent of the 1,241 children in the Strathcona public school were Japanese, 19 percent Chinese, and 30 percent white. Since 1922 the Oriental population has increased 112 percent, and the white population has decreased 24 percent. This school district includes the original business center of Vancouver, the present center being about one mile to the west. Average rates for boy and girl delinquency in Vancouver for two successive five-year periods from 1925 to 1934 give this area a rate about one-half that of the district to the east and about one-third that to the west.

In an unpublished study of "The Oriental Delinquent in Court," Judge Helen Gregory MacGill of the Vancouver Juvenile Court found that during the ten-year period from 1926 to 1935 the rate for white juvenile delinquency in the city of Vancouver was thirteen times as great as that for Orientals. Of the twenty-six Oriental children appearing in court during this period, thirteen were Chinese and thirteen were Japanese. Since there have been during the ten-year period about three times as many Japanese school children in Vancouver as Chinese, the delinquency rate for the Japanese has been about one-third that of the Chinese.

After graduation from school some of the Chinese boys of Vancouver—disdaining the menial work of their fathers and prevented by race prejudice from securing better positions—develop a grudge against society, take over the common Chinese attitude that it is all right to evade the white man's law, and forthwith get into trouble. They sometimes show a spinelessness that permits them to be supported by the wages and tips of white waitresses working in the little cafés that are the social centers of Chinatown. With the Japanese, on the other hand, rates of delinquency continue to be low for adults. Although the Japanese population of British Columbia is more than four-fifths that of the Chinese, only seven Japanese convicts were admitted to the British Columbia Penitentiary during the ten-year period from 1926 to 1935 as compared with one hundred and seventy-three Chinese.

One of the major factors that accounts for this low rate of criminality is the extent to which the Japanese are incorporated in those closely integrated families that are characteristic not only of Japan but also of China and the Philippines. The sex-age composition of the Japanese population in America shows a more normal biological group than that of the Chinese or Filipinos. According to the latest censuses there were about five Japanese males fifteen years of age and over to every three Japanese females of the same age group. Filial piety and the feeling of kinship are much stronger in this transplanted patriarchal family—more like those in the Continental family—than in the loosely integrated, democratic family of America. As long as parents are Japanese born, proper and improper conduct will be clearly defined, and this moral discipline in the home will restrain individuals from committing crimes. The use of the Japanese language in the home, the emphasis on courtesy which is praised by American friends, and the strong parental feeling of responsibility for the child help to maintain the authority of first-generation parents over their children. The family and marriage attitudes of the American-born generation are different from those of their Japanese-born parents, however, and it is probable—as in the case of Dr. Pauline Young's Molokans[3]—that Americanization will increase delinquency.

Another major factor is the efficiency and organization of the Japanese community. Language schools keep Japanese youngsters busily occupied after public-school hours. Community attitudes are so powerful that criminals discovered by the police sometimes commit suicide rather than face them. The father of a Japanese girl who had been intimate with a Filipino complained that her conduct had ostracized him from all Japanese associations. "No other foreign-language group," say Park and Miller in *Old World Traits Transplanted*, "is so completely and intelligently organized to control its members, and no other group has at all equaled them in the work of accommodating themselves to alien conditions." The Japanese community is always one of the first to reach its quota in a community-fund drive. This efficiency is related to the principle of allegiance developed during the feudal period in Japan. It is also a response to the hostility of the white community and to the barriers erected by race prejudice.

It should be remembered that the Japanese are proud. They hate to "lose face." They do everything possible to maintain a high status for their community or family. They feel that it is a disgrace to go on relief. Many of their destitute, sick, or delinquents have been sent back to Japan.

The following facts from Seattle illustrate concretely the ability of the Japanese to accommodate themselves to public opinion in this country. Police records for the five-year period 1900–1904 show 1,676 arrests of Japanese females—all but 4 for commercialized prostitution or keeping a disorderly house—and only 406 arrests of Japanese males, including 147 for keeping a disorderly house. In 1910 there were 4 female arrests and 230 male arrests—none of them for the above-mentioned offenses. Conversations with old-timers in the Japanese community revealed the fact that in 1908 the late John F. Miller, then mayor, conducted a cleanup campaign against prostitution. Several Japanese prostitutes were deported. Fear of deportation drove other prostitutes of this nationality into respectable occupations or into the hinterland. The Japanese churches, led by their pastors and encouraged by newly arrived young people from Japan,[4] achieved the complete abolition of public prostitution among the women of their race.

Many Japanese offenses suggest a lack of acquaintance with American ways. According to Professor Walter G. Beach in his study of *Oriental Crime in California*, traffic violations, offenses against miscellaneous city ordinances, gambling, drunkenness, and liquor law violations—in the order named—make up 70 percent of the Japanese offenses.

Professor Beach's study also shows that the most frequent arrests of Chinese in the cities and counties of California from 1900 to 1927 were for lottery playing (44 percent), gaming (23 percent), and violation of the opium and narcotic laws (12 percent). Chinese crime in the Pacific Northwest follows a similar pattern. During the fiscal year 1935–36 at the Oakalla Prison in British Columbia, an institution which keeps prisoners with sentences of less than two years, 24 of the 105 Chinese were received for lottery and gaming and 31 for infraction of the Opium and Narcotic Drug Act. Of the 179 Chinese received from January 1, 1931, to November 30, 1936, by the federal penitentiary at McNeil Island, which serves the western states and Alaska, all but 10 had violated the Narcotic Drug Act. Buying a lottery ticket is for the Chinese like buying a theater ticket for the American, and gambling is similar to a game of bridge. Moderate use of opium, like the tobacco habit in America, has been practiced for generations by the Chinese. But why should gambling and the violations of drug laws by Chinese in America be excessive?

In China the family is the dominant social group. All social relationships and all values are tied up with the family system. Man's social obligations toward the stranger are entirely omitted from Confucian ethics. Lin Yutang in his important book, *My Country and My People*, calls the family "a walled castle outside which everything is legitimate boot." Under the influence of recent social changes economic crimes for men are increasing in China, but it is significant that even in Chinese cities juvenile delinquency is not a problem. When the Chinese migrated to America they came as contract laborers to work on the railroads, in the mines, and on the farms. The women were left behind, and the family was absent as a factor in community life. Since the Exclusion Act of 1882 the Chinese have gradually given up camp life, and, after a period of occupational exploration they have to a large extent gone into the laundry, chop suey, and lottery businesses of the larger cities.

The Chinese lottery, originally a form of amusement within the group, has gradually acquired the status of an organized business which caters to migratory workers of all nationalities. The extent of the lottery business varies from season to season and from place to place according to the attitude of the public and the activity of the police. In some cities, however, the lottery tends to become the major form of business, as was the case in Seattle a few years ago when there were over forty Chinese lotteries in operation and tickets were purchased by the ton.[5]

Chinatown has been in the past and still remains predominantly a community of men. The proportion of Chinese males fifteen years of age and over to females of the same age for British Columbia in 1931 was still about eighteen to one. For Oregon and Washington this ratio was ten to one in 1920—five to one in 1930. It is significant that only 10 percent of the Chinese received at McNeil Island had wives living in the United States. The Chinese in China have for generations married young. By tradition they are not fitted for celibate life. For this reason, from the first period of Chinese immigration bootlegging slave-girls has been an important source of revenue. In addition, the absence of family controls in America undermined the characteristic Chinese temperance in the indulgence of their two vices of gambling and the use of opium products. In America these vices were soon seized upon by a certain class of whites who exhibited less temperance than the homeless Chinese. This situation in Chinatown was, of course, favorable for the emergence of criminal groups. Such activities as the monopoly control of the slave-girl and opium traffic and the protection of gamblers from the American police served as the economic base for the origin and development of the fighting tongs. Most tong wars had their basis in this economic factor.

As Professor C. N. Reynolds points out in his interesting article on "The Chinese Tongs,"[6] there are many indications that the problem of the fighting tongs is decreasing in importance. The hatchet could be wielded over members of the older generation, but not over the American-born Chinese. There is said to be less demand for the wares of Chinese bootleggers, the police are improving their methods of control, and many of the tongs are becoming benevolent-protective associations. In San Francisco "open tong wars have been practically nonexistent since 1921."

Vancouver, B.C., on the other hand, with its Chinatown of about eight thousand individuals—second largest on the Pacific Coast— has not been troubled with fighting tongs. The last tong murder was in 1924 and that was exceptional. More important than the greater severity of Canadian law is the fact that the Chinese in Vancouver's Chinatown, which is only about half as old as San Francisco's, have been greatly influenced by the ideas of post-revolutionary China, are more aggressive than the American Chinese, and are more sensitive to the attitudes of the dominant group. The American Chinese came in the fifties, were bitterly attacked in the seventies and eighties, and by 1900 began to be tolerated. The Canadian Chinese have experienced similar hostility much more recently, culminating in the Chinese Immigration Act of 1923. Writing in 1926, Miss Winifred Raushenbush said: "Sentiment against the Chinese is at present strong; in fact British Columbia is the only place on the coast where the Chinese are disliked. Tong wars and feuds would be so much tinder in the hands of the Vancouver Anti-Asiatic Society and the Canadian politician, so these things are not allowed to occur."[7]

As in the other groups studied, most of the Filipino offenses—disorderly conduct and gambling, for example—are minor in character, only police-court cases. The prejudice of American law-enforcement officers is, however, stronger against Filipinos than against Chinese or Japanese. The term "earwig," the name of a local insect pest, is used by the police to describe Filipinos. A special identification book in the detective division at police headquarters in Seattle, a book which includes "mugs" of all the Filipino offenders that have come to the attention of the police since 1919, is labeled "Head Hunters." The implication is that all Filipinos behave like the headhunting Igorots exhibited at the Alaska-Yukon-Pacific Exposition in 1909. Owing to a few widely publicized cases, "running amuck" is commonly regarded as a typical Filipino offense. A study of 330 convicted Filipino offenders, as indicated by Seattle police records for the period 1919 to 1935, shows that such crimes against property as larceny, burglary, and prowling are the most frequent offenses, totaling 197 or almost three-fifths. Crimes against decency and good morals—carrying concealed weapons, disorderly person, conducting gambling games, and contributing to the delinquency of a minor—total 77, or less than one-fourth. Crimes against the person, such as assault, murder, and threat to kill, total 42, or about one-eighth. There were also 12 violations of narcotic laws, which can be classed as crimes against public health.

A random sample of 100 whites, 100 Negroes, and 100 Filipinos recorded in the identification books of the King County[8] Sheriff's Office during the last twenty years shows the Filipinos a little less than the whites in percentage of crimes against property—66 and 70 respectively—and about the same as the Negroes in percentage of crimes against the person—14 and 13, respectively. A similar study of 100 Japanese—it took all the Japanese offenders for the twenty-year period to meet the quota—showed them lowest in percentage of crimes against property—35, but highest in percentage of crimes against the person—20. It will be seen from these statistics that crimes against the person, of which assault and murder are the most important items, are not peculiarly characteristic of the Filipino.

Data on criminality for eight racial groups in Hawaii, 1916–24, show the Puerto Rican, Hawaiian, and Filipino high and the Chinese and Japanese low. The criminal status of the newly arrived Filipino changed rapidly between 1915 and 1928 however. In 1915–16 the rates for convictions of Filipinos in the territorial courts per ten thousand male population eighteen years and over were three to four times as high for assault, homicide, and sex offenses as the rates for the total population. By 1925–28 these rates had diminished to only a fraction more than the average. The rates for stealing were less than the average.[9] It is significant that family life increased during this period. In 1910 one of every six Filipino men was married; in 1930 one of three. About one-quarter of these unions were across race lines.

The factors that account for the maladjustment to which Filipino crime is an index may be grouped roughly under three heads: (1) cultural heritage, (2) sex-age formation, and (3) contacts in America. Racially Oriental (Malayan), the Filipino is culturally Occidental. Although family life is closely knit in the Philippines and the sense of filial duty strong, as in China and Japan, most Filipino cultural traits—the Spanish language, the village fiesta, cockfighting, the idea of romantic love, strict chaperonage of young women—are Latin in origin. Public schools and the wide knowledge of English are American contributions. In contrast to the Chinese and Japanese the Filipino is probably too readily Americanized. The relatively free behavior of American girls is, however, a frequent source of misunderstanding. They do and say things that are done and said only by girls in the Islands who wish to encourage boys. Unless a Filipino girl is in love with a boy she avoids looking him straight in the eyes. Even if she were in love with him she would gaze steadily into his face only when no one else was present. The protective attitude toward marriageable girls in the Philippines is a factor preventing their migration to the United States.

Filipino migration to America is largely a post-war phenomenon. With the exclusion of the Chinese in 1882 came the substitute Japanese laborers, and with the exclusion of the Japanese in 1924 came the streams of Mexicans and Filipinos. As a result there were more Filipinos in the Pacific Northwest in 1930 than there were in the entire country in 1920.[10] Like the Chinese the sex ratio is abnormal. In 1930 there were in the United States as a whole fourteen Filipino males to every Filipino female. In Washington and Oregon there were thirty-two males to every female. As in the case of the Chinese this abnormal sex ratio means that the closely knit family life of the Philippines is not transplanted to America. Filipinos in this country live in mobile communities of homeless men with the disorders that are always associated with such aggregations. It is not surprising also that the few Filipino girls who migrate are more fickle than their sisters in the Islands. Owing to the strain on the wife's fidelity, marriages between Filipino men and women in the United States tend to be more unstable than those in the Philippines. The excess of males explains why many Filipino boys—usually not those sacrificing for scholastic achievement—seek the society of young American women and flirt with Indian girls in Alaska. Conflicting cultural heritages and loss of status, however, tend to make Filipino-Italian marriages, representing as they do the union of two similar cultures, seem to be more successful.

Another significant fact about Filipinos is their immaturity. Many of them left the Islands at an early age and came to America to get an education. If they fail in this they may be ashamed to go back. But most of them, thinking of themselves as transients in this country, plan to return to the Philippine commonwealth where there are many opportunities for those who have the prestige arising from travel and study in the United States. Their relative youth is shown by the fact that the average age for the 100 whites cited above was thirty-one; for the 100 Negroes, thirty-two; for the 100 Japanese, thirty-five; for 100 Chinese studied in the same way, thirty-seven; and for the 100 Filipinos, twenty-seven.

Newcomers are naturally attracted by countrymen who come from the same town or province or who speak the same dialect. Instead of guiding the greenhorn to the schools and libraries, this crowd or gang by which he is influenced may introduce him to the dance halls, houses of prostitution, and gambling joints. The novice is also influenced by the occupation which he chooses. The specialized occupation most frequently listed in the police mugbook was that of cannery worker. As a result Filipino criminality lags during the spring and summer, when more than three thousand Filipinos—mostly from the Pacific Northwest—are working in Alaskan canneries, increases during the fall, and reaches its peak in the winter. Owing in part to the practice of gambling in the Islands and in part to the exploitation of the Filipino by Chinese and Filipino contractors or by ship captains, much of his earnings is frequently lost in gambling. His employer sometimes withholds part of his wages in order to pay for his living during the winter. Returning from Alaska by September, the migratory Filipino, unencumbered by family ties, may work several weeks in the hop fields of Yakima, move south to California for the winter, return to Seattle in May, and ship for Alaska again.

If a Filipino spends the winter in Seattle and is not attending the university, he will probably live in one of the cheap, Japanese-operated hotels in cosmopolitan "Chinatown."[11] Here he finds less discrimination against Filipinos than in other areas of the city. More than two-thirds of the Filipino arrests in Seattle are made in or near the gambling resorts, dance halls, and poolrooms of this district.

In conclusion, the extent to which Orientals in America are incorporated in family groups, the closely related sex-age formation, the type of community influence, the contacts in America, and the distinctive cultural heritage are significant social factors for the explanation of variations in Oriental criminality. Generally speaking, criminality is low when a normal balance between the sexes makes possible a large amount of family life, and when a strong community organization maintains national traditions and prevents too rapid Americanization. The Japanese community represents the nearest approach to this situation. On the other hand, criminality is higher when there is an abnormal sex ratio, little family life, a weak community organization, and disorganizing contacts with Americans. In the Pacific Northwest the Chinese community of the past and the Filipino community of the present approximate this condition.

Notes

1. State and federal prisons and reformatories received during 1933 twenty times as many native-white males of native parentage fifteen years of age and over as Japanese males of the same age per ten thousand of these groups in the 1930 population.
2. See Norman S. Hayner. Delinquency Areas in the Puget Sound Region, *American Journal of Sociology*, XXXIX (November 1933), 319, 321. The Atkinson grade-school district, in the heart of Portland, Oregon, presents a similar picture. A study of 2,255 boy delinquents brought to the attention of the Multnomah County Juvenile Court during the three-year period 1932–34 gives the six other areas in the central business and industrial section of Portland rates that average more than twice as high as that in the Atkinson district. The school census for 1930 shows that 44 percent of the 324 children in this area were Japanese, 39 percent Chinese, 8 percent American-Chinese hybrids, and 9 percent white. Dominated as it is by railroad, industrial, and commercial property, the concentration of Japanese and Chinese families in this district seems to be the major factor accounting for its low rate of boy delinquency.
3. See Pauline Vislick-Young. Urbanization as a Factor in Juvenile Delinquency. *Publications of the American Sociological Society*, XXIV (July 1930), 162–66.
4. It is generally recognized that the quality of Japanese immigration to America improved after the "Gentlemen's Agreement" of 1907. The practice of sending undesirables to Japan has helped to maintain this quality.
5. R. D. McKenzie. The Oriental Finds a Job. *Survey Graphic*, IX (May, 1926), 152
6. *American Journal of Sociology*, XL (March 1935), 622–23.
7. The Great Wall of Chinatown. *Survey Graphic*, IX (May 1926), 157–58. A ruling went into effect three years ago requiring the deportation—after he has served his sentence—of any China-born Chinese convicted of violating drug laws. This regulation has cut to one-third the average number of Chinese sent to the British Columbia Penitentiary for narcotic offenses. One unfortunate effect, however, has been the use of native-born boys, who are not deportable, to deliver dope. Two such cases recently came to the attention of the Vancouver Juvenile Court.
8. King County includes Seattle.
9. See Bruno Lasker, *Filipino Immigration* (Chicago, 1931), tables, 192, 193.
10. Since the acceptance on May 1, 1934, by the Philippine Legislature of the act providing for complete independence of the Philippines, immigration from the Islands has been restricted to a quota of fifty a year.
11. See Hayner, *Hotel Life* (Chapel Hill, NC, 1936), 36.

3

Variability in the Criminal Behavior of American Indians

Norman S. Hayner

Demoralization has been the common result of the impact of civilization on primitive peoples. Diseases against which immunities have not been developed greatly reduce the native population. The old social order breaks down and the building of a new order to take its place is slow and painful. So it has been with the American Indian.

The extent and character of contacts with white civilization have an important relation to the persistence of primitive ways. Isolation encourages cultural vitality; alien stimulations facilitate tribal disorganization. Among the Hopis of the Southwest, 60 miles from a modern highway or railroad, the native culture is strong, "theft is rare, and murder is unknown." Laguna and Isleta, the two pueblos nearest Albuquerque, present the biggest law-enforcement problem to the officers of the United Pueblos Agency. Although as large as Laguna in population, Zuni Pueblo, 40 miles south of Gallup on a third-class road, had no report to the agency officers in 1937. All problems had been handled by the reservation court. Police officers have discovered that prohibition is enforced more easily and effectively in areas where Indians live apart from whites as compared with those where they are scattered among whites. The incidence of venereal disease among Indians is also higher near the population centers and lower in faraway places.

Closely related to social contacts as a factor in the criminal behavior of Indians is economic status. Quinault families that received the richest timber claims on their Washington coast reservation are today the most poverty-stricken and demoralized. In general the wealthier the tribe, the greater the offending. Money attracts predatory whites and makes it possible to buy liquor and to wander far from the reservation in automobiles. The Osage, Klamath, and Menominee tribes rank high in both unearned wealth and undesirable behavior. The Paiutes of Nevada, on the other hand, have had to labor diligently to obtain enough income for a bare existence and have rarely come to the attention of the police.

Drunkenness and sex offenses are the Indian crimes that most frequently perplex American law-enforcement officers. Since this fact sometimes leads to a biological interpretation, it calls for critical consideration. It should be clear, of course, that most Indians are peaceful, law-abiding citizens. A very high proportion of their offenses are minor misdemeanors—vices rather than systematic professional crimes. A 1932 official report on "Law and Order on Indian Reservations of the Northwest" concludes that "among Indians drinking is associated with most infringements of the law, and that sex offending closely connected with the breakdown of family life, though neglected by the courts, constitutes the other great problem."[1]

Few Indians north of Mexico had alcoholic beverages in prehistoric times. Generally speaking, the Indian of today, like many of his white associates, has not learned "to hold his liquor like a gentleman." He has not developed those traditions of moderate drinking that characterize most Italians and Greeks but too few white Americans. It should be remembered that more than half the white arrests in the United States are occasioned by intoxication and that the poor white, who is closer to the Indian economically, is more likely to come to the attention of the police for drunkenness than the wealthy "gentleman." It is also pertinent that other primitive groups have exhibited a potent reaction to alcohol. In a 1932 Report of the Native Economic Commission, Union of South Africa, is the statement: "It has always been a cardinal and very salutary principle of European administration that the Native must be protected from the stronger liquors."

Furthermore, the federal liquor law discriminates against the Indian as compared with his white neighbor. Since he is subject to arrest if liquor is found in his possession, he is likely to drink the bottle of whiskey or the jug of wine as quickly as possible, with devastating effect. In the words of a tribal leader: "The boys figure they can't take it away if it's inside!"

In the light of these facts it is not surprising that of the 1,484 Indian law violations in federal, state, and Indian courts reported by twenty-seven officers during the calendar year 1938 to Louis C. Mueller, chief special officer, Office of Indian Affairs, more than three-fourths were violations of liquor laws or drunk and disorderly cases. The territory served by these officers includes nine-tenths of the Indian population of the United States. In a letter to the writer Mr. Mueller, who has been associated with the enforcement of law on Indian reservations for sixteen years, made the following interesting comment on the relation of liquor to Indian crime:

> We are convinced that the Indian has a greater alcoholic reaction than the white race. (It may here be noted that the Finns and Irish have a greater alcoholic reaction than the Swedes or Germans.) The Indian has not, as a whole, learned temperance or moderation, and his reaction is generally a violent one. Now to break down these statements, we note that a Chippewa or an Osage does not react as violently as does a Klamath, an Apache or even a Sioux. Moreover, members of the same tribe, and for that matter, members of the same family having the same degree of Indian blood, react differently.[2]

It is obvious from Mr. Mueller's letter that the reaction of the Indian to alcohol varies not only in different tribes but also in different individuals from the same family. This calls for an explanation in situational rather than in racial terms. Just as white communities and individuals show wide variations in the extent of social or personal disorganization, so also do Indian. Some of these variations show similarities within a region; others are jurisdictional; still others are familial and personal. These last two are beyond the scope of this chapter.[3] Attention will be given here to regional and jurisdictional variability. The Plains (Montana and the Dakotas) and the Pacific Northwest (Oregon, Washington, and British Columbia) will be used to illustrate regional differences.[4] Three reservations in the Pacific Northwest will be discussed in detail to show jurisdictional contrasts.

In the days before white men slaughtered the buffalo for hides, the Plains Indians were hunters. Following the bison and fighting their enemies, they roamed over wide areas of the Great Plains. The greatest prestige was gained by the warrior who performed the bravest exploits. Life was rigorous. Chiefs got up at daylight and in winter broke the ice for their baths. Everyone had to be eternally alert against attack. A man gained both honor and wealth in his tribe by stealing horses from the enemy. "Stealing livestock was an art," says the Meriam Report, "requiring much skill and cunning, the respect for which still lingers. Cattle stealing involves the changing of brands, at which some

Indians are very skillful. It would seem from our data that this crime may in some cases be considered professional."

The old code of the buffalo hunters, with its glorification of warrior exploits, has broken down. A correlate of these declining mores is the increasing proportion of white blood. From 1890 to 1940 the proportion of mixed-bloods in the Blackfeet tribal roll increased almost ten times—from 8 to 79 percent. As the Indian becomes more like the white biologically and, as a result, associates more freely with him, his criminal behavior tends to approximate more closely the white pattern. Out of twenty-six "slick" crimes—forgery, fraudulent checks, embezzlement, jumping hotel bills—the Meriam Report found that twenty-two were committed by mixed-bloods.

The rate for Indian criminality, as indicated by the Meriam Report, was lower in the Plains region than in the Pacific Northwest. The percentage of enrolled Indians resident on reservations in the Dakotas and Montana who appeared in court as offenders during 1929 was 2.0; in Washington and Oregon, 3.6. A difference in the character of the offenses in the two regions was also found. In the wide-open spaces offenders are "younger, more vigorous and bold, less inclined to mere drunkenness, and more likely to commit outbreaking crimes," such as grand larceny or assault, and "they are not so likely to come into the courts repeatedly." The problem of the "drifter" is not serious.

Although little is left of the early religious beliefs, native games, or the old dances of the primitive Plains communities, a rugged independence and pride in solving their own problems are suggested by Mueller's experience with the Crows. It took him eleven days to set up the Court of Tribal Offenses at the Crow Reservation. Fifty of the one hundred members of the tribal council came the first day; another fifty, the second. Answers to the same questions had to be repeated. In spite of opposition from the old guard and the initial refusal of the Crows to admit that the Department of the Interior had authority to set up such an institution, the Court was finally established and is now one of the best of its kind.[5]

The Indians of the Pacific Northwest are divided into two main groups by the Cascade Mountains. To the west is a long narrow coastal strip extending from the islands and fiords of Southeastern Alaska, through British Columbia and Washington into Oregon; to the east, a semiarid plateau drained in part by the Fraser and Columbia rivers.

The aboriginal culture of the coastal strip was most highly developed among the Tlingit, Haida, Tsimshian, and Kwakiutl tribes to the north, was less clear on the Washington coast, and faded out on the coast of Oregon. In contrast to the Plains emphasis on brave deeds, the major criterion for the achievement of prestige on the coast was the accumulation of wealth. There was little "brotherly love" among Indians in the vicinity of Cape Flattery, according to Dr. Erna Gunther, University of Washington anthropologist. They were always struggling for status and fearing this and that. Murder was justified on the ground of jealousy alone. Since they were very envious of a successful person, he had to be constantly on the lookout lest he be murdered. The Makab, for example, had elaborate methods of poisoning.

Contacts with whites seem to have been more disastrous for the Indians of the Northwest coast than for those in the Southwest, Smallpox and the venereal diseases, originating from these contacts, took a heavy toll. The abolition of slavery and the banning of potlatches, which had been the chief means for gaining prestige, completely broke down the old system of classes. These Indians find it "not worth while" to compete with the more industrious and efficient Europeans and Orientals on the farms or in the canneries and logging camps. The disparity between sixteenth-century Spaniards and the Pueblo Indians, with their high achievements in government, art, and religion, was not so great as between eighteenth-century English and the coast Indians.

A study of the 1,495 Indian offenders received by the Oakalla Prison Farm in Burnaby, British Columbia, during a ten-year period ending in 1938, shows that the percentage of Indians incarcerated in this provincial prison was twice the percentage in the total population. Fifty-five percent had been convicted of offenses pertaining to liquor. A detailed analysis of the Indian offenders received at Oakalla during the calendar year 1937 indicated an economic status that was not more than semiskilled and a low educational experience. Although more than four-fifths rated themselves as semiskilled in occupation—farmers, fishermen, loggers, housekeepers, seamen, and trappers in that order—one-third were illiterate and only twelve had had over six years of education.[6]

Of the sixty-two British Columbia Indians charged with murder from 1910 to 1936, only two suffered the death penalty. Due to the conflicting testimony of Indian witnesses and the reluctance on the part of juries to hold Indians responsible to the same extent as whites, it is difficult to prove capital charges against them. "Other major crimes such as robbery are comparatively infrequent and accordingly, with the exception of these cases of homicide, criminal law enforcement on Indian Reserves is concerned chiefly with the suppression of the liquor traffic. In the vicinity of cities, logging camps, canneries, and other centers of population, prostitution of Indian women is fairly common and is difficult to control as the women leave the reserves for the purpose."[7]

Although it is evident from the material presented above that there are differences in the extent and character of Indian crime between the Plains and the Pacific Northwest, greater variability exists between specific reservations in the same region. The accompanying table, which is based on data included in the Meriam Report, shows jurisdictional crime rates for Indians of the Dakotas, Montana, Washington, and Oregon. The crude rates are the percentages of the total number of enrolled Indians in residence at their jurisdiction April 1, 1930, who appeared in a federal, state, or Indian court as offenders during the calendar year 1929. No matter how many times each Indian appeared in court he is counted but once.

Granting administrative differences among states, the contrast in rates between Standing Rock and Turtle Mountain, North Dakota, Sisseton and Rosebud, South Dakota, North Cheyenne and Flathead, Montana, Colville and Yakima, Washington, and Warm Springs and Klamath, Oregon, is probably great enough to offset local variations in the energy and efficiency of law-enforcement officials. It would have been interesting to have studied all these contrasting jurisdictions in an effort to determine the factors associated with low and high rates. Recently it was possible for the writer to spend four weeks in the field, talking with agency officials and representative Indians in the Pacific Northwest. To illustrate variability in specific areas, special attention will be given to the contrast between the Colville and Yakima jurisdictions in eastern Washington and to the unusually high rate for the Klamath Reservation in southern Oregon.

The Colville jurisdiction, which includes the contiguous Colville and Spokane reservations, illustrates very well the importance of isolation. Although its 1,385,086 acres and 4,126 Indians (1939) make it the largest jurisdiction in the Pacific Northwest, it has never been crossed by a railroad and even at the present time is cut by no interstate highway. During the last one hundred and fifty years many culture traits from the Plains Indians have been adopted by tribes on the Columbia plateau. The Sanpoil and Nespelem, Salishan peoples who are the principal tribes on the Colville jurisdiction, being more isolated, clung to the true plateau culture, which included the ideal of pacifism. Verne F. Ray in his monograph on these tribes points out that "from earliest infancy the child was drilled in the tenets of peaceful existence with his fellows. The pugnacious man was a public enemy with whom respectable people associated as little as possible." A person lost status by engaging in brawls. To some extent this is still true.

The Nez Perces, one of the smaller tribes in this jurisdiction, show how strong antagonism to whites may accentuate isolation. Long after the death of their leader at Nespelem in 1904, the influence of Chief Joseph and his hostility to white ways persisted. More than any other group on the reservation these Nez Perce folk cling to their distinctive native costumes. They seem to be less demoralized than surrounding tribes.

Table 3.1 Jurisdictional Crime Rates for Indian Enrollees

Jurisdiction	Indian Enrollees	Indian Offenders	Crude Rate	Corrected Rate*
Fort Totten, N.D.	829	17	2.1	1.9
Turtle Mountain, N.D.	2,154	60	2.8	2.4
Fort Berthold, N.D.	1,374	18	1.3	1.2
Standing Rock, N.D.	3,237	33	1.0	1.0
Sisseton, S.D.	1,811	7	0.4	0.3
Yankton, S.D.	1,464	28	1.9	1.7
Crow Creek, S.D.	1,200	23	1.9	2.1
Rosebud, S.D.	5,576	144	2.6	2.5
Pine Ridge, S.D.	7,472	81	1.1	1.0
Cheyenne River, S.D.	2,664	45	1.7	1.6
Fort Peck, Mont.	2,161	64	3.0	2.9
Fort Belknap, Mont.	1,155	34	2.9	2.6
Rocky Boy, Mont.	402	12	3.0	2.8
Blackfeet, Mont.	2,985	87	2.9	2.7
Flathead, Mont.	2,164	90	4.2	3.9
Crow, Mont.	1,720	37	2.2	2.0
North Cheyenne, Mont.	1,390	23	1.7	1.7
Colville, Wash.	3,529	32	0.9	0.9
Yakima, Wash.	2,326	109	4.7	4.7
Tulalip, Wash.	2,050	32	1.6	1.4
Taholah, Wash.	953	14†	1.5†	1.5†
Umatilla, Ore.	797	46	5.8	5.7
Warm Springs, Ore.	825	37	4.5	5.1
Klamath, Ore.	1,052	140	13.3	13.1

* Corrected for variations in the age–sex composition of the 1930 Indian population.
† Since this is based on offenders in one court only, the rate is too low.

The isolation of the Colvilles has been coupled with modest economic resources. During 1938, 385 families, for whom records were available at the agency, had an average income of $431.60. This was derived mostly from livestock. Two hundred and twenty-five Indians have been employed on C.C.C.–I.D. projects—men from seventeen to seventy are eligible—and about 35 on roads activities. Much of the rugged tribal land is covered with a forest of ponderosa pine. Each year about 2 percent of this timber is sold to the highest bidder for selective logging. The money thus acquired goes into the tribal funds.

The tremendous construction activities at Grand Coulee Dam on the southern rim of the reservation have increased the number and variety of contacts for these Indians. Since the main construction work began (July, 1934), from 150 to 200 Colvilles have held jobs for which the lowest wage is $4.50 a day. Many receive two or three times that much. Prior to the colossal undertaking of building the world's largest dam, when 14 persons lived at this strategic site rather than 16,000, as at present, both drinking and venereal disease were uncommon among the Indians. Dr. W. S. Johnston, who was physician at the Colville Agency from 1914 to 1922, reported very little drunkenness and only three or four cases of venereal disease. Indians caught drinking were given from thirty to ninety days in jail. Fourth of July celebrations in the village of Nespelem near the agency used to attract about 1,000 Indians and 50 whites. Now there are many more whites. Recently (June, 1940) Dr. and Mrs. Johnston camped with their trailer at the reservation hamlet known as New Keller during its Salmon

Days Celebration. Drunken Indians parked all around them. Only two arrests were made on this occasion, and those were for possession. With high wages received from work on the dam, drunken driving has become a problem, but Sergeant McGinn, who is in charge of the Washington State Patrol office in this district, affirms that Indians are not worse than whites in this offense. By 1935 venereal disease cases began to come to the attention of the Indian Service nurse at Nespelem. In spite of the fact that during 1937 only 54 arrests of Colville and Spokane Indians were made by Indian police on the jurisdiction and by county and city law-enforcement officers in the surrounding circle of towns, according to the official agency report, demoralization has probably been increasing.

The Yakimas, in contrast with the Colvilles, show the effect of a longer and more intense period of contact with whites. The reservation is crossed by the main line of the Northern Pacific and by U.S. 97, the principal north-south highway east of the Cascades. The leading arterial highway between Seattle and Salt Lake City skirts its eastern boundary. The city of Yakima with 27,000 inhabitants is only a few miles away. Approximately 100,000 acres, comprising 9 percent of the total land area in this big reservation, are irrigated. The verdure of thriving fruit orchards and the healthy growth of sugar beets and of hop and potato fields in this irrigated section remind one of fertile California valleys. White men and Japanese now own or lease much of the best land. In fact, out of a total population on the reservation of 16,000 less than 3,000 are Indians. Workers of many races and cultures—local and transient Indians, white fruit tramps, Filipinos, Japanese—help with the harvests.

The rate of 4.7 in Table 1—five times that of the Colville—is, of course, based on the 109 resident enrolled Indians who were offenders in 1929. It is interesting that the Meriam Report found 106 additional Indian offenders for this year who were not on the rolls of the Yakima Reservation.

About one-quarter of the Yakimas are entirely self-supporting. There are 225 farms on the reservation operated by Indians. Others that lease their land tend to "just play around." In many cases, crime seems to vary with economic prosperity. A study of the offenses of Yakima Indians by months shows the highest to be December, when money is paid them for grazing leases, then March, when spring rentals are paid for their farm land, and, third, September, when money is earned picking hops and fall rentals are paid.[8]

From spring until fall many Yakimas are on the move. They dig clams on the ocean beaches, gather roots in the mountains, pick cherries near the Dalles and huckleberries on Mount Adams, and fish with dip nets for salmon on the Columbia. From the white point of view these trips tend to "discourage habits of settled industry and promote moral irresponsibility." To the Indian, however, these journeys are in harmony with his old culture. As in the annual long house celebrations and at the local fairs, so also at transient camps like Celilo Falls, the traditional bone-gambling game is still played, but American poker is increasingly popular. Wandering may thus be a means of losing money as well as of earning it.

The weakening of the old cultures—twelve different tribes are united in the Yakima federation—has been a gradual process involving loss of status for the Indian, deterioration of the early religions, and disorganization of the family and tribal life. The old Indian custom marriage "involved some ceremony and a public sanction of the relationship." It often lasted as long as a week. Now, in many instances, to use the words of Nealey Olney, judge of the Court of Indian Offenses, "a man simply gets in bed with a woman and they call it marriage." After a detailed study of the Yakima Reservation (pp. 14410–20) the Meriam Report concludes: "Drunkenness and sex irregularities are both so common that they are no disgrace to a Yakima."

Americanization has progressed further among the Klamaths than among the Yakimas. Driving south to Klamath Agency from the much more isolated, poverty-stricken, and law-abiding Warm Springs Reservation in north central Oregon, the writer was impressed by the fine cars—few of them more than a year old—and the completely American dress. There are no "long hairs," i.e., men with long braids, or any moccasins here. Visits in representative homes showed that the furniture and the table fare for many of these Indians are similar to those of middle-class whites.

The unusually high crime rate for the Klamaths may be accounted for by the large amount of valuable timber in this 50-mile-square reservation coupled with contacts provided by seasonal workers attracted to local logging camps and sawmills. Of the 5,000 people on the Klamath Reservation less than one-fourth are now Indians. These whites are not supposed to possess or transport liquor, but many do and much of it reaches the Indians. After the first timber cutting in 1910, the Indians received so much money—$300–$400 per month—that they did not have to work. More leisure provided more opportunities to get into mischief. Many bought automobiles and started out. Of the 1,465 Indians enrolled under this agency many live in Oklahoma and elsewhere. Generally speaking, the older people have been able to make an adjustment, but for the younger generation it has been demoralizing. The picture is complicated by the fact that a "riffraff" element of Indians from other places, hearing about the easy money "on the Klamath," has come in. The local C.C.C.–I.D. employs only three Klamaths.

In spite of this general situation most of the Klamath Indians—the enrollees include a number of Modocs and a few Paiutes and Pit Rivers—are law-abiding citizens. A recent count shows that in 1938 and 1939 only 44 of the resident Indians accounted for 412 cases of drunkenness and disorderly conduct. Chiloquin, a small sawmill town 5 miles from the agency, and Sprague River on the eastern side of the reservation, are popular places to get drunk, but Klamath Falls, a frontier city of 18,000 inhabitants 31 miles south of the agency, is the bootlegger's paradise. From the Indian standpoint "they lay for the boys and charge double." In the words of Ben F. Mitchell, chairman of the Loan Board: "The first time an Indian is out of line into jail he goes. As soon as he pays the fine out he comes. Some have been in as many as 100 times. They help to support the city and the county."

Judge Ashurst of Klamath Falls was very frank in describing conditions: "The Indian is exploited here. He is regarded as fair meat. If the price of a dress is seven dollars, it is okay to charge fourteen. They have no heart about it at all."

The Indians recently won $7,500,000 in a suit against the government because the latter made the mistake some years ago of selling a large tract of reservation timber to the Long-Bell Lumber Company for only $87,000! Although the agency insists that the individual Indians buy something definite with the judgment money allowed them, it is significant that Sheriff Lowe of Klamath County noticed an increase in offending after these payments began. One Indian woman wrecked five cars in less than that many months! Following each quarterly payment, as they were formerly made, there was an increase in the jail population.

Mr. Mueller, who was for some time a law-enforcement officer on this reservation, writes that there have been sixteen murders among the Indians on the Klamath Reservation in the past ten years. This gives the Klamaths an average annual homicide rate seventeen times that of the country as a whole and six times that for the 69,294 resident enrolled Indians covered by the Meriam Report. It should be noted that murder or manslaughter is a common ground for commitment of Indians to penal institutions. Aside from sex crimes, these are practically the only offenses for which Indians are sent from Alaska to the federal penitentiary at McNeil Island. The rate for the closely related crime of assault is also high for the Klamaths. In fact the Klamath rate for offenses against the person, as indicated by Meriam Report data, was three times as high as those for its nearest competitors—the Blackfeet and Crows of Montana.

How to explain these exceedingly high rates for murder and assault is not entirely clear. There are a number of probable factors arising out of the distinctive backgrounds of the various Indian tribes enrolled at this agency. Leslie Spier in his Klamath Ethnography states that "quarrels and blood feuds were quite common." Verne F. Ray, who is studying the old Modoc culture, informs the writer that murder was not much emphasized by the early tribal code. Mr. Mueller stresses the point that because the Paiutes had been constantly at war with both the Klamaths and the Pit Rivers, "the hatchet is buried in a very shallow grave with the handle conveniently uncovered." He also writes that

> a long-present characteristic among certain tribes of the Northwest is the tendency to allow an insult, real or imaginary, to smolder for many years, sometimes as much as twenty, and then when the brain is excited from alcohol to recall the long-forgotten incident and make an effort to right the wrong by violence.

These influences from the past, operating in the demoralizing social and economic setting described above, offer at least a partial explanation.

In conclusion, the extent to which an aboriginal culture has disorganized seems to be in large part determined by the degree of isolation, on the one hand, and the source and adequacy of sustenance, on the other. Such distinctive customs as the horse-stealing of the Plains Indians or the pacifism of the Sanpoil tend to become less important factors for the explanation of criminal behavior as acculturation progresses. Some Indians, pauperized by too much easy money or unwisely administered relief, lack the incentive to work; others, including many boarding-school graduates, want to work but lack the opportunity. In so far as such enterprises as the C.C.C.–I.D. revive the fundamental drive to work, they contribute toward the reorganization of Indian society. A thoroughgoing solution of the Indian problem should include revival of some of the best traits in the old culture, education for young people that will enable them to compete with whites, and the development on the reservations of economic activities that will make self-support possible. Many interesting studies have been made of the old American cultures. A new field for research, equally challenging and more practical, is offered by the problems and processes of present-day Indian communities.

Notes

1. "Survey of Conditions of Indians in United States," Hearings before a Subcommittee of the Committee on Indian Affairs (U.S. Senate), Part 26, 14137–426. Although the study was made by Roy A. Brown, Mary L. Mark, Henry R. Cloud, and Lewis Meriam, for the sake of brevity it will be referred to in this chapter as the Meriam Report.
2. The writer is indebted to his colleagues, Jesse F. Steiner in sociology and Erna Gunther and Verne Ray in anthropology, as well as to Mr. Mueller, for critical reading of this article in its original form and for many helpful suggestions.
3. The writer is now working with Una Hayner on a study of Indian marriage and family problems.
4. A comparison between the criminal behavior of these regions and of the Southwest (Arizona and New Mexico) would be interesting. In spite of four hundred years of contacts with whites, many of the village dwellers and herdsmen of the Southwest retain their old traditions. The fact that Indians make up one-twelfth of the total population in Arizona and New Mexico—more than three times their proportion in the Plains region and more than five times their percentage in the Pacific Northwest—helps to explain this cultural vitality. It is significant that the 1930 census of Indian population reported only slightly over 2 percent of mixed blood for Arizona and New Mexico. The average percentage of mixed blood for all states was twenty times as high. Hostility against intermarriage has been accompanied by a tenacious holding to the mother-tongue. Seven-tenths of the Navajos were unable to speak English in 1930; four-tenths of the Keresans, a Pueblo linguistic stock; three-tenths of the Tanoans, another Pueblo stock; two-tenths of the Hopis. Unfortunately, complete data are not available from which a crime rate for the Southwest could be derived that would be comparable to those for the other two regions. With this degree of persistence in the old languages and traditions, however, a generally lower incidence of crime and demoralization is probable.
5. The Crow Court was organized under the law-and-order regulations approved by the Secretary of the Interior in 1935. The purpose of this type of court is to place responsibility for reservation behavior entirely on the Indians and to take it away from the superintendent and his deputy. The court has jurisdiction over Indian misdemeanors. No professional attorneys are admitted. Experience has indicated that lawyers "bulldoze" witnesses and "really mess things up." As a matter of fact, no outsider has a right to speak in Indian court unless asked to do so by the judge. Development of this institution has created much more interest on the part of Indians in law enforcement.
6. Based on an unpublished manuscript on crime among the Indians of British Columbia, prepared for this article by Stanley J. Bailey under the direction of Professor C. W. Topping, University of British Columbia.
7. Taken from a letter to the writer by A. F. MacKenzie, secretary, Department of Indian Affairs, Ottawa, October 29, 1936.
8. Based on data from an unpublished paper, "Crime among the Yakima Indians," prepared for this article by Miss Evelyn C. Wohlers of Yakima.

4
Lynching and the Status Quo

Oliver C. Cox

Quite frequently lynching has been thought of as a form of social control consisting in the taking of the life of one or more persons by a mob in retribution for some criminal outrage committed by the former. This method of unceremonial punishment is assumed to be common on the frontier where there is no constituted juridical machinery; and where, in the interest of social order, the group finds itself constrained to act spontaneously. Furthermore, it is known to occur in organized society where some crime is of such a heinous and socially revolting nature that an angry crowd gathers spontaneously and passionately mangles the criminal to death. Even in this situation, however, the police may be ineffectively organized, as is ordinarily the case in rural communities.

At any rate, these two situations do not involve significant social problems in America; in fact they hardly refer to lynching as a social institution.[1] They have no racial, nationality, or political-class significance. Justice among frontiersmen has never been a pressing social problem for the nation. Moreover, lynching must not be confused with the "hue and cry" of the general mob in medieval times. Here indeed was a recognized method of arrest, with its system of sanctuaries and sanctuary law.

Lynching may be defined as an act of homicidal aggression committed by one people against another through mob action for the purpose of suppressing either some tendency in the latter to rise from an accommodated position of subordination or for subjugating them further to some lower social status. It is a special form of mobbing—mobbing directed against a whole people or political class.[2] It is an *inter*- rather than an *intra*-group phenomenon. We may distinguish lynching from race rioting by the fact that the lynching mob is unopposed by other mobs, while it tends to be actuated by a belief that it has a constituted right to punish some more or less identified individual or individuals of the other race or nationality.

Lynching is an exemplary and symbolic act. In the United States it is an attack principally against all Negroes in some community rather than against some individual Negro.[3] Ordinarily, therefore, when a lynching is indicated, the destruction of almost any Negro will serve the purpose as well as that of some particular one. Lynchings occur mostly in those areas where the laws discriminate against Negroes; sometimes, in these areas, the administrative judicial machinery may even facilitate the act. However, the lynching attitude is to be found everywhere among whites in the United States.

A lynching, as we have defined it, is not primarily a spontaneous act of mob violence against a criminal. Where the interracial situation is not favorable, it will not occur. There seems to be a recognizable lynching cycle, which may be described as follows:

(a) A growing belief among whites in the community that Negroes are getting out of hand—in wealth, in racial independence, in attitudes of self-assertion especially as workers; or in reliance upon the law. An economic depression causing some whites to retrograde faster than some Negroes may seem a relative advancement of Negroes in some of the latter respects.
(b) Development, by continual critical discussion about Negroes among whites, of a summatory attitude of racial antagonism and tension.
(c) The rumored or actual occurrence of some outrage committed by a Negro upon some white person or persons. The ideal act is the rape of a white girl. But if the tension is very high, whites will purposely seek an incident with the Negroes.
(d) The incident having occurred, the white mob comes into action, lays hands upon the Negro, and lynches him. He is burned, hanged, or shot in some public place, preferably before the courthouse, and his remains dragged about the Negro section of the community: Ordinarily, in the heat of mob action, other Negroes are killed or flogged, and more or less Negro property is destroyed—houses are burned, places of business pillaged, and so on. There is usually a scramble among the mob for toes, fingers, bits of clothing and the like, which are kept as souvenirs of the lynching occasion.
(e) During the lynching, all Negroes within the area are driven under cover. They are terrified and intimidated. Many put themselves completely at the mercy of their nonmilitant "white friends" by cowering in the latter's homes, and pleading for protection from the enraged mob. Sometimes they leave the community altogether.
(f) Within about two or three days the mob achieves its emotional catharsis. There is a movement for judicial investigation; and some of the "best white people" speak out against lynching. On the following Sunday, one or more ministers of great courage declare that lynching is barbarous and unChristian; and in time the grand jury returns its findings that "the deceased came to his death by hanging and gunshot wounds at the hands of parties unknown."
(g) There is a new interracial adjustment. Negroes become exceedingly circumspect in their dealing with whites, for they are now thoroughly frightened. Many are obligated to their "white friends" for having saved their lives; and few will dare even to disagree with white persons on any count whatever. The man who does so is not considered a hero by the majority of Negroes; rather he earns their censure.
(h) In a more or less short period of time, Negroes begin to smile broadly and ingratiatingly over the merest whim of white men.[4] They are eager to show that they bear no malice for the horrible past.[5] The lynching has accomplished its purpose; social euphoria is restored; and the cycle is again on its way.

Some lynchings may appear to have a high degree of spontaneity. It should be remembered, however, that in the South the threat of lynching is continually impending; and this threat is a coercive force available to white people as such. Says Arthur F. Raper, "Lynching is resorted to only when the implied threat of it appears to be losing its efficacy."[6] Both the overt threat of lynching and prevented lynchings function to maintain white dominance. They provide, in fine, the sociopsychological matrix of the power relationship between the races.

Lynching in the South is not a crime, and this notwithstanding the fact that a few state statutes apparently proscribe it.[7] It is quite obvious that the constitutions of the Southern states and their supporting black codes, the system of discriminatory laws intended to keep Negroes in their place, intentionally put the Negro beyond the full protection of the law, and that the former take precedence over any contravening statute. Furthermore, it is clear that the political power of the area aims at class exclusiveness. Consider, for example, the following not uncommon public threat to Negroes of South Carolina by a United States Senator—the normal attitude of the Southern politician:

> Whenever the Constitution comes between me and the virtue of the white women of South Carolina, I say, "To hell with the Constitution"...
>
> When I was governor of South Carolina you did not hear me calling out the militia of the State to protect Negro assaulters.
>
> In my South Carolina campaigns you heard me say, "When you catch the brute that assaults a white woman, wait until the next morning to notify me."[8]

It is certainly true that all white people in the South will not thus express themselves, and some are decidedly opposed to this view. But where a leading politician could hold himself up for election on the grounds that he is a potential lyncher, the presumption is inevitable that lynching is not a crime.

The dominant opinion of the community exalts the leaders of the mob as "men of courage and action."[9] Raper reports an incident in point:

> Women figured prominently in a number of outbreaks. After a woman at Sherman had found the men unwilling to go into the courtroom and get the accused, she got a group of boys to tear an American flag from the wall of the courthouse corridor and parade through the courthouse and grounds, to incite the men to do their "manly duty."[10]

To be a crime lynching must be an offense against the local state; but the propagandized sentiment of the community registered by votes determines what offenses shall be. "Mobs do not come out of the nowhere; they are the logical outgrowths of dominant assumptions and prevalent thinking. Lynchings are not the work of men suddenly possessed of a strange madness; they are the logical issues of prejudice and lack of respect for law and personality."[11] To be sure, the law loses respect naturally when it seems to contravene the powerful interests which lynching protects.

Moreover, the sense of penal immunity which pervades the mob amounting frequently to elation in performance of a social service tends to belie the theory that lynching is criminal. A story of crime does not read like the following:

> Shortly before midnight, with an acetylene torch and high explosives, a second-story vault window was blown open and the Negro's body was thrown to the crowd below. It was greeted by loud applause from the thousands who jammed the courthouse square. Police directed traffic while the corpse was dragged through the streets to a cottonwood tree in the Negro business section. There it was burned.[12]

A person or group of persons committing crime might be expected to go to great pains in relieving themselves of any trace of the act. Lynchers, however, expect to be glorified in identifying themselves. In reviewing one case Ray Stannard Baker writes: "They scrambled for the chains before they were cold, and the precious links were divided among the populace. Pieces of the stump were hacked off, and finally one young man . . . gathered up a few charred remnants of bone, carried them uptown, and actually tried to give them to the judge."[13]

The mob, then, is seldom, if ever, apprehensive of punishment. The law stands in a peculiar relationship to lynching. Nowhere is lynching advocated on the statute books; yet there is a prepotent sanction in the South that whites may use force against any Negro who becomes overbearing. According to Raper, "The manhunt tradition rests on the assumptions of the unlimited rights of white men and the absence of any rights on the part of the accused Negro."[14] Negroes can ordinarily be taken from police custody because there is a controlling assumption that the law is not available to Negroes. The mob is composed of people who have been carefully indoctrinated in the primary social institutions of the region to conceive of Negroes as extra-legal, extra-democratic objects, without rights which white men are bound to respect.

Therefore, most Southern official criticism of mob action against Negroes must necessarily be taken largely as pretense. The jury and courts could hardly be expected to convict, since their "hands are even as dirty."[15] Mrs. Jessie Daniel Ames puts it in this way: "Newspapers and Southern society accept lynching as justifiable homicide in defense of society. When defenders of society sometimes go too far in their enthusiasm, as in the Winona, Mississippi, torch lynchings of 1937, public opinion regrets their acts, deplores them, condemns, but recognizes that too much blame must not be attached to lynchers because their provocation is great and their ultimate motives are laudable."[16]

Such functionaries as the sheriff, mayor, or prosecuting attorney have not only been known to take part in lynchings but also the court sitting formally has answered the purpose of the mob. "Mobs do not loiter around courtrooms solely out of curiosity; they stand there, armed with guns and threats, to see that the courts grant their demands—death sentences and prompt executions. Such executions are correctly termed 'legal lynchings,' or 'judicial murders.' "[17]

We should make the distinction between that which is socially pathological and that which is criminal. Although these two phenomena may converge, they are nevertheless capable of separate existence. All criminal acts indicate some form of social maladjustment, but not vice versa. In illustration, certain types of speculation on the stock and commodity-exchanges may be socially pathological and yet not crimes. If the economic system and supporting laws are such that unwholesome speculation cannot be but inevitable, then, clearly it will not be criminal. In like manner, although the lynching of a Negro involves some social wrong against Negroes besides some increment of degeneracy among the lynchers, statutory impotency or even implied encouragement may necessarily exclude it from the category of crime.

Lynching is socially pathological only in the sense that it is incompatible with the democratic, Christian spirit of the Western world. The spirit of the age is antipathetic to both the Southern system of social values and its stabilizer, lynching; but lynching happens to be the more obtrusive. Like a society of headhunters or cannibals where the individual hunter is never inculpated in terms of the values of his society, the Southern lyncher can be considered criminal and degenerate only in the judgment of an out-group.

Lynching is crucial in the continuance of the racial system of the South. From this point of view lynching may be thought of as a necessity. This is not to say, however, that lynching is "in the mores"; it is rather in the whip hand of the ruling class.[18] It is the most powerful and convincing form of racial repression operating in the interest of the *status quo*. Lynchings serve the indispensable social function of providing whites with the means of periodically reaffirming their collective sentiment of white dominance. During a lynching the dominant whites of the community ordinarily assume an explicit organization for interracial conflict. By overt acts of aggression they give emotional palpability to their perennial preoccupation with racial segregation and discrimination. Their belligerency tends to compel the conformity of possible indifferent whites in the community; and it defines opposing whites as unpatriotic and traitorous to the cause of white dominance.

Furthermore, there is an inseparable association between Negro disfranchisement and lynching. Disfranchisement makes lynching possible and lynching speedily squelches any movement among Southern Negroes for enfranchisement. In the South these two are indispensable instruments in the service of the *status quo*. Indeed, as Jessie Ames concludes: "Negroes, as a voteless people in a Democracy, [are] a helpless people."[19]

Clearly, the lynching would be of no particular concern of Negroes if custom in the South prescribed, as punishment for certain offenses, public hanging and mutilation. We should not expect

Negroes to be any more occupied with problems of such a practice than they are, say, with the current question of capital punishment. Indeed, there is a sense in which Negroes may prefer public retribution for such a crime as rape. The act of penalizing is itself a factor contributing to social cohesion.[20] If Negroes were permitted to attend in concert with whites the public execution of a white or a Negro rapist, we should expect the event to engender a degree of solidarity between them. Such interracial action, however, is not at all intended by a lynching. Lynching is not punishment; it is racial aggression.

"In the states where most lynchings have occurred, white people generally justified slavery. . . . They justified methods of terror employed to intimidate and disfranchise the Negroes; and they later enacted laws and perfected party procedures to restore and preserve 'white supremacy.'"[21] Through the instrumentality of these laws and political contrivances the Southern aristocracy returned to power and relegated the protection of the Negro to the benevolence of white people as individuals. Having defined Negroes basically as extra-legal objects, some sort of informal means of violent coercion, ranging all the way from an occasional blow to floggings, mutilations, and homicides, had to be relied upon.

Lynchings were excluded, *ipso facto*, from the category of criminal offenses when Negroes were disfranchised by the Southern state constitutions; the black codes support the constitutions. As we have attempted to show elsewhere, the type of racial situation determines the pattern of white-colored relationship, while some sort of political class interest is fundamental. The planter, exploitative class-interest dominates the social life of the South, and lynching is bound up with the latter interest.[22] In South Africa, where the racial situation is in many respects similar to that of the South, the same need for extra-legal violence against the colored people presents itself. As one writer concludes: "The history of the century [in South Africa] would hardly show an instance of a single white man awarded capital punishment for the murder of a native. But it will bring to light scores of cases in which the white murderer escaped scot-free or only with nominal punishment. . . . [The natives] get nominal wages and heaps of insults. The white farmer could . . . whip them and make them slave for him."[23] In South Africa, however, the lynching pattern is not exactly duplicated because personal violence against the natives is, to a considerable extent, permitted in the formal law.

This is a consideration of highest importance in understanding the determining force in the pattern of race relations in the South. The insistence upon a personal right of white men to control Negroes has its roots in the Southern system of slavery. The landlords had achieved such a right over their Negro slaves, and their vision of losing it was clearly the most galling aspect of the Civil War. It is this right which the counter-revolution of the aristocracy practically restored. Its brilliant self-satisfying outer covering was extended to the white commonality as a reward for their counter-revolutionary support. The aristocracy retrieved this right of personal control over the Negro at greater cost than that of any other right known to their constitutions. This class is naturally sensitive about it, and cannot be expected either to accept or to make laws which will abrogate it.[24] Then, too, the rights secured by belonging to a dominant race must necessarily be personal.

Lynching, moreover, is integral in the Southern system. To remove the threat of it is to overthrow the ruling class in the South and to change the basis of Southern economy. Where the system is functioning most effectively, lynching tends to become natural even to Negroes. Arthur F. Raper observes a case in point: "The Negroes were not greatly disturbed by the lynching, being already inured to the undisputed domination of whites. In Bolivar County, with an average of one lynching every four years, such occurrences are part of the normal picture."[25] One is in error, then, in thinking that it is possible to eradicate mob-action in the South, as it may be possible to stamp out, say, the crime of kidnapping, without also revolutionizing the Southern social order. Jessie Daniel Ames, Executive Director of the Association of Southern Women for the Prevention of Lynching, sees the alternatives thus: "to those who believe lynchers are criminal devils, inherently wicked and depraved, then punishment, swift, severe, and sure, appeals; to those who believe lynchers are born into a social and economic system which turns them to acts of brutal violence, then change of the system appeals."[26]

We have seen that lynching is a form of interracial conflict facilitated by the fundamental laws of the Southern states. By lynching, Negroes are kept in their place, that is to say, kept as a great, easily-exploitable, common-labor reservoir.[27] It is not essential, therefore, that the victim be actually guilty of crime. When the situation of interracial tension is sufficiently developed, a scapegoat will do.[28] Negroes have been lynched for such apparent trivialities as "using offensive language," "bringing suit against white men," "trying to act like white men,"[29] "frightening women and children," "being a witness," "gambling," "making boastful remarks," and "attempting to vote."[30]

Yet there is a peculiar and consistent association of the crime of rape committed by Negroes upon white women and lynching. Indeed, the arguments in favor of lynching have consistently justified it on the grounds that Negroes can be deterred from venting their vicious sexual passion upon white women only by the constant threat of lynching.[31] Our problem here is not to disprove this position (many Negro women have been lynched), but rather to indicate further the relationship between lynching and the social system.

There are two principal reasons why the accusation of rape is apparently the best available defense of lynching. In the first place, rape, especially when committed upon a child, is probably the most outrageous of crimes in modern society. Mob action against a rapist, then, tends to be excused in the mores. In fact, the lynchers of such a criminal, like the men of the New Testament who threw stones, expect some sort of social approbation as a reward for their chivalry. Hence supporters of lynching find it expedient to hold out the crime of rape to a censuring world and to focus all discussion upon it. On this ground they are able to develop any degree of eloquence and heat in justification of the institution.

In the second place, as we have attempted to show elsewhere, the white woman holds a strategic position in the interracial adjustment of the South. To the extent that the ruling interest in the South can maintain eternal watchfulness over her, to that extent also the system may be perpetuated. The belief that Negroes are surreptitiously using white women to "mongrelize" the population produces a bitter sense of frustration, calling for practically unlimited violence against Negroes. It is principally on the latter score that the white ruling class has been able to corral the white masses for expressions of mob violence. Clearly a "mongrelized" South will ultimately mean not only a non-segregated South but also a non-aristocratic South, the perennial nightmare of the Southern oligarchy.

Therefore, in order that the Negro-man-white-woman emotional set might be exploited, lynchers and their defenders always seek to manipulate the story of a lynching to include rape as a crime of the victim. Success in this would disarm almost any Southern judge, jury, or prosecuting attorney. The latter, like the majority of the propagandized population, are naturally predisposed and receptive to arguments founded upon sexual precaution. In the final analysis, then, the shibboleth of white womanhood provides the most effective rationale of the interests of the Southern aristocracy.

Since the act of lynching is directed particularly against the Negroes of the community, wide publicity and exemplary cruelty is desirable. The purpose of the lynchings is not particularly the elimination of a dangerous individual from society; rather the ideal is to make the occasion as impressive as possible to the whole population.[32] To Negroes it involves a challenge and a setting at naught of all that they might have held as rights to integrity of person and property, while to whites it is a demonstration and reaffirmation of white dominance. Sometimes outsiders wonder at the presence of women and children at lynchings. For instance, Arthur F. Raper quotes the Raleigh *News and Observer* on a 1930 lynching as follows:

> "It was quite the thing to look at the bloody dead nigger hanging from the limb of a tree near the Edgecombe-Wilson County line this morning. . . . Whole families came together, mothers and fathers bringing even their youngest children. It was the show of the countryside—a very popular show. Men joked loudly at the sight of the bleeding body . . . girls giggled."[33]

However, as a means of schooling white children in the Southern principles of race relations, there could hardly be a more effective method. On the other hand, the custom of mutilating, burning, or dragging the victim's body in the Negro community produces the obverse side of the lesson.

Recently there has been considerable discussion among statisticians and lawmakers concerning the exact definition of a lynching. Persons who tabulate the number of lynchings per year feel a great need for accuracy and reliability, while lawmakers want to be certain that the concept is limited so as to exclude other forms of violence and homicide. Thus far, however, these problems have not been settled—and for good reason. Everyone knows what an ordinary lynching is, but there are marginal cases difficult to define. What is a mob? Two or ten times two people. In Mississippi a Negro and a white man are gambling. The white man kills the Negro in a fight and goes free. Is that a lynching?

The reason why lynching is difficult to define for purposes such as those mentioned above is that the lynching, the culminating act of continuing white aggression against Negroes, cannot be completely extricated from the social matrix which produces it. In the South the lyncher is involved in the dominant theme of the society. Indeed lynching should be thought of as homicidal but not necessarily homicide. Any one of the unnumbered insults, slaps, cuffs, and kicks which white persons deal to Negroes daily in the South may be described as a lynching situation. So far as its effect upon Negroes of the community is concerned, the flogging of a Negro by a white mob is not very much different from a full-blown lynching. Specifically, we may think of a lynching situation as one in which one or more Negroes encounter one or more whites and in which they find themselves exposed to insult or violence, their reaction to which, as normal citizens, threatens to lead either to their being beaten or killed by one or by a mob of white persons; and for this impending exercise of arbitrary violence there is a consciousness on both sides that the law will not punish and that the ruling class in the community will show condonement.

We do not mean to say that every act of violence by whites against Negroes in the South, without exception, has gone unpunished. Ordinarily such acts do go unpunished; yet there are situations unfavorable to lynchers. The following are some of them: (a) a lynching motivated by a highly personal controversy in a community where the Negroes are well-behaved, that is to say, where they are working honestly and industriously for the "big white folk"; (b) where the occasion for the killing, the lynching, is clearly a "drunken prank" of "white trash" in a "peaceful" Negro community; and (c) where uninformed whites accidentally become involved with and lynch some trusted and dependable Negro leader of the community. In the border states, especially, there is some remote likelihood that such lynchers may be sentenced to prison. On the periphery of the Deep South the definition of acts of extra-legal violence, which contribute to the support of white dominance and exploitation, tends to contract.

It is sometimes believed that all the "best white people" in the South are opposed to lynching. Nothing is farther from the truth. In fact, we should expect the leading Southern citizens to be most deeply affected by a policy so significant to the continuance of the social system as mob violence. When it is possible for a sheriff in answer to an accusation of non-feasance to declare that "nearly every man, woman and child in our community wanted the Negro lynched,"[34] it is difficult to exculpate the leading citizens from the charge of mob sentiment or condonement of it. In reality lynching is an institution maintained by leading white people of the South; it serves as a powerful support of the ruling class.

The "best white people" may be classified into the following groups:

(1) Those who are convinced of the wrongness of lynching and speak directly against it. This group does not see the place of lynching in the Southern system. There are, naturally, degrees of enthusiasm among them.[35]
(2) Those who recognize that white violence and general aggression against Negroes is determined by the political class system; but who, confronted with the magnitude of the problem involved in attacking the system, remain silent.
(3) Those who understand the relation of the system to lynching, and actually speak out against the system. These constitute a very small minority of white people who live precariously in the South.[36]
(4) Those who attack lynching as a means of restoring the good name of the community in the eyes of critical outsiders. This procedure is essentially a matter of good business policy.[37]
(5) Those who are convinced about the rightness of lynching and who either silently approve of or openly justify it as inevitable. Sometimes these people actually attend the lynching ceremony. Evidently, this group is in the overwhelming majority.[38]

During a lynching it would be foolhardy for Negroes of the community to seek the protection of the police station, the sheriff's office or the courthouse; of course, they will never dream of seeking shelter in a white church. To enter the police station on the assumption that their persons would be defended against the mob is to infuriate the mob. In other words, such a course would symbolize to the white mob that Negroes expect to utilize the machinery of the law to protect their rights, which is the antithesis of the lynchers' objective. The custom of Negroes is rather to go to the homes of "white friends," who would be able to certify to the lynchers that they are "good, well-behaved niggers." In discussing one case Raper writes: "Most of the Negroes had gone to the homes of white friends, or had left town. . . . At midnight when other Negroes called the police-officers and Rangers and militia men for protection, they were told that nothing could be done for them, that they had better get out of town or stay at the homes of 'white friends.'"[89]

This act of relying upon white friends for primary security has a double significance. It demonstrates to the lynchers that the Negro is willing to accept the personal authority and guardianship of white people as the final guarantee of any possible rights which he may have. It is a sort of admission that he has divested himself of any hope of reliance upon institutions intended to safeguard the rights of citizens as such. He prostrates himself, as it were, before white men in recognition that Negroes may enjoy a degree of well being only by sufferance of their white neighbors.

In the second place, the practice is significant in that it provides an invaluable lesson to possible intractable Negroes. Negroes who have been saved by their white friends are indebted to the latter, and subsequently such Negroes tend to act as a check upon any of their fellows who might harbor ideas of revolt. Most Negroes come to know these "sympathizers" as the "good white folk" of the community. The combined effect is to make Negroes aware of their dependence upon whites and to put at rest any tendency to criticize the whites for their partiality in government, education, economic dealings, and so on. Out of this situation is produced the finally accommodated Negroes known as "Uncle Toms."

We may conclude then that lynching and the threat of lynching is the fundamental reliance of the white ruling class in maintaining the *status quo*. It is a sub-legal contrivance developed to meet a vital social need, which, because of the powerful democratic conventions of Western society, cannot be satisfied by formal law. Although lynching is directed almost entirely against Negroes, it serves to keep both Negroes and poor whites in their place. The keeping of these black and white masses antagonized leaves the exploiting class an easy opportunity to play one against the other thus stabilizing their position of sub-standard American workers.[40]

Notes

1. We may mention incidentally that a rather puerile approach to a study of the institution of lynching is to derive hypotheses from an examination of the history of *the term* lynching.
2. Recently there has been a tendency, especially among journalists, to call any kind of mobbing a lynching. This, however, gives us no basis for an understanding of lynching as an inter-group phenomenon.
3. Francis W. Coker says with some considerable degree of truth: "As violent manifestation of a racial antagonism mixed with economic rivalry the programs of tzarist Russia and the terrorist activities against Jews in Germany and the states of Southern Europe are in a class with lynching. Similarly, the conflicts between labor and capital (political class action) often give rise to what are in essence lynching." *Encyclopedia of the Social Sciences*, article, "Lynching."
4. Gunnar Myrdal makes an observation in point: "Much of the humor that the Negro displays before the white man in the South is akin to the manufactured satisfaction with their miserable lot which the conquered people of Europe are now forced to display before their German conquerors. The loud high-pitched cackle that is commonly considered as the 'Negro laugh' was evolved in slavery times as a means of appeasing the master by debasing oneself before him and making him think that one was contented." *An American Dilemma*, 960.
5. "Law and order" in the South implicitly but resolutely insist that the family, or worse still, Negroes of the community, upon whom this appalling atrocity has been committed, do nothing to show that they harbor resentment. The lynching to be successful must have so cowed the Negroes that even a gratuitous offer of possible legal assistance would be rejected by them. In a recent Mississippi lynching a white Northern reporter tactfully avoided interviewing the colored family of two lynched boys "because a man in Quitman told me quietly, 'it wouldn't do them niggers any good to be seen talking to you.'" (Victor H. Bernstein in the *Pittsburgh Courier*, Oct. 31, 1942). The overwhelming terror among Negroes in the lynching situation is evoked principally by the awareness that there is in effect no legal power presuming to question the free violence of the lynchers. It is this social attitude which Mrs. Attwood Martin, chairman of the Association of Southern Women for the Prevention of Lynching, refers when she says: "Knowing at the start that if we went too fast … it would be the Negro population that would suffer, we have refrained from overzeal until sure of our support." See Jessie Daniel Ames, *The Changing Character of Lynching*, Atlanta, 1942, 68.
6. *Preface to Peasantry*, Chapel Hill, 1936, 23. In discussing one lynching situation Raper says also: "While these seventy-five thousand people were members of actual mobs but one day in the year, they were most probably mob-minded every day in the year. Millions of others were mob-disposed, and under provocation would have joined a mob, killing or standing sympathetically by while others killed." *The Tragedy of Lynching*, Chapel Hill, 1932, 47.
7. cf.. James H. Chadbourn, *Lynching and the Law*, Chapel Hill, 1933, Chapter III; James E. Cutler, *Lynoh Law*, Longmans, Green, and Co., 1905, 1–12, and Frank Shay, *Judge Lynch*, New York, 1938, 8.
8. Cole Blease, quoted in Arthur F. Raper, *The Tragedy of Lynching*, Chapel Hill, 1933, p. 293. In November, 1942, at the national poll-tax filibuster, Senator Doxey said confidently, "Mississippi and the other southern states will uphold Anglo-Saxon supremacy until the lofty mountains crumble to dust." No one has the slightest doubt about the means which the Senator and the entire legal machinery of the Southern states employ and will continue to employ in the interest of this brand of democracy. Doxey knows that he has behind him the firmly established and effective Southern institution of interracial violence; hence he speaks to the nation with conviction. Moreover, he is able to speak with this degree of finality because he is assured that the United States Senate dares not challenge his position—at least he knows that the moral level of the Senate is far below that necessary to cope with the probable cost of instrumenting such a challenge.

   Nothing serves to bring the Southern congressmen so solidly in opposition as a national movement to pass legislation making lynching a crime. We should expect this because to make lynching a crime would be to strike at the pivot of white dominance in the South; to make lynching a crime would be to indict the political leadership of the South; indeed, to make lynching a Federal crime would be to bring before the nation the full unfinished business of the Civil War. An effective anti-lynching law must inevitably inculpate the deepest intent of Southern constitutions. Remarkable as it may seem, the most sacred and jealously guarded right of the Southern states is undoubtedly the right to lynch Negroes; consequently, any Federal law seeking to limit this right will be promptly construed to be an infringement upon the sovereignty of states. It is in this light that the impotance of the Fourteenth Amendment in protecting the life and liberty of Negroes in the South must be estimated.
9. Walter White, *Rope and Faggot, (*New York, 1929), 4.
10. Arthur F. Raper, *The Tragedy of Lynching*, 12; see also 323.
11. Ibid., 47.
12. Ibid., 7. Sometimes the scheduled lynching of a Negro is announced in the newspapers. See William H. Skaggs, *The Southern Oligarchy*, (New York, 1924), 300.
13. *Following the Color Line*, 187.
14. *The Tragedy of Lynching*, 9.
15. The tables of convictions for lynchings and attempted lynchings presented by Chadbourn, op. cit., 14–15, are not very revealing. They may include contempt cases and cases falling within the two possible meanings of lynching suggested in the introduction to this analysis. The situations may be further complicated by the lynchers' doing more or less serious violence to white persons who may attempt to protect the Negro.

16. *The Changing Character of Lynching.* Atlanta, 1942, 51.
17. Arthur F. Raper, op. cit., 46; see also 13; and Walter White, op. cit., 32. In this connection Mrs. Ames observes: "in more than one prevented lynching a bargain was entered into between officers and would be lynchers before the trial began in which the death penalty was promised as the price of the mob's dispersal." Op. cit., 12.
18. In criticizing the policy of Southern newspapers Jessie Daniel Ames declares: "They cannot defend lynching as a necessary form of violence to ensure white supremacy. All the country hold the philosophy of white supremacy . . . but nationally it is not good sales talk to advertise that white supremacy can be maintained in the South . . . only by force, coercion, and lynching." Op. cit., 54.
19. *Ibid.,*. 19.
20. For a general discussion of the nature of negative sanctions see Emile Durkheim, *The Division of Labor in Society*, trans. by George Simpson, (New York, 1933), Ch. II.
21. Arthur F. Raper, op. cit., 50.
22. "The Black Belt lynching is something of a business transaction. . . . Negroes are in least danger in these plantation counties. The whites, there, chiefly of the planter class and consciously dependent upon the Negro for labor, lynch him to conserve traditional landlord-tenant relations rather than to wreak vengeance upon his race. Black Belt white men demand that the Negroes stay out of their politics and dining rooms, the better to keep them in their fields and kitchens." Ibid., 57–58.

    This inherent requirement of southern economy tends to set the dominant theme of race relations; so that even poor whites may seem to exploit the advantage in their competitive contacts with Negroes.
23. P. S. Joshi, *The Tyranny of Colour*, (Durban, South Africa, 1942), 18, 20.
24. At a recent court hearing in Mississippi, prosecuted by the Federal Government, the southern attorney defending the lynchers of Howard Wash said: "The people of this great Southland are on trial. We may as well face the truth. This is not a trial only to convict the three defendants. . . . It is just another effort to see how much we of the South will permit invasion of state rights." The newspaper reported that "a popular subscription, conducted by leading citizens of southeastern Mississippi, was launched for a defense fund." The jury, of course, did not convict. See *Pittsburgh Courier*, May 1, 1943.
25. *The Tragedy of Lynohing*, 97.
26. Op. cit., 59.
27. In the period of early Reconstruction Judge Humphrey of Alabama expressed the fundamental economic purpose of the ruling class: "I believe," he said, "in case of a return to the Union, we would receive political cooperation so as to secure the management of that labor by those who were slaves. There is really no difference, in my opinion, whether we hold them as absolute slaves or obtain their labor by some other method." Quoted by W. E. DuBois, *Blaok Reconstruction*, New York, 1935, 140.

    Again Mrs. Ames is in point: "This peace and friendship, based on a recognition of any respect for a caste system, is the basis of good race relations. Negroes, undisturbed in the philosophical acceptance of their 'present capacity' in a white society, go along unharmed and unlynched." Op. cit., 53.
28. "Two of the 1930 mob victims were innocent of crime, (they were not even accused), and there is grave doubt of the guilt of eleven others. In six of these eleven cases there is considerable doubt as to just what crimes, if any, were committed, and in the other five, in which there is no question as to the crimes committed, there is considerable doubt as to whether the mobs got the guilty men." Arthur F. Raper, op. cit., 4–5.
29. Ibid., 36.
30. From Tuskegee Institute unpublished records on lynching.
31. "Regardless of the cause of the particular lynching there were always those who defended it by the insistence that unless Negroes were lynched, no white woman would be safe, this despite the fact that only one-sixth of the persons lynched in the last thirty years were even accused of rape. Regardless of the accusation, an example must be made of the accused Negro for the sake of womanhood." Raper, op. cit., 20. Says Walter White, "Sex and alleged sex crimes have served as the great bulwark of the lyncher." Op. cit., 55.
32. The following is a report on one lynching: "In Baker County, Ga., a Negro killed a white bootlegger at a Negro dance. When the 'right man' could not be found, two unaccused Negroes were lynched as an object lesson." See Jessie D. Ames, op. cit., 66.
33. *The Tragedy of Lynching*, 114.
34. Walter White, op. cit., 25.
35. The following excerpts are intended to represent types of reactions for these groups: "It was the average man," declares *The Maoon Telegraph* editorially, "who took the vicious Negro, James Irwin, from the sheriff and mutilated and lynched him. For their crime there is not a shadow of excuse. . . . By their deed they wiped their bloody feet on society's rule of law. By their deed they lynched justice in Georgia and did almost as terrible a thing to society as did the Negro." Quoted by Arthur F. Raper, op. cit., 154.

    For a discussion of duplicity in Southern newspaper practice concerning lynching see Jessie Daniel Ames, *The Changing Character of Lynching*, (Atlanta, 1942), 51–58.
36. Among these William H. Skaggs is typical. This critic writes: "Both social and economic conditions in the South are conducive to propagation of crime. Punishment alone will not prevent crime, so long as the economic and social causes remain. . . . "The revival of lynching after the (Civil War) was caused by economic conditions; the claim that it was for the protection of white women was an afterthought." *Southern Oligarchy*, 309, 319.
37. "Mob-law . . . struck . . . at the sensitive pocket of the business interests of the county. . . . It was just at the beginning of the cotton picking season, when labor of every sort was much needed, Negro labor especially. It will not do to frighten away all the Negroes. . . . Some of the officials and citizens of Statesboro got together, appointed extra marshals, and gave notice that there were to be no more whippings, and the mob-spirit disappeared." Ray S. Baker, op cit., 188.

38. "At Scooba, Mississippi, where a double lynching occurred, the two men reported to have organized and engineered the mob from start to finish were leading people in the community and prominently identified with the local church, school and other community activities.

"In every community where lynching occurred in 1930 there were some people who openly justified what had been done. All walks of life were represented among the apologists: judges, prosecuting attorneys, lawyers, business men, doctors, preachers, teachers." Arthur F. Raper, op. cit., 11,19. As an example of studied justification for lynching among the better class, see also David L. Cohn, *God Shakes Creation*, (Harper and Brothers, 1935), 92 ff. Here one may observe with what alfish art the case for lynching is built up; and how pointedly lynchers and those who, like this writer, provide the rationale of lynching, direct their antagonism against colored people as a whole rather than against any allegedly offending Negro person.

39. Op. cit., 438.
40. cf. Jennings Perry, "The Other South—the Unknown South," *The New York Times Magazine*, September, 3, 1944.

Race, Crime, and the Disproportionality Debate

As noted in the first section, race and crime has been a topic of interest for more than a century. For much of that period, there has been discussion as to what theories best explain offending among ethnic/racial groups. At the beginning of the century, biology was considered the most important factor; while during the mid-1940s, the University of Chicago conducted large-scale community studies that challenged such suppositions. Between these two periods, a variety of scholars began to incorporate race discrimination as a potential explanatory factor (Du Bois 1899, 1904; Sellin 1928, 1935; Johnson 1941). As outlined in the Preface, in successive decades, scholars continued to research and debate the influence of race.

During the 1980s and 1990s, scholars began to openly debate whether the over representation (also referred to as disproportionality) of racial minorities (particularly African Americans), was the product of racial discrimination or other factors. From this debate emerged two schools of thought. On the one side, scholars believed that the continuing over representation of racial minorities at all stages of the criminal justice system was an indication that discrimination was present in the system (Mann 1993). This became known as the discrimination thesis (DT). On the other side, scholars believed that the continuing overrepresentation of racial minorities was not a product of discrimination, but could be better accounted for by the frequency and nature of the offenses being committed by them (Wilbanks 1987). Those who followed this perspective adhered to the no discrimination thesis (NDT). Until the mid-1990s, the thinking was that you were either on one side of the fence or the other.

In 1996, Samuel Walker, Cassia Spohn, and Miriam De Lone, created the discrimination-disparity continuum, which provided a new way of looking at the DT/NDT conundrum (Walker, Spohn, and De Lone 1996). Moving left to right, on the one end of the continuum was systematic discrimination which suggested that there was discrimination at all stages and at all times in the criminal justice system. This was followed by institutionalized discrimination which suggested "[r]acial and ethnic disparities in [criminal justice] outcomes that are the result of the application of racially neutral factors such as prior criminal record, employment status, demeanor, etc." (Walker et al. 1996, p. 16). Contextual discrimination suggests that discrimination occurs in the criminal justice system in certain contexts. Such contexts include: regional variations, certain crimes, and victim-offender relationships (Walker et al. 1996). The fourth point on the continuum is reserved for individual acts of discrimination. Those who adhere to this line of thought believe that while there is discrimination in the criminal justice system, it is only carried out on an individual basis. Finally at the far end of the continuum is pure justice. Adherents to this thinking believe that there is no discrimination in the criminal justice system. As one can easily see, to some, the discrimination-disparity continuum created middle ground for the debate.

Today, the DT/NDT debate rages on most fervently in the racial profiling issue. As is noted later in Section IV, the heart of the debate is whether the over representation of African Americans and Latinos in traffic stops is a product of discrimination or whether African Americans and Latinos are stopped because they worse drivers than whites.

To provide further context on the debate, we include four chapters that provide contrasting viewpoints. The first chapter by noted criminologist Alfred Blumstein provides one of the benchmark studies which sought to determine how much of the over representation of Blacks in American prisons is explained by the frequency and nature of their arrests (Blumstein 1982). While Blumstein's chapter suggests that most of the disparity can be explained by such factors, he notes that a portion cannot. In addition to discrimination, he points to other avenues which can potentially explain this unexplained portion. Interestingly, an update of Blumstein's work showed that, a decade later, even more of the disparity in prison was unexplained by Black offending patterns (see Blumstein 1993). The second chapter is by two other noted criminologists, Ruth Peterson and John Hagan. Their chapter discusses what has often been considered anomalous findings in the race and crime research. For example, in past years, when scholars found that blacks were treated more leniently than whites, it was thought to be an exceptional circumstance. A closer examination, however, revealed that, in some instances, this was the case because black life was devalued in comparison to white life. Therefore, only in cases where there were interracial offenses would blacks be severely punished. Thus, the chapter argues for the contextualization of anomalous findings. Without using such an approach, certain findings will likely seem out of line with conventional wisdom.

During the 1980s and 1990s, conservative criminologists such as John DiLulio moved forward the NDT position by speaking out about the black and Hispanic "super predators" (his term) who were terrorizing inner city residents. In this chapter, DiLulio's arguments are illustrative of the types of arguments that were espoused during the period. In line with DiLulio's arguments, the chapter by DeLisi and Regoli (1999) examines several propositions related to the DT. More specifically, they look to see if discrimination exists in the following areas: police discretion, arrests, incarceration rate differentials, racial victimization, and the war on drugs. According to their analysis of several data sources, they found no support for the DT.

While there have been no definitive studies eliminating any of the perspectives, the chapters in this section are meant to simply serve as a starting point for understanding the debate.

References

Blumstein, A. 1982. On the racial disproportionality of the United States' prison populations. *Journal of Criminal Law & Criminology* 73: 1259–81.

Blumstein, A. 1993. Racial Disproportionality of U.S. Prison Populations Revisited. *University of Colorado Law Review* 63. Retrieved from Lexis-Nexis database on August 25, 2002.

Delisi, M., and Regoli, B. 1999. Race, conventional crime, and criminal justice: The declining importance of skin color. *Journal of Criminal Justice* 27: 549–57.

Du Bois, W. E. B. 1899/1996. *The Philadelphia Negro: A social study.* Philadelphia: The University of Pennsylvania Press.

Du Bois, W. E. B. ed. 1904. Some notes on Negro crime, particularly in Georgia. Atlanta: Atlanta University Press.

Johnson, G. 1941. The Negro and crime. *Annals of the American Academy of Political and Social Sciences* 217: 93–104.

Mann, C. R. 1993. *Unequal justice: A question of color.* Bloomington: Indiana University Press.

Sellin, T. 1928. The Negro criminal: A statistical note. *Annals of the American Academy of Political and Social Sciences* 140: 52–64.

Sellin, T. 1935. Race prejudice in the administration of justice. *American Journal of Sociology* 61: 212–17.

Wilbanks, W. 1987. *The myth of a racist criminal justice system.* CA: Brooks/Cole.

5

On the Racial Disproportionality of United States' Prison Populations

Alfred Blumstein

1. The Problem of Racial Disproportionality in Prisons

One of the most distressing and troublesome aspects of the operation of the criminal justice system in the United States is the severe disproportionality between blacks and whites in the composition of prison populations. Although blacks comprise roughly one-eighth of the population, they represent about one-half of the prison population. Thus, the race-specific incarceration rates (the ratio of prisoners to population within each racial group) are grossly disproportionate. This disproportionality has been a source of major concern, largely because it suggests the possibility of gross injustice in the criminal justice system.

The racial differences in imprisonment are reflected in Table 5.1, which presents demographic-specific incarceration rates (in units of prisoners per 100,000 persons within each indicated demographic group) in state prisons (not including federal prisons or local jails) for blacks and whites and their total.[1] This table highlights the great sensitivity of incarceration rates to the demographic variables of sex and age as well as race. The group with the highest incarceration rate, black males in their twenties, suffer an incarceration rate that is twenty-five times that of the total population. On any given day, one can expect to find over three percent of that group in state prisons. In view of the relatively low likelihood of imprisonment generally (about one person per 800 of the total population is in a state prison on any day), finding as many as one person out of thirty-three from any demographic group in prison is strikingly high and represents a source of considerable concern.[2]

Combining this very large incarceration rate for blacks (and especially for the young black males) with a gross disproportionality of about seven to one between black and white incarceration rates raises a serious moral challenge. These figures generate a deep concern that the disproportionality may be a consequence of profound racial discrimination within the criminal justice process. Indeed, that concern was reflected in a letter[5] that Alan Breed, the Director of the National Institute of Corrections, circulated widely in convening a seminar to address these issues. In his letter, Breed asked "whether a democratic society can continue to tolerate the flagrant racism apparently demonstrated"[6] by the racial disproportionality of prison populations. Dunbaugh[7] and Christianson[8] invoke the existence of the racial disproportionality as providing evidence of the "racism" and "discrimination"

Table 5.1 Demographic-Specific Incarceration Rates[a] in U.S. State Prisons[b]

Demographic Group	Total[c]	White	Black	Black/White Ratio
Total Population	124	72	493	6.9
Males	233	142	1,012	7.1
Males 20–29	755	425	3,068	7.2

[a]The "demographic-specific incarceration rate" is the ratio of prisoners in the indicated demographic group to the population within that demographic group, in prisoners per 100,000 population.

[b]The estimates of state prisoners within each demographic group is derived from a survey of state prisoners conducted in 1979 by the Bureau of Justice Statistics.[3] The estimates of the population within each demographic group are obtained from the United States Bureau of the Census.[4]

[c]The totals for both prisoners and population are based only on black and white groups. Other races are omitted from the calculations.

in the criminal justice system. Christianson and Dehais[9] conclude that "it is likely that racial discrimination in the criminal justice process may be a significant factor in determining why blacks are sent to prison so much more than whites."[10]

If the racial disproportionality in prisons is directly attributable to criminal justice officials' discrimination on the basis of race, a massive legal and political effort should be mobilized to redress that evil. If, however, the disproportionality results predominantly from some legally relevant difference between the races, such as a corresponding differential involvement in crime, then the charge of "racism" would not be justified. Indeed, it could be more harmful than helpful. The charge would wrongly strain even further the already troubled race relations in U.S. society. Perhaps most important, directing attention to a secondary issue rather than to the primary issue may well leave the primary problem unaddressed. This chapter explores the racial disproportionality of prison populations to discern, in at least a preliminary way, the degree to which it is likely to have emerged as a consequence of racial discrimination in the criminal justice system compared to the alternative explanation that the racial disproportionality might have emerged as a consequence of disproportionate involvement in criminal activity, and particularly in the kind of criminal activity that is most likely to lead to imprisonment and to longer sentences.

The sex ratio in prisons, for example, is far more disproportionate even than the race ratio. Ninety-six percent of prisoners are male and only four percent are female.[11] As a result, the sex-specific incarceration rates are in the ratio of twenty-four to one, more than three times the ratio between the races. Very few people, however, would argue that this disproportionality results primarily from discrimination against males (or in favor of females, even though there might well be some degree of such discrimination). It is generally accepted that males do engage in a disproportionately larger amount of crime and especially of the more serious crimes. If it is true that the very large disproportionality of males in prison compared to females fairly reflects their greater propensity to engage in serious criminal activities, then it would be unreasonable to argue that the disproportionality is unjust or discriminatory. The differential involvement might reflect sex differences in socialization, in the economic demands they face, or in other "causal factors" associated with male criminality that could explain their different propensity to commit crime. If the differential representation in prison were fully explained by the differential involvement in crime, and if one were concerned about the prison disproportionality, then one would have to focus on the causes of the differential involvement in crime rather than on discrimination in the criminal justice system as the primary means for reducing the disproportionate representation in prison.

It is fully as important—perhaps even more so in view of the inflammatory potential of the issue—that the factors associated with the racial disproportionality in prison are responsibly identified. If blacks are relatively more involved in crimes as compared to whites, and if this difference is most pronounced in the more serious crimes of homicide and robbery, then it is important to discern how much of the differential incarceration is attributable to this differential involvement. These crimes do have a greater risk of apprehension and conviction (in part at least because of the ability to develop and identify suspects). Also because these crimes are viewed by society as being the more serious, persons convicted of these offenses are more likely to go to prison and to receive more severe sentences.

II. Isolation of Discrimination Effects from Other Factors Influencing Prison Populations

Ideally, a pure test for discrimination within the criminal justice system would involve finding pairs of cases that are identical except for the race of the defendant. One might then process them through the criminal justice system in parallel, and compare the consequences of that processing. Because such controlled experiments are typically not possible, other means must be used. Some investigators have used statistical techniques, such as multiple regression analysis, that control for crime type and other case and offender attributes, and seek to discern whether a detectable effect is attributable to the race variable (i.e., whether there is a statistically significant coefficient associated with the offender's race in the presence of the other relevant variables). The issue is complicated by the fact that race is correlated with other possibly relevant variables (e.g., employment status) which might legitimately enter a sentencing decision for reasons other than racial discrimination.

In one review of twenty such studies, Hagan[12] concluded that "while there may be evidence of differential sentencing, knowledge of extra-legal offender characteristics [of which race was a principal one] contributes relatively little to our ability to predict judicial dispositions."[13] Somewhat different findings have emerged from the work of Lizotte,[14] who found that the provision of bail (and hence, economic status) had a significant influence on sentencing outcome, but that black laborers fared somewhat better than white laborers.

A review of these studies indicates the complexity of the question and the difficulty of using such statistical approaches to measure the presence—let alone the magnitude—of discrimination. The absence of an effect in the aggregate could be a result of mutually compensating discrimination, some of which may help a black suspect and some of which may penalize him. Discrimination at early stages of the criminal justice process could well mask discrimination at later stages. Much richer statistical models and individually based longitudinal data through the various processing stages of the criminal justice system will be required to be able to estimate through such statistical approaches the nature and magnitude of discrimination in the criminal justice process.

Another approach to this issue is through consideration of the consequences on prison populations of the racially differential involvement in arrest. If there were no racially differential treatment of arrestees anywhere in the criminal justice system after arrest—including prosecution, conviction, commitment to prison, and time served—then one would expect to find the racial distribution of prisoners who were sentenced for any particular crime type to be the same as the racial distribution of persons arrested for that crime type. Thus, for example, if there were no discrimination after arrest, one would expect the black fraction of persons arrested for murder. Then, the expected black fraction in prison in the absence of post-arrest discrimination can be estimated by aggregating over the various crime types based on their relative presence in prison.

A few symbols will help clarify the formula. B_j denotes the fraction of persons arrested for crime type j who are black, and F_j represents the fraction of prisoners who are serving time for crime type j. If there were no racial discrimination after arrest, one would expect that a fraction $R_j = B_jF_j$ of the prisoners will be prisoners who are black and are sentenced for crime type j. Then, by summing up the crime types represented in prison, R ($= S_jR_j$) is the expected fraction of all the prisoners who would be black if there were no discrimination after arrest.

This approach assumes that the crime-type distribution in prison, F_j, does not itself result from a discriminatory process, i.e., that it reflects the frequency of arrest, the probability of imprisonment given arrest, and the time served given imprisonment for each particular kind of crime, and that these parameters emerge as a result of a process that is not in itself racially biased. Thus, this assumption would be challenged by those who believe that the punishment for murder or robbery (say, in terms of the expected person-years of prison per arrest) is unduly severe *because* these crime types involve a disproportionate number of blacks—rather than because of the relative ease of conviction and the perceived seriousness of the crime itself.[15]

Thus, if the race ratios of arrests based on crime type (the B_j's) and the crime-type distribution in prison (the F_j's) are known, an estimate may be made of the expected racial distribution in prison (R is the expected black fraction) in the absence of discrimination subsequent to arrest. The degree to which R calculated in this way approximates the actual black fraction in prison is an indication of the degree to which the black disproportionality in prison derives from the racially differential involvement in arrest rather than from post-arrest discrimination.

The distribution of offense types in prison (the value of F_j) is available from a survey of state prison inmates.[16] The survey recorded for each of the state prison inmates in the sample the most serious offense for which he was serving time in prison. In that distribution, presented here as Table 5.2, it is seen that the three most common offenses are robbery, burglary, and murder. Their presence reflects a combination of considerations: numbers of arrests (high for burglary), probability of arrest leading to imprisonment (especially high for murder and robbery), and the time served in prison (highest for murder).

The corresponding data on the race distribution in arrests based on crime type (the values of B_j) can also be obtained from official statistics. The 1974 *Uniform Crime Reports* provides the number of white and black[17] adult (eighteen or over) arrests for each of these crime types.[18]

These two groups of numbers provide the basis for developing Table 5.3, which indicates for each of the crime types the number of white arrests, the number of black arrests, their sum (the "black + white arrests"), and the black arrest percentage (the percentage of black arrests to the total arrests). Then, if there were no other sources of differential treatment after arrest within the criminal justice system because of race, the expected proportion of total prisoners who are black and are imprisoned for each of the crime types (R_j) is obtained by multiplying the black arrest percentage for that crime

Table 5.2 Distribution of Offenses among State Prisoners: 1974 Survey

Crime Type	Number	Percent
TOTAL	187,500	100
VIOLENT		
Murder and Attempted Murder	25,000	13.8
Manslaughter	8,200	4.4
Sexual Assault	9,600	5.1
Robbery	42,400	22.6
Assault (other than sexual)	9,000	4.8
PROPERTY		
Burglary	33,800	18.0
Larceny	12,200	6.5
Auto Theft	3,200	1.7
Forgery, Fraud or Embezzlement	8,100	4.3
DRUG (major)	8,000	4.3
OTHER	27,200	14.5

Table 5.3 Estimation of Black Percentage in Prison, Assuming No Post-Arrest Discrimination

Crime Type	White Arrests	Black Arrests	Black + White Arrests	Black Arrest Percentage (B_j)	Offense Distribution Among State Prisoners (F_j)	Expected Percentage of Prisoners (by crime type) that are black (R_j)
VIOLENT						
Murder and Attempted Murder	4,457	6,407	10,864	59.0	13.8	8.1
Manslaughter	1,468	417	1,885	22.1	4.4	1.0
Sexual Assault	6,339	5,865	12,204	48.1	5.1	2.5
Robbery	22,728	37,043	59,771	62.0	22.6	14.0
Assault (other than sexual)	186,831	117,499	38.6	4.8	1.9	
PROPERTY						
Burglary	94,339	48,621	142,960	34.0	18.0	6.1
Larceny	225,710	118,848	344,558	34.5	6.5	2.2
Auto Theft	25,784	14,892	40,676	36.6	1.7	0.6
Forgery, Fraud or Embezzlement	80,236	56,833	117,069	31.5	4.3	1.4
Drug	239,673	75,276	314,949	23.9	4.3	1.0
Other	2,022,306	741,046	2,763,352	26.8	14.5	3.9
TOTAL						42.7 = R

type (B_j) by the fraction of the prison population associated with that crime type (F_j). This is the percentage indicated in the last column of Table 5.3. Thus, for example, since 59.0 percent of those arrested for murder or attempted murder are black, and since 13.8 percent of all the persons in prison were convicted of murder or attempted murder, then, if there was no post-arrest discrimination, we would expect 59.9 percent of the 13.8 percent—or 8.1 percent (the value shown in the last column of Table 5.3)—of all prisoners to be blacks imprisoned for murder or attempted murder.

Summing these percentages over the crime types provides an estimate (R) that 42.7 percent of the 1974 prison population was *expected* to be black as a result simply of the differences in arrest involvement, even if there were *no* race-related differential treatment of arrestees throughout the rest of the criminal justice system. This value of 42.7 percent is somewhat below the ratio of 48.3 percent that is reported in the 1974 survey as the black fraction of the white and black 1974 prison populations,[19] but it is certainly much closer to the actual percent black than the expected rates based merely on the racial distribution of the general population.

In order to indicate the fraction of the racial disproportionality in prison that is accounted for by the disproportionate representation in arrests, the following ratio may be formulated:

$$X = \frac{\text{ratio of expected black-to-white incarceration rates based only on arrest disproportionality}}{\text{ratio of black-to-white incarceration rates actually observed}}$$

If all the prison disproportionality were accounted for by the differential arrest involvement, X would be 1.0. We can let Q represent the *actual* black percentage in prison and R represent the *expected* black percentage in prison under the post-arrest discrimination-free assumption (as calculated above). For convenience of development, we define the following variables:

P = total number of black and white prisoners
N = total population
b = black percentage of the total population.
Then, the ratio X can be written as a percent as follows:

$$X = \frac{\text{expected (black incarceration rate/white incarceration rate)}}{\text{actual (black incarceration rate/white incarceration rate)}} \times 100$$

or that:

$$X = \frac{\frac{RP}{bN} / \frac{(100-R)P}{(100-b)N}}{\frac{QP}{bN} / \frac{(100-Q)P}{100-b)N}} \times 100$$

From that formula X = 100 (R(100 – Q)/(100 – R)Q). Applying this formula to the present case, where R = 42.7 percent, and Q = 48.3 percent, we find that X = 80.0 percent, indicating that 80 percent of the actual racial disproportionality in incarceration rates is accounted for by the differential involvement in arrest. Thus, racial differences in arrests alone account for the bulk of the racial differences in incarceration.

III. Accounting for the Other Twenty Percent

The question remains about the nature of the remaining 20 percent. Even though this is a small component of the total racial disproportionality in prison, it does not represent a small amount of differential imprisonment. In Table 5.1, the total-population black/white incarceration-rate ratio is indicated as 6.9. Twenty percent of this figure is a ratio of 1.4 that remains to be explained. Thus, even though 1.4 is small compared to 6.9, it does represent an excess of 40 percent in black incarceration rate beyond that accounted for by arrest. In other terms, among the 187,500 persons in state prisons in 1974, the difference between 42.7 percent and 48.3 percent is 10,500 prisoners to be accounted for on the basis of considerations other than differential involvement in arrest. This is certainly not a trivial number of prisoners. If it were all attributable to discrimination, that would still be a distressing level of discrimination.

Legitimate race-related variation in process through the criminal justice system that has not been accounted for in the calculations displayed in Table 5.3 may account for part of the remaining 20 percent. For example, just as blacks are disproportionately represented in the most serious offense *types*, it *may be* that they are also disproportionately represented among the more serious versions *within* each of the offense types (e.g., in the *stranger-to-stranger* homicides, in the *armed* robberies, etc.). Further exploration is needed on these issues of intra-crime-type distribution of seriousness.

Black offenders may also individually accumulate longer criminal records; this could occur, for example, even in the absence of discrimination, if the period during which they continue to be criminally active were longer. The criminal justice system treats more harshly those offenders who have prior convictions. This possibility is suggested by the observation that the peak incarceration rate for blacks occurs at a later age than for whites. *If* length of prior offense record is a significant factor distinguishing whites and blacks, then it would be important to discern whether that difference might be attributable to the lingering effects of discrimination in earlier years, even if discrimination is not a significant factor currently. Research on the nature of individual patterns of offending, or "criminal careers," is needed to shed light on these issues.

There are also aspects of discrimination in the criminal justice process which might work in the opposite direction, resulting in black offenders receiving more favorable treatment than white offenders. LaFree,[20] for example, has shown the importance in one city of the race of the victim in determining the outcome of rape cases involving black defendants. Because less certain and less severe punishment results when the victim is black, and because the victims of black offenders more often *are* black, this could result in black defendants being treated *less* severely than white defendants. Thus, this act of discrimination against black *victims* could result in discrimination in favor of the black *offenders*. In LaFree's study, the race of the victim strongly influenced the punishment received by blacks who were accused of rape.[21] Since a prior relationship between the offender and victim is sometimes taken as a mitigating factor, and since such relationships are more likely to occur in intra-racial than in inter-racial situations, it is possible that part of the influence of the victim's race could also be reflecting consideration of a prior relationship. In LaFree's study, the leniency displayed in intraracial rapes were approximately balanced by the harshness displayed in the inter-racial ones, and so the net effect on black offenders approximately balanced out.[22] The complex interaction among these various factors highlight the difficulty of isolating with precision all the factors that could be contributing to racially different treatment within the criminal justice system.

Another factor that would favor black defendants could result from the regional differences in the imposition of sanctions. Blacks, for example, comprise a larger fraction of city arrests and a relatively smaller proportion of rural arrests. In 1980, arrests for the violent crime types (murder, forcible rape, robbery, and aggravated assault) were composed of 48.7 percent blacks in the cities, 30.4 percent in the suburban counties, and 25.1 percent in the rural counties.[23] The situation is similar for the property crimes (burglary, larceny, and vehicle theft), where the corresponding ratios are 32.5 percent, 22.6 percent, and 13.4 percent.[24] If punishment is the least severe in the urban areas and the most severe in the rural areas, then, even in the absence of racial discrimination *within* any of these regions, aggregation across the regions would provide an appearance of greater leniency toward blacks compared to whites arrested for the same offense.

An arguable but understandable basis for differential treatment might also be associated with the degree to which prosecutors or judges attempt to predict an offender's recidivism on the basis of his education or other socioeconomic factors that are often associated with an offender's ability to function effectively within the legitimate economy. Because many such indicators are correlated with race, they could also be contributing to the remaining 20 percent of the disproportionality.

Even after taking into account all factors that are at least arguably legitimate and that could explain the racial disproportionality in prison, it would certainly not be surprising to find a residual effect that is explainable only as racial discrimination. The literature on discrimination and prejudice[25] suggests that such an effect will exist, and could probably be discerned with a sufficiently sensitive instrument. The previous analysis by no means argues that no discrimination exists, but it does indicate that the predominant fraction of the racial disproportionality in prison is attributable to differential involvement in arrest, leaving a much smaller residue that may be attributable to racial discrimination.

IV. Time Trends and Sensitivity Analysis

The previous analytical results showing that 80 percent of the racial disproportionality in prison is attributable to differential involvement in arrest were based on a particular year's prison population and arrest distribution. In order to guard against the possibility that 1974 may have been an anomalous year in some respects or that the situation that prevailed in 1974 has changed appreciably since then, it is desirable to include other years in the analysis. This should be done to assure that the results do not hinge on special conditions in 1974, and also to detect changes that may have occurred since then.

Fortunately, the Bureau of Justice Statistics, through the Census Bureau, conducted a second survey in 1979[26] similar to the one in 1974. Table 5.4 lists the distributions of crime types of the prisoners interviewed in the two surveys. Despite the fact that the number of persons in state prisons increased by 46 percent from 187,500 in 1974 to 274,600 in 1979, the distribution across the offenses is strikingly stable. As a sensitivity check, the 1979 crime-type distribution could be used to estimate the expected fraction R of prisoners who would be black based on the 1974 race distribution of arrestees developed in Table 5.3. Furthermore, this same approach could be applied to the arrests for any year, using the two years' estimates of the crime-type distribution in prison (the F_j's) and the arrest ratios obtained from the *Uniform Crime Reports* (the B_j's) for each year. Thus, two estimates of R are obtained for each year, one based on the 1974 distribution of crime types in prison and one based on the 1979 distribution. These results are shown in Figure 5.1.

Figure 5.1 certainly reflects the fact that the changes in the distribution of crime types in prison between 1974 and 1979 were of no significance in influencing the racial distribution of offenders. The two distributions shown in Table 5.4 are sufficiently close that the results are insensitive to any differences that do exist. Figure 5.1 also indicates a slight downward trend in the expected black fraction in prison, but that trend might be an artifact of changes in the arrest reporting process. Reporting on arrests to the *Uniform Crime Reports* is less complete than is the more familiar reporting of "crimes known to the police." During the period 1970 to 1979, as shown in Table 5.5, the jurisdictions reporting represented a population that ranged from 142,000,000 in 1970 to 206,000,000 in 1978 with a striking drop in 1974[27] to 125,000 and a slight drop in 1979 to 204,000,000. If the jurisdictions that were included for only a portion of the decade (probably the smaller communities) had disproportionately white populations, then their participation in the later years may account for the observed slight decline from 1971 in the expected fraction of prisoners who are black.

The principal observation from Figure 5.1 is that the expected fraction of black prisoners, R, is very stable, ranging from 44 percent to 39 percent over the ten years. The average value of R over the ten years, and averaged over the two surveys is 42.1 percent. This figure can be compared with 47.7

Table 5.4 Percent Distribution of Offenses among State Prisoners 1974 and 1979 Surveys

Crime Type	1974	1979
VIOLENT		
Murder and Attempted Murder	13.8	13.6
Manslaughter	4.4	4.0
Sexual Assault	5.1	6.2
Robbery	22.6	24.9
Assault (other than sexual)	4.8	6.4
PROPERTY		
Burglary	18.0	18.1
Larceny	6.5	4.8
Auto Theft	1.7	1.9
Forgery, Fraud or Embezzlement	4.3	4.4
DRUG (major)	4.3	5.7
OTHER	14.5	10.1
TOTALS	100.0	100.0
NUMBER OF PRISONERS	187,.500	274,.564

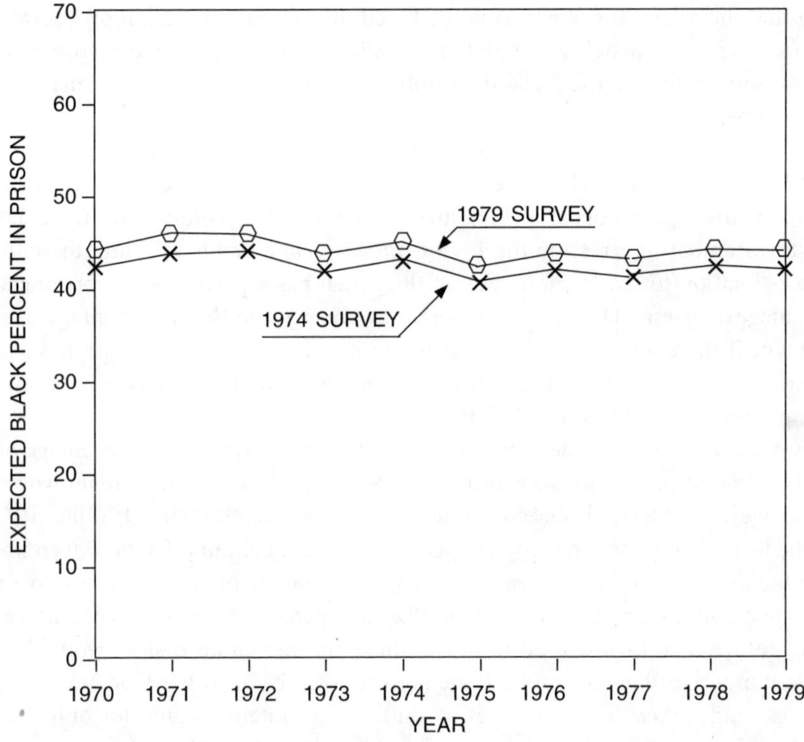

Fig. 5.1 Expected Black Percent in Prison Based on Race Ratios in Arrest and Discrimination-Free Processing after Arrest.

percent, which is the actual black fraction in prison the Bureau of Justice Statistics reported for 1978, and 47.4 percent reported for 1979.[28] Thus, here again, the expected black fraction based on arrest ratios accounts for 80 percent of the racial disproportionality in the actual prison populations.

V. Crime-Type-Specific Rates

The previous analyses, which examined the aggregate racial composition in prison, found that 80 percent of the black disproportionality was attributable to differential involvement in arrest and

Table 5.5 Population in Police Jurisdictions Reporting Arrests to the Uniform Criminal Reports

Year	Reporting Populations (millions)
1970	142
1971	147
1972	151
1973	145
1974	125
1975	169
1976	173
1977	197
1978	206
1979	204

recognized that the other 20 percent could be based on some combination of discrimination and legitimate factors not adequately addressed in the estimates. A sharper focus on some of these issues might result from exploring the racial distribution in arrest and in imprisonment for each individual crime type.

Preliminary data on the racial distribution of prisoners based on crime type were made available from the 1979 inmate survey. These are presented in the first two columns of Table 5.6, using the crime-type classification reported in that survey. The next two columns of Table 5.6 report the corresponding number of arrests in the 1978 *Uniform Crime Reports.*[29] Thus, these four columns permit the estimation for each crime type of the actual black percentage of prisoners and of the black percentage of arrests. This latter number is also the *expected* black percentage of prisoners for that crime type if there is no post-arrest discrimination. These actual and expected black fractions in prison are also displayed in Table 5.6. It can be seen that, for all crime types but one,[30] the black fraction in prison is larger than the black fraction in arrest.

These two columns provide the basic data to enable us to estimate the percentage of the crime-type-specific racial disproportionality in prison that is explained by differential involvement in arrest. For this, we use the formula developed in Section II, $X = 100\,R\,(100 - Q)/(100 - R)Q$, where the values in the formula now are crime-type-specific.[31] The last column of Table 5.6 contains for each crime type the complement of X, the racial disproportionality in prison that arrest does not explain. The aggregate amount unexplained is the familiar 20.5 percent. Some of the crime types are composed of aggregates, and their composition is sufficiently ambiguous that we would be reluctant to attribute very much to their structure; these are the offenses of "other violent," "other property," "public order," and "other." These offenses of ambiguous content account for only 14.2 percent of the prison population, and so a focus on the other defined offenses, whose definition at arrest and in prison is less ambiguous, does account for 86 percent of the prison population.

It is interesting to list these offenses in order of the fraction of disproportionality remaining unexplained by arrest alone:

homicide	2.8%
aggravated assault	5.2%
robbery	15.6%
aggregate	20.5%
forcible rape	26.3%
burglary	33.1%
larceny/auto theft	45.6%
drugs	48.9%

This ordering suggests that the magnitude of this unexplained disproportionality seems directly related to the discretion permitted or used in handling each of the offenses, which tends to be related to offense seriousness—the less serious the offense, the greater the amount of the disproportionality in prison that must be explained on grounds other than differences in arrest. Homicide, aggravated assault, and robbery, three of the most serious offenses, which together account for a majority (51.1 percent) of the prison population, display very small values of disproportionality unaccounted for (2.8 percent, 15.6 percent, and 5.2 percent respectively). Arrest accounts for a much smaller fraction of the disproportionality, however, for the more discretionary offenses of forcible rape (26.3 percent), burglary (33.1 percent), larceny and auto theft (45.6 percent), and drug offenses (48.9 percent). Thus, the magnitude of the disproportionality unaccounted for seems strongly related to the degree to which discretion regarding prosecution and imprisonment is used: serious offenses require vigorous prosecution and certain and severe sentences, whereas the less serious offenses permit more

Table 5.6 Comparison of Crime-Type-Specific Percentages of Blacks in Prison and in Arrests

Crime Type	Prisoners Black	Prisoners White	Arrests Black	Arrests White	Crime Type Distribution in Prison (Fj)	Black Percentage Prisoners (Actual =Qj)	Black Percentage Arrests[a] (Expected =Rj)	Percent Dispro-portionality Unexplained (100-Xj)
Murder and Non-negligent Manslaughter	24,577	22,399	8,413	7,882	17.7	52.3	51.6	2.8
Forcible Rape	6,261	4,852	11,134	11,709	4.2	56.3	48.7	26.3
Robbery	41,022	26,003	51,401	38,604	25.2	61.2	57.1	15.6
Aggravated Assault	9,193	12,516	85,236	123,210	8.2	42.3	41.0	5.2
Other Violent	2,924	3,310	237,932	370,621	2.3	46.9	39.1	27.3
Burglary	20,383	27,765	74,676	152,396	18.1	42.3	32.9	33.1
Larceny/Auto Theft	8,678	8,916	235,519	445,710	6.6	49.3	34.6	45.6
Other Property	7,313	13,239	127,464	240,986	7.7	35.6	34.6	4.3
Drugs	5,966	9,141	110,518	331,629	5.7	39.5	25.0	48.9
Public Order	4,028	6,413	81,331	183,938	3.9	38.6	30.7	29.5
Other	234	592	452,870	889,380	.3	28.3	33.7	–28.7
Total	130,579	135,146				49.14	43.45[b]	20.5

[a] The black percentage of arrests is also the *expected* black fraction in prison if there is no post-arrest discrimination.
[b] The *expected* black percentage in prison, 43.45 percent, is calculated by the method used in Table 5.3.

room for discretion and the weighing of considerations other than the offense itself. These other considerations could include socioeconomic considerations like employment which are correlated with race. Also, in these relatively less serious offenses, greater weight is likely to be given to the offender's prior record, and the length of the prior record could be related to race, perhaps because the duration of criminal careers may be related to race, or perhaps because of residual effects of discrimination from an earlier time. And, of course, these other considerations that enter in the decisions in the relatively less serious offenses could also include the illegitimate consideration of race itself.

Much of the earlier research,[32] and especially earlier litigation, on the subject of racial discrimination in the criminal justice system was focused on capital punishment, which is associated with the most serious offenses. Perhaps because of the intensity of those prior efforts, the offenses at that high end of the seriousness scale do not appear to offer major potential opportunity for purging of racial discrimination that leads to imprisonment. The potential, however, does appear to be appreciably greater among the less serious offenses. Subsequent research, therefore, should focus on those offenses to discern the factors contributing to the larger percentage of blacks imprisoned for those offenses compared to the percentage arrested for them.

Clearly, whatever part of the excess black imprisonment in these offenses that is due to discrimination should be eliminated. It must be recognized, however, that accomplishing that will not result in dramatic changes in the racial composition of prisons. Black prisoners charged with drug offenses, larceny and auto theft, burglary, and rape together comprise 15.6 percent of the 1979 prison population.[33] If the black fraction of the prisoners charged with these offenses were reduced to the black fraction of arrests in each crime type, the black prisoners charged with these offenses would instead comprise 12.2 percent of the reduced prison population. Such a change would, of course, be most important to the more than 10,000 persons involved, but it would still have only a small influence on the racial mix in prisons: the black fraction of prisoners would be reduced from 49.14

percent to 47.12 percent, a reduction of only 2.02 percentage points. This small effect is a consequence of the fact that the offense types involved account for only a small fraction of the total prison population—even though they do account for a large fraction of reported crimes.

VI. Racial Differences in Arrest Vulnerability

Even if we conclude that the racial differences in prison cannot be predominantly attributable to discrimination after arrest, there could still be a strong racial difference in arrest vulnerability. Differences in arrest vulnerability, leading to inappropriately large values of the B_j's, are, of course, difficult to estimate. While demographic information such as race is reasonably easy to determine for those who the criminal justice system actually arrests and subsequently processes, it is very difficult to obtain the same information for all those who actually commit the crimes. It is well recognized, for example, that there is more police patrol in poorer, more crowded and more crime-prone neighborhoods. This difference in patrol intensity could account for some of the disproportionality in black arrest rates. That difference, however, is much more likely to affect arrests for minor offenses like disorderly conduct which involve on-sight arrests and police discretion than in the more serious cases that appear in state prisons.

To determine the degree of demographic bias in the arrest process, Michael Hindelang compared the demographic characteristics of persons the police arrested with the characteristics of offenders crime victims reported.[34] The results showed a very consistent relationship between the racial distribution reported in police arrest statistics (in the 1974 *Uniform Criminal Reports*) and that reported by victims of robbery, rape, and assault (where there was direct contact with the offender) when they were interviewed in the 1974 Victimization Survey. For robbery, the modal offense in prison, the results were virtually identical; in the National Crime Panel Victimization Survey, 62 percent of the victims reported that the robber was black, and blacks comprised 62 percent of the robbery arrestees reported in the *Uniform Criminal Reports.* For rape and aggravated assault, which together comprised 9.0 percent of the prison population (compared to 22.6 percent for robbery), there was a difference, with blacks comprising 48 percent of the arrests for rape (compared to 39 percent of the victim reports), and 41 percent of the arrests for aggravated assault (compared to 30 percent of the victim reports).[35]

These results were consistent with Hindelang's similar comparison of victim reports and arrests based on data from eight individual cities.[36] Here, the results for forcible rape and aggravated assault were very close. (For rape, whites represented 43 percent of the arrests and 40 percent of the victim reports, and for aggravated assault, whites were involved in 47 percent of the arrests and 44 percent of the victim reports.[37]) This *over*-representation of whites in arrest was even more exaggerated for robbery, where whites comprised 29 percent of the arrestees but only 19 percent of the victim reports.[38]

While these results are certainly short of definitive evidence that there is no bias in arrest, they do strongly suggest that the arrest process, whose demographics we can observe, is reasonably representative of the crime process for at least these serious crime types, and that whatever racial bias does exist in the arrest process is far less than sufficient to account for the major contribution that differential involvement in arrest makes in explaining the large disproportionality in prison incarceration rates. If there is no large arrest bias, that would leave differential involvement in crime as the principal factor contributing to the racial disproportionality in prison populations.

VII. Crime Type Emphases

The other factor contributing to the high value of the expected black percentage in prison is associated with the F_j distribution and the relatively large representation in prison of the crime types (especially homicide and robbery) for which blacks are most disproportionately arrested. It might be argued that some of the disproportionality in incarceration rates results from the fact that the criminal justice system places more emphasis on the crimes in which blacks tend to predominate, and that the system could or should do more to apprehend and punish offenders who engage in the crimes in which whites are more prevalent. Perhaps the more severe punishment imposed for the more "violent" crimes might be reduced compared to that for the property crimes, for the disproportionate involvement of blacks within the violent crimes is a significant factor in creating their disproportionate representation in prison. This argument would involve a major reconsideration of the seriousness which society attaches to the different offenses, possibly leading to a significant reordering of the severity of punishment assigned to them. The scaling work by Sellin and Wolfgang,[39] and by Rossi, Waite, Bose, and Berk,[40] and especially the more recent national survey by Wolfgang,[41] should help to illuminate that possibility. Blumstein and Cohen[42] compared the public's view of the appropriate time to be served by offense and the actual time served. Their results show a strong ordinal consistency between the two times.

More vigorous pursuit of the kinds of crimes more often associated with whites (e.g., fraud, corporate crime, white collar crime, etc.) might serve to redress the disproportionality to some degree. Such crimes, of course, are much more difficult to detect and to solve, but some additional resources could undoubtedly be applied to them. These crimes, however, represent a small fraction of prison populations. For example, fraud, embezzlement, and forgery comprise only 4 percent of the 1974 prison population and have a black arrest fraction of 31.3 percent. Thus, even if the number of whites imprisoned for these offenses were *trebled*, their proportion of the white prison population would go from about 2.75 percent to about 8 percent, certainly well short of enough white prisoners to revise in any meaningful way the racial composition of prison populations. Furthermore, it is reasonable to anticipate that intensive pursuit of those offenses would serve to deter their commission, since these offenses tend to be more carefully planned and premeditated, and so be more vulnerable to deterrence signals. Any such deterrent response is thus likely to mitigate any intended effect on the prison-population mix.

VIII. Effects of Aggregation

The research approach pursued in this chapter involves considerable aggregation across the various processing stages of the criminal justice system and over the United States as a whole. One of the benefits of such an approach is the fact that it avoids the necessity to collect the difficult and often incompatible data that account for the detailed decisions made at all the intermediate processing stages between arrest and prison. On the other hand, this approach cannot discern offsetting racial discrimination, some of which may aid a black defendant and some injure him. Thus, for example, if there were discrimination in the prosecutor's charging decision, it could be partially or fully compensated in the judge's sentencing decision or in the parole board's release decision. These offsetting effects could also result, for example, from discrimination based on the race of the victim; if the black defendant is treated leniently when the victim is black, but harshly when the victim is white, these two effects could well offset each other and mask practice that *is* racially discriminatory. The analyses considered here reflect only the *net* discrimination effect. Thus, they do not preclude the possibility of discrimination at some of the processing stages, or discrimination based on some inappropriate attributes of a case, but with those effects offset by other factors or decisions that could favor black defendants.

Similarly, the aggregation over jurisdictions represents a net national effect. Thus, to the extent that some regions may discriminate against blacks, other regions may be more lenient toward blacks. This effect, for example, could also result from rural-urban differences in sentencing patterns, if sentences in urban areas, which have a relatively larger black population, are more lenient. If that is the case, it is even possible that there could be discrimination against blacks in both urban and rural areas, but that the greater leniency in the urban areas (which would tend to benefit black defendants) could mask the discrimination which injures them. A more detailed and disaggregated analysis of the individual processing stages and jurisdictions than reported in this article should be pursued to test the degree to which compensating discriminatory effects exist.

IX. Conclusion

This chapter has explored the troubling question of the gross disproportionality between black and white incarceration rates, which stand at a ratio of more than seven to one. It was found that the differential involvement of blacks as arrestees, particularly for the offenses of homicide and robbery, which together comprise a major fraction (over 40 percent) of prison populations, accounts for 80 percent of the disproportionality between black and white incarceration rates. These observations hold generally for the race ratios in arrest and the crime-type distributions in prison that prevailed throughout the decade of the 1970's.

The remaining 20 percent of the disproportionality may be attributable to a variety of other explanations that are at least arguably legitimate, but may also reflect some unknown degree of discrimination based on race. Exploration of crime-type-specific racial distributions at arrest and in prison indicates that, as the seriousness of the offense decreases, blacks are disproportionately represented in prison. This does suggest that blacks become increasingly disadvantaged as the amount of permissible criminal-justice discretion increases, and discrimination must remain a plausible explanation for an important fraction of that effect. Other possible explanations include the greater saliency in such cases of socioeconomic considerations about the defendant, such as his employment status, and the fact that many such factors are correlated with race. Even if the relatively large racial differences in handling these offenses were totally eliminated, however, that would not result in a major shift in the racial mix of prison populations.

Certainly, so important an issue warrants far more detailed analysis, both to verify the degree to which the arrest process is indeed representative of the crime process, and also to discern any factors that might be contributing to discrimination. Such research requires studies in individual jurisdictions, much more careful tracking of individual cases longitudinally through the criminal justice system, and major emphasis on the relatively less serious offenses like drug offenses, larceny, and burglary that offer more room for discretion and thus, more opportunity for discrimination.

The results presented in this chapter certainly do not argue that discrimination is absent from the criminal justice system, or even that the amount of discrimination is negligibly small or unimportant. Nor should the results in this chapter provide an excuse for impeding any efforts to discover and to eliminate discrimination wherever it exists. The results do suggest, however, that the finding of racial disproportionality does not by itself demonstrate the existence of discrimination, and further, that attacking the discrimination in the criminal justice system to redress the disproportionality is not likely to have the desired effect on prison populations. Any significant impact on the racial mix in our prisons will have to come from addressing the factors in our society that generate the life conditions that contribute to the different involvement between the races in serious person crimes.

Notes

1. The data on age, race, and sex of the prisoners were obtained from a survey of state prison inmates conducted in 1979 by the Bureau of the Census for the U.S. Bureau of Justice Statistics. From that survey, for example, there were estimated to be 74,150 black males in their twenties in state prisons. The ratio of this number to the corresponding U.S. population (2,384,000 black males in their twenties) is the incarceration rate of 3068 per 100,000. Population data were obtained from U.S. Bureau OF Census, *1980 Census of Popularation Supplementary Report, No. PC80-31-1, Age, Sex, Race, and Spanish Origin of* THE /SC *Populations by Region, Divisions, and States: 1980* (1981) [hereinafter cited as 1980 *Census of Population Report*].

2. If one includes federal prisons and local jails, this incarceration rate would reach about 4.5 percent. Lawrence Greenfeld, in Measuring the Application and Use of Punishment, a paper presented at the American Society of Criminology meeting (Nov. 12, 1981), explored the prevalence (i.e., the fraction ever to have served) of "confinement" in a juvenile or adult prison or jail, and the racial differences in that prevalence. He found that 18.2 percent of black males would expect to serve in such an institution sometime in their lives, whereas only 2.7 percent of white males would have a similar expectation. The black/white ratio of these prevalence expectations is 6.7, fairly close to the ratio of 7.1 for the male race-specific incarceration rates shown in Table 5.1. Greenfeld also found that the confinement recidivism probability (i.e., the chance of one or more additional commitments for those once committed) was very similar for blacks and whites. This finding of major differences between the races in prevalence and very similar recidivism probabilities is consistent with the Blumstein and Graddy results found for index arrests in large U.S. cities. Blumstein & Graddy, "Prevalence and Recidivism in Index Arrests: A Feedback Model Approach," *Law & Soc'y Rev.*16 (1981–82): 265.
3. U.S. Bureau of Just. Statistics, Bureau of the Census, State Correctional Populations and Facilities, 1979—Advance Report (unpublished report) [hereinafter cited as State Correctional Populations and Facilities].
4. 1980 *Census of Population Report, supra* note 1.
5. Letter from Alan Breed (Dec. 7, 1979).
6. Id.
7. Dunbaugh, "Racially Disproportionate Rates of Incarceration in the United States," *Prison Law Monitor* 1 (1979): 205.
8. Christianson, "Our Black Prisons," *Crime & Delinq.* 27 (1981): 364.
9. Christianson, and Dehais, The Black Incarceration Rate in the United States, a Nationwide Problem, (Draft Report) (Training Program in Criminal Justice Education, Graduate School of Criminal Justice, State University of New York at Albany (August, 1980).
10. Id., 35.
11. For example, on December 31, 1979, there were 301,080 male prisoners and 12,926 female prisoners in U.S. state and federal prisons. *U.S. Dep't of Just, National Prisoner Statistics, Prisoners in State and Federal Institutions* (1979) [hereinafter cited as *Prisoners in State and Federal Institutions*].
12. Hagan,"Extra-Legal Attributes and Criminal Sentencing: An Assessment of Sociological View-point," *Law & Soc'y Rev.* 8 (1974): 357.
13. Id., 379.
14. Lizotte, "Extra-Legal Factors in Chicago's Criminal Courts: Testing the Conflict Model of Criminal Justice," *Soc. Probs.* 25 (1977): 564
15. In more technical terms, the basic assumption is that F_j and B_j are independent, so that if B_j were to increase (holding total arrests for j constant), F_j would not also increase.
16. The data were obtained from *U.S. Dep't of Just., National Prisoner Statistics Report No. SD-NPS-SR-2, Survey of Inmates of State Correctional Facilities, 1974: Advance Report (1976).* More detailed information from that survey is available in *U.S. Dep't of Just., National Prisoner Statistics Special Report No. SD-NPS-SR-4, Profile of State Prison Inmates: Sociodemographic Findings from the 1974 Survey of Inmates of State Correctional Facilities (1979)* [hereinafter cited as *1974 Profile*].
17. *U.S. Dep't of Just., Uniform Crime Reports*, 1974, 193 (1975) [hereinafter cited as *Uniform Criminal Reports*].
18. 1974 Profile, *supra* note 16, at 193. To be more precise, earlier years' arrest statistics should be used. If the distribution of time that prisoners of each crime type had already served were available, then each of the previous years' black arrest percentage should be included, weighted by the fraction of prisoners whose time served began in that year; also, an extra year should be subtracted to account for the time from arrest until the sentence begins. The arrest fractions (the values of B_j) in the major crime types are sufficiently stable from year to year that this correction is not likely to change any of the results appreciably.
19. Id., 45. There the estimated state-prison populations were 95,000 white and 88,628 black, for a black percentage of 48.3 percent.
20. LaFree, "The Effect of Sexual Stratification by Race on Official Reactions to Rape," *Am. Soc. Rev.* 45 (1980): 842.
21. Id., 851–52.
22. Id., 848.
23. *Uniform Criminal Reports* (1980), *supra* note 17; 216, 228, 240.
24. Id.
25. See, e.g., Crosby, Bromley & Saxe, "Recent Unobtrusive Studies of Black and White Discrimination and Prejudice: A Literature Review," *Psychological. Bull.* 37 (1980): 546, for a review of that literature.
26. State Correctional Populations and Facilities, *supra* note 2. The data used in Table 5.4 were taken from Table 4 of the Jan. 28, 1981 Review Draft.
27. In 1974, the Uniform Criminal Reports reporting system switched from annual police department reporting to monthly reporting, and that transition may account for the large drop in participation.
28. Prisoners in State and Federal Institutions (1978 and 1979), *supra* note 11.
29. For the crime types in the inmate survey that do not correspond to the Uniform Criminal Reports' arrest categories, arrests for "other violent" offenses were based on the Uniform Criminal Reports' categories of "other assault" and arson; "other property" were based on the sum of arrests for forgery and counterfeiting, fraud, embezzlement, and stolen property; "public order" arrests were based on the sum of arrests for vandalism, weapons offenses, and sex offenses; and "other" were based on the categories not otherwise counted.
30. The only exception is the "other" offenses; the uncertainty over the specific crime types involved, as well as the small absolute numbers, make this category of minor relevance.

31. More precisely, the formula should read $X_j = 100\ R_j\ (100 - Q_j)/(100 - R_j)\ Q_j)$, where X_j, R_j, and Q_j refer to the respective ratios for crime-type j.
32. See, e.g., Johnson, "Selective Factors in Capital Punishment," *Soc. Forces* 36 (1957): 165 (1957), and Wolfgang & Reidel, *Race,* "Judicial Discretion, and the Death Penalty," *The Annals of the Am. Acad. of Pol. and Soc. Science* 407 (1973): 119.
33. This total is derived from Table 6 for those four crime types.
34. Hindelang, "Race and Involvement in Common Law Personal Crimes," *Am. Soc. Rev.* 43 (1978): 93.
35. Id., 100.
36. M. Hindelang, *Criminal Victimization in Eight American Cities: A Descriptive Analysis of Common Theft and Assault* (1976).
37. Id., 197.
38. Id.
39. T. Sellin & M. Wolfgang, *The Measurement of Delinquency* (1964).
40. Rossi, Waite, Bose & Berk, "The Seriousness of Crime: Normative Structure and Individual Differences," *Am. Soc. Rev.* 39 (1974) 224..
41. Wolfgang, Crime and Punishment, *New York Times*, March 2, 1980, at E21, col. 2.
42. Blumstein & Cohen, "Sentencing of Convicted Offenders: An Analysis of the Public's Views," *Law & Soc. Rev.* 14 (1980): 223.

6

Changing Conceptions of Race

Toward an Account of Anomalous Findings of Sentencing Research

Ruth D. Peterson and John Hagan

Theories based on static and simplistic conceptions of the social significance of race fail to account for anomalous research findings and confuse our understanding of race-related outcomes. To substantiate this argument, an analysis is presented of the effects of changing conceptions of race and drugs on sentencing outcomes during a modern anti-drug crusade. This crusade involved a compromise between conservative and liberal impulses in which "big dealers" were identified as villains, while middle-class youth and nonwhites (but the latter only insofar as they were rarely big dealers in a racially stratified drug trade) were reconceived as victims. The results of our contextualized analysis allow us to make sense of otherwise anomalous findings and suggest that while there may be a trend toward equality in American criminal sentencing, there are also patterns of differential leniency and severity that can only be revealed when changing conceptions of race and crime are taken into account.

Conceptions of race are closely linked to the settings in which they operate. Through time and across situations, then, conceptions of race change. Failure to consider fully this variability undermines our understanding of race relations, confusing debates over the "declining significance of race" (Wilson, 1978) and obscuring the "changing significance of race" (Pettigrew, 1980) in the determination of social and economic outcomes. For example, and as we illustrate further below, our tendency to treat the meaning of race as a constant has often made findings of sentencing research seem anomalous. Our premise is that the meaning of race must be understood in historical, contextual terms. With such an understanding, anomalous research findings come to make sense. Without such understanding, sociological theories of race relations are often as static as the genetic explanations they seek to replace.

Of course scholars do not always fail to consider the specific social and historical context in examining the social significance of race. Contextual considerations are apparent in some works on racial inequality (in education, income, employment, occupations, etc.) such as that by Wilson (1978) cited above and Farley (1977), and in analyses of certain trends (marriage, divorce, remarriage) in family patterns (e.g., Cherlin, 1981). In the criminal justice area, such considerations are sometimes apparent in research on the social origins of law. These examples notwithstanding, in much social research race is treated as if the direction and level of its impact should always be the same.

The Anomalous Findings of Sentencing Studies

Sentencing studies provide an example of an area of sociological research in which a static, simplistic understanding of race has impeded theoretical development. Thus while the most popular theory of criminal sentencing, conflict theory, traditionally has predicted that non-white offenders would receive more severe sentences than whites (Quinney, 1970; Chambliss and Seidman, 1971), and while much of the American public has shared this expectation (see Hagan and Albonetti, 1982), recent reviews of sentencing research provide little support for this perspective (Green, 1961; Hindelang, 1969; Hagan, 1974; Kleck, 1981; see also Hagan and Bumiller, 1983). Indeed, Kleck (1981, 799) goes so far as to call special attention to anomalous findings of differential lenience in the sentencing of black offenders.

For a variety of specific crimes, jurisdictions, and judges, various researchers have produced data indicating more lenient treatment of black defendants than whites, although the admittedly scattered findings were usually deemphasized or discounted as merely anomalous results. . . . For example, Bullock (1961) found significantly shorter prison sentences were assigned to blacks convicted of murder; Levin's (1972) Pittsburgh data indicate that blacks received more lenient dispositions than whites for eight of nine offense categories; and Bernstein and her colleagues (1977) found that blacks received significantly less severe sentences than whites. Gibson (1978, 469) studies sentences given by individual judges and found that seven of eleven judges gave a higher percentage of severe sentences to whites than to blacks.

Making sense of such findings is the current challenge of sentencing research. One possibility is that they are simply random fluctuations from a trend toward equality. Such a trend may exist, but these findings are not random in appearance. We believe that a more convincing explanation of differential lenience *and* severity in sentencing is to be found in race-related conceptions of offender–victim relationships, conceptions that are specific to the contexts in which they operate.

For example, homicide and assault are characteristically *intra*racial offenses. When black offenders assault or kill black victims, the devalued status of the black victims and the paternalistic attitudes of white authorities can justify lenient treatment (Kleck, 1981; see also Myrdal, 1944; Garfinkel, 1949). Rape, on the other hand, is more frequently *inter*racial. When blacks violate white victims, the high sexual property value attached to the white victims and the racial fears of authorities can justify severe treatment (LaFree, 1980; see also Wolfgang and Riedel, 1973). Robbery is also becoming increasingly interracial. The higher value attached to white property and persons and the fears of white authorities may here also lead to more severe sentences for black offenders (Thomson and Zingraff, 1981).

However, the above studies only consider crimes involving victims of interpersonal violence (homicide, assault, rape), or the threat of it (robbery). Such offenses constitute an important, but only a small part of the American crime problem. If race-related conceptions of offender–victim relationships like those highlighted above are to provide a more general explanation of sentencing disparities, they must be relevant to a broader range of offenses, including the so-called "victimless" crimes. Using drug law violations as an example, we argue below that a recent, historically specific tendency to see certain kinds of non-white offenders as victims may explain the anomaly of some nonwhite offenders receiving more lenient sentences than whites.

The Victims and Villians of Drugs

Through most of this century the issue of race has been manifest in the American moral crusade against drugs (Musto, 1973; Reasons, 1974). Musto (1973, 5) observes that as early as ". . . the nineteenth century addicts were identified with foreign groups and internal minorities who were already actively feared and the objects of elaborate and massive social and legal constraints." However, conceptions of deviant behavior are not static. As Gusfield (1967, 187) notes, "... deviance designations have histories.... What is attacked as criminal today may be seen as sick next year and fought over as possibly legitimate by the next generation." Our interest is in demonstrating how such changes may have influenced the sanctioning of drug offenders. To do so, it is necessary to focus on a time and a setting that allow detailed analysis of changing conceptions of offenders and offenses. Temporally, we have chosen the period of the 1960s and 1970s because it includes the most recent and concerted national effort to mobilize criminal justice resources against drug crimes, a period which culminated with the Nixon Administration's 1970 reform of federal drug laws. As a setting, we have selected the Southern Federal District of New York because it is widely recognized as the "premier" prosecution office in the country (e.g., Katz, 1980), among other reasons, for its pursuit of major drug cases (Moore, 1977).

An analysis of public opinion, media materials, and legislative activities summarized below suggests a subdivision of the time period we consider into three parts (1963–68, 1969–73, 1974–76), the most interesting of which is the middle interval. During this middle period public interest in drugs seemed to peak. This point can be made first through a consideration of Gallup Poll data providing national opinion rankings of "the most important problem the country faces today." Drugs were not among ranked social problems in these data prior to 1970, and were not consistently ranked after 1973. However, from February 1971 to August 1973, through six Gallup pollings, drugs were never less than fifth in the national rankings, and were usually ranked second or third in importance behind the Vietnam War and economic issues (see Gallup, 1972, 1978a, 1978b, 1979).

The treatment of an issue in the mass media is another index of shifts in public interest (Berk et al., 1977). Quantitative measures of such changes are presented elsewhere (see Peterson, 1983). Here we simply note that there was a rather dramatic increase in the coverage of drug problems in the New York print media that began in the late 1960s and declined dramatically by the mid-1970s: drug use, abuse, and trafficking were issues of much greater interest in the late 1960s and early 1970s than during either the early and mid-1960s or the mid- to late 1970s.

The qualitative changes in the nature of public opinion about drugs that accompanied these quantitative shifts are of even greater interest and importance. These changes are apparent in the content of drug-related editorials appearing in the *New York Times* between 1960 and 1978. The most important qualitative change over these eighteen years was the distinction increasingly made between dealers and users of drugs. This distinction became particularly salient during the Nixon Administration, as the former group became the villains, and the latter victims, in the changing imagery of America's drug problems. The significance of this distinction lies in its origins and race-related nature and consequences. As we have seen, in the earlier part of this century it was sufficient to condemn drug offenders, who were presumed to be mostly of minority status, in an undifferentiated fashion. However, in the 1960s the composition of the drug-abusing population changed. Whether this change was linked to the growing popularity of the anti-war movement, or to a more general "morals revolution" (Gusfield, 1975), its consequence was clear: "... for the first time in the twentieth century, the objects of the drug control laws were persons from the dominant middle class whose value system served as the basis for the development and enforcement of the criminal code" (Susman, 1975, 23–24).

During the late 1960s and early 1970s, the legitimacy of the criminal justice system was threatened almost as much by the public's view that it was inappropriate to subject their children to criminal punishment as it was by youthful drug and protest behavior itself (Glaser, 1974; Susman, 1975). A solution to this problem seemed to lie in what Gusfield might refer to as altered deviance designations (i.e., in a redefinition of what constituted the "real" drug problem). Pushers, especially high-level dealers, became the designated villains in this new portrayal of the problem. Perceived as part of organized drug networks with ties to the underworld, professional traffickers were designated as the real source of the drug problem. They were assigned responsibility for the street crimes of addicts forced to steal to pay the high price of drugs, and for the acts of violence committed by addicts under the influence of drugs so acquired. Their sins also included preying upon innocent victims, especially middle-class youth. "For material gain, he corrupted the young and introduced them to the joys and horrors of addiction. Thus the concept of the innocence of youth could be preserved and the source of corruption focused on the pusher" (Lidz and Walker, 1980, 80).

These new deviance designations were reflected during 1969–73 in editorial coverage of drug-related events in the *New York Times*, as well as in the penalty provisions and intent of the Nixon Administration's Comprehensive Drug Abuse Prevention and Control Act of 1970. Beginning with the former, *Times* editors repeatedly called for a scaling down of penalties for "soft" drugs, users and youthful offenders. Indeed, judges who imposed overly harsh penalties on these types of offenders were criticized openly (*New York Times*, July 15, 1969, 38; October 22, 1969, 46; December 8, 1969, 46; January 24, 1970, 30; August 30, 1970, V, 12; September 26, 1970, 28; January 25, 1971, 42; January 22, 1972, 28; February 20, 1972, IV, 12; August 2, 1972, 36; January 15, 1973, 28; February 9, 1973, 34; April 17, 1973, 40). In sharp contrast to these liberal views, *Times* editors supported "throwing the book" at veteran pushers and dealers in hard drugs. As one editorial noted, "The penalties for those who prey on the innocent by peddling drugs can hardly be too severe" (*New York Times*, July 15, 1969, 38; see also, January 9, 1973, 38; January 10, 1973, 40; March 7, 1973, 42; April 30, 1973, 30).

We turn now to the relevant legislation. On October 27, 1970, President Nixon signed into law the Comprehensive Drug Abuse Prevention and Control Act. In the legislative debates leading to the 1970 Act, Congress also focused on two target populations: young middle- and upper-class drug users, now seen as victims of drugs; and traffickers and professional drug criminals, now seen as the hardcore villains. Speaking of young middle- and upper-class drug users. Senator Dodd noted that "these people arrested for one drug offense or another are not hardened criminals . . . they are young people on the road to professional careers as lawyers and teachers" (United States Senate, 1969, 2–4). Dodd's concern was that the "cream of American youth" not be sent off to prison ". . . where it is now obvious they will get worse rather than better." Representative Koch cogently summarized this commonly held view:

> I believe that if we are to condemn and punish our young people, we ought to be sure that the cure is not worse than the disease . . . , it seems to me that the severe federal and state criminal penalties only exacerbate the problem. . . . (United States Senate, 1969,562)

On the other hand, severe penalties were widely seen as essential for the hardcore villains—the traffickers, pushers and big dealers. Representative Hunt asserted:

> There is nothing wrong with imposing a mandatory sentence on a hard-headed pusher. Mitigating circumstances should not apply to a person of this nature. The only way you can handle narcotics and get rid of the situation is to incarcerate those main pushers and help those who have unfortunately become addicted. (United States Congress, 1970:33629)

The penalties that emerged from Congressional hearings and debates reflected compromises reached to "properly" deal with these two target populations. Reduction of first offense possession and of distribution of small amounts of marihuana for no remuneration from felonies to misdemeanors, removal of mandatory minimum penalties, and a provision for special first offender treatment served to minimize the possibility of subjecting middle- and upper-class youth to criminal penalties and their presumed negative consequences. On the other hand, the retention of a possession offense for the purpose of bargaining with informants, the relatively minor reductions in maximum penalties for trafficking offenses, the provision of mandatory special parole terms, the provision of extreme sanctions for two new offense categories of questionable constitutionality (Continuing Criminal Enterprise and Dangerous Special Drug Offender), and the passage of supplementary criminal enforcement provisions provided the coercive policies required for handling (and warning) the second targeted population: major drug traffickers.

We suggest that the distinction drawn, by the public and lawmakers, between users as victims and dealers as villains could well account for the more lenient treatment of minorities. A factual premise that underwrites this suggestion is that the opportunity structure of the drug trade in America, like more conventional opportunity structures, is racially stratified. Most big dealers are white (Ianni, 1974).[1] Also, media sources (e.g., the *New York Times*) and interviews with U.S. Attorneys from the Southern District confirm that operating assumptions of the public and criminal justice officials include the views that nonwhites (1) are more likely to be users than dealers, (2) are very unlikely to be big dealers, and (3) commit their drug crimes in part because of their victim status in society.

Our point then is not simply that minority offenders might be treated more leniently *because* they are in fact users, but rather that as an identifiable population, minority drug offenders may well have been "typed" or characterized as victims in a more *generalized* fashion (Sudnow, 1965; Swigert and Farrell, 1977). Coming as it did on the heels of the high point of the Civil Rights Movement, our expectation is that this otherwise anomalous form of equity held sway in the formation of the new drug strategy. Indeed, we believe that it was this coalition of conservative purpose (i.e., a moral crusade against the big dealers of the drug trade) and liberal impulse (i.e., the recognition and treatment of youthful, better educated, and minority offenders as victims of the world of drugs) that best accounts for the emergence of a new drug strategy. As indicated above, our expectation is that this strategy became most pronounced in the context represented by the years 1969–73: during these years we expect well-educated youth, minority offenders and users of drugs to have received the most lenient treatment, while big drug dealers are expected to have experienced particularly harsh treatment.

One final point should be made. The lenience we expect for minority drug offenders is premised on their designation as victims. However, in those infrequent instances when minority offenders are clearly big dealers, it is unlikely that the designation as victim would apply. If the perspective we offer is correct, then we would not expect in these instances to encounter the anomaly of more lenient treatment for minority offenders. This implied interaction of race and dealer status is explored in the last part of our analysis.

The Measurement of Change and the Correction of Selection Bias

To demonstrate the kind of social change we have described, it is necessary to have information on joint variations in dependent and independent variables within varied contexts. Duncan (1975) notes that analysis of this kind permits identification of social change of a "structural" form, that is, social change ". . . in a deeper sense of the term." The data considered in this study allow this kind of analysis: they include crucial information on all drug offenders (N = 4371) sentenced between 1963 and 1976 in the Southern Federal District of New York. The analysis considers sentencing decisions within the three contexts derived from the above discussion: 1963–68, 1969–73, and 1974–76.

Sentencing can be thought of as a two-stage process (Wheeler et al., 1982), involving first a decision as to whether to imprison, and second, if imprisonment is selected, a decision about the length of sentence. However, there are three problems with simply treating these two decisions as separate occurrences: (1) the two phases of the sentencing process are left disconnected, while in practice they are not; (2) the separate results make it difficult to reach summary judgments about the overall influence of explanatory variables; and (3) the parameter estimates for the separate analysis of length of imprisonment will be biased. The last point requires elaboration (see also Heckman, 1974, 1975; Berk et al., 1981).

As we have noted, the decision about length of imprisonment follows the decision to imprison. The initial decision results in a selected pool of offenders who have exceeded a threshold on the criteria that determine the choice of the prison sanction. When such selection occurs length of imprisonment will be a function not only of the linear combination of regressors ordinarily considered, but also of what Heckman (1975) terms the "hazard rate," or risk of not being selected into the imprisoned population, i.e., the risk of exceeding or not exceeding the threshold. Estimation procedures, such as ordinary regression, which fail to take into account the "hazard rate" will yield biased and inconsistent estimates of the structural coefficients (see Berk, 1983).

To avoid these problems a procedure is required that provides information about the two decisions, type and length of sentence, but that also allows us to combine this information in a meaningful way. Heckman (1974, 1975) outlines such a procedure that for our purposes will involve two equations: the first is a probit equation that estimates whether a drug offender receives an institutional sentence, and the second an OLS equation for sentence length that is corrected for selection bias. The first equation is:

$$\text{Probit (Pi)} = \text{Xi B}^*, \tag{1}$$

where P_i is the probability of the ith drug offender being sentenced to prison; X_i is a row vector of covariates: and B* the corresponding column vector of parameters. The second equation is:

$$Z_i = A_i n + f_0 l_i + E_i, \tag{2}$$

where Z_i is months of imprisonment, $A_i n$ is a set of explanatory variables and parameters: l_i is a regressor (a new covariate) derived from equation (1) and defined as the "hazard" or risk that the ith offender will be sentenced to a prison term, with f_0 as its regression coefficient (i.e., the estimator of the covariance between the errors in the equation predicting imprisonment and the errors in the equation predicting length of imprisonment); and E_i is an error term. Because this correction procedure is not widely used or its consequences widely recognized, we will also estimate a prison sentence length equation using OLS regression without a correction for selection bias.

The Analysis

We now apply Heckman's estimation procedures in analyzing the impact of 22 explanatory variables on sentences received by federal drug offenders for the three periods previously identified. Although the coding of most of the variables is straightforward (see Table 6.1), several require comment. The last of the offender characteristics, "status," is a composite measure coded (1) if the defendant is 22 years of age or less, high school educated and white, and (0) if otherwise. Since age, education and race are all included separately in the analysis as well, significant status effects represent interactions that persist beyond the main effects of the component measures. The legally relevant offender characteristics include number of prior convictions, distinctions between prosecution under pre- and post-1970 statutes, as well as indicators of whether the offender is a user and/or big dealer. Users were identified as such in the court records. We identified big dealers when they were designated as "prime movers" in marginal notes in court records, or when their drug-related criminal activities involved 100 pounds or more of a narcotic substance.[2] Characteristics of judges include whether they were appointed to the bench during the Nixon administration and a measure of the average severity of the sentences given by individual judges in nondrug cases over the period of the study. Our expectation is that Nixon appointees will be more punitive than non-Nixon appointees, especially between 1969 and 1973.

Table 6.1 Variables, Means, and Standard Deviations for the Total Population of Drug Offenders and for the Population of Imprisoned Offenders

Variables	Value	Total Population (N = 4371) Mean	Total Population (N = 4371) Standard Deviation	Imprisoned Population (N = 3056) Mean	Imprisoned Population (N = 3056) Standard Deviation
A. Offender's Status Characteristics					
1. Male Sex: Yes	1	.908	.289	.940	.238
No	0				
2. Age:	In Years	33.370	9.371	35.148	8.829
3. Race: Nonwhite	1	.350	.477	.365	.482
White	0				
4. Education: < High School Graduate	1	.637	.481	.701	.458
≥ High School Graduate	0				
5. Marital Status: unattached	1	.511	.500	.464	.499
attached	0				
6. Status: Middle-Status Youth	1	.038	.191	.009	.092
Non-Middle Status Youth	0				
B. Legally Relevant Offender and Case Characteristics					
7. Prior Convictions	Total Number	3.781	5.101	4.346	5.230
8. Pre-1970 Trafficking: Yes	1	.298	.457	.379	.485
No	0				
9. Post-1970 Trafficking: Yes	1	.321	.467	.321	.467
No	0				
10. Pre-1970 Importing: Yes	1	.017	.127	.020	.140
No	0				
11. Post-1970 Importing: Yes	1	.005	.069	.004	.063
No	0				
12. Conspiracy: Yes	1	.198	.399	.192	.394
No	0				
13. Illegal Communication: Yes	1	.012	.108	.011	.103
No	0				
14. Charge Seriousness:	Months Maximum Possible Prison	177.7	53.730	189.45	47.006
15. Gun Used: Yes	1	.063	.242	.074	.262
No	0				
16. Narcotic Drug: Yes	1	.432	.495	.436	.496
No	0				
17. Drug User: Yes	1	.300	.458	.292	.455
No	0				
18. Big Dealer: Yes	1	.014	.116	.018	.135
No	0				
C. Characteristics of the Judge					
19. Nixon Judge: Yes	1	.215	.411	.209	.407
No	0				
20. Judge Severity	Average Sentence in Non-Drug Cases	45.543	8.109	45.996	8.126
D. Legal Process Variables					
21. Plea: Not Guilty	1	.355	.478	.447	.497
Guilty	0				
22. Pre-sentence Report: Yes	1	.800	.400	.761	.427
No	0				

The legal process variables include measures of whether the offender pleaded guilty or went to trial, and of whether a pre-sentence report was prepared (the recommendations contained in these reports were not available in our data). It has been argued that independent of the specific sentence recommendation, the contents of pre-sentence reports are used to justify sentences judges wish to impose for other reasons (Rothman, 1980, Chap. 3). For example, in light of prevalent victim/villain designations during the 1969–73 period, a pre-sentence investigation for big dealers might be associated with more severe sanctions, but for drug users and middle-class youth, with less severe sanctions.

Before presenting our corrected regression analysis, we first consider uncorrected results of the length of imprisonment equation for the three separate time periods (see Table 6.2). These results indicate that big dealers receive substantially more severe treatment than other drug offenders in all time periods, with their most harsh sentences coming between 1969 and 1973; while nonwhite offenders receive more lenient treatment than white offenders in all time periods, with this disparity again being most pronounced during the middle years. Nixon-appointed judges are more punitive

Table 6.2 Uncorrected Regression of Length of Imprisonment (in Months) on Independent Variables for Different Social Contexts

	Period I 1963–68			Period II 1969–73			Period III 1974–76		
Variable	**b**	**β**	**Standard Error**	**b**	**β**	**Standard Error**	**b**	**β**	**Standard Error**
Male Sex	6.210	.033	5.580	11.045	.042	7.334	9.662	.028	9.554
Age	1.267***	.235	.171	.798**	.103	.231	.972**	.123	.245
Race (nonwhite)	–5.769*	–.064	2.915	–16.528**	–.119	4.175	–10.405*	–.063	4.722
Marital Status (unattached)	.411	.005	2.905	–16.446***	–.122	3.905	–10.441*	–.069	4.285
Education	–6.216	–.048	3.994	4.842	.035	4.026	7.875	.051	4.584
Status	–12.634	–.020	19.204	–11.418	–.018	17.477	5.893	.007	22.327
Prior Convictions	.045	–.005	.300	1.762***	.133	.390	2.033***	.148	.432
Pre-1970 Trafficking	10.808*	.097	5.389	45.152***	.308	11.426	49.255	.169	31.996
Post-1970 Trafficking	—	—	—	16.874	.125	10.275	21.014	.139	25.239
Pre-1970 Importing	–.592	–.003	8.128	35.713	.037	28.815	—	—	—
Post-1970 Importing	—	—	—	18.439	.017	30.823	67.178*	.079	34.015
Conspiracy	—	—	—	17.068	.100	10.722	23.457	.151	25.276
Illegal Communication	—	—	—	16.803	.036	15.317	–29.656	–.041	25.446
Charge Seriousness	.107**	.136	.033	–.051	–.036	.060	–.239	–.088	.157
Gun Use	—	—	—	–.870	–.003	8.197	5.116	.025	6.048
Narcotic Drug	—	—	—	7.038	.052	5.051	18.955*	.085	7.089
Drug User	–3.321	–.035	3.162	–9.631*	–.059	4.682	–18.839***	–.118	4.666
Big Dealer	45.707*	.065	21.192	88.567***	.135	17.903	54.779***	.145	10.970
Nixon Judge	—	—	—	17.973**	.100	5.436	2.832	.019	4.282
Judge Severity	.077	.014	.166	.027	.003	.234	–.128	–.013	.284
Plea (Not Guilty)	11.115**	.124	2.905	31.541***	.235	3.885	35.828***	.235	4.432
Pre-sentence Report	2.774	.029	3.077	25.438*	.074	9.965	–17.835	–.041	13.748
	R^2 =.159			R^2 =.254			R^2 =.276		
	Intercept = –12.006			Intercept = 24.634			Intercept = 29.167		
	Mean Sentence = 69.525			Mean Sentence = 69.138			Mean Sentence = 66.380		

*p ≤ .05.
**p ≤ .01.
***p ≤ .001.

than other judges, specifically during the Nixon years, 1969–73. Our most direct measure of victim status, being a drug user, results in increasingly more lenient treatment across the three time periods. The age, education and status variables do not act entirely as expected, but their effects do not particularly conflict with our viewpoint either. The effect of plea jumps dramatically in the second period, and increases again, albeit slightly, in the final period.

We now correct for selection bias. The probit equations are estimated first, with the decision between a prison and nonprison sentence as the dependent variable (see Table 6.3). We discuss the probit results only briefly because they are built into the corrected regression analysis.

Our most direct measures of villain and victim status influence imprisonment in expected ways. Users are *more* likely than others to go to jail between 1963 and 1968, but *less* likely to do so between

Table 6.3 Probit Regression of Type of Sentence (Prison/Nonprison) on Independent Variables for Different Social Contexts

	Period I 1963–68			Period II 1969–73			Period III 1974–76		
Variable	**Co-efficient**	**Standard Error**	**Correl-ation With Risk Factor**	**Co-efficient**	**Standard Error**	**Correl-ation With Risk Factor**	**Co-efficient**	**Standard Error**	**Correl-ation With Risk Factor**
Male Sex	.449**	.167	.283	.727***	.124	.748	.818***	.131	.698
Age	.018**	.006	.345	.025***	.005	.652	.036***	.005	.749
Race (nonwhite)	–.233*	.112	–.218	–.084	.091	–.123	–.210*	.089	–.330
Marital Status (unattached)	.010	.111	.019	–.071	.083	–.232	–.075	.081	–.199
Education	.138	.138	.211	.261**	.084	.565	.175*	.083	.305
Status	–.858*	.396	–.345	–1.006***	.215	–.771	–.734**	.208	–.566
Prior Convictions	.039**	.012	.431	.019	.010	.354	.026*	.010	.355
Pre-1970 Trafficking	1.407***	.157	.883	.528**	.160	.545	.966	.634	.240
Post-1970 Trafficking	—	—	—	.609**	.160	.678	.405	.484	.257
Pre-1970 Importing	1.661***	.375	.799	–.082	.458	.053	—	—	—
Post-1970 Importing	—	—	—	.122	.563	.132	-.088	.605	.057
Conspiracy	—	—	—	.550**	.174	.640	.395	.485	.256
Illegal Communication	—	—	—	1.368***	.321	.762	.668	.360	.295
Charge Seriousness	.003**	.001	.319	.004***	.001	.687	.004	.003	.195
Gun Use	—	—	—	–.042	.201	–.037	.196	.133	.193
Narcotic Drug	—	—	—	.109	.106	.184	.394**	.109	.527
Drug User	.426**	.129	.383	–.278*	.094	–.517	.027	.082	.013
Big Dealer	1.484	2.692	.114	2.015	1.603	.245	.950	.503	.161
Nixon Judge	—	—	—	–.259*	.119	–.391	–.300**	.080	–.512
Judge Severity	.008	.008	.053	.027***	.006	.689	.026***	.005	.620
Plea (Not Guilty)	.440**	.142	.364	.666***	.093	.840	.520***	.089	.708
Pre-sentence Report	–.457***	.111	–.526	.211	.206	.132	–.072	.217	–.100

* $p \leq .05$.
** $p \leq .01$.
*** $p \leq .001$.

1969 and 1973. It is difficult to interpret these effects in any way other than the altered deviance designations of drug users that we have described. Although the effect of the big dealer variable is not significant during any of the three periods, its influence is largest during the middle interval. And, while we were unable to find any significant status effects in the above analysis, we now find that middle-class status decreases significantly the likelihood of imprisonment in all time periods, and, again as expected, this effect is strongest during 1969–73. Education and age also affect imprisonment, with education having the larger impact, and with the likelihood of high school educated offenders being jailed lowest for 1969–73. Nixon-appointed judges show a greater reluctance to imprison offenders than other judges during the last two periods, while judges with high severity scores for nondrug cases are more willing in drug cases to use imprisonment as a sanction. Pleading not guilty has a significant impact on the likelihood of imprisonment in all periods, with that impact being largest for 1969–73. The latter findings are discussed further below. Finally, although nonwhite offenders are less likely than white offenders to receive jail sentences in all three periods, counter to our expectations, this effect is smallest and statistically nonsignificant for 1969–73. The above findings are all taken into account through the incorporation of a risk-factor variable in the corrected regression equations (see Table 6.4).

Inclusion of the risk factor l_i as a regressor in the corrected equations alters many of the coefficients and standard errors. The tendency is for the coefficients to become larger when selection bias is taken into account. For example, the effects of race increase by two months in the first and second periods, and three months in the third period. Thus while non-whites received sentences (net of 21 other variables and l_i) nearly eight months (b = –7.745) shorter than whites during 1963–68, this difference jumped to more than 18 months (b = –18.320) during 1969–73, and remained close to this level (b = –16.920) during 1974–76. The t-tests reported in Table 6.5 indicate that the differences between periods I and II, and I and III, are statistically significant. Again, our explanation of this pattern is that our data cover a period in which the historical association of the drug problem with minority and low income populations was declining. These offenders were now seen more as victims, while big drug dealers were seen as the villains.

Including l_i in the prison sentence length equation also augments the influence of the big dealer variable: by seven additional months each period. The corrected coefficients are 52.8 (1963–68), 95.9 (1969–73), and 62.4 (1974–76). The between-period differences are all statistically significant (see Table 6.5). We view the unique and severe sentences for big dealers during the period of heightened attention to drugs as substantiating our argument that big dealers were the villains of the anti-drug crusade from 1969 through 1973.

When the uncorrected equations were estimated, users did not appear to receive substantially different sentences than other offenders in periods I and II. In contrast, the corrected equations reveal a substantial 13.3 months difference in length of sentences for users versus other offenders when periods I and II are compared. This difference is statistically significant, as is the difference (16.46 months) between the effect parameters for periods I and III (see Table 6.5). Furthermore, the corrected equation suggests that, in the earliest years, drug users received *more* rather than less severe sentences than nonusers, although this pattern is neither substantial (b = .528) nor statistically significant. In contrast, drug users in the later periods received sentences that were substantially and significantly *less* severe than those received by nonusers (for the corrected equations, b = –13.9 for 1969–73, and b = –16.99 for 1974–76). We interpret this new-found lenience as reflecting the altered designation of users as victims.

Controlling for selection bias, however, has the most important impact on the findings for the status variable. The uncorrected equation (Table 6.2) indicated a decline over time in the impact of this variable. This suggests that middle-class youth received the least break in sentencing (compared

Table 6.4 Corrected Regression of Length of Imprisonment (in Months) on Independent Variables for Different Social Contexts

	Period I 1963–68			Period II 1969–73			Period III 1974–76		
Variable	**b**	**β**	**Standard Error**	**b**	**β**	**Standard Error**	**b**	**β**	**Standard Error**
Male Sex	10.970	.059	5.821	24.710*	.095	10.990	49.870**	.145	12.950
Age	1.449***	.268	.183	1.115**	.150	.307	2.277***	.288	.359
Race (nonwhite)	–7.745*	–.086	3.007	–18.320***	–.137	4.209	–16.920**	–.102	4.863
Marital Status (unattached)	.438	.005	2.923	–17.740***	–.138	4.007	–15.000**	–.099	4.250
Education	–3.704	–.029	4.126	9.780*	.073	4.880	13.130*	.085	4.679
Status	–38.290	–.055	22.800	–45.590	–.076	27.330	–59.400*	–.074	26.270
Prior Convictions	.370	.042	.333	1.800***	.141	.423	2.584***	.188	.449
Pre-1970 Trafficking	40.020**	.682	11.480	56.750***	1.458	13.590	85.800*	2.212	31.980
Post-1970 Trafficking	—	—	—	32.280*	.830	13.980	58.680*	1.513	25.380
Pre-1970 Importing	31.770*	.541	14.050	39.320	1.010	28.730	—	—	—
Post-1970 Importing	—	—	—	25.350	.651	30.970	84.590*	2.181	34.140
Conspiracy	—	—	—	31.490*	.809	13.950	61.190*	1.578	25.410
Illegal Communication	—	—	—	49.170*	1.263	23.900	32.240	.831	26.190
Charge Seriousness	.139***	.177	.034	.049	.036	.083	.030	.011	.157
Gun Use	—	—	—	–.842	.003	8.241	9.374	.046	5.983
Narcotic Drug	—	—	—	10.040	–.078	5.152	41.030*	.184	8.115
Drug User	.528	.006	3.425	–13.900*	–.090	5.470	–16.990***	–.106	4.540
Big Dealer	52.750*	.075	21.360	95.990***	.153	18.380	62.410***	.165	10.780
Nixon Judge	—	—	—	12.370*	.073	5.921	-9.550	–.063	4.843
Judge Severity	.112	.018	.194	.687	.083	.347	.961*	.092	.367
Plea (Not Guilty)	14.450***	.161	3.140	41.320***	.322	7.128	55.360***	.364	6.095
Pre-sentence Report	2.726	–.028	3.635	27.850*	.085	10.010	–26.570	–.062	13.420
Risk of Imprisonment (λ_1)	41.310*		14.290	41.280		25.090	97.080***		21.700
	R^2 =.159			R^2 =.250			R^2 =.285		
	Intercept = –69.33			Intercept = –134.8			Intercept = –248.9		

* p ≤ .05.
** p ≤ .01.
*** p ≤ .001.

to traditional offenders) during the period when sources of public and elite opinion were converging in advocating more lenient handling of such offenders; and, when legislative provisions (e.g., discretionary sentencing and special first offender provisions) should have facilitated the awarding of lenient penalties to middle-class youth. Correcting for selection bias eliminates this puzzling finding. The corrected equations show that middle-status youth received substantially larger breaks in sentencing during the final two periods. We should also note that a significant change in the main effect of education precedes the status effect: between 1969 and 1973, better-educated drug offenders received more than nine months shorter sentences (b = 9.780) than the less educated; between 1974 and 1976 this difference widened to more than thirteen months (b = 13.130). Finally, the corrected model indicates that the penalty received by those pleading not guilty was greater in each period (than for those pleading guilty), and substantially and significantly greater in the latter two periods: b = 14.4 for 1963–68. 41.3 for 1969–73, and 55.3 for the 1974–76 period.

Table 6.5 t-Statistics for Differences in the Value of Beta Coefficients Comparing the Effects of Independent Variables on the Corrected Model of Prison Sentence Length Across Social Contexts

	Period I Compared with Period II		Period I Compared with Period III		Period II Compared with Period III	
Variable	**Difference**	**t**	**Difference**	**t**	**Difference**	**t**
Male Sex	–13.740	–4.710**	–38.890	–12.630**	–25.150	–7.270**
Age	.334	.672	–.828	–1.586	–1.162	2.010*
Race (nonwhite)	10.580	5.540**	9.175	4.610**	–1.400	–.657
Marital Status (unattached)	–17.300	–9.250**	–14.560	–7.660**	–2.740	1.350
Education	–13.480	–6.330**	–16.830	–8.020**	–3.350	–1.530
Status	7.300	1.450	21.110	4.260**	13.810	2.670**
Prior Convictions	–1.430	–3.760**	–2.210	–3.540**	–.784	–1.190
Pre-1970 Trafficking	–16.730	–4.710**	–45.780	–9.780**	–29.050	–6.100**
Post-1970 Trafficking	—	—	—	—	–26.400	–5.970**
Pre-1970 Importing	–7.550	–1.620	—	—	—	—
Post-1970 Importing	—	—	—	—	–59.240	–10.390**
Conspiracy	—	—	—	—	–29.670	–6.710**
Illegal Communication	—	—	—	—	16.930	3.390**
Charge Seriousness	.090	.370	.109	.350	.019	.055
Gun Use	—	—	—	—	–10.216	–3.830**
Narcotic Drug	—	—	—	—	–30.990	-12.060**
Drug User	–13.370	–6.310**	–16.460	–8.210**	3.090	1.380
Big Dealer	–43.240	–9.720**	–9.660	–2.420*	33.580	8.770**
Nixon Judge	—	—	—	—	2.820	1.220
Judge Severity	–.575	–1.100	–.849	–1.600	–.274	–.459
Plea (Not Guilty)	–26.870	–11.790**	–40.910	–18.940**	–14.040	–5.460**
Pre-sentence Report	–30.580	–11.580**	23.840	8.110**	54.420	15.910**
Risk of Imprisonment (λ_i)	.030	.007	–55.770	–13.120**	-55.800	–11.530**

* $p \leq .05$.
** $p \leq .01$.

Further Test

Above we argued that an important contributor to the leniency expected for nonwhite drug offenders derived from their tendency to be restricted to the lower levels of the drug trade and therefore characterized as victims. However, on those rare occasions when nonwhites do rise to the position of big dealers, the predicted leniency should according to our reasoning, disappear.

To examine this possibility, we have combined the data for the last two time periods and regressed sentence length, separately for big dealers and for ordinary drug offenders, on those independent variables (race, marital status, pre-1970 trafficking, drug user, plea, and pre-sentence report) which were substantively and statistically related to this criterion variable (see Table 6.6).[3] The decision to combine the data for the last two periods follows from the fact that the number of big dealers was too small to permit a reliable regression analysis within each period. Since our prior analysis revealed considerable carryover of the effects of the second period into the third, this approach seems justified. No correction for selection bias is attempted in this part of our analysis because for big dealers there is none: they are all imprisoned.

First the findings for race: the unstandardized coefficient for ordinary offenders indicates dicates that nonwhites received sentences that are on average about six and one-half months shorter than those received by whites (b = –6.686). In contrast, nonwhite big dealers received prison sentences

Table 6.6 Regression of Length of Prison Sentence (in Months) on Significant Independent Variables for Ordinary Drug Offenders and Big Dealers, 1969–76

Independent Variables	Ordinary Offenders (N = 2025) b	Big Dealers (N = 53) b	Difference	t
Race (nonwhite)	–6.686*	19.385	–26.071	–13.254***
Marital Status (unattached)	–18.290***	–13.789	–4.501	2.425*
Pre-1970 Trafficking	20.502***	50.380	–29.878	–14.344***
Drug User	–15.700***	–18.489	2.759	1.340
Plea (Not Guilty)	36.271***	126.796***	–90.525	–48.203***
Pre-sentence Report	13.119	57.767	–44.648	–14.045***
	R^2 =.155	R^2 =.342		
	Intercept = 48.317	Intercept = 11.074		
	Mean Sentence = 65.265	Mean Sentence = 164.151		

* $p \leq .05$.
** $p \leq .01$.
*** $p \leq .001$.

that average more than 19 months longer than those received by white big dealers. While the racial differential in the latter finding in itself is not statistically significant (a not surprising outcome given the small number of nonwhite big dealers), the *difference* in the impact of race on the sentences received by ordinary drug offenders versus big dealers is significant beyond the .001 level. In a period when big dealers were viewed as the source of the drug problem, *nonwhite big dealers* may have been seen as even more suspect and villainous since they in particular were likely to be perceived as inflicting their evil on an already victimized population: nonwhite users. Additional qualitative evidence for this conclusion is offered below. Meanwhile, the regression coefficients for the plea variable indicate that this is the single most important predictor of sentence length for both ordinary offenders and big dealers, but that plea has a much greater (and significantly so) impact for big dealers than for ordinary offenders. Ordinary drug offenders who plead not guilty are subject to average prison sentences that are more than 36 months longer than their counterparts who plead guilty. By comparison big dealers who plead not guilty are subject to average prison sentences that are more than 126 months longer than those received by big dealers who plead guilty. These findings are also discussed further below.

Some Conclusions

Prior theorizing and research on sentencing (and in some other areas as well) have tended to treat the meaning of race as a constant. Explicit in our analysis is the premise that the meaning of race varies, and that, despite simplistic interpretations of conflict theory, both differential severity and leniency are possible. There are hints of such an understanding in prior sentencing studies of inter- and intraracial crimes with victims. However, we have suggested that race can influence societal reactions to the more frequent victimless crimes as well. The key, we have argued, is an understanding of changing race-related conceptions of offender–victim relationships.

For example, American drug prohibition began with the portrayal of minorities as the villains behind a growing drug menace. However, with the increasing nonmedical use of drugs by middle-class youth in the 1960s, this conception of the drug problem became problematic. A general shift occurred in the social image of the different types of parties involved, and a new strategy of control was required. Big dealers became the new villains, while middle-class youth *and* nonwhites (the latter insofar as they rarely were big dealers in a racially stratified drug trade) were reconceived as victims. We have argued that inclusion of nonwhites in the latter category was the product of a compromise between conservative and liberal impulses that facilitated a more specialized allocation of penal sanctions. The modern anti-drug crusade reached its peak between 1969 and 1973, a period that included the passage of a new drug law spearheaded by the Nixon Administration.

We were able to identify a series of outcomes consistent with the above perspective. The most dramatic of these effects included a peak in the punitive treatment of big dealers between 1969 and 1973. Lenient treatment of nonwhite offenders also peaked during these years. The latter ultimately was revealed to be a lenience restricted to *ordinary* nonwhite drug offenders, not big dealers. Indeed, there were signs that *nonwhite big dealers* received the most severe sentences of all.

These findings were reinforced by a series of follow-up interviews we conducted with three former heads of the drug enforcement division of the U.S. Attorney's Office of the Southern District of New York. When asked to explain the general pattern of leniency we found for nonwhite drug offenders, one former prosecutor answered with the immediate response that, "Sure, three blacks equal one Italian, and three Italians equal one Corsican." Asked to elaborate, the former U.S. Attorney noted that the world of drugs is not only racially, but also ethnically stratified. The remainder of this interview and the others we conducted are best characterized as reflecting a casual, jaded, and sometimes paternal indifference to nonwhite drug crime that is well captured in contemporary American films like "Prince of the City," which not coincidentally was set in the same time and place as the current study.

There is, however, a more ominous side to the new drug strategy that is reflected in the race-period-big dealer interaction noted above. Indeed, there are dramatic examples of the extremely severe treatment of nonwhite big dealers. The case of Leroy "Nicky" Barnes offers a vivid illustration. On January 19, 1978, Barnes was sentenced to life imprisonment *without* parole on drug conspiracy charges *and* under the seldom used Continuing Criminal Enterprise provision of the 1970 Federal Drug Act.[4] Regarded as possibly Harlem's biggest drug dealer, Barnes was listed in the New York Police Department's Blue Book of "Black Major Violators." In imposing such a severe sentence, the judge in the case explained that Barnes "is 'a great danger' to the community. . . . His narcotics trafficking affected 'the lives of thousands of people.' And the saddest part of all . . . is that the great majority of people he is affecting are people in his own neighborhood [Harlem]" (*New York Times*, January 20, 1978). This latter comment is consistent with our suggestion that nonwhite big dealers are seen as more villainous, and therefore as deserving more severe penalties, because they offend against an already victimized population. The following comment from a *New York Times Magazine* article (written prior to Barnes's 1978 conviction) is also noteworthy in light of our perspective.

> Whatever the reasons, the failure to make an arrest stick has earned Barnes the street name "Mr. Untouchable." He is not a retiring man. Of medium height, he projects a presence larger than his size. He is muscular and recently shaved the beard he sported for years. He prefers luxurious motor cars and elaborate custom clothing. To the street people, he is a presence. To the police, this symbolic quality is as significant as the crimes they allege he has committed. To them he embodies the new trend in drug trafficking, in which blacks and Hispanics, the new ethnic successors in organized crime, have taken over from their predecessors, the Italian street gangsters. (*New York Times Magazine*, June 5, 1977, 16).

Not all of our findings are entirely consistent with our expectations. For example, we found race and status effects that persisted from the second into the third period. These effects may have been more persistent than we anticipated because the increased involvement of middleclass populations in drug crimes produced not only a more liberal, but also an *enduring* change in public attitudes toward drug use. If so, these lasting changes in the perception of drugs might well be reflected in a continuation, during the 1974–76 period, of relatively lenient treatment of minorities and middle-status youth.

There may be organizational pressures operating as well, particularly pressures having to do with court caseloads and the use of prisons. These pressures may have helped shape and mediate the influence of the changing conceptions we have discussed, while also exercising their own independent effects. For example, the decline in prison sentence length for big dealers during the third period may reflect not only a decrease in public anxiety about drugs, but also a recognition that the policy was doing little more than adding to the overcrowding of prisons. This concern with overcrowding may also explain the continuing increase in leniency for users in the third time period. Meanwhile, the overcrowding of the courts probably best explains the strong effect of the plea variable throughout our analysis: high caseloads are a common explanation for plea bargaining and the severe treatment of offenders who insist on trials. Particularly interesting, however, is the strength of the effect of the plea variable during the second period, the peak of the anti-drug crusade, and among big dealers. We suggest that it was within this context that the organizational need for plea bargaining was particularly well supported by the kinds of conceptions we have discussed. That is, it was during the second period that the demand for severe treatment was at its peak, with big dealers singled out for particular disdain. Who better could have served as an organizational example of the costs of refusing to plea bargain than a big dealer during the anti-drug crusade who demanded a trial and had his sins paraded before an open court? Nicky Barnes is a clear example.

More generally, we offer this study as an example of, and argument for, sociological research that takes context-specific conceptions of race into account. Our results suggest that there are patterns of advantage and disadvantage that only contextualized analyses can reveal. The role of race is more variable and more complicated than previously acknowledged.

Notes

1. As one might expect, in our data only a small percentage of whites (1.5%, n = 2840) or nonwhites (0.7%, n = 1529) are big dealers. More relevant to our argument are the results of tables percentaged in the alternative direction. Nonwhites are proportionately twice as large a part of the user population (41.2%, n = 1310) as they are of the big dealer population (20.7%, n = 53). Particularly likely to have stood out in the observations of control agents was that nearly 80 percent (79.3%) of the big dealers are white. These tables are available upon request.
2. While the use of 100 pounds as a cut-off is somewhat arbitrary, selection of this amount was based on the minimum volume of drugs typically involved in major drug cases as indicated in the *Annual Reports* of the U.S. Attorney for the Southern District.
3. Initially, we included in the above analysis only those independent variables that overall accounted for at least six months difference in prison sentence length. (This is consistent with the tendency of judges to assign prison sentences in intervals of six months, e.g., 6, 12, 18, 24 months.) Our reason for limiting the number of independent variables was the small number of big dealers (N = 53) in our data, and the desire, therefore, to conserve degrees of freedom. Nonetheless, we also regressed sentence length for big dealers on the full set of 22 explanatory variables. The results of doing so are substantively similar to the above results, except that when prior convictions and other independent variables are included, the disadvantage to nonwhite big dealers increases (b = 37.87) as does the advantage to nonwhite ordinary offenders (b = –11.40). Because of the reduction in degrees of freedom, the f value for the nonwhite big dealers remains statistically nonsignificant. However, note that the difference in the effect of race for big dealers and ordinary offenders is now even larger than reported above, as well as statistically significant.
4. Under the 1970 Act, a person is considered to be engaging in a continuing criminal enterprise if she or he (1) commits a felony which is part of a continuing series of drug offenses, (2) acts in concert with at least five other persons to commit these offenses, (3) commands some organizational or supervisory position with respect to the group, and (4) obtains substantial income from the enterprise. None of the big dealers in our population of drug offenders was sentenced for this offense. While the Barnes case was not processed until 1977, it is not irrelevant to the present analysis. Indeed, the 1978 conviction represented the culmination of efforts, begun in 1973, to criminally sanction Mr. Barnes for drug trafficking. Earlier attempts to prosecute him under state laws were unsuccessful.

References

Berk, Richard A. 1983. An introduction to sample selection bias in sociological data. *American Sociological Review* 48:386–98.

Berk, Richard A., Harold Brackman, and Selma Lesser. 1977. *A measure of justice: An empirical study of changes in the California penal code, 1955–1971.* New York: Academic Press.

Berk, Richard A., Ray C. Subhash, and Thomas F. Cooley. 1981. Selection biases in sociological data. Mimeographed Paper. Department of Sociology, University of California, Santa Barbara.

Bernstein, Ilene, William Kelly, and Patricia Doyle. 1977. Societal reactions to deviants: the case of criminal defendants. *American Sociological Review* 42:743–55.

Bullock, Henry. 1961. Significance of the racial factor in the length of prison sentences. *Journal of Criminal Law, Criminology and Police Science* 52:411–17.

Chambliss, William, and Robert Seidman. 1971. *Law, order and power.* Reading, MA: Addison-Wesley.

Cherlin, Andrew J. 1981. *Marriage. Divorce. Remarriage.* Cambridge: Harvard University Press.

Duncan, Otis Dudley. 1975. *Introduction to structural equation models.* New York: Academic Press.

Farley, Reynolds. 1977. Trends in racial inequalities: Have the gains of the 1960s disappeared in the 1970s? *American Sociological Review* 42:189–208.

Gallup, George H. 1972. *The Gallup poll: Public opinion 1935–1971.* Volume Three, 1959–1971. New York: Random House.

——. 1978a. *The Gallup poll: Public opinion 1972–1977.* Volume One, 1972–1975. Wilmington, DE: Scholarly Resources.

——. 1978b. *The Gallup poll: Public opinion 1972–1977.* Volume Two, 1976–1977. Wilmington, DE: Scholarly Resources.

——. 1979. *The Gallup poll: Public opinion 1978.* Wilmington, DE: Scholarly Resources.

Garfinkel, Harold. 1949. Research note on inter- and intra-racial homicides. *Social Forces* 27:369–81.

Gibson, James L. 1978. Race as a determinant of criminal sentences: a methodological critique and a case study. *Law and Society Review* 12:455–78.

Glaser, Daniel. 1974. Interlocking dualities in drug use, drug control, and crime. In James Inciardi and Carl Chambers, eds., *Drugs and the criminal justice system,* 39–56. Beverly Hills: Sage.

Green, Edward. 1961. *Judicial attitudes in sentencing: A study of the factors underlying the Sentencing Practices of the Criminal Court of Philadelphia.* New York: St. Martin's Press.

Gusfield, Joseph R. 1967. Moral passage: the symbolic process in public designations of deviance. *Social Problems* 15:175–88.

——. 1975. The (f)utility of knowledge?: The relation of social science to public policy toward drugs. *The Annals* 417:1–15.

Hagan, John. 1974. Extra-legal attributes and criminal sentencing: an assessment of a sociological viewpoint. *Law and Society Review* 8:357–83.

Hagan, John and Celesta Albonetti. 1982. Race, class and the perception of criminal injustice in America. *American Journal of Sociology* 88:329–55.

Hagan, John and Kristen Bumiller. 1983. Making sense of sentencing: A review and critique of sentencing research. In *Research on sentencing: The search for reform,* Volume 2, eds. Alfred Blumstein, Jacqueline Cohen, Susan Martin, and Michael Tonry, 1–54. Washington, DC: National Academy Press.

Heckman, James J. 1974. Shadow prices, market wages, and labor supply. *Econometrics* 42:679–94.

——. 1975. "Shadow prices, market wages, and labor supply: some computational and conceptual simplifications and revised estimates." Mimeographed Paper, Department of Economics, University of Chicago.

Hindelang, Michael J. 1969. Equality under the law. *Journal of Criminal Law, Criminology and Police Science* 60:306–13.

Ianni, Francis. 1974. *The black mafia.* New York: Simon & Schuster.

Katz, Jack. 1980. The social movement against white-collar crime. In *Criminology review yearbook,* Volume 2,, eds., Egon Bittner and Sheldon Messinger, 161–84 Beverly Hills: Sage.

Kleck, Gary. 1981. Racial discrimination in criminal sentencing: a critical evaluation of the evidence on the death penalty. *American Sociological Review* 46:783–804.

LaFree, Gary. 1980. The effect of sexual stratification by race on official reactions to rape. *American Sociological Review* 45:842–54.

Levin, Martin A. 1972. Urban politics and judicial behavior. *Journal of Legal Studies* 1: 193–221.

Lidz, Charles W. and Andrew L. Walker. 1980. *Heroin, deviance and morality.* Beverly Hills: Sage.

Moore, Mark. 1977. *Buy and bust: The effective regulation of an illicit market in heroin.* Lexington, MA: Lexington Books.

Musto, David F. 1973. *The American disease: Origins of narcotic control.* New Haven: Yale University Press.

Myrdal, Gunnar. 1944. *An American dilemma.* New York: Harper.

New York Times. January 20,1978. "Barnes is sentenced to life in drug case."

New York Times Magazine. June 5, 1977 " 'Mister Untouchable.' "15–17ff.

New York Times Editors 1969. Various Issues (see 1973 text for dates and pages).

Peterson, Ruth. 1983. The Sanctioning of Drug Offenders: Social Change and the Social Organization of Drug Law Enforcement. Unpublished PhD Dissertation, Department of Sociology, University of Wisconsin–Madison.

Pettigrew, Thomas. 1980. "The changing—not declining—significance of race." *Contemporary Sociology* 9:19–21.

Quinney, Richard. 1970. *The social reality of crime.* Boston: Little, Brown.

Reasons, Charles. 1974. "The politics of drugs: an inquiry in the sociology of social problems." *Sociological Quarterly* 15:381–404.

Rothman, David J. 1980. *Conscience and convenience: The asylum and its alternatives in progressive America.* Boston: Little, Brown.

Sudnow, David. 1965. "Normal crimes: sociological features of the penal code in a public defender office." *Social Problems* 12:255–76.

Susman, Ralph M. 1975. "Drug abuse, Congress and the fact-finding process." *The Annals* 417:16–26.

Swigert, Victoria L. and Ronald A. Farrell. 1977. "Normal homicides and the law." *American Sociological Review* 42:16–32.

Thomson, Randall J. and Matthew T. Zingraff. 1981. Detecting sentencing disparity: some problems and evidence. *American Journal of Sociology* 86:869–80.

United States Congress. 1970. *Congressional Record—House Volume 116* (daily edition, September 23, 1970).

——. 1970. *Congressional Record—House Volume 116* (daily edition, September 24, 1970).

United States Senate 1969 Narcotics Legislations. Hearings Before the Subcommittee to Investigate Juvenile Delinquency of the Committee of the Judiciary, 91st Congress—1st Session. Washington, DC: United States Government Printing Office.

Wheeler, Stanton, David Weisbord, and Nancy Bode, 1972. Sentencing the white-collar offender: rhetoric and reality. *American Sociological Review* 47:641–59.

Wilson, William Julius. 1978. *The declining significance of race: Blacks and changing American institutions.* Chicago: University of Chicago Press.

Wolfgang, Marvin E., and Marc Riedel. 1973. Race, judicial discretion, and the death penalty. *The Annals* 407:119–33.

7

My Black Crime Problem, and Ours

John J. DiIulio, Jr.

Violent crime is down in New York and many other cities, but there are two big reasons to keep the champagne corked. One is that murder, rape, robbery, and assault remain at historic highs: the streets of Manhattan, like those of Houston, Philadelphia, Detroit, Chicago, and Los Angeles, remain much less safe today than in the 1950s and 1960s. Worse, though policing and prison policies matter, nothing affects crime rates more than the number of young males in the population—and by the year 2010, there will be about 4.5 million more males age 17 or under than there were in 1990: 8 percent more whites and 26 percent more blacks. Since around 6 percent of young males turn out to be career criminals, according to the historical data, this increase will put an estimated 270,000 more young predators on the streets than in 1990, coming at us in waves over the next two decades. Numerous studies show that each succeeding generation of young male criminals commits about three times as much serious crime as the one before it: the occasional fatal knife fight of 1950s street gangs has given way to the frequent drive-by shootings of 1990s gangs.

The second reason to keep the champagne corked is that not only is the number of young black criminals likely to surge, but also the black crime rate, both black-on-black and black-on-white, is increasing, so that as many as half of these juvenile super-predators could be young black males. But just when we need to think most earnestly about black crime, the space for honest discourse about race and crime is shrinking. The evidence of that shrinkage is everywhere: in the lickety-split O.J. verdict and its racially polarized aftermath, in the utter certitude of many blacks that the justice system is rigged against them, in the belief of many whites that violent crime is synonymous with black crime and the fear they feel of every young black male passerby not wearing a tie or handcuffs.

What has made our views on race and crime so polarized—and often so out of touch with reality? What *are* the facts about race and crime? And what are Americans, blacks and whites together, to do about it?

Many blacks, and some whites, believe that the justice system is biased against blacks, at worst purposefully racist or even "genocidal." Take a recent *New Yorker* article, in which Henry Louis Gates Jr., leader of Harvard University's black studies program, chronicled "Thirteen Ways of Looking at a Black Man," namely, the acquitted O.J. Simpson. Gates writes: "Perhaps you didn't know that Liz Claiborne appeared on *Oprah* and said she didn't design her clothes for black women—that their hips were too wide. Perhaps you didn't know that the soft drink Tropical Fantasy is manufactured by the Ku Klux Klan and contains a special ingredient to sterilize black men. . . . Perhaps you didn't know these things but a good many black Americans think they do. . . . Never mind that Liz Claiborne has never appeared on *Oprah*, [or] that the beleaguered Brooklyn [soft drink] company has gone as far as to make an FDA assay of its ingredients. . . . If you wonder why blacks seem particularly susceptible to rumors and conspiracy theories, you might take a look at a history in which the official story was a poor guide to anything that mattered much, and in which rumor sometimes verged on the truth. Heard the one about the L.A. cop who hated interracial couples, fantasized about making a bonfire of black bodies, and boasted of planting evidence?"

Gates, like the renowned sociologist William Julius Wilson, one of the prominent black Americans whose views of the O.J. verdict he cites, was convinced that O.J. was guilty. But he recounts a story Wilson told him about once being stopped near a small New England town by a policeman who wanted to know what he was doing in those parts: "There's a moving violation that many African-Americans know as DWB: Driving While Black," notes Gates. As "older blacks like to repeat," when "white folks say 'justice,' they mean 'just us.'" In other words, blacks really do experience enough casual, reflexive racism from law enforcement officers to make them understandably fearful that racism permeates the criminal justice system.

A point well taken. But then Gates's article goes astray: it never makes plain that, in spite of these reasonable anxieties and resentments, some ways of "looking at a black man"—at any man—are right and reasonable while others are wrong and malicious. Some of the people who burst into jubilation over the O.J. verdict were celebrating the release of a man whom they believed to be innocent. With due regard for the fact that two families have lost loved ones, that's okay. But other blacks partied to a he-killed-the-blonde-and-got-away-with-it tune. For example, a sign held by a woman whose picture appeared in the *New York Times Magazine* read: "Guilty or Not We Love You O.J." Gates quotes film director Spike Lee as follows: "A lot of black folks said, 'Man, O.J. is *bad*, you know. This is the first brother in the history of the world who got away with murder of white folks, and a blonde, blue-eyed woman at that.' " Lee, Gates reports, "wasn't happy" at the verdict. But some black folks were thrilled—and for morally indefensible reasons that Gates needs to condemn, not artfully explain.

Nevertheless, the ambivalence and mistrust that many blacks feel toward the justice system is a social reality that whites can't ignore. *The Weekly Standard's* deputy editor, John Podhoretz, wrote in the magazine about the O.J. verdict and race relations under the double-meaning heading "Yes, We Do Understand": "How can most black Americans believe (or say they believe) that O.J. Simpson is innocent of a crime science tells us there is a one-in-a-billion chance he did not commit? . . . We—that is, we upper-middle-class whites—must, by a process of study and observation, come to *understand*. And it will be 'white' institutions, from the Ford Foundation to the *New York Times* to America's corporations, that will insist on fostering this *understanding*. . . . For the American liberal establishment, this has become the stock response after a public outrage that divides Americans by color. . . . Is black America so lost in its own resentment . . . that they feel closer kinship to a killer because of his skin color than to the killer's victims? I can understand how this has happened, but it makes me sick."

Like Gates, Podhoretz never arrives at the right moral point. The point is that to *understand* is neither to forgive any criminal his crime nor to sit still when "racism" is used as an all-purpose excuse for morally abhorrent or socially pathological behavior. Like Podhoretz, I have little patience with liberal elites of whatever color who are nothing better than well-funded nihilists. I could not care less about understanding what they have to say, and I would not be the least bit concerned—if they were the only ones saying it.

But they aren't. All of us, "upper-middle-class whites" included, are morally required to understand and ponder what so many black folks have to say—not only the knee-jerk liberal pundits and politicians, but also world-class professors (like Wilson), plumbers, postal workers, paramedics, prosecutors, preachers, and (in my case) former students. Many of them are saying that they feel the justice system is as much a foe as a friend. As I will summarize below, I find almost nothing in the empirical research literature on racial disparities in sentencing to justify their fears and frustrations. But that does not mean their fears and frustrations are without any sort of empirical basis, including the kind that, for most of us, counts more than any other—our own lived experiences and those of our family and friends.

As Gates recalls, Norman Podhoretz, the father of John Podhoretz and until recently the editor of *Commentary*, wrote a famous soul-searching 1963 essay, "My Negro Problem, and Ours." Gates describes the essay as "one of the frankest accounts we have of liberalism and race resentment," a. plainspoken tale of "a Brooklyn boyhood spent under the shadow of carefree, cruel Negro assailants, and of the author's residual unease when he passes groups of blacks in his Upper West Side neighborhood." In one key passage, the elder Podhoretz noted: "I know now, as I did not know when I was a child, that power is on my side, that the police are working for me and not for them."

But I knew. Growing up in rough-edged, white-ethnic, working-class neighborhoods of Philadelphia in the 1960s and 1970s, I knew—as all the kids I grew up with knew—that when push literally came to shove, the police would be "working for me and not for them." Each morning on my way to high school, I stood by myself at a bus stop, surrounded mainly by black teenagers from adjacent neighborhoods. I was by myself, but I was not alone. I knew that the cop in the cruiser was looking out for me in case "they" started trouble that I could not handle.

My old neighborhood had its biracial, but strictly segregated, parks and playgrounds. When interracial fights did break out, everyone ran when the cops came. But we white boys knew that if we got caught and showed due deference to the officers (*never* mouth off to a panting cop), we'd get lectured, get our hair pulled, or (at most) get our fathers called. We also knew the black boys would get that and worse—slapped, clubbed, and maybe arrested.

Once when I was unloading 100-pound flour bags at a downtown pizzeria where I worked, the cops came zooming up the sidewalk, got out of their cruiser, and pushed my pal and co-worker, Willie Brown, against the wall. They did not touch me. Willie, an illiterate black man then in his forties, had done nothing. I protested, and the cops sped off as quickly as they had come: "Sorry, kid, we got a call that somebody was stealing." But the only "somebody" they grabbed was the black man, and the only apology they issued was to the white boy.

I recall the second time my father, a retired deputy sheriff, ran a citywide race for sheriff and appointed me his manager (mainly to teach me something about politics before I "bought whatever they think they know about it at Harvard"). He ran on a real rainbow-coalition ticket with former deputy mayor Charles Bowser, Philly's first major black mayoral candidate. We lost the election (no surprise) as well as good relations with some neighbors (sad surprise), one of whom loudly scolded me that "we'll never be safe from crime if *they're* in charge of it."

Even though I am now a card-carrying elite professor and "upper-middle-class white," I have stayed close to home. I hang out with the same white working-class relatives and friends I've known all my life. I live a few minutes by car from some of Philadelphia's worst black neighborhoods. So I have a very different perspective from that of most white intellectuals, both on the white ethnics who turn into the cops blacks fear and on the everyday reality of life in black communities. And as little as the white policy elites, liberal or conservative, know about "the black experience," believe me, they know less about what race means in the lives of those Italian-American bricklayers, Irish-American gas pumpers, and Polish-American salesclerks whom the U.S. Census bureaucrats have baptized "non-Hispanic whites." We need to understand these folks, too—and especially how their experience of black-white relations leaves a tangle of powerful contradictions and ambivalences, as I know vividly from my own experience.

I indelibly remember taking a jump shot on the playground when I was ten. As the ball left my hand, instead of invoking, for luck, the name of a white star (as was customary), I unthinkingly shouted the name of a black star. "Nigger lover!" snapped a scandalized playmate. But the following week, the same kid punched out a white schoolyard bully for bothering a black girl who wandered by. I'll never forget how much, when my frail grandmother got kicked, punched, and robbed in broad daylight for the third time (on her way to church, no less), the fact that her assailants were (once again) black boys got under my white skin. The memory of the anger is still there—along with the image of her in her hospital bed, imploring her strapping grandsons, some of us cops, to "love all God's people."

So it's no mystery to me that blacks tense when they see a white cop coming: they know the Willie Brown experience well enough, and how could they possibly know the sense of justice regardless of race, even the Christian *caritas* transcending race, that can lie beneath the blue uniform and the white skin? Just that white ambivalence is as familiar territory to me as it was to Norman Podhoretz. I grew up with it; I know that casual racism is there; I know the anger and shame you feel at seeing it all around you—and I know the competing anger, no less familiar: the anger at the knowledge that when real violence erupts, all too often the assailants are (once again) black.

Honest blacks know this, too. In a recent issue of *The New Republic*, Boston University economist Glenn Loury writes of inner-city black communities: "'What manner of people are you who live like this?' The question is unavoidable. . . . It does no good to say that these are a minority of black persons; that there are good and sufficient reasons for their troubling behaviors; that others, who are not black, have also fallen short." Of middle-class blacks, he admits: "We are afraid to go into these communities. We do not recognize these kids as us; the distance is great and difficult to bridge."

My black crime problem, and ours, is that for most Americans, especially for average white Americans, the distance is not merely great but almost unfathomable, the fear is enormous and largely justifiable, and the black kids who inspire the fear seem not merely unrecognizable but alien. Not that we can't understand where they come from, when we stop to consider. After all, the child is father to the man: and think how many inner-city black children are without parents, relatives, neighbors, teachers, coaches, or clergymen to teach them right from wrong, give them loving and consistent discipline, show them the moral and material value of hard work and study, and bring them to cherish the self-respect that comes only from respecting the life, liberty, and property of others. Think how many black children grow up where parents neglect and abuse them, where other adults and teenagers harass and harm them, where drug dealers exploit them. Not surprisingly, in return for the favor, some of these children kill, rape, maim, and steal without remorse. And around goes the negative feedback loop: reasonable fear feeds unreasonable white race hostility, whose reality in turn feeds unreasonable black paranoia about the justice system.

Is there anything social science research can do to help dispel all the ambivalence and confusion crowding around the subject of race and crime? At least it can tell the truth, as the data disclose it, about the reality of black crime and black punishment. The bottom line of most of the best research is that America's justice system is *not* racist, not anymore, not as it undoubtedly was only a generation ago—in spite of the Driving While Black experience. If blacks are overrepresented in the ranks of the imprisoned, it is because blacks are overrepresented in the criminal ranks—and the violent criminal ranks, at that. Yes, there are ways in which the justice system is failing all Americans, including black Americans. But to the extent that the justice system hurts, rather than helps, blacks more than it does whites, it is not by incarcerating a "disproportionate" number of young black men. Rather, it is by ignoring poor black victims and letting convicted violent and repeat black criminals, both adult and juvenile, continue to victimize and demoralize the black communities that suffer most of their depredations.

Consider the data. A 1993 study of the racial impact of federal sentencing guidelines found that the imposition between 1986 and 1990 of stiffer penalties for drug offenders, especially cocaine traffickers, did not result in racially disparate sentences. The amount of the drug sold, the seriousness of the offender's prior criminal history, whether weapons were involved, and other such valid characteristics of criminals and their crimes accounted for *all* the observed interracial variations in prison sentences.

Similarly, a 1991 RAND Corporation study of adult robbery and burglary defendants in 14 large U.S. cities found that a defendant's race or ethnic group bore almost no relation to conviction rates, sentencing severity, or other key measures. In 1995, federal government statistician Patrick A. Langan analyzed data on 42,500 defendants in the nation's 75 largest counties and found "no evidence that, in the places where blacks in the United States have most of their contacts with the justice system, that system treats them more harshly than whites."

A 1985 study by Langan of black–white differentials in imprisonment rates demonstrated that "even if racism exists, it might explain only a small part of the gap between the 11 percent black representation in the United States adult population and the now nearly 50 percent black representation among persons entering state prisons each year in the United States." An otherwise typically liberal-leaning 1993 National Academy of Sciences study voiced the same basic conclusion.

It is often asserted that the 1980s war on drugs resulted in a more racially "disproportionate" prison population. The data tell a different story. In 1980, 46.6 percent of state prisoners and 34.4 percent of federal prisoners were black; by 1990, 48.9 percent of state prisoners and 31.4 percent of federal prisoners were black. In 1988, the median time served in confinement by black violent offenders was 25 months, versus 24 months for their white counterparts. The mean sentence lengths were 116 months for blacks and 110 for whites, while the mean times actually served in confinement were 37 months for blacks, 33 months for whites. These small differences are explained by the fact that black violent crimes are generally more serious than white ones (aggravated rather than simple assaults, weapon-related crimes rather than weaponless ones).

Indeed, the evidence on the race-neutrality of incarceration decisions is now so compelling that even topflight criminologists who rail against the anti-drug regime, mandatory sentencing laws, three-strikes laws, and other policies with which they disagree are nonetheless careful to contend that racial biases are "built into the law," are "America's dirty little secret," or constitute "malign neglect." In other words, they do everything but challenge the proposition that blacks and whites who do the same crimes and have similar criminal records are now handled by the system in the same ways.

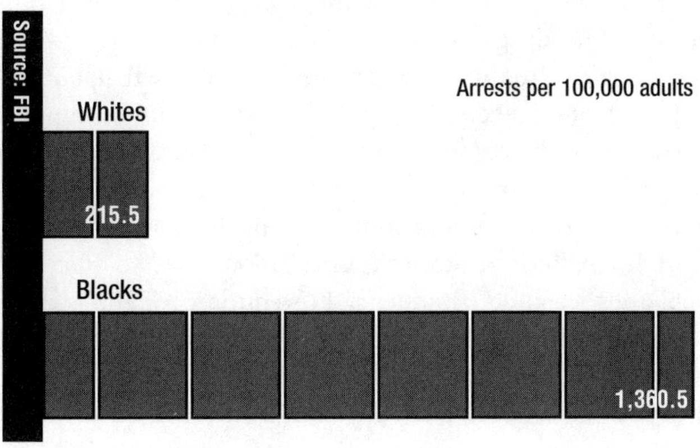

Fig. 7.1 Violent Crimes Arrest Rates, 1992.

In this vein, liberal experts contend that the penalties for crack cocaine possession and sale are excessive compared with powder cocaine penalties. I concur. And liberals are also right that blacks are far more likely than whites to use and sell crack instead of powder cocaine. But they go badly wrong on two key counts. First, they feed the conspiratorial myth that federal anti-crack penalties were born of a white conspiracy led by right-wing Republicans. Go check the *Congressional Record:* in 1986, when the federal crack law was debated, the Congressional Black Caucus (CBC) supported it, and some CBC members pressed for even harsher penalties. A few years earlier it was CBC members and other Democrats in Congress who pushed President Reagan, against his considered judgment, to create ate the Office of National Drug Control Policy (better known as the drug czar's office). And it was President Clinton who recently refused in no uncertain terms to change the federal penalty structure for drug crimes.

Second, liberal experts and advocates of drug legalization cloud the facts about who really goes to prison for drug crimes. As I and several other researchers have concluded, society gets little return on its investment in locking up low-level offenders who possess or even traffic in small amounts of drugs and commit no other crimes. But most drug offenders, both those behind bars and those who have served their time, do *not* fit that description.

As a recent study funded by the National Institute of Justice and other federal agencies acknowledged, in "an important sense the label 'drug offender' is a misnomer." Few "drug offenders" are in prison for mere possession. In 1991, for example, only 2 percent of the 36,648 persons admitted to federal prisons were in for drug possession. Moreover, as for imprisoned drug *traffickers*, most have long and diversified criminal records—only their latest and most serious conviction offense is a drug-trafficking offense. Even in the much-maligned federal system, few convicted drug traffickers, whether they handle crack, powder cocaine, or pot, are black college kids or white white-collar types arrested on the interstate by a state trooper who found a small stash under the driver's seat. The average quantity of drugs involved in federal cocaine trafficking cases is 183 pounds, while the average for marijuana traffickers is 3.5 tons.

In an ongoing study of who really goes to prison in Wisconsin, George Mitchell and I are examining the complete criminal records, adult and juvenile, of a randomly selected sample of imprisoned felons from Milwaukee County. We are finding that the imprisoned "drug offenders," black and white, like most of the rest of the sample, have committed many times more property, drug, and violent crimes than the latest entries on their prison rap sheets would indicate. This is not to mention all the crimes swept completely under the official-records rug by plea bargaining, or all the wholly undetected, unprosecuted, and unpunished crimes the prisoners have committed while free.

Of course, there are cases of truly petty drug dealers, black and white, being hit with long, hard time. But such cases are the exception that proves the rule, and the rule is that the system is neither harsh nor racist in dealing with "drug offenders" or other criminals.

Some experts will come *almost* to the point of agreement with all that, but still will insist that the system is anything but color-blind when it comes to two important tasks: punishing juveniles and dishing out death sentences. But here, too, the evidence does more to exonerate than to indict the system.

Out of hundreds of post-1969 studies of minorities in the juvenile justice system, barely two dozen offer evidence of any pattern of racial discrimination. Even so, liberal strongholds like the federal Office of Juvenile Justice and Delinquency Prevention (OJJDP)—which made a cavalierly fragmentary and outdated examination of only 46 of the 250 relevant studies—continue to purvey the myth that young black offenders are treated more severely than young white ones. Notwithstanding OJJDP and its race-baiting minions, the truth is not that the juvenile system is racist, or that the states incarcerate too many minority juvenile offenders—or, indeed, too many juvenile offenders of whatever background.

Rather, as the National District Attorneys Association and other law enforcement officials have said for years, the juvenile system is an even worse revolving door than the adult system. For example, in 1991 fewer than 20,000 male juvenile violent offenders were in public juvenile facilities—but in 1992 alone there were more than 110,000 juvenile arrests for violent crimes, and more than 1.6 million juvenile arrests for other crimes. In most states, police, prosecutors, and judges do not even have complete access to juvenile records, and some states still forbid fingerprinting juveniles, including kids charged with weapons offenses that would be grade-A felonies if committed by adults.

Over the coming decade, juvenile arrests in California and many other states are projected to increase by some 25 percent, even more for minority juveniles. By the year 2005 we will probably have 200,000 convicted juvenile criminals, half of them black males, in secure confinement, including adult prisons and jails—over three times more than the number of incarcerated juveniles today. The reason for this will not be racism or what OJJDP calls "disproportionate minority confinement." The reason will be that more black boys grew up without adults who were willing and able to save them—and their victims—from tragedy.

What should be done with cold-blooded killers of whatever race? Like most other Americans, the majority of black Americans favor the death penalty. Yet around that punishment swirls the most acrimonious of all racial disparity controversies. Here too, though, the data disclose no trace of racism.

Reviewing the evidence in 1994, Professors Stanley Rothman and Stephen Powers concluded that after controlling for all relevant variables, one finds simply no evidence of racial disparities in post-1972 capital sentencing. The crucial variable is the severity of the crime. Though the vast majority of murders are committed by someone of the same race as the victim, black-on-white murders are more likely than black-on-black murders to be cases of strangers killing strangers and to "involve kidnapping and, rape, mutilations, execution-style murders, tortures, and beatings," according to Rothman and Powers. "These are all aggravating circumstances that increase the likelihood of a death sentence."

Even the raw statistics don't show much sign of racism. From the day the U.S. Supreme Court reinstated the death penalty in 1976 through the end of 1993, more than 400,000 Americans were murdered. Over the same period, only 226 killers were executed, 38 percent of them black. In 1993, blacks were 40 percent of the 2,716 prisoners on death row and 36 percent of the 38 convicted murderers executed. The scandalous truth is, most of the thousands of murderers behind bars don't face too harsh but too lenient a punishment. Most get out of prison. Murderers released from state prisons in 1992 served an average of only 5.9 years. There is no evidence that black murderers get out any less quickly than comparable white ones.

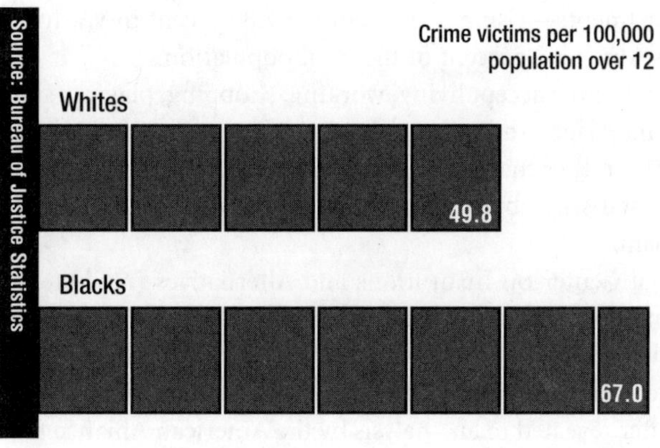

Fig. 6.2 Violent Crimes Victimization Rates, 1993.

Yet, as with juvenile justice, anti-death penalty partisans, including congressmen, promote racially charged falsehoods like those that flew during the 1994 debate in Congress over the so-called Racial Justice Act (RJA). Though this disgraceful bill, which would have established a de facto racial quota system in murder cases, was defeated, it got very serious consideration. It was based on the shoddiest possible research, purporting to show that because of racism, more blacks than whites are executed for similar crimes, and that the law values white victims' lives more than black victims' lives. But in fact, contrary to the fevered fantasies of the RJA's supporters that we have hardly progressed beyond the days of racist lynchings, we actually have arrived at a day when in murder cases generally, and in black-on-white murder cases in particular, "going for the death penalty" has become such a political, judicial, and media nightmare for big-city prosecutors that many urban DAs do not even try. Many, like L.A. District Attorney Gil Garcetti—the man who spared O.J. a death sentence even faster than the jury spared him any sentence at all—not only avoid the death penalty but seem more concerned with preempting any possibility of false but damaging accusations of racism than in following the rule of law, protecting the public, doing the work, and taking the heat.

Recently a page-one story in the *Wall Street Journal* tackled the question of "jury nullification" in cases involving black defendants. It is increasingly common for black jurors to "side with African-American defendants against a mostly white-dominated justice system," even to the point of acquitting black defendants whom the jurors know to be guilty on the legal merits—and even when the victims are black. More black jurors "are choosing to disregard the evidence, however powerful, because they seek to protest racial injustice and to refrain from adding to the already large number of blacks behind bars." The story noted that in the Bronx, where juries are more than 80 percent black and Hispanic, black defendants are acquitted in felony cases 47.6 percent of the time—three times the national acquittal rate of 17 percent for all races. In Washington, D.C., where virtually all defendants and 70 percent of jurors are black, 28.7 percent of all felony trials end in acquittals. Similar patterns hold in Detroit and several other cities where black jurors predominate. Paul Butler, a black criminal-law professor at George Washington University, was quoted as arguing that in cases involving black defendants charged with nonviolent crimes, black jurors should "presume in favor of nullification."

A response to racism? Something more is at issue, for this isn't happening just in cases where black jurors are hearing white cops testify against black criminals. Black jurors' resistance to police witnesses has grown even as virtually every big city has increased the percentage of blacks on its police force, moved the force ever nearer to mirroring the racial composition of its citizenry, and seen blacks become precinct captains, deputy chiefs, commissioners, and mayors. Between 1983 and 1992, the percentage of blacks on big-city police forces increased in each and every one of the nation's ten biggest police departments—rising 50 percent to 67.8 percent in Washington, D.C., to take one example, where blacks were 65.8 percent of the local population.

Most whites and blacks now accept living, working, shopping, playing, side by side—every inter-racial interaction save marriage. And yet on crime, America seems closer than ever to becoming two nations separated by race rather than one nation under God. Why? At least part of the reason is that we are inundated with statistics about race, crime, and punishment that needlessly fan black concerns about white racism.

In 1993 the National Center on Institutions and Alternatives (NCIA), an advocacy group that opposes mandatory sentencing and favors making a greater use of probation, parole, and rehabilitation programs, publicized its finding that "43 percent of all young black men in Washington, D.C.—and 56 percent in Baltimore—are firmly in the grip of the justice system." The press broadcast the numbers far and wide. As was later revealed in an analysis by the American Alliance for Rights and Responsibilities, the statistics were a bit inflated, but even after appropriate correction, the NCIA study would still have found about 35 percent of Washington's young black men in prison, in jail, on probation, or on parole. Indeed, in a highly publicized 1995 report, the Sentencing Project, a Washington-based counterpart of NCIA, found that nationwide about one in three black males age 20 to 29 was under some form of correctional supervision. As the Sentencing Project reported, in 1989 about 610,000 black males in their twenties—23 percent of the cohort—were in custody. But by 1995 that number had risen to over 827,000—32.2 percent of the nation's twenty-something black males. One could quibble with the estimates, but the finding is valid; in fact, my own estimates would indicate that the number is already closer to 50 percent in some places, and that nationally it will be nearer to a half than a third by the year 2000.

As the Sentencing Project boasts, "the report has had a major impact in the media and among policymakers." Oddly, however, its "major impact" has been to divert attention from the big truth that one in three young black males is under correctional supervision because young black male rates of serious crime are so high. Instead it has focused attention on the half-truths and outright distortions long purveyed by the Sentencing Project, other anti-incarceration advocacy groups, and their funders and allies in the drug legalization movement, the liberal foundations, the politically correct universities, and the elite media. The mantra goes like this: how shameful to America that one in three young black males is in custody . . . most of those in custody are in for petty drug crimes . . . revolving-door justice is a right-wing myth . . . the justice system is racist . . . America has been on an imprisonment binge . . . prisons don't cut crime in the least . . . imprisonment is not only an ineffective response to crime but a racist one.

Predictably, the Sentencing Project and its turn-'em-loose comrades-in-arms have now begun to dig for more such racially polarizing pay dirt. For example, the Center for Juvenile and Criminal Justice in San Francisco recently "found" that 40 percent of black men in their twenties in California were under some form of correctional supervision. Representative Maxine Waters held a news conference in which she declared the study proof that in California "the color of your skin dictates whether you will be arrested or not, prosecuted harshly or less harshly, or receive a stiff sentence or gain probation or entry into treatment." The report itself called for a moratorium on prison construction in California until the state's penal code is "overhauled." It also called for mandating "racial impact statements" in all new crime legislation, and for a state commission to study black "overrepresentation." Except for a very few dissenting voices, including the nation's leading crime-policy scholar, UCLA's James Q. Wilson, virtually all the published and broadcast "expert" commentary on this report followed the radical–liberal party line.

The Sentencing Project and its supporters can pretend all they want that racism and the "war on drugs" have put too many harmless young black males in prison. But are racist drug laws responsible for the fact that *weapons arrest rates* during 1993 were five times greater for blacks than for whites? Do they explain the fact that 47 percent of all black men in prison in 1995 were in for a *violent crime*, and that most black state prisoners, like most state prisoners, have committed one or more violent crimes in the past? Do they explain the fact that the black men in prison for a drug crime were, like virtually all prisoners, *repeat offenders* with non-drug crimes on their rap sheets?

There are Washington monument-sized fallacies and contradictions in what the Sentencing Project and its allied spin doctors have argued about "1 in 3." For example, the system is supposedly "racist" because it hammers black drug dealers. But who wants them hammered? Look at the survey data on decriminalizing or legalizing drugs. Without fail, blacks are every bit as opposed to weakening anti-drug enforcement efforts as whites. Only 30 percent of blacks would even consider legalizing marijuana; virtually none will even debate legalizing harder drugs. My dear friend and former colleague Ethan Nadelmann is director of the Lindesmith Center and the country's leading proponent of turning down the volume on the drug war. His most vehement, unyielding critics are not middle-class whites led by right-wing Republicans. Rather, they are poor and working-class blacks led by folks like New York's black Democratic Representative Charles Rangel.

What if, for argument's sake, one swallows the notion that the system now "over-punishes" black drug dealers, and that most of these "drug dealers" are not, in fact, plea bargain-gorged persons with long adult and juvenile records of criminal mischief against persons and property? What then? Which drug-crime 911 calls from black neighborhoods are the police to ignore? Which black drug dealers should be released back to their communities tomorrow morning?

You can't have it both ways—protesting that police are less responsive to black crime victims than to white ones in one breath, charging that "too many" black victimizers get caught, convicted, and sentenced, in the next; spinning out conspiratorial theories of white acquiescence in letting drugs flow into black communities in the morning, complaining that efforts to crack down on the drug trade are motivated by racism in the afternoon.

Take a look at Fig. 7.3. Based on its latest crime victimization surveys, the U.S. Bureau of Justice Statistics estimates that in 1993 alone blacks committed 1.29 million violent crimes against other blacks—80 percent of all violent crimes against blacks. Blacks also committed 1.54 million violent crimes against whites—18 percent of all violent crimes against whites.

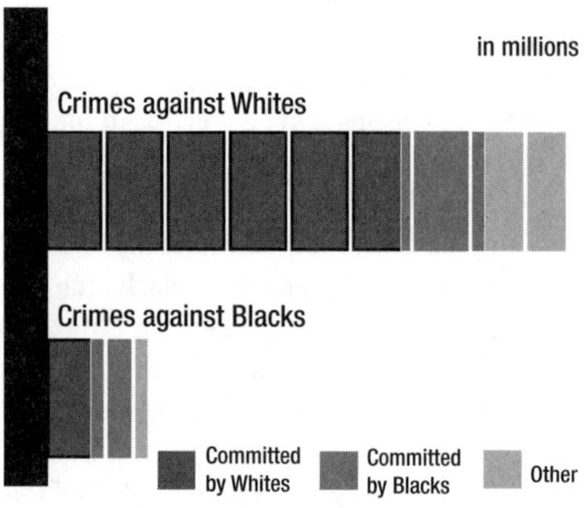

Fig.7.3 Violent Crimes, 1993.

As a number of analysts have begun to notice, blacks are about 50 times more likely to commit violent crimes against whites than whites are to commit violent crimes against blacks. Like the Sentencing Project's "1 in 3" number, this "50 to 1" statistic is technically correct. If you divide the total number of black-on-white violent crimes in 1993 (1.29 million) by the number of black males age 20 to 29 in the population in 1993 (3.94 million), you get a ratio equal to 1,013 violent crimes against whites per 10,000 young black males. If you do the same calculation for the total number of white-on-black crimes (186,000) divided by the total number of twenty-something white males (22.9 million), you get a ratio of 17.6 violent crimes committed by whites against blacks for every 10,000 young white males. Thus, the incidence of interracial black-on-white violent crime by young black males (1,013) is 57.5 times the incidence of interracial white-on-black crime by young white males (17.6). Using different denominators (for example, white versus black males age 15 to 29) moves the statistic down a bit (in the example given, to 48 to 1). But it clusters around "50 to 1."

In his recent essay in *The New Republic*, Glenn Loury explains that "there are roughly eight times as many whites as blacks; and there are about six times as many violent criminals per capita among blacks as among whites. So, if criminals chose their victims at random, without regard to race, one would expect the black-on-white victimization rate per black person to be 48 times as large as the white-on-black rate per white person. Thus, it does not appear that black criminals take affirmative action to find white victims."

Loury is absolutely right, and he or I or any other competent analyst could fashion a half-dozen fancier ways of minimizing the "50 to 1" statistic. In the end, however, nothing we could produce would be other than cold comfort to white victims of black criminals. For every such "explanation" merely underlines the reality behind *both* "1 in 3" and "50 to 1": namely, that young black males *do* commit serious crimes at a much higher rate than whites. Worse, where the growing problems of black juvenile and "wolf pack" crimes are concerned, it may well be that young black criminals really are targeting white victims. For example, as even OJJDP has noted, while about 95 percent of all violent crimes committed by white juveniles in 1991 were against whites, 57 percent of all violent crimes committed by black juveniles also were against whites.

The simple if unpalatable truth, therefore, is that even if we decriminalized black drug-dealing, there would still be racial "disproportionalities" in the justice system. Even if we also decriminalized all black crime save black-on-black violent crime, racial "disproportionalities" would persist.

Here's a suggestive calculation. In 1991, 372,200 black men were in prison, along with 363,600 white men. About 60 percent of all prisoners in 1991 had committed one or more violent crimes in the past. Suppose that we released 40 percent of the black prisoners—the 40 percent, say, with either no official history of violence or the least severe records of it. That would leave 223,320 black men behind bars. Then, because slightly more than half of the violent crimes committed by blacks are committed against whites, let's release, say, 55 percent of the remaining black violent male offenders. That would leave 100,494 black males in prison, 27 percent of 1991's actual total. They would be doing time with 3.6 times as many white males. But since whites in the general population still would outnumber blacks by roughly 8 to 1, the racial "disproportionality" would persist. To make it disappear completely—to get an 8-to-1 white–black ratio in prison—we would have to release all but 45,450 of the 372,200 black men in prison in 1991.

Similarly, 605,062 black adults were on probation in 1993, compared with 1,132,092 white adults, and 240,767 black adults were on parole, compared with 236,083 white adults. Thus, the total black adult community-based corrections population (probation plus parole) numbered 845,829, compared with 1.36 million whites. Let's say we believed that fully 70 percent of all black probationers and parolees, but none of the white ones, were innocent victims of a racist "war on drugs" and should never have been arrested. That would leave 253,749 black adults on probation and parole. We would still have only 5.3, not eight, times as many white adults as blacks "in custody" in the community. To eliminate entirely the racial "disproportionalities" in probation and parole, all but about 170,000 of the more than 800,000 black adults under community-based supervision in 1993 would have to be expunged from the rolls.

Even if, therefore, the justice system punished only those blacks who commit violent crimes—indeed, even if it punished only black violent criminals whose victims were themselves black—blacks would still be "overrepresented" in prison, in jail, on probation, and on parole. Thus, instead of all the ideological nonsense about "1 in 3" and the like, we should begin to focus in common on how revolving-door justice harms all Americans, most especially blacks. As the bipartisan Council on Crime in America has reported: "America's violent crime problem, especially the rage of homicidal and near-homicidal violence, is extremely concentrated among young urban minority males. . . . A study of murders committed in the nation's 75 most populous counties found that blacks were 52 percent of all murder victims and 62 percent of all murder defendants," but "they were only 20 percent of the general population in these metropolitan jurisdictions. . . . Between 1985 and 1992 the rate at which males ages 14 through 17 committed murder increased by about 50 percent for whites and over 300 percent for blacks. Between 1973 and 1992 the rate of violent victimizations of black males ages 12 to 24 increased about 25 percent; for example, black males ages 16 to 19 sustained one violent crime for 11 persons in 1973 versus one for every six in 1992."

For God's sake, let's be truthful. Especially in urban America, white fears of black crime—like black fears of black crime—are rational far more than reactionary or racist. If Americans are to learn how to deal in common with black crime as a problem of "sin, not skin," as Glenn Loury puts it—as a correctable moral defect of individuals, not some ineradicable racial fate—then we must hear and heed those leaders, black and white, liberal and conservative, who are speaking and doing something about it.

Hear Robert L. Woodson Sr., leader of the National Center for Neighborhood Enterprise. A veteran of the civil rights movement and an organizer of community- and faith-based groups that reach poor blacks and their children, Woodson speaks not of white racism but of "moral vagrants" in the black community who prey upon their disadvantaged neighbors.

Hear John W. Gillis, another prominent black, who heads California's parole board and is a member of the Council on Crime in America. On the day the council's first report was released to the press, Gillis stared into the cameras and implored responsible journalists to remember who normally puts black convicted criminals where they are, and why: black victims, black witnesses, and black communities—in order to do justice and to protect themselves from murder, mayhem, and deadly drug dealing.

Hear the grief-stricken family of Philadelphia police officer Lauretha Vaird, the city's first female cop—and first black woman—to be killed in the line of duty. Officer Vaird was murdered in cold blood, execution-style. Two of her three alleged killers are 26-year-old local black "gangsta" rappers who apparently practice the hate they sing. Vaird's family members are calling for justice—life in prison or the electric chair for the killers.

Hear Debra Dickerson, the self-described liberal black sister of a young black man paralyzed from the waist down in a drive-by shooting. Read her intensely gripping, highly personal essay published in *The New Republic*, "Who Shot Johnny?" Therein she rages at the black assailant who shot her brother and left him for dead. His "crime?" Waving hello at a car full of boys whom he mistakenly thought he knew. The assailant stood over his bleeding, barely conscious body and said, "Betch'ou won't be doin' nomo' wavin', motha'-fucker." The vicious attacker was never caught.

Hear Harvard law professor Randall Kennedy, who in a 1994 *Wall Street Journal* op-ed described as "dangerous" the response "that cries 'racism' as part of an all-out defense of any black accused of wrongdoing by 'white' authorities, regardless of the facts of the case," and as "troubling" the "position of some blacks that they will refuse to help send any black person to prison."

Hear the Reverend Jesse Jackson. For over a decade, no national black leader has argued more eloquently against policies that offer blacks jails instead of jobs—and none was quicker to make hay of the Sentencing Project's "1 in 3" finding. But recall Jackson's own tortured words on November 27, 1993: "There is nothing more painful for me at this stage of my life than to walk down the street and hear footsteps and start to think about robbery and then look around and see it's somebody white and feel relieved. How humiliating."

Above all, hear the Reverend Eugene Rivers of Boston. In the 1960s, Rivers was a member of one of Philadelphia's most violent black street gangs. Then the Reverend Ben Smith, a legend in the City of Brotherly Love, set him on the right path. As the Harvard-educated Rivers preaches: "For the people of God, every crisis, no matter how grim, presents a unique opportunity that can only be seen with the eyes of faith. For example, in racially war-torn Boston, black, Roman Catholic, and Jewish clergy have come together by faith to develop concrete strategies" for reducing crime and violence among black youth. In particular, under Rivers's leadership, dozens of black churches have begun moving together to look after abused or neglected inner-city black children, to stand up to drug dealers and gangsters, to spark local business development, and to reclaim the streets and end the terrors.

Rivers, his wife, and his two young children live in the Four Corners section of Dorchester, one of Boston's most violent black neighborhoods, where in 1991 three bullets from a gang shoot-out flew into Rivers's three-year-old son's bedroom. In 1993, Rivers grabbed a local crack merchant by the collar and told him not to deal at the local playground. "I told him, brother, I'll get you a job, I'll get you up for college—the whole nine yards," he says. "He told me to kiss his ass. So I did like I promised: I busted him—called the cops and probation and said, come get him now. They did." A week later, back on the streets and out for revenge, the kid drove by Rivers's house at 2 AM and pumped it with gunfire. No one was hurt.

As Rivers recalled: "The question from all the hoodlums in the neighborhood after that was, 'Is the minister going to cut and run?' " He stayed. He reformed the kid who shot up his home. He branched out, developing alliances with other churches, setting up neighborhood crime-watch programs, and developing a host of practical, tough-love programs, including "adopting a gang" for evangelistic outreach, and commissioning "missionaries" to go to court with juveniles, to make sure both that they get a fair shake and that they comply with the court's requirements. Rivers and his small group of talented volunteers work closely with city officials, the local police, the Catholic Church and schools, and just about everyone else who might make a positive difference in the lives of the kids he's trying to save.

Rivers styles himself a "Christian black nationalist." No one in America is less romantic about the record of inner-city black churches; no one is more realistic about their dwindling congregations, often near-empty coffers, and negative attraction to today's angry young black males. At the same time, no one understands better that when you get right down to it, a resurrection of the inner-city black churches is the one and only key to the resurrection of civil society in crime-and-drugs-ravaged black inner-city neighborhoods. A moral problem—a deficit of conscience, of values, of connectedness—requires a moral solution, and only a moral institution that comes out of the black community, such as the black church, can bring to bear the moral authority to solve it. "It's barbed wire and more black juvenile super-predators," observes Rivers, "or civil society and stronger black churches. It's that simple."

Since November 1994, conservatives have been talking lots about civil society. Now, however, comes the test. Rivers, Smith, and others aren't out there talking; they're out there doing. In Smith's case, he's been doing it for 50 years, a textbook example of the self-reliant, family-centered, church-based, community-strengthening, not-a-penny-from-government approach today's conservative theorists applaud. Conservative elites who are pushing welfare cuts should be putting their own money and influence into supporting the Riverses and the Smiths of inner-city America.

As Rivers exhorts, we must "together embrace the youth, disciplining our young people." In particular, he implores Christians to remember that "whatever you do for the least of these brothers and sisters, you do for Jesus." Amen.

8

Race, Conventional Crime, and Criminal Justice

The Declining Importance of Skin Color

Matt DeLisi and Robert Regoli

Introduction

The relationship between race, conventional or street crime, and the criminal justice system in the United States has been studied for many years.[1] Research studies reported that Blacks were more likely than Whites to commit conventional crimes. The arrest ratios by race (Black/White) were particularly significant for the violent crimes of murder (8:1), forcible rape (5:1), robbery (10:1), and aggravated assault (4:1) (U.S. Department of Justice, 1997a). Official data indicated the incarceration rate per 100,000 adults in 1996 was 289 for Whites and 1860 for Blacks (Kennedy, 1997). The chance of a Black male going to prison during his lifetime was greater than one in four (29 percent), while a White male only had a one in twenty-three (4 percent) chance of being incarcerated. The Black/White ratio for women serving prison time was roughly the same. Black women were seven times more likely than White females to be incarcerated sometime during their lives (U.S. Department of Justice, 1997b).

The disproportionate involvement of Blacks, particularly young males, in the criminal justice system may constitute a national crisis (Chiricos, Eschholz, and Gertz, 1997; Dilulio, 1994; Noguera, 1997). Some criminologists blamed the disparities on racial discrimination (Baer and Chambliss, 1997; Gordon, 1988; Hogan, 1995; Lynch and Patterson, 1991; 1996; Maden, 1993; Morris, 1988; Petersilia, 1985; Short, 1997), while others asserted that social class biases accounted for the differences (Blau and Blau, 1982; Hagan, Gillis, and Simpson, 1985; Tittle, Villimez, and Smith, 1978). The latter believed that the greater involvement of Blacks in street crime was due to their abject poverty. The statistical evidence in support of this last argument was substantial. At every level of educational attainment, Whites earned more money than Blacks. A greater percentage of Whites than Blacks earned high school diplomas, college degrees, and advanced degrees.[2] Nearly 9 percent of Whites lived below the poverty line, compared to 28 percent of Blacks. Blacks were more than twice as likely as Whites to be classified as working poor (U.S. Bureau of the Census, 1997).

Fueling the racial/social class discussion was the controversy over which data best described the relationship, since the manner in which variables were measured would influence a study's findings (Farnworth and Leiber, 1989; Menard, 1995). Official data indicated that Blacks were overwhelmingly more likely to be arrested for street crimes than were Whites. On the other hand, self-report data demonstrated sharp reductions in race differentials. Even self-report data indicated that Blacks were more involved in conventional crime than Whites (Elliott, 1994; 1995). Victimization surveys reported large race differentials in offending (Hindelang, 1978; 1981; Hindelang, Hirschi, and Weis, 1979; Laub and McDermott, 1985), as well as in criminal victimization. Blacks were more likely to be crime victims than were Whites, particularly for the violent crimes of murder and non-negligent homicide, forcible rape, robbery, and aggravated assault (U.S. Department of Justice, 1997c).

Each method of data production has its own unique strengths and weaknesses, though criminologists are puzzled about which source of data is best for explaining the problem at hand. If official data involve inflated race differences, perhaps that is because of invalid or biased police reporting practices. If self-report and victimization studies point to fewer racial differences in offending, some possible explanations may be that: (1) people do not recall when and whether they were an offender or victim (despite the visceral nature of criminal victimization), (2) respondents remember events as occurring more recently than they did because the events remain fresh in their memories (increasing measurement error), and, most simply, (3) offenders and victims lie to criminologists. For example, Hindelang, Hirschi, and Weis (1981) reported that Blacks minimized self-reports of criminal offending, thereby reducing reported race differentials. Self-reported error may also vary by age. Elliott (1994) discovered that during the adult years, self-reported race differentials were similar to official arrest data for serious criminal crimes.

Regardless of the technique used to produce the data, Blacks were found to be more involved in conventional crime than Whites (Elliott, 1994). The authors of the current study were uncomfortable assuming, *prima facie*, that a racist criminal justice system explains race differentials.[3] Such an explanation is problematic for three reasons. First, conceptions of the criminal justice system as racist retard the implementation of policies, such as community policing, which may improve the criminal justice system generally. Racial antagonism complicated the implementation of community policing (see Skogan, 1990). Second, the perception of the criminal justice system as racist, aggravates the relationship between the public and those criminal justice agents whose job it is to serve the community. Third, the allegation of racism diverts attention from crime victims who are disproportionately Black.

Methods and Propositions

Secondary analysis of the extant criminological literature was used to examine five hypotheses. The literature included studies employing official data (e.g., *Uniform Crime Reports*), self-report data (e.g., National Youth Survey), and victimization data (e.g., National Crime Victimization Survey).[4] The analysis was used to address questions that these original data sets never intended, incorporate several different data sets and studies in order to address a complex research question, and examine, in a larger scope, a criminological phenomenon (Senese, 1997, p. 200).

1. Police discretion is racially biased, resulting in higher Black arrest rates.
2. The arrest setting is an example of the practice of racial bias.
3. Incarceration rate differentials indicate racial bias.
4. If racial bias does occur, racial victimization rates should not be commensurate with racial arrest rates.
5. The "war on drugs" is biased against Blacks.

Findings

Little evidence was found to support the assertion that the criminal justice system exercises systematic racial discrimination against Blacks.

Proposition 1: Police Discretion

Do police discriminate against Blacks who are suspected of a criminal offense? A common perception is that police generally discriminate against Blacks. For example, 31 percent of Blacks, compared to only 8 percent of Whites, believed police had very low moral or ethical standards (U.S. Department of Justice, 1997a), which may manifest in discriminatory practices. To assess whether the police discriminate against Blacks, the current study examined arrest data for a crime where police exercise extraordinary discretion and, implicitly, have tremendous opportunity to discriminate: driving under the influence of alcohol (DUI). Seemingly benign infractions, such as expired plates, disengaged taillights, nonilluminated license plates, obstructed view, swerving, driving too slow, and speeding offer probable cause for police to stop a motorist.

If police were intent on a racist application of the law, Blacks should constitute a disproportionate number of DUI offenders. They do not. In two separate studies, with more than 5,000 people participating, it was reported for both adults and juveniles, that Whites were nine times more likely than Blacks to be arrested for DUI offenses (U.S. Department of Justice, 1992a; 1997a). It is plausible that motor vehicle ownership and registration, as a function of socioeconomic status, were greater among Whites than Blacks.[5] For a crime where it would be very easy for police to discriminate, Whites, not Blacks, were disproportionately arrested.

Proposition 2: Arrest Setting

The validity of arrestee accusations of police bias may be challenged since police often are responding (via 911 emergency calls) to highly volatile situations where offenders are frequently under the influence of drugs and alcohol. For example, 75 percent of spousal abuse victims reported that the arrestee was drinking alcohol. Thirty-six percent of the more than five million convicted offenders in the United States were drunk at the time of their arrest (U.S. Department of Justice, 1998a). Alcohol use by the offender, victim, or both preceded 50 percent of all violent criminal events (Roth, 1993).

The drug–crime link presents a logical dilemma for criminologists who blame race differentials in criminal offending on racial discrimination. First, police usually react to victim and/or witness calls for service; police do not typically patrol to exact a racist agenda. Claims that they do are largely anecdotal. Second, the arrest suspect's interpretation of what occurred during a police-citizen encounter is often clouded by drugs and alcohol. Who is more likely to misreport, the intoxicated offender or the police? Third, claims that police (at the point of arrest) exaggerated, inflated, or overcharged Blacks compared to Whites (e.g., Baer and Chambliss, 1997; Huizinga and Elliott, 1987) lacked empirical evidence, and, again, were largely anecdotal. Finally, what is the motivation for police to discriminate against Blacks? If the arrest scenario is a chaotic, visceral event almost always aggravated by drug and alcohol use, do police really have much of an opportunity to be racially selective in who they arrest? The current study does not dispute that some police discriminate against some Blacks, though whether they do varies among individual officers and by jurisdictions (Black and Reiss, 1970; Piliavin and Briar, 1964).

Proposition 3: Incarceration

In his presidential address to the American Society of Criminology, Charles Wellford (1997) cautioned that a mostly Black prison population was evidence of racial bias in the criminal justice system. In a study of the interaction between race and sentencing, Jendrek (1984) found that Blacks received longer sentences than did Whites. Petersilia (1983) reported that minorities in Texas and California (states with the two largest prison populations) served longer sentences than Whites convicted of identical crimes.[6] Bias may also be practiced behind prison walls. In a study of a medium-security prison, Poole and Regoli (1980) discovered that Black inmates were stereotyped by corrections officers as more dangerous and subsequently more likely to be officially reported for rule infractions than were White inmates.

Other evidence suggested that the criminal justice system is more lenient with Blacks than with Whites. Blacks were more likely than were Whites to receive nonfinancial release from jail for felony offenses despite anecdotal claims to the contrary (see Zatz, 1987, p. 84). Of all personal recognizance bonds received for felony cases, Blacks received 61 percent of them and Whites received 38 percent. Of all unsecured, nonfinancial felony releases from jail, 63 percent were Black and 37 percent were White. Of those rearrested for new felony cases while on felony bond, 12 percent were Black and 8 percent were White (U.S. Department of Justice, 1994a). Bond release was contingent on seriousness of offense (Lynch and Patterson, 1991), and Blacks were more likely than Whites to be arrested for serious violent crimes.

The administration of the death sentence is profoundly marked by alleged racial inequalities, yet Whites are executed more quickly than Blacks. The average elapsed time from conviction to execution from 1977–96 for Whites was 110 months; for Blacks it was 117 months. The evidence presented here suggests that when it comes to the contemporary application of the death penalty, Blacks are not discriminated against.[7]

Proposition 4: Criminal Victimization

One fact often lost in statistics, reporting an overrepresentation of Black criminal offenders, is that there are relatively more Blacks than Whites who also are crime victims, particularly at younger, more criminogenic ages. In 1993, the homicide rate for Black males 12–24 years old was 115 per 100,000; the comparable rate for Whites was 12 per 100,000. For Black males age 25 and older, the homicide rate was 68 per 100,000; for the comparable group of Whites the homicide rate was only 8 per 100,000 (U.S. Department of Justice, 1994b). For handgun victimizations, Black males were four times more likely than Whites to be victims. Black females were almost four times more likely than White females to be crime victims. For Blacks of all ages, homicide was the fourth leading cause of death. For 15–24-year-old Black males, homicide was the leading cause of death (U.S. Department of Justice, 1994b). Nearly 80 percent of Blacks, compared to 59 percent of Whites, felt handgun laws should be more strict (U.S. Department of Justice, 1997a).

Substantial race differentials exist not only in criminal victimization, but also in concerns about becoming a crime victim. In 1997, it was reported that 24 percent of Blacks but only 6 percent of Whites worried about being murdered. Twenty-six percent of Blacks but 9 percent of Whites expressed concern about being seriously assaulted, stabbed, or shot. Thirty-two percent of Blacks, compared to 14 percent of Whites, experienced some distress about being sexually assaulted. Finally, 23 percent of Blacks and 18 percent of Whites worried about their homes being burglarized. For every year from 1982 to 1996 (except 1985), Blacks were more likely than Whites to report that they did not believe enough money was being allocated to reduce the rising crime rate (U.S. Department of Justice, 1997a).

Criminologists are often too busy worrying about criminal offenders to notice that "racist" policies, such as mandatory crack-cocaine laws (see Proposition 5 following), actually benefit crime victims who are disproportionately Black. Criminologists generally ignore the racial epidemiology of criminal victimization, though the general public does not. Among others, present and former Black police chiefs in Baltimore, New York City, Cleveland, Detroit, Chicago, Philadelphia, and Houston have expressed concern about Black victimization. Former Washington, D.C., Mayor Sharon Pratt Kelly asked President Clinton to employ the National Guard in the nation's capital to control the crime problem. In a recent national poll, 25 percent of Blacks reported crime to be the fundamental

American social problem, while only 8 percent of Blacks stated that racism was the most serious social problem (Kennedy, 1997). Research has shown a drastic racial (Black/White) convergence in punitive attitudes toward crime and justice measures (DiMaggio, Evans, and Bryson, 1996).

Proposition 5: The War on Drugs

The impact of the war on drugs on Black neighborhoods has been substantial (Palermo, 1996). In each year from 1982 to 1996 (except 1985 and 1987), Blacks were more likely than Whites to report that more spending was needed to address the nation's drug problem (U.S. Department of Justice, 1997a). Some criminologists (Chambliss, 1994; 1995; Tonry, 1994; 1995) pointed to the sentencing of persons to mandatory prison terms in federal prisons, as evidence of racial bias in the criminal justice system. Offenders in federal prison were almost three times as likely to be incarcerated for drugs than were state inmates (U.S. Department of Justice, 1992b).

The "casualties" of the war on drugs, primarily federal inmates, were typically older, better educated, and from more stable home environments than were state inmates. Fifty-eight percent of federal inmates were drug offenders (21 percent of state inmates were drug offenders). Forty-three percent of federal inmates had never been incarcerated or on probation prior to their current sentences, while 47 percent of state inmates were incarcerated for violent convictions. Casualties of the war on drugs appeared to be less dangerous than state prison inmates (U.S. Department of Justice, 1992b).

An additional debate regarding the war on drugs revolves around the disparity in sentencing for offenses involving powder cocaine (most often used by Whites) and crack-cocaine (most often used by Blacks). The penalties for possession of crack-cocaine are much greater than are the penalties for powder cocaine. Federal mandates established a 100:1 quantity ratio between the amount of powder and crack-cocaine needed to trigger mandatory minimum sentences (Kennedy, 1997). The average possession amount of powder cocaine for federal inmates was 183 pounds, for crack-cocaine, it was only 2 pounds (U.S. Department of Justice, 1992b). Some criminologists interpreted this disparity as proof of racial bias (Tonry 1994; 1995). Perhaps a different interpretation should be considered. First, the sizable weight disparity between powder and crack-cocaine was illustrative of the differences in how the two drugs were purchased and distributed. Crack is cheaper, sold in smaller quantities, and often sold in more volatile settings than powder cocaine (U.S. Sentencing Commission, 1995). Second, though no pharmacological differences exist between powder and crack-cocaine, the effects of the drugs are very different. Smoking crack immediately affects the lungs and brain, while intranasal ingestion of powder cocaine takes three to five minutes before psychoactive effects occur. The duration of the "high" from powder cocaine is approximately 20 minutes, for crack it is only about 10 to 12 minutes (U. S. Department of Justice, 1998b). Once the psychoactive effect is over, a dysphoric crash occurs characterized by fatigue, depression, and most importantly, the insatiable need to have more of the drug. Crack is a more transitory and compulsive drug than powder cocaine. Third, crack, not powder cocaine, is a criminological enterprise for the most criminogenic group in the United States, young males. From 1985 to 1992, the juvenile homicide rate, number of juvenile handgun homicides, and non-White juvenile drug arrest rate doubled (Blumstein, 1995; Travis, 1998). As crack-cocaine use proliferated in American cities, young males became more involved in an illicit drug economy characterized by violent crime and guns (Blumstein and Cork, 1996). The disparity between powder and crack-cocaine may not be a consequence of race, but of the criminogenic differences between the drugs. Drug sales and consumption patterns depend on the substance. Crack-cocaine users are more likely than powder cocaine users to know numerous dealers, to be transient, and to purchase the drug in their own neighborhoods. These differences shaped the way police, service providers, and policymakers addressed the problem (Riley, 1997).

After all this discussion of racial disparities in drug sentencing, who actually was in federal prison? The racial composition of federal prisons was 38 percent White, 30 percent Black, and 28 percent Latino (compared to state prisons which were 35 percent White, 46 percent Black, and 17 percent Latino). More than 80 percent of the Latinos in federal prison were drug offenders and 18 percent of federal inmates were not United States citizens. Whites and Latinos were most victimized by the war on drugs (because of their disproportionate numbers in federal prison), therefore, it may be argued the greatest casualties of the war on drugs were Latinos and Whites, not Blacks.

Discussion

Many criminologists assumed racial disparities in the criminal justice system were the product of racism, however, three viable alternative explanations existed. First, the overinvolvement of Blacks in the criminal justice system reflected actual offending patterns, not systematic racial bias (Cohen and Kluegel, 1978; Hindelang, 1978; LaFree, 1995; cf. Chambliss, 1994; 1995). Myriad studies (e.g., Blau and Blau, 1982; Hagan, Gillis, and Simpson, 1985; Short, 1997; Tittle, Villimez, and Smith, 1978) demonstrated that the Black involvement in conventional crime was largely a function of class position and poverty, yet, at the same time, many criminologists refused to believe that Blacks were actually committing various street crimes. They believed instead that a racially biased criminal justice system was systematically and unscrupulously forcing Blacks into jails and prisons. Second, racial involvement in conventional crime was not an essentialism argument. The epidemiological data indicated that crime was primarily the activity of young males (Hirschi and Gottfredson, 1983). Discussions of "Black crime" ostensibly denoted young, Black male crime. The same holds for "White crime," "Latino crime," and "Asian crime." Crime is neither a Black problem nor a White problem, it is a young male problem. Even though a distinct segment of any racial or ethnic population is more involved in crime, would not systematic racism on the part of the criminal justice system punish all segments of a minority population equally? Or, are young males (of any race or ethnic group) over-represented in official crime data because, as previously mentioned, they commit more crime? Third, racial disparities in the administration of justice should be greatest during periods of American history when racial discrimination has been most virulent. Such disparities were common during the slave era, the period of Reconstruction, and Jim Crow segregation. For example:

- In slave-era Virginia, Black slaves were subject to the death penalty for seventy-three separate capital offenses. Whites were subject to the death penalty for one offense, first-degree murder (Kennedy, 1997, p. 77).
- During the Reconstruction, the Mississippi Black Code made it a criminal offense for Blacks to make "insulting gestures" or to function as ministers of the Gospel without a license from some regularly organized (i.e., White) church (Kennedy, 1997, p. 85).
- In 1936, the Supreme Court ruled in *Brown v. Mississippi* that Blacks had the right to be free of torture used to coerce forced confession (Kennedy, 1997, p. 104).

The racial gap (Black/White) in state prisons in 1932 was approximately 4 to 1, in 1979 the gap was 8 to 1 (Wilbanks, 1987). Today there are more Blacks (506,950) than Whites (394,760) in state prisons despite the fact Whites comprise over 82 percent of the U.S. population and Blacks comprise only 13 percent (U.S. Department of Justice, 1997a). Does this mean the contemporary United States is more racist than it was during the Great Depression? Similarly, the state prison racial gap varies by region. Minnesota had the greatest Black/White ratio (23:1) while Mississippi had the second lowest (3:1) (Stark, 1987; Wilbanks, 1987). Does this mean Minnesota is roughly eight times more racially biased than Mississippi? It is naive to look at race differentials in arrest rates (Huizinga and Elliott,

1987) or incarceration rates (Wellford, 1997) and hastily conclude that racial bias accounts for the unexplained variation in any given research study. The evidence reported here suggests that racism does not pervade the American system of criminal justice to the degree suggested by some criminologists (Arrigo, 1998; Morales, 1978; Skolnick, 1996).

This study hesitates to conclude that racism is not practiced *at all* by the criminal justice system. There are reasonable alternative interpretations of this study's findings. For example, even though Blacks were proportionally less likely than Whites to be arrested for DUI offenses, Blacks were more likely than Whites to be stopped and questioned by police (Kennedy, 1997), as well as stereotyped and suspected of more serious violent crimes (LaFree, 1995). For these reasons, Blacks may be deterred from driving under the influence of alcohol or drugs since research indicates that increasing the certainty of apprehension deters unwanted behavior (Reynolds, 1996).

Though Whites were executed more quickly than Blacks, the crimes they committed may have been more heinous, thereby reducing the amount of time needed for appeals. For example, nearly all serial killers were White (Hickey, 1997). What this suggests is that there may be less doubt about the guilt of Whites convicted of death penalty crimes than there is for Blacks.

Some criminologists (Baer and Chambliss, 1997; Chambliss, 1994; Quinney, 1970) conceptualized racism as dichotomous, though the authors of this article believe racism is a continuous variable (Hindelang, 1978). In this sense, racial bias has continuous, qualitatively different levels of measurement. In earlier historical periods, racial bias in all social institutions, including the criminal justice system, was quite pronounced, however, this has changed. Racial bias in the criminal justice system and racial differences between Blacks and Whites have experienced a sharp diminution (Crank, 1998; DiMaggio, Evans, and Bryson, 1996; Hall and McLean, 1998; Kennedy, 1997; Pruitt and Wilson, 1983; Zatz, 1987). The findings presented here indicate the criminal justice system does not systematically discriminate against Blacks.

Notes

1. The present discussion of race was restricted to Blacks and Whites. Latinos were excluded because of the low reliability in criminal justice classification of persons of Hispanic heritage. Asian/Pacific Islanders and American Indians were excluded due to their low numbers in arrest and incarceration data. The present discussion of "crime" was confined to conventional or street crime. Political, organized, and white-collar or corporate crime were not included. The authors of this study acknowledge that offender and victim epidemiological data for these other types of crime are different from street crime.
2. The race-education gap, however, is converging. For example, from 1973–93, the high school dropout rate for Whites fell from 5.7 to 4 percent, while the high school dropout rate for Blacks fell from 10 percent to 5.4 percent (U.S. Bureau of the Census, 1995).
3. A racist criminal justice system was defined as the systematic discrimination against Blacks when compared to the nondiscriminatory practices against Whites.
4. This article is descriptive in the sense that it is not concerned with causality, rather with the empirical operation of the criminal justice system. This article is exploratory because it examines a rather uncommon, if not unpopular, idea of a nonracist criminal justice system. As a consequence, the study is methodologically incapable of generalization in a statistical sense. Analyzing existing statistics and extant literature has validity and reliability limitations (see Babbie, 1992, p. 329–36), though the substantive benefits of such a method are useful.
5. This study was unable to find vehicle registration data for Blacks and Whites and thus could not control for population representation. It should be noted, however, that the purchasing power of Blacks has doubled since 1990 (Sewell, 1998), therefore, the lack of Black DUI arrests were not necessarily a function of socioeconomic status. For example, Blacks were less likely to be involved in automobile accidents than Whites, Asian/Pacific Islanders, Latinos (regardless of race), and American Indians (U.S. Department of Transportation, 1998).
6. Klein, Petersilia, and Turner (1990) later found prior record was the best indicator of prison sentencing when controlling for a variety of demographic variables such as race. Hindelang, Hirschi, and Weis (1981) also found prior criminal record, not race, was most important in predicting prison sentencing. Others found legal factors, not race, best explained prison racial disparities (Spohn, Grohl, and Welch, 1981).
7. For a review of the historically racist application of the death penalty, see Kennedy (1997). Research on racial victim-offender pairings has shown systematic bias against Black offenders killing Whites. The majority of these executions, however, have occurred in the "Death Belt" stretching from Texas to Virginia. This article mentions and acknowledges the historically racist practices of states in the southern United States.

References

Arrigo, B. (1998). Justice with prejudice. *Justice Quarterly* 15: 199–205.

Babbie, E. (1992). *The practice of social research* 6th ed. Belmont, CA: Wadsworth Publishing Company.

Baer, J., and Chambliss, W. (1997). Generating fear: The politics of crime reporting. *Crime, Law, and Social Change* 27: 87–107.

Black, D., and Reiss, A. (1970). Police control of juveniles. *American Sociological Review* 35: 63–77.

Blau, J., and Blau, P. (1982). The cost of inequality: Metropolitan structure and violent crime. *American Sociological Review* 47: 114–29.

Blumstein, A. (1995). Youth violence, guns, and the illicit drug industry. *Journal of Criminal Law and Criminology* 86: 10–36.

Blumstein, A., and Cork, D. (1996). Linking gun availability to youth gun violence. *Law and Contemporary Problems* 59: 5–24.

Chambliss, W. (1994). Policing the ghetto underclass: The politics of law and law enforcement. *Social Problems* 41: 177–94.

Chambliss, W. (1995). Another lost war: The costs and consequences of drug prohibition. *Social Justice* 22: 101–24.

Chiricos, T., Eschholz, S., and Gertz, M. (1997). Crime, news, and fear of crime. *Social Problems* 44: 342–57.

Cohen, L., and Kluegel, J. R. (1978). Determinants of juvenile court dispositions: Ascriptive and achieved factors in two metropolitan courts. *American Sociological Review* 43: 162–76.

Crank, J. (1998). *Understanding police culture.* Cincinnati, OH: Anderson Publishing Co.

Dilulio, J. (1994). The question of Black crime. *Public Interest* Fall:3.

DiMaggio, P., Evans, J., and Bryson, B. (1996). Have Americans' social attitudes become more polarized? *American Journal of Sociology* 102: 690–755.

Elliott, D. (1994). Serious violent offenders. *Criminology* 32: 1–21.

Elliott, D. (1995). *Lies, damn lies, and arrest statistics.* Unpbl. ms. University of Colorado, Boulder, CO 80309-0327.

Farnworth, M., and Leiber, M. (1989). Strain theory revisited. *American Sociological Review* 54: 263–74.

Gordon, P. (1988). Black people and the criminal law: Rhetoric and reality. *International Journal of the Sociology of Law* 16: 295–313.

Hagan, J., Gillis, A. R., and Simpson, J. (1985). The class structure of gender and delinquency. *American Journal of Sociology* 90: 1151–78.

Hall, C., and McLean, E. (1998). Civil rights progress rated. *USA TODAY.* July(8): 1A.

Hickey, E. (1997). *Serial murderers and their victims.* 2d ed. Pacific Grove, CA: Brooks/Cole Publishing.

Hindelang, M. (1978). Race and involvement in common law personal crimes. *American Sociological Review* 43: 93–109.

Hindelang, M. (1981). Variations in sex, race, age specific incidence rates of offending. *American Sociological Review* 46: 461–74.

Hindelang, M., Hirschi, T., and Weis, J. (1979). Correlates of delinquency: The illusion of discrepancy between self report and official measures. *American Sociological Review* 44: 995–1014.

Hindelang, M., Hirschi, T., and Weis, J. (1981). *Measuring delinquency.* Beverly Hills, CA: Sage Publications.

Hirschi, T., and Gottfredson, M. (1983). Age and the explanation for crime. *American Journal of Sociology* 88: 552–84.

Hogan, M. (1995). Unequal justice: A question of color [Review essay]. *Social Pathology* 1: 270–6.

Huizinga, D., and Elliott, D. (1987). Juvenile offenders: Prevalence, offender incidence, and arrest rates by race. *Crime and Delinquency* 33: 206–23.

Jendrek, M. (1984). Sentence length: Interactions with race and court. *Journal of Criminal Justice* 12: 567–78.

Kennedy, R. (1997). *Race, crime, and the law.* New York: Pantheon Press.

Klein, S., Petersilia, J., and Turner, S. (1990). Race and imprisonment decision in California. *Science* 247: 812–16.

LaFree, G. (1995). Race and crime trends in the United States, 1946–1990. In *Ethnicity, race, and crime: Perspectives across time and space,* ed. D. Hawkins. Albany, NY: State University of New York Press.

Laub, J., and McDermott, M. (1985). An analysis of serious crime by young Black women. *Criminology* 23: 81–98.

Lynch, M., and Patterson, E. (1991). *Race and criminal justice.* Albany, NY: Harrow and Heston.

Lynch, M., and Patterson, E. (1996). *Justice with prejudice.* Guilderland, NY: Harrow and Heston.

Maden, T. (1993). Crime, culture, and ethnicity. *International Journal of Psychiatry* 5: 281–9.

Menard, S. (1995). A developmental test of Mertonian anomie theory. *Journal of Research in Crime and Delinquency* 32: 136–74.

Morales, A. (1978). Institutional racism in mental health and criminal justice. *Social Casework* 59: 387–95.

Morris, N. (1988). Race and crime: What evidence is there that race influences results in the criminal justice system? *Judicature* 72: 111–13.

Noguera, P. (1997). Reconsidering the "crisis" of the Black male in America. *Social Justice* 24: 147–64.

Palermo, G. (1996). The city under siege: Drugs and crime. *Journal of Interdisciplinary Studies* 8: 1–18.

Petersilia, J. (1983). *Racial disparities in the criminal justice system.* Santa Monica, CA: RAND.

Petersilia, J. (1985). Racial disparties in the criminal justice system: A summary. *Crime and Delinquency* 31: 15–34.

Piliavin, I., and Briar, S. (1964). Police encounters with juveniles. *American Journal of Sociology* 70: 206–14.

Poole, E., and Regoli, R. (1980). Race, institutional rule breaking, and disciplinary response. *Law and Society Review* 14: 931–46.

Pruitt, C., and Wilson, J. Q. (1983). A longitudinal study of the effect of race on sentencing. *Law and Society Review* 7: 613–35.

Quinney, R. (1970). The social reality of crime. Boston, MA: Little, Brown & Company.

Reynolds, M. (1996). *Why does crime pay—Update.* Dalias, TX: National Center for Policy Analysis.

Riley, J. (1997). *Crack, powder cocaine, and heroin: Drug purchase and use patterns in six U.S. cities.* Washington, D.C.: National Institute of Justice and Office of National Drug Control Policy.

Roth, J. (1993). Psychoactive substances and violence. In *Understanding and preventing violence*, eds. A. J. Reiss, Jr., and J. A. Roth. Washington, D.C.: National Academy Press.

Senese, J. (1997). *Applied research methods in criminal justice.* Chicago, IL: Nelson-Hall Publishers.

Sewell, D. (1998). African Americans' buying clout rises. *Daily Camera* Jul(30): 1B, 4B.

Short, J. (1997). *Poverty, ethnicity, and violent crime.* Boulder, CO: Westview Press.

Skogan, W. (1990). *Disorder and decline: Crime and the spiral of decay in American neighborhoods.* New York: The Free Press.

Skolnick, J. (1996). Passions of crime. *American Prospect* 25: 89–96.

Spohn, T., Grohl, H., and Welch, R. (1981). The effect of race on sentencing. *Law and Society Review* 71: 16–18.

Stark, R. (1987). Deviant places: A theory of the ecology of crime. *Criminology* 25: 893–909.

Tittle, C., Villimez, W., and Smith, D. (1978). The myth of social class and criminality: An empirical assessment of the empirical evidence. *American Sociological Review* 43: 643–56.

Tonry, M. (1994). Racial politics, racial disparities, and the war on crime. *Crime and Delinquency* 40: 475–94.

Tonry, M. (1995). *Malign neglect.* New York: Oxford University Press.

Travis, J. (1998). Declining crime and our national research agenda. [Speech given at the School of Public Policy and Social Research]. University of California, Los Angeles.

U.S. Bureau of the Census. (1995). *Current population reports.* Washington, D.C.: U.S. Government Printing Office.

U.S. Bureau of the Census. (1997). *Current population reports.* Washington, D.C.: U.S. Government Printing Office.

U.S. Department of Justice. (1992a). *Prior records common among drunk drivers.* Washington, D.C.: U.S. Government Printing Office.

U.S. Department of Justice. (1992b). *Comparing federal and state prison inmates.* Washington, D.C.: U.S. Government Printing Office.

U.S. Department of Justice. (1994a). *Pretrial release of felony defendants.* Washington, D.C.: U.S. Governtment Printing Office.

U.S. Department of Justice. (1994b). *Guns and crime.* Washington, D.C.: U.S. Government Printing Office.

U.S. Department of Justice. (1997a). *Sourcebook of criminal justice statistics.* Washington, D.C.: U.S. Government Printing Office.

U.S. Department of Justice. (1997b). *Lifetime likelihood of going to state or federal prison.* Washington, D.C.: U.S. Government Printing Office.

U.S. Department of Justice. (1997c). *National crime victimization survey: Criminal victimization 1973–1996.* Washington, D.C.: U.S. Government Printing Office.

U.S. Department of Justice. (1998a). *Prison and jail inmates at midyear 1997.* Washington, D.C.: U.S. Government Printing Office.

U.S. Department of Justice. (1998b). "Cocaine." *Drugs of abuse.* Washington, D.C.: Drug Enforcement Agency.

U.S. Department of Transportation. (1998). *Motor vehicle crashes as a leading cause of death in 1994.* Washington, D.C.: U.S. Government Printing Office.

U.S. Sentencing Commission. (1995). *Special report to Congress: Cocaine and federal sentencing policy.* Washington, D.C.: U.S. Government Printing Office.

Wellford, C. (1997). Controlling crime and achieving justice. *Criminology* 35: 1–12.

Wilbanks, W. (1987). *The myth of a racist criminal justice system.* Monterey, CA: Brooks/Cole Publishing.

Zatz, M. (1987). The changing forms of racial/ethnic bias in sentencing. *Journal of Research in Crime and Delinquency* 24: 69–92.

Women, Race, and Crime

Compared to other topics in criminology and criminal justice, females and their involvement in crime garnered very little attention until the latter part of the twentieth century. As the number of females arrested increased and as a cadre of female scholars, including feminist criminologists, emerged more interest in female crime resulted in substantive research on women and crime. Early writings about female criminality were theoretical and narrowly focused on female prisoners. For example, in the late nineteenth century Lombroso and Ferrero (1894) published *The Female Offender.* Cesare Lombroso, often referred to as the "Father of Criminology," and Ferrero believed that women were not as evolved as men, and that female criminals had more masculine characteristics than other women. Although there were few studies of female criminals early in the century, most scholars asserted that these women were anomalies with biological or psychological deficiencies. Rarely did researchers consider the sociological context of women and their involvement in crime. Instead, emphasis was usually placed on their sexual deviance. After the 1960s, female criminologists called attention to the need to consider how societal and cultural factors contribute to female crime. Liberal, radical, and Marxist criminologists emphasized the importance of greater opportunities for women, patriarchy, and capitalism in explaining women's participation in criminal behavior. Since the 1970s, more attention has been devoted to other aspects of female criminality including sexual abuse victimization, domestic violence victimization, children of female offenders, and female involvement in serious crime. Today, in spite of increased interest, there is still limited research on women and crime generally, and women, race, and crime specifically.

Throughout most of the twentieth century research on women, race, and crime focused on black females. These females have comprised a majority of female offenders for at least three decades. In 2002, there were 36,000 black, 15,000 Hispanic, and 35,400 white female prisoners under state and federal jurisdiction (Harrison and Beck 2003). In spite of increased interest in female criminality there is very little research about the experiences of other women of color (Asians, Latinas, Native Americans). There is also a need for researchers to acknowledge that within racial/ethnic groups cultural diversity should be taken into consideration.

Adler (1975) (perhaps inadvertently) sparked interest in black women and crime when she made comparisons between black females and black males and black females and white females in an effort to understand female crime. Adler asserted that the "(B)lurring of social boundaries among blacks and its influence in making black females statistically more equal partners in crime with black males has interesting and important criminogenic implications for white women (1975, 140)." Adler, who studies under Marvin Wolfgang, relied heavily on his research on homicide offenders (Wolfgang 1958) and generalized his findings to other black and white female offenders. However, she rather naively overlooked the fact that white females were involved in crime in the nineteenth and twentieth centuries as "sexual deviants," and other types of offenders. Instead she posited that as white females' sex roles converged with those of white males (as did those of black females with those of black males) their involvement in crime would increase. Young (2002, [1980]), in one of the first empirical studies of women, race, and crime, used victimization data to test some of Adler's propositions. She concluded, "that there is no simplistic answer to the question of whether female offenders differ by race" (174).

The first chapter in this section is by Hans von Hentig. Originally published in 1942, it is one of the first of its kind to focus on "colored women." Like other scholars of the time, von Hentig examines biological and psychological factors to understand female criminality. In a rather unique manner, he examines several factors including age, sex ratios, mortality rates, and admission to state institutions (for the insane), in a structural and cultural context. Unlike other early writers, he noted that the interaction of biological and psychological factors must be viewed in the context of environmental conditions including economics and marital status. He also noted that fear of the colored race by the white race could lead to discriminatory practices by the police. Von Hentig's telling comment about such fear is directly related to the importance of images.

Zatz and Mann (1998) examined how images of color and images of crime are racialized and gendered. They point to the role of images in perpetuating stereotypic perceptions. The second chapter in this section by Lynch and Huey examines how historical negative images of Black women impact criminological theories, social policies, and are passed on to future criminal justice academicians and practitioners. These distorted stereotypes of Black women as mammies, matriarchs, welfare moms, and jezebels are directly related to their experiences in the United States since slavery. The authors argue that these images are incorporated into criminological theories. For example, in the family, black women are often perceived to be either welfare moms or single parents who are unable to effectively socialize their children. They note that these stereotypes often go unchallenged and that factual information about mothers and their children is often omitted. For example, most black youth are lawabiding. The chapter concludes with an explanation of the importance of challenging these distorted images.

The third chapter in this section is by Jodi Miller, a female criminologist, well known in the discipline for her contributions to understanding female crime and delinquency. Increased concern with female participation in violent crimes such as robbery motivated Jodi Miller to examine female robbers in an urban environment. Miller examines and critiques several explanations for female participation in robbery including whether or not females desire to be masculine, are responding to either their victimization, (sub)cultural norms, or to the strain that results from race, gender, or economic oppression. Miller explores both why and how females and males engage in robbery to better understand the role of gender.

The final chapter in this section addresses women and domestic violence. West, Kantor, and Jasinski provide an interesting analysis of female responses to battering by examining, race, ethnicity, and cultural contexts. Unlike most research on this topic, the chapter provides a study of Latina women with different cultural backgrounds Mexican, Mexican American, and Puerto Rican. The chapter calls attention to the need to understand sociocultural differences in womens' responses to battering and how these differences impact service providers.

References

Adler, F. 1975. *Sisters in Crime: The Rise of the New Female Criminal.* New York: McGraw-Hill.

Harrison, P. M., & Beck, A. J. 2003. *Prisoners in 2002.* Washington, DC: US Department of Justice, Bureau of Justice Statistics.

Lombroso, C., and Ferrero, W. (1920 [1984]). *The female offender.* New York: Appleton
Wolfgang, M. 1958. *Patterns in criminal homicide.* Philadelphia: University of Pennsylvania Press.
Young, V. 2002. Women, race, and crime. In *African American classics in criminology and criminal justice*, eds. S. Gabbidon, H. Greene, & V. Young, 171–75. Thousand Oaks, CA: Sage Publications
Zatz, M. S., and Mann, C., R. 1998. The power of images. In *Images of color, images of crime*, eds. C. Mann & M.S. Zatz, 1–12. Los Angeles, CA: Roxbury Publishing.

9
The Criminality of the Colored Woman

Hans von Hentig

I

Our ideas concerning racial groups come from a common belief that certain physical characteristics are linked with distinct psychic traits. We follow exactly the same course in discriminating, in the animal world, between a cat and a tiger. We think that among human races, just as among different animal groups, physically differentiated races tend to respond differently to outside stimuli, such as climatic, social, and other forces, and conversely that physically similar groups tend to respond similarly to such stimuli. Of these multifarious and measurable tendencies, one should be the readiness of a racial group to commit crime. It must be, so we think, rather simple to read these tendencies from compiled criminal statistics.

The problem is, however, not as simple as the mere reading of figures. We would certainly not be wrong in discovering "tendencies" to commit certain crimes; but in criminology these "tendencies" have a life of their own. They occur or disappear according to the degree of pressure exercised by forces of environment on the individuals possessing them, and the greatest difficulty encountered in a study of race criminality rests in the fact that race is considered to be merely dispositional, whereas any actual crime is a complex combination of these predispositions and of intricately blended inside and outside forces.

Another difficulty must not be overlooked. All racial pictures are abstractions gained by comparison. What are the races which have been investigated by English, German, or French scholars? Have they examined the unpleasant traits of their own racial compounds? They never have. There are only a few, mostly partisan and therefore not very reliable, investigations of the criminality of the Jews and other minorities.

To be faced by a minority must not necessarily blind our judgment. We have minority groups in our own midst, children and women, for instance. These minorities, however, make up for their numerical weakness by developing a different pattern of power. Children have turned their physical inferiority into a victorious demand upon our support and indulgence. The social history of all colonial countries has proved that the larger the minority of female beings, the greater their superiority.

It is true that it is quite different with other minorities. These minorities differ fundamentally from the groups just mentioned, and are not natural and constituent parts of a homogeneous social composite, but mostly autonomous and neoplastic formations. They are competitors, present or future. The more rigid the morals of such compound groups, and the better their biological equipment, the more menacing they seem to be. The persecution starts with a conscious or unconscious "repacking" of our common and fixed views. Virtues become vile characteristics when invested in our enemies. Our moral ideas, or at least our moral practices, lose color in the presence of danger. Fear acts upon our glands, and glands have a peculiar way of shaking off the loosely rooted, most recent moral acquisitions.

Arrests, trials, convictions, releases, statistical surveys, and statements are human acts. We must expect them to be thoroughly imbued with the problem of minorities which are opposed and which strike back.

In former studies of the criminality of the Negro[1] involving an examination of the delinquent colored woman, the writer became aware that the female Negro probably profited somewhat from the universal trend to favor women.[2] He was, however, certain that a comparative study of the women of the dominant race would cause this error to disappear in view of the privileges extended to each of the racial groups.

II

Complete data on the criminality of females according to race are lacking. The *Judicial Criminal Statistics* do not give the number of defendants nor the procedural outcome by sex, and still less, by race. The figures covering arrests, as presented by the *Uniform Crime Reports*, originate mostly from urban surroundings,[3] and do not cover all sections of the country, and certainly not the rural criminality in its totality. In addition to these, there are other handicaps, some of them mentioned by the *Reports*.[4] The statistics on *Prisoners in State and Federal Prisons and Reformatories* give satisfactory information on sex and race of the prisoners received and discharged and are most valuable in this respect. No reports however were received from Georgia, Alabama, and Mississippi prisons,[5] a deficiency which might not affect seriously the general crime picture but which, however, impairs considerably a survey of Negro delinquency. The data, finally, on *Federal Offenders*, issued by the Bureau of Prisons in Washington, D.C., fortunately do not disregard the discrimination by race although the field of federal offenses is rather limited.

Criminal procedures start with investigation and arrest. Arrest, considered separately, does not mean very much, and the frequently used term "cleared by arrest" cannot easily be accepted by scientific research if not specified by a definite form of procedural outcome.

We shall first reproduce arrest figures[6] and annex some critical remarks.

Table 9.1 Arrests, 1935–1938; Females, per 100,000 Population, 15 Years and Over

Offense	White	Negro
Homicide	0.6	10.2
Aggravated assault	1.4	44.6
Robbery	0.9	6.1
Burglary	0.9	4.6
Larceny	6.5	46.1
Embezzlement and fraud	1.4	3.9
Forgery	0.9	2.0
Prostitution	7.4	25.0
Disorderly conduct	3.8	25.1
Drunkenness	6.6	22.9
Vagrancy	5.1	15.6
Suspicion	7.7	30.7

The picture presented by these arrest figures is very dark. Even if we take into consideration that "homicide" is of a very complex and heterogeneous legal structure[7] and that the notion of "intent," which is difficult to determine, enters into the legal suppositions of "aggravated assault"[8], the predominance of arrests of colored women is striking. This predominance is still very considerable in robbery[9] and larceny, although pronouncedly smaller in burglary, embezzlement and fraud, and forgery; however, figures mount again with disorderly conduct, drunkenness, prostitution, and vagrancy. Suspicion very clearly falls on the colored woman to a great extent.

We have tried to obtain more arrest figures. The New York Police Department does not segregate white and Negro arrests; the Commissioner of Police of Chicago, however, was kind enough to give us the Chicago arrest figures for the last six years so that we were able to compute the following table:

Table 9.1a Chicago Arrests, 1933–1938, per 100,000 Population of Each Group

	White	Negro
Male	4,716.5	14,322.0
Female	416.6	3,795.7

We are not concerned in the present investigation with the criminality of the colored male. The unfavorable proportion of arrests of colored females is manifest. However, do these figures actually have the same intrinsic value as numerical magnitude? It is true that these figures demand an explanation more fundamental than a purely technical one, and we shall attempt such an analysis later on. Some factors of technical or quasi-technical nature, however, have to be mentioned here.

Some studies have been made in which, the authors not satisfied with arrest figures, have followed the further disposition of such cases by the police. We have a few such statistics which, although not very recent, are probably still valid; they pertain to the cities of Philadelphia, Pittsburgh, and Denver.

Table 9.2 Discharges of Arrested Negroes

	Percent
Philadelphia (1924)	31.1[10]
Pittsburgh (1924)	36.7[11]
Denver (1928)	35.5[12]

The Negro Survey of Pennsylvania is therefore probably correct in contending "that the number of arrests does not give an accurate picture of crime."[13] The *Uniform Crime Reports* did not overlook another very important point[14] which is also raised by an author in analyzing the Negro crime statistics for Minneapolis and who declares: "The total number of such women (Negro prostitutes arrested) is considerably less than the total number of arrests indicates, since probably 30 to 50 percent of the cases are repeaters."[15]

Some figures gathered on arrests of colored people in Minneapolis (unfortunately they are not segregated into males and females) prove that but a very small number of these arrests signifies a serious form of delinquency. This, at least, seems to be the judgment of the courts.

Table 9.3 Disposition of Arrested Negroes; Minneapolis, 1923–1925[16]

	Percent
Dismissed, found not guilty[17]	11.5
Suspended sentence, placed on probation	8.2
Committed to workhouse, fined	66.3
Other dispositions	8.0
	94.0
Held to Grand Jury or District Court	6.0
Total of 1,384 arrests of colored people	100.0

This picture is completed by a glance at the type of offense for which Negroes are customarily arrested. It is obvious that these offenses are, to an overwhelming degree, the minor criminality of the destitute and helpless groups of society.

Table 9.4 Charges against Arrested Negroes; Minneapolis, 1923–1925[18]

	Percent
Disorderly conduct, drunkenness, gambling	65.6
Vagrancy	11.3
Prostitution	7.8
Miscellaneous (fighting, petit larceny, adultery, illegitimacy, etc.)	10.7
Minor delinquency	95.4
Felonies, major crimes	4.6
Total of 1,374 arrests[19]	100.0

The statistics of *Federal Offenders* do not neglect the race problem and even permit a discrimination between males and females of each race. The commitments of colored females to federal institutions are, however, minimal (1935–36—54 individuals)[20] and statistically useless.

Table 9.5 Jail Commitments,[21] 1933–36; Females, Percent

	Native White	Negro
All commitments	100.0	100.0
Liquor and drug law violations	56.1	70.5

The jail commitments are somewhat higher, and we have reckoned out three-year averages. It would not be of much value to present the corresponding figures by offense, since Customs Act violations, Immigration Act violations, crimes on government and Indian reservations, high seas, military, naval, and territorial cases do not concern the Negro very much and still less the colored woman. Liquor laws are violated to a considerable extent by Negroes, and the relatively high percentage of colored females sentenced for violation of the Narcotic Drug Act becomes explicable when we consider the close connection between prostitution and drug consumption.

Table 9.6 Jail Commitments,[22] Female Federal Offenders, 1933–1936, Per 100,000 Population 15 Years and Over of Each Racial Group

	Native White	Negro
All commitments	2.2	5.9
Liquor law violations	0.8	3.5
Drug act violations	0.5	0.9
All other offenses	0.9	1.5

In view of the fact that Liquor and Drug Law violations dominate the picture of colored females and that these offenses are the deeds of poor people, and in view further that there might be a somewhat different treatment in Federal courts, the ratio of white and Negro received into jails for Federal crimes does not present the enormous racial disparity we met in state prisons.

The high counterfeiting rate for colored females is striking and demands explanation. For the period 1933–1936 per 100,000 of population, it was:[23]

Table 9.7

Native white females	1.9
Colored females	4.4

Federal jurisdiction covers relatively small ground and refers to highly specialized topics. We meet the great bulk of delinquency proper when we turn to state laws and state prisons. Total commitments to state prisons during a five-year period show a very large preponderance of colored commitments:

Table 9.8 Women Received in Prisons,[24] 1932–1936, per 100,000 Population 15 Years and Over

Native white females	5.85
Colored females	20.52

Such totals, however, have little significance when they are composed of dissimilar elements which are but mathematically equivalent. From the sociological and practical point of view, "commercialized vice" cannot possibly be compared with "rape," nor "carrying weapons," with "murder." We have, therefore, to break down such vague and crude generalities. For the sake of clarity we use a rate of one million population for each racial group in this table:

Table 9.9 Female Prisoners Received from Courts,[25] by Race and Selected Offenses, 1932–1936, per 1,000,000 Population of Each Racial Group 15 Years and Over

Selected offenses	Native White	Negro
Homicide	2.8	46.4
Aggravated assault	0.8	21.8
Robbery	1.8	8.9
Burglary	2.1	11.5
Larceny	5.9	38.1
Embezzlement and fraud	1.8	1.4
Forgery	3.6	4.4
Prostitution[26]	4.4	13.4
Disorderly conduct[27]	6.9	8.9

The most striking result is the exorbitant figures for colored females received for having committed homicide and aggravated assault. This angle of race delinquency should receive special and careful study.

An intermediate group is formed by robbery, burglary, and larceny cases. Commitments are still very high, but these figures do not reach by far the enormous disparity shown by crimes against the person. The predatory crimes of the two races committed by other means than force or manual dexterity differ but slightly. Prostitution and disorderly conduct again show a preponderance among colored cases which is much more pronounced in prostitution. Prison commitments, however, cover but a small number of all cases of prostitution and disorderly conduct.

These are the facts concerning the delinquency of the colored woman. They are not numerous, although the writer took pains to produce the most recent figures and to avoid data covering only a one-year period. To the surveyor who stops here and does not look behind the mere numerical magnitude the picture appears extremely gloomy. We shall, however, make an attempt to go further than the delusive surface of figures.

III

Each group of a given population consists of numerical units—inhabitants. We are accustomed to relating certain phenomena, such as insanity, suicide or criminality, with inhabitants or members of a group. Although figures for such cases are mathematically equivalent, they differ widely from the dynamic point of view. An "inhabitant" is a conception which covers the most diverse forms and stages of activity and, therefore, might be a much-varied generator of social modifications. Such wide abstractions cannot be used by criminology without being further broken down. If possible we have to arrive at more simple and primitive elements.

The shapeless block of population rises on two great substructures—age and sex. By age we mean the moving of the individual through that long curve from an ineffectual child up to the climax of mature vital power, and down again to the feebleness and passivity of old age. It is obvious that a man of thirty might be dynamically equivalent in all social relations to a hundred small children or the same number of very old men. Yet in a mere calculation by inhabitants, the children and old men are numerically one hundred and the man of thirty is but one.

The same is true when we consider the substructure, sex. Sex is linked with the phenomena of age, but it has its own centers of gravity and its own problems. But that is not all. Sex means a correlation, a reference to another sex. Separation deprives sex of its essential virtues. In the civilized world sexual contacts are, officially at least, monogamous. One partner of each sex is entitled to one sole partner of the other sex at one time. Separation by space has practically the same inhibitory results as numerical disparity of the sexes. Irregularities in the even distribution of sex must necessarily cause personal difficulties and breed social conflicts.

In age distribution, too, the successive age groups should be balanced. The preponderance of certain age groups, especially the dependent ones, is undesirable, just as is their massing together in definite geographical areas. If one were to shuffle some age groups in an uneven way and to disjoin them geographically, grave disorders and disturbances would follow. Little attention has been paid by criminologists to the problem of these altered mechanics of the population structure.

There are crime-free age zones, let us say from one to fifteen years of age and again from forty years of age and upward. There are age groups of high crime frequency. Very much depends upon whether or not these minus or plus groups are equally distributed in both races.

Table 9.10 Crime-Free Age Zones,[28] 1 to 15 Years, and 40 Years and Over; Percentages

	White females	Negro females
Under 15 years of age	28.9	31.1
40 years of age and over	29.9	21.9
Total	58.8	54.0

The crime-free age groups are proportionately larger among white females than among Negroes. It is likely that the higher mortality of the colored race leaves decimated older age groups.

If we reverse the picture we arrive at the age zone of highest crime frequency.

Table 9.11 Age Zone of High Crime Frequency,[29] 15 to 39 Years, Percentages

	White females	Negro females
15 to 39 years of age	41.4	46.2

When females of the colored race have a larger share in that specific and crime-disposed age group, more delinquency would be, to some degree, the function of age and not of race.

All these figures of nationwide age variations are numerical averages and differ in time as well as in space. It is very difficult to watch short and often changing, sometimes periodical, migratory currents. Migrations are performed by certain age groups and these migrants are responsible for many of the crimes attributed to such groups. The number of female transients, and especially of colored women, it is true, is small.[30] There are, however, migratory movements of a more invisible and imperceptible kind. Females flock to the great southern winter resorts of Florida and California; they follow the movements of an increasing army and navy; they are not missed at great fairs and other occasions where people of wealth and leisure meet.

More sizable by statistical means are the permanent migratory trends. We shall soon describe more amply the war and post-war migration of the colored population from the South to the East and to the North. These mass movements, too, decompose the normal age structure of a population; like an earthquake they disrupt the old established order and give rise to new and uneven age strata. That the age group from 15 to 40 years surpasses by far the average of the United States in some large and important cities can be shown by the figures of New York, Chicago, Detroit, Pittsburgh, and Philadelphia:

Table 9.12 Percent Distribution of White and Negro Females,[31] 1930, 15 to 39 Years of Age

	New York	Chicago	Detroit	Pittsburgh	Philadelphia
White	45.0	46.3	47.8	43.2	42.4
Negro	57.9	56.1	58.6	51.0	53.5

Should we be disposed to consider life in these immense and turbulent cities unhealthy, socially speaking, and should we be certain that the age group from fifteen to forty years includes the period of greatest vital expansivity, we would be forced to the conclusion that the Negro woman is twice handicapped.

The sex ratio, usually assumed to be the number of males per 100 females, is bound to influence deeply all human relations. A serious deviation from this fundamental ratio creates physiological disturbances, mental incongruities, and social disarrangement. There have been few or no investigations concerning the effects of a considerable surplus on the male or the female side. The terrible human losses of the last world war created a numerical superiority of women in the age class, 20 to 40 years, which certainly affected millions of European women deleteriously. The unceasing unrest in the following twenty years might be attributable partly to the disturbed equilibrium of essential human relations.

The United States did not suffer to such a great extent from war losses. However, other powerful factors intervene in the Western Hemisphere. The conditions differ widely in the white and colored populations. Males prevail in the United States, a result of immigration which is largely male. In contrast, the colored race presents a sex ratio with a preponderance of females. The scope is not excessive; nevertheless, there are 1,463,501 white males and 179,805 colored females—more than members of the opposite sex. The gravity of the problem increases when we turn to the age distribution of the sexes.

Table 9.13 Sex Ratio, 1930

White	102.7
Negro	97.0

By reducing the general sex ratio into distinct age groups new conditions make themselves apparent. In the important period from 20 to 29 years of age, the numerical superiority of females among the whites vanishes and gives room to a slight male surplus. In the colored race, however, the preponderance of females is apparent up to 45 years. It is then reversed and makes way for a rather large surplus of males.

Table 9.14 Sex Ratio,[32] 1930

Age group	White	Negro
15–19 years	100.3	91.0
20–24 years	97.2	85.2
25–29 years	98.2	87.6
30–34 years	100.2	93.1
35–39 years	104.0	93.5
40–44 years	107.8	97.5

It is not difficult to figure out what it means that in the stormy twenties, 12 to 14 percent of the colored females—theoretically—do not find mates of their own race. Other factors, too, tend to render the situation even more unfavorable.

The numerical discrepancy is enlarged by geographical diversities. The surplus of young colored females is already large in a mathematical total of the United States. It is still more striking when we look at an important industrial town of the Midwest—Detroit, for example—and compute the sex ratio of the significant age period, 15 to 29 years.

Table 9.15[33] Sex Ratio of the Age Group 15 to 29 Years, Detroit; by Racial Groups, Males per 100 Females

	Males	Females	Sex Ratio
White	203,141	199,464	101.8
Negro	18,718	20,287	90.8

From this table we see that in the city of Detroit there are approximately nine female Negroes in 100 in the age group from 15 to 29 years who have no possibility of legally sanctioned sexual relations and a regularly established household. Similar conditions prevail in some states, regardless of urban surroundings and age, whereas other states show an abnormal surplus of males. Table 9.16 presents such plus and minus states.

Table 9.16[34] Sex Ratio by States, 1930; Number of Males Per 100 Females (Negroes)

Maxima	
West Virginia	112.7
Michigan	110.5
Ohio	106.0
Maryland	103.4
Pennsylvania	102.6
Minima	
South Carolina	91.5
Georgia	92.1
New York	93.5
Alabama	93.7
Tennessee	94.9

It is obvious that this disparity of sexes which forces a race to undergo such serious maladjustments cannot possibly be beneficial. It is therefore not surprising that investigations carried out in the western and the eastern cotton belt complain that the migration of the young male Negro to the North has left the aged female Negro in the South. "The Negro population," says an elaborate report,[35] "receiving relief in both cotton areas, included more aged persons, especially aged women, than any other group. In the Western cotton arcas counties, persons 65 years of age and older were almost two and one-half times as numerous in the relief as in the general population."

IV

Mortality and criminality are closely connected. Mortality may affect delinquency in two very different ways. First, a high mortality at a certain age diminishes the number of possible delinquents and thus checks criminality somewhat. Second, and much more significant, death is not brought about suddenly, but mostly is the final result of a long pathological process. In the course of this process, the mind is affected as well as the organism. Disease, in its first stages, often changes the character and the moral reactions of man. The morbidity of the Negro is much higher than that of the white race. The following table presents diseases in which sub-febrile stages are frequent. Although little studied, these stages mean that many individuals affected show a different kind of behavior from that of normal persons.

Table 9.17 Mortality Rates,[36] 1933–1935, Females; Per 100,000 Population of Each Race

	White	Colored
All death causes	1111.0	1380.6
Influenza	8.4	15.1
Tuberculosis, respiratory	41.2	130.1
Syphilis	3.6	30.9
Lobar pneumonia	37.1	55.3
Pellagra	2.2	20.4

There are other causes of death which are not attributable to microscopic enemies and a diminished resistance of the colored race, but to human interference.

Table 9.18 Mortality Rates,[37] 1933–1935, Females; Per 100,000 Population of Each Group

Death cause	White	Colored
Homicide	2.6	15.5
Suicide	7.6	2.4
Ill-defined causes	2.3	15.5[38]
Not specified or unknown	5.8	54.4

It seems that the Negro child is exposed to a much harder process of selection than the white child.[39] The mortality of the female colored child under one year of age is almost double the mortality of the female white child.

Table 9.19 Mortality,[40] Female Children One Year of Age and Under, 1935, Per 100,000 Population of Each Racial Group

	White	Negro
United States	77.3	153.1
Urban	75.5	146.3
Rural	80.0	158.5

In certain southern states, however, the mortality rises considerably above the average for the United States. We have selected three states—Georgia, Mississippi, and South Carolina:

Table 9.20 Mortality,[41] Females, 1935, Per 100,000 Population of Each Race

	White	Negro
United States	1111.0	1380.6
Georgia	2039.2	2799.2
Mississippi	1874.9	2365.2
South Carolina	1944.8	2699.3

All these figures mean that before they die thousands of Negro women undergo a slow process of physical weakening, of moral collapse and social decline. Disease is an economic catastrophe to innumerable men who are accustomed to winning their bread by manual labor. This weight rests much more heavily on the shoulders of the colored race which is less able to support it. It is not the morality itself, but all the stages of ailment preceding the final exit which are of consequence to criminology. Mortality stops all human activity, but before this occurs, physical and mental changes combined dismember bit by bit the normal personality. Out of trifling dislocations, a criminal deed often arises.

Insanity figures unfortunately cannot be obtained for the most recent years. We have to go back to 1933, since for unknown reasons the statistical surveys on *Patients in Hospitals for Mental Disease* have grown smaller and do not record racial diversities in more recent years.

In 1933, the first admissions of colored females surpassed the figures of white women. We have, of course, to exclude the foreign-born white women who are mostly adult and aging people and who are to a large extent submitted to the unfamiliar strain of city life.

Table 9.21 Admissions to State Hospitals[42] by Race, Females, 1933, Per 100,000 Population of Each Race

White	46.5
Negro	51.4

Doubtless large numbers of white patients are cared for in private hospitals, and we should be able to establish that number. Insane persons, however, are not admitted except for a minority of cases when they become troublesome or burdensome or endanger themselves or their surroundings. The large and essential differences of the admission practice by states seem to prove that colored women are sometimes well-cared for, sometimes neglected, but always present a high insanity rate. We would, of course, expect variations in this or in that state. The magnitude, however, of this disparity renders it probable that rather the mind of the admitting than the brain of the admitted has shaped these figures.

In some southern states the first admissions of female Negroes in state institutions are considerably lower than those of white women.

Table 9.21a First Admissions,[43] Females, 1933, Per 100,000 of Each Group

State	Native White	Negro
South Carolina	49.3	37.9
Mississippi	57.0	37.7
Arkansas	53.8	50.1

The southern states, however, seem to have different admission practices, since the figures for native whites correspond approximately in some northern states, although the figures for Negroes are radically different as shown by the following table:

Table 9.21b First Admissions,[44] Females, 1933, Per 100,000 of Each Group

State	Native White	Negro
New York	60.8	191.7
Illinois	53.3	138.6
Ohio	36.5	81.1

In these northern states the admissions of female Negroes surpass by 250 to 300 percent the admissions of native white females. The terrible strain of the new climatic conditions, and the new social surroundings to which the Negroes are not yet sufficiently adjusted takes its toll. There are different forms of this painful process of adjustment. Mortality is a kind of negative adjustment, as are insanity and criminality. Although the average for the whole United States does not present a greater disparity than 42.2 per 100,000 population of native white women and 51.4 of colored women for the whole nation,[45] the difference is much greater when we compile figures by single states. In New York more than three times as many Negro women succumb to the pressure of urban surroundings than native white women.

No one will doubt that insanity has much to do with the high Negro criminality in homicide and aggravated assault which we noticed in the beginning of our survey. It seems safe to assume that some southern states do not separate Negroes to the same extent as they separate insane whites from the outside world. Insane or weak-minded Negroes roving about without sufficient protection are bound to commit crimes which otherwise would not be committed.

That only the graver cases of insanity are admitted in Negroes appears to be proved by the mortality of colored female insane patients:

Table 9.22 Deaths of Patients in State Hospitals[46] 1933, Females, Per 100 First Admissions

White	40.7
Colored	48.3

It is well known that more time elapses before a family decides to send a female member to an asylum than a male; the mortality of females thus is considerably higher than the mortality of male patients.[47] They are mostly old and serious cases.

Wealthy people can afford to keep their insane either at home under fit supervision or to have them sent to a private hospital. Native white females and colored females come from fundamentally different economic strata as shown by the following table:

Table 9.23 Percent Distribution[48] by Economic Status of First Admissions, by Race, Females, 1933

	Native White	Negro
Dependent	27.7	52.2
Marginal	58.5	46.0
Comfortable	13.8	1.8

These conditions lead us to the great problem of the economic status of the colored woman.

V

There was a time when education was believed to be a major factor in preventing criminality. We have since abandoned such exaggerated hopes, and we now know that the emotional set-up is much more important in the genesis of human actions than the intellectual equipment. Nevertheless, it is true that many better paid jobs require some kind of education and that illiteracy, for instance, automatically excludes many otherwise fit candidates from many occupations.

The situation is exceptionally unfavorable in the colored race. Although Negro females seem to be better equipped with certain fundamental rules of reading and writing,[49] there are still states in which a third of the adult Negro population is illiterate. Figures are presented in the following table.

Table 9.24 Illiterates[50] 21 Years and Over, 1930, Percent of Population

	Native White	Negro
United States	1.8	20.0
South Carolina	6.5	35.3
Alabama	6.2	33.3
Mississippi	3.3	30.3

It would make considerable difference if illiterates were to be found mostly in the age group which plays but a trifling role in the delinquency of a nation. High figures for the Negro race appear to justify such assumption, but a look at figures for whites shows that the older age group is much more illiterate, so that the conditions compensate.

Table 9.24a Illiterates[51] 10 Years Old and Over by Race and Age Groups, 1930, Percent

Age	White	Negro
All classes	2.7	16.3
10–14 years	0.5	5.3
15–19 years	0.8	8.9
20–24 years	1.1	12.2
25–34 years	1.7	13.0
35–44 years	3.6	16.8
45–54 years	4.6	24.2
55–64 years	4.9	34.4
65 and over	6.5	55.7
Unknown	4.2	18.6

In New York and Chicago the illiteracy of whites is considerably greater than that of Negroes;[52] the writer is sorry not to be able to present figures distributed by sex.

The greater literacy of the colored female is apparent throughout all geographical sections:

Table 9.24b Illiteracy,[53] Negroes, 10 Years Old and Over, 1930, Percent

	Males	Females
United States	17.6	15.1
The North	4.9	4.5
The South	21.4	18.1
The West	3.1	3.6

The foreign-born white is more illiterate than the American Negro in urban areas: unfortunately, however, separate figures are not available for the females, so that conclusions cannot be drawn.

VI

The sociological significance of the marital status has two aspects: on the one hand, psychological weight should doubtless be attached to the fact that an individual remains single or even widowed; on the other hand, marriage undubitably involves an attempt to adjust oneself to new and difficult forms of a group life. Quite apart from the physiological demands of marriage, many psychic entanglements are possible and probable. The death of a marital partner often is a formidable nervous shock to the survivor.

Marital status has an economic meaning as well. To many women the death of the breadwinner is an economic catastrophe. The married woman is implicated in the economical welfare of the husband. They both are an economic unity, often bound together by common children, and it is well known that saving devices in times of distress first affect the food and other necessities of the mother.

Marital status is closely linked with the age grouping of a given society. Although, therefore, the marital status of the whole population is under consideration, criminological conclusions can be drawn only according to the marital status of certain age groups. These vary among white and colored females as follows:

Table 9.25 Marital Condition,[54] Females, 15 to 34 Years of Age, Percent Distribution, 1930

	Single		Married		Widowed		Divorced	
	White	Negro	White	Negro	White	Negro	White	Negro
15–19 years	88.1	77.9	11.5	20.5	0.1	0.9	0.2	0.6
20–24 years	48.0	33.1	50.3	60.4	0.6	4.1	1.0	2.3
25–29 years	22.6	15.9	74.3	73.5	1.3	7.4	1.6	3.1
30–34 years	13.7	9.9	82.0	76.0	2.4	10.8	1.8	3.2

One would expect that in a sound population the rate of married persons should correspond. But the troubles of life have disorganized the family life of the colored race to such a degree that urban areas present a surplus of married females and the western states an excess of married males. The following figures show this astounding and unwholesome disparity and present at the same time varying conditions in the correlation of single, widowed, and divorced males and females.

Table 9.26 Ratio of Males to Females[55] of the Negro Population 15 Years Old and Over, by Urban, Rural and Geographical Divisions, 1930, Males Per 1,000 Females

	Single	Married	Widowed	Divorced	Total
Urban	1,267	960	315	562	899
Rural-farm	1,304	994	492	711	1,011
Rural-non-farm	1,605	1,026	433	758	1,049
The South	1,261	980	376	570	943
The North	1,591	993	390	830	1,022
The West	2,054	1,001	378	792	1,056

The considerable excess of single colored males in the North and in the West is not balanced by the surplus of females, widowed and divorced, and could be produced as a partial explanation of the prostitution figures.

There is an interesting relation between marital status and insanity.

Table 9.27 First Admissions,[56] 1933, by 100,000 of Each Group 15 Years and Over

	Single	Married	Widowed	Divorced	Total
White females	62.4	53.6	111.3	236.2	65.4
Negro females	82.8	62.1	88.7	185.7	75.6

The writer does not believe that the single colored woman is more disposed to become insane than the married woman; probably married insane women are more likely to be kept in their families as long as possible. The difference between the high rate of white widowed and the low rate of Negro widowed is easily explained by the younger age of the colored widows. In addition, white widows have a better chance of remarrying than have Negro widows. Here again the different sex ratio is operative. Since more white widows remarry, those remaining unmarried are probably biologically and sociologically less desirable and more inclined to failures of all sorts.

The problem of the criminal widow, which was discussed by the writer many years ago,[57] cannot be separated from the age problem. The statement that there are many more Negro widows than white is, *per se*, without significance.[58] From a certain age on, three quarters of the entire female population consists of widowed women,[59] but these age groups are criminologically non-essential. What we should do is to examine the young widows and, since there are but few of these, the middle-aged widows as well. An attempt to calculate marital status ratios of white and female prisoners received from courts was futile; the prison statistics do not give figures of the marital status by age groups. There are, it is true, certain agglomerations in the figures of colored widows concerning homicide, aggravated assault, larceny, prostitution, and liquor law violations, but larceny, liquor law violations and that indirect form of prostitution, keeping a disorderly house, could theoretically be committed by older women. The writer has, therefore, attempted two different ways of approach. He has reckoned out figures of native white females and of colored females per 100,000 *of each form of marital status*, for all felonies, homicide and larceny. He has then taken a middle-aged group of white and colored *widows*. The figures thus obtained are much less erroneous than a comparison of widowed prisoners with the widows of the total population, regardless of the fact that in both races the age grouping varies considerably and that age is an essential circumstance in the genesis of crime.

Table 9.28 Female Prisoners Received from Courts,[60] 1932–1936, per 100,000 of Each Form of Marital Status

	All admissions		Admissions for homicide		Admissions for larceny	
Marital status	**Native White**	**Negro**	**Native White**	**Negro**	**Native White**	**Negro**
Total	5.81	21.4	0.24	4.96	6.0	40.0
Single	6.28	34.0	0.12	6.58	6.6	70.5
Married	4.78	17.0	0.17	3.69	4.9	32.1
Widowed	5.17	11.2	0.60	3.90	3.6	13.8
Divorced	36.06	26.2	0.16	6.74	40.6	39.4
Unknown	117.11	790.8	16.41	33.77	228.5	1,037.9

The high figures for the single colored women in homicide are striking. Negro widows have a relatively low criminality, and the figures are even smaller when only middle-aged widows are considered.

Table 9.28a Female Prisoners Received from Courts,[61] 1932–1936, per 100,000 of Population and of 100,000 Widows 30 to 44 Years of Age

	Per 100,000 of all widows		Per 100,000 widows 30 to 44	
	Native White	**Negro**	**Native White**	**Negro**
All prisoners	5.17	11.2	31.6	38.8
Larceny	3.6	13.8	2.2	4.7
Homicide	0.6	3.9	4.9	13.6

VII

The occupational division of the United States places the Negro in the lowest layers of the economic structure. When we divide the totality of occupations into two large groups we see that the Negro belongs almost exclusively to the one group, the white population to the other. It must further be remembered that agriculture has a very different meaning, according as one is owner or tenant of a farm, wage worker, or unpaid family worker.

Table 9.29 Primitive Professional Group,[62] per 1,000 Gainfully Occupied Females, 1930

	Negro	Native White	Foreign-born White
Total	1,000	1,000	1,000
Agriculture	361	214	91
Domestic and personal service	287	66	127
	648	280	218

Table 9.29a Higher Professional Group, per 1,000 Gainfully Occupied Females, 1930

	Negro	Native White	Foreign-born White
Total	1,000	1,000	1,000
Manufacturing and mechanical industries	186	275	441
Transportation, etc.	72	82	66
Trade	33	137	127
Professional service	25	79	44
Extraction of minerals	14	19	31
Public service	9	19	16
Clerical occupations	7	104	41
Forestry, fishing	6	5	6
	352	720	772

Such a division obviously is full of dangerous possibilities. The lowest occupations are the least accommodated to modern industrial life and the most exposed to the attack of newly invented mechanical devices. They have not yet passed the critical stage which the deadly machine competition prepares for every manual laborer. They are unadjusted and therefore menaced occupations.

On the other hand, have these primitive occupations always been carried on by women? A crisis was bound to hit the gainfully occupied woman with all force and directness.

I shall try to describe the occupational tragedy of the colored woman as briefly as possible. The main bulk of our data goes back to the 1930 census, so that the effects of the depression are not yet visible and computable.[63]

When we look at the figures of gainfully occupied females by racial groups, we notice that the colored woman always was to a high degree more gainfully occupied than either the native white or the foreign-born white woman. We should expect that the rate of occupation would follow the tendencies of (a) giving the woman a larger share in the professional life and (b) the increase of population ten years old and over. This trend, although not very strongly expressed, is noticeable in the case of the native white woman. In the case of the colored woman, however, the rate dips strikingly in 1920 and painfully maintains itself in 1930 as the following figures clearly show:

Table 9.30 Gainfully Occupied Females,[64] Percent

	Native White	Negro
1910	19.2	54.7
1920	19.3	38.9
1930	20.5	38.9

What is the reason that the poorest section of our Negro population has had its occupational status sensibly lowered during the last twenty years? During this time a tremendous change has taken place in the sort and the number of occupations into which women have entered. There were new and swiftly developing occupations; there were dying occupations. A few figures will suffice to illustrate this process which could but affect deeply the fate of millions of women.

These occupations have grown rapidly. They are a part of the modern industrial structure and, except in the occupations of teacher and waitress, admit but a few colored women.

Table 9.31 Selected Growing Occupations,[65] 1910–1930, Females

	1910	1920	1930	Negro
Population	34,552,712	40,449,346	48,773,249	4,727,866
Gainfully occupied	8,075,772	8,549,511	10,752,116	1,840,642
Clerks (exc. in stores)	122,665	472,163	706,553	4,926
Stenographers, typists	263,315	564,744	775,140	3,225
Bookkeepers, etc.	187,155	359,124	482,711	1,983
Saleswomen, clerks in stores	313,929	535,730	723,897	6,027
Teachers (school)	476,864	633,207	853,967	45,672
Trained nurses	76,508	143,664	288,737	5,581
Telephone operators	88,262	178,379	235,259	331
Waitresses	85,798	116,921	231,972	15,312

Other occupations like those of semi-skilled operative, servant, and cook are only feebly progressing; the Negro rate is rather large in domestic and personal service. In the manufacturing group there was a striking increase from 1910 to 1920 due to the great temporary demand which came with the World War, then a moderate decline from 1920 to 1930.[66] The figures are still comparatively low, comprising only about 100,000.

A third group of occupations is declining, and this decrease partly assumes the proportions of a social catastrophe. The following table shows the conditions of farm labor and of three non-agricultural pursuits:

Table 9.32 Declining Female Occupations,[67] 1910–1930

	1910	1920	1930	Net Change 1910–1930	Negroes 1930
A. Agricultural pursuits					
Farm laborers:					
Unpaid family workers	1,176,585	576,642	475,008	–701,577	298,727
Wageworkers	349,122	226,587	171,323	–177,799	120,114
B. Non-agricultural pursuits					
Laundresses (not in laundry)	520,004	385,874	356,468	–163,536	268,214
Dressmakers and seamstresses (not in factory)	447,700	235,519	157,928	–289,772	20,433
Milliners, millinery dealers	122,447	69,598	40,102	–82,345	441
Servants	976,113	743,515	1,263,868	287,775[68]	455,696

Farm laborers, laundresses, and dressmakers had a loss of 872,149 during the 20 years, 1910–1930; servants were oscillating, presenting sharp fluctuations. A really desperate attempt is being made by the colored woman to regain the ground lost in other dying occupations. The number of Negro women in domestic and personal service, 1,150,000, represented a gain of nearly 50 percent from 1920 to 1930.

The depression found the Negro and especially the Negro woman in "two of the great occupational groups which have suffered severely: agriculture and personal and domestic service;" it has "led to a larger amount of unemployment among the colored than among the whites and has forced them to appear in disproportionate numbers among the seeker of relief."[69] To this cyclic movement were added more permanent trends. The disappearance of the laundress presents such a more or less immutable tendency,[70] and we may pause here for a moment.

Of colored laundresses[71] there were:

		Per 100,000 population
In 1910	356,275	7,229
In 1920	281,761	5,573
In 1930	269,098	4,459

The rate of decrease has been lessened, but at what cost! We must, further, not overlook the fact that the decrease of laundresses coincides with an increase in the female population during the last twenty years.

We omit some statements of statistical technique mentioned in the census monographs.[72] They cannot possibly affect the figures to a significant degree, and are contradicted by the rising figures of laundry operatives.[73] They are contradicted further by the fact that the decrease has not been considerable in the North and the West, but was most marked in the South.[74] Why should the census enumerators have followed a different line of registering in different sections of the country? In any case these inconsistencies are comparatively negligible. There are other and deeper causes.

It is the power laundry which has taken away the job of the home laundress. In return it has provided work for a much smaller number of women, as the following table shows, to which we add the figures of dressmakers and of operatives in the clothing industries:

Table 9.33 Negro Females[75] in Some Declining Occupations

	1910	1920	1930	*Negroes*
Laundresses (not in laundry)	520,004	385,874	356,468	268,214
Laundry operatives	76,355	80,747	160,475	44,963
Dressmakers and seamstresses (not in factory)	447,700	235,519	157,928	20,433
Clothing industry operatives	237,270	265,643	346,751	15,635

Although a tremendous effort has been made by the eliminated women to win a place in power laundries, more than 250,000 laundresses have been thrown out of work. But before giving way, the Negro woman has put up a terrible fight for her existence, and 75 percent of all laundresses are colored.

In a study of laundries by the Women's Bureau in 1935,[76] the competitive struggle between power laundries and the Negro washwoman came to light through the comments of laundry employers in the South and other informed persons. We reproduce a few of these comments:

> Since the depression servants are required to do laundry as well as maid work; most of them get only $3.00 a week on the average.
>
> Greatest competition in colored washwomen. Will take a 30 pound bundle for a dollar. Some of them do a week's washing for 50 cents.
>
> The washwoman charges only 60 to 75 percent of what the laundry charges for the same size bundle.

The manager knew a number of washwomen who were glad to get a day's work for carfare, lunch, and an old dress.

Other factors have contributed in reducing the number of washwomen.

The modern household employs more and more mechanical devices for washing and ironing.[77] Modern apartment houses are furnished with running warm water and thus permit short washing operations. Women's underwear has undergone changes in the kind of material used (silk) and by reducing it to small and separate fragments. Millions of girls have developed the habit of taking care of their own linen and eliminating the washwoman.

Many factors of our industrial and social evolution combine in rendering the washwoman's an obsolete and outmoded type of occupation. She is on the way, without the slightest fault of her own, to becoming a social fossil.

At the same time the colored woman who succeeded in entering a power laundry or a clothing factory underwent all the pernicious influences of an enforced mass existence during most hours of the day, instead of home life. The children during the daytime had no mother at all and at nighttime an exhausted, uninterested, nervous, and impatient mother.

Health being the Negro's main instrument in his struggle for life, the economic importance of the high morbidity and mortality of the colored working race becomes self-evident. Health is economically much more important to the colored woman than to the white woman, notwithstanding the fact that for the age group 15 to 25 years the mortality among colored girls "is more than two and three-quarters times as high as for young white women."[78]

We speak of an individual having an occupation and we imagine such an occupation to be firm ground on which to make an adequate living. We think of an occupation as removing the individual from need. This does not hold true in many cases with the Negro woman. Wherever we look into relief statistics of colored people we find unemployment, acute illness, old age, blindness, and tuberculosis, along with "insufficient earnings" as a relief cause,[79] and I am afraid that many times insufficient earnings are but the first steps to acute illness, tuberculosis, prostitution, and minor forms of property criminality.

A Women's Bureau investigation of tobacco stemmeries in 1934 revealed that "weekly earnings are very low. Of all employees included, one-tenth earned less than $5.00 for the week, not far from half earned less than $10.00 and about 87 percent received less than $12.00."

"That many workers," the report goes on, "in the tobacco plants have failed to earn a livelihood and required supplementary aid from relief agencies was evident from the firms' pay-roll data and facts from the emergency relief agencies. In a tobacco manufacturing center the emergency relief administration reported in one month that slightly more than 10 percent of its case load consisted of experienced tobacco factory workers."[80]

"Gainfully occupied" workers who work all day long and need partial relief complete the somber picture of the economic status of the Negro woman. It is obvious that among the desperate attempts to make a marginal living[81] are some minor forms of criminality which form the bulk of the Negro delinquency.

VIII

It is not easy to verify the numerous complaints of colored people that they are unnecessarily maltreated by the police in many communities[82] and that colored girls are not safe in jails and in prisons.[83] The high release figures of arrested Negroes indicated in Table II seem to confirm many of these charges. In the South, it is true, the general population and its violent outbursts are more feared than excesses of the police.

We possess, however, some means of checking racial discrimination by the practice of police, courts, and prisons.

Can we quote homicide figures in this connection? I think we could cite them with some limitations. It has been stated that in Chicago during the years 1926 and 1927, one percent of all female white victims were supposed to have been slain in self-defense, but four percent of the colored female victims were believed to have been killed by justifiable homicide.[84] We do not hear of the race of the killer in relation to the race of the murdered victim. But I am inclined to believe that the use of certain weapons is a reliable indication of the race which handled it. From this point of view we are justified in assuming that the great majority of killings is to be attributed to white men who, in contrast to the knife-loving colored man, in most cases use firearms.

Table 9.34 White and Negro Women Victims of Homicide,[83] 1933–35, per 100,000 Population of Each Racial Group

	Homicide (All weapons)	Homicide (By firearms)	Homicide (By cutting or piercing instruments)
White females	22.6	11.0	1.6
Negro females	153.7	80.3	48.5

Thorsten Sellin has quoted Alabama reports showing the acquittal rates of whites and Negroes as being considerably higher for whites.[80] We regret that separate figures for white and colored females are not available. According to Detroit figures quoted by the same author,[87] the average fine was

	White females	Colored females
In felonies	$55.66	$66.66
In misdemeanors	30.80	29.15

This fact should be considered in connection with the low economic status of the Negro as it renders the misdemeanor average of $29.00 relatively much higher than the $30.00 for whites.

Whereas material on colored females is extremely rare, prison statistics offer a good insight into release procedures as the following table shows.

Table 9.35 Female Prisoners Discharged,[88] 1933–36

	Total	White	Negro
Expiration	100.0	27.4	42.7
Parole	100.0	60.1	46.7
Pardon	100.0	1.4	2.3
Other methods	100.0	11.1	8.3

It is apparent that the law is more strictly enforced against a colored woman, who is less able to secure adequate legal advice or to make use of "fixing" opportunities. Her only way of "fixing" would be that bitterly complained of surrender to some more or less influential male person in order to obtain a pardon, a parole, or some other method of release. Naturally these circumstances do not lend themselves to exact statistical methods. We could, perhaps, get an indirect insight if we had pardon and parole statistics by sex, race, and age groups, since we could expect the young Negro women to profit from such release procedures.

I think that two tendencies are in conflict in the case of the Negro woman: racial discrimination against her as a Negro, and favoritism for her as a woman, as happens commonly throughout our man-dominated criminal jurisdiction. The execution statistics point in the same direction. In proportion to population ten times as many colored men as native white men are executed.

Table 9.36 Prisoners Executed,[89] Male, per 1,000,000 of Corresponding Group 1932–1936

	Native White	Negro
18 to 24 years	2.9	39.6
25 and over	2.0	19.1
18 years and over	2.3	24.3

The age distribution is most interesting: the young Negro is executed—the competitor is eliminated. The young colored woman is spared. Although figures which distinguish by race are lacking, the trifling number of 6 females executed leaves no room for many executions of colored women when we compare this number with an average of 172 male executions a year (1932–1936), and when we remember the high homicide figures of the colored woman. There is apparently discrimination, but a sex-limited discrimination.

IX

These are a few of the facts which lie behind that unshaped numerical quantity known as the colored female population. They change the problem by introducing qualitative distinctions. Many angles had to be omitted. I did not mention the conflict-laden atmosphere of crowded Negro-ghettos.

Following the studies of E. W. Burgess, Woofter concluded from his survey of several cities that "the density of Negro areas in most cities is much greater than the density of white areas. In some cities it is four times as great."[90] The housing problem, apart from being a considerable psychological factor,[91] affects the sex criminality, and the inescapable altercations lead to fighting, aggravated assault, and manslaughter. The high tuberculosis mortality of the colored race is directly connected with vicious housing conditions.

The writer has attempted in a prior publication[92] to present a short psychological and evolutionary history of the Negro, showing that the white man has intentionally selected and bred a definite physical and mental type of man; he has forced him to become warped, and has driven out mental traits which are indispensable in modern life.

This study should be extended by examining the—probably—different selective maxim which the white race, represented by men, has applied to colored women. As far as I can see, the colored woman has been permitted to survive better the disfiguring interferences of the white race. Perhaps she has saved the colored race from destruction by keeping and transmitting the more desirable attributes of her race. Some important facts, however, have been proved: the altered age distribution of the colored woman and the profoundly disturbed sex ratio, the high mortality and insanity rate of the Negro woman. All these conditions are closely connected with delinquency; there are intimate inter-relations between age distribution and crime as well as between illness preceding death and delinquency. It is of the utmost importance whether a race suffers from early originating diseases as, for instance, tuberculosis,[93] or syphilis,[94] or from ailments which occur later in the life span such as cancer. In one case human behavior is affected and altered during the time of greatest activity, in the other the weary and aging individual is affected.

A race presenting numerous cases of epilepsy[95] or syphilitic insanity[96] will have a larger criminality than a race in which senile psychoses play an important role. Before an insane person is certified as such and admitted to an institution he generally has endured long years of latent psychosis. It is just this unrecognized interval between full health and full malady which is dangerous to the order and peace of society, and everything depends on whether the disease happens to start between the ages of 20 and 30 or between 50 and 60. In the case of the Negro, his organism is damaged by over-exertion even before this critical period begins.[97] He enters adult life biologically and socially with a grave handicap, and this probably holds more true with the colored girl than with the colored boy.

The economic status of the colored woman cannot be held separate from disease, insanity, death, and crime even in textbooks; in real life, however, there is a continuous and pitiless interaction. Pellagra, for instance, is a hunger ailment or, more cautiously expressed, it can be prevented and cured by proper diet. It has been estimated that in 1934 there were 30,000 pellagra victims in North Carolina—300 in state institutions.[98] Table XVII of this report shows that ten times as many colored women died during the period 1933–1935 from pellagra as white women. Like a maelstrom the modern industrial development attacks their old occupations and robs them legally of their jobs.

Colored women are tolerated chiefly in dangerous, unhealthful, and crisis-endangered occupations. Wherever heat must be endured, as in cooking or washing; wherever unpleasant odors or dust must be borne, as in the tobacco factories, the slaughter and packing houses, the cotton mills, the fish packing plants, we meet the colored woman. And it cannot be said which is worse: the eternally menacing unemployment[99] or the insufficient week's earnings. Depression struck the Negro woman a terrible blow and produced a downward shift from white-collar to skilled, semi-skilled, and unskilled positions.[100]

All these charges would suffice to explain the delinquency figures of the colored woman. Another powerful factor, however, presents itself. The Negro's adjustment to African conditions had probably reached a high degree of perfection, physically, mentally, and socially. The Negro slaves who were imported into the United States had to start anew, not only to adjust themselves to new climatic and social conditions, but to a world which was to them artificial and unreal. Polygamous institutions of their native continent were relieved by two hundred and fifty years of compulsory promiscuous sex relations. Initiative was suppressed, obedience and submission were bred, and since enforced submission always creates a split mentality, certain characteristics were imposed and overemphasized: laziness (which we find in all prisons), improvidence, supersensitiveness,[101] excitability,[102] and other traits which the writer has tried in his former study to explain partly as necessary and useful adjustments to life in the primitive forests and under the climatic conditions of Africa.

That the colored race is feared seems incredible in view of its continuous numerical decrease,[103] but it has been mentioned again and again in interviews of white persons.[104] From this obscure fear it is but one step to the discriminatory practice of many law-enforcing agencies.[105]

It is difficult to give these diverse handicaps the same short and simple statistical expression which is afforded by the calculation that so many arrests have been effected or that so many prisoners have been received per 100,000 of population. The writer, however, could not resist the temptation, in concluding, to select a condition which probably represents a low cultural and economic status as well, and to substitute these more qualitative traits for mere population figures.

Table 9.37 Women Received in Prisons, 1932–1936

	Per 100,000[106] (15 years and over)	Per 100,000[107] gainfully occupied (10 years and over)	Per 100,000[108] families having no radio set*	Per 100,000[109] illiterates†
Native White	5.8	24.5	16.1	410.0
Colored	20.5	46.7	32.5	120.8

* By color of head of family.
†10 years and over.

It may be interesting to add arrest figures per 100,000 illiterates:

Table 9.38 Arrests, Females, 1936–1938

	Per 100,000[110] population, 15 years and over		Per 100,000[111] illiterates, 10 years and over	
	White	Negro	White	Negro
Homicide	0.6	10.3	18.8	59.3
Robbery	0.8	6.4	26.3	36.8
Aggravated assault	1.4	46.5	45.8	267.2
Burglary	0.9	4.7	28.1	26.8
Larceny	6.4	47.3	204.6	271.7
Embezzlement and fraud	1.4	4.2	45.9	24.0
Prostitution	7.9	27.0	253.9	155.1
Disorderly conduct	4.0	26.7	128.0	153.7
Total arrests	57.5	314.2	184.9	180.6

When this probably more adequate relation is used, the arrest figures for the colored woman shrink to such a degree that in some offenses (burglary, embezzlement and fraud, prostitution) white arrests surpass Negro arrests.

In important offenses such as larceny and disorderly conduct, the arrests come strikingly close for the two races.

The writer is not satisfied that the references to illiterates, or to families having no radio set, or to females gainfully occupied, 10 years of age or over, is the ideal and the ultimate relation attainable.[112] It is but an attempt to come closer to the realities behind the delinquency of the colored woman, and it is certainly a truer and a more significant standard than that sphinx: "population."

Notes

1. "Die Kriminalitaet des Negers," *Schweizerische Zeitschrift fuer Strafrecht*, 1938, pp. 34–61; and "La criminaliu dei Negri," *Giuslizia Penale*, 1938, 1–35.
2. The combination of less fear of a woman and sex appeal changes the aspect considerably. A resident of Chicago has given this sentiment a naive and instructive expression. "A colored family lives next door north of me, and you'll be surprised when I tell you that I have not been able to open my bedroom window on that side to air that room for three years. I couldn't think of unlocking the windows because their window is so near somebody could easily step across into this house. It's awful to have to live in such fear of your life." When asked if she considered her neighbors so dangerous as that, she said: "Well, no, the woman seems pretty nice. I see her out in the backyard occasionally and bid her the time of day out of charity. You can't help but pity them, so I am charitable and speak. . . ." *The Negro in Chicago*, (Chicago, 1922), 453.

3. Crime reports were received during the calendar year 1938 from 2,662 city and village departments, from 1,61; sheriffs and state police organizations, and 9 agencies in territories and possessions of the United States. The population covered by these reports totaled 67,555,972 in 1938. The report does not say what population is covered by its fingerprint records, from which arrest statistics are obtained. *Uniform Crime Reports, 1938*, 126.
4. Fingerprint cards representing arrests for violation of federal laws are excluded from the tabulation. "The tabulation of data from fingerprint cards obviously does not include all persons arrested, since there are individuals taken into custody for whom no fingerprint cards are forwarded to Washington." *Uniform Crime Reports, 1938*, 157.
5. *Prisoners in State and Federal prisons and reformatories*, 1936, (Washington, DC, 1938), 1.
6. Compiled from figures in *Uniform Crime Reports*; 1935, 44; 1936, 168; 1937, 236; 1938, 178.
7. Homicide includes murder and non-negligent manslaughter, and further, manslaughter by negligence, only however, "those cases in which death is caused by culpable negligence which is so clearly evident that if the person responsible for the death were apprehended he would be prosecuted for manslaughter." *Uniform Crime Reports*, 1938, 125.
8. Aggravated assault includes assault with intent to kill; assault by shooting, cutting, stabbing, maiming, poisoning, scalding, or by use of acids. Does not include simple assault, assault and battery, fighting, etc." *Uniform Crime Reports*, 1938, 125. The reports in giving arrest figures mention only "assault" but certainly mean "aggravated assault." See *Uniform Crime Reports*, 1938, 158.
9. "Includes assault to rob and attempt to rob." *Uniform Crime Reports*, 1938, 125.
10. *Negro survey of Pennsylvania* (Harrisburg, 1927), 70.
11. Ibid.
12. Computed from figures in *The Negro population of Denver, Colorado*, Ira De A. Reid (New York, 1929), 21.
13. *Negro survey of Pennsylvania*, 70.
14. "Data pertaining to persons arrested should not be treated as information regarding the number of offenses committed, since two or more persons may be involved in the joint commission of a single offense, and on the other hand one person may be arrested and charged with the commission of several separate crimes." *Uniform Crime Reports*, 1938, 157, 158.
15. Maurine Boie, "An analysis of negro crime statistics for Minneapolis for 1923, 1924 and 1925," *Opportunity*, 1923, vol. VI, 173.
16. Figures quoted and computed from M. Boie, op. cit.
17. For an unknown reason the Minneapolis police are more careful in arresting colored people than were the Philadelphia, Pittsburgh, and Denver police some years ago.
18. M. Boie, op. cit.. 172.
19. M. Boie gives 1,384. Our computation arrives at a slightly smaller number, 1,374.
20. *Federal Offenders*, 1935–36, (Washington, DC, 1937), 186.
21. Computed from figures in *Federal Offenders*; 1933–34, 212, 213; 1934–35, 308, 309; 1935–36,. 252, 253.
22. Ibid.
23. Ibid.
24. Computed from figures in *Prisoners in State and Federal prisons and reformatories*, 1932, 20; 1933, 23; 1934, 30; 1935, 35; 1936, 35.
25. Ibid.
26. Four-year average.
27. Four-year average.
28. Figures calculated from Fifteenth Census, 1930, *Population. Age Distribution* (Washington, 1933), 581, 582. In following the official statistics we arrive at small excesses of 0.2 percent.
29. Ibid.
30. See John N. Webb, *The Transient Unemployed* (Washington, DC, 1935), 34, 102.
31. Computed from figures in *Age Distribution*, 726, ff.
32. *Age Distribution*, 583.
33. Computed from figures in *Age Distribution*, 729.
34. *Abstract of the Fifteenth Census of the United States, 1930* (Washington, 1933), 91. There are states with much greater maxima (New Hampshire with 197.0 for instance), but their small figures do not permit a conclusion. Some cities too show a wider range (San Francisco, 135.8, and Atlanta, 79.6); here apparently the conditions are approaching the degree of a pathological state.
35. P. G. Beck and M. C. Forster, *Six Rural Problem Areas*, (Washington, DC, 1935), 48.
36. *Mortality Statistics*, 1933, 112–150; 1954,. 160–202; 1935, 200–249.
37. Ibid.
38. Is the close resemblance to the homicide figures purely accidental?
39. Diarrhea killed 10.8 children under 2 years of age, and 19.4 Negro children per 100,000 population in 1935.
40. Figures computed from *Mortality Statistics*, 1935, 62, 63.
41. Computed from figures in *Abstract*, 91; and *Mortality Statistics*, 1935, 22, 25.
42. *Patients in Hospitals for Mental Disease*, 1933, (Washington, DC, 1935), 26.
43. Computed from figures in *Abstract*, 92, and *Patients in Hospitals for Mental Disease*, 1933, (Washington, DC, 1935), 29.
44. Ibid.
45. *Patients in Hospitals for Mental Disease*, 1933, (Washington, DC, 1935), 26.
46. Ibid., 92.
47. Ibid., 93.

48. Ibid,. 55.
49. Illiteracy in Negro population 10 years old and over by sex, 1930 (United States): male Negro 17.6 percent, female Negro 15.1 percent. *Negroes in the United States, 1920–1932* (Washington, DC, 1935), 231. In the older age groups there are more female than male illiterates. This relation, however, is reversed in the age period, 10 to 44 years, so that improvement is visible, more pronounced on the female side than on the male.
50. *Abstract*, 253.
51. *Negroes in the United States, 1930–1932* (Washington, DC, 1935), 230.
52. Ibid., 237.
52. Ibid., 243.
53. Ibid., 231. On the comparative illiteracy of Negroes and foreign-born see 251.
54. Ibid., 147.
55. Ibid.
56. Figures computed from *Negroes*, p. 147; and *Patients in Hospitals for Mental Disease*, 1933, (Washington, DC, 1935), 38.
57. "Die Kriminalitaet der Verwitweten und Geschiedenen," *Ocsterreichische Zeilschrift fuer Strafrecht*, 1913,. 365–387.
58. 15.9 percent of all colored women, 15 years and over, and only 10.5 percent of all white women of that age are widowed. *Negroes*, 147.
59. *Negroes*, 147. This means that the married men have a greater and earlier mortality; they have no time (or not of may we say, opportunity) to become widowed since they die first. The widows survive and present by that very much greater vitality a sociological problem.
60. Computed from figures in *Prisoners*, etc.; 1932, 20; 1933, 28; 1934, 30; 1935, 35; and 1936, 35.
61. Computed from figures in *Prisoners, loc. cil.* and *Abstract*, 234.
62. *Negroes*, 289.
63. Unfortunately, *Women in Gainful Occupations, 1870–1920*, has not been issued for the following decade. Many trends have changed somewhat since 1920 so that the conclusions of this able study do not apply to 1930.
64. *Negroes*, 288.
65. Fifteenth Census, 1930, *Population*, vol. IV, 7–16, 25–34.
66. "Why this decrease took place cannot be explained. One possible cause is that in 1920 there still were many Negro women employed in the jobs they had taken on during the war-time period of labor scarcity, and that by 1930 most of these jobs would have reverted to white men or women. Another explanation concerns the tremendous technological changes in industry, which have been focussed largely on the elimination of low-skilled jobs, the jobs in which the majority of Negro women are employed." *The Negro Woman Worker*, United States Department of Labor, Bell No. 165 (Washington, DC,1938), 8.
67. Figures in *Population*, vol. IV, *loc. cit.*
68. This increase has certainly changed since 1930. In a survey of employment and unemployment in Louisville, Ky., conducted by the State Department of Labor in the spring of 1933, it was found that "more than three-fourths of the Negro women wage earners in the survey depended on domestic and personal service for their livelihood, but the depression had thrown 56 percent of these out of work." *The Negro Woman Worker*, (Washington, DC, 1938), 3. In the southern cities covered by a survey of persons on relief, "there were only 5,000 white women, as against 52,000 Negro women, classed as servants and allied workers" on relief. Ibid.
69. *Handbook of Labor Statistics*, (1936 ed.), 569.
70. There are other such tendencies, an interesting instance being the decline of the birth rate which eliminated the midwife. Births with midwife attendance in Connecticut were, in 1931, 5.3 percent: in 1936, 2.1 percent. *[??252] Connecticut, Report of the State Dept. of Health*, 1937, 308. 50.1 percent of all midwives are colored. *Negroes*, 289.
71. Fifteenth Census, vol. IV, 34; *Abstract*, 82.
72. *Women in Gainful Occupations*, 109.
73. Ibid.
74. In Denver the number of colored laundresses decreased from 296 to 194 (that is, by 34.4 percent) during the period 1910 to 1920. The number of colored laundry operatives increased only from 10 to 20. Ira De A. Reid, *The Negro Population of Denver, Colorado* (New York, 1929), 12.
75. Fifteenth Census, *Population*, vol. IV, 7–16, 25–34.
76. Jean Collier Brown, *The Negro Woman Worker*, United States Department of Labor, *Bull. No. 165*, (Washington, DC, 1938), 4.
77. *Women in Gainful Occupations*, (Washington, DC, 1929), 113.
78. Lots I. Dublin, "The health of the Negro" in *Annals of the American Academy for Political and Social Science* (1928), 78.
79. Ira De A. Reid. *The Negro Population of Denter, Colorado* (New York, 1929), 42. The three relief are: unemployment (46), insufficient earnings (39), acute illness (35). *Ibid.*
80. In one city . . . relief of tobacco workers in this city was averaging a few thousand dollars a month." *The Negro Woman Worker*, 9.
81. Marriage is one of them, although racial precocity may play an additional role. Married females in the age group 15 to 19 years in 1930 were: White, 11.5 percent; Negro, 20.5 percent. *Negroes*, 147. Since the single Negro can scarcely make his living, the colored married woman goes to work. Gainfully occupied women 15 years old and over in 1930 were: Native White, 9.8 percent; Negro, 33.2 percent. (These figures are for married women.) *Negroes*, 297. The possible economic support of a marriage again might turn out to be a new source of personal conflict and physiological harm.

82. "The antagonism of the Irish policeman to the Negro in general is the basis for many jokes around City Hall."—A. Thompson, "A survey of crime among Negroes in Philadelphia," *Opportunity*, 1926, vol. IV, 254.
83. "When a girl is sent to prison, she becomes the mistress of the guards and others in authority. . . ." Quoted from the *Defender* by *The Negro in Chicago* (Chicago, 1922), 88.
84. *The Illinois Crime Survey*, 1929, 607.
85. *Moriality Statistics*, 1933, 146; 1934, 202; 1935,. 240.
86. Thorsten Sellin, "The Negro criminal" in *Annals*, 1928, 58.
87. Ibid., 61. January 1 to June 30, 1926, is much too short a statistical period.
88. Computed from figures in *Prisoners in State and Federal prisons and reformatories*, 1933, 59; 1934, 68; 1935, 74; 1936, 72.
89. Ibid. 1932, 45; 1933, 61; 1934, 70; 1935, 76; 1936, 74.
90. Quoted by L. V. Kennedy, *The Negro Peasant turns Cityward*, (New York, 1930), 154.
91. Some of the chief answers to the question "What difficulties do you think a person from the South meets in coming to Chicago?" "Change in climate, crowded living conditions, lack of space for gardens, etc.; adjusting myself to the weather and flat life; rooming and 'closeness' of the houses." *The Negro in Chicago*, by the Chicago Commission on Race Relations, 101.
92. *Die Kriminalitaet des Negers.*
93. Tuberculosis is the cause of the sudden increase in the mortality rate between 15 and 25 years, which was previously mentioned.
94. . . . "Jamison of New Orleans in a series of medical cases in colored women, found 16.6 percent syphilitic. Young of Louisville found that 25 percent of the Negro women attending the obstetric clinic were positive for syphilis; Scherman and Barnes of Philadelphia General Hospital found 27.8 percent in the same class of patients."—Wm. R. R. Granger, "A neglected Health Problem," *Opportunity*, 1928, 72. Granger himself made a routine test on 1,040 consecutive colored patients seen by him in his private practice; 15.6 percent were undoubtedly positive for syphilis, 10.7 percent were doubtful . . . Ibid.
95. For the high epilepsy figures for Negroes, see *Patients*, 1933, 30.
96. The admissions into North Carolina state hospitals for paresis and cerebral syphilis, 1930–1934, were: Raleigh (White)—1.6 percent of total; Morganton (White)—3.2 percent; Goldsboro (Negro)—33.6 percent.—*A Study of Mental Health in North Carolina*, (Ann Arbor, 1937), 127.
97. Gainfully occupied female children 10 to 15 years, U. S.: Native White (1920) 3.9 percent. (1930) 1.8 percent; Negro (1920) 17.1 percent, (1930) 12.0 percent. *Abstract*, (Washington, 1933), 339. The gainfully occupied native white girls decreased 46.5 percent; Negro girls, 28 percent.
98. *A Study of Mental Health in North Carolina*, 131.
99. "It is because of the Negro's place in agriculture, because of his place as a newcomer in industry together with his predominance in domestic pursuits that he has had to suffer the full brunt of the depression."—Lawrence A. Oxley, "Occupations, Negroes, and Labor Organizations," *Occupations*, March, 1936, 3.
100. *The Negro Women Worker*, U. S. Dept. of Labor, *Bull. No. 165*, (Washington, DC, 1938), 11.
101. "The employment manager said that misunderstandings had arisen occasionally, due to the colored girl being over-sensitive and suspicious. . . . Another characteristic of Negro girls, in the opinion of the employment manager, was an 'excitable nature' which made it possible for a good leader to influence them readily." *The Negro in Chicago*, 381.
102. A trait which probably explains the high killing and wounding figures.
103. In 1790 the Negro population made up 19.3 percent of the total population of the United States; in 1930, 9.7 percent. *Negroes*, 1.
104. See *The Negro in Chicago*, 452, 453.
105. How can a destitute colored man or woman secure a medical expert in support of an insanity plea?
106. Computed from figures in *Age Distribution*, 584; *Prisoners*, 1932, 19; 1933, 33; 1934, 30; 1935, 33; 1936, 42.
107. *Abstract*, 332, and *Prisoners*, loc. cit.
108. *Abstract*, 431, and *Prisoners*, loc. cit.
109. Ibid., 275.
110. For obvious reasons, 1930 population figures have always been used. *Uniform Crime Reports*, 1936, 168; 1937, 236; 1938, 178.
111. *Abstract*, 275, and *Uniform Crime Reports*, loc, cit.
112. The writer has lately suggested other such relations in his paper "A statistical test of causal significance" in *American Sociological Review*, Vol. V, 1940, 930–936.

10

The Image of Black Women in Criminology

Historical Stereotypes as Theoretical Foundation

Jacklyn Huey and Michael J. Lynch

The purpose of this chapter is to examine how prejudices and stereotypes embedded in history, tradition and culture affect modern criminological theory. Specifically, this chapter will examine common stereotypes about Black females found in popular culture and criminological theory. We will assess whether or not and how popular culture stereotypes are incorporated into modern criminological theory.

Part of the reason we are investigating this problem is that theory construction is not an objective process (Mills 1959; Messerschmidt 1988). Rather, theorists often incorporate cultural biases and values into the theories they construct. Thus, like theorists in other fields, criminologists may unwittingly reproduce derogatory cultural stereotypes and images in their work.

Many different stereotypes are reproduced in theories examining crime and justice. Typically, we are most concerned about stereotypes that tend to include negative characteristics and images, as well as those which focus on excluded and disadvantaged groups. The inclusion of stereotypes in theories about crime and justice that focus on minority groups reinforce exclusion and powerlessness, and serve as a tool of oppression.

For these reasons, this chapter focuses on Black women and criminological theory. As a group, Black women are disadvantaged and excluded from power as a consequence of their race and gender. They also constitute a group which is the focus of many negative stereotypes. Consequently, if the images criminologists draw upon are distorted, then so too will be the images of Black women that appear in modern criminological theory.

The replication of distorted images concerning Black women in criminological theory is important in several ways. First, distorted images can generate inappropriate policies (i.e., policies about crime that won't work). Second distorted images are often passed on to the next generation of criminologists in the classroom. If these images are taught noncritically, students "may react to these differences . . . with differential treatment of women and minorities in all areas of criminal justice administration" (Dorworth and Henry 1992, 258). Thus, criminologists need to expose these derogatory stereotypes to shortcircuit the intergenerational transfer of misleading and harmful views concerning Black women. To develop this idea further, some background concerning the stereotyping of Black women in American culture is needed. It is to such an overview that we now turn.

Background

For centuries, images of Black women in the United States have been distorted, ignored and trivialized. Even with the momentum behind multiculturalism, many academic fields continue to operate under the old stereotypes and assumptions about Black women; assumptions that undermine the Black woman as subject (as a thinking actor), as well as theorist. Patricia Morton (1991, 153) comments on the consequences of the continued use of historically inaccurate representations of Black women:

> To explore how Afro-American women have figured in a century of American historiography is largely to discover a history of disfigured images. While these may be interpreted in various ways, it is clear that they remain just that—images—not facts.

Aside from Black women scholars, few scholars have thought it necessary or even desirable to challenge the historical and theoretical distortions of Black women in popular culture or academic literature. Most scholars seem willing to accept Black female stereotypes, and fail to see the detrimental consequences these images have on Black women. However as more Black women enter academia, they increasingly expose and address such issues. Black female scholars and authors are especially sensitive to the need to address: (1) the inclusion of Black women in theory, especially feminist theory; (e.g., Collins 1990; hooks 1981, 1984, 1989; Hull et al. 1982; Joseph and Lewis 1981; King 1988; Martin and Hall 1992; Wallace 1990); and (2) the roles assigned to and the absence of Black women from America's recorded history (e.g., Giddings 1984; Lerner 1992; Morton 1991; White 1985; Neverdon-Morton 1989).

In short, academic disciplines have tended to: (1) exclude or omit Black women from consideration; (2) include Black women only by proxy, as an extension of a general theory about women; and (3) present distorted images of Black women. These tendencies, though diminished in some fields in recent years, remain the norm in academic circles. For example, most criminological research that is "women centered" focuses upon White women. Further, much criminological research done on Blacks in particular has been male-centered. In addition, when Black women are addressed, it is largely in reference to theory generated by studying White females.

In sum, little research has been done on Black women in criminology (i.e., Von Hentig 1942; French 1978; McClain 1982; Simpson 1991; Laub and McDermott 1985; C. Mann 1989; Young 1980). The few studies that have examined the images of women in criminology texts, for example, demonstrated a tendency to depict Black women as "vamps and tramps" (Wright 1992). In addition, early textbooks and theorists (i.e. Lombroso and Ferrero 1930; Thomas 1924; Pollak 1950) used traditional (i.e., negative) stereotypes that blamed Black women's criminal activity and victimization on their inferiority or sexual promiscuity (for review see: Steffensmeier and Clark 1980; Wright 1992). In sum, these archaeological histories (Foucault 1970) of Black women in criminology still define Black women negatively, or erase them from the text completely (e.g., see Lynch et al. 1992).

Criminological depictions of Black women are also important because of the impact these images sometimes have upon social policy. Stereotypical images of Black women, since they contain inaccurate information can lead to a misdiagnosis of the problem under study. If the problem is misdiagnosed, policies based upon such theory will not yield appropriate (useful) solutions.

To illustrate these contentions, the following section examines the origins or history of stereotypes that relate to Black women. From there, we will move to an in depth examination of criminological distortions of Black women. The implications of this research will be discussed in the concluding section to this chapter.

Distorted Images of Black Women

Black women's particular history within the United States has generated some interesting and debilitating stereotypes. During the period in which White women were confronted with and were attempting to accommodate the popular ideas of "True Womanhood" (i.e., an image that defined how "good" women acted and appeared), Black women were emerging from slavery. Black women's most immediate problem centered upon survival in a world they were unfamiliar with—a free world.

In the late 1800s, "True Womanhood" was defined by the virtues of "piety, purity, submissiveness and domesticity" (Welter 1966). Often times these virtues were defined by characteristics White women were assumed to possess. In fact, many Whites believed that Black women could not attain "True Womanhood," even by behaving properly. These beliefs undermined Black women's concept of femininity, beauty and worth (Guy-Sheftall 1990; hooks 1992). As a result, the womanhood of Black women was frequently challenged. In general, Black women were devalued relative to White women (Guy-Sheftall 1990), and were considered "less than women."

In essence, Black woman fell short of the Victorian era's hero-worshipping, nonsexual, obedient, dimwitted housewife image. Slavery required Black women to work, which contradicted one of the more fundamental tenets of womanhood: domesticity (Dill 1979; S. Mann 1989). And, even though the definition of "True Womanhood" changed over time, it usually excluded Black women since womanhood was defined to fit the desires of White men.

By White-sanctioned definition, Black women could not meet the criteria for "True Womanhood:" Black women's failure to attain this status translated into occupying a position within America's strict gender hierarchy of something less than woman. Accordingly, a set of externally defined images, shaping the public's attitudes, emerged to control Black women. As a sexualized beast of burden, Black women were viewed as something to be used and abused, rousing none of the chivalry or respect "real women" deserve (Guy-Sheftall 1990). These early cultural images of Black women "by meshing smoothly with systems of race, class, and gender oppression, . . . provide effective ideological justifications for racial oppression, the politics of gender subordination, and the economic exploitation inherent in capitalist economies" (Collins 1990, 78).

Stereotypes of Black women fall into one of several categories. The four most popular depictions have been the "mammy," the "matriarch," the "welfare mom" and the "Jezebel" or "whore" (Collins 1990; Gilkes 1983; Bogle 1973; Sims-Wood 1988; Morton 1991). These images emphasize contradictory attitudes toward Black women. Black women have been treated as chattel in slavery (the epitome of the commodification of women), yet martyred for her strength and long-suffering demeanor; castigated for her inability to properly rear her children, she was employed as a wet nurse for White families' children; ridiculed for her ugliness, she was desired for her sexual animalism; currently chastised for an inability to control her fertility, she was once bought, sold, and borrowed for that same ability. For all she has achieved, Black women are still reduced to two-dimensional stereotypes. The next section examines these stereotypes more completely. As we shall see in a later section, many of these stereotypes continue to find their way into modern criminological theory.

Stereotyping Black Women in America

In this section we analyze four predominant stereotypes about Black women found in American society and its popular culture. These stereotypes include the "mammy," the "matriarchy," the "welfare mom," and the "Jezebel." These stereotypes are important to the extent that they are responsible for affecting the images of Black women found in criminological theory. Each will be discussed separately in the remainder of this section.

The Mammy

The mammy characterization generates an image of the dark, fat, jolly, nurturing, faithfully obedient domestic servant who happily serves the White folks. The asexual mammy (e.g., Aunt Jemima) can easily occupy a nonthreatening role in the dominant group's idea of family, that is as long as she knew her place (Sims-Wood 1988; Jewell 1976). The "mammy" image is so entrenched within White society that figurines, cookie jars and other collectibles have been made in her honor. There have even been attempts to immortalize her (The Black Mammy Movement 1923). In short, the mammy "symbolizes the dominant group's perceptions of the ideal Black female relationship to elite White male power" (Collins 1990, 71).

The Matriarch

The matriarch is the strong Black woman often depicted as ruling her family with an iron first and castrating her men (Harris 1982; Sims-Wood 1988; Jewell 1976). This image of the Black woman was popularized by social sciences "observations" and writings by "experts" such as Daniel Moynihan in the 1960s (Weitz and Gordon 1993). According to the social scientists who legitimized this image, the Black matriarch embodied all the ills of the Black community. This view was seeped in a misunderstanding of the history of Black family structure (see Bailey 1996) which examined Black women's roles and behaviors from the perspective of dominant White males. The resulting image recast strong Black women as aggressive, overbearing, tyrants who chased their men away or browbeat them into total submission. This, in turn resulted in the destruction of the natural hierarchy of patriarchy, undermined the family and caused poverty. More immediately, poverty itself caused other ills in the Black community such as crime (Blau and Blau 1982). But, by tracing the chain backwards, social scientists linked all these ills to Black matriarchical control of the family.

The Black matriarch was assailed in other ways as well. Her behavior drove her man away, which in itself created an inappropriate atmosphere in which to raise children. In addition, without a male provider, it became economically necessary for Black women to work. Because they were forced to work, Black women could not supervise their children properly.

As a result, Black children would likely "go astray." In effect, Black women's position in the family was viewed as instituting a cycle of poverty and lack of control over children which led to crime. This cycle was passed on from generation to generation. In theory, this occurred because Black women stubbornly rejected their womanly role within traditional gender and family structures. In essence, Moynihan and others' myth of the matriarch blamed the Black woman's inability to remain in her proper place for the desolation of the Black community.

The Welfare Mom

The welfare mom image arose as Black women became more dependent on the state welfare system. Unlike the hardworking mammy, the welfare mom image depicts a lazy ignorant mother who refuses to work (Dill 1979). Unable to control her sexual urges, she has a number of children she cannot support, which serves to increase her welfare benefits. Although she has no job other than rearing her children, she miserably fails at that task. Her sons become criminals and her daughters repeat the welfare cycle.

In some ways, this stereotype reflects the use of Black women as "breeders" during slavery. In this way, a role that helped to build empires in the South is now blamed for undermining the American work ethic and unraveling the social fabric. This myth blames Black women for "their own poverty and that of the African-American communities [and] shifts the angle of vision from structural sources of poverty" (Collins 1990, 77) to individuals and Black women more generally.

The Jezebel

One of the most persistent images of Black women is the Jezebel, sexpot, or whore. Throughout history, the Jezebel has had her special talents extolled and condemned; they have sparked desires and inspired envy. She has intrigued observers as the "exotic," and threatened them as the "sex animal." Men have salivated over her by associating her with edibles: "hot chocolate," "brown sugar," "dark meat," "honey," "mocha," and "caramel" (Allen 1990). Her purported insatiable sexual appetites functioned to justify sexual assaults by White men (Collins 1990; White 1985; Davis 1981; hooks 1981). The "super" sexuality associated with the Jezebel was in direct opposition to expected chastity norms associated with "True womanhood." The Jezebel image justifies the sexual exploitation of Black women, devalues them, and makes them "unworthy" (Jordan 1968).

Regardless of the image she was given, Black women have had their womanhood and sexuality assaulted and devalued. Although the attitudes embodied within these images are centuries old, they are continuously repackaged in more popular forms and terminology. Despite increased interest in examining the plight of Black women today, she is still treated as "other."

The ideologically controlling images of Black women reviewed above have surreptitiously found their way into modern social and biological theories (Wallace 1990; hooks 1984). And criminology is no exception.

Distorted Images of Women in Crimonology

Criminology, like other disciplines, relies upon historical distortions of Black women's images as the foundation for its theories that concerned Black women (when Black women were mentioned at all!). Historically, criminology has been dominated by White males who are unfamiliar with Black culture and Black women in particular. Consequently, the assumptions criminologists made (and still make) about Black women were (are) informed by popular or stereotypical cultural images.

Rarely, however, are these assumptions and images overtly expressed within the text. Rather, the images embedded within the criminological text must be closely examined to expose stereotypes about Black women. This can be accomplished by analyzing the absence of Black women in the criminological text (e.g., see Lynch et al. 1992), the inferred relationship of Black women to the family, and the treatment of Black women as offenders and victims.

Background: Black Women as Criminological Subjects

The last 20 years has witnessed increased interest in women in criminology and criminal justice (Adler 1975; Ageton 1983; Baskin and Sommers 1989; Box and Hale 1984; Daly and Chesney-Lind 1988). Despite this increased interest, few studies explicitly include Black women. Rather criminologists seem to assume that theories created in reference to White women are generalizable to Black women. In short, Black women are almost nonexistent in criminological and criminal justice theory and research (Hill and Crawford 1990; Laub and McDermott 1985; Young 1980). And, until recently no one missed them or speculated about the implications of their absence.

Historically, images of Black women in criminological theory have incorporated the stereotypes outlined earlier. These images are subsumed within criminological theory in a number of ways:

1. Black women are implicitly blamed for the Black crime problem
2. Black women are morally corrupt so they engage in crime more often than White women
3. Black women's elevated sexual appetites make them prone to sexual exploitation including prostitution and sexual assault.

These images are examined further below.

Implicitly Blaming the Black Women: Black Women as Matriarch and Welfare Mom

In criminological theory, poverty, family structure, and childrearing practices have all been examined as causes of crime. For example, control subculture and lower class theories point to family variables as predictors of criminality in young men (see Cohen 1955; Wolfgang and Ferracuti 1967; Miller

1958; Matsueda and Heimer 1987; Sampson 1987; Johnson 1986; Wells and Rankin 1986; McLanahan 1985; Rankin 1983; Toby 1957). The key here is that the type of family a person is raised in is believed to affect the criminality of children. With these background assumptions in mind, it is easy to expose the negative effects criminologists have attributed to Black women and Black families. Borrowing from the matriarch and welfare mom stereotypes, many criminological theories implicitly argue that Black women "cause" crime to the extent that their roles in the family effect men's criminality, children's criminality and Black-on-Black crime. The explanation runs as follows.

As either a welfare mom or a matriarch, the Black woman is responsible for the "tangle of poverty" within the Black community. As a welfare mom, her refusal to work is indicative of a failed work ethic that is passed on to her offsprings. The family is caught in a cycle of poverty that keeps them out of the loop of the American dream. Her children lack academic motivation and are exposed to dangerous living conditions.

As a matriarch, the Black woman has emasculated the men around her. The son she is attempting to rear alone does not have a role model after whom to pattern his behavior. The son fails to understand the dynamics of being a man, which includes taking responsibility for his family. The matriarch's daughter has no guidelines on appropriate male-female relationships, especially sexual relationships, and learns emasculation techniques that become intergenerational.

In either incarnation, the Black woman fails to provide her children with adequate supervision, proper socialization, good role models, work ethics, and value systems. Her inability to properly rear her children, especially her male children, makes them vulnerable to illicit behaviors. In short, the Black woman and the context of her family are believed to be directly responsible for most social ills associated with criminal activity.

In general, family structure theories operate on the assumption that the family, as the primary agent of social control and transmitter of values, is the first defense for the prevention of criminal behavior in people. Only "proper" (i.e., mother/father, male-headed) families can fulfill this function. Female-headed households fail to provide an appropriate family environment, which circumvents attempts at proper socialization, and diminishes the ability of the family to provide the first line of defense against crime and deviance. In fact, in this view, female-headed households could lay the foundation for the growth and development of positive attitudes towards crime and delinquency.

Many of the theories that use family structure (i.e., female-headed households) and poverty as predictors of criminal behavior, especially for young Black men, are in fact blaming Black mothers for crime. For example, using this view, it can and has been argued that Black men are disproportionately involved in crime because Black females failed in her most fundamental womanly duties: motherhood.

The limitations of this view should be quite clear. First, it is basically ridiculous to attempt to trace the ills of the Black community to Black women. Whether she is a matriarch or a welfare mom. Black women are not responsible for creating the conditions conducive to crime or poverty. Those conditions exist independently of the actions of Black women. In effect, the prevalence of matriarchy or welfare mom's in Black communities and the association between these variables and crime (if it really exists at all), is spurious.

Second, we need to make a related point: while family-oriented research attempts to pinpoint the ways in which families generate crime, such research rarely goes beyond family structure in its search for the cause(s) of crime. Where Black women are concerned, criminological researchers and others have attempted to describe the ways in which her skills as mother and household head are deficient. However, there is no attempt to go beyond appearances, to ask if poor economic conditions, lack of employment, poor educational facilities, community and neighborhood factors, etc., that are prevalent in Black communities across America are the real culprits. Even the efforts of the best mothers can be offset by the extremely deficient social and economic circumstances that exist in some American communities.

Our third and final objection deals with the reality of welfare moms and matriarchy in Black communities. In reality, most Black welfare moms raise conforming children. Similarly, Black matriarchy also seems to generate far fewer deviants than it does law abiding citizens. Again, the problem is not Black matriarchy or the Black welfare mom per se, but the conditions in which Black women live their lives and raise their families.

Moral Corruption and Stereotypes of Black Women

Another prime example of distortion in criminological assessments of Black women and their role in crime relates to the theme of moral corruption. The Black woman is not only stereotyped, but vilified as a morally corrupt person. In the welfare mother and matriarch approach, we saw that Black women were blamed for contributing to the moral corruption of their children and the community. In other words, in the welfare mother approach, the mother is not necessarily deviant—she simply establishes the type of family structure that generates deviance among her children.

The moral corruption view is quite different. In this view, the Black mother is the morally corrupt person. In popular culture and in theory, it is easy to justify such a view since the Black woman is popularly characterized as overbearing, loud, aggressive, argumentative, and bitchy (Weitz and Gordon 1993)—she has already stepped beyond the realm of proper moral behavior for women. Recall from our discussion that a "True Woman" is passive and obedient, not aggressive and rebellious. What, then, are the supposed results of Black women's immoral character?

In theory, lacking morality and piety, the bonds that hold Black women to legitimate behavior are not as strong as those White women establish. Thus it is easier for Black women to engage in criminal behavior with little or no remorse. And, it seems that criminal statistics justify such an explanation.

Black women have been disproportionately represented in violent crime statistics (von Hentig 1942; Ageton 1983; Mann, C. 1989; McClain 1982) Although some have called for further research to determine the cause of these statistical difference (McClain 1982; Young 1980; Hill and Crawford 1985; Laub and McDermott 1985), few have questioned the underlying attitudes and assumptions that justify the use of stereotypical "moral character" explanation for Black female criminality.

Biased cultural attitudes concerning the morality of Black women have been reflected in some of the most influential writings on female criminality. For instance, Otto Pollak noted that "the social position of the negro woman seems to be much freer than that of the White woman" (1950, 118). Twenty-five years later, Freda Adler went even further to explain Black women's disproportionate participation in crime by stating that "bankrupt by fortune and with no reputation to lose, the Black woman became well versed in deviant methods" (1975, 138).

In both instances, theorists assumed that the bonds that restrained and individual from criminal behavior was weaker in Black women than in White women; that the Black women was "free" to engage in criminal activity while White women were not. The Black women's refusal to acquiesce demonstrates that she is less submissive to the letter of the law, less ladylike than the White woman, and lacking the moral fortitude to avoid crime.

In a longer litany of the position of Black women, Adler sums up the historical position of Black women in criminology:

> But in the center of this cultural chaos, assailed by the demands of economically castrated consorts, burdened by unwanted, unruly, and unmanageable children, impoverished and uneducated, stood the Black female, the chief bulwark against the social and financial catastrophes constantly threatening to engulf her family. In a role which history and economics had thrust upon her, and with a strength born of necessity—a strength, incidentally, which her White sisters would later emulate—she sallied uncertainly into the White man's

> world. When survival is at stake, the legitimacy of its attainment is not ordinarily a primary consideration. Necessity knows no law and Black women were neither in the mood nor the position to have their struggles hobbled by legalities (1975: 138).

Thus in the literature explaining higher rates of criminal activity among Black women, there was the tendency to disparage the womanhood of Black women, asserting that Black women were more like men (i.e., Lombroso and Ferrero 1930; Mulvihill et al. 1969; Sutherland and Cressey 1966). Laub and McDermott (1985, 84) comment on this:

> The assumptions regarding the criminal propensities of the Black woman seem to be that her femaleness lessens the effects of the criminogenic factors associated with her race (she is less criminal than the Black male), and that her Blackness operates to counteract the other wise low rate of offending associated with her sex (she is more criminal, especially more violently criminal, than the White female).

Adler's convergence theory updated this view to suggest that as women became more like men socially and economically (i.e., as female roles undergo masculinization), the crime rates of men and women will converge. More importantly, by introducing social and economic considerations, Adler's view began to lessen criminologists' reliance on popular culture stereotypes concerning women. This was a particularly salient consideration for Black women, who were typically viewed (in popular culture and in criminological theory) as masculine in a biological sense.

As noted above, attitudes toward Black female criminals are often biased by stereotypical images. Assumptions based on the beliefs in a mythical "True Womanhood" are quite evident. Thus the lingering stereotypes of inherent immorality sustains the explanations for Black women's participation in crime: they were immoral and could not attain "True Womanhood."

Hypersexuality: The Myth Built to Devalue and Stigmatize

Beliefs about the moral corruption of Black women also lead directly into myths concerning their hypersexuality. This myth covers both the offender and the victim. To understand the origin of this myth, it must be located within an existing economic and social environment of sexual exploitation.

Perhaps America's and criminology's most obvious and enduring image of the Black woman is the sexually exotic Jezebel/whore/slut/prostitute. This image personifies Lombroso's precocious "fallen" woman, who sells her body for personal gratification. Culturally, the exploitation of Black women's sexuality was necessary to justify the ideology of "True Womanhood." A Collins (1990, 176) notes, "Black 'whores' make White 'virgins' possible." This Madonna/Whore dichotomy, which became a Black/White dichotomy as well, was one that Westerners have cherished. Since purity in the female was valued, soiling devalued her. Therefore, if a woman was sexually promiscuous or passionate, she was impure: as such she did not deserve the same treatment as real women. She could be used with little regard to her humanity. Thus, the conceptualization of Black women's animal sexuality assuaged the guilt feelings of the exploiter—such as slaveowners. The slaveowner could absolve himself of guilt by believing that Black women were active participants in their own exploitation (hooks 1981)—that their "animal-like" sexual desires were out of control.

Jordan (1968, 150) explains the necessity and function of these myths "sexually-oriented beliefs about the Negro in America derived principally from the psychological needs of men and were to a considerable extent shaped by specifically masculine modes of thought and behavior." hooks (1981, 59) notes that the continued "devaluation of Black womanhood after slavery ended was a conscious, deliberate effort on the part of Whites to sabotage mounting Black female self-confidence and self-respect."

Thus, the use of these myths functioned as both neutralizers of guilt and mechanisms of social control of Black women.

And, indeed, the long history of sexual assault upon Black women is well established in the research literature. From the raping of Black women by slaveholders, to the tiptoeing of White male patrons to Black townships for prostitutes, to having affairs with the help, White men have sought the "wild animal lust" of passion believed to exist in the nether world of Black women (Hernton 1988; Collins 1990; hooks 1992).

What is startling is the prevalence of this subject within Black feminist literature assessing the devaluation of Black womanhood (see hooks 1981 1992; Giddings 1984; Christian 1985; Guy-Sheftall 1990; Collins 1990; Morton 1990; Gilkes 1983). This indicates that the wanton exploitation of Black women is still a point of contention today. It underscores the feeling of continued victimization and tradition experienced by Black women in modern American society.

The history of popular cultural and theoretical images of Black women's moral character and sexuality can be traced through the writings of Whites. Guy-Sheftall (1990, 48) explains how this image was used in historical and popular literature:

> White writers thought that this animal sexuality that Black women possessed did not result in criminal behavior on their parts, but could be used to justify their sexual exploitation at the hands of White men.

Jordan (1968, 151) extends this justification by stating:

> For by calling the Negro woman passionate they were offering the best possible justification for their own passions. Not only did the Negro woman's warmth constitute a logical explanation for the White man's infidelity, but, much more important, it helped shift responsibility from himself to her.

The pitting of White women's femininity and chastity against those of Black women can be found as far back in the criminological literature as Lombroso. For example, in considering virility as a "special feature of the savage women," Lombroso and Ferrero refer the reader to "portraits of Red Indian and Negro beauties, whom it is difficult to recognize for women, so huge are their jaws and cheek-bones, so hard and coarse their features" (1895, 112). The dominant culture's standards of beauty, femininity, and womanhood, as well as the economic system, continue to impugn the Black woman.

In terms of political economy, popular hypersexuality images of Black women serve to devalue their labor, and undermines Black women's self-esteem. Destruction of Black women's self-esteem and the value of their labor on the open market made occupations such as prostitution a viable alternative. This view may help explain the historical participation of female ethnic-minorities in prostitution (Mann 1993; Budros 1983). Today, prostitution has reached a new dimension, with the trading of sex for crack, a practice that has hit Black women addicts especially hard (Maher and Curtis 1992; Ratner 1993). It is a new level of powerlessness for women.

Popular images of prostitutes have also been racialized. Take for instance, the immediate idea of the streetwalker and the call girl. The stereotype of the streetwalker is a Black woman, blonde wig, leather skirt, in spiked heels wearing a boa. In contrast, the call girl, working for an escort service run by a "Madame," is a college co-ed working her way through school.

The other part of this sexual myth is victimization. Sexual violence is another method that was used to control Black women. From the legitimization of sexual assault against Black women within a slave economy to the contemporary failure to successfully prosecute rapists, sexual violence threatens all women. As this threat is conveyed to women, it in turn effects the reporting of sexual assault to the police (Brownmiller 1975; Giacopassi and Dull 1986), for women have internalized the belief that the officers will blame them for their victimization and nothing will be done. Criminology only confirms these disillusions with research that indicates the existence of a set of cultural rape myths that effect the attitudes of victims, rapists, criminal justice personnel and the general public (Feild 1978; Jones and Aronson 1973; Burt 1980; Berger 1977; Brownmiller 1975; Giacopassi and Dull 1986; Hall et al. 1986; LaFree 1989).

The most sinister of these myths blames the victim for her victimization: "only bad girls get raped"; "they asked for it." These myths effect how the victim is viewed. An issue that directly responds to this is the admission of victim's prior sexual history in rape trials (Spohn and Horney 1991; Estrich 1987; Berger 1977). Permitting such evidence fosters the "assumption that chastity was a character trait" (Spohn and Horney 1991,137); an assumption that is crucial to the "True Womanhood" doctrine and the Madonna/whore ideology.

These attitudes are not freestanding; they are culturally ingrained. Burt (1980,229) writes that "rape attitudes are strongly connected to other deeply held and pervasive attitudes such as sex role stereotyping, distrust of the opposite sex and acceptance of interpersonal violence." These attitudes create an environment that is conducive to sexual assaults. Some have speculated that adoption of these myths may "encourage" offenders to rape (Giacopassi and Dull 1986); whereas the rapist believes there is little chance that there will be sanctions taken against him.

These myths are particularly harmful to Black women. Because Black women are viewed as impure, loose, sexually active, etc., they are more likely to be seen as "asking for it" as far as rape mythology is concerned. Thus, as empirical evidence demonstrates, Black women who are raped are less likely to be protected by law than a White female (Lafree 1980, 1982, 1989). In one sense, the history of cultural oppression directed at Black women seems to claim that they cannot be raped: popular culture (and some criminological theories) depicts them as the common sexual property of all men.[1]

The most prevalent form of rape is the Black-on-Black (Black offender, Black victim) rape. Yet, news stories, public myths, criminal justice punishment, and even academic research has traditionally focused more closely on the Black (male) on White (female) rape. This emphasis is driven by a "fear" of the Black male (rapist). In recent decades, greater attention has been paid to the unequal treatment Black males who rape White women receive in the criminal justice system (Curtis 1974, 1975; LaFree 1980, 1982; Wolfgang and Riedel 1975; Schulman 1974). Though the trend has shifted in one sense (i.e., the focus has become whether Black males receive justice or equal treatment under law), the Black female victim has continued to be omitted from study. The question is why?

Black women are victimized, ignored by the criminal justice system and by academics as a result of sexism, racism, and patriarchy. The act of rape is first and foremost an act of power, domination and control in which men exert power over women; in which the system of sexual stratification is reinforced (e.g., Brownmiller 1975; LaFree 1989). However, when Black women are raped, the message involves racial dimensions of domination and control as well. As Burt (1980, 229) explains, "rape is the logical and psychological extension of a dominant–submissive, competitive, sex role stereotyped culture" (Burt 1980, 229). In turn, through the act of ignoring the Black female victim, academic criminologists also contribute to reinforcing sexual and racial hierarchies and myths about Black women, their behavior and roles in society.

As demonstrated above, degrading images can be found within criminology. Although the connections are not explicit, manifestations of their use can be traced. Their use has failed to create a foundation for credible explanations for disparities in the rates of Black female criminality. Fortunately, more recent writings on the Black female criminal have noted the scarcity of literature and suggested that more tenable explanations for the disproportionate representation in crime statistics should be sought (Mann, C. 1989; Young 1980; McClain 1982; Laub and McDermott 1985, Hill and Crawford 1990; Simpson 1991). Sally Simpson has explored more radical theories such as Neo-marxist approaches (Colvin and Pauly 1983), power–control theory (Hagan et al. 1985), and socialist feminist approaches (Messerschmidt 1986) for some insight into to the relationship.

Conclusion

Until recently any consideration of the Black woman within criminology has been driven by centuries old stereotypes of the identities of Black women. Because these images were part of America's cultural pattern, they were not challenged. When these images were challenged by Blacks, the challenges were ignored by the general racialization of academia.

This essay has attempted to present a historical context for the paucity of literature and theory on Black women in criminology. In doing so, we have brought numerous stereotypes about Black women to the forefront so that they might be challenged and disavowed. We must first exorcise our demons before we can administer the sacrament of our chosen profession. This purging is necessary if we are to get on with the business of theory construction. For as long as any of these stereotypes remain unchallenged, even if (publicly) dismissed by most scholars, they hinder progress.

The treatment of Black women in criminology is indicative of the interplay of patriarchy and racism that has dominated Western thought in the United States. Theoretical distortions are not accidental, but are a function of and necessity of domination. We need to be cognizant of the fact that criminologists, like others, influenced by systems of domination, reproduce these relations and myths in theoretical explanations involving Black female offenders and victims.

Our approach here emphasizes that nontraditional, qualitative methods are needed to expose biased treatment of Black women in criminological theory. We must not restrict ourselves, for instance, to taking an "empirical look" at a subculture of violence, etc. It may be necessary to examine the history of violence remembered and passed on within the oral tradition of African-Americans. It is this history that formulates responses to threats to Black women's womanhood, self-esteem, mental and physical health. This history determines their relationships within a socio-political economy; a relationship and experience that differs from those of White women (Palmer 1983; King 1974; duCille 1994).

The answer lies not in the structural or individual level of analysis, but rather in a holistic, interactive context. It is necessary: that we know the history and conditions of existence of Black women in American society; comprehend Black women's perceptions of their situation and the coping mechanisms available for use in particular situations; and, it is as important to know their socio-economic status and how that status impacts their choices and roles in society, as it is to know the individuals' perception of their position and opportunity structure. In addition, we must also examine the treatment of the Black woman by others who subscribe to or believe in certain images, and we must examine and understand the Black women's attitudinal and behavioral reactions to that treatment. Buried here may be a cycle of internalization, defense mechanism, and preemptive strikes.

For example, take the common description of Black women as being "loud, talkative, and aggressive." Consider the necessity of being aggressive in an environment where you have been historically invisibility to those in power; in an environment where crime is more prevalent; where you need to protect your children and keep them from socially created harms. If you do not "scream and holler" no one would listen; if you do not act aggressively, your children may fall victim to the streets, etc.

Black women must challenge traditional criminology on the most fundamental levels of theory construction in order to transcend many of its gender and racially-biased paradigms. We must realize that the distorted images of Black women are not only reflected in the writings of criminologists, but that stereotypes can affect the treatment of their Black female students. As more Black women enter the academic field of criminology, they can provide the foundation and mentoring necessary for theory construction. However, the fear of being labeled a "feminist criminologist" or a "Black criminologist" may direct many, especially Black women, away from the issues of women and Blacks. Given these circumstances, it is understandable why many Black female theorists assert that Black women are in "multiple jeopardy" (i.e., Gilkes 1989; King 1988; Mann, C. 1989).

Note

1. Given the myths and stereotypes reviewed above, if we asked a fictitious criminologist to construct a theory about Black women that employed these distorted images, it would quite possibly resemble the following description:

   Fictitious Criminologist: Collectively, the oversexed, emasculating Black women, failing in their womanly duties, have led the Black community into ruins. Their iron-fisted matriarchal rule has led them into a tangle of poverty. In addition, their inability to rear their children properly has created a subculture of violence, in which they have very little respect for the law. Morally corrupt, the women are free to engage in prostitution and other criminal behavior. Because of their hypersexuality, they do not demand or deserve the respect due "proper ladies." And everybody knows "good girls" simply do not get raped. Ladies and gentleman, that is the reason you have a disproportionate number of Blacks as offenders and victims; the women simply did not do their job. And you know how sensitive these people are these days, so we did not explicitly include them in our theories.

   Not surprisingly, this "fictitious" explanation resembles many of the discussions of Black women found in the criminological literature, in popular culture, and by criminal justice workers and officials.

References

Adler, F. (1975). *Sisters in crime.* New York: McGraw-Hill.

Ageton, S. (1983). The dynamics of female delinquency, 1976–1980. *Criminology, 21,* 555–583.

Allen, I. (1990). *Unkind words: Ethnic labeling from Redskin to Wasp.* New York: Bergin and Garvey.

Bailey, F. Y. (1996). The 'tangle of pathology' and the lower classAfrican-American family: Historical and social science perspectives. In M. J. Lynch & E. Britt Patterson (Eds.), Justice with prejudice: Race and criminal justice in America (pp. 49–71). Albany, NY: Harrow and Heston Publishers.

Baskin, D., & Sommers, I. (1989). The gender question in research on female criminality. *Social Justice, 17,* 148–156.

Berger, V. (1977). Man's trial, woman's tribulation: Rapes case sin the courtroom. *Columbia Law Review, 77,* 1–103.

Blau, P., & Blau, J. (1982). The cost of inequality: Metropolitan structure and violent crime. *American Sociological Review, 47,* 114–129.

Bogle, D. (1973). *Toms, coons, mulattoes, mammies, and bucks: An interpretive history of Blacks in American films.* New York: Viking Press.

Box, S., & Hale, C. (1984). Economic crisis and the rising prisoner population in England and Wales. *Crime and Social Justice, 17,* 20–35.

Brownmiller, S. (1975). *Against our will: Men, women and rape.* New York: Simon and Schuster.

Budros, A. (1983). The ethnic vice industry revisited. *Ethnic and Racial Studies, 6,* 438–456.

Burt, M. R. (1980). Cultural myths and supports for rape. *Journal of Personality and Social Psychology, 38,* 217–230.

Christian, B. (1985). *Black feminist criticism.* New York: Pergamon Press.

Cohen, A. (1955). *Delinquent boys.* New York: Free Press.

Collins, P. H. (1990). *Black Feminist thought.* Boston: Unwin Hyman.

Colvin, M., & Pauly, J. (1983). A critique of criminology: Toward an integrated structural Marxist theory of delinquency production. *American Journal of Sociology, 89,* 513–551.

Curtis, L. (1974). *Criminal violence.* Lexington, MA: Heath.

Curtis, L. (1975). *Violence, rape and culture.* Lexington, MA: Heath.

Daly, K., & Chesney-Lind, M. (1988). Feminism and criminology. *Justice Quarterly, 5,* 497–538.

Davis, A. Y. (1981). *Women, race & class.* New York: Vintage.

Dill, B. T. (1979). The dialectics of Black womanhood. *Signs, 4,* 543–555.

Dorworth, V. E., & Henry, M. (1992). Optical illusions: The visual representations of Blacks and women in introductory criminal justice textbooks. *Journal of Criminal Justice Education, 3,* 251–260.

DuCille, A. (1994). The occult of true Black womanhood: Critical demeanor and Black feminist studies. *Signs, 19,* 591–629.

Estrich, S. (1987). *Real rape.* Cambridge, MA: Harvard University Press.

Feild, H. S. (1978). Attitudes toward rape: A comparative analysis of police, rapists, crisis counselors, and citizens. *Journal of Personality and Social Psychology, 36,* 156–179.

Foucault, M. (1970). *Madness and civilization: A history of insanity in the age of reason.* New York: Pantheon Books.

French, L. (1978). The incarcerated Black female. *Journal of Black Studies, 8,* 321–335.

Giacopassi, D. J., & Dull, R. T. (1986). Gender and racial differences in the acceptance of rape myths within a college population. *Sex Roles, 15,* 63–75.

Giddings, P. (1984). *When and where I enter: The impact of Black women on race and sex in America.* New York: Bantam Books.

Gilkes, C. T. (1983). From slavery to social welfare: Racism and the control of Black women. In A. Swerdlow & H. Lessinger (Eds.), *Class, race, and sex: The dynamics of control.* Boston: G. K. Hall.

Gilkes, C. T. (1989). Dual heroisms and double burdens: Interpreting Afro-American women's experience and history. *Feminist Studies, 15,* 573–590.

Guy-Sheftall, B. (1990). *Daughters of sorrow: Attitudes toward Black women, 1880–1920.* New York: Carlson Publishing.

Hagan, J., Gillis, A. R., & Simpson, J. (1985). The class structure of gender and delinquency: Toward a power-control theory of common delinquent behavior. *American Journal of Sociology, 90,* 1151–1178.

Hall, E. R., Howard, J. A., & Boezio, S. (1986). Tolerance of rape: A sexist or antisocial attitude? *Psychology of Women Quarterly, 10,* 101–118.

Harris, T. (1982). *From mammies to militants: Domestics in Black American literature.* Philadelphia: Temple University Press.

Herton, C. (1988). *Sex and racism in America.* New York: Grove Weidenfield.

Hill, G., & Crawford, E. (1990). Women, race, and crime. *Criminology, 28,* 601–626.

hooks, b. (1981). *Ain't I a woman: Black women and feminism.* Boston: South End Press.

hooks, b. (1984). *Feminist theory: From margin to center.* Boston: South End Press.

hooks, b. (1989). *Talking back: Thinking feminist, thinking Black.* Boston: South End Press.

hooks, b. (1992). *Black looks: Race and representation.* Boston: South End Press.

Hull, G., Scott, P. B., & Smith, B. (Eds.). (1982). *All the women are white, all the Blacks are men, but some of us are brave.* New York: The Feminist Press.

Jewell, K. S. (1976). *An analysis of the visual development of stereotype: The media's portrayal of mammy and Aunt Jemima as symbols of Black womanhood.* PhD. Dissertation, Ohio State University.

Johnson, R. (1986). Family structure and delinquency: General patterns and gender differences. *Criminology, 24,* 65–80.

Jones, C., & Aronson, E. (1973). Attribution of fault to a rape victim as a function of respectability of the victim. *Journal of Personality and Social Psychology, 26,* 415–419.

Jordon, W. (1968). *White over Black: American attitudes toward the Negro, 1550–1812.* Chapel Hill: University of North Carolina Press.

Joseph, G., & Lewis, J. (1981). *Common differences: Conflicts in Black and white feminist perspectives.* New York: Anchor.

King, M. (1974). Oppression and power: The unique status of the Black woman in the American political system. *Social Science Quarterly, 55,* 116–127.

King, D. (1988). Multiple jeopardy, multiple consciousness: The context of a Black feminist ideology. *Signs, 14,* 42–72.

LaFree, G. D. (1980). The effect of sexual stratification by race on official reactions to rape. *American Sociological Review, 45,* 842–854.

LaFree, G. D. (1982). Male power and female victimization: Toward a theory of interracial rape. *American Journal of Sociology, 88,* 311–328.

LaFree, G. D. (1989). *Rape and criminal justice.* Belmont, CA: Wadsworth Publishing.

Laub, J., & McDermott, M. J. (1985). An analysis of serious crime by young Black women. *Criminology, 23,* 81–98.

Lerner, G. (1992). *Black women in White America.* New York: Vintage Books.

Lombroso, C., & Ferrero, W. (1930). *The female offender.* New York: Appleton.

Lynch, J. P., & Sabol, W. J. (1992). *Macro-social changes and their implications for prison reform: The underclass and composition of prison populations.* Presented at the meetings of the American Society of Criminology (November).

Maher, L., & Curtis, R. (1992). Women over the edge of crime: Crack cocaine and the changing contexts of street-level sex work in New York City. *Crime, Law, and Social Change, 18,* 221–258.

Mann C. R. (1989). Minority and female: A criminal justice double bind. *Social Justice, 16,* 95–114.

Mann, C. R. (1993). *Unequal justice: A question of color.* Bloomington, IN: Indiana University Press.

Mann S. A. (1989). Slavery, sharecropping, and sexual inequality. *Signs, 14,* 774–798.

Martin, J. K., & Hall, G. K. (1992). Thinking Black, thinking internal, thinking feminist. *Journal of Counseling Psychology, 39,* 509–514.

Matsueda, R. L., & Heimer, K. (1987). Race, family structure, and delinquency: A test of differential association and social control theories. *American Sociological Review, 52,* 826–840.

McClain, P. (1982). Black females and lethal violence: Has time changed the circumstances under which they kill? *Omega, 13,* 25.

McLanahan, S. (1985). Family structure and the reproduction of poverty. *American Journal of Sociology, 90,* 873–901.

Messerschmidt, J. (1986). *Capitalism, patriarchy, and crime.* Totowa, NJ: Rowman and Littlefield.

Messerschmidt, J. (1988). From Marx to Bonger: Socialist writings on women, gender and crime. *Sociological Inquiry, 58,* 378–392.

Miller, W. (1958). Lower class culture as a generating milieu of gang delinquency. *Journal of Social Issues, 14,* 5–19.

Mills, C.W. (1959). *The sociological imagination.* New York: Oxford.

Morton, P. (1991). *Disfigured images: The historical assault on Afro-American women.* New York: Praeger.

Mulvihill, D. P., Tumin, T. M., & Curtis, L. (1969). *Crimes of violence, Volume 12.* A Staff Report submitted to the National Commission on the Causes and Prevention of Violence. Washington, DC: USGPO.

Neverdon-Morton, C. (1989). *Afro-American women of the South and the advancement of the race, 1895–1925.* Knoxville, TN: The University of Tennessee Press.

Palmer, P. M. (1983). White women, Black women: The dualism of female identity and experience in the United States. *Feminist Studies, 9,* 151–170.

Pollak, O. (1950). *The criminality of women.* Philadelphia: University of Pennsylvania Press.

Rankin, J. (1983). The family context of delinquency. *Social Problems, 30,* 466–479.

Ratner, M. S. (1993). Sex, drugs, and public policy: Studying and understanding the sex-for-crack phenomenon. In M. S. Ratner (Ed.), *Crack pipe as pimp: An ethnographic investigation of sex-for-crack exchanges.* New York: Lexington Books.

Sampson, R. J. (1987). Urban Black violence: The effect of male joblessness and family disruption. *American Journal of Sociology, 93*, 348–382.

Schulman, G. I. (1974). Race, sex, and violence: A laboratory test of the sexual threat of the Black male hypothesis. *American Journal of Sociology, 79*, 1260–1277.

Simpson, S. S. (1991). Caste, class, and violent crime: Explaining the difference in female offending. *Criminology, 29*, 115–135.

Sims-Wood, J. (1988). The Black female: Mammy, Jemima, Sapphire, and other images. In J.C. Smith (Ed.), *Images of Blacks in American culture: A reference guide to information sources.* New York: Greenwood Press.

Spohn, C., & Horney, J. (1991). The law's the law, but fair is fair: Rape shield laws and officials' assessments of sexual history evidence. *Criminology, 29*, 137–161.

Steffensmeier, D. J., & Clark, R. (1980). Sociocultural vs. biological/sexist explanations of sex differences in crime: A survey of American criminology textbooks, 1918-1965. *The American Sociologist, 15*, 245–255.

Sutherland, E., & Cressey, D. (1966). *Principles of criminology* (7th ed.). Philadelphia: Lippincott.

Thomas, W. I. (1924). *The unadjusted girl.* Boston: Little, Brown.

Toby, J. (1957). The differential impact of family disorganization. *American Sociological Review, 22*, 505–512.

Von Hentig, H. (1942). *The criminality of the colored woman.* University of Colorado Studies, Series C, 231–260.

Wallace, M. (1990). *Invisibility blues: From pop to theory.* New York: Verso.

Weitz, R., & Gordon, L. (1993). Images of Black women among Anglo college students. *Sex Roles, 28*, 19–34.

Wells, I. E., & Rankin, J. (1986). The broken homes model of delinquency: Analytic issues. *Journal of Research in Crime and Delinquency, 23*, 68–93.

Welter, B. (1966). The cult of true womanhood, 1920-1860. *American Quarterly, 18*, 151–174.

White, D. (1985). *Ar'n't I a woman?: Female slaves in the Ante-Bellum South.* New York: Norton.

Wolfgang, M. E., & Ferracuti, F. (1967). *The subculture of violence.* London: Tavistock.

Wolfgang, M. E., & Riedel, M. (1975). Rape, race, and the death penalty in Georgia. *American Journal of Orthopsychiatry, 45*, 658–667.

Wright, R. (1992). From vamps and tramps to tease and flirts: Stereotypes of women in criminology textbooks, 1956 to 1965 and 1981 to 1990. *Journal of Criminal Justice Education, 3*, 223–236.

Young, V. (1980). Women, race, and crime. *Criminology, 18*, 26–34.

11
Up It Up
Gender and the Accomplishment of Street Robbery

Jody Miller

Attempts to understand women's participation in violence have been plagued by a tendency either to overemphasize gender differences or to downplay the significance of gender. The goal of this research is to reconcile these approaches through an examination of the experiences of female and male street robbers in an urban setting. Based on in depth interviews with active offenders, the study compares women's and men's accounts of why they commit robbery, as well as how gender organizes the commission of the crime. The research suggests that while women and men articulate similar motives for robbery, their enactment of the crime is strikingly different—a reflection, in part, of practical choices women make in the context of a gender-stratified street setting.

With the exception of forcible rape, robbery is perhaps the most gender differentiated serious crime in the United States. According to the Federal Bureau of Investigation's Uniform Crime Report for 1995, women accounted for 9.3% of robbery arrestees, while they were 9.5%, 17.7%, and 11.1% of arrestees for murder/manslaughter, aggravated assault, and burglary, respectively (Federal Bureau of Investigation, 1996). And while recently there has been considerable attention among feminist scholars to the question of why males are more violent than females, there have been few attempts to examine women's participation in these "male" crimes. Though their numbers are small, women who engage in violent street crime have something significant to teach us about women's place in the landscape of the urban street world.

Simpson (1989, 618; see also Kelly, 1991; White and Kowalski, 1994) recently noted that feminist scholars' "reticence [to address issues concerning women's criminality] leaves the interpretive door open to less critical perspectives." Nowhere is this more the case than with the issue of women's participation in violent street crime. Sensational accounts of the "new violent female offender" (e.g., Sikes, 1997; see Chesney-Lind, 1993), which draw heavily on racial imagery of young women of color, must be countered with accurate, nuanced accounts of women's use of violence in the contexts of racial and economic inequalities. This research compares the experiences of male and female robbers active in an urban underclass environment with the goal of expanding understanding of women's use of violence in nondomestic street settings.

Masculinities and Crime: Robbery as Gender Accomplishment

In the late 1980s, feminist sociologists began theorizing about gender as situated accomplishment (West and Fenstermaker, 1995; West and Zimmerman, 1987). According to these authors, gender is "much more than a role or an individual characteristic: it is a mechanism whereby situated social action contributes to the reproduction of social structure" (West and Fenstermaker, 1995, 21). Women and men "do gender" in response to normative beliefs about femininity and masculinity. These actions are "the interactional scaffolding of social structure" (West and Zimmerman, 1987, 147) such that the performance of gender is both an indication and a reproduction of gendered social hierarchies.

This approach has been incorporated into feminist accounts of crime as a means of explaining differences in women's and men's offending (Messerschmidt, 1993, 1995; Newburn and Stanko, 1994; Simpson and Elis, 1995). Here, violence is described as "a 'resource' for accomplishing gender—for demonstrating masculinity within a given, context or situation" (Simpson and Elis, 1995, 50). Further, it is suggested that although some women may engage in violent behavior, because their actions transgress normative conceptions of femininity, they will "derive little support for expressions of masculine violence from even the most marginal of subcultures" (Braithwaite and Daly, 1994, 190).

Several authors suggest that robbery epitomizes the use of crime to construct masculine identity (Katz, 1988; Messerschmidt, 1993). Messerschmidt argues as follows:

> The robbery setting provides the ideal opportunity to construct an "essential" toughness and "maleness"; it provides a means with-which to construct that certain type of masculinity—hardman. Within the social context that ghetto and barrio boys find themselves, then robbery is a rational practice for "doing gender" and for getting money (Messerschmidt, 1993, 107).

Moreover, given the disproportionate use of robbery by African-American versus white men (Federal Bureau of Investigation, 1996), the masculinity that robbery constructs may be one that fits particularly well in urban underclass settings, which are unique from areas in which poor whites live (see Sampson and Wilson, 1995). Katz, in fact, suggests that "for some urban, black ghetto-located young men, the stickup is particularly attractive as a distinctive way of being black" as well as male (1988, 239).

Examining violence as masculine accomplishment can help account for women's lack of involvement in these crimes, just as this approach offers explanation for women's involvement in crime in ways scripted by femininity (e.g., prostitution). However, it leaves unexplained women's participation in violent street crime, except as an anomaly. Perhaps this is because femininity in this approach is conceived narrowly—specifically "within the parameters of the white middle class (i.e., domesticity, dependence, selflessness, and motherhood)" (Simpson and Elis, 1995, 51). Given urban African-American women's historical patterns of economic self-sufficiency and independence, this passive feminine ideal is unlikely to have considerable influence and is "much more relevant (and restrictive) for white females" (Simpson and Elis, 1995, 71).

Messerschmidt himself has recently recognized this oversight. Given that urban African-American females are involved in violent street crime at higher rates than other females, he suggests that "theory must not universalize female crime" (1995, 171) and must consider significant women's involvement in presumably "male" crime. Simpson (1991, 129; see also White and Kowalski, 1994) concludes: "The simplistic assertion that males are violent and females are not contains a grain of truth, but it misses the complexity and texture of women's lives."

Women's Violence as Resistance to Male Oppression

Feminist scholars who address the use of street violence by women often suggest that women's violence differs from that of men's—women use violence in response to their vulnerability to or actual victimization in the family and/or at the hands of men (Campbell, 1993: Joe and Chesney-Lind, 1995; Maher, 1997; Maher and Curtis, 1992; Maher and Daly, 1996). In her ethnography of a Brooklyn drug market, Maher notes that women adopt violent presentations of self as a strategy of protection. She explains, "'Acting bad' and 'being bad' are not the same. Although many of the women presented themselves as 'bad' or 'crazy,' this projection was a street persona and a necessary survival strategy" (1997, 95; see also Maher and Daly, 1996). These women were infrequently involved in violent crime and most often resorted to violence in response to threats or harms against them. She concludes that "unlike their male counterparts, for women, reputation was about, 'preventing victimization'" (Maher, 1997, 95–96; see also Campbell, 1993). In this account, even when women's aggression is offensive, it can still be understood as a defensive act, because it emerges as resistance to victimization.

Maher's research uncovered a particular form of robbery—"viccing"—in which women involved in the sex trade rob their clients. Although the phenomenon of prostitutes robbing tricks is not new, Maher's work documents the proliferation of viccing as a form of resistance against their greater vulnerability to victimization and against cheapened sex markets within the drug economy. Comparing viccing with traditional forms of robbery, Maher and Curtis conclude, "The fact that the act [of viccing] itself is little different to any other instrumental robbery belies the reality that the motivations undergirding it are more complex and, indeed, are intimately linked with women's collective sense of the devaluation of their bodies and their work" (1992, 246). However, it is likely that not all of women's street violence can be viewed as resistance to male oppression; instead, some women may be motivated to commit violent crimes for many of the same reasons some men are. In certain contexts, norms favorable to women's use of violence may exist, and they are not simply about avoiding victimization, but also result in status and recognition.

Race, Class and Gender: Women's Violence as Situated Action

It is necessary to consider that some of women's participation in violent street crime may stem from "the frustration, alienation, and anger that are associated with racial and class oppression" (Simpson, 1989, 618). The foregrounding of gender is important; however, there are structural and cultural underpinnings related to racial and economic inequalities that must simultaneously be addressed when one considers women's involvement in violent street crime (Simpson, 1991).

Research suggests that urban African-American females are more likely to engage in serious and violent crime than their counterparts in other racial groups and/or settings (Ageton, 1983; Hill and Crawford, 1990; Laub and McDermott, 1985; Mann, 1993). Ageton's analysis of the National Youth Survey found little difference across race or class in girls' incidence of crimes against persons, but she reports that "lower class females report . . . the greatest involvement in assaultive crime . . . [and] a consistently higher proportion of black females are involved in crimes against persons for all five years surveyed" (1983, 565). This is not to suggest that African-American women's participation in these offenses parallel or converge with that of urban African-American males (see Chesney-Lind and Shelden, 1992, 21–24; Laub and McDermott, 1985). Rather, my point is to highlight the contexts in which these women negotiate their daily lives. Violence is extensive in the lives and communities of African-American women living in the urban underclass. As a result, some women in these circumstances may be more likely than women who are situated differently to view violence as an appropriate or useful means of dealing with their environment. As Simpson (1991, 129) notes,

> Living daily with the fact of violence leads to an incorporation of it into one's experiential self. Men, women, and children have to come to terms with, make sense of, and respond to violence as it penetrates their lives. As violence is added to the realm of appropriate and sanctioned responses to oppressive material conditions, it gains a sort of cultural legitimacy. But not for all.

Evidence of the significance of the link between underclass conditions and African-American women's disproportionate involvement in violence may be found in recent research that examines factors predicting women's criminal involvement. Hill and Crawford (1990) report that structural indicators appear to be most significant in predicting the criminal involvement of African-American women, while social-psychological indicators are more predictive for white women. They conclude that "the unique position of black women in the structure of power relations in society has profound effects not shared by their white counterparts" (Hill and Crawford, 1990, 621). In fact, Baskin et al. (1993, 413) suggest that "women in inner city neighborhoods are being pulled toward violent street crime by the same forces that have been found to affect their male counterparts. As with males, neighborhood, peer and addiction factors have been found to contribute to female initiation into violence."

This is not to suggest, however, that gender does not matter. Gender remains a salient aspect of women's experiences in the urban street milieu, and must remain—along with race and class—at the forefront of attempts to understand their involvement in violent crime. Some research that stresses race and economic oppression as factors in women's criminality overlooks the significance of gender oppression in these contexts. For instance, Baskin et al. (1993, 415) argue that "women's roles and prominence have changed in transformed neighborhoods" such that there exist "new dynamics of crime where gender is a far less salient factor" (417).

However, there is overwhelming evidence that gender inequality remains a salient feature of the urban street scene (Anderson, 1994; Maher, 1997; Maher and Curtis, 1992; Maher and Daly, 1996; Oliver, 1994; Steffensmeier, 1983; Steffensmeier and Terry, 1986; Wilson, 1996). As Maher notes, for scholars who suggest that gender has lost its relevance, women's "activity is confused with [their] equality" (1997, 18). Research that examines women's participation in violent street crime without paying sufficient attention to the gendered nature of this participation or the ways in which "gendered status structures this participation" (Maher, 1997, 13) cannot adequately describe or explain these phenomena.

The strength of the current study is its comparative analysis of women's *and* men's accounts of the accomplishment of one type of violent crime—street robbery. In comparing both the question of *why* women and men report engaging in robbery, and *how* gender organizes the commission of robbery, this research provides insight into the ways in which gender shapes women's involvement in what is perhaps the typification of "masculine" street crime. As such, it speaks to broader debates about women's place in the contemporary urban street world.

Methodology

The study is based on semistructured in depth interviews with 37 active street robbers. The sample includes 14 women and a comparative sample of 23 men, matched approximately by age and age at first robbery.[1] The respondents range in age from 16 to 46; the majority are in their late teens to mid-twenties.[2] All of the men are African-American; 12 of the women are African-American and 2 are white.[3] See the appendix for a fuller description of each respondent.

Respondents were recruited on the streets through the use of snowball sampling (Watters and Biernacki, 1989) in impoverished urban neighborhoods in St. Louis, Missouri. An ex-offender was hired to serve as a street ethnographer; he culled from his former criminal associates in order to generate the initial respondents for the study (see also Decker and Van Winkle, 1996; Wright and Decker, 1994). These respondents were then asked to refer other friends or associates who might be willing to be interviewed, and the process continued until an appropriate sample was built.

Criteria for inclusion in the sample included the following: the individual had committed a robbery in the recent past, defined him or herself as currently active, and was regarded as active by other offenders.[4] Though it is not possible to determine the representativeness of this sample of active offenders (see Glassner and Carpenter, 1985), the approach nonetheless overcomes many of the shortcomings associated with interviewing ex-offenders or offenders who are incarcerated (see Agar, 1977). In fact, in the current study snowball sampling allowed for the purposive oversampling of both female and juvenile robbers.

Perhaps the greatest limitation of the sample is the overrepresentation of African-American robbers and the near absence of white offenders. According to the St. Louis Metropolitan Police Department's (1994) *Annual Report*, whites were 18% of robbery arrestees in that year. As Wright and Decker (1997, 11) explain,

> No doubt the racial composition of our sample is a reflection of the social chasm that exists between blacks and whites in the St. Louis underworld. Black and white offenders display a marked tendency to "stick to their own kind" and seldom are members of the same criminal networks. Successfully making contact with active black armed robbers proved to be of almost no help to us in locating white offenders.

This problem was exacerbated because the hired street ethnographer was African-American and was unable to provide any initial contacts with white robbers. In fact, both of the white females interviewed in the study were referred by their African-American boyfriends.

Each respondent was paid $50 for participation in the research and was promised strict confidentiality.[5] Respondents were paid an additional $10 for each successful referral (i.e., a cooperative participant who was currently an active robber). Interviews lasted one to two hours and included a range of questions about the respondents' involvement in robbery, with particular focus on "their thoughts and actions during the commission of their crimes" (Wright and Decker, 1997, 8). Respondents were asked to describe their typical approach when committing robbery, as well as to describe in detail their most recent offense; the goal was to gain a thorough understanding of the contexts of these events (see Wright and Decker, 1997, for a full discussion of the research process).

Because this research is concerned with the situational accomplishment of robbery, it does not provide a means to explore fully the contexts of offending as they relate to respondents' life circumstances. Nonetheless, it is worthwhile to situate their discussions with a brief description of the milieu from which they were drawn. As noted above, respondents were recruited from impoverished urban neighborhoods in St. Louis. St. Louis typifies the midwestern city devastated by structural changes brought about by deindustrialization. With tremendous economic and racial segregation, population loss, and resulting social isolation, loss of community resources, and concentrated urban poverty among African-Americans, the neighborhoods the respondents were drawn from are characteristic of "underclass" conditions (Sampson and Wilson, 1995; Wilson, 1996). These conditions no doubt shape respondents' offending through the interactive effects of structural barriers and resulting cultural adaptations (see Sampson and Wilson, 1995). Thus, they should remain in the foreground in examining the accomplishment of robbery.

Motivations to Commit Robbery

In this study, active robbers' articulation of the reasons they commit robbery is more a case of gender similarities than differences. What they get out of robbery, why they choose robbery instead of some other crime, why particular targets are appealing—the themes of these discussions are overlapping in women's and men's accounts. For both, the primary motivation is to get money or material goods. As Libbie Jones notes, "You can get good things from a robbery." For some, the need for money comes with a strong sense of urgency, such as when the individual is robbing to support a drug addiction—a situation more prevalent among older respondents than younger ones. But for the majority of women and men in this sample, robberies are committed to get status-conferring goods such as gold jewelry, spending money, and/or for excitement.[6] For instance, T-Bone says he decides to commit robberies when he's "tired of not having money." When the idea comes about, he is typically with friends from the neighborhood, and he explains, "we all bored, broke, mad." Likewise, CMW says she commits robberies "out of the blue, just something to do. Bored at the time and just want to find some action." She explains, "I be sitting on the porch and we'll get to talking and stuff. See people going around and they be flashing in they fancy cars, walking down the street with that jewelry on, thinking they all bad, and we just go get 'em." For both males and females, robberies are typically a means of achieving conspicuous consumption.

If anything, imperatives to gain money and material goods through robbery appear to be stronger for males than females, so that young men explain that they sometimes commit robberies because they feel some economic pressure, whereas young women typically do not. Masculine street identity is tied to the ability to have and spend money, and included in this is the appearance of economic self-sufficiency. Research has documented women's support networks in urban communities, including among criminally involved women (see Maher, 1997; Stack, 1974). This may help explain why the imperative for young men is stronger than for young women. Community norms may give women wider latitude for obtaining material goods and economic support from a variety of sources, including other females, family members, and boyfriends; whereas the pressure of society's view of men as breadwinners differentially affects men's emotional experience of relying on others economically. This may explain why several young men specifically describe that they do not like relying on their parents in order to meet their consumer needs. As Mike J. notes, "My mother, she gives me money sometimes but I can't get the stuff like I want, clothes and stuff . . . so I try to get it by robbery." Though both males and females articulate economic motives for robbery, young men, more than young women, describe feeling compelled to commit robberies because they feel "broke."

Asked to explain why they commit robberies instead of other crimes with similar economic rewards, both women and men say that they choose robberies, as Cooper explains, because "it's the easiest." Libbie Jones reports that robbery provides her with the things she wants in one quick and easy step:

> I like robbery. I like robbery cause, I don't have to buy nothing. You have a herringbone. I'm gonna take your herringbone and then I have me a herringbone. I don't have to worry about going to the store, getting me some money. If you got some little earrings on I'm gonna get 'em.

The ease with which respondents view the act of robbery is also reflected in their choice of victims—most frequently other street-involved individuals, who are perceived as unlikely to be able to go to the police, given their own criminal involvement. In addition. these targets are perceived as likely to have a lot of money, as well as jewelry and other desirable items. Less frequently, respondents report targeting individuals who are perceived as particularly easy marks, such as older citizens. However, most robberies, whether committed by females or males, occur in the larger contexts of street life, and their victims reflect this—most are also involved in street contexts, either as adolescents or young adults who hang out on the streets and go to clubs, or as individuals involved (as dealers and/or users) in the street-level drug economy. Because of this, it is not uncommon for robbers to know or at least know of their victims (for more on target selection, see Wright and Decker, 1997, Ch. 3).

In addition to the economic incentives that draw the respondents toward robbery, many also derive a psychological or emotional thrill from committing robberies. Little Bill says, "when my first robbery started, my second, the third one, it got more fun . . . if I keep on doing it I think that I will really get addicted to it." Likewise, Ne-Ne's comment illustrates the complex dynamics shaping many respondents' decisions to commit robberies, particularly the younger ones: "I don't know if it's the money, the power, or just the feeling that I know that I can just go up and just take somebody's stuff. It's just a whole bunch of mixture type thing." Others describe a similar mixture of economic and emotional rewards. Buby notes, "you get like a rush, it be fun at the time."

When individuals on the street are perceived as "high-catting" or showing off they are viewed by both male and female robbers as deserving targets. Ne-Ne describes the following dialogue between herself and a young woman she robbed: "[The girl] said 'if you take my money then I'm gonna get in trouble because this is my man's money. He told you to keep it, not showboat. You talking 'nigger I got $800 in my pocket,' pulling it out. Yeah, you wanted us to know." Likewise, describing a woman he robbed at a gas station, Treason Taylor says, "really I didn't like the way she came out. She was like pulling out all her money like she think she hot shit." A few respondents even specifically target people they don't like, or people who have insulted or hurt them in the past.

For both women and men, then, motivations to commit robbery are primarily economic—to get money, jewelry, and other status-conferring goods, but they also include elements of thrill seeking, attempting to overcome boredom, and revenge. Most striking is the continuity across women's and men's accounts of their motives for committing robbery, which vary only by the greater pressure reported by some young men to have their own money to obtain material goods. As discussed in the next sections there are clear differences in the accomplishment of robbery by gender; however, these differences are apparently not driven by differences in motivation.

Men's Enactments of Street Robbery

Men accomplish street robberies in a strikingly uniform manner. Respondents descriptions of their robberies are variations around one theme—using physical violence and/or a gun placed on or at close proximity to the victim in a confrontational manner. This is reflected in Looney's description, of being taught how to commit his first robbery, at the age of 13, by his stepbrother:

> We was up at [a fast food restaurant] one day and a dude was up there tripping. My stepbrother had gave me a 22 automatic. He told me to walk over behind him and put the gun to his head and tell him to give me all his stuff. That's what I did. I walked up to him and said man, this is a jack, man, take off all your jewelry and take you money out of your pockets, throw it on the ground and walk off. So that's what he did. I picked up the money and the jewelry and walked away.

By far the most common form of robbery described by male respondents entails targeting other men involved in street life—drug dealers, drug users, gang members, or other men who look "flashy" because of their clothes, cars, and/or jewelry. Twenty-two respondents (96%) report committing robberies in these contexts, which involve accosting people on the streets or accosting them in their cars. Only Little Bill, who is an addict, does not describe engaging in these types of robberies. Instead, he only targets non-street-involved citizens, whom he feels safer confronting.[7] Seven men (30%) describe robbing women as well as men.

All of the men in this sample report using guns when they rob, though not everyone uses a gun every time.[8] The key is to make sure that the victim knows, as Syco says, "that we ain't playing." This is accomplished either through the positioning of the gun or by physically assaulting the victim. If the victim appears to resist, the physical assault is more severe, a shot is fired in the air or to the side of the victim, or the victim is shot—typically in the foot or the leg. Again, what is striking across men's interviews is the continuity of their approach toward street robberies. Upon spotting a target, they swiftly run up on the victim and physically confront him or her telling the victim "up it up," "come up off it," or some similar phrase. These robberies frequently are committed with partners, but sometimes are committed alone.

For many male robbers, cooperation is achieved simply by the presence and positioning of the gun. Bob Jones confronts his victims by placing the gun at the back of their head, where "they feel it," and says, give it up, motherfucker, don't move or I'll blow your brains out." Explaining the positioning of the gun, he says, "when you feel that steel against your head ... that pistol carries a lot of weight." Describing one of his robberies, Looney says, "I creeped up behind him, this time I had a 12 gauge, I pointed it to the back of his head, told him to drop it." Big Prod notes that he will "have the gun to his head, can't do nothing but respect that." Likewise Treason Taylor explains that he will "grab [the victim] by the neck and stick the gun to they head. Sometimes I don't even touch them I just point the gun right in front of they face. That really scares people." Prauch says. "I don't even have to say nothing half the time. When they see that pistol, they know what time it is."

A number of respondents report using some measure of physical confrontation, even when using a weapon, in order to ensure the victim's cooperation and/or the robber's getaway. Cooper says, "you always got to either hit'em, slap'em or do something to let them know you for real." T-Bone says: "I just hit them with the gun and they give it up quick." Likewise, Mike J. says, "you might shake them a little bit. If there is more than one of you, can really do that kind of stuff like shake them up a little bit to show them you're not messing around." Sometimes physical confrontation is simply part of the thrill. Damon Jones says that while he typically doesn't physically assault his victims, a friend he often robs with "always do something stupid like he'll smash somebody with the pistol, you know what I'm saying. He'll hit them in the head or something just. I guess, just to do it."

When the victim hesitates or is seen as uncooperative, the respondents describe using a variety of physical measures to ensure, the completion of the robbery. The mildest version is described by Carlos Reed: "If I have a revolver, I'll cock it back that will be the warning right there. If I run up to you like this and then you hesitate I'm gonna cock it back." Others use physical violence to intimidate the victim. Redwood says. "if they think I'm bullshitting I'll smack them up in they motherfucking head." Likewise. Tony Wright notes, "you would be surprised how cooperative a person will be once he been smashed across the face with a 357 Magnum." Other respondents describe shooting the gun, either past the victim or in the leg or foot, in order to ensure cooperation. Prauch says, "one gun shot, they ass in line. If I hit them a couple of times and that don't work one gun shot by they ear and they in line." And Cooper notes, "If I see he just trying to get tough then sometimes I just straight out have to shoot somebody, just shoot 'em."

Though most robberies involve the use of a weapon, several men also report engaging in strong-arm robberies, sometimes when an opportunity presents itself and there is no time to retrieve a weapon. These robberies involve a great deal of physical violence. Taz says, "if it's a strong-arm, like I'll just get up on them and I'll just hit 'em and [my partner] will grab them or like he will hit them and I'll grab 'em and we keep on hitting them until they fall or something . . . we just go in his pockets, leave him there, we gone." Likewise, Swoop describes a strong-arm robbery he was involved in:

> Me and my two partners saw this dude and he had on a lot of jewelry. I wanted them chains and my partner wanted the rings. We didn't have a weapon. We strong-armed him. . . . He was coming from off the lot [at a fast food restaurant], he actually was going to his car so I ran up on him . . . and I hit him in the face. He tried to run. My partner ran and kicked him in the mouth. He just let us, I took the chains off of him, my partner took his rings, my partner took his money, we split the money and that was all it took.

Seven men describe robbing women as well as men. However, male respondents—both those who have robbed women and those who have not—clearly state that robbing women is different from robbing men. Robbing women is seen as less dangerous, and women are believed to be less likely to resist. The following dialogue with Looney is illustrative:

Interviewer: Do you rob men or women more?
Looney: I rob men.
Interviewer: Why?
Looney: They got money.
Interviewer: Do men behave differently than women?
Looney: Nope. Men gonna try to act like the tough guy, when they see the gun, then they give it up quick. But a lady, I just tell them to give it up and they give me they whole purse or whatever they got.

While physical violence is often used in men's robberies of other men, respondents do not describe assaulting women routinely, typically only if they are seen as resisting. It appears not to be deemed a necessary part of the transaction with female victims. Taz, whose robberies of men typically involve a great deal of physical violence (see above), says, "I did a girl before but I didn't hurt her or nothing we just robbed her. She was too scared." Having women present is also seen as making male targets more vulnerable. Swoop explains: "If he like by himself or if he with a girl then that's the best time, but if he with two dudes, you know they rolling strapped so you wait." Unlike when a street-involved target is with other males and needs to maintain an air of toughness, Swoop says "you know they ain't gonna try to show off for the little gals, they gonna give it all up."

It is notable that women are widely perceived, as C-Loco says, as "easy to get," and yet as a rule they are not targeted for street robberies. Partly this is because women are perceived as less likely to have a lot of money on them. Moreover, women are not viewed as real players in the action of the streets; they are peripheral, and thus not typically part of the masculine game of street robbery. Antwon Wright sums this up in the following dialogue about the use of physical violence:

Interviewer: Do you hit everybody?
Antwon Wright: It depends. It depends on who is there and how many. If it's a dude and a gal we might hit the dude and leave the girl.
Interviewer: Why?
Antwon Wright: Cause a girl is no threat for real to us. A girl is no threat. We just worry about dudes. Girls is no threat. But if it's about six dudes, man we gonna hit everybody. We gonna get everybody on the ground bam, bam. Then if they want to get back up we just keep on hitting.

Male robbers, then, clearly view the act of robbery as a masculine accomplishment in which men compete with other men for money and status. While some rob women, those robberies are deviations from the norm of "badass" against "badass" that dominates much of men's discussions of street robbery (see Katz, 1988). The routine use of guns physical contact, and violence in male-on-male robberies is a reflection of the masculine ideologies shaping men's robberies. Women's enactment of robbery is much more varied than that of men's and provides a telling contrast about the nature of gender on the streets.

Women's Enactments of Street Robbery

The women in the sample describe three predominant ways in which they commit robberies: targeting female victims in physically confrontational robberies, targeting male victims by appearing sexually available and participating with males during street robberies of men. Ten women (71%) describe targeting female victims, usually on the streets but occasionally at dance clubs or in cars. Seven (50%) describe setting up men through promises of sexual favors, including two women who do so in the context of prostitution. Seven (50%) describe working with male friends, relatives, or boyfriends in street robberies; three (21%) report this as their exclusive form of robbery.

Robbing Females

The most common form of robbery reported by women in the study is robbing other females in a physically confrontational manner. Ten of the 14 female respondents report committing these types of offenses. Of those who do not, three only commit robberies by assisting men, whose targets are other males (see below), and one only robs men in the context of prostitution. Typically, women's robberies of other females occur on the streets, though a few young women also report robbing females in the bathrooms or parking lots of clubs, and one robs women in cars. These robberies are sometimes committed alone, but usually in conjunction with one or several additional women, but not in conjunction with men. In fact, Ne-Ne says even when she's out with male friends and sees a female target, they don't get involved: "They'll say 'well you go on and do her.'"

Most robberies of females either involve no weapon or they involve a knife. Four women report having used a gun to rob women, only one of whom does so on a regular basis.[9] Women are the victims of choice because they are perceived as less likely to be armed themselves and less likely to resist or fight back. CMW explains, "See women, they won't really do nothing. They say, 'oh, oh, ok, here take this.' A dude he might try to put up a fight." Yolanda Smith reports that she only robs women because "they more easier for me to handle." Likewise, Libbie Jones says, "I wouldn't do no men by myself," but she says women victims "ain't gonna do nothing because they be so scared." The use of weapons in these assaults is often not deemed necessary. Quick explains that she sometimes uses a knife, "but sometimes I don't need anything. Most of the time it be girls, you know, just snatching they chains or jewelry. You don't need nothing for that." Quick has also used a gun to rob another female. She and a friend were driving around when they spotted a young woman walking down the street with an expensive purse they liked. "We jumped out of the car. My friend put a gun up to her head and we just took all of her stuff." However, this approach was atypical.

On occasion, female victims belie the stereotype of them and fight back. Both Janet Outlaw and Ne-Ne describe stabbing young women who resisted them. Janet Outlaw describes one such encounter:

> This was at a little basketball game. Coming from the basketball game. It was over and we were checking her out and everything and she was walking to her car. I was, shit fuck that, let's get her motherfucking purse. Said let's get that purse. So I walked up to her and I pulled out the knife. I said "up that purse." And she looked at me. I said "shit, do you think I'm playing? Up that purse." She was like "shit, you ain't getting my purse. Do what you got to do." I was like "shit, you must be thinking I'm playing." So I took the knife, stabbed her a couple of times on the shoulder, stabbed her on the arm and snatched the purse. Cut her arm and snatched the purse. She just ran, "help, help." We were gone.

Ne-Ne describes a similar incident that occurred after an altercation between two groups of young women. When one young woman continued to badmouth her, she followed the girl to her car, pulled out a knife, "headed to her side and showed the bitch [the knife]." The girl responded, "I ain't giving you shit," and Ne-Ne said, "please don't make me stick you." Then, "She went to turn around and I just stuck it in her side: She was holding her side, just bleeding. And so when she fell on the ground one of my partners just started taking her stuff off of her. We left her right there."

As with pulling guns on women stabbing female victims is a rare occurrence. Nonetheless, women's robbery of other women routinely involves physical confrontation such as hitting, shoving, or beating up the victim. Describing a recent robbery, Nicole Simpson says, "I have bricks in my purse and I went up to her and hit her in the head and took her money." Kim Brown says that she will "just whop you and take a purse but not really put a gun to anybody's face." Libbie Jones says she has her victims throw their possessions on the ground, "then you push 'em, kick 'em or whatever, you pick it up and you just burn out." Likewise, CMW describes a recent robbery:

> I was like with three other girls and we was like all walking around: walking around the block trying to find something to do on a Saturday night with really nothing to do and so we started coming up the street, we didn't have no weapons on us at the time. All we did was just start jumping on her and beating her up and took her purse.

According to Janet Outlaw, "We push 'em and tell them to up their shit, pushing 'em in the head. Couple of times we had to knock the girls down and took the stuff off of them." She explains the reason this type of physical force is necessary: "It's just a woman-to-woman thing and we just like, just don't, just letting them know like it is, we let them know we ain't playing." As discussed below, this approach is vastly different from women's approaches when they rob men, or when they commit robberies with males. It appears to be, as Janet Outlaw says, "a woman-to-woman thing."

As noted above, sometimes female-on-female robberies occur in or around night clubs, in addition to on the streets. Libbie Jones explains, "you just chill in the club, just dance or whatever, just peep out people that got what you want. And then they come out of the club and you just get them." Likewise, Janet Outlaw says, "we get a couple of drinks, be on the blow, party, come sit down. Then be like, damn, check that bitch out with all this shit on." Libbie Jones came to her interview wearing a ring she had gotten in a robbery at a club the night before, telling the interviewer, "I like this on my hand, it looks lovely." She describes the incident as follows:

> This girl was in the bathroom. I seen the rings on her hands. Everybody was in there talking and putting their makeup on, doing their hair. So I went and got my godsister. She came back with her drink. She spilled it on her and she was like, "oh, my fault, my fault." She was wiping it off her. I pulled out my knife and said "give it up." The girl was taking the rings off her hand so when we got the rings we bounced up out of the club.

Though most of the women who rob females are teenagers or young adults and rob other young women, two women in the sample—Lisa Wood and Kim Brown—also describe targeting middle-aged or older citizens. It is notable that both are older (in their late 30s) and that both describe robbing in order to support drug habits, which make them more desperate.[10] As with the younger women who choose to rob other young women because they believe them unlikely to resist, both of these women choose older targets because they won't fight back. Lisa Wood says sometimes they accomplish these robberies of non-street-involved citizens by getting victims to drop their guard when they are coming out of stores. She describes approaching the person, "say 'hi, how you doing,' or 'do you need any help?' A lot of times they will say yeah. They might have groceries to take to they car and get it like that." She says once they drop their guard she will "snatch they purse and take off running."

To summarize, notable elements of women's robberies of other women are that they most frequently occur within street-oriented settings, do not include male accomplices, and typically involve physical force such as hitting, shoving and kicking, rather than the use of a weapon. When weapons are used, they are most likely to be knives. In these contexts, women choose to rob other females rather than males because they believe females are less likely to fight back; they typically do not use weapons such as guns because they perceive female targets as unlikely to be armed.

Setting Up Males by Appearing Sexually Available

Women's robberies of men nearly always involve guns.[11] They also do not involve physical contact. Janet Outlaw, who describes a great deal of physical contact in her robberies of other women (see above), describes her robberies of men in much different terms: "If we waste time touching men there is a possibility that they can get the gun off of us, while we wasting time touching them they could do anything. So we just keep the gun straight on them. No touching, no moving, just straight gun at you." The circumstances surrounding the enactment of female-on-male robberies differ as well. The key, in each case, is that women pretend to be sexually interested in their male victims, whose guard drops, providing a safe opportunity for the crime to occur. Two women—Jayzo and Nicole Simpson—rob men in the context of prostitution. The other five typically choose a victim at a club or on the streets, flirt and appear sexually interested, then suggest they go to a hotel, where the robbery takes place. These robberies may involve male or female accomplices, but they are just as likely to be conducted alone.

Nicole Simpson prostitutes to support her drug habit, but sometimes she "just don't be feeling like doing it," and will rob her trick rather than complete the sexual transaction. Sometimes she does this alone, and other times has a female accomplice. She chooses tricks she feels will make safe victims. She explains, "like I meet a lot of white guys and they be so paranoid they just want to get away." When Nicole Simpson is working alone, she waits until the man is in a vulnerable position before pulling out her knife. As she explains, "if you are sucking a man's dick and you pull a knife on them, they not gonna too much argue with you." When she works with a female partner, Nicole Simpson has the woman wait at a designated place, then takes the trick "to the spot where I know she at." She begins to perform oral sex, then her partner jumps in the car and pulls a knife. She explains, "once she get in the car I'll watch her back, they know we together. I don't even let them think that she is by herself. If they know it's two of us maybe they won't try it. Because if they think she by herself they might say fuck this, it ain't nothing but one person." Jayzo's techniques parallel those of Nicole Simpson, though she uses a gun instead of a knife and sometimes takes prospective tricks to hotels in addition to car dating.

Young women who target men outside the context of prostitution play upon the men's beliefs about women in order to accomplish these robberies—including the assumptions that women won't be armed, won't attempt to rob them, and can be taken advantage of sexually. Quick explains, "they don't suspect that a girl gonna try to get 'em. You know what I'm saying? So it's kind of easier 'cause they like, she looks innocent, she ain't gonna do this, but that's how I get 'em. They put they guard down to a woman." She says when she sets up men, she parties with them first, but makes sure she doesn't consume as much as them. "Most of the time, when girls get high they think they can take advantage of us so they always, let's go to a hotel or my crib or something.'" Janet Outlaw says, "they easy to get, we know what they after—sex." Likewise, CMW and a girlfriend often flirt with their victims: "We get in the car then ride with them. They thinking we little freaks: whores or something." These men's assumptions that they can take advantage of women lead them to place themselves at risk for robbery. CMW continues: "So they try to take us to the motel or whatever we going for it. Then it's like they getting out of the car and then all my friend has to do is just put, the gun up to his head, give me your keys. He really can't do nothing, his gun is probably in the car. All you do is drive on with the car."

Several young women report targeting men at clubs, particularly dope dealers or other men who appear to have a lot of money. Describing one such victim, Janet Outlaw says she was drawn to him because of his "jewelry, the way he was dressed, little snakeskin boots and all: I was like, yeah, there is some money." She recounts the incident as follows:

> I walked up to him got to conversating with him. He was like, "what's up with you after the club?" I said "I'm down with you, whatever you want to do." I said "we can go to a hotel or something." He was like "for real?" I was like, "yeah, for real." He was like, "shit, cool then." So after the club we went to the hotel. I had the gun in my purse. I followed him, I was in my own car, he was in his car. So I put the gun in my purse and went up to the hotel, he was all ready. He was posted, he was a lot drunk. He was like, "you smoke weed?" I was like, "yeah shit, what's up." So we got to smoking a little bud, he got to taking off his little shit, laying it

> on a little table. He was like, "shit, what's up, ain't you gonna get undressed?" I was like "shit, yeah, hold up" and I went in my purse and I pulled out the gun. He was like "damn, what's up with you gal?" I was like, "shit, I want your jewelry and all the money you got." He was like, "shit, bitch you crazy. I ain't giving you my shit." I said, "do you think I'm playing nigger? You don't think I'll shoot your motherfucking ass?" He was like, "shit, you crazy, fuck that, you ain't gonna shoot me." So then I had fired the thing but I didn't fire it at him, shot the gun. He was like "fuck no." I snatched his shit. He didn't have on no clothes. I snatched the shit and ran out the door. Hopped in my car.

Though she did this particular robbery alone, Janet Outlaw says she often has male accomplices: who follow her to the hotel or meet her there. While she's in the room, "my boys be standing out in the hallway," then she lets them in when she's ready to rob the man. Having male backup is useful because men often resist being robbed by females, believing that women don't have the heart to go through with what's necessary if the victim resists. Janet Outlaw describes one such incident. Having flirted with a man and agreed to meet him, she got in his car then pulled her gun on him:

> I said "give me your stuff." He wasn't gonna give it to me. This was at nighttime. My boys was on the other side of the car but he didn't know it. He said "I ain't gonna give you shit." I was like, "you gonna give me your stuff." He was like "I'll take that gun off of your ass." I was like, "shit, you ain't gonna take this gun." My boy just pulled up and said, "give her your shit." I got the shit.

In the majority of these robberies, the victim knows that the woman has set him up—she actively participates in the robbery. Ne-Ne also describes setting up men and then pretending to be a victim herself. Her friends even get physical with her to make it appear that she's not involved. She explains:

> I'll scam you out and get to know you a little bit first, go out and eat and let you tell me where we going, what time and everything. I'll go in the restroom and go beep them [accomplices] just to let them know what time we leaving from wherever we at so they can come out and do their little robbery type thing, push me or whatever. I ain't gonna leave with them 'cause then he'll know so I still chill with him for a little while.

Only Ne-Ne reports having ever engaged in a robbery the opposite of this—that is, one in which her male partners flirted with a girl and she came up and robbed her. She explains:

> I got some [male friends] that will instigate it. If I see some girl and I'm in the car with a whole bunch of dudes, they be like "look at that bitch she have on a leather coat." "Yeah, I want that." They'll say "well why don't you go get it?" Then you got somebody in the back seat [saying] "she's scared, she's scared." Then you got somebody just like "she ain't scared, up on the piece" or whatever and then you got some of them that will say well, "we gonna do this together." It could be like two dudes they might get out like "what's up baby," try to holler at her, get a mack on and they don't see the car. We watching and as soon as they pulling out they little pen to write they number, then I'll get out of the car and just up on them and tell them, the dudes be looking like, damn, what's going on? But they ain't gonna help cause they my partners or whatever.

Street Robberies with Male Robbers

As the previous two sections illustrate, women's accomplishment of robbery varies according to the gender of their victims. As a rule women and men do not rob females together, but do sometimes work together to set up and rob males. In addition, half of the women interviewed describe committing street robberies—almost always against males—with male accomplices. In these robberies, women's involvement either involves equal participation in the crime or assisting males but defining their role as secondary. Three women in the sample—Buby, Tish, and Lisa Jones—describe working with males on the streets as their only form of robbery, and each sees her participation as secondary. The rest engage in a combination of robbery types, including those described in the previous two sections, and do not distinguish their roles from the roles of male participants in these street robberies.

Lisa Jones and Tish each assist their boyfriends in the commission of robberies; Buby goes along with her brother and cousins. Lisa Jones says "most of the time we'll just be driving around and he'll say 'let's go to this neighborhood and rob somebody.'" Usually she stays in the car while he approaches the victim, but she is armed and will get out and assist when necessary. Describing one such incident, she says, "One time there was two guys and one guy was in the car and the other guy was out of the car and I seen that one guy getting out of the car I guess to help his friend. That's when I got out and I held the gun and I told him to stay where he was." Likewise Buby frequently goes on robberies with her brother and cousins but usually chooses to stay in the car "because I be thinking that I'm gonna get caught so I rather stay in the back." She has never done a robbery on her own and explains. "I know what to do but I don't know if I could do it on my own. I don't know if I could because I'm used to doing them with my brother and my cousins." Though her role is not an active one, she gets a cut of the profits from these robberies.

Tish and Lisa Jones are the only white respondents in the study. Each robs with an African-American boyfriend, and—though they commit armed robberies—both reject the view of themselves as criminals. Lisa Jones, for instance, downplays her role in robberies, as the following dialogue illustrates:

Interviewer: How many armed robberies have you done in your life?
Lisa Jones: I go with my boyfriend and I've held the gun, I've never actually shot it.
Interviewer: But you participate in his robberies?
Lisa Jones: Yeah.
Interviewer: How many would you say in your whole life?
Lisa Jones: About fifteen.
Interviewer: What about in the last month?
Lisa Jones: Maybe five or six.
Interviewer: What other crimes have you done in your life, or participated with others?
Lisa Jones: No, I'm not a criminal.

It is striking that this young woman routinely engages in robberies in which she wields a weapon, yet she defines herself as "not a criminal." Later in the interview, she explains that she would stop participating in armed robberies "if I was to stop seeing him." She and Tish are the only respondents who minimize the implications of their involvement in armed robbery, and it is probably not coincidental that they are young white women—their race and gender allow them to view themselves in this way.

Both also describe their boyfriends as the decision makers in the robberies—deciding when, where, and whom to rob. This is evident in Tish's interview, as her boyfriend, who is present in the room, frequently interjects to answer the interviewer's questions. The following dialogue is revealing:

Interviewer: How do you approach the person?
Tish: Just go up to them.

Interviewer: You walk up to them, you drive up to them?

Boyfriend: Most of the time it's me and my partner that do it. Our gals, they got the guns and stuff but we doing most of the evaluating. We might hit somebody in the head with a gun, go up to them and say whatever. Come up off your shit or something to get the money. The girls, they doing the dirty work really, that's the part they like doing, they'll hold the gun and if something goes wrong they'll shoot. We approach them. I ain't gonna send my gal up to no dude to tell him she want to rob him you know. She might walk up to him with me and she might hit him a couple of times but basically I'm going up to them.

These respondents reveal the far end of the continuum of women's involvement in robbery, clearly taking subordinate roles in the crime and defining themselves as less culpable as a result. Tish's boyfriend also reveals his perception of women as secondary actors in the accomplishment of robbery. For the most part, other women who participate in street robberies with male accomplices describe themselves as equal participants. Older women who rob citizens to support their drug habits at times do so with male accomplices. For instance, Lisa Woods sometimes commits her robberies with a male and female accomplice and targets people "like when they get they checks. Catch them coming out of the store, maybe trip 'em, go in they pocket and take they money and take off running." Among the younger women, robberies with male accomplices involve guns and typically come about when a group of people are driving around and spot a potential victim. Janet Outlaw describes a car jacking that occurred as she and some friends were driving around:

> Stop at a red light, we was looking around, didn't see no police, we was right behind them [the victims] . . . So one of my boys got out and I got out. Then the other boy got up in the driver's seat that was with them. My boy went on one side and I went on the other side and said "nigger get out of the car before we shoot you." Then the dudes got out. It was like, shit, what's up, we down with you all. No you ain't down with us, take they jewelry and shit off. It was like, damn, why you all tripping? Then my boy cocked the little gun and said take itoff now or I'm gonna start spraying you all ass. So they took off the little jewelry, I hopped in, put it in drive and pulled on off.

Likewise, Ne-Ne prefers committing street robberies with males rather than females. She explains:

> I can't be bothered with too many girls. That's why I try to be with dudes or whatever. They gonna be down. If you get out of the car and if you rob a dude or jack somebody and you with some dudes then you know if they see he tryin' to resist, they gonna give me some help. Whereas a girl, you might get somebody that's scared and might drive off. That's the way it is.

It is not surprising, then, that Ne-Ne is the only woman interviewed to report having ever committed this type of street robbery of a male victim on her own. Her actions parallel those of male-on-male robbers described above. Ne-Ne explicitly indicates that this robbery was possible because the victim did not know she was a woman. Describing herself physically, she says, "I'm big, you know." In addition, her dress and manner masked her gender. "I had a baseball cap in my car and I seen him . . . I just turned around the corner, came back down the street, he was out by hisself and I got out of the car, had the cap pulled down over my face and I just went to the back and upped him. Put the gun up to his head." Being large, wearing a ballcap, and enacting the robbery in a masculine style (e.g., putting a gun to his head) allowed her to disguise the fact that she was a woman and thus decrease the victim's likelihood of resisting. She says, "He don't know right now to this day if it was a girl or a dude."

Discussion

Feminist scholars have been hesitant to grapple with the issue of women's violence, both because a focus on women's violence draws attention away from the fact that violence is a predominantly male phenomenon and because studying women's violence can play into sensationalized accounts of female offenders. Nonetheless, as this and other studies have shown, "gender alone does not account for variation in criminal violence" (Simpson, 1991, 118). A small number of women are involved in violent street crime in ways that go beyond "preventing victimization," and appear to find support among their male and female peers for these activities. To draw this conclusion is not to suggest that women's use of violence is increasing, that women are "equals" on the streets, or that gender does not matter. It does suggest that researchers should continue developing feminist perspectives to address the issue.

What is most notable about the current research is the incongruity between motivations and accomplishment of robbery. While a comparison of women's and men's motivations to commit robbery reveals gender similarities, when women and men actually commit robbery their enactments of the crime are strikingly different. These differences highlight the clear gender hierarchy that exists on the streets. While some women are able to carve out a niche for themselves in this setting, and even establish partnerships with males, they are participating in a male-dominated environment, and their actions reflect an understanding of this.

To accomplish robberies successfully, women must take into account the gendered nature of their environment. One way they do so is by targeting other females. Both male and female robbers hold the view that females are easy to rob, because they are less likely than males to be armed and because they are perceived as weak and easily intimidated. Janet Outlaw describes women's robbery of other women as "just a woman to woman thing." This is supported by Ne-Ne's description that her male friends do not participate with her in robberies of females, and it is supported by men's accounts of robbing women. While women routinely rob other women, men are less likely to do so, perhaps because these robberies do not result in the demonstration of masculinity.

At the same time that women articulate the belief that other women are easy targets, they also draw upon these perceptions of women in order to rob men. Two of the women describe committing robberies much in keeping with Maher's (1997) descriptions of "viccing." In addition, a number of women used men's perceptions of women as weak, sexually available, and easily manipulated to turn the tables and manipulate men into circumstances in which they became vulnerable to robbery—by flirting and appearing sexually interested in them. Unlike women's robberies of other women, these robberies tend not to involve physical contact but do involve the use of guns. Because they recognize men's perceptions of women, they also recognize that men are more likely to resist being robbed by a female, and thus they commit these robberies in ways that minimize their risk of losing control and maximize their ability to show that they're "for real."

West and Zimmerman (1987, 139) note that there are circumstances in which parties reach an accommodation that allow[s] a woman to engage in presumptively masculine behavior." In this study, it is notable that while both women and men recognize the urban street world as a male-dominated one, a few of the women interviewed appear to have gained access to male privilege by adopting male attitudes about females, constructing their own identities as more masculine, and following through by behaving in masculine ways (see also Hunt, 1984). Ne-Ne and Janet Outlaw both come to mind in this regard—as women who completed robberies in equal partnerships with men and identified with men's attitudes about other women. Other women, such as Lisa Jones and Tish, accepted not only women's position as secondary, but their own as well. While Ne-Ne and Janet Outlaw appeared to draw status and identity from their criminality in ways that went beyond their gender identity. Lisa Jones and Tish used their gender identity to construct themselves as non-criminal.

In sum, the women in this sample do not appear to "do robbery" differently than men in order to meet different needs or accomplish different goals. Instead, the differences that emerge reflect practical choices made in the context of a gender-stratified environment—one in which, on the whole, men are perceived as strong and women are perceived as weak.

Motivationally, then, it appears that women's participation in street violence can result from the same structural and cultural underpinnings that shape some of men's participation in these crimes, and that they receive rewards beyond protection for doing so. Yet gender remains a salient factor shaping their actions, as well as the actions of men.

Though urban African-American women have higher rates of violence than other women, their participation in violent crime is nonetheless significantly lower than that of their male counterparts in the same communities (Simpson. 1991). An important line of inquiry for future research is to assess what protective factors keep the majority of women living in underclass settings from adopting violence as a culturally legitimate response. While research shows that racial and economic oppression contribute to African-American women's greater participation in violent crime, they do not ensure its occurrence. Daly and Stephens (1995, 208) note: "Racism in criminological theories occurs when racial or cultural differences are over-emphasized or mischaracterized *and* when such differences are denied." Future research should strive to strike this balance and attend to the complex issues surrounding women's participation in violence within the urban street world.

Notes

Thanks to Richard Wright and Scott Decker for so generously allowing me to re-read their data with a feminist eye; to Richard Wright for his feedback throughout the writing process; and to the anonymous reviewers at *Criminology* for their helpful suggestions on an earlier draft. The research on which the article is based was funded jointly by the Harry Frank Guggenheim Foundation and the National Institute of Justice (NIJ grant 94-IJ-CX-0030). Opinions expressed are those of the author and do not necessarily reflect those of the funding agencies.

1. The original study (Wright and Decker, 1997) contained 86 interviews, 72 of which were with males. From these the matched sample of males for the current study was drawn prior to data analysis to avoid sampling biases.
2. This age distribution differs from that of the larger sample, which included a sizable number of older male robbers. Eighteen of the males in the current sample were under 25 (78%), while only 35 of the 72 males in the larger sample (49%) were under 25.
3. One white male was interviewed for the original study but was excluded from this analysis because he didn't fit the matching criteria (age, age at first robbery) and had only committed one robbery, which was retaliatory in nature. He was 30 years old and had recently been ripped off by someone, whom he robbed in order to get his money back. Notably though, the physicality of his style in committing the robbery—"I had my left hand on his neck and the gun on his cheekbone"—paralleled the predominant style of the male robbers included.
4. All but five of the respondents reported that they had committed at least one robbery within the month prior to being interviewed. These five included three men (Woods, C-Loco, and Tony Wright) and two women (Quick and Kim Brown). All nonetheless considered themselves active robbers.
5. Because the project was partially supported by funds from the National Institute of Justice, respondents' confidentiality was protected by federal law. In addition, completed interviews were kept in a locked file cabinet. For a fuller discussion of human subjects' protections, see Wright and Decker (1997). In regard to confidentiality, one clarification is in order. One of the young women (Tish) was referred by her boyfriend, who had previously been interviewed for the project. They insisted that he be present during her interview, and he occasionally interjected to offer his own clarifications of her responses. Though his presence may have made her more hesitant or self-conscious in answering, his own comments were illuminating regarding the gendered nature of their robberies, as both of them downplayed the seriousness of her involvement.
6. This pattern is somewhat different from that of the larger sample of 86 active robbers, more of whom described robbing with a greater sense of desperation for money (Wright and Decker; 1997). This difference results from the differences in age structure of the current sample compared to the original sample. Because the majority of female respondents were teenagers or young adults (10 of the 14), the matched sample of males drawn for this study was younger than the larger sample of males (see note 2). Older robbers were more likely to be supporting drug habits and were more likely to have children or family that they made efforts to provide for.

   Sommers and Baskin's (1993) study of female robbers offers much the same conclusion regarding motivation. In their study of 44 female robbers, 89% describe committing the crime for money, and 11% for noneconomic reasons such as excitement or vengeance. Of women who committed robbery for money, 81% did so to support drug habits, and only 19% did so to get commodities such as jewelry and clothes. These differences are likely the case because their sample is older than the current sample and because they were incarcerated at the time of the interview and thus likely represent less successful robbers (perhaps because of their drug habits). In fact when giving life-history history accounts, two-thirds of Sommers and Baskin's sample reported that their initial reasons for committing robbery were less economic and more oriented toward thrill seeking and excitement.

7. This may be a low estimate. Sometimes it is difficult to discern whether victims are street involved: robbers simply view them as an individual likely to have money because of their physical appearance, dress, and jewelry. In the larger sample. Wright and Decker estimated that 30 of the 86 robbers (35%) targeted citizens.
8. In the larger sample, approximately 90% of respondents used guns to commit robberies.
9. This is Yolanda Smith, who robs older women by offering to give them rides in her car. Describing a typical robbery, she says: "I asked her did she need a ride. I said 'if you give me one dollar for gas I'll take you to work.' So she jumped in the car. I took her about three or four blocks and then I said 'do you have any more money?' She had this necklace on so I put a gun up to her head and said 'give it up.'" Her approach was unlike any other woman's in the sample, both in terms of how she approached the victim and in her routine use of a firearm.
10. These two are also the only women who report having had male accomplices when robbing women in this way.
11. The only exception to this pattern was Nicole Simpson, who used a knife to rob tricks in the context of prostitution. These findings parallel those of Sommers and Baskin (1993:147) who found that women were not likely to rob men without weapons, but were likely to rob other women without them.

References

Agar, Michael H. 1977. Ethnography in the streets and in the joint: A comparison. In *Street ethnography: Selected studies of crime and drug use in natural settings*, ed. Robert S. Weppner. Beverly Hills, CA: Sage.

Ageton, Suzanne S. 1983. The dynamics of female delinquency. 1976–1980. *Criminology* 21(4): 555–584.

Anderson, Elijah. 1994. The code of the streets. *Atlantic Monthly* 273:81–94.

Baskin, Deborah, Ira Sommers, and Jeffrey Fagan. 1993. The political economy of violent female street crime. *Fordham Urban Law Journal* 20:401–417.

Braithwaite, John and Kathleen Daly. 1994. Masculinities, violence and communitarian control. In *Just boys doing business?,* eds. Tim Newburn and Elizabeth A. Stanko. . New York: Routledge.

Campbell, Anne. 1993. *Men, women and aggression*. New York: Basic Books.

Chesney-Lind, Meda. 1993. Girls, gangs and violence: Anatomy of a backlash. *Humanity & Society* 17(3):321–344.

Chesney-Lind, Meda and Randall G. Shelden. 1992. *Girls, delinquency and juvenile Justice*. Pacific Coves, CA: Brooks/Cole.

Daly, Kathleen and Deborah J. Stephens. 1995. The "dark figure" of criminology: Towards a black and multi-ethnic feminist agenda for theory and research. In *International feminist perspectives in criminology: Engendering a discipline*, eds. Nicole Hahn Rafter and Frances Heidensohn. Philadelphia: Open University Press.

Decker, Scott and Barrik Van Winkle. 1996. *Life in the gang*. New York: Cambridge University Press.

Federal Bureau of Investigation 1996 Crime in the United States, 1995. Washington. DC: U.S. Government Printing Office.

Glassner, Barry and Cheryl Carpenter. 1985. The feasibility of an ethnographic study of adult property offenders. Unpublished report prepared for the National Institute of Justice. Washington, DC.

Hill, Gary D. and Elizabeth M. Crawford. 1990. Women, race, and crime. *Criminology* 28(4):601–623.

Hunt, Jennifer. 1984. The development of rapport through the negotiation of gender in field work among police. *Human Organization* 43(4): 283–296.

Joe, Karen A. and Meda Chesney-Lind. 1995. Just every mother's angel: An analysis of gender and ethnic variations in youth gang membership. *Gender & Society* 9(4): 408–430.

Katz, Jack. 1988. *Seductions of crime*. New York: Basic Books.

Kelly, Liz. 1991. Unspeakable acts. *Trouble and Strife* 21: 13–20.

Laub, John H. and M. Joan McDermott. 1985. An analysis of serious crime by young black women. *Criminology* 23(1): 81–98.

Maher, Lisa. 1997. *Sexed work: Gender, race and resistance in a Brooklyn drug market*. Oxford: Clarendon Press.

Maher, Lisa and Richard Curtis. 1992. Women on the edge of crime: Crack cocaine and the changing contexts of street-level sex work in New York City. *Crime, Law and Social Change* 18:221–258.

Maher, Lisa and Kathleen Daly. 1996. Women in the street-level drug economy: Continuity or change? *Criminology* 34(4): 465–492.

Mann, Coramae Richey. 1993. Sister against sister: Female intrasexual homicide. In *Female criminality: The state of the art*, ed. C.C. Culliver. New York: Garland Publishing.

Messerschmidt, James W. 1993. *Masculinities and crime*. Lanham, Md.: Rowman & Littlefield.

——— 1995 From patriarchy to gender: Feminist theory, criminology and the challenge of diversity. In Nicole Hahn Rafter and Frances Heidensohn (eds.). International Feminist Perspectives in Criminology: Engendering a Discipline. Philadelphia: Open University Press.

Newburn, Tim and Elizabeth A. Stanko (eds.) 1994. *Just boys doing business?* New York: Routledge.

Oliver, William. 1994. *The violent social world of black men*. New York: Lexington Books.

Sampson, Robert J. and William Julius Wilson. 1995. Toward a theory of race, crime, and urban inequality. In *Crime and Inequality*, eds. John Hagan and Ruth D. Peterson. Stanford, CA: Stanford University Press.

Sikes, Gini. 1997. *8 ball chicks: A year in the violent world of girl gangsters*. New York: Anchor Books.

Simpson, Sally. 1989. Feminist theory, crime and justice. *Criminology* 27(4): 605–631.

——— 1991 Caste, class and violent crime: Explaining difference in female offending. *Criminology* 29(1): 115–135.

Simpson, Sally and Lori Elis. 1995. Doing gender: Sorting out the caste and crime conundrum. *Criminology* 33(1): 47–81.

Sommers, Ira and Deborah R. Baskin. 1993. The situational context of violent female offending. *Journal of Research on Crime and Delinquency* 30(2): 136–162.

St. Louis Metropolitan Police Department 1994 Annual Report–1993/1994.

Stack, Carol B, 1974, *All our kin: Strategies for survival in a black community.* New York: Harper & Row.

Steffensmeier, Darrell J. 1983 Organization properties and sex-segregation in the underworld: Building a sociological theory of sex differences in crime. *Social Forces* 61: 1010–1032.

Steffensmeier, Darrell J. and Robert Terry. 1986. Institutional sexism in the underworld: A view from the inside. *Sociological Inquiry* 56: 304–323.

Watters, John and Patrick Biernacki. 1989. Targeted sampling: Options for the study of hidden populations. *Social Problems* 36:416–430.

West, Candace and Sarah Fenstermaker. 1995. Doing difference. *Gender & Society* 9(1): 8–37.

West, Candace and Don H. Zimmerman. 1987. Doing gender. *Gender & Society* 1(2): 125–151.

White, Jacquelyn W. and Robin M. Kowalski. 1994. Deconstructing the myth of the nonaggressive woman: A feminist analysis. *Psychology of Women Quarterly* 18: 487–508.

Wilson, William Julius. 1996. *When work disappears: The world of the new urban poor.* New York: Alfred A. Knopf.

Wright, Richard T. and Scott Decker. 1994. *Burglars on the job: Streetlife and residential break-ins.* Boston: Northeastern University Press. 1997 Armed Robbers in Action: Stickups and Street Culture. Boston: Northeastern University Press.

12

Sociodemographic Predictors and Cultural Barriers to Help-Seeking Behavior by Latina and Anglo American Battered Women

Carolyn M. West, Glenda Kaufman Kantor, and Jana L. Jasinski

Data from a national survey were used to investigate the help-seeking efforts of Latinas (Mexican, Mexican American, Puerto Rican) and Anglo American women who experienced battering by intimate partners. The findings revealed that battered Latinas were significantly younger, less educated, and more impoverished than Anglo women. Additionally, Latinas more often categorized their marriages as male dominated and their husbands as heavy drinkers. Bivariate analyses showed that Latinas who sought help were significantly more acculturated and more likely to have a heavy-drinking husband than those who did not seek help. Although battered women were active help seekers, Latinas underutilized both informal and formal resources relative to Anglo women, with Mexican women least likely to seek assistance. When sociodemographic predictors of help seeking were analyzed, being youthful and Anglo significantly increased the odds of help-seeking efforts. Low acculturation, as measured by preference for the Spanish language, was the only significant cultural barrier to help seeking by Latinas. Implications for treatment include improved outreach and advocacy to underserved groups.

Although much has been published on the prevalence of partner violence (e.g., Straus & Gelles, 1990), few studies have investigated the extent and nature of battered women's help-seeking efforts (Gordon, 1996). Even less of the literature has focused specifically on the help-seeking efforts made by battered women of color. This is an oversight because Latinos are the second largest and fastest growing minority group in the United States (U.S. Bureau of the Census, 1993). Moreover, there is substantial economic, demographic, and cultural diversity among Latino ethnic groups (see Kaufman Kantor, Jasinski, & Aldarondo, 1994; West, 1998 for a detailed discussion of the influence of socio-cultural status on Latino family violence). These Latino ethnic group differences may have implications for the help-seeking process (Keefe, 1982). Nevertheless, most previous researchers have treated Latinos as a homogeneous group. This study will address the lack of research by investigating the amount and type of help sought as well as sociodemographic and cultural factors that may influence help-seeking efforts of Latinas and Anglo battered women. Ethnic group differences in help seeking among Mexican, Mexican American, and mainland Puerto Rican women also will be considered.

Patterns of Help Seeking

Despite prior assumptions concerning battered women's passivity, researchers have found that more than half the women in their samples sought some type of assistance (Grayson & Smith, 1981; Horton & Johnson, 1993). An analysis of battered women's help-seeking patterns shows that they initially turned to their informal support network of friends and relatives (Horton & Johnson, 1993; Gondolf & Fisher, 1988). As the violence escalated in severity, victims more frequently consulted formal help sources (Harris & Dewdney, 1994) such as the criminal justice system, followed by social service agencies, medical services, crisis hotlines, mental health services, clergy members, support groups, and battered women's shelters (Bowker, 1988; Gordon, 1996; Hamilton & Coates, 1993). However, much of this research has been limited to small community-based samples drawn from varying geographic areas (Bowker, 1988; Bowker & Maurer, 1986; Donato & Bowker, 1984). Unlike previous scholars, we used data from a national probability sample of families to examine help-seeking behavior among Latinas and Anglo battered women.

Ethnic Differences in Help-Seeking Behavior

Using shelter samples, researchers have found ethnic differences in help-seeking efforts. For example, O'Keefe (1994) discovered that Latinas in her sample reported receiving less help from family and friends than did Anglo women, though not significantly so. Ethnic differences in the use of formal help sources also have been reported. Specifically, battered Latinas in two shelter samples, when compared to Anglo women, were more likely to call the police and less likely to contact a clergy member or social service agency (Gondolf, Fisher, & McFerron, 1991; Torres, 1991).

These findings should be interpreted with caution for several reasons. First, shelter samples may not represent the general population of battered women with regard to severity of violence experienced (Gondolf & Fisher, 1988). In addition, "ethnic lumping," or using one group, for example, Mexican Americans, to represent the experiences of other Latino ethnic groups is potentially misleading (Fontes, 1997). Another research limitation is the failure to consider cultural resources that are unique to Latinas, for example, the practice of visiting healers who use herbs, prayers, and rituals (Torres, 1987). Despite the research limitations, previous studies point to a pattern of service underutilization by battered Latinas.

Predictors and Barriers to Help Seeking

As one might expect, severity of abuse has been associated with increased help-seeking efforts (Harris & Dewdney, 1994), but there is a need to consider other dimensions of outreach. For instance, although sociodemographic and culturally based factors have been shown to be predictors of medical and mental health service utilization (Horwitz, 1987; Rodriguez & O'Donnell, 1995; Woodward, Dwinell, & Arons, 1992), few studies have investigated these factors as predictors or barriers to the help-seeking efforts of battered women.

Sociodemographic Predictors

The general health care utilization literature demonstrates that young, educated, Anglo women with greater economic resources were more likely than Latinos to seek medical and mental health care (Horwitz, 1987; Woodward et al., 1992). We expect that these same sociodemographic disparities will influence the help-seeking behavior of battered Latinas. In both national (Kaufman Kantor et al. 1994; Straus & Smith, 1990) and shelter samples (Gondolf et al., 1991; O'Keefe, 1994; Torres, 1991) Latino families who reported wife assaults were more educationally and economically disadvantaged when compared to Anglo families. Consequently, Latinas may have less access to telephone service or transportation which may result in greater difficulty using formal resources. Moreover, Mexicans often had even fewer economic resources than their Mexican American counterparts. Therefore, Mexican women may be even less likely than Mexican American and Anglo women to seek assistance after being battered.

Cultural Barriers

Level of acculturation, as measured by language preference, has often been identified as an obstacle to obtaining assistance. That is, individuals who are not proficient in English are less able to access formal help sources (Altarriba & Santiago-Rivera, 1994; Woodward et al., 1992). Kanuha (1994) proposed that more acculturated, second- and third-generation battered Latinas may be more familiar with and accepting of mental health services and thus more likely to seek assistance. However, she reported no empirical tests of her hypothesis. Therefore, additional research needs to investigate acculturation level as a potential barrier to help seeking among Latinas.

Regardless of ethnicity, culturally linked values and behaviors such as male-dominated marriages (Coleman & Straus, 1990), the endorsement of cultural norms sanctioning partner assaults (Kaufman Kantor et al., 1994), and husbands' heavy drinking (Kaufman Kantor, 1997) have been associated with an increased risk of wife assaults. These factors may potentially pose barriers to the help-seeking efforts of battered women. For example, the social isolation enforced by a dominant and controlling husband may restrict a battered woman's mobility and thus her opportunity to contact help. Women who believe that abuse is acceptable under some circumstances may not perceive themselves as victims and therefore may be less likely to seek assistance when assaulted (Torres, 1991). Furthermore, fear of escalating violence or feelings of obligation toward an alcoholic husband may prevent some women from seeking assistance. There is evidence that Latinas are more likely than Anglo women to be in male-dominated marriages (Jasinski, 1996), experience conflict with their husbands around decision making, express a more tolerant attitude toward wife abuse (Torres, 1991), and have heavy drinking husbands (Kaufman Kantor, 1997). However, more empirical evidence is needed to determine if these cultural factors also impede the help-seeking behavior of both Latinas and Anglo women. Unlike previous researchers who have taken a race comparative approach, this study also will investigate within-ethnic group differences. For example, we will consider sociodemographic and cultural differences between Latinas who seek help and Latinas who do not.

Goals of the Study

Taken together, the research suggests that there is an underutilization of services by battered Latinas, particularly by Mexican women. These findings lead to the following research questions: (a) To what extent do battered Latinas and Anglo women differ on sociodemographic and cultural factors?; (b) How much and what types of help are sought by Latinas and Anglo battered women? How does help-seeking behavior differ by ethnic group and among the various Latina ethnic groups?; (c) Are there within-ethnic group differences in help seeking?; (d) What sociodemographic factors predict help seeking?; and (e) What cultural factors act as barriers to help seeking?

Method

Sample

The data used for this paper were obtained in 1992 as a part of a national study on alcohol-family violence relationships (National Alcohol and Family Violence Survey) (Kaufman Kantor & Asdigian, 1997; Kaufman Kantor et al., 1994). Face-to-face interviews were conducted with a national probability sample of 1,970 persons, including an oversample of 846 Latinos, who were living as a couple with a member of the opposite sex. One member of each household, either the husband or the wife, was randomly selected and interviewed. Bilingual interviewers were utilized in oversample areas and respondents had the choice of taking the interview in English or Spanish. The overall response rate for all eligible individuals was 75.4%. The response rate for Latinos in oversample areas was 80.3%.

Measures

Ethnicity The ethnicity of respondents was assessed by the question "Which of these racial and ethnic groups do you consider yourself: Pacific Islander; Asian; Native American or Alaskan Native; White but not Latino; Black but not Latino; Latino or Hispanic, or some other group?" The analyses for this paper focused on those respondents who indicated that their race/ethnicity was either White but not Latino, or Latino or Hispanic. Latinos from the major United States ethnic groups included in this paper were those who self-identified as Mexican, Mexican American, and Puerto Rican. Cuban American women were excluded because the numbers reporting wife assaults were too low for reliable analyses.

Dependent Variables

Help-Seeking Behavior To measure help-seeking behavior, respondents were asked about both formal and informal types of help seeking based on Gottlieb's (1978) classification of helping behavior. The following question was asked: "Was there ever a time when you contacted any of the following because of your disagreements?" Possible responses included friends, relatives, shelter, psychologist, clergy, healer, lawyer, police, and others.

Wife Assault Physical aggression was measured with the Conflict Tactics Scale (CTS) (Straus, 1990). Respondents were asked to think of situations in the past year when they disagreed or were angry with a spouse or partner and then to indicate how often they engaged in each of the acts included in the CTS. The same questions were repeated and respondents were asked to report on their partner's behavior. In this study the husband-to-wife assault variable included the following violent acts (e.g., threw something at the other; pushed, grabbed, or shoved; slapped or spanked; kicked, bit or hit with fist; hit or tried to hit with something; beat up the other; threatened with a knife or gun; used a knife or gun). The husband-to-wife assault variable was coded as a dichotomy where a value of 1 indicated the presence of any violence that occurred during the course of the marital or cohabiting relationship. Respondents were categorized as severely battered if they experienced one or more of the acts of violence included in the severe violence index (i.e., the last five CTS items listed above, "kicked" through the "use of a knife or gun").

Independent Variables

Education To measure educational attainment, respondents were asked the following question about themselves and their partner: "What is the last year of school that you have completed?"

Poverty The measure used to assess poverty was based on an income-to-needs ratio of family economic status and was calculated by dividing household income by its corresponding poverty threshold specified by the U.S. Bureau of the Census (1992). The poverty threshold, which varies by family size, is based on the expenses considered necessary for minimally acceptable amounts of food and other necessities (Duncan & Rodgers, 1991).

Acculturation The measure assessing acculturation for the respondents and their spouse was composed of four items adapted from Szapocznik, Scopetta, Kurtines, and Aranalde (1978) and the National Health and Nutrition Examination Survey (National Center for Health Statistics, 1985).

The items refer to language preference and utilization of Spanish versus English in a variety of situations: (a) "What language do you (your partner) prefer to speak?"; (b) "What language do you (your partner) prefer to speak at home?"; (c) "What language do you (your partner prefer to speak with friends?"; (d) "What language do you (your partner) prefer to speak at work?" The response categories were: "Spanish all the time"; "Spanish most of the time"; "Spanish and English equally"; "English most of the time"; "English all the time." Items were combined into a summative scale ranging from 4 to 21. High scores indicated greater English proficiency.

Marital Power Structure The balance of power between spouses was measured by questions based on the work of Blood and Wolfe (1960) that asked the respondents to indicate "Who has the final say" in making decisions about the following six issues: buying a car, having children, what house or apartment to take, what job either partner should take, whether a partner should go to work or quit work, and how much money to spend each week for food. The responses for each issue are: "husband only," "husband more than wife," "husband and wife exactly the same," "wife more than husband," and "wife only." The pattern of responses to these six questions was used to classify couples in a dichotomous manner as male-dominant or other marital power structure based on final say for different gender-typed decisions. The work of Blood and Wolfe (1960) has been used in other nationally representative samples to measure marital power in violent relationships (e.g., Coleman & Straus, 1990).

Approval of Violence To measure norms tolerating wife abuse, we replicated the measure first employed in a 1968 survey conducted for the President's Commission on the Causes and Prevention of Violence: "Are there situations that you can imagine in which you would approve of a husband slapping his wife?" (Kaufman Kantor & Straus, 1987; Owens & Straus, 1975).

Husband's Drinking Husband's drinking behavior was measured by asking women respondents about their partner's quantity and frequency of drinking. The responses were categorized as heavy and nonheavy according to a manner previously utilized by Kaufman Kantor, and Straus (1987) (see also Kaufman Kantor, & Asdigian, 1997). The heavy drinking category included all husbands who were classified by the respondents as either high daily drinkers (four or more drinks per occasion, drunk on average four to seven days a week in the previous year), or binge drinkers (five or more drinks per occasion, drunk from less than once a month up to three days a week on average in the previous year). Nonheavy drinkers included those husbands who were classified as abstinent, low, or moderate drinkers.

Results

Sample Descriptives

Analyses included women who reported ever experiencing any battering by their current partner during the course of their marital relationship, regardless of their help-seeking patterns. The sample of battered women consisted of 76 Latinas who identified as Mexican ($n = 40$), Mexican American ($n = 19$), or Puerto Rican ($n = 17$), and 117 Anglo American women.

Part I of Table 12.1 presents data on sociodemographic and cultural factors for battered Latinas, regardless of ethnic group membership, and Anglo women. Section A of the table shows that battered Latinas were significantly younger, less educated, and more likely to live below the poverty level than Anglo battered women. However, there were no ethnic differences in severity of abuse.

With regard to culturally linked factors, Section B of Table 12.1 reveals that almost twice as many Latinas, when compared to Anglo women, could be characterized as living in male-dominated relationships, a difference that is statistically significant at the bivariate level. Consistent with the research literature on the higher prevalence of problem drinking by Latino men relative to Anglo

Table 12.1 Sociodemographic and Cultural Differences Between Battered Women by Ethnicity and Latina Ethnic Groups Based on T-Tests, Chi-squares, and ANOVAs.

Part I. Ethnicity	**Latinas ($n = 76$)**	**Anglos ($n = 117$)**	
A. Sociodemographic Factors			
M Age	35	41**	
M Years of Education	9	12***	
% Below Poverty Level	44	13***	
% Severely Battered	37	34	
B. Cultural Factors			
% Male-Dominated Marriage	26	15*	
% Approve Husband-Wife Slapping	21	19	
% Husband Heavy Drinker	41	26*	
Part II. Latina Ethnic Groups	**Mexican ($n = 40$)**	**Mexican American ($n = 19$)**	**Puerto Rican ($n = 17$)**
A. Sociodemographic Factors			
M Age	34	37	32
M Years of Education	8	11	10***
% Below Poverty Level	54	33	33
% Severely Battered	41	26	41
B. Cultural Factors			
% Male-Dominated Marriage	28	21	25
% Approve Husband-Wife Slapping	17	21	29
% Husband Heavy Drinker	33	63	35
M Acculturation Score	9	15	14***

* $p < .05$, **$p < .001$, ***$p < .0001$.

men (Kaufman Kantor, 1997), the data show that a significantly higher percentage of battered Latinas reported heavy drinking by their husbands.

Although Latinas were not significantly more approving of wife slapping than their Anglo counterparts, a substantial number in both groups asserted approval.

Part II of Table 12.1 presents the sociodemographic and cultural factors among Mexican, Mexican American, and Puerto Rican battered women. Overall, there were few significant differences. Part II A indicates that Mexican battered wives reported significantly fewer years of education than Mexican American and Puerto Rican battered wives. Although there were no significant ethnic group differences in age, poverty level, and the experience of severe abuse, Mexican and Puerto Rican women reported high levels of severe abuse relative to Mexican American women.

Part II B of Table 12.1 reveals few cultural differences among Latina groups. Abused Mexican women were less acculturated, as measured by their English language preference, than both Mexican American and Puerto Rican women. Although Mexican American wives were twice as likely to have heavy drinking husbands as their Mexican and Puerto Rican counterparts, these differences were not statistically significant. Additionally, there were no ethnic group differences in marital power structure (male dominated) and approval of husband-to-wife slapping. It should be noted that small sample sizes may contribute to the lack of significant ethnic group differences.

Amount and Types of Help Sought

Table 12.2 shows the pattern and frequency of help seeking. When the total amount of help sought is considered, slightly less than half of the abused Latinas in this sample sought one or more types of help, while two thirds of Anglo women did so. Significant differences also were found in the types of help sought. Although the general patterns of help seeking were similar across ethnic groups, with friends and relatives the most likely source of support, Latinas sought less help from both informal and formal help sources. Specifically, Anglo battered women were almost twice as likely to contact friends and family members, and were five times more likely than Latinas to use psychologists. There were no statistically significant ethnic differences in the use of battered women's shelters, clergy members, or lawyers. Although not significant, it should be noted that more Latinas contacted the police, while more Anglo women consulted attorneys. With regard to the use of culturally specific resources, only one Mexican and one Mexican American woman sought help from a healer (not shown in table).

As illustrated in Table 12.2, Part II, we next explored the amount and types of help sought among the various Latina ethnic groups. The only statistically significant ethnic differences were in the utilization of informal help sources, with Mexican American battered women turning to friends and family members more often than to their Puerto Rican and Mexican counterparts. While not statistically significant, most likely because of the small sample sizes within groups, variations in help-seeking patterns across ethnic groups can be discerned. Less acculturated Mexican women were more likely to consult clergy members. However, they generally used fewer help sources relative to Mexican American and Puerto Rican women.

Bivariate within Group Differences

In order to determine what group characteristics might be associated with the likelihood of help seeking, we first conducted bivariate analyses. Chi-square and t-tests of significance were utilized, as

Table 12.2 Results of Chi-Square Analyses of Types of Help Sought by Ethnicity and Latina Ethnic Groups

	Percent Who Sought Help		
Part I. Ethnicity	**Latinas ($n = 76$)**	**Anglos ($n = 117$)**	
Source of Help	%	%	
Friend/Relative	35	61***	
Shelter	4	2	
Psychologist	4	20**	
Clergy	16	14	
Lawyer	4	9	
Police	12	7	
Others	—	2	
Total[a]	48	66*	
Part II. Latina Ethnic Groups	**Mexican ($n = 40$)**	**Mexican American ($n = 19$)**	**Puerto Rican ($n = 17$)**
Source of Help	%	%	%
Friend/Relative	20	58	47*
Shelter	3	10	—
Psychologist	5	—	6
Clergy	20	17	6
Lawyer	3	5	6
Police	8	26	6
Others	—	—	—
Total[a]	38	63	53

[a] Total percentage of respondents who sought help from at least one source.
* $p < .01$, ** $p < .001$, *** $p < .0001$.

Table 12.3 Test and Chi-Square Results of Sociodemographic and Cultural Factors by Ethnicity and Help Seeking Behavior

	Latinas No Help ($n = 39$)	Any Help ($n = 36$)	No Help ($n = 39$)	Anglos Any Help ($n = 77$)
A. Sociodemographic Factors				
M Age	36	33	47	38**
M Years of Education	9	10	12	12
% Below Poverty Level	50	35	11	15
% Severely Battered	33	40	28	37
B. Cultural Factors				
M Acculturation Score	10	13**	NA	NA
% Male-Dominated Marriage	22	31	18	13
% Approve of Husband–Wife Slapping	13	28	15	21
% Husband Heavy Drinker	31	54*	28	26

* $p < .05$ ** $p < .001$.

appropriate to the level of measurement, for each sociodemographic and cultural factor by ethnicity and help-seeking status. Part A of Table 12.3 shows that Latinas who sought help did not differ significantly from Latinas who did not seek help based on age, years of education, poverty level, and severity of abuse. However, it can be seen that poorer women were less likely to get any help. The help-seeking status for Anglo women was not associated with most of these sociodemographic variables. Age was the only significant exception. Anglo women who sought help were significantly younger than their nonhelp-seeking Anglo counterparts. The data also showed that severity of battering increased the likelihood of help seeking for all women regardless of ethnicity, but severity was not a significant discriminator of any occurrence of help seeking.

Part B of Table 12.3 examined the question of whether cultural determinants of help seeking are present for battered women. The findings revealed that Latinas who sought assistance were significantly more acculturated and more likely to have a heavy drinking husband compared to Latinas who did not seek help. It should be noted that the latter characteristics were more consistent with those of Mexican American women in this study. Cultural norms that support violence toward women and a male dominant relationship structure were more common among help-seeking battered Latinas, but the associations were not statistically significant. Among Anglo women, none of the culturally based factors differed by help-seeking status. Although like Latinas, cultural norms reflecting violence approval appear to increase help-seeking behavior.

Sociodemographic Predictors and Cultural Barriers to Help Seeking

To test our research question concerning the relative contribution of sociodemographic predictors to the likelihood of help seeking, we next conducted multivariate analyses. Because of the dichotomous nature of the help-seeking variable in this study, logistic regression analysis was selected to analyze the data. Although it would be desirable to conduct multivariate analyses for each Latina ethnic group, reliable analyses were not possible because of small sample size. The dependent variable was a dichotomy measuring any occurrence of help seeking related to the abuse (1 = any type of help sought). The dependent variables were ethnicity (1 = Anglo); age and education (both continuous variables), poverty as assessed by the income-to-needs measure (1 = below the poverty level), and severity of violence (1 = any severe violence).

The results presented in Table 12.4 show that our predictions are partially supported. Help seeking differed by ethnicity. Specifically, being Anglo tripled the probability of help seeking (by a factor of 3.08). Youthfulness also was associated with increased odds of getting help. Alternatively stated, as

Table 12.4 Logistic Regression Results of Help-Seeking Status (1 = Any Help Sought) by Sociodemographic Factors (N = 175)

	B[a]	Odds Ratio
Ethnicity	1.12*	3.08
(1 = Anglo)	(.40)	
Age	–.04**	.95
	(.01)	
Education	.00	1.00
	(.06)	
Poverty Level	–.38	.68
(1 = Below Poverty Level)	(.41)	
Severely Battered	.29	1.34
(1 = Severe)	(.34)	
Constant	1.26	
–2 Log Likelihood	216.951	
Model Chi-Square	21.46	
df	5	
Sig.	$p < .0001$	

[a]Standard errors are in parentheses.
* $p < .005$.
** $p < .001$.

a woman's age increased, the odds of her seeking help decreased. Years of education, poverty level, and severity of abuse were not significant net of the effects of the other variables in the equation.

In order to examine the effects of cultural barriers to help seeking, we next conducted a logit analysis by regressing these factors on help seeking. We estimated a logit equation for each ethnic group separately so that different patterns might be identified. The dependent variable was a dichotomy-measuring help seeking related to battering. The independent variables were acculturation (a continuous variable) (Latina model only), marital power structure (1 = male dominant), approval of wife slapping (1 = yes for approval), and husband's heavy drinking (1 = heavy).

The results presented in Table 12.5 demonstrate partial support for cultural barriers to help seeking among battered Latinas. Level of acculturation increased the odds of help seeking by Latinas. The greater the preference for English, the greater the probability that the respondent sought assistance. A male-dominated marriage, normative approval of violence, and husband's heavy drinking were not significant predictors of help seeking among Latinas net of the other factors in the model. Similarly, none of these cultural factors significantly influenced the odds of help seeking among Anglo women.

Discussion

Data from a national survey were used to investigate the help-seeking efforts of Latinas and Anglo battered women. One concern was the extent to which Latinas and Anglo battered women differ on socioeconomic and cultural factors. Consistent with previous findings (Gondolf & Fisher, 1988; O'Keefe, 1994; Straus & Smith, 1990), battered Latinas in this sample are significantly younger and more likely than their Anglo counterparts to be educationally and economically disadvantaged. In addition, when compared to Anglo women, Latinas more often categorized their marriages as male dominated and their husbands as heavy drinkers. While Latinas and Anglo women are equally likely to experience severe violence, poverty and lack of resources may further exacerbate the abuse for Latinas. Moreover, the combination of lower educational attainment, income, and acculturation makes Mexican battered women more vulnerable and isolated.

Table 12.5 Logistic Regression Results of Help-Seeking Status (1 = Any Help Sought) by Cultural Barriers

	Latinas ($n = 72$)		Anglos ($n = 115$)	
	B[a]	Odds Ratio	B[a]	Odds Ratio
Male-Dominated Marriage	.40	1.49	–.45	.63
(1 = male dominated)	(.61)		(.54)	
Approve Husband-Wife	.94	2.57	.37	1.46
Slapping (1 = approve)	(.71)		(.53)	
Husband Heavy Drinker	.34	1.41	–.10	.90
(1 = Heavy)	(.56)		(.44)	
Acculturation Score	.18*	1.20	NA	
	(.07)			
Constant	–2.68		.73	
–2 Log Likelihood	85.90		144.75	
Model Chi-Square	13.85		1.18	
df	4		3	
Sig.	$p < .05$		$p < .75$	

[a] Standard errors are in parentheses.
* $p < .05$.

Although battered women in this sample are active help seekers, there is a tendency for Latinas to underutilize informal resources. Specifically, they are less likely than Anglos to seek help from friends and relatives. This seems surprising because the general help-seeking literature suggests that family members are a common source of emotional support for Mexican Americans (Keefe, 1982). However, this emotional support may not extend to battered women. Using a shelter sample, Torres (1991) found that Mexican American women were more likely than Anglo women to be battered in the presence of relatives. This may explain why some Mexican American women might be reluctant to seek assistance from family members. The reasons why Latinas seek less help than Anglos from relatives and friends awaits further investigation. Among the various ethnic groups, Mexican women are less likely than Mexican American and Puerto Rican women to seek help from intimates. These findings may reflect the limited informal social support system available to immigrant women. For example, after relocating to the United States Mexican women may have fewer friends, family members, neighbors, and coworkers in which to confide (Keefe, 1982).

Although Anglo women are five times more likely to seek assistance from psychologists, Latinas are less likely to utilize formal help sources. Keefe (1982) argues that the use of mental health services is not consistent with the cultural values of Latinas. Instead, Latinas may more often turn to clergy members for support, particularly if they are immigrant women with limited support systems. Although Mexican women in this sample are not significantly more likely to turn to religious leaders, there is a slight tendency for them to seek help from the clergy more than Mexican and Puerto Rican women would. However, few Latinas in this study consulted healers.

Although not significant, battered Latinas in this sample more frequently turned to the police for assistance, while Anglo women more often consulted lawyers. Battered Latinas may be fearful of the discrimination that their partners will face in the criminal justice system (Rasche, 1988), but the police may be one of the few legal options available to lower-income women. When ethnic group differences were considered, fewer Mexican women sought help from the police. As a result of limited education and English-speaking skills, Mexican women may be less knowledgeable of their legal rights. In contrast, the combination of battering and a husband's heavy drinking may contribute to the greater willingness of Mexican American women to contact the police. In addition, Mexican

American women, because they are more educated and acculturated, may be somewhat better able to negotiate the legal system.

When sociodemographic predictors of help seeking are considered, we find that being young and Anglo are predictors of help-seeking efforts, a finding that is similar to previous research (Woodward et al., 1992). Although education and poverty level are not significant predictors of help seeking in this study, they are correlated with ethnicity and are likely to play a role in the ability or willingness of victims to obtain assistance. Similarly, severity of battering was not associated with seeking assistance in this study. However, the potential lethality of abuse has been found to be predictive of help seeking in other studies (Harris & Dewdney, 1994).

An advantage of this study is that within-ethnic group differences are considered. Age is the only difference between help-seeking and nonhelp-seeking Anglo women. Specifically, Anglo women who sought help are more likely to be under age forty. In contrast, help-seeking Latinas, when compared to Latinas who did not seek assistance, are more acculturated as defined by a greater preference for English and are more likely to have heavy drinking husbands. However, based on multivariate analysis, level of acculturation is the only significant predictor of help seeking by battered Latinas. Consistent with previous research (Altarriba & Santiago-Rivera, 1994; Woodard et al., 1992), individuals who are proficient in English appear to have greater access to formal help sources.

This study has some limitations, however. First, reliable analyses of Latina ethnic group differences were not possible because of small sample size. Based on our findings there are important differences between Mexican, Mexican American, and Puerto Rican battered women that warrant further investigation. Second, acculturation was measured by English preference. Although the validity of language preference as a way to measure cultural adoption may be questioned, language proficiency and preference have been shown to account for the largest proportion of variance in measures of acculturation (Domino, 1992; Cueller, Harris, & Jasso, 1980). Finally, we do not know how many battered women in this sample sought medical attention for injuries related to their abuse. It is not uncommon for Mexican Americans to consult physicians for emotional problems (Keefe, 1982). Future research needs to explore this important help source. In addition, we could not assess the perceived usefulness of these services to battered women. It could be that services are not used because victims have found them to be insensitive.

Implications for Treatment

Although addressing the problem of abuse may not be their primary role, many professionals will confront the needs of battered women. Based on our research, it can be concluded that certain groups of women may benefit from increased outreach efforts. Service providers must make their assistance relevant to middle-aged and older Anglo women. This may entail addressing the stigma of seeking assistance for marital problems, including partner violence.

As the Latino population increases, helping professionals must be more aware of the sociocultural experiences that differentially impact battering among the various Latino ethnic groups (Kaufman Kantor et al., 1994). For example, service providers may need to help a Mexican American battered woman escape her abuser as well as deal with his heavy drinking. Less educated and acculturated Mexican women may require greater help negotiating various help sources.

In addition, the institutional barriers that make it difficult for Latinas to gain access to services must be addressed. For instance, agencies may lack translators, bilingual professionals, and reading materials in the client's native language. Other structural barriers include rules against treating non-English speaking or immigrant clients, geographic distance from minority communities and prohibitive fee structures (Williams & Becker, 1994; West, 1998). Increased attention to both sociodemographic and cultural barriers may enable Latinas and Anglo battered women to have greater access to resources.

Acknowledgment

Support for this research was provided by the Family Research Laboratory of the University of New Hampshire, NIMH Training Grant No. T32-MN15161 and Research Grant No. RO1AA09070 from the National Institute on Alcohol Abuse and Alcoholism.

References

Altarriba, J. and Santiago-Rivera, A. L. (1994). Current perspectives on using linguistic and cultural factors in counseling the Hispanic client. *Professional Psychology: Research and Practice* 25(4): 388–397.

Blood, R. O. and Wolfe, D. M. (1960). *Husband and wives.* Glencoe: Free Press.

Bowker, L. H. (1988). The effect of methodology on subjective estimates of the differential effectiveness of personal strategies and help sources used by battered women. In *Coping with family violence: Research and policy perspectives*, eds., G. T. Hotaling, D. Finkelhor, J. T. Kirkpatrick, and M. A. Straus. Newbury Park, CA: Sage Publications.

Bowker, L. H. and Maurer, L. (1986). The effectiveness of counseling services utilized by battered women. *Women & Therapy* 5: 65–82.

Coleman, D. H. and Straus, M. A. (1990). Marital power, conflict, and violence in a nationally representative sample of American couples. In *Physical violence in American families: Risk factors and adaptations to violence in 8,145 families*, eds., M. A. Straus and R. J. Gelles, 287–304. New Brunswick, NJ: Transaction.

Cueller, I., Harris, L. C., and Jasso, R. (1980). An acculturation scale for Mexican American normal and clinical populations. *Hispanic Journal of Behavioral Sciences* 2: 199–217.

Domino, G. (1992). Acculturation of Hispanics. In *Hispanics in the workplace,* eds., S. B. Knouse, P. Rosenfeld, and A. L. Cubertson, 56–74. Newbury Park, CA: Sage Publications.

Donato, K. M. and Bowker, L. H. (1984). Understanding the helpseeking behavior of battered women: A comparison of traditional service agencies and women's groups. *International Journal of Women's Studies* 7: 99–109.

Duncan, G. J. and Rodgers, W. (1991). Has children's poverty become more persistent? *American Sociological Review* 56: 538–550.

Fontes, L. A. (1997). Conducting ethnical cross-cultural research on family violence. In *Out of the darkness: Contemporary perspectives on family violence*, eds., G. Kaufman Kantor and J. L. Jasinski. Thousand Oaks, CA: Sage.

Gondolf, E. W. and Fisher, E. R. (1988). *Battered women as survivors: An alternative to treating learned helplessness.* Lexington, MA: Lexington Books.

Gondolf, E. W., Fisher, E., and McFerron, R. (1991). Racial differences among shelter residents: A comparison of Anglo, Black, and Hispanic battered women. In *Black family violence: Current research and theory*, ed., R. L. Hampton, 103–113. Lexington, MA: Lexington Books.

Gordon, J. S. (1996). Community services for abused women: A review of perceived usefulness and efficacy. *Journal of Family Violence* 11(4): 315–329.

Gottlieb, B. (1978). The development and application of a classification scheme of informal helping behaviors. *Canadian Journal of Behavioural Science* 10(2): 105–115.

Grayson, J., and Smith, G. (1981). Marital violence and help seeking patterns in a micropolitan community. *Victimology: An International Journal* 6: 188–197.

Hamilton, B. and Coates, J. (1993). Perceived helpfulness and use of professional services by abuse women. *Journal of Family Violence* 8(4): 313–324.

Harris, R. M. and Dewdney, P. (1994). *Barriers to information: How formal help systems fail battered women.* Westport, CT: Greenwood Press.

Horton, A. L. and Johnson, B. L. (1993). Profile and strategies of women who have ended abuse. *Families in Society* 74: 481–491.

Horwitz, A. V. (1987). Help-seeking processes and mental health services. In *Improving mental health services: What the social sciences can tell us*, ed., D. Mechanic, 33–45. San Francisco, CA: Jossey-Bass.

Jasinski, J. L. (1996). Structural inequalities, family and cultural factors, and spousal violence among Anglo and Hispanic Americans. Doctoral Dissertation, University of New Hampshire, Durham.

Kanuha, V. (1994). Women of color in battering relationships. In *Women of color: Integrating ethnic and gender identities in psychotherapy, eds.,* L. Comas-Diaz & B. Greene, 428–454. New York: Guilford Press.

Kaufman Kantor, G. (1997). Alcohol and spouse abuse: Ethnic differences. In M. Galanter ed., *Recent developments in alcoholism.* New York: Plenum.

Kaufman Kantor, G., and Asdigian, N. (1997). Gender differences and alcohol-related spousal aggression. In *Gender and alcohol: Individual and social perspectives*, eds., R. W. Wilsnack and S. C. Wilsnack (Eds.). New Brunswick, NJ: Rutgers University Press.

Kaufman Kantor, G., Jasinski, J., and Aldarondo, E. (1994). sociocultural status and incidence of marital violence in Hispanic families. *Violence and Victims* 9(3): 207–222.

Kaufman Kantor, G. and Straus, M. A. (1987). The "drunken bum" theory of wife beating. *Social Problems* 34: 213–230.

Keefe, S. E. (1982). Help-seeking behavior among foreign-born and native-born Mexican Americans. *Social Science Medicine* 16: 1467–1472.

National Center for Health Statistics (1985). *Plan and operation of the Health and Nutrition Examination Survey*, 1982–84. Vital Health Statistics (Series 1, No. 19, DHHS Publication No. PHS 85-1321). Washington, DC: U.S. Government Printing Office.

O'Keefe, M. (1994). Racial/ethnic differences among battered women and their children. *Journal of Child and Family Studies* 3(3): 283–305.

Owens, D. and Straus, M. A. (1975). The social structure of violence in childhood and approval of violence as an adult. *Aggressive Behavior* 1: 193–211.

Rasche, C. E. (1988). Minority women and domestic violence: The unique dilemmas of battered women of color. *Journal of Contemporary Criminal Justice* 4: 150–171.

Rodriguez, O. and O'Donnell, R. M. (1995). Help-seeking and use of mental health services by the Hispanic elderly. In *Handbook on ethnicity, aging, and mental health*, eds., D. K. Padgett, 165–184. Westport, CT: Greenwood Press.

Straus, M. (1990). New scoring methods for violence and new norms for the Conflict Tactics Scales. In *Physical violence in American families* (Appendix B), eds., M. A. Straus and R. J. Gelles. New Brunswick, NJ: Transaction Publishers.

Straus, M. A. and Gelles, R. J. (1990). How violent are American families? Estimates from the national family violence resurvey and other studies. In *Physical violence in American families* (Appendix B)., eds., M. A. Straus and R. J. Gelles, 95–112. New Brunswick, NJ: Transaction Publishers.

Straus, M. and Smith, C. (1990). Violence in Hispanic families in the United States: Incidence rates and structural interpretations. In *Physical violence in American families: Risk factors and adaptations to violence in 8,145 families,* eds., M.A. Straus and R. J. Gelles, 341–368). New Brunswick, NJ: Transaction.

Szapocznik, J., Scopetta, M. A., Kurtines, W., and Aranalde, M. (1978). Theory and measurement of acculturation. *Interamerican Journal of Psychology* 12: 113–130.

Torres, S. (1987). Hispanic-American battered women: Why consider cultural differences? *Response* 10(3): 20–21.

Torres, S. (1991). A comparison of wife abuse between two cultures: Perceptions, attitudes, nature, and extent. *Issues in Mental Health Nursing* 12: 113–131.

U.S. Bureau of the Census (1992). *Statistical abstract of the United States* (112 ed.). Washington, DC: U.S. Government Printing Office.

U.S. Bureau of the Census (1993). *Current population reports. Hispanic Americans today* (P23–183). Washington, DC: U.S. Government Printing Office.

West, C. M. (1998). Lifting the "political gag order": Breaking the silence around partner violence in ethnic minority families. In *Partner violence: A comprehensive review of 20 years of research*, eds., J. L. Jasinski and L. M. Williams, 184–209. Thousand Oaks, CA: Sage Publications.

Williams, O. J. and Becker, R. L. (1994). Domestic partner abuse treatment programs and cultural competence: The results of a national survey. *Violence and Victims* 9(3): 287–296.

Woodward, A. M., Dwinell, A. D., and Arons, B. S. (1992). Barriers to mental health care for Hispanic Americans: A literature review and discussion. *The Journal of Mental Health Administration* 19(3): 224–236.

Race, Crime, and Communities

The terms neighborhoods and communities are often used interchangeably to refer to places where we reside. Most of us live in communities and neighborhoods that are located either in urban, suburban, or rural areas. While some citizens live in communities where their homes are in close proximity to their jobs, religious institutions, and the schools their children attend, many Americans travel outside of their residential neighborhoods for these activities. Regardless of where we live, and where we go, safety is important. Most Americans are privileged to live in communities where there are very little crime, and they have a sense that their person and property is safe. Others live in a great deal of fear in communities characterized by hypersegregation and social disorganization. Although some citizens might travel through blighted urban areas, at the end of the day, many cities are deserted after the mass exodus of workers from their jobs to their homes in the suburbs. Those remaining are often trapped in communities where crime is accepted as a normal part of their community. Of course, it does not have to be like this. The community justice model emphasizes the importance of involving community residents in improving the quality of life and in preventing crime (Karp and Clear 2002).

Even though Americans are relatively safe and protected from crime, there is a great deal of fear about race and crime. This carries over to communities in several ways. First, many whites do not want to reside in black communities (and vice versa), and do not want blacks residing in their communities. Some whites do not want blacks in their communities at all. If they see blacks (or other minorities) they have an uneasiness about their safety and they fear victimization. It is hard to believe that governmental officials actually implemented policies and often turned their heads when practices such as redlining (the illegal practice of financial institutions to deny loans based on where an applicant lived) were clearly racist. Unfortunately, many inner city communities have more crime than most suburban communities. This has resulted in a "blame the victim" mentality that points to the criminality of African Americans and not to the conditions that foster hypersegregation and social disorganization that are related to crime.

The chapters in this section address several common themes related to race, crime, and communities including race and violent crime, the importance of communities, how structural and cultural contexts effect race and crime, racial profiling, hate crimes, and interracial violence. The first chapter by Sampson and Wilson utilizes the ecological approach, and the community as the unit of analysis, to lend new understanding to the controversial issue of race and crime. They argue that macrostructural factors such as deindustrialization and the exodus of middle- and upper-class black families have resulted in inner cities with high concentrations of poverty and family disruption. Residents of these socially disorganized communities are isolated and exposed to conditions that foster rather than prevent violence.

The next chapter by Meehan and Ponder examines the community context (ecological dimension) of racial profiling. The authors contend that for the police, race and place are closely related and tied to organization and societal contexts. In some racially segregated communities citizens expect the police to monitor community boundaries and protect community members from outsiders. Racial profiling is examined utilizing query data generated by Mobile Data Terminals (MDTs) located inside police vehicles, and stop data from a Roadway Observation Study. The authors conclude that racial profiling of African American drivers increases as these drivers travel into white neighborhoods. They discuss the implications of MDT technology for profiling and the limitations of relying on police recorded stops to study racial profiling.

The next chapter entitled, "Crime and Racial Profiling by U.S. Police: Is There an Empirical Basis?," by Taylor and Whitney, purports to lend support to an issue also presented in the previous chapter by Meehan and Ponder. One of the primary rationales for racial profiling is the belief that African Americans are more criminal. Therefore, many police officers believe that if more African Americans are stopped there will be more "hits" (Meehan and Ponder)—queries that will result in legal problems. Taylor and Whitney circuitously argue in favor of racial profiling by analyzing victimization data and hate crime statistics to support their argument that blacks are more criminal than whites or other groups. They describe interracial violence and hate crime violence for blacks and whites and conclude that blacks are more likely to be arrested and are more dangerous than whites. They argue further that there is more black on white crime than white on black crime. The treatment of Hispanics in crime statistics is also addressed in an effort to refine the nonHispanic white arrest rates for comparative purposes.

The final chapter in this section by Perry, also examines interracial violence and hate crimes. Although not a rejoinder to Taylor and Whitney, Perry views the issue of interracial violence differently. After analyzing Hate Crime Statistics for 1991–1998, Perry concludes that racial bias accounts for about one-third of all hate crimes, that African Americans are the most likely victims, and that whites are the usual suspects. Unlike Taylor and Whitney, Perry places ethnoviolence in the structural and cultural context of racism. She includes in her discussion the topics of racialized sexuality and the economics of race.

References

Karp, D. R. and Clear, T. 2002. *What is community justice?* Thousand Oaks, CA: Sage.

13

Toward a Theory of Race, Crime, and Urban Inequality

Robert J. Sampson and William Julius Wilson

Our purpose in this chapter is to address one of the central yet difficult issues facing criminology—race and violent crime. The centrality of the issue is seen on several fronts: the leading cause of death among young black males is homicide (Fingerhut and Kleinman 1990, 3292), and the lifetime risk of being murdered is as high as 1 in 21 for black males, compared with only 1 in 131 for white males (U.S. Department of Justice 1985). Although rates of violence have been higher for blacks than whites at least since the 1950s (Jencks 1991), record increases in homicide since the mid-1980s in cities such as New York, Chicago, and Philadelphia also appear racially selective (Hinds 1990; James 1991; Recktenwald and Morrison 1990). For example, while white rates remained stable, the rate of death from firearms among young black males more than doubled from 1984 to 1988 alone (Fingerhut et al. 1991). These differentials help explain recent estimates that a resident of rural Bangladesh has a greater chance of surviving to age 40 than does a black male in Harlem (McCord and Freeman 1990). Moreover, the so-called drug war and the resulting surge in prison populations in the past decade have taken their toll disproportionately on the minority community (Mauer 1990). Overall, the evidence is clear that African-Americans face dismal and worsening odds when it comes to crime in the streets and the risk of incarceration.

Despite these facts, the discussion of race and crime is mired in an unproductive mix of controversy and silence. At the same time that articles on age and gender abound, criminologists are loath to speak openly on race and crime for fear of being misunderstood or labeled racist. This situation is not unique, for until recently scholars of urban poverty also consciously avoided discussion of race and social dislocations in the inner city lest they be accused of blaming the victim (see W. J. Wilson 1987). And when the topic is broached, criminologists have reduced the race–crime debate to simplistic arguments about culture versus social structure. On the one side, structuralists argue for the primacy of "relative deprivation" to understand black crime (e.g., Blau and Blau 1982), even though the evidence on social class and crime is weak at best. On the other side, cultural theorists tend to focus on an indigenous culture of violence in black ghettos (e.g., Wolfgang and Ferracuti 1967), even though the evidence there is weak too.

Still others engage in subterfuge, denying race-related differentials in violence and focusing instead on police bias and the alleged invalidity of official crime statistics (e.g., Stark 1990). This in spite of evidence not only from death records but also from survey reports showing that blacks are disproportionately victimized by, and involved in, criminal violence (Hindelang 1976, 1978). Hence, much like the silence on race and inner-city social dislocations engendered by the vociferous attacks on the Moynihan Report in the 1960s, criminologists have, with few exceptions (e.g., Hawkins 1986; Hindelang 1978; Katz 1988), abdicated serious scholarly debate on race and crime.

In an attempt to break this stalemate we advance in this chapter a theoretical strategy that incorporates both structural and cultural arguments regarding race, crime, and inequality in American cities. In contrast to psychologically based relative deprivation theories and the subculture of violence, we view the race and crime linkage from contextual lenses that highlight the very different ecological contexts that blacks and whites reside in—regardless of individual characteristics. The basic thesis is that macrosocial patterns of residential inequality give rise to the social isolation and ecological concentration of the truly disadvantaged, which in turn leads to structural barriers and cultural adaptations that undermine social organization and hence the control of crime. This thesis is grounded in what is actually an old idea in criminology that has been overlooked in the race and crime debate—the importance of communities.

The Community Structure of Race and Crime

Unlike the dominant tradition in criminology that seeks to distinguish offenders from nonoffenders, the macrosocial or community level of explanation asks what it is about community structures and cultures that produce differential rates of crime (Bursik 1988; Byrne and Sampson 1986; Short 1985). As such, the goal of macrolevel research is not to explain individual involvement in criminal behavior but to isolate characteristics of communities, cities, or even societies that lead to high rates of criminality (Byrne and Sampson 1986; Short 1985). From this viewpoint the "ecological fallacy"—inferring individual-level relations based on aggregate data—is not at issue because the unit of explanation and analysis is the community.

The Chicago School research of Clifford Shaw and Henry McKay spearheaded the community-level approach of modern American studies of ecology and crime. In their classic work *Juvenile Delinquency and Urban Areas*, Shaw and McKay (1942) argued that three structural factors—low economic status, ethnic heterogeneity, and residential mobility—led to the disruption of local community social organization, which in turn accounted for variations in crime and delinquency rates (for more details see Kornhauser 1978).

Arguably the most significant aspect of Shaw and McKay's research, however, was their demonstration that high rates of delinquency persisted in certain areas over many years, regardless of population turnover. More than any other, this finding led them to reject individualistic explanations of delinquency and focus instead on the processes by which delinquent and criminal patterns of behavior were transmitted across generations in areas of social disorganization and weak social controls (1942; 1969, 320). This community-level orientation led them to an explicit contextual interpretation of correlations between race/ethnicity and delinquency rates. Their logic was set forth in a rejoinder to a critique in 1949 by Jonassen, who had argued that ethnicity had direct effects on delinquency. Shaw and McKay countered:

> The important fact about rates of delinquency for Negro boys is that they, too, vary by type of area. They are higher than the rates for white boys, but it cannot be said that they are higher than rates for white boys in comparable areas, since it is impossible to reproduce in white communities the circumstances under which Negro children live. Even if it were possible to parallel the low economic status and the inadequacy of institutions in the white community, it would not be possible to reproduce the effects of segregation and the barriers to upward mobility (1949, 614).

Shaw and McKay's insight almost a half century ago raises two interesting questions still relevant today. First, to what extent do black rates of crime vary by type of ecological area? Second, is it possible to reproduce in white communities the structural circumstances in which many blacks live?

The first question is crucial, for it signals that blacks are not a homogeneous group any more than whites are: Indeed, it is racial stereotyping that assigns to blacks a distinct or homogeneous character, allowing simplistic comparisons of black-white group differences in crime. As Shaw and McKay recognized, the key point is that there is heterogeneity among blacks in crime rates that correspond to community context. To the extent that the causes of black crime are not unique, its rate should thus vary with specific ecological conditions in the same way that the white crime rate does. As we shall now see, recent evidence weighs in Shaw and McKay's favor.

Are the Causes of Black Crime Unique?

Disentangling the contextual basis for race and crime requires racial disaggregation of both the crime rate and the explanatory variables of theoretical interest. This approach was used in recent research that examined racially disaggregated rates of homicide and robbery by juveniles and adults in over 150 U.S. cities in 1980 (Sampson 1987). Substantively, the theory explored the effects of black male joblessness and economic deprivation on violent crime as mediated by black family disruption. The results supported the main hypothesis and showed that the scarcity of employed black males relative to black females was directly related to the prevalence of families headed by women in black communities (W. J. Wilson 1987). In turn, black family disruption was substantially related to rates of black murder and robbery, especially by juveniles (see also Messner and Sampson 1991). These effects were independent of income, region, density, city size, and welfare benefits.

The finding that family disruption had stronger effects on juvenile violence than on adult violence, in conjunction with the inconsistent findings of previous research on individual-level delinquency and broken homes, supports the idea that the effects of family structure are related to macro-level patterns of social control and guardianship, especially for youth and their peers (Sampson and Groves 1989). Moreover, the results suggest why unemployment and economic deprivation have had weak or inconsistent direct effects on violence rates in past research—joblessness and poverty appear to exert much of their influence indirectly through family disruption.

Despite a tremendous difference in mean levels of family disruption. among black and white communities, the percentage of white families headed by a female also had a large positive effect on white juvenile and white adult violence. In fact, the predictors of white robbery were shown to be in large part identical in sign and magnitude to those for blacks. Therefore, the effect of black family disruption on black crime was independent of commonly cited alternative explanations (e.g., region, density, age composition) and could not be attributed to unique cultural factors within the black community given the similar effect of white family disruption on white crime.

To be clear, we are not dismissing the relevance of culture. As discussed more below, our argument is that if cultural influences exist, they vary systematically with structural features of the urban environment. How else can we make sense of the systematic variations *within* race—for example, if a uniform subculture of violence explains black crime, are we to assume that this subculture is three times as potent in, say, New York as in Chicago (where black homicide differs by a factor of three)? In San Francisco as in Baltimore (3:1 ratio)? These distinct variations exist even at the state level. For example, rates of black homicide in California are triple those in Maryland (Wilbanks 1986). Must whites then be part of the black subculture of violence in California, given that white homicide rates are also more than triple the rates for whites in Maryland? We think not. The sources of violent crime appear to be remarkably invariant across race and rooted instead in the structural differences among communities, cities, and states in economic and family organization.

The Ecological Concentration of Race and Social Dislocations

Having demonstrated the similarity of black-white variations by ecological context, we turn to the second logical question. To what extent are blacks as a group differentially exposed to criminogenic structural conditions? More than 40 years after Shaw and McKay's assessment of race and urban ecology, we still cannot say that blacks and whites share a similar environment—especially with regard to concentrated urban poverty. Consider the following. Although approximately 70 percent of all poor non-Hispanic whites lived in non-poverty areas in the ten largest U.S. central cities (as determined by the 1970 census) in 1980, only 16 percent of poor blacks did. Moreover, whereas less than 7 percent of poor whites lived in extreme poverty or ghetto areas, 38 percent of poor blacks lived in such areas (W. J. Wilson et al. 1988, 130). In the nation's largest city, New York, 70 percent of poor blacks live in poverty neighborhoods; by contrast, 70 percent of poor whites live in non-poverty neighborhoods (Sullivan 1989, 230). Potentially even more important, the majority of poor blacks live in communities characterized by high rates of family disruption. Poor whites, even those from "broken homes," live in areas of relative family stability (Sampson 1987; Sullivan 1989).

The combination of urban poverty and family disruption concentrated by race is particularly severe. As an example, we examined race-specific census data on the 171 largest cities in the United States as of 1980. To get some idea of concentrated social dislocations by race, we selected cities where the proportion of blacks living in poverty was equal to or less than the proportion of whites, *and* where the proportion of black families with children headed by a single parent was equal to or less than that for white families. Although we knew that the average national rate of family disruption and poverty among blacks was two to four times higher than among whites, the number of distinct ecological contexts in which blacks achieve equality to whites is striking. In not one city over 100,000 in the United States do blacks live in ecological equality with whites when it comes to these basic features of economic and family organization. Accordingly, racial differences in poverty and family disruption are so strong that the "worst" urban contexts in which whites reside are considerably better than the average context of black communities (Sampson 1987, 354).

Taken as a whole, these patterns underscore what W. J. Wilson (1987) has labeled "concentration effects," that is, the effects of living in a neighborhood that is overwhelmingly impoverished. These concentration effects, reflected in a range of outcomes from degree of labor force attachment to social deviance, are created by the constraints and opportunities that the residents of inner-city neighborhoods face in terms of access to jobs and job networks, involvement in quality schools, availability of marriageable partners, and exposure to conventional role models.

The social transformation of the inner city in recent decades has resulted in an increased concentration of the most disadvantaged segments of the urban black population—especially poor, female-headed families with children. Whereas one of every five poor blacks resided in ghetto or extreme poverty areas in 1970, by 1980 nearly two out of every five did so (W. J. Wilson et al. 1988, 131). This change has been fueled by several macrostructural forces. In particular, urban minorities have been vulnerable to structural economic changes related to the deindustrialization of central cities (e.g., the shift from goods-producing to service-producing industries; increasing polarization of the labor market into low-wage and high-wage sectors; and relocation of manufacturing out of the inner city). The exodus of middle-and upper-income black families from the inner city has also removed an important social buffer that could potentially deflect the full impact of prolonged joblessness and industrial transformation. This thesis is based on the assumption that the basic institutions of an area (churches, schools, stores, recreational facilities, etc.) are more likely to remain viable if the core of their support comes from more economically stable families in inner-city neighborhoods (W. J. Wilson 1987, 56). The social milieu of increasing stratification among blacks differs significantly from the environment that existed in inner cities in previous decades (see also Hagedorn 1988).

Black inner-city neighborhoods have also disproportionately suffered severe population and housing loss of the sort identified by Shaw and McKay (1942) as disrupting the social and institutional order. Skogan (1986, 206) has noted how urban renewal and forced migration contributed to the wholesale uprooting of many urban black communities, especially the extent to which freeway networks driven through the hearts of many cities in the 1950s destroyed viable, low-income communities. For example, in Atlanta one in six residents was dislocated by urban renewal; the great majority of those dislocated were poor blacks (Logan and Molotch 1987, 114). Nationwide, fully 20 percent of all central-city housing units occupied by blacks were lost in the period 1960–70 alone. As Logan and Molotch (1987, 114) observe, this displacement does not even include that brought about by more routine market forces (evictions, rent increases, commercial development).

Of course, no discussion of concentration effects is complete without recognizing the negative consequences of deliberate policy decisions to concentrate minorities and the poor in public housing. Opposition from organized community groups to the building of public housing in their neighborhoods, de facto federal policy to tolerate extensive segregation against blacks in urban housing markets, and the decision by local governments to neglect the rehabilitation of existing residential units (many of them single-family homes), have led to massive, segregated housing projects that have become ghettos for the minorities and disadvantaged (see also Sampson 1990). The cumulative result is that, even given the same objective socioeconomic status, blacks and whites face vastly different environments in which to live, work, and raise their children. As Bickford and Massey (1991, 1035) have argued, public housing is a federally funded, physically permanent institution for the isolation of black families by race and class and must therefore be considered an important structural constraint on ecological area of residence.

In short, the foregoing discussion suggests that macrostructural factors—both historic and contemporary—have combined to concentrate urban black poverty and family disruption in the inner city. These factors include but are not limited to racial segregation, structural economic transformation and black male joblessness, class-linked out-migration from the inner city, and housing discrimination. It is important to emphasize that when segregation and concentrated poverty represent structural constraints embodied in public policy and historical patterns of racial subjugation, notions that individual differences (or self-selection) explain community-level effects on violence are considerably weakened (see Sampson and Lauritsen 1994).

Implications

The consequences of these differential ecological distributions by race raise the substantively plausible hypothesis that correlations of race and crime may be systematically confounded with important differences in community contexts. As Testa has argued with respect to escape from poverty:

> Simple comparisons between poor whites and poor blacks would be confounded with the fact that poor whites reside in areas which are ecologically and economically very different from poor blacks. Any observed relationships involving race would reflect, to some unknown degree, the relatively superior ecological niche many poor whites occupy with respect to jobs, marriage opportunities, and exposure to conventional role models (quoted in W. J. Wilson 1987: 58–60).

Regardless of a black's individual-level family or economic situation, the average community of residence thus differs dramatically from that of a similarly situated white (Sampson 1987). For example, regardless of whether a black juvenile is raised in an intact or single-parent family, or a rich or poor home, he or she will not likely grow up in a community context similar to that of whites with regard to family structure and income. Reductionist interpretations of race and social class camouflage this key point.

In fact, a community conceptualization exposes the "individualistic fallacy"—the often-invoked assumption that individual-level causal relations necessarily generate individual-level correlations. Research conducted at the individual level rarely questions whether obtained results might be spurious and confounded with community-level processes. In the present case, it is commonplace to search for individual-level (e.g., constitutional) or group-level (e.g., social class) explanations for the link between race and violence. In our opinion these efforts have largely failed, and so we highlight contextual sources of the race-violence link among individuals. More specifically, we posit that the most important determinant of the relationship between race and crime is the differential distribution of blacks in communities characterized by (1) *structural social disorganization* and (2) *cultural social isolation*, both of which stem from the concentration of poverty, family disruption, and residential instability.

Before explicating the theoretical dimensions of social disorganization, we must also expose what may be termed the "materialist fallacy"—that economic (or materialist) causes necessarily produce economic motivations. Owing largely to Merton's (1938) famous dictum about social structure and anomie, criminologists have assumed that if economic structural factors (e.g., poverty) are causally relevant it must be through the motivation to commit acquisitive crimes. Indeed, "strain" theory was so named to capture the hypothesized pressure on members of the lower classes to commit crime in their pursuit of the American dream. But as is well known, strain or materialist theories have not fared well empirically (Kornhauser 1978). The image of the offender stealing to survive flourishes only as a straw man, knocked down most recently by Jack Katz, who argues that materialist theory is nothing more than "twentieth-century sentimentality about crime" (1988, 314). Assuming, however, that those who posit the relevance of economic structure for crime rely on motivational pressure as an explanatory concept, is itself a fallacy. The theory of social disorganization *does* see relevance in the ecological concentration of poverty, but not for the materialist reasons Katz (1988) presupposes. Rather, the conceptualization we now explicate rests on the fundamental properties of structural and cultural organization.

The Structure of Social (Dis)Organization

In their original formulation Shaw and McKay held that low economic status, ethnic heterogeneity, and residential mobility led to the disruption of community social organization, which in turn accounted for variations in crime and delinquency rates (1942; 1969). As recently extended by Kornhauser (1978), Bursik (1988), and Sampson and Groves (1989), the concept of social disorganization may be seen as the inability of a community structure to realize the common values of its residents and maintain effective social controls. The *structural* dimensions of community social disorganization refer to the prevalence and interdependence of social networks in a community—both informal (e.g., the density of acquaintanceship; intergenerational kinship ties; level of anonymity) and formal (e.g., organizational participation; institutional stability)—and in the span of collective supervision that the community directs toward local problems.

This social-disorganization approach is grounded in what Kasarda and Janowitz (1974, 329) call the "systemic" model, where the local community is viewed as a complex system of friendship and kinship networks, and formal and informal associational ties are rooted in family life and ongoing socialization processes (see also Sampson 1991). From this view social organization and social *dis*-organization are seen as different ends of the same continuum of systemic networks of community social control. As Bursik (1988) notes, when formulated in this way, social disorganization is clearly separable not only from the processes that may lead to it (e.g., poverty, residential mobility), but also from the degree of criminal behavior that may be a result. This conceptualization also goes beyond the traditional account of community as a strictly geographical or spatial phenomenon by focusing on the social and organizational networks of local residents (see Leighton 1988).

Evidence favoring social-disorganization theory is available with respect both to its structural antecedents and to mediating processes. In a recent paper, Sampson and Lauritsen (1994) reviewed in depth the empirical literature on individual, situational, and community-level sources of interpersonal violence (i.e., assault, homicide, robbery, and rape). This assessment revealed that community-level research conducted in the past twenty years has largely supported the original Shaw and McKay model in terms of the exogenous correlates of poverty, residential mobility, and heterogeneity. What appears to be especially salient is the *interaction* of poverty and mobility. As anticipated by Shaw and McKay (1942) and Kornhauser (1978), several studies indicate that the effect of poverty is most pronounced in neighborhoods of high residential instability (see Sampson and Lauritsen 1994).

In addition, recent research has established that crime rates are positively linked to community-level variations in urbanization (e.g., population and housing density), family disruption (e.g., percentage of single-parent households), opportunity structures for predatory crime (e.g., density of convenience stores), and rates of community change and population turnover (see also Bursik 1988; Byrne and Sampson 1986; Reiss 1986). As hypothesized by Sampson and Groves (1989), family disruption, urbanization, and the anonymity accompanying rapid population change all undercut the capacity of a community to exercise informal social control, especially of teenage peer groups in public spaces.

Land et al. (1990) have also shown the relevance of *resource deprivation, family dissolution*, and *urbanization* (density, population size) for explaining homicide rates across cities, metropolitan areas, and states from 1960 to 1980. In particular, their factor of resource deprivation/affluence included three income variables—median income, the percentage of families below the poverty line, and the Gini index of income inequality—in addition to the percentage of population that is black and the percentage of children not living with both parents. This coalescence of structural conditions with race supports the concept of concentration effects (W. J. Wilson 1987) and is consistent with Taylor and Covington's finding (1988) that increasing entrenchment of ghetto poverty was associated with large increases in violence. In these two studies the correlation among structural indices was not seen merely as a statistical nuisance (i.e., as multicolinearity), but as a predictable substantive outcome. Moreover, the Land et al. (1990) results support Wilson's argument that concentration effects grew more severe from 1970 to 1980 in large cities. Urban disadvantage thus appears to be increasing in ecological concentration.

It is much more difficult to study the intervening mechanisms of social disorganization directly, but at least two recent studies provide empirical support for the theory's structural dimensions. First, Taylor et al. (1984) examined variations in violent crime (e.g., mugging, assault, murder, rape) across sixty-three street blocks in Baltimore in 1978. Based on interviews with 687 household respondents, Taylor et al. (1984, 316) constructed block-level measures of the proportion of respondents who belonged to an organization to which coresidents also belonged, and the proportion of respondents who felt responsible for what happened in the area surrounding their home. Both of these dimensions of informal social control were significantly and negatively related to community-level variations in crime, exclusive of other ecological factors (1984, 320). These results support the social-disorganization hypothesis that levels of organizational participation and informal social control—especially of public activities by neighborhood youth—inhibit community-level rates of violence.

Second, Sampson and Groves's analysis of the British Crime Survey in 1982 and 1984 showed that the prevalence of unsupervised teenage peer groups in a community had the largest effects on rates of robbery and violence by strangers. The density of local friendship networks—measured by the proportion of residents with half or more of their friends living in the neighborhood—also had a significant negative effect on robbery rates. Further, the level of organizational participation by residents had significant inverse effects on both robbery and stranger violence (Sampson and Groves 1989, 789). These results suggest that communities characterized by sparse friendship networks, unsupervised teenage peer groups, and low organizational participation foster increased crime rates (see also Anderson 1990).

Variations in these structural dimensions of community social disorganization also transmitted in large part the effects of community socioeconomic status, residential mobility, ethnic heterogeneity, and family disruption in a theoretically consistent manner. For example, mobility had significant inverse effects on friendship networks, family disruption was the largest predictor of unsupervised peer groups, and socioeconomic status had a significant positive effect on organizational participation in 1982. When combined with the results of research on gang delinquency, which point to the salience of informal and formal community structures in controlling the formation of gangs (Short and Strodtbeck 1965; Sullivan 1989; Thrasher 1963), the empirical data suggest that the structural elements of social disorganization have relevance for explaining macrolevel variations in crime.

Further Modifications

To be sure, social-disorganization theory *as traditionally conceptualized* is hampered by a restricted view of community that fails to account for the larger political and structural forces shaping communities. As suggested earlier, many community characteristics hypothesized to underlie crime rates, such as residential instability, concentration of poor, female-headed families with children, multi-unit housing projects, and disrupted social networks, appear to stem directly from planned governmental policies at local, state, and federal levels. We thus depart from the natural market assumptions of the Chicago School ecologists by incorporating the political economy of place (Logan and Molotch 1987), along with macrostructural transformations and historical forces, into our conceptualization of community-level social organization.

Take, for example, municipal code enforcement and local governmental policies toward neighborhood deterioration. In *Making the Second Ghetto: Race and Housing in Chicago, 1940–1960*, Hirsch (1983) documents in great detail how lax enforcement of city housing codes played a major role in accelerating the deterioration of inner-city Chicago neighborhoods. More recently, Daley and Mieslin (1988) have argued that inadequate city policies on code enforcement and repair of city properties contributed to the systematic decline of New York City's housing stock, and consequently, entire neighborhoods. When considered with the practices of redlining and disinvestment by banks and "block-busting" by real estate agents (Skogan 1986), local policies toward code enforcement—that on the surface are far removed from crime—have in all likelihood contributed to crime through neighborhood deterioration, forced migration, and instability.

Decisions to withdraw city municipal services for public health and fire safety—presumably made with little if any thought to crime and violence—also appear to have been salient in the social disintegration of poor communities. As Wallace and Wallace (1990) argue based on an analysis of the "planned shrinkage" of New York City fire and health services in recent decades: "The consequences of withdrawing municipal services from poor neighborhoods, the resulting outbreaks of contagious urban decay and forced migration which shred essential social networks and cause social disintegration, have become a highly significant contributor to decline in public health among the poor" (1990, 427). The loss of social integration and networks from planned shrinkage of services may increase behavioral patterns of violence that may themselves become "convoluted with processes of urban decay likely to further disrupt social networks and cause further social disintegration" (1990, 427). This pattern of destabilizing feedback (see Skogan 1986) appears central to an understanding of the role of governmental policies in fostering the downward spiral of high crime areas. As Wacquant has recently argued, federal U.S. policy seems to favor "the institutional desertification of the urban core" (1991, 36).

Decisions by government to provide public housing paint a similar picture. Bursik (1989) has shown that the planned construction of new public housing projects in Chicago in the 1970s was associated with increased rates of population turnover, which in turn were related to increases in crime. More generally, we have already noted how the disruption of urban renewal contributed disproportionately to housing loss among poor blacks.

Boiled down to its essentials, then, our theoretical framework linking social-disorganization theory with research on urban poverty and political economy suggests that macrosocial forces (e.g., segregation, migration, housing discrimination, structural transformation of the economy) interact with local community-level factors (e.g., residential turnover, concentrated poverty, family disruption) to impede social organization. This is a distinctly sociological viewpoint, for it focuses attention on the proximate structural characteristics and mediating processes of community social organization that help explain crime, while also recognizing the larger historical, social, and political forces shaping local communities.

Social Isolation and Community Culture

Although social-disorganization theory is primarily structural in nature, it also focuses on how the ecological segregation of communities gives rise to what Kornhauser (1978, 75) terms *cultural* disorganization—the attenuation of societal cultural values. Poverty, heterogeneity, anonymity, mutual distrust, institutional instability, and other structural features of urban communities are hypothesized to impede communication and obstruct the quest for common values, thereby fostering cultural diversity with respect to nondelinquent values. For example, an important component of Shaw and McKay's theory was that disorganized communities spawned delinquent gangs with their own subcultures and norms perpetuated through cultural transmission.

Despite their relative infrequency, ethnographic studies generally support the notion that structurally disorganized communities are conducive to the emergence of cultural value systems and attitudes that seem to legitimate, or at least provide a basis of tolerance for, crime and deviance. For example, Suttles's (1968) account of the social order of a Chicago neighborhood characterized by poverty and heterogeneity supports Thrasher's (1963) emphasis on age, sex, ethnicity, and territory as markers for the ordered segmentation of slum culture. Suttles found that single-sex, age-graded primary groups of the same ethnicity and territory emerged in response to threats of conflict and community-wide disorder and mistrust. Although the community subcultures Suttles discovered were provincial, tentative, and incomplete (Kornhauser 1978, 18), they nonetheless undermined societal values against delinquency and violence. Similarly, Anderson's (1978) ethnography of a bar in Chicago's Southside black ghetto shows how primary values coexisted alongside residual values associated with deviant subcultures (e.g., hoodlums), such as "toughness," "getting big money," "going for bad," and "having fun" (1978, 129–30; 152–58). In Anderson's analysis, lower-class residents do not so much "stretch" mainstream values as "create their own particular standards of social conduct along variant lines open to them" (1978, 210). In this context the use of violence is not valued as a primary goal but is nonetheless expected and tolerated as a fact of life (1978, 134). Much like Rainwater (1970), Suttles (1968), and Horowitz (1987), Anderson suggests that in certain community contexts the wider cultural values are simply not relevant—they become "unviable."

Whether community subcultures are authentic or merely "shadow cultures" (Liebow 1967) cannot be resolved here (see also Kornhauser 1978). But that seems less important than acknowledging that community contexts seem to shape what can be termed *cognitive landscapes* or ecologically structured norms (e.g., normative ecologies) regarding appropriate standards and expectations of conduct. That is, in structurally disorganized slum communities it appears that a system of values emerges in which crime, disorder, and drug use are less than fervently condemned and hence expected as part of everyday life. These ecologically structured social perceptions and tolerances in turn appear to influence the probability of criminal outcomes and harmful deviant behavior (e.g., drug use by pregnant women). In this regard Kornhauser's attack on subcultural theories misses the point. By attempting to assess whether subcultural values are authentic in some deep, almost quasi-religious sense (1978, 1–20), she loses sight of the processes by which cognitive landscapes rooted in social ecology may influence everyday behavior. Indeed, the idea that dominant values become existentially irrelevant in certain community contexts is a powerful one, albeit one that has not had the research exploitation it deserves (cf. Katz 1988).

A renewed appreciation for the role of cultural adaptations is congruent with the notion of *social isolation*—defined as the lack of contact or of sustained interaction with individuals and institutions that represent mainstream society (W. J. Wilson 1987, 60). According to this line of reasoning, the social isolation fostered by the ecological concentration of urban poverty deprives residents not only of resources and conventional role models, but also of cultural learning from mainstream social networks that facilitate social and economic advancement in modern industrial society (W. J. Wilson 1991). Social isolation is specifically distinguished from the culture of poverty by virtue of its focus on adaptations to constraints and opportunities rather than internalization of norms.

As Ulf Hannerz noted in his seminal work *Soulside*, it is thus possible to recognize the importance of macrostructural constraints—that is, avoid the extreme notions of the culture of poverty or culture of violence, and yet see the "merits of a more subtle kind of cultural analysis" (1969, 182). One could hypothesize a difference, on the one hand, between a jobless family whose mobility is impeded by the macrostructural constraints in the economy and the larger society but nonetheless lives in an area with a relatively low rate of poverty, and on the other hand, a jobless family that lives in an inner-city ghetto neighborhood that is influenced not only by these same constraints but also by the behavior of other jobless families in the neighborhood (Hannerz 1969, 184; W. J. Wilson 1991). The latter influence is one of culture—the extent to which individuals follow their inclinations as they have been developed by learning or influence from other members of the community (Hannerz 1969).

Ghetto-specific practices such as an overt emphasis on sexuality and macho values, idleness, and public drinking are often denounced by those who reside in inner-city ghetto neighborhoods. But because such practices occur much more frequently there than in middle-class society, largely because of social organizational forces, the transmission of these modes of behavior by precept, as in role modeling, is more easily facilitated (Hannerz 1969). For example, youngsters are more likely to see violence as a way of life in inner-city ghetto neighborhoods. They are more likely to witness violent acts, to be taught to be violent by exhortation, and to have role models who do not adequately control their own violent impulses or restrain their own anger. Accordingly, given the availability of and easy access to firearms, knives, and other weapons, adolescent experiments with macho behavior often have deadly consequences (Prothrow-Stith 1991).

The concept of social isolation captures this process by implying that contact between groups of different class and/or racial backgrounds either is lacking or has become increasingly intermittent, and that the nature of this contact enhances effects of living in a highly concentrated poverty area. Unlike the concept of the culture of violence, then, social isolation does not mean that ghetto-specific practices become internalized, take on a life of their own, and therefore continue to influence behavior no matter what the contextual environment. Rather, it suggests that reducing structural inequality would not only decrease the frequency of these practices; it would also make their transmission by precept less efficient. So in this sense we advocate a renewed appreciation for the ecology of culture, but not the monolithic and hence noncontextual culture implied by the subculture of poverty and violence.

Discussion

Rejecting both the "individualistic" and "materialist" fallacies, we have attempted to delineate a theoretical strategy that incorporates both structural and cultural arguments regarding race, crime, and urban inequality in American cities. Drawing on insights from social-disorganization theory and recent research on urban poverty, we believe this strategy provides new ways of thinking about race and crime. First and foremost, our perspective views the link between race and crime through contextual lenses that highlight the very different ecological contexts in which blacks and whites reside—regardless of individual characteristics. Second, we emphasize that crime rates among blacks nonetheless vary by ecological characteristics, just as they do for whites. Taken together, these facts suggest a powerful role for community context in explaining race and crime.

Our community-level explanation also departs from conventional wisdom. Rather than attributing to acts of crime a purely economic motive springing from relative deprivation—an individual-level psychological concept—we focus on the mediating dimensions of community social organization to understand variations in crime across areas. Moreover, we acknowledge and try to specify the macrosocial forces that contribute to the social organization of local communities. Implicit in this attempt is the incorporation of the political economy of place and the role of urban inequality in generating racial differences in community structure. As Wacquant observes, American urban poverty is "preeminently a *racial poverty* … rooted in the *ghetto* as a historically specific social form and mechanism of racial domination" (1991, 36, emphasis in original). This intersection of race, place, and poverty goes to the heart of our theoretical concerns with societal and community organization.

Furthermore, we incorporate culture into our theory in the form of social isolation and ecological landscapes that shape perceptions and cultural patterns of learning. This culture is not seen as inevitably tied to race, but more to the varying structural contexts produced by residential and macroeconomic change, concentrated poverty, family instability, and intervening patterns of social disorganization. Perhaps controversially, then, we differ from the recent wave of structuralist research on the culture of violence (for a review see Sampson and Lauritsen 1994). In an interesting methodological sleight of hand, scholars have dismissed the relevance of culture based on the analysis of census data that provide no measures of culture whatsoever (see especially Blau and Blau 1982). We believe structural criminologists have too quickly dismissed the role of values, norms, and learning as they interact with concentrated poverty and social isolation. In our view, macrosocial patterns of residential inequality give rise to the social isolation and concentration of the truly disadvantaged, engendering cultural adaptations that undermine social organization.

Finally, our conceptualization suggests that the roots of urban violence among today's 15- to 21-year-old cohort may stem from childhood socialization that took place in the late 1970s and early 1980s. Consider that this cohort was born between 1970 and 1976 and spent its childhood in the context of a rapidly changing urban environment unlike that of any previous point in U.S. history. As documented in detail by W. J. Wilson (1987), the concentration of urban poverty and other social dislocations began increasing sharply in about 1970 and continued unabated through the decade and into the 1980s. As but one example, the proportion of black families headed by women increased by over 50 percent from 1970 to 1984 alone (W. J. Wilson 1987, 26). Large increases were also seen in the ecological concentration of ghetto poverty, racial segregation, population turnover, and joblessness. These social dislocations were, by comparison, relatively stable in earlier decades. Therefore, the logic of our theoretical model suggests that the profound changes in the urban structure of minority communities in the 1970s may hold the key to understanding recent increases in violence.

Conclusion

By recasting traditional race and poverty arguments in a contextual framework that incorporates both structural and cultural concepts, we seek to generate empirical and theoretical ideas that may guide further research. The unique value of a community-level perspective is that it leads away from a simple "kinds of people" analysis to a focus on how social characteristics of collectivities foster violence. On the basis of our theoretical framework, we conclude that community-level factors such as the *ecological concentration of ghetto poverty, racial segregation, residential mobility* and population turnover, *family disruption*, and the dimensions of local *social organization* (e.g., density of friendship/acquaintanceship, social resources, intergenerational links, control of street-corner peer groups, organizational participation) are fruitful areas of future inquiry, especially as they are affected by macrolevel public policies regarding housing, municipal services, and employment. In other words, our framework suggests the need to take a renewed look at social policies that focus on prevention. We do not need more after-the-fact (reactive) approaches that ignore the structural context of crime and the social organization of inner cities.

References

Anderson, E. (1978). *A place in the corner.* Chicago: University of Chicago Press.

Anderson, E. (1990). *Streetwise: Race, class and change in an urban community.* Chicago: University of Chicago Press.

Bickford, A., & Massey, D. (1991). Segregation in the second ghetto: racial and ethnic segregation in American public housing, 1977. *Social Forces, 69,* 1011–1036.

Blau, J. R., & Blau, P. M. (1982). The cost of inequality: Metropolitan structure and violent crime. *American Sociological Review, 47,* 114–129.

Bursik, R. J., Jr. (1988). Social disorganization and theories of crime and delinquency: Conflict and consensus. In S. Messner, M. Krohn, & A. Liska (Eds.), *Theoretical integration in the study of deviance and crime.* Albany, NY: State University of New York Press.

Byrne, J., & Sampson, R. J. (1986). Key issues in the social ecology of crime. In J. Byrne & R. J. Sampson (Eds.), *The social ecology of crime.* New York: Springer-Verlag.

Daley, S., & Mieslin, R. (1988). New York City, the landlord: A decade of housing decay. *New York Times,* February 8.

Fingerhut, L. A., & Kleinman, J. C. (1990). International and interstate comparisons if homicide among young males. *Journal of the American Medical Association, 263,* 3292–3295.

Fingerhut, L. A., Kleinman, J., Godfrey, E., & Rosenberg, H. (1991). Firearms mortality among children, youth, and young adults, 1–34 years if age, trends and current status: United states, 1979–88. *Monthly Vital Statistics Report, 39,* 11, 1–16.

Hagedorn, J. (1988). *People and folks: Gangs, crime and the underclass in a rustbelt city.* Chicago: Lake View Press.

Hannerz, U. (1969). *Soulside: Inquiries into ghetto culture and community.* New York: Columbia University Press.

Hawkins, D. (Ed.). (1986). *Homicide among Black Americans.* Lanham, MD: University Press of America.

Hindelang, M. J. (1976). *Criminal victimization in eight American cities.* Cambridge, MA: Ballinger.

Hindelang, M. J. (1978). Race and involvement in common law personal crimes. *American Sociological Review, 43,* 93–109.

Hinds, M. (1990). Number of killings soars in big cities across U.S. *New York Times,* July 18, 1.

Hirsch, A. (1983). *Making the second ghetto: Race and housing in Chicago, 1940–1960.* Chicago: University of Chicago Press.

Horowitz, R. (1987). Community tolerance of gang violence. *Social Problems, 34,* 437–450.

James, G. (1991). New York killings set record in 1990. *New York Times,* A14.

Jencks, C. (1991). Is violent crime increasing? *The American Prospect, Winter,* 98–109.

Jonassen, C. (1949). A reevaluation and critique of the logic and some methods of Shaw and McKay. *American Sociological Review, 14,* 608–614.

Kasarda, J., & Janowitz, M. (1974). Community attachment in mass society. *American Sociological Review, 39,* 328–339.

Katz, J. (1988). *Seductions of crime: The sensual and moral attractions of doing evil.* New York: Basic Books.

Kornhauser, R. (1978). *Social sources of delinquency.* Chicago: University of Chicago Press.

Land, K., McCall, P., & Cohen, L. (1990). Structural covariates of homicide rates: Are there any invariances across time and space? *American Journal of Sociology, 95,* 922–963.

Leighton, B. (1988). The community concept in criminology: Toward a social network approach. *Journal of Research in Crime and Delinquency, 25,* 351–374.

Liebow, E. (1967). *Tally's corner.* Boston: Little, Brown.

Logan, J., & Molotch, H. (1987). *Urban fortunes: The political economy of place.* Berkeley: University of California Press.

McCord, M., & Freeman, H. (1990). Excess mortality in Harlem. *New England Journal of Medicine, 322,* 173–175.

Mauer, M. (1990). *Young Black men and the criminal justice system: A growing national problem.* Washington, DC: The Sentencing Project.

Merton, R. (1938). Social structure and anomie. *American Sociological Review, 3,* 672–682.

Messner, S., & Sampson, R. (1991). The sex ratio, family disruption, and the rates of violent crime: The paradox of demographic structure. *Social Forces, 69,* 693–714.

Prothrow-Stith, D. (1991). *Deadly consequences.* New York: Harper Collins.

Rainwater, L. (1970). *Behind ghetto walls: Black families in a federal slum.* Chicago: Aldine.

Recktenwald, W., & Morrison, B. (1990). Guns, gangs, drugs make a deadly combination. *Chicago Tribune,* July 1, Section 2, 1.

Reiss, A. J., Jr. (1986). Why are communities important in understanding crime? In A. J. Reiss, Jr., & M. Tonry (Eds.), *Communities and crime.* Chicago: University of Chicago Press.

Sampson, R. J. (1987). Urban Black violence: The effect of male joblessness and family disruption. *American Journal of Sociology, 93*, 348–382.

Sampson, R. J. (1990). The impact of housing policies on community social disorganization and crime. *Bulletin of the New York Academy of Medicine, 66*, 526–533.

Sampson, R. J. (1991). Linking the micro and macrolevel dimensions of community social organization. *Social Forces, 70*, 43–64.

Sampson, R. J., & Groves, W. B. (1989). Community structure and crime: Testing social-disorganization theory. *American Journal of Sociology, 94*, 774–802.

Sampson, R. J., & Lauritsen, J. (1994). Violent victimization and offending: Individual, situational, and community-level risk factors. In A. J. Reiss, Jr., & J. Roth (Eds.), *Understanding and preventing violence: Social Influences, Vol. 3*, Committee on Law and Justice, National Research Council. Washington, DC: National Academy Press.

Shaw, C., & McKay, H. (1942). *Juvenile delinquency and urban areas.* Chicago: University of Chicago Press.

Shaw, C., & McKay, H. (1969). *Juvenile delinquency and urban areas* (rev. ed.). Chicago: University of Chicago Press.

Short, J. F., Jr. (1985). The level of explanation problem in criminology. In R. Meir (Ed.), *Theoretical methods in criminology.* Beverly Hills: Sage Publications.

Short, J. F., Jr., & Strodtbeck, F. L. (1965). *Group process and gang delinquency.* Chicago: University of Chicago Press.

Skogan, W. (1986). Fear of crime and neighborhood change. In A. J. Reiss, Jr., & M. Tonry. (Eds.), *Communities and crime.* Chicago: University of Chicago Press.

Stark, E. (1990). The myth of Black violence. *New York Times*, July 18, A21.

Sullivan, M. (1989). *Getting paid: Youth crime and work in the inner city.* Ithaca, NY: Cornell University Press.

Suttles, G. (1968). *The social order of the slum.* Chicago: University of Chicago Press.

Taylor, R., Gottfredson, S., & Brower, S. (1984). Black crime and fear: Defensible space, local social ties, and territorial functioning. *Journal of Research and Crime and Delinquency, 21*, 303–331.

Taylor, R., & Covington, J. (1988). Neighborhood changes in ecology and violence. *Criminology, 26*, 553–590.

Thrasher, F. (1963). *The gang: A study of 1,313 gangs in Chicago* (rev. ed.). Chicago: University of Chicago Press.

US Department of Justice. (1985). *The risk of violent crime.* Washington, DC: Government Printing Office.

Wacquant, L. (1991). *The specificity of ghetto poverty: A comparative analysis of race, class, and urban exclusion in Chicago's Black belt and the Parisian Red Belt.* Paper presented at the Chicago Urban Poverty and Family Life Conference, University of Chicago.

Wallace, R., & Wallace, D. (1990). *Origins of public health collapse in New York City: The dynamics of planned shrinkage, contagious urban decay and social disintegration.* Bulletin of the New York Academy of Medicine, 66, 391–434.

Wilbanks, W. (1986). Criminal homicide offenders in the U.S. In D. Hawkins (Ed.), *Homicide among Black Americans.* Lanham, MD: University Press of America.

Wilson, W. J. (1987). *The truly disadvantaged: The inner city, the underclass, and public policy.* Chicago: University of Chicago Press.

Wilson, W. J. (1991). Studying inner city social dislocations: The challenge of public agenda research. *American Sociological Review, 56*, 1–14.

Wilson, W. J., & Aponte, R., Kirschenman, J., & Wacquant, L. (1988). The ghetto underclass and the changing structure of American poverty. In F. Harris & R. Wilkins (Eds.), *Quiet riots: Race and poverty in the United States.* New York: Pantheon.

Wolfgang, M., & Ferracuti, F. (1967). *The subculture of violence.* London: Tavistock.

14

Race and Place

The Ecology of Racial Profiling African American Motorists

Albert J. Meehan and Michael C. Ponder

We propose an ecological dimension to racial profiling by comparing the distribution of drivers on the roadways with officers' proactive surveillance and stop behavior in a predominantly white suburban community bordering a predominantly African American community. African Americans are subject to significant racial profiling, as reflected in disproportionate surveillance and stopping by the police when driving through whiter areas. Officers' behavior is not explained by African Americans' criminality because the "hit rates" for African American drivers are lower in whiter areas. Profiling is sensitive to race and place and manifests itself organizationally, reflecting community patterns of residential segregation.

Minority motorists, particularly African Americans, have long complained that the police, especially in suburban areas, stop them for no legitimate reason but solely because they are black: a practice referred to as racial profiling. Furthermore, they have reported that during such stops, they have been subjected to detailed questioning and searches and given no explanation, or only a vague explanation, of why they were stopped. The phenomenon has achieved such notoriety among African Americans that it is called "driving while black" (Harris, 1997). A national survey of police-citizen contacts indicated that African American drivers *are* more likely than white drivers to be stopped, have their vehicles searched, and be ticketed by the police (U.S. Bureau of Justice Statistics 2001, 15–19).[1] Nationally, four out of ten African Americans report having been "profiled" by the police, and even a majority of white Americans believe that the problem is widespread (Gallup Organization, 1999).[2]

Research suggests that police behavior varies by ecological or neighborhood context (Klinger, 1997). That is, disparate treatment by the police may not be the product of race alone—the racial *and* class composition of a neighborhood influences police behavior and citizens' perceptions of that behavior (Alpert & Dunham, 1988; Smith, Graham, & Adams, 1991; Weitzer, 2000). Weitzer (1999) found that the class composition of a neighborhood can have a positive impact on police-citizen relations, for instance, between middle-class African Americans and the police in a middle-class African American neighborhood. Neighborhood racial composition can also have a negative effect when African American middle-class citizens are outside their neighborhood and in a predominantly white area (Weitzer, 2000). Williams and Murphy (1990) noted that modern police patrol had its origins in southern slave patrols, which legally sanctioned the routine monitoring of all blacks, not just slaves.[3] That current police practice may function in the same way is not lost on many African Americans (Feagin, 1991; Walker, 1997; Weitzer & Tuch, 1999), reinforcing the perception in the African American "collective consciousness" (DuBois, 1903/1989; Rawls, 2000) that the police serve an oppressive function.

In this chapter, we present data that reveal an ecological dimension to racial profiling. African Americans are subject to disproportionate *surveillance* and *stopping* by the police when they drive through white areas of the community under study. Furthermore, profiling significantly increases as African Americans move farther from stereotypically "black" communities and into wealthier, whiter areas: a phenomenon we call the *race-and-place* effect. Being an African American driver in a whiter area has more negative consequences than being an African American driver in a blacker area of the same community.

Race and Place

Police conceptions of place constitute a vital part of police work—orienting officers toward physical and social surroundings. As Gieryn (2000, 466–467) observed:

> Place is, at once, the building, streets, monuments and open spaces assembled at a certain geographic spot *and* actor's interpretations, representations and identifications. Both domains, the material and the interpretive, the physical and the semiotic, work autonomously and in a mutually dependent way.

Police officers develop and use an intricate knowledge of place: "area knowledge" (Bittner, 1970), "territorial knowledge" (Brown, 1981; Rubenstein, 1973), and knowledge of "hot spots" (Sherman, 1989). Conceptions of place and the people who occupy places are critically linked to the police assessment of moral character (Sacks, 1972). A patrol officer's sector assignment (place) is not simply a geographic designation; it is the territory over which the officer exerts jurisdictional claims about acceptable and unacceptable behavior (Manning, 1997; VanMaanen, 1974).

Police conceptions of place do not exist in a social vacuum. The police orient toward place in ways that are shared by the community, yet framed by their occupational and professional demands and experiences (Alpert & Dunham, 1988; Brown, 1981). That police attitudes reflect the community (Banton, 1964; Brown, 1981; Reiss, 1971) is not merely a truism, but a feature of the occupational character of police work. By its very nature, police work is divisive and reflects the prejudices of the community and individual officers (Bittner, 1970; Matson & Duncombe, 1992). It is those citizens they must satisfy. Writing about the differential treatment of minorities, Bittner (1970, 9–10) observed that in treating a poor African American differently from an affluent white person,

> the policeman [is not] merely expressing personal or institutional prejudice by according the two characters differential treatment. Public expectations insidiously instruct him to reckon with these "factors." . . . Indeed, the differential treatment they accord them reflects only the distribution of esteem, credit and desserts in society at large.

For the police, race is strongly tied to their conception of place. Officers know which communities are whiter, blacker (or more minority), or some combination of the two and where in their own community racial, ethnic, and class composition differ (Brown, 1981). Such "commonsense geography" is a resource for constructing the meaning of "place." Officers develop "typifications" of vehicles, persons, and spaces on the basis of their experience (Sacks, 1972; VanMaanen, 1978). These form the background expectancies against which typifications of race and place are produced in the lived, embodied experience of patrol work. They include assumptions and expectations about the criminality of African Americans.

Social psychological studies provide evidence that the police, when compared to nonpolice, apply a "cognitive schema" that views the ambiguous behaviors of African Americans as suspicious and potentially criminal (Ruby & Brigham, 1996; Vrij, 1993). Indeed, officers are acutely—though uncritically—aware that official statistics show that African Americans are disproportionately represented as offenders throughout the criminal justice process. The police often associate an imagined propensity toward criminality with blackness, and hence many police officers (Cleary, 2000) and citizens (Weitzer, 1999) rationalize the profiling of African Americans as "good police work" that is likely to be productive (e.g., produce arrests). The practice of racial profiling is inextricably tied not only to race, but to officers' conceptions of place, of what *should* typically occur in an area and *who belongs*, as well as *where they belong*.

The linkage of race and place does not evolve within police departments without tacit or explicit community support. For example, research on social threats has demonstrated that communities respond to the greater residential presence of minorities by increasing police expenditures (P. Jackson, 1989, 1992; Liska, 1992). Community support is also reflected in gatekeeping practices that have produced patterns of residential segregation of African Americans that are deeply entrenched throughout the United States (Alba & Logan, 1993; Darden & Kamel, 2000; Massey & Denton, 1993). Although patterns of residential segregation have changed over the past 30 years—statistics show that 1 in 3 African Americans now live in suburbs—American suburbs are still predominantly white (Baldassare, 1992; Thernstrom & Thernstrom, 1997). While community members, real estate agents, and lending institutions are important gatekeepers at strategic points in maintaining or changing a community's racial composition (Gotham, 1998; Massey & Denton, 1993; Pearce, 1979), the everyday monitoring of community boundaries is the responsibility of the police. Indeed, citizens expect the police to protect them from minority outsiders (Weitzer, 1999).[4]

Therefore, we consider racial profiling to be a practice embedded within the police organizational context and emphasize its relationship to the larger societal context from which discrimination, whether intentional or unintentional, emanates (Feagin & Eckberg, 1980). Profiling, viewed this way, is a form of *side-effect institutional discrimination* that "involves practices in one institutional or organizational arena that have an adverse impact because they are linked to intentionally discriminatory practices in another" (Feagin & Eckberg, 1980, 13). Specifically, profiling African Americans is linked to the larger context of the community under study, which, like many American communities, is residentially segregated and whose citizens fear African Americans and what "they" symbolize (i.e., danger, criminality, property devaluation). In short, we propose that underlying the police practice of racial profiling is the contested preservation of *place*.

Racial Profiling

Racial profiling is typically defined as the police use of race as the *sole* basis for initiating law enforcement activity (e.g., stopping, searching, and detaining a person) (Ramirez, McDevitt, and Farrell, 2000). By this definition, for an action to constitute racial profiling, the officer's motivation or intent to discriminate by race must be demonstrable. It is extremely difficult to prove racial profiling, particularly in cases involving traffic offenses, which the Supreme Court has ruled can be used as a pretext for investigating other offenses (Abramovsky & Edelstein, 2000; Harris, 1997). Ramirez et al. (2000,3) defined racial profiling more broadly as

> any police initiated action that relies on the race, ethnicity or national origin *rather than the behavior* of an individual *or information* that leads the police to a particular individual who has been identified as being, or having been, engaged in criminal activity." [italics added]

Justification for police action requires the presence of "suspicious" behavior or law enforcement information that leads the police reasonably to conclude that a specific person is engaged in or is about to engage in criminal behavior.

Obviously, racial profiling can occur in contexts other than driving—while walking, bicycling, taking a bus, boarding a plane, and moving through customs (Ahmed & Rezmovic, 2001; Cole, 1999; Russell, 1998). However, profiling in the context of driving—the focus of this research—has drawn the most public attention. The reasons for this focus reflect important structural changes in American society related to the automobile's impact on daily life, combined with law enforcement tactics and legal rulings that grew from the U.S. preoccupation with the war on drugs.

First, the growth of the automobile as the primary mode of transport, coupled with the decline of rail transport, led to an increase of vehicles on roadways and the broader ecological distribution of persons to places (Felson, 1998; Hawley, 1971; Kay, 1997). Thus, private vehicles, subject to constitutional protections of private property, have become the primary means of transporting persons and goods (legal and illegal) that are not always visible to the police.

Second, the shift of the economy—white-collar and light industrial work, shopping, and leisure venues—from urban to suburban locations (K. T. Jackson, 1985; Kowinski, 1985; Ward, 1994) has necessarily brought minorities into traditionally white areas, although not, for the most part, to reside there.

Third, in the 1980s, the war on drugs became the primary concern of law enforcement, and with it came important court decisions limiting constitutional protections against unreasonable search and seizure (Skolnick, 1994). The "result-oriented" focus of this "war" created an atmosphere in which stereotypes about African Americans' drug use and drug dealing contributed to disproportionate police enforcement of drug laws against African Americans (Allen-Bell, 1997; Currie, 1993), despite research that found that drug use among African Americans is proportionate to their number in the general population (Miller, 1996; the Sentencing Project, 1999).

The most significant case involving the automobile was the 1996 U.S. Supreme Court decision in *Whren vs. the United States* (hereafter *Whren*). The focus on racial profiling in traffic stops emerged in numerous legal analyses of *Whren*, most notably by Harris (1997). Although *Whren* affirmed that racially motivated stops are unconstitutional, it nonetheless permitted the police to use the pretext of a traffic violation to stop a vehicle and investigate (i.e., search and seize evidence) for possible criminal behavior without meeting the standard of reasonable suspicion or probable cause for that specific offense. Thus, a traffic violation is a legitimate pretext for the officer's "real" motivation (i.e., trying to find evidence of some crime; conducting a fishing expedition; or, worse, harassing the driver). Harris argued that discretionary enforcement and harassment using traffic offenses had disproportionately fallen upon minorities before *Whren* and that this disparity would increase after this decision. Thus, in 1997, the focus on "driving while black" received considerable national attention among legal and social science scholars, the mass media, and federal and state legislatures.[5]

While most researchers agree that racial profiling is a problem, the extent of profiling is essentially unknown and difficult to measure (Police Executive Research Forum, 2001; U.S. Bureau of Justice Statistics, 2001; U.S. General Accounting Office, GAO, 2000). As lawmakers debate methods of reducing racial profiling, researchers attempt to measure the extent of the practice and understand its complexities. Most research to date has compared proxy measures of roadway usage (e.g., residential racial composition) with the recorded stops of motorists using traffic tickets issued or stop events recorded in written patrol logs. This procedure seems logical because a statistical database can be derived from these police records (e.g., traffic tickets and patrol logs).

However, measuring the extent of stops, let alone *who* the police stop, on the basis of tickets and log entries is problematic because a significant portion of patrol activity—including traffic stops and field interrogations—is never recorded (Cooney, 1997; Meehan, 1986, 2000; U.S. Commission on Civil Rights, 2000; Weiss & Freels, 1996). This creates an important source of measurement error for research that depends on records created by officers.

More important, studies based on written records of stops, interrogations, or searches overlook a crucial step in the decision-making process: The police use their in-car computers to surveil the population of drivers.[6] Such surveillance may or may not result in a stop—either recorded or not recorded. However, the in-car computer leaves an electronic trail of officers' query behavior that *can* be used to examine this police activity. This heretofore unexamined, technologically based, aspect of profiling behavior provides a record of who the police surveil, when and where they surveil, and what information is requested.

In-car computers (called Mobile Data Terminals, or MDTs) give police officers immediate access to national (the FBI's National Crime Information Computer), state (Department of Motor Vehicles, state police), and local databases from their patrol cars. Depending on the type of query, information on the vehicle and the driver's (or passenger's) criminal and traffic-violation history are available to determine if a car is stolen or the person has outstanding arrest warrants. If a person is on probation or parole, the conditions are also provided (e.g., no driving except to and from work).

Prior to computers in patrol cars, officers were dependent upon radio communication with the dispatcher who conducted a record check for them. Research suggests this practice was also influenced by race, social class, and place considerations (Brown, 1981; Muir, 1977; Skolnick, 1994). However, the MDT enhances an officer's autonomy by eliminating the dispatcher in this record-checking process—making the officer's surveillance activity virtually invisible to coworkers, supervisors, and dispatchers (Meehan, 1998).[7] The use of computer technology in this capacity illustrates what Marx (1988, 2) called the *new surveillance*, whereby "the state's power to seek out violations, even without specific grounds for suspicion, has been enhanced." Marx observed that the new surveillance fosters more "proactive, diffuse, and open-ended investigations of individuals, groups, and property" (9–10). Computer technology figures prominently in this process (see also Gordon, 1990; Lyon, 1994). Marx also noted that "computers qualitatively alter the nature of surveillance—routinizing, broadening, and deepening it. Organizational memories are extended over time and across space" (208). The new surveillance is virtually invisible, hard to evade, and subject to database error,[8] or worse—manipulation (Marx, 1988).

Another limitation of research on profiling is that the organizational and ecological contexts studied have concentrated on specialized units, such as drug enforcement teams, or traffic units that are responsible for patrolling specific stretches of highway, rather than on patrol officers in suburban communities.[9] African Americans report that when they are driving through suburban communities or areas outside where they live, they are profiled because they are presumed to be "out of place" (Ramirez et al., 2000). This suggests an ecological distribution to the profiling experience *and* to profiling behavior by suburban police—a logical assumption given that police behavior varies by ecological and neighborhood context (Alpert & Dunham, 1988; Klinger, 1997).

To our knowledge, no study of racial profiling has focused on an *entire* suburban police department, which, in addition to traffic duties, engages in delivering a broad range of police services. If racial profiling is a significant and consistent experience of African Americans traveling in suburban areas, it should be broadly reflected in the practices of a whole department. Furthermore, if there is a place effect, it can be demonstrated only by comparing police behavior in different areas of the same community.

Description of the Data

Data were collected from a medium-sized suburban police department with over 100 sworn officers. This department has no minorities and few women. The city has over 75,000 residents, can be characterized as blue collar and predominantly white (98%), and has a mix of industrial and technological industries. It is among the larger cities in the state and shares one border with a city of predominately African American residents (more than 75%), hereafter called "Black City."[10] Thus, these two communities reflect the pattern of racially segregated communities that is found throughout the United States.

There is considerable variation as one travels through the community, and it is reflected in the pattern of patrol assignments. Patrol assignments use eight sector designations that we labeled A–H, which correspond to geographic boundaries that the officers are responsible for patrolling. Sectors are not all equal in size, but are configured according to levels of crime and citizens' calls for police service. Each of the border sectors (A–D), which constitute about one-third of the square mileage in this community, cover smaller areas because they are densely populated, generate the most calls for service, and have the highest rates of reported property and violent crimes.

The two middle sectors (E–F) and the farthest sectors (G–H) from the border are equal in size and cover one-third of the city each. They contain larger property lots with wealthier residents and businesses. These sectors have less population density, fewer calls for police service, and less reported violent and property crimes. Thus, officers in these sectors (E–F, G–H) have more space to patrol and fewer calls for service.

We used both qualitative and quantitative data in our analysis. In fact, our initial interest in the MDT as an investigative and surveillance tool had its origin in field observations and discussions of this practice with officers in this (and one other) department. Field research conducted over four years (1996–99) prior to the collection of the MDT and roadway data reported here, included extensive ride-alongs[11] with patrol officers (240 hours) and 25 interviews at all levels of the command staff (from the chief to sergeants) and specialized units (e.g., detective bureau, internal affairs). Knowledge of police practices in the field and how different records of these practices are constructed by officers and stored electronically informed the design of two different and unique quantitative data sets: an MDT query database and data from our Roadway Observation Study.

When officers conduct an MDT query, the information they request and receive is preserved electronically. Officers can receive information about a vehicle (e.g., year, make, and model; the name and address of the registered owner; and the status of the vehicle—stolen or unregistered) or of an individual (e.g., criminal career history, outstanding warrants, and probation/parole restrictions). In our data set, each officer's query was compared with subsequent queries the officer made to construct a query's event history. For example, when a plate query (the most common type of query) was processed and the name of the vehicle's owner was subsequently queried for a criminal career history, these queries were coded as continuations of the first query event. The MDT also records which officer is making the query, his or her patrol assignment (place), and time of query. Combining this query information with patrol officers' logs and police dispatchers' records, we could determine an outcome for each query. In sum, we could correlate information about the driver with the place of the query, time of day, officer's characteristics (i.e., age, years of experience on the force, and use of the computer) and outcome of the query.

Data on race are not available in the information the police receive from MDT queries.[12] Thus, we used a proxy measure, like the police do when they use knowledge of community composition to link race with place. Given distinct patterns of residential segregation in the metropolitan area we studied, we assigned a racial identity (African American, white, or other) for each driver, by inference, using the residence of the vehicle owner. A driver was coded as white if the vehicle owner lived in a community whose population was 97% or more white. A driver was coded as African American if the vehicle owner lived in a community whose population was 75% or more African American. The remaining drivers who did not meet either 97% white or < 75% African American residence thresholds were not included in the analysis of race.

This approach assumes (1) that the registered vehicle owner is usually driving the car and (2) that when owners lend their vehicles, they usually do so to family members or friends who reside in the same community and/or are most likely to be the same race. According to our definition, the MDT data indicated that 27% of the drivers (owners) were African American and 73% were white: That is, they lived in communities meeting our definitions of primarily white or primarily African American.

Although this approach leaves room for error, it is in the direction of *undercounting* African Americans. We tested this assumption by comparing race as assigned by residence (a variable we call "resrace") to the actual race observed in three related data sets. In the pilot test of the Roadway Observation protocol, we recorded the license plates, race, and gender of 526 randomly selected drivers. Then, using all African American drivers observed ($N = 76$) and a random sample of the 450 white drivers observed ($N = 78$), the police department conducted a computerized search of those plates similar to what officers do with an MDT. We also compared the residence recorded for all tickets ($N = 339$) and arrests ($N = 258$) during the two weeks of our study with the race recorded by the officer on tickets and arrest reports. In these data sets, the race of the driver or the ticketed or arrested person was known (or, at least, observed and recorded by someone), not merely inferred.

Table 14.1 compares race as observed to race as inferred (resrace) for each data set. It indicates that resrace reliably predicts race, as observed for both whites and African Americans, across each data set. For example, resrace predicts observed African American drivers 100% of the time in the Roadway Observation pilot data, 92% of the time in the ticket data, and 89% of the time in the arrest data. While there is error because some whites may live in a predominantly African American community and be incorrectly coded as African American and some African Americans may live in a predominantly white community and be incorrectly coded as white, the error is in the direction of undercounting African American drivers. The rate of true positives for African Americans is consistently greater than our assumption of 75%. If anything, African Americans are more likely to be incorrectly coded as white using resrace. Thus, the rate of profiling indicated in our analysis may actually be higher, but not lower, than reported. Furthermore, across each data set, race as assigned by residence is positively and highly correlated with race as observed. We interpret this finding as confirmation of the high degree of residential segregation in the study region. In general, we conclude that, for the purpose of measuring racial profiling of African American drivers, residence reliably serves as a proxy for race.

Table 14.1 Percentage of Drivers Predicted to Be African American and White Using Residence (Resrace) Who Are Actually African American and White Using Roadway Observations,[a] Ticket,[b] and Arrest Data[c]

	Resrace Predicts White			**Resrace Predicts African American**		
	Roadway	**82**	**($N = 59$)**	**Roadway**	**0**	**($N = 0$)**
White	Ticket	98	($N = 275$)	Ticket	8	($N = 5$)
	Arrest	93	($N = 173$)	Arrest	11	($N = 8$)
	True Positive: Percent of Time Resrace Predicts a White as a White Using Residence			False Positive: Percent of Time Resrace Predicts a White as an African American Using Residence		
	Roadway	**18**	**($N = 13$)**	**Roadway**	**100**	**($N = 47$)**
African American	Ticket	2	($N = 5$)	Ticket	92	($N = 54$)
	Arrest	7	($N = 14$)	Arrest	89	($N = 63$)
	False Positive: Percent of Time Resrace Predicts an African American as a White Using Residence			True Positive: Percent of Time Resrace Predicts an African American Using Residence		

[a] All African Americans and a random sample of whites observed in the Roadway Pilot Study ($n = 119$). Correlation of resrace and race =.80, $p < .001$ (two-tailed test).

[b] All tickets issued during the study period in which race was identified ($N = 339$). Correlation of resrace and race =.90, $p < .001$ (two-tailed test).

[c] All arrests during the study period in which race was identified ($N = 258$). Correlation of resrace and race =.80, $p < .001$ (two-tailed test).

The MDT query database consists of all 5,604 MDT queries made by 111 patrol officers working during seven days (24-hour periods) spanning two weeks in April 2000. In this article, we analyze the 3,716 queries that occurred in *proactive* time windows during which, we argue, officers have more discretion whether to query the MDT. That is, we eliminated all reactive events (and queries) in which the officer was either required, or was more likely, to run a plate or a name (e.g., traffic accidents; calls for service, such as "suspicious vehicles"; or when an arrest was made).[13] Hence, the analysis focuses on the queries that officers *chose* to initiate when they were not engaged in reactive work.

Furthermore, to analyze officers' "pure" surveillance activities, we excluded proactive queries associated with recorded police stops from the analysis. We assumed that when officers decided to record a stop, these proactive events were *more likely* to have been based on an observed violation or suspected illegal activity that could be later justified if necessary. From our perspective, the question is to what extent do police act solely on the basis of race? When officers ran plates and did not stop drivers, we assumed that they did not observe violations that *would have* warranted stops. Therefore, if significantly more queries *not* related to stops involved African Americans than whites, we had some confidence that those queries were influenced by race. If race is a factor in query behavior, we would also conclude that it is a factor in stops. By focusing on queries that did not result in stops, however, we controlled for possible legal justifications for actions. Thus, we examined the proactive surveillance behavior (measured by queries) of officers who, for the record, did not record stops.

Using an MDT query database offers two advantages. First, officers make more queries than stops, and query behavior is far more prevalent than recorded stops. For example, during these seven days, 3,716 proactive queries were made by 111 officers. By contrast, on the same days, only 333 recorded traffic stops were made by 73 of these officers.[14] Only 9% of the 3,716 proactive queries were related to recorded stops. Thus, there was more query behavior than recorded stops to analyze.

Second, focusing on query behavior uses the "informating" capacity of computers, which record police actions automatically, rather than relying on the memories or note-taking/reporting skills of officers, drivers, or other observers. Zuboff (1987, 9) noted that unlike earlier machine technologies that substituted for human labor, "the devices that automate by translating information into action also register data about those automated activities, thus generating new streams of information." Thus, the MDT not only automates the processing of queries, it records that processing as an *action of the user*. As such, MDT technology is a more consistent recorder of police surveillance behavior than are recorded stops.

Roadway Observation Data

On the same seven days during this two-week period, we conducted a rolling Roadway Observation Study in this community. Racial profiling can be assessed reliably only if one compares police data with the racial composition of drivers who are actually using the roadways.[15] Our decision to use a rolling method versus observation of intersections was based on several factors. First, officers typically do not remain in one location for an extended time during their shifts; they roam their sectors. Thus, our observation method mimics patrol practice. Second, given the size of the city, coverage of the 50 major intersections, or even sampling them, was impractical because of the lack of personnel. Third, a rolling observation car is less obtrusive to both the citizenry and the police.

Vehicles were sampled on the 15 major roads that run north to south and east to west in this community. A two-person team in an observation car was randomly assigned one of eight designated travel routes (called sorties) that they drove for three-hour time windows. Observation time windows spanned 24 hours a day excluding 3 a.m. to 6 a.m. because of the low traffic volume. Each sortie entailed citywide coverage, and the starting points were randomly chosen.

Using a stopwatch and a tape recorder, an observer recorded information on randomly selected passenger vehicles, vans, and trucks within one-to-three car lengths of the observation vehicle at 30-

second intervals. Vehicles already recorded, commercial vehicles, and buses were excluded. Each observation recorded the following data: sortie observation number, license plate, the driver's race (African American, not African American) and gender, the observation location (i.e., main street and cross streets), the target position (e.g., front left) and the time of the observation.

The observer and driver had 60 seconds to observe and record this information. Any information not obtained within 60 seconds was noted (e.g., unable to determine race). If no target vehicle was available at the 30-second interval, this observation was recorded as "no target vehicle available," and the time and location were noted.

A total of 35 sorties, spanning 105 hours, yielded 6,269 observations of this community's roadways. A target vehicle was available in 61% (n = 3,840) of the observations; thus no target vehicle was available, within one to three car lengths, in 39% (n = 2,429) of the observations. The race and gender composition of drivers using these roadways was calculated from these 3,840 observations and mapped according to time and location.

The analysis compared the rates at which African American and white drivers were the objects of officers' proactive MDT query behavior with the racial composition of drivers on the roadway during the same seven-day period. Our goal was to answer two questions: (1) Do police officers proactively surveil African American drivers at a rate that is significantly higher than their proportion of the actual population of drivers on the road? and (2) Does police behavior vary by place?

Race and Place Matter

To determine whether African Americans and whites are equally likely to have proactive MDT queries made about their vehicle or person, we compared the racial composition of the roadway to the racial composition of proactive police queries. Tables 14.2 and 14.3 show that the race and gender composition of the roadways varies by place and time. African American drivers tend to use roads

Table 14.2 Race and Gender of Drivers Observed by Place: Patrol Sector and Type of Street (Percentages; Numbers in Parentheses)

	African American			White		
	Male	Female	Total	Male	Female	Total
Grand Mean	7 (269)	6 (238)	13 (507)	53 (1,981)	34 (1,274)	87 (3,261)
Patrol Sector						
Borders Black City						
A	11 (22)	12 (25)	23 (47)	50 (100)	27 (55)	77 (155)
B	15 (31)	8 (18)	23 (49)	54 (114)	23 (50)	77 (164)
C	12 (56)	14 (64)	26 (100)	48 (216)	26 (118)	74 (334)
D	12 (49)	10 (41)	22 (90)	48 (198)	30 (123)	78 (321)
Middle sectors						
E	6 (38)	6 (38)	12 (76)	54 (353)	34 (224)	88 (577)
F	5 (29)	3 (19)	8 (48)	55 (349)	38 (241)	92 (590)
Farthest from Black City						
G	4 (27)	2 (15)	7 (42)	57 (346)	36 (221)	93 (567)
H	3 (17)	3 (18)	6 (35)	52 (305)	42 (242)	94 (547)
Type of Street						
Borders Black City	26 (65)	24 (59)	49 (124)	39 (97)	12 (30)	51 (127)
Interior streets	6 (193)	5 (148)	11 (341)	53 (1,623)	35 (1,070)	89 (2,693)
Farthest border—Black City	2 (3)	1 (2)	3 (5)	59 (92)	37 (92)	97 (150)

Source: Data from the Roadway Observation Study: Drivers (N = 3,840) observed during 35 sorties on 7 days over a 14-day period in April 2000.

Table 14.3 Race and Gender of Drivers Observed by Time: Police Shift and Type of Day (Percentages; Numbers in Parentheses)

	African American			White		
	Male	Female	Total	Male	Female	Total
Grand Mean	7 (269)	6 (238)	13 (507)	53 (1,981)	34 (1,274)	87 (3,261)
Police Shift						
Midnights						
(12–8 a.m.)	8 (41)	7 (37)	16 (78)	58 (288)	26 (131)	84 (419)
Days						
(8 a.m.–4 p.m.)	6 (91)	7 (111)	13 (202)	52 (799)	34 (525)	87 (1,324)
Afternoons						
(4 p.m.–12 a.m.)	8 (137)	5 (90)	13 (227)	51 (894)	36 (618)	87 (1,512)
Type of Day						
Weekdays	7 (184)	6 (167)	13 (351)	53 (1,456)	34 (951)	87 (2,407)
Weekends	8 (85)	7 (71)	16 (156)	52 (525)	32 (323)	84 (848)

Source: Data from the Road Observation Study: Drivers ($N = 3,840$) observed during 35 sorties on 7 days over a 14-day period in April 2000.

closer to the border of Black City and are slightly more likely to drive at night (12 a.m.–8 a.m.) and on weekends. The distribution of men (60%) and women (40%) on the roadway remains relatively stable across place and time except that women are less likely to drive after midnight.[16]

Overall, African Americans constitute 13% of the drivers on the roadways but only less than 3% of the residential population. Clearly, more African Americans are employed in or pass through this city than reside there. However, the distribution of African American drivers on these roadways is not a uniform 13% throughout the city.

Sectors (A–D), which border Black City, contain the largest percentage of African American drivers (an overall average of 24%). (See Table 14.4.) As one moves to the middle sectors (E–F) and sectors (G–H) farthest from Black City, there are significantly fewer African Americans driving these roads. Each border sector (A–D) includes the border road between this city and Black City: About half (49%) the drivers on this border road are African American, whereas the distribution of African Americans on other city border roads, which adjoin predominantly white communities, is much lower. As one compares this border road to the interior roads, one sees that the proportion of African American drivers drops precipitously to an average of 11% overall for interior roadways. The border-sector pattern is dramatically magnified when one compares the Black City border road with the road farthest from this border, where African American drivers constitute only 3% of the drivers.

Overall, a comparison of the roadway data to the MDT data indicates that the most significant finding is the race variable: 13% of the drivers were African American, whereas 27% of all proactive police queries were about African American drivers. Whites, who constituted 87% of the drivers, made up only 73% of the proactive police queries. In other words, if one assumes that the percentage of African American and white drivers on the road should be the same as the percentage of African American and white drivers queried, the ratios in Table 14.4 should be at or near 1:1. However, this is clearly not the case: African American drivers are twice as likely as are white drivers to be queried (2.1 versus 0.8).

This effect is not constant; it changes as African Americans move from one sector of the city to another. In general, African Americans who are traveling in three of the four sectors (A, B, and D) bordering Black City have query rates that are slightly, but significantly, higher than their number in the driver population. Only in Sector C is the ratio slightly less than 1:1. Given that these sectors

Table 14.4 Racial Composition of Drivers on the Roadways Compared to Proactive Mobile Data Terminal (MDT) Queries by Individual Patrol Sectors (Percentages; Numbers in Parentheses)

	African American			White		
	Drivers	Queries	D-Q Ratio[a]	Drivers	D-Q Queries	Ratio
Grand Mean	13 (507)	27 (572)	1:2.1***	87 (3,261)	73 (1,581)	1:0.8
Borders Black City						
Sector A	23 (47)	32 (115)	1:1.4***	77 (156)	68 (241)	1:0.9
Sector B	23 (49)	35 (57)	1:1.6**	77 (164)	64 (103)	1:0.8
Sector C	26 (120)	26 (99)	1:0.9	74 (335)	76 (311)	1:1.0
Sector D	22 (90)	25 (113)	1:1.1	78 (322)	75 (331)	1:1.0
Middle Sectors						
Sector E	12 (76)	28 (62)	1:2.4***	88 (579)	71 (154)	1:0.8
Sector F	8 (48)	26 (49)	1:3.3***	92 (590)	74 (141)	1:0.8
Farthest from Black City						
Sector G	7 (42)	16 (15)	1:2.0*	93 (568)	86 (95)	1:0.9
Sector H	6 (35)	22 (62)	1:3.8***	94 (547)	77 (205)	1:0.8

Source: Data on drivers based on data from the Roadway Observation Study for one week in April 2000 ($N = 3,840$). Data on police queries based on 3,716 proactive MDT queries made by the police during this same one-week period.

[A] D–Q ratio equals the percentage of police queries divided by the percentage of drivers and is expressed as a ratio.

*$p < .01$, **$p < .001$, ***$p < .0001$ (two-tailed tests).

include the largest percentage of African American drivers on the roadways, this finding requires an explanation.

Border streets between poorer–wealthier or blacker–whiter communities in police departments are often referred to as "demilitarized" or "combat" zones. Because there are more African American drivers in these sectors, one might predict a higher rate of African American queries. But here, the reverse is the case. In all four border sectors, the police operate with a concept of who belongs in this zone. African American drivers are not considered out of place and receive slightly more queries than do whites.

Within border sectors, Sector C stands out for the police. It generates the highest load of calls and official crime rates in the city. Census data show that it contains the greatest concentration of poor whites, with lower income and educational levels compared to other parts of the city. In short, in this sector, police officers deal with the city's *white criminal element.* While the differences are small, the lowest rates of African American queries and the highest rates of white queries are found here. Officers' concern in this area is not the presence of African Americans but, rather, the activity of whites. Thus, a different conception of race and place operates here: Poor whites in this place (Sector C) require more watching.

As African American drivers move from these border sectors to the farthest sectors of this white community, their chances of being the subject of a query increase dramatically. African Americans who travel in Sectors F and H, which are adjacent and contain the largest pockets of wealthier white neighborhoods, have query rates that are 325% and 383% greater than their number in the driver population. To put this finding in perspective, to achieve such high query rates with fewer African American drivers on these roadways, officers must be "hunting" for, or clearly noticing, African American drivers in these sectors. By comparison, whites have about the same chance of being the subject of a query *throughout* the whole city.

If surveillance behavior varies by ecological context, does stop behavior display a similar pattern? Table 14.5 compares the recorded stops of African American persons by place. The African American stop rates of officers in the nonborder sectors are three times greater than African American

Table 14.5 African American Drivers on the Roadways Compared to Recorded Stops of African Americans, by Patrol Sectors (Percentages; Numbers in Parentheses)

	African American Drivers	African American Stops	Driver–Stop Ratio[a]
Grand Mean	13 (507)	25 (62)	1:1.9***
Borders Black City			
Sectors A–D	24 (306)	26 (41)	1:1.1
Middle Sectors			
Sectors E–F	10 (124)	32 (12)	1:3.2**
Farthest from Black City			
Sectors G–H	6 (77)	18 (9)	1:3.0***

Source: Data on drivers based on data from the Roadway Observation Study for one week in April 2000 ($N = 3{,}840$). Data on recorded stops based on 3,716 proactive MDT queries made by the police during this same one-week period.

[a] The driver–stop ratio equals the percentage of stops of African Americans divided by the percentage of African American drivers and is expressed as a ratio.

* $p < .01$, ** $p < .001$, *** $p < .0001$ (two-tailed tests).

drivers on these roads. African American drivers are not only surveilled because they are out of place (i.e., in whiter areas), but are also more likely to be stopped in these areas. By contrast, border-sector officers stop African American drivers at rates equal to their number on those roadways. Thus, a race-and-place effect is also evident in the stop behavior of officers.

Race, Place, and the "Hit" Rate

A common defense of racial profiling is the claim that African Americans are more criminal and that when the police profile by race, they engage in "rational discrimination" (Taylor & Whitney, 1999). As evidence of African Americans' criminality, this position typically cites the disproportionate number of African Americans who are arrested and incarcerated and ignores studies of discriminatory decision making by criminal justice officials that makes disproportionate "outcomes" a self-fulfilling prophecy. Furthermore, research has consistently found that targeting African Americans and other minorities does not support arguments of greater criminality. For example, a review of police success rates in searches concluded that although the police tend to search minorities more often than whites, "Blacks and Latinos are no more likely than Whites to be in possession of narcotics or other contraband" (Ramirez et al., 2000, 10).

Whether or not it has any empirical basis, many officers *believe* that querying vehicles with African Americans produces more "hits"—that is, the computer returns information indicating legal problems with the vehicles or drivers. The expectation of productivity and its attendant rewards motivate officers' behavior (Mastrofski, Ritti, & Snipes, 1994). Although there is scant empirical research on the MDT as a tool for generating hits, police officers and administrators generally believe that the MDT makes officers more effective crime fighters (c.f., Meehan, 1998; Nunn, 1994). In the police department under study, officers receive no information about their overall hit-to-query ratio to assess or challenge such beliefs.[17] However, because our data links an officer's query to a hit, we could test the claim that querying African Americans is more productive.

We restricted our analysis to the first query an officer made on a license plate. Unlike the earlier analysis, which excluded recorded stops, we *included* recorded stops to represent fairly all possible hits associated with first queries. By examining the *first query* only, we tested the officer's initial hunch or suspicion about a vehicle—it is closest to testing the value of pure surveillance. Furthermore, we included first queries only of *license plates* because the occurrence of a name or operator license as a first query in these data indicates that the officer most likely stopped the person or vehicle, even if no record was made of this stop.[18]

Table 14.6. Hit Rate for Officers' First Queries of License Plates (N = 2,004) by Border and Nonborder Sectors

	Number of Plate Queries	Number of Hits	Hit Rate[a]
All Drivers (total)	2,004	144	7.2
Border sectors A–D	1,280	83	6.4
Nonborder sectors E–H	724	61	8.4
African American Drivers (total)	541	47	8.6
Borders sectors A–D	365	35	9.6
Nonborder sectors E–H	176	12	6.8
White Drivers (total)	1,463	97	6.6
Border sectors A–D	915	48	5.2
Nonborder sectors E–H	548	49	8.9

[a] The hit rate equals the number of hits divided by the number of plate queries.

Table 14.6 indicates a hit rate of 7.2% for first queries of license plates: 144 of the 2.004 plates queried returned a hit; expired plates comprised 78% ($N = 113$) of these hits. The plates of African American drivers are more likely to return a hit than are the plates of white drivers (86% versus 66%)—although this difference is not statistically significant.[19]

When we analyzed the hit rate by border and nonborder sectors, however, important differences emerged. Officers in border sectors have a higher hit rate for African Americans than do officers in nonborder sectors (9.6% versus 6.8%). The hit rate for whites in nonborder sectors is 8.9%, higher than the 6.8% hit rate for African Americans. Yet, officers in nonborder sectors query African American can plates at levels that are consistently higher than those of officers in border sectors. If the justification for racial profiling were African American criminality, then the lower hit rates for African Americans in nonborder areas should discourage disproportionate surveillance. The African American drivers in these whiter nonborder sectors, who are subject to the higher levels of query surveillance, are the *least* likely to have legal problems (i.e., hits). Thus, although African American hit rates are somewhat higher overall, an analysis by place shows that *queries are the highest for African Americans where hits are the lowest.* Therefore, considerations of place, not the productivity from hits, drives the African American query rate.

The Role of MDT Technology in Racial Profiling

The availability of MDT technology in police cars has the obvious consequence of increasing officers' proactive surveillance via various databases. However, officers' use of MDT varies widely: Some officers use it a lot, whereas others do so only occasionally. We found that the level of MDT use was a significant predictor of higher levels of racial profiling.

We assigned officers to three groups of high, medium, and low MDT users on the basis of their average number of proactive queries. Each group accounted for one-third of all proactive queries. Twelve officers, who averaged 64.5 queries, were categorized as high users and accounted for one-third (774) of all proactive queries. A second group of 23 officers, who averaged 33.3 queries, were labeled medium users. The remaining 76 officers, labeled low users, averaged 10.3 queries and accounted for the remaining 34% of all proactive queries.

Table 14.7 shows the racial distribution of queries by high, medium, and low MDT users. As MDT use increased, the proportion of African American queries also increased significantly. The 12 high-MDT users accounted for 43% ($n = 219$) of all proactive African American queries. The African American query rate of these 12 high-MDT users was 1.6 times greater than the African American query rate of the 75 low-MDT users and 1.4 times greater than the 23 medium-MDT users.

Table 14.7 Racial Distribution of Proactive Mobile Data Terminal (MDT) Queries of High-, Medium-, and Low-Level MDT Users (Percentages; Numbers in Parentheses)

Type of MDT User	African American Queries	White Queries
Low user	26 (134)	36 (527)
Medium user	31 (160)	35 (512)
High user	43 (219)	30 (443)
Total	100 (513)	100 (1,482)

Note: $X^2 = 30.334$, $df = 2$, $p < .0001$.

Table 14.8 shows the percentage of African American queries of high, medium, and low MDT users by place (border versus nonborder sectors). Once again, the race-and-place effect is demonstrated. Officers patrolling in whiter areas had a higher percentage of African American queries. But the effect is also related to officers' use of MDT. High-MDT users consistently and disproportionately surveilled African Americans in both the border (34%) *and* nonborder (37%) sectors. Their rate in the border sectors was 1.4 times greater than the number of African Americans driving in those sectors, and in the nonborder sectors, it was 4.6 times greater than the number of African Americans driving in those sectors. Thus, we found that this small group of high MDT-using officers had the highest levels of profiling, regardless of where they were located.

By contrast, low- and medium-MDT users queried African Americans in the border sectors at rates in proportion to the number of African Americans who were driving in these sectors. But consistent with the race-and-place effect already observed, in the nonborder sectors, the query rates of low- and medium-MDT users were disproportionate to the number of African Americans in the driving population but not at the same levels as those of the high MDT users.

Furthermore, the rates of *recorded* stops of African American by high MDT users were significantly *higher* than those of the low and medium-MDT users. Table 14.9 indicates that high-query officer recorded more stops for African Americans (36%) than did low query officers (19% of recorded stops). So, this small group of officers were not only surveilling but also stopping more African Americans.

Table 14.8 African American Drivers on the Roadways Compared to Proactive (MDT) Queries of African Americans by High-, Medium-, and Low-Level MDT Users, by Border and Nonborder Sectors (Percentages; Numbers in parentheses)

		Low-Level MDT Users		Medium-Level MDT Users		High-Level MDT Users	
	African American Drivers	African American Queries	African American D–Q Ratio[a]	African American Queries	African American D–Q Ratio	African American Queries	African American D–Q Ratio[a]
Borders Black City (Sectors A–D)	24 (306)	24 (70)	1:1.0	26 (131)	1:1.0	34 (142)	1:1.4***
Nonborder sectors (Sectors E–H)	8 (201)	18 (62)	1:2.2***	19 (25)	1:2.3*	37 (77)	1:4.6***
Grand mean	13 (507)	21 (132)	1:1.6***	24 (156)	1:1.8***	35 (219)	1:2.7***

Source: Data on drivers based on data from the Roadway Observation Study for one week in April 2000 ($N = 3,840$). Data on police queries based on 3,716 proactive MDT queries made by the police during this same one-week period.

[a] The D–Q ratio equals the percentage of police queries divided by the percentage of drivers and is expressed as a ratio.

* $p < .01$, ** $p < .001$, *** $p <. 0001$ (two-tailed tests).

Table 14.9 Racial Distribution of Recorded Stops of High-, Medium-, and Low-Level MDT Users (Percentages; Numbers in Parentheses)

	Recorded Stops		
Type of MDT User	**African American**	**White**	**Total**
Low user	19 (23)	81 (100)	100 (123)
Medium user	22 (19)	78 (66)	100 (85)
High user	36 (22)	64 (39)	100 (61)

Note: X^2 6.925, df = 2, $p < .01$.

Discussion

Our analysis suggests that racial profiling has an important ecological distribution. Profiling, as measured by the proactive surveillance of African American drivers, significantly increases as African Americans travel farther from "black" communities and into whiter neighborhoods. We also found that MDT technology may facilitate profiling. That is, while most officers queried African Americans at a higher rate than they did whites, a small group of high-MDT users, who represented only about 10% of the patrol force during the period under study, accounted for a significant proportion of all proactive queries of African Americans. These officers also had higher levels of recorded stops of African Americans.

Thus, on the one hand, we found a systemic effect of race-and-place profiling reflected in the behavior of most of the police officers and characterized by greater surveillance of African Americans in whiter areas. Conceptions of place reflect stereotypically negative and prejudicial judgments about the presence of African Americans in a community. Such perceptions are not unique to the police profession. They are typical of American society in which citizens, both white and African American, fear African Americans, whom they perceive as out of place or whose mere presence invokes the fear of victimization.

On the other hand, a small group of officers, characterized by greater levels of MDT use, produced higher levels of surveillance and stops of African American drivers. Although we suggest that the officers overall were responding to institutionalized conceptions of place, which mirror patterns of residential segregation, this group of high-MDT users seemed more responsive to the presence of African Americans regardless of place. The technology, in combination with conceptions of race and place, appears to heighten this effect.

Because racial profiling is a product of pervasive and institutionalized patterns of racial segregation in American society, it is not helpful to treat racial profiling as an effect of individual officers, consciously or unconsciously taking advantage of their occupational positions to act on their individual prejudices. That police officers are often socially conservative in attitude and lifestyle and express prejudices against minorities does not, ipso facto, translate into discrimination against minorities (Black & Reiss, 1967). In fact, findings in the police literature on discrimination have reinforced the classic gap between such prejudicial attitudes and behavior (Chen, 1996; Waddington, 1999).

Discussions of racial profiling must move beyond a consideration of the intent or motivation of police officers in individual cases, which dominates legal thinking, to an examination of its embeddedness as a practice within the organizational (institutional) context of the police and their relationship to the larger societal context from which discrimination, whether intentional or unintentional, emanates (Feagin & Eckberg, 1980). If racial profiling reflects society-wide patterns of segregation and a generalized attitude about who belongs where, focusing on police "attitudes" or "cultural sensitivity" will not solve the problem.

Sensitivity training for officers, for example, is designed to increase cultural awareness of the historical and contemporary plight of minorities in the United States, as well as to sensitize officers to their own covert (unintentional), and even overt (intentional) forms of prejudice and discrimination. However, our findings suggest that a focus on individual attitudes and behavior misses the underlying societal and occupational *structural* problems that produce racial profiling. Racial profiling in our study was a department-wide phenomenon—responsive to place. We propose that even the most racially sensitive officers engaged in it. And although a small group of officers engaged in a higher rate of profiling than the others, it is not clear that prejudicial attitudes or intentions motivated their behavior either. It seems that their behavior was closely linked to the available technology.

Set against the reality of a biased society, a police officer's recourse is an appeal to professional ideals. In response to accusations of racism and discrimination, officers often respond by stating that they are trained to be "color blind." This term is meant to convey conformity to the "professional" ideal of universality and the legal principle that the *behavior* of people—not *who* they are or *what* racial, ethnic, age, or social-class group they belong to—affects the officer's decision to stop; question; arrest; or, in our data, to surveil and query. It is important to note that many officers in the department we studied sincerely believed this to be true of their behavior such that efforts to persuade them otherwise through cultural awareness seminars gnawed at the core of their professional belief system and training.

However, as we noted earlier, the work of the police, by its very nature and consequences, precludes their ability to act in such a color-blind or nonprejudicial manner. Put more strongly, society expects police officers to preserve the boundaries of place. Add to this structural occupational characteristic and the contradiction it engenders, the following irony: Against the backdrop of police professionalism, various court rulings have supported the legal justification of using race as a proxy for criminality and dangerousness by creating legal precedents in which race can be used either as the *sole* consideration or in *combination* with other contextual factors to trigger "suspicion," thus justifying police intervention (Kennedy, 1997). So, color blindness need no longer be invoked as a defense or explanation by officers or be considered a professional ideal. Legal precedent already permits a full color pallet to enter into police decision making.

As court rulings make challenges to racial profiling more difficult, profiling has been added to the list of those police behaviors that occur when too much discretion is afforded the police (Ramirez et al., 2000). This approach aims to reduce discretion by requiring officers to record traffic-stop information in patrol logs (or some electronic equivalent). The documentation of stops, now legally mandated in three states with legislation pending in others, is considered a method of documenting the "profiling" problem and a means of curtailing highly discretionary stops. That is, if the police know they are accountable via record keeping, they will reduce such stops. Critics of this proposal suggest that monitoring police behavior may discourage police aggressiveness and lead to an increase in crime or have a negative impact on police morale (c.f. Cleary, 2000).

However, there is another predictable police response to consider: The police will continue to conduct such stops but not record them—thus constructing their records to reflect no bias. In our data, about 25% of the stops were not recorded. This is not to suggest a simple argument that the police will purposely distort reality through their record-keeping practices, although there are certainly occasions when they do. Rather, the argument has more to do with the fundamental nature of discretion and attempts to control it and some essential features of police record-keeping practices.

In his classic exposition on the police, Bittner (1970, 2) argued: "While the proposal that discretion should be reviewable is meritorious, the hope that its scope can be curtailed by the formulation of additional norms is misguided. Contrary to the belief of many jurists, new rules do not restrict discretion but merely shift its locus." Bittner called attention to a philosophical argument regarding the fundamental defeasibility of rules. Rules are open ended, and although they offer a "core of clarity," their application is surrounded by uncertainty and contingency. The task of fitting rules to cases *necessarily* entails discretion, that is, judging "the correctness of the fit."

Officers already manage a variety of realities through their patrol logs (Meehan, 1986), and recording requirements for traffic stops are no exception. It is well known that the police do not *call out* all traffic stops over the radio (a rule in most police organizations), let alone *record* all traffic stops they make (another organizational rule). Currently, patrol logs are primarily internal organizational documents whose uses are primarily actuarial (i.e., used to generate statistics on officers' activities, such as the number and type of calls for service answered and the number of traffic stops sans race and gender). Logs are used to generate internal measures of patrol activity, typically for supervisors, and are constructed with this internal organizational career in mind. They do not represent all activity, nor do they necessarily represent "real" activity because officers often construct their logs to conform to bureaucratic expectations (Meehan, 2000). As such, they have a fictive character.

The new traffic stop-reporting requirements will alter the organizational career and uses of patrol log records. Data on traffic stops will be produced with these projected external organizational careers in mind (i.e., courts assessing profiling behavior). Thus, the use of the logs will become primarily contractual, rather than actuarial (Garfinkel & Bittner, 1967; Meehan, 1986). This change, in turn, will affect how the records are constructed.

Arrest reports illustrate contractual uses of records. The organizational career of an arrest report is primarily external (i.e., sent to the court and available to the defense). It is contractual in that it documents police treatment of persons in accordance with specified bureaucratic and legal constraints. Once patrol logs have the projected external career and contractual use proposed by legislation, the police can fashion their logs to make racial differences invisible. That is, they may continue to stop African Americans, but will not record the stops unless formal actions (i.e., tickets or arrests) are taken. The "harassment" will continue, but no record of it will exist.[20]

Conclusion

The surveillance and stopping behavior of the police is sensitive to race and place. This effect manifests itself systemically and organizationally and reflects community patterns of residential segregation. Being African American and out of place is noticed. A small group of officers magnify this pattern through their use of MDT technology.

Although this was a case study of one police department's practices in a large, racially segregated suburban community, we think that this community and its police are not unlike many suburban communities bordering urban areas with a substantial population of African Americans. Torn by racial conflict in the 1960s, waves of whites fled the urban cities to the "safety" of the suburbs. Preservation of place shapes the thinking of suburban residents and officers alike. We suggest that our findings are generalizeable to suburban communities in which racial tension between urban and suburban communities exists and the police are responsive to these community concerns.

The current focus on stops and tickets, while important, overlooks an important data source that is less easy for officers to manipulate. We have developed an alternative methodology focusing on the proactive surveillance of patrol officers via MDT technology. These data provide insights into the surveillance and investigative activities of officers, moving the focus to earlier stages in the profiling process.

Finally, proposed remedies for racial profiling must take into account a more complete sociological understanding of the phenomenon. Sensitivity training that is targeted at the attitudes of individual officers and efforts to structure discretion will not have much impact on a practice that reflects the values of the community to which the police are accountable.

Acknowledgments

The authors acknowledge the generous assistance of the anonymous police department that provided research access. The Roadway Observation Study was supported by the Oakland University Research Committee and Vice-Provost Randy Hanson.

Notes

1. However, in this survey, 75% of African Americans who were stopped reported that the police had a legitimate reason for the stops, and 82% reported that the police behaved properly during the stops. By comparison, whites were more likely to report that the police had a legitimate reason to stop them (86%) and behaved properly (91%).
2. While whites acknowledge the existence of profiling, they do not necessarily oppose the practice, Weitzer (2000) found that white middle-class respondents justified the racially disparate treatment of African Americans as rational discrimination, citing stereotypical beliefs about the criminality, dangerousness, and disproportionate representation of African Americans in the criminal justice system.
3. Research on discriminatory behavior toward African Americans by the police has a long and somewhat controversial history (Mann, 1993; Weitzer, 1996). Some studies have suggested bias (e.g., Brown, 1981; Chambliss, 1994), while others have argued that the offender's demeanor, criminal history, and/or seriousness of the instant offense accounts for police decision making that produces higher rates of arrests for minorities (Black, 1971; Black & Reiss, 1967; c.f., Smith & Visher, 1981; Smith, Visher, & Davidson, 1984).
4. Community support for police protecting community boundaries can be quite explicit. A *Detroit Free Press* analysis of ticketing practices in a predominantly white suburb found that African American drivers from Detroit were disproportionately ticketed. At the next city council meeting, " 'keep it up' was the phrase enthusiastically announced . . . by residents and council members alike . . . [in] phone calls to city leaders, the police department and the Free Press, about 100 Harper Woods residents have defended the department's ticketing practices, outweighing critics more than 5–1" ("Harper Woods Supports Its Cops," 2000, 7).
5. Additional support for 1997 as a watershed year is reflected in our Lexus-Nexus database search using the keywords "racial profiling" and "driving while black." Prior to 1994, these topics are not mentioned in law reviews, wire services, newspaper articles, and radio and television broadcasts. Between 1994 and 1996, a total of 15 articles or stories were about these topics. From 1997 to 2000, the total number of articles or stories increased exponentially each year—from 45 in 1997 to 14,804 in 2000. Also, federal legislation requiring mandatory reporting of data on traffic stops was also introduced in 1997.
6. The police do not need any particular reason or level of suspicion to conduct a query. For example, Illinois courts have upheld the random running of license plates, ruling that a plate is a public record, not a private one. Current proposals argue that a higher standard, such as probable cause, should be required to prevent unwarranted police access to information on drivers (see Amirante, 1997; Cedres, 1997; Prime, 1996).
7. The fact that these computer records exist and can be analyzed may appear to contradict the claim that computer usage increases an officer's autonomy and invisibility. While the computer trail of officers' computer *queries* to various databases does exist, to date, it has not been systematically used by the police department under study or other departments routinely to monitor officers' behavior. It is common practice for departments to report that officers' *car-to car* computer communications—not officers' *queries* of databases—are routinely monitored by supervisors, particularly in the aftermath of the Christopher Commission's investigation of the Rodney King beating. Indeed, officers orient to this possible monitoring even though, in the department under study, supervisory review is infrequent and undertaken only when some "problem" has arisen with a specific officer (e.g., a female dispatcher complains that a male officer is "hitting" on her). Query behavior is not monitored, partly because one would need to create a merged database from various records (MDT queries, patrol logs, and dispatcher records) and have an accurate estimate of roadway composition like we undertook to analyze proactive surveillance behavior. Generally, departments have not constructed such databases, nor have they conceived of the need to do so.
8. Database error is particularly serious, since evidence suggests that the "benefit of the doubt" in questionable circumstances is usually given to the computer. Gordon (1990, 73) reported that fewer than half the 50 states require updating criminal history files to include dismissals and acquittals and that only 13 states require random audits to ensure accuracy. Yet, all the states require the entry of arrests. Given that African Americans are more likely to be released after arrest without prosecution (Petersillia, 1983), database errors specifically disadvantage them. Zonderman (1990, 164–165) also found that about 11% of arrest warrants in the FBI database had either been cleared, were inaccurate, or invalid and that 7,000 reports of stolen cars and license plates were errors.
9. For example, studies of the New Jersey State Police and the sheriffs' departments in Florida and Maryland have focused on agencies whose primary function is traffic enforcement on major highways or roads that are considered drug-transport corridors (Harris, 1997; Verniero, 1999). Some research has examined precinet-level behavior in cities like Philadelphia (GAO, 2000) and New York City (U.S. Commission on Civil Rights, 2000). But this research cannot address the suburban racial profiling experience of being out of place.
10. We selectively altered aspects of the community and the description of the department to preserve anonymity.
11. During ride-alongs, a semistructured interview about current information technology was used and observations were made of how the officers used information technology (e.g., in-car computers and cameras) during their patrols. Field notes were written upon leaving the setting.
12. Race is not even included for a query about an operator's license. Only criminal career history (CCH) queries provide information on race, but this information is usually incomplete. In our data, only 154 (4%) of the CCH queries identified the person's race. Furthermore, most persons do not have criminal records.
13. For this seven-day period, officers made 5,604 queries, of which 3,963 were first queries. Of the 3,963 first queries, 2,673 (67%) were proactive. These 2,673 proactive queries resulted in an additional 1,043 follow-up queries that originated from the first proactive queries. Thus, the total number of proactive queries was 3,716. Our analysis focuses on the 2,673 first proactive queries. The data from the 1,043 proactive follow-up queries were included as a part of the record of the first queries.

14. We used officers' logs and dispatchers' records to identify all *recorded* traffic stops and coded outcomes reported on the logs (i.e., warn, issue ticket, arrest). These data do not reflect the *actual* number of traffic stops because officers do not record all stops in their logs or call them into the dispatcher who records stops in the dispatch database.
15. In addition to roadway composition, some have argued that comparable rates of violators and the seriousness of violations are necessary to prove profiling (U.S. Bureau of Justice Statistics, 2001, 15). However, no satisfactory method of ascertaining this rate has been agreed upon (GAO, 2000, 2).
16. Discussions of racial profiling generally gloss over the issue of gender. Studies of racial discrimination typically focus on the overrepresentation of African American men in the system. However, recent studies have suggested that the war on drugs has had a disproportionate impact on African American women (Sentencing Project, 1999). In our data, women made up 40% of the drivers on the road, and their distribution was uniform throughout the city. White women used interior roads and roads farthest from the Black City border, whereas African American women use roads closer to the Black City border. Our analysis indicates that where gender differences occur, it is African American women who are the target of MDT queries.
17. While officers extol the value of the MDT's crime-fighting capacity, the hit-rate question strains their belief system. Officers readily cite examples of the computer identifying a stolen vehicle or person with a warrant leading to an arrest. However, some officers, particularly supervisory personnel, complain that many MDT arrests for minor traffic violations (e.g., driving with a suspended license) pad an officer's productivity statistics, increase overtime opportunities, and that officers waste time going after these "easy" arrests and miss opportunities to catch serious criminals. Many older officers complain that the computer deskills younger officers in this regard (Meehan, 1998). Nonetheless, officers maintain the belief that the computer enhances their detection abilities.
18. This analysis assumes the officer initiated the query at the time as opposed to using information collected at some previous point in time. Nonetheless, it is possible to estimate the number of unrecorded stops. In our data, there were 333 recorded stops. Among the first queries, there were 6 operator-license and 91 name queries. These 97 queries suggest that the number of unrecorded stops was 97—bringing the total number of stops to 430. So, 23% or, about 1 in 4 stops, were not recorded by officers. This is a conservative estimate; it does not include officers who made a stop and did not use the MDT. Also, officers told us that they estimate that between 30% and 50% of all stops are not recorded.
19. The possible hits an officer can receive from a plate query include (1) the plate is expired because the registration is not updated; (2) there is no title information recorded for the vehicle; (3) the license plate is not valid; (4) the plate is reported stolen; (5) the vehicle assigned to this plate is reported stolen; (6) the registered owner of this vehicle has a warrant for his or her arrest outstanding; (7) there is no record of this plate, indicating that the plate has not been registered for five or more years; and (8) the vehicle attached to this plate has been impounded or abandoned.
20. Such record keeping was part of a consent agreement with the Maryland State Police (Harris, 1997). When the data subsequently reported to the court showed continued patterns of discrimination, litigation was reopened. Clearly, then, such a record-keeping requirement is not effective for preventing profiling. The police may have thought that despite having to log these data, there would be no repercussions (i.e., supervisors would not monitor it, and the court would not revisit the issue). However, once the police *do* orient to the external career of any record, they are more careful in crafting that record. The legal and political implications of traffic-stop reporting are not lost on officers.

References

Abramovsky, A. and Edelstein, J. I. 2000. Pretext stops and racial profiling after *Whren v. United States*. *Albany Law Review* 63: 725–748.

Ahmed, W. and Rezmovie, E. 2001. Racial profiling: A policy issue in need of better answers. *Chance* 14: 40–41.

Alba, R. D. and Logan, J. R. 1993. Minority proximity to whites in suburbs: An individual-level analysis of segregation. *American Journal of Sociology* 98: 1388–1427.

Allen-Bell. A. 1997. The birth of the crime: Driving while black (DWB). Southern University Law Review 25: 195–225.

Alpert G. P. and Dunham, R. G. 1988. *Policing multi-ethnic neighborhoods*: Westport, CT: Greenwood Press.

Amirante, S. L. 1997. People v. Barnes—George Orwell's *1984* revisited: Unbridled and impermissible police use of computer power in the modern age. *Loyola University Chicago Law Journal* 28: 667–684.

Baldassare, M. 1992. Suburban communities. *Annual Review of Sociology* 18: 475–494.

Banton, M. 1964. *The policeman and the community*. New York: Basic Books.

Bittner, E. 1970. *The functions of the police in modern society*. Chevy Chase, MD: National Institute of Mental Health.

Black, D. 1971. The social organization of arrest. *Stanford Law Review* 23: 63–77.

Black, D. and Reiss, A. J. 1967. Patterns of behavior in police and citizen transactions. In *Studies in crime and law enforcement in major metropolitan areas*. Washington, DC: U.S. Government Printing Office.

Brown, M. K. 1981. *Working the street: Police discretion and the dilemmas of reform*. New York: Russell Sage Foundation.

Cedres, D. 1997. Mobile data terminals and random license plate checks: The need for uniform guidelines and reasonable suspicion requirement. *Rutgers Computer and Technology Law Journal* 23: 391–417.

Chambliss, W. 1994. Policing the ghetto underclass: The politics of law and law enforcement. *Social Problems* 41: 177–195.

Chen, J. 1996. Changing police culture. *British Journal of Criminology* 36: 109–134.

Cleary, J. 2000. *Racial profiling studies in law enforcement: Issues and methodology*. St. Paul: Minnesota House of Representatives Research Department.

Cole, D. 1999. *No equal justice*. New York: New York Press.

Cooney, M. 1997. Hunting among police and predators: The enforcement of traffic law. *Studies in Law, Politics and Society* 16: 165–188.

Currie, E. 1993. *Reckoning: Drugs, the cities and the American future.* New York: Hill & Wang.
Darden, J. T. and Kamel, S. M. 2000. Black residential segregation in the city and suburbs of detroit: Does socioeconomic status matter? *Journal of Urban Affairs* 22: 1–13.
DuBois, W. E. B. 1989. *The souls of black folk.* New York: Penguin. (Original work published 1903)
Feagin, J. R. 1991. The continuing significance of race: Antiblack discrimination in public places. *American Sociological Review* 56: 101–116.
Feagin, J. R. and Eckberg, D. (1980). Discrimination: Motivation, action, effects, and context. *Annual Review of Sociology* 6: 1–20.
Felson, M. 1998. *Crime and everyday life* (2nd ed.). Thousand Oaks, CA: Pine Forge Press.
The Gallup Organization. 1999, December 9. *Racial profiling is seen as widespread, particularly among young black men.* Princeton, NJ: Author.
Garfinkel, H. and Bittner, E. 1967. Some good organizational reasons for bad clinic records. In *Studies in ethnomethodology,* ed. H. Garfinkel, 186–207. Englewood Cliffs, NJ: Prentice Hall.
Gieryn, T. F. 2000. A space for place in sociology. *Annual Review of Sociology* 26: 463–495.
Gordon, D. 1990. *The justice juggernaut: Fighting street crime, controlling citizens.* New Brunswick, NJ: Rutgers University Press.
Gotham, K. F. 1998. Race, mortgage leading and loan rejections in a U.S. city. *Sociological Focus* 31: 391–405.
Harper Woods supports its cops. 2000, June 6. *Detroit Free Press,* 7.
Harris, D. 1997. "Driving while black" and all other traffic offenses: The Supreme Court and pretextual traffic stops. *Journal of Criminal Law and Criminology* 87: 544–582.
Hawley, A. H. 1971. *Urban society: An ecological approach.* New York: Ronald Press.
Jackson, K. T. 1985. *Crabgrass frontier: The suburbanization of the United States.* New York Oxford University Press.
Jackson, P. 1989. *Minority group threat, crime and policing: Social context and social control.* New York: Praeger.
——— 1992. Minority group threat, social context and policing. In *Social threat and social control ed.,* A. Liska,. 89–101. Albany: State University of New York Press.
Kay, J. H. 1997. *Asphalt nation: How the automobile took over America and how we can take it back.* New York: Crown.
Kennedy, R. 1997. *Race, crime, and the law.* New York: Vintage Books.
Klinger, D. A. 1997. Negotiating order in patrol work: An ecological theory of police response to deviance. *Criminology* 35:277–306.
Kowinski, W. S. 1985. *The malling of America.* New York: William Morrow.
Liska, A. ed. 1992. *Social threat and social control.* Albany: State University of New York Press.
Lyon, D. 1994. *The Electronic eye: The rise of surveillance society.* Minneapolis: University of Minnesota Press.
Mann, C. R. 1993. *Unequal justice: A question of color.* Bloomington: Indiana University Press.
Manning, P. K. 1997. *Police work: The social organization of policing* (2nd ed.). Prospect Heights, IL: Waveland Press.
Marx, G. T. 1988. *Undercover: Police surveillance in America.* Berkeley: University of California Press.
Massey, D. S., and Denton, N. A. 1993. *American apartheid: Segregation and the making of the underclass.* Cambridge, MA: Harvard University Press.
Mastrofski, S. D., Ritti, R. R., and Snipes, J. B. 1994. Expectancy theory and police productivity in DUI enforcement. *Law and Society Review* 28: 113–147.
Matson, A. O., and Duncombe, S. R. 1992. Public space, private place: The contested terrain of Tompkins Square Park. *Berkeley Journal of Sociology* 37: 129–161.
Meehan, A. J. 1986. Recordkeeping practices in the policing of juveniles. *Urban Life* 15: 70–102.
Meehan, A. J. 1998. The impact of Mobile Data Terminal (MDT) information technology on communication and recordkeeping in patrol work. *Qualitative Sociology* 21: 225–254.
Meehan, A. J. 2000. The organizational career of gang statistics: The politics of policing gangs. *Sociological Quarterly* 41: 337–370.
Miller, J. G. 1996. *Search and destroy: African-American males in the criminal justice system.* New York: Cambridge University Press.
Muir, W. 1977. *The police: Streetcorner politicians.* Chicago: University of Chicago Press.
Nunn, S. 1994. How capital technologies affect municipal service outcomes: The case of police Mobile Digital Terminals and stolen vehicle recoveries. *Journal of Policy Analysis and Management* 13: 539–559.
Pearce, D. 1979. Gatekeepers and homeseekers: Institutional patterns in racial steering. *Social Problems* 26: 325–342.
Petersillia, J. 1983. *Racial disparities in the criminal justice system.* Santa Monica, CA: RAND.
Police Executive Research Forum. 2001. *Racially biased policing: A principled response.* Washington, D.. Author.
Prime, J. S. 1996. A double-barreled assault: How technology and judicial interpretations threaten public access to law enforcement records. *Federal Communications Law Journal* 48: 341–369.
Ramirez, D., McDevitt, J., and Farrell, A. 2000. *A resource guide on racial profiling data collection: Promising practices and lessons learned.* Washington, DC: U.S. Department of Justice.
Rawls, A. W. 2000. "Race" as an interaction order phenomena: W. E. B. DuBois's "Double consciousness" thesis revisited. *Sociological Theory* 18: 241–274.
Reiss, A. J. 1971. *The Police and the public.* New Haven, CT: Yale University Press.
Rubenstein, J. 1973. *City police.* New York: Random House.
Ruby, C. L. and Brigham, J. C. 1996. A criminal schema: The role of chronicity, race, and socioeconomic status in law enforcement officials' perception of others. *Journal of Applied Social Psychology* 26: 95–112.
Russell, K. K. 1998. *The color of crime.* New York: New York University Press.
Sacks, H. 1972. Notes on the police assessment of moral character. In *Studies in social interaction,* ed. David Sudnow, 280–293. New York: Free Press.

The Sentencing Project. 1999. *Drug policy and the criminal justice system.* Washington, DC: Author.

Sherman, L. 1989. Hot spots of predatory crime: routine activities and the criminology of place. *Criminology* 27: 27–55.

Skolnick, J. 1994. *Justice without trial.* New York: John Wiley & Sons.

Smith, D. A., Graham, N., and Adams, B. 1991. Minorities and the police: Attitudinal and behavioral questions. In *Race and criminal justice,* eds. M. J. Lynch & E. B. Patterson (22–35). New York: Harrow & Heston.

Smith, D. A. and Visher, C. 1981. Street-level justice: Situational determinants of police arrest decisions. *Social Problems* 29: 167–177.

Smith, D. A., Visher, C., and Davidson, L. A. 1984. Equity and discretionary justice: The influence of race on police arrest decisions. *Journal of Criminal Law and Criminology* 75: 234–249.

Taylor, J. and Whitney, G. 1999. Crime and racial profiling by U.S. police: Is there an empirical basis? *Journal of Social, Political and Economic Studies* 24: 485–510.

Thernstrom, S. and Thernstrom, A. 1997. *America in black and white.* New York: Simon & Schuster.

U.S. Bureau of Justice Statistics. 2001. *Contacts between the police and the public: Findings from the 1999 national survey.* Washington, DC: U.S. Department of Justice.

U.S. Commission on Civil Rights. 2000. *Police practices and civil rights in New York City.* Washington, DC: Author.

U.S. General Accounting Office. 2000. *Racial profiling: Limited data available on motorist stops.* Washington, DC: Author.

VanMaanen, J. 1974. Working the street: A Developmental view of police behavior. In *The potential for reform of criminal justice,* ed. H. Jacob, 83–130. Beverly Hills, CA: Sage.

VanMaanen, J. 1978. The asshole. In *Policing: A view from the street,* eds. P. K. Manning and J. VanMaanen, 221–238. Santa Monica, CA: Goodyear.

Verniero, P. 1999. *Interim report of the state police review team regarding allegations of racial profiling.* Trenton: New Jersey Department of Law and Public Safety.

Vrij, A. 1993. An impression formation framework on police prejudice. An overview of experiments on perceptual bias in police-citizen interaction. *Police Studies,* 16: 28–32.

Waddington, P. A. J. 1999. Police (canteen) sub-culture: An appreciation. *British Journal of Criminology* 39: 287–309.

Walker, S. 1997. Complaints against the police: A focus group study of citizen perceptions, goals, and expectations. *Criminal Justice Review* 22: 207–226.

Ward, S. K. 1994. Trends in the location of corporate headquarters: 1969–1989. *Urban Affairs Quarterly* 29: 468–478.

Weiss, A. and Freels, S. 1996. The effects of aggressive policing: The Dayton Traffic Enforcement Experiment. *American Journal of Police* 15:45–64.

Weitzer, R. 1996. Racial discrimination in the criminal justice system: Findings and problems in the literature. *Journal of Criminal Justice* 24: 309–322.

Weitzer, R. 1999. Citizen perceptions of police misconduct: Race and neighborhood context. *Justice Quarterly* 16: 820–846.

Weitzer, R. 2000. Racialized policing: Residents' perceptions in three neighborhoods. *Law and Society Review* 34: 129–155.

Weitzer, R. and Tuch, S. A. 1999. Race, class, and perceptions of discrimination by the police. *Crime and Delinquency* 45: 494–507.

Williams, H. and Murphy, P. V. 1990, January. The evolving strategy of police: A minority view. *Perspectives on Policing.* No. 13. Bethesda, MD: National Institute of Justice

Zonderman, J. 1990. *Beyond the crime lab.* New York: John Wiley & Sons.

Zuboff, S. 1987. *In the age of the smart machine: The future of work and power.* New York: Basic Books.

15

Crime and Racial Profiling by U.S. Police

Is There an Empirical Basis?

Jared Taylor and Glayde Whitney

Introduction

One of the strangest phenomena in contemporary criminology in the United States is the treatment of race and ethnicity. On the one hand there is a long history of academic attention to differences among racial and ethnic groups in involvement in various sorts of criminality (Hooton, 1939; Wilson & Herrnstein, 1985). On the other hand there today appears to be media and political pressure to avoid acknowledgment of the differences and possible consequences of the differences. Recently the New Jersey State Police Superintendent Col. Carl Williams was fired by Gov. Christie Whitman after he said in an interview that some minority groups were more likely to be involved in certain crimes (AP, 1999). The Governor is quoted as having said that Williams' comments were "inconsistent with our efforts to enhance public confidence in the State Police." The same article reports that Williams said he did not condone racial profiling, and has never condoned racial profiling, but at the same time he said "it is naïve to think race is not an issue" in some sorts of crime (AP, 1999). While Col. Williams claims not to condone racial profiling, the American Civil Liberties Union (ACLU) reported in June, 1999, that it was a widespread practice: "Citing police statistics, case studies from 23 states and media reports, the organization asserts that law enforcement agencies have systematically targeted minority travelers for search . . . based on the belief that they are more likely than whites to commit crimes." (Drummond, 1999).

Although reports such as that of the ACLU which criticize the practice of racial profiling and criticize the "belief" that there may be race differences in criminality get wide media coverage, even being featured in national news magazines such as *Time*, (Drummond, 1999), other reports that deal with the actual incidence of crimes as related to race get short shrift. The nationally syndicated columnist Samuel Francis recently wrote:

> Black Americans commit 90 percent of the 1.7 million interracial crimes that occur in the United States every year and are more than 50 times more likely to commit violent crimes against whites than whites are against blacks. These facts were the main findings of a study released earlier this month by the New Century Foundation, but they're not the really big news.

> The big news is that the report, despite having been made available to virtually all newspapers and news outlets in the United States as well as to most major columnists and opinion writers, has been almost totally ignored by the national news media. The study was released on June 2 of this year. To date, all of one single news story about it has appeared. (Francis, 1999).

It does indeed seem strange for there to be a great disparity between media reports and the subsequent public apperception, and the actual data concerning one of the more important issues in criminology today.

The inconsistency between media reports and criminological data concerning race is not a new phenomenon. About a decade ago we reviewed the literature dealing with race differences in criminal behavior. Taylor (1992) largely reviewed media reports, while Whitney (1990) reviewed the scientific literature. A main finding of the review of media accounts of race and crime was the existence of a double standard with regard to reports of crime that mentioned race of perpetrator or race of victim, with white victimization of blacks receiving considerably more prominent coverage than black victimization of whites. (Taylor, 1992). The review of scientific literature was remarkable for both the quantity and consistency of prior literature (Whitney, 1990). Furthermore, the racial differences were accentuated when one considered more serious offenses and offenses that were variously described as victimful or predatory crimes. In a major review Ellis (1988) had reported that for serious victimful crimes, whenever comparisons had been made, blacks had *always* had higher rates than whites. Whenever blacks or whites had been compared with Orientals in roughly the same geographical areas, Orientals had always had the lowest serious victimful crime rates. The results were much less consistent for minor and/or victimless offenses. Overall, an order of blacks > whites > Orientals prevailed, with racial differences being larger the more serious and clearly victimful the offenses (Whitney, 1990).

In their classic *Crime and Human Nature*, Wilson and Herrnstein (1985, 461) reviewed some literature on race and crime. They mentioned that blacks then constituted about one-eighth of the population of the United States and about one-half of arrestees for murder, rape, and robbery, and from one-fourth to one-third of arrestees for burglary, larceny, auto theft, and aggravated assault. Even with adjustments for other demographic variables, such as age and urban residence, in comparison to whites, blacks were overrepresented about four to one with regard to violent crimes and about three to one with regard to property crimes. Rushton (1985) pointed out that experience in England was consistent with that in the United States: blacks then constituted about 13 percent of the population of London and accounted for 50 percent of the crime. Indeed, violent crime by blacks had been mentioned as a factor contributing to the rearming of London's Metropolitan Police (Gould & Waldren, 1986). Blacks were similarly overrepresented with regard to white-collar crimes such as fraud and embezzlement. Blacks were underrepresented only with regard to offenses, such as securities violations, that usually required access to high-status occupations in which they were at that time underrepresented (Wilson & Hernstein, 1985, 462).

Whitney (1990) analyzed the race-specific arrest rates for various offenses that had been compiled for the years 1965 to 1986 (UCRP, 1988). For 19 categories listed in each of 22 years (418 comparisons), the rate for nonwhites *always* exceeded the rate for whites in the same year, typically by a factor of four to ten. For example, averaged across years, the nonwhite murder rate was nine times the white rate. Considerations of rate of crime combine prevalence (individuals who participate in crime) and incidence (recidivism, number of crimes by individuals who participate). Prevalence has been estimated through accumulation of first arrests across age (Blumstein & Graddy, 1981–1982; Blumstein & Cohen, 1987). Blumstein's results suggest that incidence is not strongly different among participants of different races. Rather, the race differences in crime rates are largely attributable to differences in the proportion of individuals of various races that participate in crime (Blumstein & Cohen,

1987). Among urban males the probability that by age 55 a black had been arrested for an FBI index crime was about 0.51; for whites it was 0.14 (Blumstein & Graddy, 1981–1982). Comparable age accumulated participation rates are not available for Orientals due primarily to their very low overall participation rates. Conversion of percentages to areas under a normal curve can be useful for comparing populations. These individual participation rates suggest about a one-standard-deviation difference between male urban blacks and whites for criminal liability (Whitney, 1990). The apologist argument that arrest data are inappropriate for documentation of race differences in crime rates due to bias in arrests was thoroughly considered, and essentially debunked in Wilbank's 1987 book *The Myth of a Racist Criminal Justice System.* More recently Dilulio (1996) has also presented data concerning crime disparities among races, and the suggestion that the disparities are real in that they do not reflect differential law enforcement.

For regions within the United States, Whitney (1995) pointed out that the best predictor of local murder rate was simply the percent of the population that was black. Across all of the 170 cities in the United States that had a 1980 population of at least 100,000, the correlation between murder rate and percent of the population that was black was $r = +0.69$. With data from 1980 aggregated for the 50 states of the United States, the simple correlation between murder rate and percent of the population that was black was $r = +0.77$. More recently Hama (1999) used data from 1995 to calculate the correlation across the 50 states between percent of the population that is black and violent crime rate, where violent crime rate was an aggregate of murder, non-negligent manslaughter, rape, robbery, and aggravated assault. Hama (1999) reported the correlation to be $r = +0.76$.

Clearly the existing data briefly reviewed above are quite consistent. They are also somewhat limited in scope. There are two areas of criminality related to race that are not considered above, but which have become of interest in recent years. One is the question of hate crime categorization, and the other is that of interracial crime. In crimes where the perpetrator and the victim are of different races, are there any patterns in incidence, and what amount of interracial crime gets included in hate crime statistics? The analyses reported in the present chapter were conducted to obtain information concerning the questions of interracial crime and hate crimes, as well as to update the investigation of incidence of crime as related to race in the United States.

Sources and Methods

The primary sources of data for consideration were governmental compilations of statistical information having to do with crime. The major sources are described here. One of the most important sources is the *National Crime Victimization Survey* (NCVS). Every year since 1972, the U.S. Department of Justice has carried out what is called the NCVS to ascertain the frequency of certain kinds of crimes. The NCVS sample is large, upward of 80,000 people from about 50,000 households, and carefully stratified on the basis of census data to be representative of the nation as a whole. The NCVS is unique as a record of criminal victimization as reported directly by Americans, not filtered through police reports. It is the only significant nationwide measure of interracial crime. The NCVS is carried out annually, but the Department of Justice does not issue full reports every year; 1994 is the most recent year for complete data.

Ever since passage of the Hate Crime Statistics Act of 1990, The FBI has been charged with collecting national statistics on criminal acts "motivated, in whole or in part, by bias." The law does not compel local law enforcement agencies to supply the FBI with this information, but many do. In 1997, the most recent year for which data are available, the FBI received hate crime information from 11,211 local agencies serving more than 83 percent of the United States population.

Uniform Crime Reports (UCR), published annually by the FBI, is the standard reference work for crime and crime rates in the United States. The UCR is a nationwide compilation of criminal offenses and arrest data, reported voluntarily by local law enforcement agencies. In the most recent

UCR, which covers 1997, the FBI included reports from 17,000 law enforcement agencies, covering 95 percent of the country's population. The UCR is unquestionably the most comprehensive and authoritative report on crimes brought to the attention of the police. News stories about rising or falling crime rates are almost always based on the UCR.

Our primary methodology throughout this study is to calculate rates of various offenses as a function of victim and offender characteristics. Such calculations are straightforward, but can appear arcane to investigators experienced with other analytical approaches. Therefore we here provide a detailed example.

The most recent complete NCVS data are for the year 1994 (USDJ, 1997). In that report Table 42 lists categories of single offender interracial violent crimes. The various numbers at the top of the table represent totals calculated for single-offender violent crimes reported for that year. They are extrapolated from the actual crimes reported by the survey sample. We find that in 1994 6,830,360 whites were victims of violent crimes, and that 16.7 percent (1,140,670) reported that the perpetrator was black. Blacks were victims of 1,100,490 violent crimes, of which 12.3 percent (135,360) were committed by whites. Summing these figures for interracial crime (1,140,670 plus 135,360) we get a total of 1,276,030 interracial crimes, of which 1,140,670 or 89 percent were committed by blacks.

To get the *rates* at which blacks and whites commit interracial crime we divide the number of crimes by the population to get crimes per 100,000 population. The Census Bureau reports that the 1994 white and black populations were 216,413,000 and 32,653,000 respectively. Whites therefore committed acts of interracial violence at a rate of 62.55 per 100,000 while the black rate was 3,493.63 per 100,000, a figure that is 55.85 times the white rate. Put in the most straightforward terms, the average black was 56 times more likely to commit criminal violence against a white than was a white to commit criminal violence against a black. The multiple of 56 does *not* mean that blacks commit 56 times as much interracial violence as whites. What it means is that if whites commit interracial violence at a rate of 10 crimes per 100,000 whites, the rate for blacks is 560 per 100,000, or 56 times the white rate. This is the kind of calculation that is represented in most of the analyses in this report.

Results and Discussion

Calculations from the NCVS similar to those detailed above indicate that in the U.S. the black rate for interracial robbery, or "mugging," was 103 times the white rate. The single-offender robbery rates, as well as the single-offender overall violence rates explicated above, are illustrated in Figure 15.1.

Again using the NCVS (USDJ, 1997), we calculate the total number of crimes committed by perpetrators of each race, and the percentage that is committed against the other race. The 1,140,670 acts of violence committed by blacks against whites constitute 56.3 percent of all violent crimes committed by blacks. That is to say that when blacks commit violent crimes they target whites more than half the time or, put differently, there is more black-on-white crime than black-on-black crime. Similar calculations for whites show that of the 5,114,692 acts of criminal violence committed by whites, only 2.6 percent were directed at blacks. Although homicide is a violent crime, the NCVS does not include it because victims cannot be interviewed. The number of interracial homicides is rather small and does not substantially affect the percentages and ratios presented here.

It may be suggested that American blacks commit violence against whites because whites are more likely to have money and are therefore more promising robbery targets. However, of the 1,140,670 black-on-white acts of single-perpetrator violence reported in 1994, only 173,374 were robberies. The remaining 84.8 percent were aggravated assaults, rapes, and simple assaults, which presumably were not motivated by profit. Rape, in particular, has nothing to do with the presumed wealth of the victim. More than 30,000 white women were raped by black men in 1994, while about

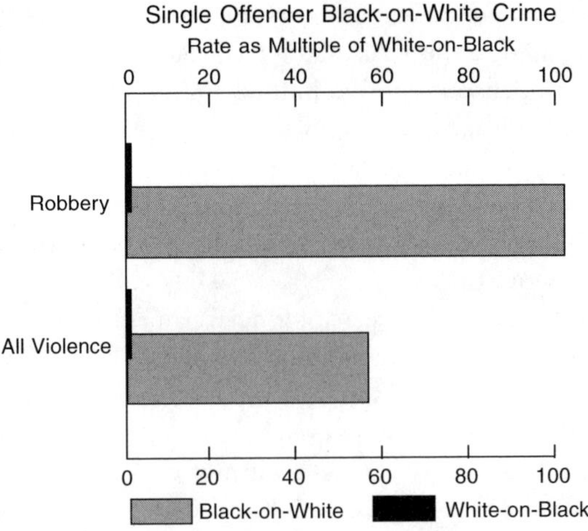

Fig. 15.1 Single Offender Black-on-White Crime.

5,400 black women were raped by white men. The black interracial rape rate was thus 38 times the white rate.

The NCVS (USDJ, 1997) Table 48 contains interracial crime data for acts of violence committed by multiple offenders. By doing calculations as before, we determine how much group or "gang" violence (not in the sense of organized gangs) is interracial and how much is committed by blacks and by whites. Of the total of 490,266 acts of multiple-offender interracial violence, no fewer than 93.9 percent were committed by blacks against whites. Robbery, for which there is a monetary motive, accounted for fewer than one-third of these crimes. The rest were gang assaults, including rapes, presumably for motives other than profit. Rates of group violence for each race can be calculated as before, and the difference between the races is stark. The black rate of overall interracial gang violence is 101.75 times the white rate; for robbery it is 277.31 times the white rate.

"Hate Crimes" in Perspective

In 1997, the most recent year for which data are available, there were a total of 9,861 "hate" offenses, of which 6,981 represented bias crimes based on race or ethnic origin (USDJ, 1999). The remainder was for reasons of religion, sexual orientation, or disability.

The FBI reports 8,474 suspected offenders whose race was known. Of that number, 5,344 were white and 1,629 were black. Their offenses—which included all categories of hate crime, not just racial bias—can, in turn, be divided into violent and nonviolent offenses, and in then calculating the rate of offense by race we find that blacks were 1.99 times more likely than whites to commit hate crimes in general and 2.24 times more likely to commit violent hate crimes.

As for cases of racial bias, there were 718 blacks charged with anti-white (as opposed to anti-homosexual, anti-Semitic, etc.) crimes and 2,336 whites charged with anti-black hate crimes. Although the number of whites charged was larger, the black rate per 100,000 was twice as high. A larger number of whites are charged with these crimes, but blacks are 2.0 times more likely to be charged with similar offenses. This overrepresentation of blacks in hate crimes, not just in race bias cases but in all categories, runs counter to the common impression that whites are the prime perpetrators of hate crimes and are certainly more likely to commit them than blacks.

But perhaps of even greater significance is the relatively small number of bias crimes to begin with. Of the 6,981 offenses based on race or ethnicity, only 4,105 were violent, involving murder, rape, robbery, or assault. The rest included such offenses as vandalism and intimidation. These numbers are almost insignificant compared to the 1,766,000 interracial crimes of violence (combining both single- and multiple-offender offenses) reported in the NCVS.

Needless to say, part of this huge disparity in numbers is explained by the fact that the NCVS covers all crimes—whether reported to police or not—whereas for a crime to be included in the FBI's hate crime statistics it must first be reported to police and then be officially classified as a hate crime. No doubt there is some number of crimes never reported to the police that authorities would consider hate crimes if they knew about them.

However, how important is the distinction between interracial crimes that are officially designated as hate crimes and those that are not? For a crime to be considered a hate crime, the perpetrator must make his motive clear, usually by using racial slurs. It is not hard to imagine that of the 1,766,000 interracial crimes committed in 1994, some—perhaps even a great many—were "motivated in whole or in part, by bias" but the perpetrators did not express their motives.

Given the realities of race in the United States, would it be unreasonable for a person attacked by someone of a different race to wonder whether race had something to do with the attack, even if his assailant said nothing? Such suspicions are even more likely in the case of the 490,266 acts of group violence that crossed racial lines in 1994. What is the psychological effect on a victim set upon by a gang of people of a different race? A white woman gang raped by blacks or a black man cornered and beaten by whites can hardly help but think she/he was singled out at least in part because of race, even if the attackers used no racial slurs.

Many states have passed laws that increase penalties for people convicted of hate crimes. These laws recognize the harm done to society when people are attacked because of race or other characteristics. However, one might ask which does more damage to society: the few thousand violent acts officially labeled as hate crimes or the vastly more numerous interracial crimes of violence that go virtually unnoticed?

Hate Crimes Committed by Hispanics

The government's treatment of hate crimes is misleading in another, even more obvious way, in that the FBI reports hate crimes *against* Hispanics but not *by* Hispanics. The FBI's "Hate Crime Incident Report" includes Hispanics as a victim category but not as a perpetrator category. In effect this forces local law enforcement agencies to categorize most Hispanic offenders as "white" and the values for 1997 reflect this. The total number of hate crimes for that year—9,861—includes 636 crimes of anti-Hispanic bias, but not one of the 8,474 known offenders is "Hispanic" because the designation is not included on the FBI form.

If a Mexican is assaulted for reasons of ethnicity he is officially recorded as Hispanic. However, he becomes white if he commits a hate crime against a black. Even more absurdly, if a Mexican commits a hate crime against a white, both the victim and the perpetrator are reported as white. And, in fact, the 1997 FBI figures duly record 214 "white" offenders who committed anti-white hate crimes (USDJ, 1999, 12). The offenders were probably Hispanic, but if that is the case the report should say so. If some of the "whites" who are reported to have committed crimes against blacks are also Hispanic, the report should indicate that, too.

An examination of specific crimes shows that official reports can be misleading. Murder is the most serious of hate crimes, and the FBI lists five cases of racially motivated murder for 1997—three "anti-black" and two "anti-white." The FBI report does not provide details about the perpetrators or the circumstances of the killings, but the local police departments that reported the crimes to the FBI have this information.

Two of the anti-black killings took place in the same town, a largely Hispanic suburb of Los Angeles called Hawaiian Gardens. Hawaiian Gardens has a history of black–Hispanic tension that is so bad many blacks have decided to leave. In one of the murders, a 24-year-old black man was beaten to death by 10 to 14 Hispanics who took turns smashing his head with a baseball bat. In the other, a Hispanic gang member challenged a 29-year-old black man's right to be in the neighborhood. A few minutes later he returned and shot the man in the chest. In both cases, the victims and killers did not know each other and the motivation appears to have been strictly racial (Russel & Mejia, 1998). These crimes are typical of what we think of as hate-crime murders, and because no Hispanics are identified as perpetrators in the FBI data, it is safe to assume the killers were classified as white.

The third anti-black killing took place in Anchorage, Alaska. According to press reports, a white man, 33-year-old Brett Maness, killed his neighbor, a 32-year-old black man, Delbert White, after a brief struggle (Sullivan, 1997). Mr. Maness, who was growing marijuana in his apartment and kept an arsenal of weapons, had been shooting a pellet gun at Mr. White's house, and the black man had come over to complain. Interestingly, a jury found that Mr. Maness killed Mr. White in self-defense, but convicted him of weapons and drug charges. The incident was designated a hate crime because Mr. Maness had brandished weapons and shouted racial slurs at Mr. White in the past (Porco, 1998).

The remaining two killings were classified as anti-white, but only one fits the usual conception of such crimes. Four white men were walking on a street in Palm Beach, Florida, when a car came to a stop not far from them. Two black men got out with their hands behind their backs and one said "What are you crackers looking at?" One of the white men replied, "Not you, nigger," whereupon one of the blacks brought a gun from behind his back and fired several times, killing one white and wounding another. Attackers and victims did not know each other, and the criminal motivation appears to have been purely racial (Offense Report, 1997). The other anti-white killing involved a Texas businessman from India, who shot his Mexican daughter-in-law because his son had divorced an Indian wife to marry her. He was incensed that his son should marry anyone who was not Indian (Padilla, 1997). Presumably this crime should have been classified as anti-Hispanic rather than anti-white.

These five racially motivated murders reported for 1997 do not fit the popular image of hate crimes, namely, of whites brutalizing non-whites. In fact, only one perpetrator was "white" in the usually accepted sense. What was the nature of the thousands of other officially reported hate crimes? Without examining all 9,861 of them it is impossible to say.

It is clear, however, that the FBI report gives a false impression. It inflates the number of hate crimes committed by "whites" by calling Hispanics white. At the same time it gives the impression that Hispanics never commit hate crimes. The reason for gathering these data is to arrive at a better understanding of the extent of racial friction and violence in the United States. If statistics are to have any meaning they must reflect American reality, namely, that most Hispanics think of themselves as a separate group, distinct from non-Hispanic whites, and are perceived by others as a different group. It is impossible to understand or alleviate group friction without recognizing this. If the FBI wants to collect meaningful data, it must recognize Hispanics as a perpetrator category as well as a victim category.

Race and Crime

Different racial groups in the United States commit crimes at different rates. Most Americans have a sense that non-white neighborhoods are more dangerous than white neighborhoods—and they are correct. However, it is very unusual to find reliable information on just how much more dangerous some groups are than others.

The *Uniform Crime Reports* (UCR) from the FBI is the standard reference for crime and crime rates in the United States. In trying to determine crime rates for different racial groups, it is important to be aware of the differences between the UCR and the NCVS referenced above. The NCVS contains only one kind of information: crimes Americans say they have suffered. The UCR includes two different kinds of data: crimes reported to the police and arrests of perpetrators. Even for the same year and for the same crime, these three sets of numbers are different. The largest numbers are in the NCVS, because they include crimes not reported to the police. Somewhat smaller are the UCR figures on offenses reported to authorities, and smaller still are arrest figures, which represent offenses for which a suspect is arrested.

For example, in the 1997 NCVS Americans say they suffered a total of 1,883,000 cases of aggravated assault (USDJ, 1998a), but according to the UCR, only 1,022,000 were reported to the police. During that same year, there were only 535,000 arrests for aggravated assault (UCR, 1998). Racial data enter the UCR numbers only when an arrest is made, so it can be argued that racial comparisons should not be based on UCR data. Different racial groups may report crime to the police at different rates, some groups may be more successful at escaping arrest, and the police may discriminate between racial groups in their arrest efforts. However, although racial bias in arrests is frequently discussed, when investigated the data suggest that arrest rates actually track perpetrator rates (Dilulio, 1996; Wilbanks, 1987). Furthermore, there is an advantage to using UCR data because its racial categories are more detailed. Unlike the NCVS, which reports only "black," "white," and "other," the UCR compiles arrest data on "black," "white," "American Indian/Eskimo," and "Asian/Pacific Islander." These are the only national crime data that make these distinctions. Also, as will be explicated below, UCR arrest data can be compared to other data sources in ways that make it possible to treat Hispanics as a separate ethnic category.

Another good reason to use UCR arrest data (race of persons arrested) is that the racial proportions are actually quite close to those from NCVS survey data (race of perpetrator as reported by victims). For example, according to the UCR, 57 percent of people arrested for robbery in 1997 were black, as were 37 percent of those arrested for aggravated assault (UCR, 1998). According to NCVS data on single-offender crimes, 51 percent of robbers were reported by their victims to be black as were 30 percent of those who committed aggravated assault (USDJ, 1997). Since there is a greater overrepresentation by blacks in NCVS-reported multiple offender crimes, combining the two sets of figures brings the racial proportions in the NCVS figures extremely close to the racial proportions in UCR arrest numbers. Put differently, police are arresting criminals of different races in very close to the same proportions as Americans say they are victimized by people of those races.

By this measure, who is committing crime in America? In Figure 15.2 are presented arrest rates as multiples of the white arrest rate for various crimes.

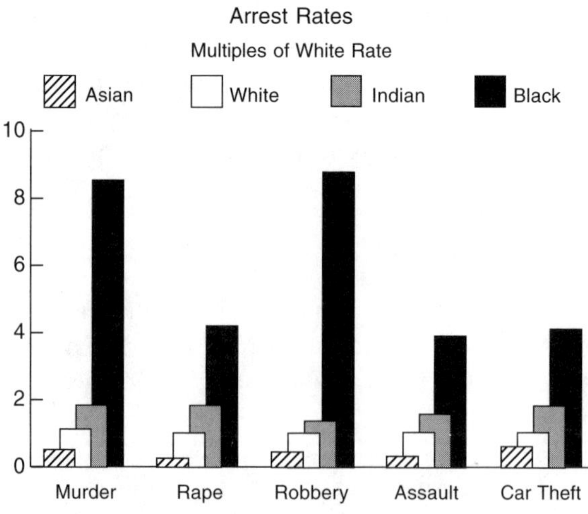

Fig. 15.2 Arrest Rates Multiples of White Rate.

The white rate is always set to one, so if the black rate is three, for example, it means that blacks are arrested at three times the white rate. Once again, it does not mean that three times as many blacks as whites were arrested; it means that if 100 of every 100,000 whites were arrested for a crime, 300 of every 100,000 blacks were arrested for the same crime. The data show a consistent pattern: Blacks are arrested at dramatically higher rates than other racial groups. American Indians and Eskimos (hereinafter "Indians") are arrested at slightly higher rates than whites, and Asians/Pacific Islanders (hereinafter "Asians") are arrested at consistently lower rates. The popular conception of crime in America is correct: rates are much higher among blacks than among whites or other groups.

To return to the view that arrest data reflect police bias rather than genuine group differences in crime rates, police actually have very little discretion in whom they arrest for violent crimes. Except for murder victims, most people can tell the police the race of an assailant. If a victim says she was mugged by a white man, the police cannot very well arrest a black man even if they want to. For this reason, many people accept that police have little discretion in who they arrest for violent crime, but still believe drug laws are enforced unfairly against minorities. Drug offenses are beyond the scope of this investigation, but here, too, there is independent evidence that arrest rates reflect differences in criminal behavior, not selective law enforcement. The U.S. Department of Health and Human Services keeps records by race of drug-related emergency room admissions. It reports that blacks are admitted at 6.67 times the non-Hispanic white rate for heroin and morphine, and no less than 10.49 times the non-Hispanic white rate for cocaine (the rates for Hispanics are 2.82 and 2.35 times the white rates; information is not provided for American Indians or Asians) (USDJ, 1998b). There is only one plausible explanation for these rates: Blacks are much more likely to be using drugs in the first place. Finally, if racist white police were unfairly arresting non-whites we would expect arrest rates for Asians to be higher than those for whites. Instead, they are lower for almost every kind of crime.

Measuring Hispanic Crime Rates

Any study of crime rates in America is complicated by the inconsistent treatment of Hispanics by different government agencies. For example, the Census Bureau's official estimate for the 1997 population of the United States divides all 268 million Americans into four racial groups: white, black, Indian and Eskimo, and Asian and Pacific Islander. The bureau then explains that among these 268 million people there are 29 million Hispanics who "can be of any race." However, it also counts *non-Hispanic* whites, *non-Hispanic* blacks, Indians, etc. Thus we find that although according to the strictly racial classification, there are 221 million whites in the United States, there are only 195 million *non-Hispanic* whites. When American Hispanics, approximately half of whom are Mexican, are apportioned to the four racial categories, the Census Bureau considers 91 percent to be white, six percent black, one percent American Indian, and two percent Asian.

The treatment of Hispanics can make for odd results. For example, according to the 1990 census, the 3,485,000 people of Los Angeles were 52.9 percent white, 13.9 percent black, 0.4 percent American Indian, and 22.9 percent Asian—which adds up to 100 percent. This makes the city appear to be majority white. However, Los Angeles was also 39.3 percent Hispanic, and if we subtract the 91 percent of them who are classified as whites, the non-Hispanic white population drops to only 16.6 percent.

What does this mean for crime statistics? Because the UCR figures do not treat Hispanics as a separate category, almost all the Hispanics arrested in the United States go into official records as "white." This is contrary to the usual cultural understanding of the term, which is not normally thought to include most Mexicans and Latinos.

If violent crime rates for Hispanics are different from those of non-Hispanic whites, putting Hispanics in the "white" category distorts the results. This is not as serious as in the case of hate

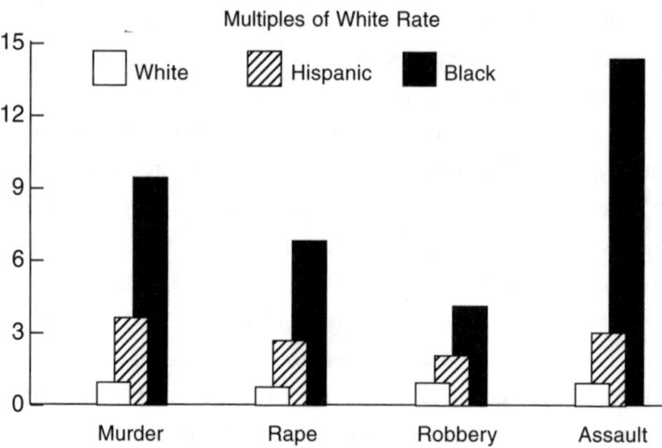

Fig. 15.3 California Arrests by Race.

crimes, in which the crime itself has to do with the very personal characteristics that are being omitted from the records, but there is no legitimate reason not to make ethnic and racial comparisons as accurate as possible. The UCR tabulates separate data on American Indians and Eskimos—who are less than 1 percent of the population—but it ignores Hispanics, who are 12 percent of the population.

Some data-gathering agencies do treat Hispanic and non-Hispanic whites separately. The California Department of Justice, which records all arrests within the state, consistently makes this distinction (although it lumps Asians and American Indians into the "other" category) (Calif., 1998). In conjunction with Census Bureau population figures for Hispanics, non-Hispanic whites, and non-Hispanic blacks living in California in 1997, we can calculate the arrest rates for the different groups for various crimes. In Figure 15.3 these rates are once again presented as multiples of the white rate. As is the case with national UCR data, blacks are arrested at much higher rates than whites, but Hispanics are also arrested at considerably higher rates.

The different rates at which Hispanics and non-Hispanic whites are held in prisons and jails are another indicator of the differences in crime rates between the two groups. Although the UCR does not treat Hispanics as a separate category for arrest purposes, some government reports on the prison population do consider them separately. For example, the Department of Justice has calculated incarceration rates per 100,000 population for non-Hispanic whites (193), Hispanics (688), and non-Hispanic blacks (1,571) (USDJ, 1998b). Expressed as multiples of the white rate, the Hispanic rate is 3.56 and black rate is 8.14. These multiples are close to those from the California arrest data, and justify the conclusion that Hispanics are roughly three times more likely than non-Hispanic whites to be arrested for various crimes. By accepting this assumption, we can use the following formula to incorporate this differential into the UCR racial data on white arrests so as to calculate more accurate arrest rates for non-Hispanic whites:

R (Number of non-Hispanic whites) + 3R (Number of white Hispanics)
= Actual Number of Arrests

Here, R is the arrest rate for non-Hispanic whites and 3R is the arrest rate for Hispanics who are categorized as white when they are arrested. Calculations of this sort show that if Hispanics are broken out as a separate ethnic category with an arrest rate three times the non-Hispanic rate, the rate for non-Hispanic whites decreases by 19.5 percent. In Figure 15.4 are shown arrest rates (as multiples of the white arrest rate) adjusted for the Hispanic reduction. Due to lack of precise information, the multiple for Hispanics is set to three times the white rate for all crimes even though there is certain to be some variation in the multiples for different types of crimes. A graph of unadjusted arrest rates is also presented for purposes of comparison. Because the evidence from national incarceration rates and California arrest rates suggests that Hispanics commit violent crimes at some multiple of the white rate, the adjusted graph in Figure 15.4 is probably a more accurate indicator of group differences. Both graphs are on the same scale and show the extent to which separating out Hispanics raises arrests rates for other groups when compared to whites.

It should be noted here that the NCVS survey data on interracial crime also includes most Hispanics in the "white" category. It is therefore impossible to know how many of the "whites" who committed violent crimes against blacks were actually Hispanic or how many of the "whites" against whom blacks committed violent crimes were Hispanic. If Hispanics commit violent crimes against blacks at a higher rate than whites—and judging from their higher arrest and incarceration rates for violent offenses this seems likely, the NCVS report also inflates the crime rates of non-Hispanic whites.

Men vs. Women, Blacks vs. Whites

Many people resist the idea that different racial groups have substantially different rates of violent crime. However, there are several group differences in crime rates that virtually everyone accepts and, indeed, takes for granted. Men in their late teens and 20s, for example, are much more prone to violence than men beyond their 50s. When young men are arrested more frequently for violent offenses, no one doubts that it is because they commit more violent crime. Likewise, virtually no one disputes the reason for higher arrest rates for men than for women: men commit more violent crime than women (Wilson & Herrnstein, 1985). This is the case for racial groups as well: Asians are arrested at lower rates than whites because they commit fewer crimes; blacks and Hispanics are arrested at higher rates because they commit more crimes (Levin, 1997; Rushton, 1995; Whitney, 1990).

When it comes to violent crime, blacks are approximately as much more likely to be arrested than whites, as men are more likely to be arrested than women. The multiples of black vs. white arrest rates are very close to the multiples of male vs. female arrest rates, suggesting that blacks are as much more dangerous than whites as men are more dangerous than women.

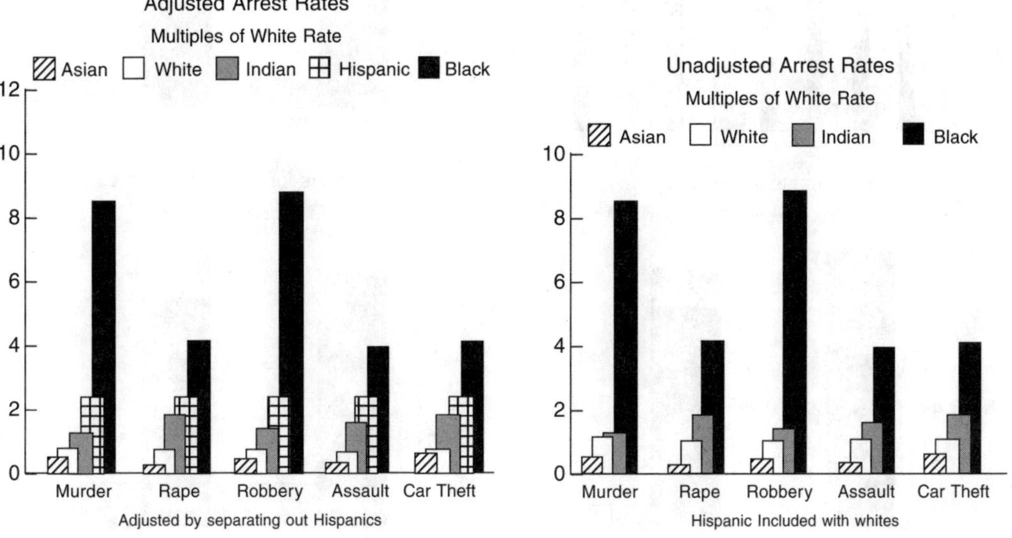

Fig. 15.4 Arrest Rates with Hispanic Separate/Included with Whites.

The first panel in Figure 15.5 has arrest rates for men as multiples of arrest rates for women for the same crimes (UCR, 1998). The differentials are roughly similar to those between blacks and whites. The next two panels compare arrest rates for murder and robbery, and illustrate that the black/white arrest multiple is almost as great as the male/female multiple. The fourth panel of Figure 15.5 makes the same comparison for arrest rates for all violent crimes (these figures have *not* been adjusted for the fact that Hispanics are included with whites. As we have shown, adjustment would lower the white arrest rate by nearly 20 percent, and would make the black/white multiple greater than the male/female multiples).

What does this mean? Although most people have no idea what the arrest rate multiples may be, they have an intuitive understanding that men are more violent and dangerous than women. If someone in unfamiliar circumstances is approached by a group of strange men she feels more uneasy than if she is approached by an otherwise similar group of strange women. No one would suggest that this differential uneasiness is "prejudice." It is common sense, born out by the objective reality that men are more dangerous than women.

Likewise, there is now much controversy about so-called "racial profiling" by the police, that is, the practice of questioning blacks in suspicious circumstances in disproportionate numbers in the expectation that they are more likely than people of other races to be criminals. The philosophical, legal and rational case for racial profiling has been elaborated by the philosopher Michael Levin (Levin, 1997). "Racial" profiling is just as rational and productive as "age" or "sex" profiling. Police would be wasting their time if they stopped and questioned as many little old ladies as they do young black men. It is the job of the police to catch criminals, and they know from experience who is likely

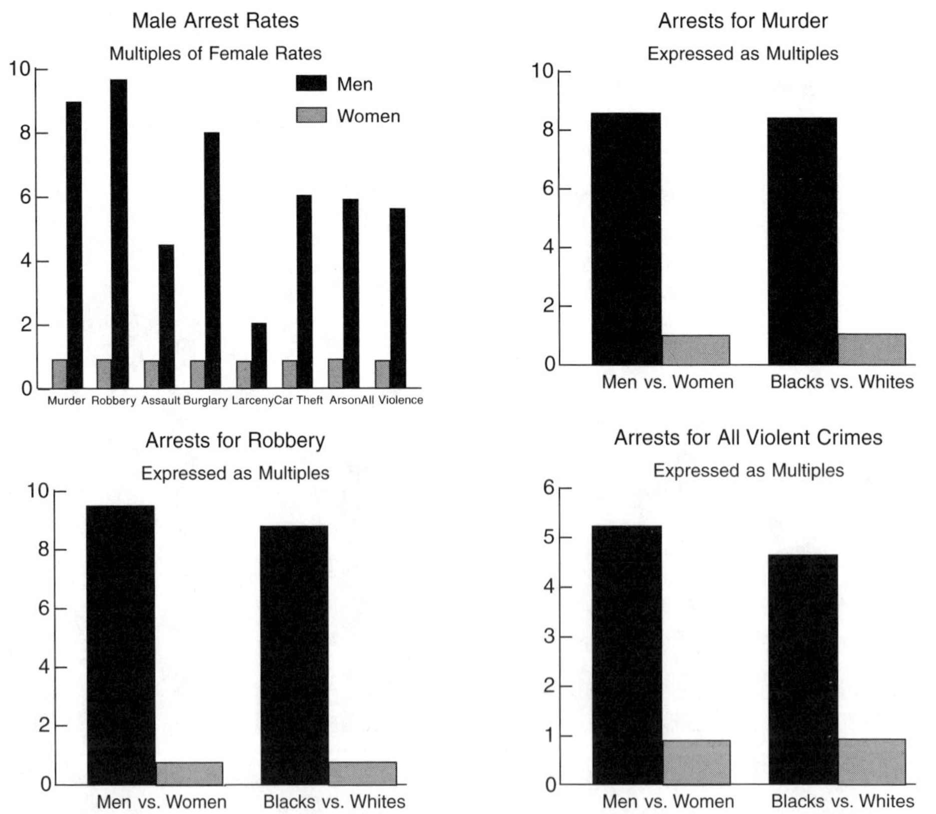

Fig. 15.5 Sex Differences and Race Differences.

to be an offender. Americans who do not question the wisdom of police officers who notice a possible suspect's age and sex should not be surprised to learn those officers also notice race.

Conclusions

Two things can be said about most of the information in this investigation: It is easily discovered but little known. Every year, the FBI issues its report on hate crimes, and distributes thousands of copies to scholars and the media. Why does no one find it odd that hundreds of whites are reportedly committing hate crimes against whites? And why does no one question the wisdom of calling someone white when he is a perpetrator but Hispanic when he is a victim?

For some years there has been an extended national discussion about the prevalence of black-on-black crime—and for good reason. Blacks suffer from considerably more violent crime than do Americans of other races. And yet, amid this national outcry over the extent of black-on-black crime, there appears to be little concern about the fact that there is actually more black-on-white crime. Nor does there seem to be much interest in the fact that blacks are 50 to 200 times more likely than whites to commit interracial crimes of violence. Differences as great as this are seldom found in comparative studies of group behavior, and they cry out for causal investigation and explanation. It is probably safe to say that if the races were reversed, and gangs of whites were attacking blacks at merely four or five times the rate at which blacks were attacking whites the country would consider this a national crisis that required urgent attention.

Everyone knows that young people are more dangerous than old people, and that men are more dangerous than women. We adjust our behavior accordingly and do not apologize for doing so. Why then must we pretend that statistics regarding race differences in violent crime, are to be ignored? It is surely understandable that police should take these statistics into account when searching for suspects, and that they may wish to take more precautions when entering some neighborhoods than others.

References

Associated Press, 1999. "Whitman fires State Police superintendent over remarks to newspaper." Trenton, NJ: March 1.

Blumstein, A. and J. Cohen. 1987. Characterizing criminal careers. *Science* 237: 985–991.

Blumstein, A. and E. Graddy. 1981–1982. Prevalence and recidivism in index arrests: a feedback model. *Law and Society Review* 16:265–290.

California Department of Justice Division of Criminal Justice. April 15, 1998. Adult and juvenile arrests reported. Race/ethnic group by specific offense statewide, January through December 1997. California Department of Justice Division of Criminal Justice, Criminal Justice Statistics Center, 5939.

Dilulio, John J., Jr. 1996. My black crime problem and ours. *City Journal*, Spring: 14ff.

Drummond, Tammerlin. June 14, 1999. It's not just in New Jersey. *Time* 153(23): 61.

Ellis, Lee. 1988. The victimful—victimless crime distinction, and seven universal demographic correlates of victimful criminal behavior. *Personality and Individual Differences* 9: 525–548.

Francis, Samuel. June 30, 1999. Media blackout on black-on-white crime. *Conservative Chronicle*, 23.

Gould, R. W. and M. J. Waldren. 1986. *London's armed police: 1829 to the present.* London: Arms & Armour Press.

Hama, Aldric. 1999. Demographic changes and social breakdown: The role of intelligence. *The Mankind Quarterly*, vol. 40, no 2. Winter .

Hooton, Earnest Albert. 1939. *Crime and the man.* Cambridge MA: Harvard University Press.

Levin, Michael. 1997. *Why race matters: Race differences and what they mean.* Westport CT: Praeger.

Offense Report: Case no. 97123655, Palm Beach, Florida Sheriffs Office.

Padilla, Gloria. 1997. Murder trial defendant misses court appearance. *San Antonio Express-News*, March 11.

Porco, Peter. 1998. Murder suspect acquitted. *Anchorage Daily News*, Dec. 12: E1.

Rushton, J. Philippe. 1985. Differential K theory: The sociobiology of individual and group differences. *Personality and Individual Differences* 6:441–452. *Race, Evolution, and Behavior: A life history perspective.* New Brunswick NJ: Transaction.

Russel, Ron and Victor Mejia. 1998. City of fear. Los Angeles: *New Times*, February 12–18: 13.

Sullivan, Patty. 1997. Anchorage man gunned down in Spenard. *Anchorage Daily News*, November 22: D1.

Taylor, Jared. 1992.*Paved with good intentions: The failure of race relations in contemporary America.* New York: Carroll & Graf.

UCR *Crime in the United States.* 1997. [known as *Uniform Crime Reports*, or UCR]. Washington, DC: U.S. Department of Justice, Federal Bureau of Investigation, USGPO.
UCRP *Age-Specific Arrest Rates and Race-Specific Arrest Rates for Selected Offenses, 1965–1986.* Washington, DC: U.S. Department of Justice, Federal Bureau of Investigation. Uniform Crime Reporting Program, USGPO.
USDJ *Criminal Victimization in the United States.* 1994. Washington, DC: U.S. Department of Justice, Bureau of Justice Statistics, USGPO.
USDJ. 1998a. *Criminal Victimization in the United States, 1997.* Washington, DC: U.S. Department of Justice, Bureau of Justice Statistics, USGPO.
USDJ. 1998b. *Sourcebook of Criminal Justice Statistics, 1997.* Washington, DC: U.S. Department of Justice, Bureau of Justice Statistics, USGPO.
USDJ. *Hate Crime Statistics, 1997.* Washington, DC: U.S. Department of Justice, Federal Bureau of Investigation, USGPO.
Whitney, Glayde. On possible genetic bases of race differences in criminality. In *Crime in biological, social, and moral contexts,* eds. Lee Ellis and Harry Hoffman, 134–149. Westport CT: Praeger.
Whitney, Glayde. 1990. Ideology and censorship in behavior genetics. *The Mankind Quarterly* 35: 327–342.
Wilbanks, William. *The myth of a racist criminal justice system.* Monterey CA: Brooks/Cole.
Wilson, James Q. and Richard J. Hermstein. 1985. *Crime and human nature.* New York: Simon & Schuster.

16

Defending the Color Line

Racially and Ethnically Motivated Hate Crime

Barbara Perry

Drawing on structured action theory, the author examines the ways in which racially and ethnically motivated hate crime emerges as a forceful means of constructing identity and difference within the institutional settings of culture, labor, sexuality, and power. The author summarizes the trends in racially and ethnically motivated violence nationwide and then explores hate crimes as a readily available means of doing difference. The author argues that racially motivated violence is not an aberration associated with a lunatic or extremist fringe. Instead, it is a normative means of asserting racial identity relative to the victimized other; it is an enactment—of the racism that allocates privilege along racial lines.

As with any human activity, hate crime takes its meaning and its impact from the broader array of social and institutional patterns. It is mediated by and enacted within culturally available forms. Each of us is held accountable to our race or ethnic category as we perform in diverse settings. Our identity performances "can be used to justify or discredit other actions; accordingly, virtually any action can be assessed in relation to its race category" (West & Fenstermaker, 1995, p. 22). So, for example, a Hispanic youth who excels in school is perceived by the majority to be crossing established racial boundaries. He is discredited to the extent that he has forgotten his place. Consequently, a White youth who victimizes this upstart will be justified and in fact rewarded for his efforts to reestablish the racialized boundaries between himself and his victim. Both actors have been judged for their actions, with predictable and reconstitutive consequences. Race and ethnicity—for both actors—have been (re)accomplished, the boundaries preserved through the mechanism of hate-motivated violence. Therefore, hate crime can be seen as a coherent racial project (Omi & Winant, 1993) in that it connects the structural meanings and organization of race with the cultural construction of racialized identity. It occurs within the institutional contexts of what is known to be the appropriate place of victim and victimizer. In this chapter, I explore those structured patterns that tell us where we belong. I will address the racialized contours of culture, sexuality, power, and labor and their implications for "doing race" (Connell, 1987; Martin & Jurik, 1996; Messerschmidt, 1993) and how racially and ethnically motivated hate crime emerges as a supplementary means of constructing identity and difference within those institutional settings. First, however, I will preface this analysis with a brief discussion of the trends in racially and ethnically motivated violence nationwide.

In this chapter, I deal specifically with White violence against racial and ethnic minorities. It is important to recognize, however, that minority on minority violence can also be viewed within the framework of *doing difference* because it too reeks of hierarchical conflict. Interethnic violence among and between subordinate groups "becomes a 'field of possibilities' for transcending class and race discrimination" (i.e., a critical resource for doing race, in particular) (Messerschmidt, 1993, p. 103). But it is important to interpret such violence within the master narrative of White, heterosexual, and masculine hegemony. As Ikemoto (1995) contended, "If you experience racism as one marginalized by it, then you may use racism to explain your relationship with other groups and their members" (p. 307). Even in their relationships with one another, members of subordinate groups are "dependent on the will and leftovers of a dominant group" (p. 308). Ultimately, hegemonic constructions of race or gender identity infuse the experiences and interactions of subordinate groups as well. Nonetheless, the dynamics of violent interactions differ substantially from White on non-White violence. So distinct are these patterns that I have taken them up separately in other contexts (see Perry, 2000, 2001) and will not address them here.

Similarly, in this chapter I do not take up the issue of minority on majority violence (i.e., violence perpetrated against White Euro-Americans) although that too must be understood within the context of the struggle for recognition and identity. Although statistics suggest that White racial victimization does occur (see below), there is reason to question these data. First, we do know that minority group members dramatically underreport their bias-motivated victimization for reasons that range from fear to a lack of confidence in the likely response of law enforcement (Herek, Gillis, & Cogan, 1999). Second, and conversely, is the possibility that White victims are more likely to report what they perceive as racially motivated violence. From their perspective, it may be seen as a serious affront to their status and authority. Of course, these suggestions are speculative at best because there is virtually no scholarly literature on anti-White violence.

Counting Racial and Ethnic Violence

Although both academic and media reports make the claim that ethnoviolence represents a rising tide, the truth is we do not know whether in fact this is the case. For the most part, existing methodologies are both too new and too flawed to give us an accurate picture of changes over time. For example, because the hate crime data are collected in the same way as the other data from the Uniform Crime Reporting (UCR) program, they are fraught with the same well-documented deficiencies (Bureau of Justice Assistance, 1997). In fact, some argue that hate crimes are even more dramatically underreported than other UCR offences (Berrill, 1992; Weiss, 1993). Reasons for underreporting are varied. The undocumented Mexican laborer may fear the repercussions of his or her status being revealed. Moreover, victims may well fear secondary victimization at the hands of law enforcement officials. At the very least, they may perceive that police will not take their victimization seriously. Moreover, the hate crime data collected by the FBI count only officially designated criminal offences, not other forms of violence and harassment, and thus those incidents go undocumented (e.g., racial slurs, pamphleteering, and so forth).

In spite of the limitations, the UCR data are of some use. They represent the most comprehensive database in the country in terms of geographical coverage and in terms of the motivations they reflect. Although inaccurate in absolute numbers, the data may nonetheless be useful as a source of information on general trends and patterns.

Table 16.1 provides a summary of UCR data from 1991 to 1998. The data seem to confirm a number of trends that anecdotal evidence has long suggested:

1. The most frequent motivation consistently is race. Racial bias typically accounts for nearly one third of all incidents; when ethnicity is included, the proportion rises to more than 70%.
2. African Americans are the most likely victims of racially motivated violence. Although making up less than 15% of the population, they represent approximately one-third of the victims of hate crime.
3. Jews are the second most frequently victimized cultural group, representing the vast majority of religious bias victims, and well over 10% of all victims.

Turning to Table 16.2, we get a sense of the other side of the equation (i.e., characteristics of the suspected offenders). As one might expect, White offenders are in the majority. However, we must take these data with a grain of salt because such a large proportion of offenders are typically unknown.

Table 16.3 reveals a number of trends associated specifically with racially and ethnically motivated violence. Most intriguing here are the disparities between crimes against the person and crimes against property. It is apparent that hate crime—relative to normal street crime—is much more likely to involve physical threat and harm to individuals rather than property.

Table 16.1 Hate Crime by Bias Motivation, 1991 to 1998

Description	1991	1992	1993	1994	1995	1996	1997	1998
Race	2,963/62.3	4,025/60.8	4,732/62.4	3,545/59.8	4,831/60.8	5,396/61.6	5,898/59.9	5,360/58.3
Anti-White	888/18.7	1,342/20.3	1,471/31.1	1,010/17.0	1,226/15.4	1,106/12.6	1,267/12.9	989/10.8
Anti-Black	1,689/35.5	2,296/34.7	2,815/59.5	2,174/36.6	2,988/37.6	3,674/41.9	3,838/39	3,573/38.9
Anti-American Indian	11/0.2	26/0.4	27/0.5	22/0.4	41/0.5	51/0.6	44/0.4	66/0.7
Anti-Asian/Pacific islander	287/6.0	217/3.3	258/5.4	211/3.6	355/4.5	355/4.1	437/4.4	359/3.9
Anti-multiracial group	88/1.9	144/2.2	161/3.5	128/2.2	221/2.8	210/2.4	312/3.2	373/4.1
Ethnicity	450/9.5	669/10.1	697/9.2	638/10.8	814/10.2	940/10.7	1,083/11	919/10.0
Anti-Hispanic	242/5.1	369/5.6	472/6.2	337/5.7	516/6.5	564/6.4	636/6.5	595/6.5
Anti-other ethnicity	208/4.4	300/4.5	225/3.0	301/5.1	298/3.7	376/4.3	447/4.5	324/3.5
Religion	917/19.3	1,162/17.5	1,298/17.1	1,062/18.0	1,277/16.1	1,401/16.0	1,483/15.1	1,475/16.0
Anti-Jewish	792/16.7	1,017/15.4	1,143/15.1	915/15.4	1,058/13.3	1,109/12.7	1,159/11.8	1,145/12.5
Anti-Catholic	23/0.5	18/0.3	32/0.4	17/0.3	31/0.4	35/0.4	32/0.3	62/0.7
Anti-Protestant	26/0.5	28/0.4	30/0.4	29/0.5	36/0.5	75/0.9	59/0.6	61/0.7
Anti-Islamic	10/0.2	15/0.2	13/0.2	17/0.3	29/0.4	27/0.3	31/0.3	22/0.2
Anti-other religion	51/1.0	69/1.0	63/0.8	67/1.1	102/1.2	129/1.5	173/1.8	138/1.5
Anti-multireligious group	11/0.2	14/0.3	14/0.3	14/0.2	20/0.3	24/0.3	26/0.3	45/0.5
Anti-atheist/agnostic	4/0.1	1/0.0	3/0.1	3/0.1	1/0.0	2/0.0	3/0.0	2/0.0
Sexual orientation	425/8.9	767/11.6	860/11.3	685/11.5	1,019/12.8	1,016/11.6	1,375/14	1,439/15.7
Anti-homosexual	421/8.9	750/11.3	830/10.9	664/11.2	984/12.4	991/11.3	1,351/13.7	1,407/15.3
Male	NA	557/8.4	516/8.1	501/8.4	735/9.2	757/8.6	912/9.3	972/10.6
Female	NA	93/1.4	121/1.6	100/1.7	146/1.8	150/1.7	229/2.3	265/2.9
Anti-heterosexual	3/0.1	14/0.2	28/0.4	14/0.2	17/0.2	15/0.2	14/0.1	13/0.1
Anti-bisexual	1/0.0	3/0.1	2/0.1	7/0.1	18/0.2	10/0.1	10/0.1	19/0.2
Total	4,755	6,623	7,587	5,932	7,947	8,759	9,839	9,193

Source: Federal Bureau of Investigation, 1992, 1993, 1994, 1995, 1996, 1997, 1998, 1999.

Noted: The first number indicates total number of crimes reported in the United States. The second number indicates the percentage of the sample.

Table 16.2 Reported Number of Incidents of Racially/Ethnically Motivated Violence by Suspected Offender's Race, 1991 to 1998

Description	1991	1992	1993	1994	1995	1996	1997	1998
White	1,679	2,612	2,813	2,939	3,361	4,892	NA	2,988
Black	769	1,381	1,312	1,139	1,209	1,258	NA	759
American Indian	12	14	30	32	40	50	NA	55
Asian/Pacific islander	47	36	53	51	97	106	NA	61
Multiracial	77	98	133	135	98	177	NA	164
Other/unknown	1,974	1,773	3,246	2,966	2,377	2,211	NA	2,252

Source: Federal Bureau of Investigation, 1992, 1993, 1994, 1995, 1996, 1997, 1998, 1999.

Overall, the UCR program provides a starting point for any discussion of hate crime. However, we are well advised to supplement this information with that available from the growing number of nongovernmental bodies devoted to tracking and responding to hate crime. Generally, these agencies tend to gather information specific to one target group, as is the case with the Anti-Defamation League (ADL), for example.

Anti-Semitic Violence

Since 1979, the ADL has generated annual audits of anti-Semitic violence, not only in the United States but worldwide. The mandate of the ADL goes much further than does the FBI's UCR program. ADL includes among its data incidents that may not fit the traditional definition of crime. The ADL tracks murder, assaults, and arsons to be sure, but this is supplemented with attention paid to harassment, petty and serious vandalism, anti-Semitic slurs, and the distribution of neo-Nazi literature.

Table 16.3 General Trends in Racially/Ethnically Motivated Violence

Description	1991	1992	1993	1994	1995	1996	1997	1998
Participating agencies	2,771	6,181	6,551	7,356	9,584	11,355	11,211	10,730
Total incidents	4,558	6,623	7,587	5,932	7,947	8,734	8,049	7,755
Incidents motivated by race/ethnicity								
Incidents	3,413	4,694	4,732	3,545	5,645	5,396	5,898	5,075
Offences	NA	5,914	5,786	4,431	7,192	6,767	9,861	9,235
Victims	NA	6,078	6,011	4,540	7,482	6,994	10,255	9,722
Known offenders	NA	6,939	6,258	4,356	6,709	6,122	8,474	7,489
Crimes against person	3,321	4,695	4,415	3,382	5,539	4,953	6,873	6,305
Crimes against property	1,434	1,219	1,371	1,049	1,639	1,814	2,973	2,905
Racial/ethnic bias motivation								
Anti-White	888	1,342	1,471	1,010	1,226	1,106	1,267	989
Anti-Black	1,689	2,296	2,815	2,174	2,988	3,674	3,838	3,573
Anti-American Indian/ Alaskan native	11	26	27	22	41	51	44	66
Anti-Asian/Pacific islander	287	217	258	211	355	355	437	359
Anti-Hispanic	242	369	472	337	516	564	636	595
Anti-multiracial group	88	144	161	128	221	210	312	373
Anti-other ethnicity	208	300	225	301	298	376	447	324

Source: Federal Bureau of Investigation, 1992, 1993, 1994, 1995, 1996, 1997, 1998, 1999.

Table 16.4 Anti-Semitic Violence by Selected Offense Type, 1990 to 1998

Description	1990	1991	1992	1993	1994	1995	1996	1997	1998
Anti-Defamation League Data Harassment, threats, assaults	758	950	874	1,079	1,197	1,116	941	898	715
Vandalism	927	929	856	788	869	727	781	673	896
Total	1,685	1,879	1,730	1,867	2,066	1,843	1,722	1,571	1,611
Campus anti-Semitic incidents	95	101	114	122	143	NA	NA	NA	NA
FBI (Uniform Crime Report) data	NA	792	1,017	1,143	915	1,058	1,109	1,159	1,145

Source: Anti-Defamation League, 1991, 1992, 1993, 1994, 1995, 1996, 1997, 1998, 1999; Federal Bureau of Investigation, 1992, 1993, 1994, 1995, 1996, 1997, 1998, 1999.

Looking at Table 16.4, one especially disturbing fact leaps immediately to the fore: Since 1991, anti-Semitic violence has been increasingly more likely to involve personal rather than property crimes. Historically, this has been a group victimized by crimes against property, such as synagogue or cemetery desecrations. However, the tide has turned in recent years. In addition, the decline in the number of anti-Semitic incidents beginning in 1995 has corresponded to an increase in the intensity of the violence associated with the incidents. In 1995, for example, an arson in New York City resulted in several deaths. In November of that year, the FBI fortunately stopped an attempt by the TriState Militia to bomb several ADL offices.

Racially Motivated Violence

In contrast to the case of anti-Semitic violence, there is no national, coherent audit of racially motivated violence in the United States. The Southern Poverty Law Center's (SPLC) *Intelligence Report* includes "For the Record," a catalog of bias incidents drawn from media sources, public reports, and initial police reports. The primary value of the SPLC report is that it offers brief narratives describing the incidents. The reports offer a qualitative supplement to the UCR data.

There are some regional organizations committed to collecting hate crime data in their area or state—for example, North Carolinians Against Racist and Religious Violence and the Northwest Coalition Against Malicious Harassment. Alternatively, some local and national organizations have been involved in survey research oriented toward hate crime. The National Institute Against Prejudice and Violence has been at the forefront of these initiatives, publishing reports on workplace and campus ethnoviolence, for example. Indeed, the institute has discovered that violence in both of those settings is more widespread than was anticipated. More narrowly, the Los Angeles County Office of Education recently released a research report documenting a 53% increase in racial hate crime between 1989 and 1992. Although valuable to their immediate constituents, such localized data are obviously limited in the extent to which their findings might be generalized.

The Arab American Anti-Discrimination Committee and the National Asian Pacific American Legal Consortium (NAPALC) are two national organizations that have emerged in recent years as a response to the perceived increase in anti-Asian violence specifically. The annual audits of both agencies are veritable treasure troves of information. They provide summary numbers, synopses of cases, information on legal actions, analyses of regional and national trends, and extensive policy recommendations. The data uncovered by each confirm what anecdotal evidence and intuitive observations have suggested: Riding the wave of anti-immigrant and anti-Asian sentiment, anti-Asian violence was consistently on the rise in closing years of the 20th century (see Table 16.5).

Table 16.5 Anti-Asian Violence by Selected Offense Type, 1993 to 1998

Description	1993	1994	1995	1996	1997	1998
Total incidents (National Asian Pacific American Legal Consortium)	335	452	355	370	144	295
% Vandalism	17	9	16	29	32	31
% Threats/intimidation	9	5	13	16	17	15
% Police abuse	7	4	3	NA	NA	NA
% Harassment	4	12	7	22	19	17
% Assault	28	26	28	33	31	32
FBI (Uniform Crime Report) data	258	211	355	355	437	359

Source: National Asian Pacific American Legal Consortium, 1995, 1999; Federal Bureau of Investigation, 1994, 1995, 1996, 1997, 1998, 1999.

As the data provided here suggest, racially and ethnically motivated violence, although relatively rare, is nonetheless a daily possibility for minority group members. Moreover, I posit that this violence is the physical expression of the endemic racism that pervades race relations in the United States.

The Culture of Racism

Although racism constitutes a structured pattern of relationships between groups, it might simultaneously be understood as a cultural field of discourse in support of that structure. The practices of racism encompass exclusion, marginalization, subordination, and not least of all, violence (Young, 1990). But these patterns are predicated on legitimating ideologies and images that mark the *other*, and the boundaries between self and other, in such a way as to normalize the corresponding inequities. Racist discourse, then, provides "a reservoir of procedural norms that not only tacitly inform routine activity, but are also able to legitimate more purposive, explicitly racist practices" (S. Smith, 1989, p. 150). It is within the cultural realm that we find the justifications for inequities and for ethnoviolence.

At the heart of this cultural field of discourse, one discovers *the American*—a deep seated (albeit often contested) presumption of what it is to be American. For the dominant majority, this invariably suggests Whiteness (Frankenberg, 1993; Wellman, 1993). Or perhaps Wellman's (1993) characterization is more precise because he suggests that the American identity revolves around "a conception of America that defines what it is not" (p. 245). Culturally, White Americans construct themselves in negative relational terms. Their normative Whiteness is created on the backs of the other. The American is not raced, is not Black or Asian, is not even ethnic. Language reinforces this exclusive categorizing to the extent that the norm of Whiteness is implicit in such terms as *Black author, Pakistani doctor*, or the distinction between White *hired hands* and Black *servants*. Simultaneously, White Americans stand on this self-perception as a means of both constructing their identity and marginalizing, even denigrating, that of non-Whites.

Ethnoviolence becomes understandable in this context as an arena in which the primacy of Whiteness can be recreated and in which the boundaries between what is and is not American can be reaffirmed. Xenophobic violence is especially acute with respect to immigrants and their descendants. Chinese, Koreans, Indians, and other people of color are perceived as *perpetual foreigners* who will never assimilate and become American. They will forever be outsiders. The NAPALC (1995, p. 4) cited a talk show host's complaints that world-class figure skaters Kristi Yamaguchi and Michelle Kwan—both second generation Americans—were not "real" Americans. A New York City police officer acted on these sentiments when he beat a Pakistani cab driver. The assault was accompanied by the exclamation that "You immigrants think we're stupid. . . . This is my country, I'll teach you a lesson" (NAPALC, 1995, p. 7).

But what is the basis for such exclusionary conceptions of American-ness and belongingness? Why and how are the racialized others distinct from White America? We might look for a response to these questions in the realm of stereotypes and popular images. It is these portrayals that justify and underlie the hostile treatment of racial minorities.

Stereotypes that distinguish the racialized other from White subjects are grounded in what are held to be the identifying features of racial minorities. They help to distance White from not White. The latter are to be feared, ridiculed, and loathed for their differences as recognized in the popular psyche. Almost invariably, the stereotypes are loaded with disparaging associations, suggesting inferiority, irresponsibility, immorality, and nonhumanness, for example. Consequently, they provide both motive and rationale for injurious verbal and physical assaults on minority groups. Acting on these interpretations allows dominant group members to re-create Whiteness as superiority, while castigating the other for their presumed traits and behaviors. The active construction of Whiteness, then, exploits stereotypes to legitimate violence.

Individuals enter each social interaction carrying with them the baggage that holds these stereotypical images. Whether a particular member of a minority group corresponds to these is almost immaterial. It is assumed—via gross generalizations—that all Blacks are criminal, or all Asians are submissive, or all Jews are greedy. Violence motivated by these preconceptions becomes an effort to prove one's Whiteness—racial solidarity—relative to the defiled other. It is a claim to superiority, which is meant to establish once and for all that the White perpetrator is not Black, is not Asian, is not Jewish. Rather, the perpetrator removes himself from the victim group by engaging in violence directed against it—surely one would not seek to harm the self, only the other.

When the youths of Bensonhurst and Howard Beach, New York, attacked their victims, they did so within the context of a mind-set that distinguished *us* from *them*. The Black youths were to be excluded from the neighborhood because they were presumed to be looking for trouble. In contrast to the White defenders of the race, the Black victims were constructed as threats to the physical and economic security of the White residents of the neighborhoods—of course, they had robbery or murder or sexual assault on their minds because "all Black men" are criminals. Again, attacking these youths provided the offenders with proof of their masculine role of defenders to be sure; but it also provided them with proof of their racial purity and solidarity. They were not like their victims. Rather, they were the virtuous ones: Their actions were inscribed with the mark of the moral supremacy of Whiteness. As Fine (1997) commented in another context,

> Among these white adolescent men, people of color are used consistently as a foil against which acceptable moral, and particularly sexual, standards are established. The goodness of white is always contrasted with the badness of Black—blacks are involved in drugs, Blacks are unacceptable sexually, Black men attempt to "invade" white sexual space. . . . The binary translates in ways that compliment white boys. (p. 57)

And violence is an important mechanism through which these translations are made. It helps to reestablish the natural hierarchy of goodness and evil, strength and weakness, morality and immorality. It ensures that Whites and people of color will inhabit their appropriate places in physical and cultural terms.

Racialized Sexuality

As the preceding quote implies, from the perspective—historical and contemporary—of White Americans, one of the most palpable realms of difference between *us* and *them* lies in sexuality. And it is in this context that people of color are often subject to the most vicious opprobrium and hostility precedent to racial violence. Non-White male sexualities are constructed as "dangerous, powerful, and uncivilized force[s] that [are] hazardous to White women and a serious threat to White men" (Daniels, 1997, p. 93). Consequently, people of color are most at risk when they visibly cross the racialized sexual boundaries by engaging in interracial relationships.

On the basis of these controlling images of people of color, White women, and especially White men, are fearful and suspicious of the sexualities of the other. Speaking of the White fear of Black bodies in particular, West (1993) contended that this

> fear is rooted in visceral feelings about black bodies and fueled by sexual myths of black men and women . . . either as threatening creatures who have the potential for sexual power over whites, or as harmless, desired underlings of a white culture. (p. 119)

In this context, hate crime functions to reinforce the normativeness of White sexuality while punishing people of color for their real or imagined sexual improprieties. It is a means of degrading the bodies of the other, with an eye to controlling them. Hate crime emasculates the sexual threat, thereby firmly establishing the essential boundaries between groups.

Nowhere have White fears been more palpable than in their historical relationship with Black males. No other group has been so narrowly defined by their sexuality than have Black males. This was clear under slavery, where *bucks* were valued for their breeding capacity, but also where Black male subordination was justified on the grounds of his savage and beastly nature. As Messerschmidt (1997) contended, Black masculinity was irrevocably defined in terms of Black sexuality, which in turn, was seen as "animalistic and bestial" (p. 23). Thus, the unrestrained instincts and desires of Black men could be reined in only through the use or threat of violence.

The sexualized image of Black males was reproduced in postbellum culture. In fact, to the extent that Black sexual independence was correlated with their economic and political freedom, they presented an even greater threat to White masculine superiority. The fact that alleged Black rapists were as often castrated as lynched suggests an attempt to emasculate the "savage" by symbolically (and literally) erasing his identity—much as one would control a wild dog. The vicious forms of punishment meted out to Black males served to highlight their animal nature at the same time that it reinforced the power and hegemony of White males.

The presumption of Black male as sexual predator continues to underlie racial difference and racial violence in the contemporary era. In fact, the myth of lascivious, rapacious, and insatiable Black sexuality is perhaps one of the most enduring themes in U.S. culture. It emerged in the 1988 Willie Horton ads; it was also evoked by Clarence Thomas's claim that he was the victim of a "hi-tech" lynching; and it ensured Mike Tyson's conviction for sexual assault. The image of the Black sexual predator is the cultural lens through which Whites perceive Blacks. As such, it provides the context for racially motivated violence: Violent people are worthy of violent repression.

Fine and her colleagues (1997) uncovered contemporary evidence of this dichotomization in their interviews with White male high school students, who proclaimed both their right and duty to preserve the chastity of White girls for themselves.

> Much expressed racism centers on white men's entitled access to white women, thus serving the dual purpose of fixing black men and white women on a ladder of social relations. . . . This felt need to protect white girls translates as a code of behavior for white male students. It is the fact that *Black* men are invading *White* women, the property of *White* men, that is at issue here. (pp. 57–58)

In defending their White girls from the unrestrained sexuality of Black boys, the White boys are also defending themselves—that is, the sanctity of their own carefully restrained, "civilized," normative sexuality. These youths are reacting to messages received from the broader culture.

Moreover, these codes of behavior often rest on violence as a means of policing the relative identities. Yusuf Hawkins, for example, was a proxy for 18-year-old Keith Mondello, evidently aggravated by the revelation that a former girlfriend had dated Black and Hispanic men. Mondello was further disturbed on the night he formed the group that killed Hawkins when the girl told him that she had planned to celebrate her birthday with a group of Black and Puerto Rican friends. The anger and hostility of Mondello and his predominantly Italian peers were so evident that the party was canceled. Deprived of direct targets of their wrath—the potential partygoers—Mondello and his friends turned their anger on three other, interchangeable Black youths who had happened into the neighborhood. One of Mondello's accomplices is said to have exclaimed, "Let's not club the niggers, let's shoot them and show Gina," presumably as a means of reminding Gina and any Black males with an interest in White women that their "unnatural" desires would not be tolerated.

Boundary crossing is perceived as not only unnatural but threatening to the rigid hierarchies that have been built around these presumed differences. This sentiment is evident in a letter to the editor (cited in Mathabane & Mathabane, 1992) written in response to a photo of Black and White youths dancing together:

> Interracial marriages are unbiblical and immoral. God created different races of people and placed them amongst themselves. . . . There is nothing for white Americans to gain by mixing their blood with blood of other peoples. There will only be irreversible damage for us. (p. 186)

The rhetoric of antimiscegenation is especially common among White supremacists. How else could the White race maintain its supremacy other than by maintaining its purity? Any "contamination" by non-White blood introduces into the White bloodline all of those reviled deficiencies characteristic of the "mud people." Supremacists look with disgust and hostility on those race traitors who seek out non-White mates, as is the case for the Klansman overheard by Ezekiel (1995) at a Klan rally: "What is the worst, to see a couple—to see some White woman and some Black man—ugh! It just turns my stomach" (p. 10).

For White racialists such as Alfred Strom, race mixing constitutes part of the genocidal agenda of non-White races. Strom (retrieved from www.com/FREESP) links the rhetoric of White supremacy with that of antimiscegenation, arguing that the White race's

> continued existence would undoubtedly [sic] be assumed by our superior intelligence and unmatched technology, if it were not for those who practice and promote the genocide of our people through racial mixing. By their actions they are killing us. . . . They kill infinite generations of our future. Their crime—the crime of racial mixture—is far, far worse than mere murder.

Race mixing is deemed to be yet another symptom of the loss of White power and identity because it violates the sacred order of the established hierarchy. It muddies the boundaries between the races in such a way that the politicized superiority of Whites is thrown into question. Consequently, miscegenation elicits calls for enforced racial purity as a means of correcting the emerging imbalance in the relationship between Whites and non-Whites. The latter must be put back in their place, by force, if necessary.

(Dis)Empowering Race

An obvious hallmark of racism as a structure of domination is the restriction of the power of non-White racial groups. To this end, racial minorities have historically been limited in terms of social, political, and economic power (the latter will be explicitly addressed in the next section). The sorts of racial constructions and categorizations discussed earlier are the stuff of which social exclusions are built, to the extent that they legitimate discrepancies in access to opportunities and privilege. The power that is wielded—physically and socially—by Whites is exercised in such a way as to "develop, evolve, nurture, spread, impose, and enforce the very myths . . . that underlie racism" (Fernandez, 1996, p. 160).

Historically in the United States, power has been cautiously guarded by imposing restrictions on citizenship and its correspondent rights. Whether through formal policy or informal practice, racialized minorities have consistently been disenfranchised as a means of limiting their voice and position in the United States. Although no ethnic or racial group is legally excluded from attaining U.S. citizenship at this time, it does not necessarily follow that all groups are able to enjoy the privileges associated with this status. Racial minorities continue to be marginalized by their inability to gain full access to political, civil, and social rights, such that inclusion is still constituted of and by Whiteness, not color. Civil rights violations of an array of racial and ethnic groups are endemic. The 1992 beating of Rodney King, and the 1997 sodomization of Abner Louima—both by police officers—are but the tip of the iceberg. The 1997 sweep of Chandler, Arizona, constituted a dramatic breach of the civil rights and liberties of the dozens of apparently Hispanic citizens—people randomly stopped and ordered to produce their papers, solely on the basis of their presumed ethnicity. Similarly, housing and mortgage discrimination continues to be a determining factor in the persistence of racial and ethnic segregation (Hacker, 1995; R. Smith, 1995). And, although the political power of minorities has increased somewhat over the past couple of decades, all such groups are still underrepresented in the formal machinery of politics (Hacker, 1995; Young, 1990).

Racially motivated violence is directly implicated in efforts to maintain these unequal relations of power. It is itself a mechanism of social power by which White males in particular assert a particular version of hegemonic Whiteness. It is not difficult to trace the history of racially motivated violence during periods when the power of Whites was perceived to be at risk—periods in which this identity was reconstructed through the exercise of violence as a resource for doing race. Nor is it difficult to identify contemporary illustrations.

Violence is empowering for its users: Physical dominion implies a corresponding cultural mastery. Gunner Lindberg boasted in a letter of his killing of a Vietnamese man, Thien Minh Ly:

> Oh I killed a jap a while ago. I stabbed him to death at Tuslin High School . . . I walked right up to him and he was scared . . . he got happy that he wasn't gona get jumped. Then I hit him . . . I stabbed him about 7 or 8 times. (Phan, "Another Senseless Hate Crime," retrieved from www.avl.umd.edu/staff/nowk/hate_crime.html)

The murderer's use of the derogatory label *jap* implies the racial distancing and animosity that underlie Lindberg's motive. He signifies his dominant Whiteness by derogating Ly's Asian identity. That Ly was in fact Vietnamese and not Japanese further confirms Lindberg's presumption of superiority and hauteur. It is enough to know that Ly was Asian—no need to discern his true ethnicity or national origin. Any Asian could be at risk. Thus, the entire community is put on notice. Moreover, Lindberg's awareness that his racial identity was reinforced by his acts is clear in his pretentious statement within the letter: "Here's the clippings from the newspaper we were on all the channels." Lindberg assumes that his audience—on learning of his exploits in the media—will judge his Whiteness and not find him lacking. He is appropriately accountable to his race, given his eagerness to destroy the other. No race traitor there, rather Lindberg announces through his actions that he is in solidarity with the White race, thereby preserving White privilege and position.

Such racial constructions, however, are dynamic and relational. Not only does this example illustrate how perpetrators empower Whiteness through violence. It is also suggestive of the opposite: disempowering the victims' communities. Ly's death—like other hate-motivated assaults—also represents an effort to render impotent the targeted group. Individual assaults are warning signs to others like the victim—you could be next. Richard Wright, in his now classic *Black Boy*, speaks to the vicarious experience of racial violence:

> The things that influenced my conduct as a Negro did not have to happen to me directly; I needed but to hear of them to feel their full effects in the deepest layers of my consciousness.

A Black person or a Korean person or a Hispanic person need not have been a victim personally. Like Wright, they are all too aware of their consistent vulnerability because of their race. The immutability of their racial identity invokes hopelessness—they are victimized for reasons they cannot change. In the midst of the "Dot Busters" campaign of terror against Asian Indians in Jersey City, an open letter made clear the generalized vulnerability of a group: "If I'm walking down the street and I see a Hindu and the setting is right, I will just hit him or her" (cited in Harvard Law Review, 1993). Thus, hate crimes have the potential to throw an entire community into paralysis, forcing them to withdraw further into themselves. Marovitz (1993) observed that

> By making members of minority communities fearful, by making them suspicious of other groups and of the power structure that is supposed to protect them, these incidents can damage society and polarize our communities. (p. 50)

Such violence reaffirms the subordinate status of minority communities. At its extreme, it discourages social and political participation by keeping potential victims off the streets and out of the public eye.

Paradoxically, efforts to render minority communities impotent—whether through the mechanism of hate crime or other repressive means—can backfire. Rather than hobbling the victim group, they may in fact mobilize the community. This was the case in New York City, for example, in which Haitians, accompanied by other Caribbeans, demonstrated angrily, vocally, and visibly against the racist violence represented by Louima's brutal beating at the hands of police officers. Although innumerable victims had previously remained silent out of fear and intimidation, the publicity surrounding Louima's victimization galvanized the community into action.

A decade earlier, other New York neighborhoods witnessed similar rallies. The racially motivated murders of Michael Griffith in Howard Beach and Yusuf Hawkins in Bensonhurst both resulted in flurries of organizing and demonstrating. An organization created after the first murder—New York City Civil Rights Coalition—was still available to lend its support to those involved in prosecuting the Hawkins case. Both incidents inspired widespread demonstrations condemning the racism of the perpetrators' communities, as well as the racist culture of New York City generally. Clearly these cases stimulated rather than disabled the communities.

Unfortunately, this posture of empowerment is often seen as an affront to White dominance. The victim community is perceived to be violating the anticipated rules of behavior. Instead of accepting their subordination, they resist it. In such a context, incidents of hate crime may escalate in retaliation. Consider the case of Farmington, New Mexico, in the mid-1970s. In response to the vicious murders of three Indian men, local Navajo activists established the Coalition for Navajo Liberation. Although the immediate purpose of the coalition was to see justice done in the prosecutions for the offense, it soon expanded to address the broader patterns of discrimination and victimization experienced by natives in the border town. As the coalition dug in its heels and intensified its demands for justice, the antagonism of the White community became clear. Rather than discourage anti-Navajo violence, the activism of the Coalition for Navajo Liberation seemed to inspire it, as evident in the increase in the number of drive-by shootings of Navajo people (Barker, 1992). This case typifies how activism—a sign of strength—can beget animosity. It may in fact elevate the level of hostility already existing in a community.

Seen in this light, hate crime is a reactionary tool, a resource for the reassertion of Whiteness over color. It is a form of "resistance to any diminishment in the authorial claims of a particular White identity" (Hesse, Rai, Bennett, & McGilchrist, 1992, p. 172). Racially motivated violence, then, is available as an albeit violent and extreme response to the other who is out of control, who has overstepped his or her social or political boundaries, thereby challenging the entrenched hierarchies.

The Economics of Race

The presumption of racial hierarchies has had, and continues to have, a profound impact on the place of minority groups within the labor process. In particular, people of color have traditionally been marginalized and exploited as cheap and malleable labor (Young, 1990). Thus, although the political and social gains made by minorities in recent years threaten White cultural identity, economic gains represent a more direct and tangible threat to White economic security. People of color who presume to advance on the economic ladder are perceived as unfair and undeserving competitors and as takers of "White" jobs. People of color are seen to have overstepped the economic boundaries that have long contributed to their marginalization. Consequently, White fear and resentment are frequently and viciously translated into racial violence in the context of labor activities.

Many White men now picture and present themselves as the *new minority*. They experience a sense of displacement and dispossession relative to people of color. This imagery of White-man-as-victim gives voice to the insecurity of White men in a weakened economy. It also provides an ideological rationale for re-creating people of color as legitimate victims. Thus, perpetrators of ethnoviolence are akin to the young White men interviewed by Fine (Fine et al. 1997), who act or "speak for a gendered and racial group whose privilege has been rattled and whose wrath is boiling over" (p. 66).

Where have all the jobs gone? From the perspective of many disaffected White workers, the answer is clear enough. They have not been relocated off-shore or replaced by technology. Rather, they have been stolen from them by lesser and unfit beings: Those uppity others who have won the ears of politicians and employers alike. The most visible manifestation of this inverted preference for minorities is the bogey of affirmative action. There is a widespread consensus emerging that affirmative action policies have resulted in the displacement of qualified White workers by unqualified minority workers (Fine et al. 1997). In a curious inversion of history, many White males imagine an array of signs stating "Whites Need Not Apply." This is particularly frustrating in the context of the cultural constructions of Blacks, Hispanics, and Native Americans, for example, as lazy and undisciplined. Where White workers imagine themselves at the opposite pole—hardworking and dedicated—the backdrop is set for a volatile response.

Perceptions of reverse discrimination provide the motive and rationale for harassment and assaults of minority workers. This has become evident in the studies of workplace ethnoviolence carried out by the Prejudice Institute (Ehrlich, 1989), which found relatively high rates of harassment and defamation of people of color (i.e., those who "don't belong"). Successive reports of the U.S. Commission on Civil Rights (1990, 1992a, 1992b) also reveal the links between hostility toward affirmative action and violence against minorities. For example, a 1990 Commission on Civil Rights summary report observed that

> most of the historical episodes of anti-democratic action occurred in times, in places, and among people who suffered from economic dislocation. . . . Their grievances in those circumstances tend to focus on the Federal government and on minorities . . . because they are believed to receive unfair advantage from Government programs. (pp. 15–16)

Ethnoviolence is an attempt to reclaim the advantages of Whiteness. It is an assertion of racial superiority and, more important, proprietorship: To the White man belongs the spoils, not some "third-world invader." Violence motivated by the resentment of labor competition provides the perpetrator with the opportunity to publicly announce his indignation, and correspondingly, his right to work. This is the essence of White masculinity after all: the ability to provide. If he is to distinguish himself from minorities of color, he must forcibly resist the latter's access to equitable conditions of employment.

There is an abundance of examples to illustrate the link between job competition and racially motivated violence. An especially brutal illustration of this connection occurred in Novato, California, in 1995. Robert Page attacked Eddy Wu, a Chinese American male, at a supermarket. Page stabbed Wu twice in the parking lot, then followed him back into the store where he stabbed him several times more. Wu was left with multiple injuries, including a punctured lung. Page later testified (NAPALC, 1995) that he had consciously set out to "kill me a Chinaman" because "they got all the good jobs" (p. 8).

Regardless of their diversity and uneven performance in the United States, Asians are inscribed with the mantle of prosperity in spite of their perpetual foreignness. Because they are not seen as Americans, Asians risk reprisal when they become viable, if not superior, competitors. The months of violence, harassment, and intimidation experienced by Vietnamese shrimpers in Texas illustrates the point. Supported by the KKK, local White shrimpers engaged in a campaign of violence from 1979 to 1980, which included sinking the boats belonging to the Vietnamese, cutting their fishing nets, assaults, and harassment. Gilbert Pampa (cited in U.S. Commission on Civil Rights, nd), then director of the federal Community Relations Service, observed that

> there was displeasure on the part of the other fishermen concerning the overindulgence of refugees. [The American fishermen] did not feel that the refugees were competing in the American way. The refugees worked on Sundays, stayed longer hours on the bay, and sometimes caught shrimp outside certain demarcated areas of the bay. [The Americans] felt that this was unfair to them, and the competition turned to open conflict. (p. 51)

It is not only individual immigrants and Americans of Asian descent who are held responsible for this loss of place. Asian nations (often interchangeable) represent a global economic threat. The lengthy trade deficit with Japan has had serious repercussions on industry, employment, and intercultural relationships. In his statement to the U.S. Commission on Civil Rights (nd), Congressman Robert Matsui argued that

> In recent years, most of the industries that have suffered the worst have been hurt by imports from countries in South East Asia. As anger develops against nations of Asia that anger is transferred to Americans of Asian ancestry who appear to be quick and "easy" targets. (p. 63)

The 1982 murder of Vincent Chin in Detroit is but the most extreme in an ongoing series of such attacks on Asian Americans. Two White men engaged Chinese American Chin in an argument in a bar, referring to him as "nip" and "chink." After leaving the bar, the men chased Chin with a baseball bat. When they caught up with him, they delivered a series of blows to his head, knee, and chest that resulted in Chin's death 4 days later. That this example fits the pattern is evident in the following two facts of the case: The assailants were laid-off autoworkers, and one was reported to have said, "It is because of you that we are out of work" (U.S. Commission on Civil Rights, nd, p. 43).

Fearing a loss of domestic and global hegemony, White perpetrators of racially motivated violence seek to redeem their status through repressive and retaliatory acts of violence. The viciousness of both the verbal and physical attacks attests to their rage at the loss of relative advantage. Rather than appear meek and accepting—the very antithesis of hegemonic White masculinity—White males assert themselves through misdirected violence. Better to be seen as active agents of their own destiny than victims of the encroachment of inferior others.

Conclusion

In a culture in which the color line is subject to increasing challenges and blurring, racial violence is a pervasive threat. Moreover, it is not the exclusive weapon of white-hooded or brown-shirted rednecks. Rather, it is shared by those without a rigid ideological dogma or without White supremacist group affiliation. In other words, racially motivated violence is not an aberration associated with a lunatic or extremist fringe. It is a normative means of asserting racial identity relative to the victimized other; it is a natural extension—or enactment—of the racism that allocates privilege along racial lines.

The cultural and structural contexts that condition hate crime are many and varied: Stereotypes, language, legislation, and differential employment practices are but a few. Stereotyping Native Americans as savages, and excluding Asians from citizenship have served to maintain the stigmatized outsider identity of these others. These same others have been defined negatively in terms of their relationship to some dominant norm—that is, Black is defined as inherently inferior to White, Jewish inferior to Christian. Racial violence has been described here as a primary site for enacting these differences, as well as acting on them.

However, there is reason for hope: Because difference is socially constructed, it can also be socially reconstructed. In other words, as a society, we can redefine the ways in which difference matters. We can strive for a just and democratic society in which the full spectrum of diversity addressed here is reevaluated in a positive and celebratory light that would preclude violence motivated by racial or ethnic difference.

We would do well to heed Young's (1990) advice that we embrace a positive politics of difference. This would involve much more than efforts to assimilate others, or merely tolerate their presence. Rather, it challenges us to celebrate our differences. Of course, this requires that much of our current way of ordering the world would be radically altered. It means that we must cease to define *different* as inferior and see it instead as simply not the same.

To engage in such a powerful politics is to resist the temptation to ask all others to conform to an artificial set of norms and expectations. It is to reclaim and value the natural heterogeneity of this nation rather than force a false homogeneity. It is to refuse to denigrate the culture and experiences of Black people, Jews, or Native Americans. It is to learn and grow from the strength and beauty that alternate cultures have to offer.

References

Anti-Defamation League. 1991. *Hate crime laws.* New York: Author.
Anti-Defamation League. 1992. *Hate crime laws.* New York: Author.
Anti-Defamation League. 1993. *Hate crime laws.* New York: Author.
Anti-Defamation League. 1994. *Hate crime laws.* New York: Author.
Anti-Defamation League. 1995. *Hate crime laws.* New York: Author.
Anti-Defamation League. 1996. *Hate crime laws.* New York: Author.
Anti-Defamation League. 1997. *Hate crime laws.* New York: Author.
Anti-Defamation League. 1998. *Hate crime laws.* New York: Author.
Anti-Defamation League. 1999. *Hate crime laws.* New York: Author.
Barker, R. 1992. *The broken circle.* New York: Simon & Schuster.
Berrill, K. 1992. Anti-gay violence and victimization in the United States: An overview. In., *Hate crimes: Confronting violence against lesbians and gay men,* eds. G. Herek & K. Berrill, 19–45. Newbury Park, CA: Sage.
Bureau of Justice Assistance. 1997. *A policy maker's guide to hate crimes.* Washington, DC: Government Printing Office.
Connell, R. 1987. *Gender and power.* Stanford, CA: Stanford University Press.
Daniels, J. 1997. *White lies: Race, class, gender and sexuality in White supremacist discourse.* New York: Routledge.
Ehrlich, H. 1989. Studying workplace violence. *International Journal of Group Tensions* 19: 69–80.
Ezekiel, R. 1995. *The Racist Mind.* New York: Penguin.
Federal Bureau of Investigation. 1992. *Hate crime statistics, 1991.* Washington, DC: Government Printing Office.
Federal Bureau of Investigation. 1993. *Hate crime statistics, 1992.* Washington, DC: Government Printing Office.
Federal Bureau of Investigation. 1994. *Hate crime statistics, 1993.* Washington, DC: Government Printing Office.

Federal Bureau of Investigation. 1995. *Hate crime statistics, 1994.* Washington, DC: Government Printing Office.

Federal Bureau of Investigation. 1996. *Hate crime statistics, 1995.* Washington, DC: Government Printing Office.

Federal Bureau of Investigation. 1997. *Hate crime statistics, 1996.* Washington, DC: Government Printing Office.

Federal Bureau of Investigation. 1998. *Hate crime statistics, 1997.* Washington, DC: Government Printing Office.

Federal Bureau of Investigation. 1999. *Hate crime statistics, 1998.* Washington, DC: Government Printing Office.

Fernandez, J. 1996. The impact of racism on Whites in corporate America. In *Impacts of racism on White Americans,* eds. B. Bowser and R. Hunt. Thousand Oaks, CA: Sage.

Fine, M. 1997. Witnessing Whiteness. In *Off White: Readings on race, power and society,* eds. M. Fine, L. Weis, L. Powell, and L. M. Wong, 57–65. New York: Routledge.

Fine, M., Weis, L., and Addelston, J. 1997. (In) secure times: Constructing White working class masculinities in the late twentieth century. *Gender and Society* 11(1): 52–68.

Frankenberg, R. 1993. *White women, race matters: The social construction of Whiteness.* Minneapolis: University of Minnesota Press.

Hacker, A. 1995. *Two nations: Black and White, separate, hostile, unequal.* New York: Ballantine.

Harvard Law Review. 1993. Racial violence against Asian Americans 106: 1926–1943.

Herek, G. M., Gillis, J. R., and Cogan, J. C. 1999. Psychological correlates of hate crime victimization among lesbian, gay, and bisexual adults. *Journal of Consulting and Clinical Psychology* 67(6): 945–951.

Hesse, B., Rai, D., Bennett, C., and McGilchrist, P. 1992. *Beneath the surface: Racial harassment.* Aldershot, UK: Avebury.

Ikemoto, L. 1995. Traces of the master narrative in the story of African American/Korean American conflict: How we constructed Los Angeles. In *Critical race theory,* ed. R. Delgado, 305–315. Philadelphia: Temple University Press.

Marovitz, W. 1993. Hate or bias crime legislation. In *Bias crime,* ed. R. Kelly, 48–53. Chicago: Office of International Criminal Justice.

Martin, S. and Jurik, N. 1996. *Doing justice, doing gender.* Thousand Oaks, CA: Sage.

Mathabane, M. and Mathabane, G. 1992. *Love in Black and White: The triumph of love over prejudice and taboo.* New York: HarperPerennial.

Messerschmidt, J. 1993. *Masculinities and crime.* Lanham, MD: Rowman & Littlefield.

Messerschmidt, J. 1997. *Crime as structured action.* Thousand Oaks, CA: Sage.

National Asian Pacific American Legal Consortium (NAPALC). 1995. *Audit of violence against Asian and Pacific Americans.* Washington, DC: NAPALC.

National Asian Pacific American Legal Consortium (NAPALC). 1999. *Audit of violence against Asian and Pacific Americans.* Washington, DC: NAPALC.

Omi, M. and Winant, H. 1993. The Los Angeles "race riots" and contemporary U.S. polities. In *Reading Rodney King, reading urban uprisings,* ed. R. Gooding-Williams, 97–114. New York: Routledge.

Perry, B. 2000. Beyond Black and White: Interethnic minority violence. *Sociology of Crime, Law and Deviance* 2: 301–324.

Perry, B. 2001. *In the name of hate: Understanding hate crime.* New York: Routledge.

Smith, R. 1995. *Racism in the post-civil rights era.* Albany: State University of New York Press.

Smith, S. 1989. *The politics of "race" and residence: Citizenship, segregation, and White supremacy in Britain.* Cambridge: Polity.

U.S. Commission on Civil Rights. 1990. *Intimidation and Violence: Racial and religious bigotry in America.* Washington, DC: Government Printing Office.

U.S. Commission on Civil Rights. 1992a. *Civil rights issues facing Asian Americans.* Washington, DC: Government Printing Office.

U.S. Commission on Civil Rights. 1992b. *Racial and ethnic tensions in American communities: Poverty, inequality and discrimination.* Washington, DC: Government Printing Office.

U.S. Commission on Civil Rights. (nd). *Recent actions against citizens and residents of Asian descent.* Washington, DC: Government Printing Office.

Weiss, J. 1993. Ethnoviolence's impact upon and response of victims and the community. In *Bias crime,* ed. R. Kelly, 174–185. Chicago: Office of International Criminal Justice.

Wellman, D. 1993. *Portraits of White racism.* Cambridge: Cambridge University Press.

West, C. 1993. Learning to talk race. In *Reading Rodney King, reading urban uprisings,* ed. R. Gooding-Williams, 255–260. New York: Routledge.

West, C. and Fenstermaker, S. 1995. Doing difference. *Gender and Society* 9(1): 8–37.

Young, I. M. 1990. *Justice and the politics of difference.* Princeton, NJ: Princeton University Press.

Explaining Race and Violent Crime

More so than any other area of the race and crime debate, criminologists unanimously agree that, while whites commit the majority of the violent crimes in America, racial minorities (particularly African Americans), are acutely overrepresented in those arrested for the FBI's *Uniform Crime Reports* four violent index crimes (murder, forcible rape, robbery, and aggravated assault). For example, in 2002, African Americans were arrested for 50 percent of the murders, 33.7 percent of rapes, 52.7 percent of robberies, and 33.8 percent of aggravated assaults (*Uniform Crime Reports* 2002). Because these figures have remained consistently high over the past century, scholars have sought plausible explanations for this trend. While the initial scholarship centered almost exclusively on African Americans, in past years, it has broadened to include scholarship on violence in the Native American, Latino, and Asian American communities. This section provides readings related to each of these groups.

In contrast to some of the early race and crime scholarship which suggested that minority criminality (including violent crime) was attributable to their physical and biological make up, during the 1950s, pioneering research by Marvin Wolfgang (1958), pointed to a consistent pattern of violent behavior among urban males. While it took over a decade to formalize his thoughts, when they were published in collaboration with a colleague (Wolfgang and Ferracuti 1967), the resulting subculture of violence thesis became one of the leading explanations for accounting for the pronounced levels of violence in urban communities which were, and continue to be, heavily populated by racial minorities.

Seventeen years after the publication of the classic work of Wolfgang and Ferracuti, the author of the first chapter, Darnell Hawkins, provided a detailed critique as to why the theory was inadequate for explaining violence in the African American community. Pointing to the lack of empirical grounding for the theory as well as an underappreciation for the economic, political, and social disadvantages of African Americans, Hawkins presents his own model for explaining homicide among African Americans. Included in his model are notions about the low value placed on black life, the differential handling of pre-homicidal behaviors (i.e., assaults) among African Americans and whites, and the role of economic deprivation.

In line with Hawkins's work, the second chapter in the section examines the vastly understudied topic of homicide among American Indians. Bachman's pioneering work examines the role of social disorganization and economic deprivation in the etiology of homicides on reservations. Looking at over one hundred counties where reservations were located, her analysis showed that both perspectives have utility in explaining homicides on reservations.

The third chapter provides an analysis of homicides in Miami. This chapter is significant because it illustrates the power of stereotypes. As the authors note, the Mariel Cuban refugees were made famous by the media's portrayal of them as being violent criminals exiled to the United States. This image was further perpetuated with the release of the American movie classic *Scarface*. Al Pacino's depiction of a Mariel Cuban who, as a result of his ruthlessness, rises to the top of the South Florida drug trade, unfortunately left an indelible negative image in the minds of millions of Americans. The chapter presented here shatters the prevailing stereotypical views. Analyzing data from over 1,600 homicides committed between 1980 and 1990, the authors show that, in contrast to conventional wisdom, the Mariels were not involved in homicides involving strangers. On the contrary, the data showed that they were primarily engaging in homicides related to relationships.

The final chapter in the section takes a look at attitudes toward marital violence in several Asian American communities. While it is widely accepted that Asian Americans are underrepresented in crime statistics, this chapter provides context for such figures in a study of domestic violence. Noting the endorsement of male privilege in some Asian communities, the authors point to the connections between these attitudes and the acceptance of wife abuse. Further, the authors show how tradition results in the under reporting of wife abuse. Finally, the authors point to the influence of educational attainment on the attitudes toward marital violence.

References

Uniform Crime Reports, 2002. Washington, DC: Federal Bureau of Investigation.

Wolfgang, M. 1958. *Patterns in criminal homicide*. Philadelphia: University of Pennsylvania Press.

Wolfgang, M., and Ferracutti, F. 1967. *The subculture of violence: Towards an integrated theory in criminology*. London: Tavistock.

17

Black and White Homicide Differentials

Alternatives to an Inadequate Theory

Darnell F. Hawkins

Rates of homicide among blacks in the United States have been consistently higher than those of white Americans and of other American nonwhites. Subculture of violence theory has been the most widely accepted explanation for these differences. In this chapter, I argue that subculture theory ignores or underemphasizes a variety of historical-structural, situational, and economic factors that might explain high rates of black homicide. Seldom examined is the behavior of the law. Three theoretical propositions are offered as guides for future research. These propositions suggest that (1) the historical devaluing of black life, (2) official responses of the criminal justice system to prehomicide behavior among blacks, and (3) the direct effects of economic deprivation are important causal factors.

Over the last 50 years or more, social science studies and official crime statistics have shown consistently higher rates of homicide among American blacks than among whites. Recent data suggest that the black homicide rate is also substantially higher than that of other disadvantaged minority groups such as Hispanics (Silberman, 1978).[1] Indeed, given the fact that white American rates of homicide are higher than those of many other countries, the black American rate of homicide may be among the highest in the world. Bohannon (1960) showed that they far exceed those found in African societies.

Somewhat surprisingly, social scientists have not done much about assessing and explaining black criminal violence (in comparison to other areas of actual or perceived sociopathology among blacks). There may be several reasons for the relative neglect of this question. First, during the last two decades, criminologists have shown decreasing interest in the study of crime etiology. Labeling and conflict theory have shifted attention to the society's part in defining crime and deviance, and in the identification and processing of criminal offenders. Thus, social researchers have chosen to study such topics as patterns of racial discrimination in arrest and sentencing rather than the causes of pathological behavior. Second, black-white crime difference has been a socially and politically sensitive topic during the last 20 years. Some researchers have tended to underemphasize such differences. Finally, it appears that the preeminence of subcultural theory among criminologists has prevented the kind of critical discourse and analysis needed for the study of this topic and many others. Subculture of violence theory has remained the most widely used sociological explanation for the etiology of criminal homicide.

Today there is renewed interest in the etiology of crime, especially crimes of violence. In this regard, Hindelang (1981) has suggested that sociological theorists of crime must begin to use clues provided by known correlates of criminal behavior as a basis for generating and modifying theory. However, it is also obvious that the traditional notions of crime causation must be reconceptualized to include a variety of concerns raised by labeling and conflict theorists and by current and historical studies of crime and criminal justice.[2]

In this chapter, I present a theoretical framework for the study of homicide among blacks in the United States. First, I assess the statistical evidence. Next, I discuss and criticize competing theories that are designed to explain disproportionately high rates of black homicide—particularly the concept of a subculture of violence. Finally, I offer three theoretical propositions, along with conclusions and hypotheses, as supplementary or alternative to subculture of violence theory for the disproportionately high rate of homicide offending and victimization among American blacks.

Incidence of Homicide—Blacks and Whites

Studies conducted by Brearley (1932), Wolfgang (1958), Pokorny (1965a), Voss and Hepburn (1968), Boudouris (1970), Block (1975), Lundsgaarde (1977), and Farley (1980) are among those which have provided data on the extent of black homicide in the United States. Shin, Jedlicka, and Lee (1977) provide one of the most comprehensive recent summaries of national trends in homicide victimization. They note that during the twentieth century, homicide rate trends have been different for blacks and whites. From 1910 to 1930, the white rate was relatively stable at about 4 to 5 per 100,000 population. By 1940, the rate was around 2. The pre-World War II rates for blacks were more irregular. The rate was 22 in 1910, 43 during the middle 1920s, and down to 26 in 1940. The downward trend continued for both blacks and whites until 1955 when rates began to increase considerably. However, it is shown that for blacks, the proportional increases were less than for whites through 1974, when the researchers end their investigation.

Shin et al. (1977) also provide sex- and age-specific data that show more clearly the patterns of black homicide victimization. From 1940 to 1974, the black male homicide rate had increased from 57 to 78 per 100,000. They report that in 1973, nonwhite males between the ages of 25 and 34 had a homicide rate of 153 compared to 15 for white males in this age range. Rates for black men in this age range have shown a decline since 1973; however, recent data supplied by the Public Health Service show that homicide has replaced accidents as the leading cause of death for young, nonwhite men.[3] In addition, the homicide offense and victimization rates among black women have ranged from two to four times the rates of white men (Wolfgang, 1958; Shin et al., 1977).

Since homicide is primarily an intraracial phenomenon, high rates of black victimization indicate similarly high rates of black offending. However, as in the study of other types of crime, official homicide offense statistics vary in quality and reliability. The *Uniform Crime Reports* (UCR) of the Federal Bureau of Investigation provide arrest data for homicide offenders and for the last 20 years also provide some victimization data. Because of the methods for reporting crime used by the FBI, race-, sex-, and age-specific offense data have not always been readily available. Though the proportion of all homicides committed by nonblacks has decreased over the last 20 years, the incidence among blacks is still four to five times greater than what one would expect given the relative size of the black population, that is, 10% to 12% during those decades (see UCR, 1960–1980).

While these statistics raise a number of social, political, and moral questions, the social scientist's task has been to provide an explanation for the disproportionately high rates of criminal homicide among black Americans.[4] Are the rates accurate? If they are, what factors account for the black-white differentials observed? Many commentators have urged caution in using aggregate crime rates to propose a causal link between race and crime despite the obvious racial imbalance in statistics (for example, Bonger, 1943, and Wolfgang (1964).

Patterning of Black Homicide

The notes of caution raised by Bonger (1943) and Wolfgang (1964) emphasize the need for more detailed examination of homicide patterns among blacks. Which segments of the black population have the highest rates? Is the social patterning of homicide in the black community similar to that found among whites? While the black rate of arrests for all crimes is higher than the white rate, residential patterns are evident. *Uniform Crime Reports* data for 1975 show that blacks living in rural areas constituted 10%of the rural population and made up 10%of arrests for all types of crimes. The black suburban population was 15%, while only 12% of all suburban arrestees were black. A large discrepancy between population figures and arrest rates was evident only in urban areas.[5] While this was not an analysis of homicide rates, a further examination of homicide statistics may yield similar findings.

Pettigrew and Spier (1962) found that black homicide rates differed by regions of the country. They conclude that a ranking of states on the basis of black homicide rates is similar to a ranking based upon white rates. A recent analysis of homicide rates in Atlanta found blacks and whites of similar socioeconomic status (SES) to have similar rates of family and acquaintance homicide (Centerwall, 1982). Blau and Blau (1982) report that while poverty, per se, does not explain rates of violent crime in urban areas, such rates are significantly related to income inequality between blacks and whites and to SES inequality among blacks themselves.

All of the studies reported above are ecological analyses. Consequently, they provide no data on the characteristics of individual offenders and victims, such as those required to examine the social patterning of black homicide in the United States. Indeed, a few nonecological studies do exist (Pokorny, 1965a; Boudouris, 1970; Lundsgaarde, 1977). However, the amount of data they provide on variables, such as the SES of black or white homicide offenders and victims, goes little beyond the kind of data provided in the pioneering work of homicide in Philadelphia by Wolfgang (1958). Most studies generally conclude that homicide victims and offenders are more likely to be black, poor, undereducated, and to reside in the South.

The Subculture of Violence: American Blacks

Analysts in the subcultural tradition appear to have proceeded on the basis of two rather plausible assumptions. First, they have noted that criminals' homicide statistics in contrast to data for other types of crime are less subject to distortion by police and other criminal justice officials, for example, by differing patterns of detection and prosecution. There are also high clearance rates for homicide cases in comparison to other crimes. Thus, they conclude that consistently high rates of black homicide represent a *real* phenomenon. Further, to the extent that whites and other racial groups do not display similar levels of violence, the cause does not lie within the whole of American culture.

Wolfgang and Ferracuti (1967) were among the first to propose the idea of a subculture of violence as a potentially integrating theory for explaining and predicting various patterns of criminal homicide. Certain subgroups in America are said to live in a cultural and social milieu that encourages physical aggression, or at least does not actively discourage it. Wolfgang and Feracutti noted that on the basis of an awareness of social, economic, and political disparities between whites and blacks, any diligent researcher would propose that the black crime rate would be higher than the white rate and that there would be a "large spread to the learning of, resort to and criminal display of the violence value among minority groups such as Negroes" (1967, p. 264).

Subculture of violence theory, therefore, tends to identify the value system of a given subculture as the locus of crime causation. Emphasis is also placed upon the role of social learning as the principal process by which aggressive behavior is acquired. While there is some attention paid to the social, economic, and political deprivation within subcultures, such deprivation itself is seldom seen as a direct cause of crime. That is, the impact of deprivation on crime is mediated by social values—in particular, the existence of a positive attitude toward the use of violence. Most subculture of violence theorists have focused on explaining the northern-southern differentials in homicide rather than black-white differentials. Hackney (1969), Gastil (1971), Erlanger (1974), Loftin and Hill (1974), Reed (1971), and Doerner (1975) have sought to provide explanations for the higher-than-average violent crime rates of the southern United States.

The high rates of both southern and black homicide have led to additional speculation. For example, it has been suggested that the high homicide rates of blacks may be related to their lower-class, Southern heritage. That is, blacks share with lower-class Southern whites a common subculture of violence (Pettigrew & Spier, 1962). Block (1975) found not race but the percentage of residents who had migrated from the South to be the stronger correlate of violent crime in an analysis of Chicago data. City areas with large concentrations of Southerners, whether black or white, tended to have higher rates of violent crime than those populated by non-Southerners. Others have questioned this explanation for black homicide rates (Gastil, 1971), since black–white differentials appear to persist across regions and within similar socioeconomic strata (Wolfgang, 1958).

Recent studies have begun to look more specifically at the relationship between race, the history of blacks in the United States, and criminal violence, but often continue to rely upon traditional subcultural explanations. Both Curtis (1974, 1975) and Silberman (1978) suggest that slavery and other slavery-linked factors may produce the observed high rates of black criminal violence. Like earlier analysts, Curtis (1975) linked black criminal violence to "a black poverty subculture" that potentially has both African and American slave origins. He relies partly on the subculture of poverty thesis of Lewis (1959). Silberman (1978), on the other hand, takes a subcultural approach, but quotes Bohannan (1960) to argue that the propensity to violence is not part of the cultural heritage American blacks brought from Africa. Rather, he concluded that "violence is something black Americans learned in this country" (1978, p. 123). Silberman goes on to attribute present rates of criminal violence among blacks to the violence used by whites to perpetuate slavery and later violence used to maintain discrimination and white economic superiority. Like Blauner (1972), Silberman argues that the black experience has been different in kind, not just degree, from other American racial-ethnic groups.

Critique of Subculture of Violence Theory and an Alternative Model

The empirical basis for subculture of violence theory has been extremely limited and unpersuasive. While it has often asserted that blacks or white Southerners possess distinct criminogenic subcultural values, few efforts have been made to adequately assess the nature of such values. In an empirical study of value orientations toward violence, Erlanger (1974) and Blumenthal, Kohn, Andrews, and Head (1971) found no support for the idea that the poor or nonwhites are more favorable toward violence than are more affluent persons and whites. Such evidence of a lack of empirical grounding has caused Loftin and Hill (1974) to assert that the idea of a cultural basis of regional variations in homicide is the result of an uncritical assessment of questionable research.

Fine and Kleinman (1979) have offered a general critique of the notion of subculture as it is used by social scientists. Many of their criticisms are relevant for understanding the limitations of subculture of violence theory. They note that problems in previous subculture research include (1) a confusion of the ideas of subculture and subsociety, (2) the lack of a meaningful referent for subculture, (3) the homogeneity and stasis associated with the concept, and (4) the emphasis on defining subcultures in terms of values and central themes. They suggest that the subculture construct, to be of maximal usefulness, needs to be linked to processes of interaction among members of groups.

The usual problems of separating concepts of SES subculture have also been evident in subculture of violence theory and research. That is, how much of a given homicide rate is attributable to each of these variables? How might one empirically separate the effects of each of these dimensions in a meaningful way? Wolfgang (1958) offered some limited evidence that black homicide rates in Philadelphia could not be accounted for on the basis of social class alone; but he could only speculate as to other possible causal factors. Though economic factors often determine the contours and boundaries of a given subculture, subcultural theorists have seldom attempted to link such conditions to homicide as Bonger (1969) has done.

The concerns raised above point out several major weaknesses of the subculture of violence theory: (1) There is an extreme emphasis on mentalistic value orientations of individuals—orientations that in the aggregate are said to produce a subculture. (2) The theory lacks empirical grounding and indeed is put in question by some empirical findings. (3) Much of the theory has tended to underemphasize a variety of structural, situational, and institutional variables that affect interpersonal violence. For blacks, these variables range from historical patterns developed during slavery, to the immediate social context of an individual homicidal offense, to the operation of the criminal justice system, past and present. (4) Subcultural theory underemphasizes the effects of the law on patterns of criminal homicide. (5) There are other plausible ways apart from the inculcation of values by which the economic, political, and social disadvantages of American blacks may produce high rates of homicide.

Gouldner (1974) has suggested that the study of criminology involves the critical understanding of both the larger society and of the broadest social theory, as well as phenomena and theory peculiar to crime. Yet, on the whole, criminological theory, including subculture of violence theory, has relied upon a rather limited subset of the broader body of social theory and research; for example, see Taylor, Walton, and Young (1974, 1975).

In the next part of the chapter, I propose a series of general theoretical concepts that draw upon a variety of social science theories to explain rates of black criminal homicide. Figure 17.1 is a summary of these concepts and provides a guide to the remainder of the chapter. I begin with an historical-structural framework and rely upon studies of American race relations. This historical analysis is supplemented by a consideration of present situational, legal and sociocultural factors thought to affect rates of criminal violence. The framework as proposed will not meet all of the theoretical and methodological requirements demanded of a fully explanatory model and is not intended to do so. Rather, I attempt to integrate some of the important theoretical concerns raised by past studies of criminal homicide with those derived from non-crime research and theory in order to suggest plausible topics for future research.

Proposition 1: American Criminal Law: Black Life Is Cheap, But White Life Is Valuable

Criminal violence is a legally defined and regulated phenomenon. The importance of that fact is most often underemphasized in sociological theories of crime etiology. Criminal violence and other categories of crime cannot be understood without consideration of the part played by criminal law and the criminal justice system in the attempted regulation of criminal behavior. Subcultural theory has ignored the historical and present day interaction between legal and extra-legal factors that affect crime. There appears to be an assumption made in such theory that the official treatment of black and white crime and criminals is the same. Yet, an abundance of historical and contemporary data and theory refutes that assumption even for so serious an offense as criminal homicide.

Black (1976, 1979) argues that law is a form of governmental social control. It is also a variable and quantifiable aspect of social life. How the law behaves in any given situation is a function of the location of victims and offenders in the stratification system, organization, culture, and so forth. He notes that law is affected by the distance between victims and offenders along various social dimensions such as social class, race, ethnicity, and other similar factors. If criminal law and criminal justice in the United States are viewed in historical perspective, Black's theory is well grounded.

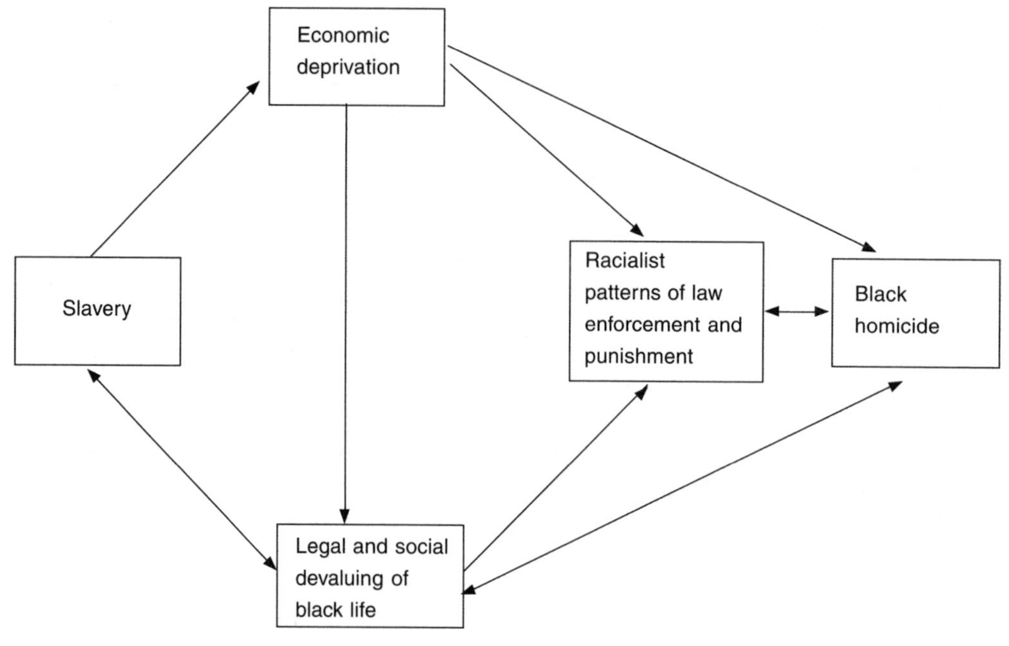

Fig. 17.1 A Causal Model of Black Homicide.

At the beginning of the slavery era, the killing of a slave by his master was not considered a criminal offense. Whites, including nonslaveowning whites, were permitted to injure slaves with impunity. At the same time, the killing of a white person by a black slave was considered one of the most heinous offenses. The constant fear of black insurrection led to swift and cruel punishment for blacks who offended against whites (see Hindus, 1980). Of course, since slaves were an economic investment, there was some incentive on the part of slavemasters to refrain from large-scale executions or excessive punishment of offending slaves (see Fogel & Engerman, 1974; and David, Gutman, Sutch, Temin, and Wright, 1976).

By the 1850s, most southern states still had state statutes and local ordinances that made certain acts crimes only if they were perpetrated by slaves. Where crimes were not racially defined, there were nevertheless explicit, statutorily defined differences in punishment (Mangum, 1940). Capital offenses such as murder and rape were usually covered by such statutes. Murder was differentially punished based upon the racial identity of the victim and offender. Though there is some question regarding the extent to which these laws were actually implemented in given cases, the codified law was undeniably racist.

The legal cheapening of black life and the concomitant valuing of white life was not based primarily on racist ideas of inferiority and superiority. Rather, offenses against whites by black slaves were punished more severely because they came to represent an attack on the social order. The symbolic and nonsymbolic structures of authority in the antebellum South were ones in which whites, regardless of their social status, had the right to control many aspects of the lives of black slaves.

Many analysts would suggest that the historical patterns described above are legal and social anachronisms today and have no impact upon the way the criminal law currently defines and punishes criminal behavior.[6] The various civil acts of the 1860s and 1870s, and the 14th Amendment, specifically addressed the issue of differential punishment for crime. Despite legal reforms of that era and later, which removed many of the obviously racist definitions of criminal behavior and provisions for punishment, there is evidence that some of these historical patterns have not been completely changed.

Even where changed, they may have set in motion certain historical–structural forces that affect the lives of blacks today. Consider, for example, the rank order of the seriousness of black and whites homicides.

A Hierarchy of Homicide Seriousness

The idea of a racial hierarchy for the treatment of homicide offenders is not new in social science research. As early as 1941, Johnson proposed such a model. Follow-up studies have been conducted by Garfinkel (1949), Green (1964), Farrell and Swigert (1978), and Radelet (1981). These have been primarily studies of the extent to which the race of the offender and victim affect the amount of punishment administered. These studies assume the existence of antebellum origins for this racial hierarchy, but only Johnson attempts specifically to link it to pre-twentieth century social values. None of these studies suggests that such a hierarchy many be linked to rates of black homicide, as I do in the present discussion. That is, the legal cheapening of black life is seen to affect the behavior of the criminal justice system, but not to have a causal effect on criminal behavior.

Johnson (1941) studied racial differences in sentencing in three states of the South during the 1930s and 1940s. He proposed that in the South black-versus-black homicides would be treated with undue leniency, while black-versus-white offenses would be treated with undue severity. The following ranking from most serious to least serious was hypothesized: "(1) Negro versus white, (2) white versus white, (3) Negro versus Negro and (4) white versus Negro." Data from courts in Virginia, North Carolina, and Georgia tended to support this rank order of seriousness. A greater proportion of blacks who killed whites were executed once sentenced than was true of whites who killed whites. Least likely to be executed were blacks who murdered blacks. Only a small number of cases of whites murdering blacks were noted, thus few conclusions could be reached as to the seriousness of this offense.[7] Garfinkel (1949) reported similar findings.

Kleck (1981) found racial bias to exist only in the South, and asks whether previous findings apply to the non-South. Other researchers have warned that observed black-white differences in punishment for murder may be caused by a variety of unexamined factors. Among such factors are the social status of the offender and victim (Farrell & Swiggert, 1978); the legal seriousness of the offense, such as degree of premeditation or the commission along with another felony (Green, 1964); and whether victim and offender are acquainted (Parker & Smith, 1979; Smith & Parker, 1980). Lundsgaarde (1977) reported that Houston murderers charged with killing family persons (primary homicide) received less severe punishment than those charged with killing nonfamily persons (nonprimary homicide). Radelet (1981) controlled for some of these factors in his recent study of homicide sentencing.

Radelet found that overall there were no strong racial differences for his sample of 637 homicide cases in either the probability of being indicted for first-degree murder or in the overall probability of being sentenced to death. However, blacks accused of murdering whites were more likely to be sentenced to death than blacks who were accused of murdering other blacks. This trend was due to the higher probability for those accused of murdering whites (whether black or white offenders) to be indicted for first-degree murder. Significantly, nonprimary (Stranger) homicides in which there were white victims were more likely to result in a first-degree indictment than those nonprimary homicides with black victims. He concludes that the race of the victim, as well as that of the offender, must be considered in studies of sentencing disparities.

These studies suggest that a variety of factors converge to determine the seriousness of a homicide. Many of these factors are not considered in recent studies of crime seriousness such as that of Rossi, Bose, and Berk (1974). They also suggest that in a racially stratified society, such as that in the United States, race remains a crucial determining variable. The response of the legal system toward black offenders and victims of homicide has created a racial hierarchy of homicide offenses. I suggest that such a hierarchy has direct and indirect effects on the etiology of homicide among blacks. These are discussed under the second proposition. Below, I suggest a scale of seriousness of homicide offenses that emerged from historical patterns of race relations in the American South. This scale assumes that where legally relevant factors, such as prior record and the brutality of the act, are controlled for, racial differences will still be evident. There is also an assumption that social class differences alone will not fully explain levels of the hierarchy.

Rating	*Offense*
Most serious	Black kills white, in authority
	Black kills white, stranger
	White kills white, in authority
	Black kills white, friend, acquaintance
	Black kills white, intimate, family
	White kills white, stranger
	White kills white, friend, acquaintance
	White kills white, intimate, family
	Black kills black, stranger
	Black kills black, friend, acquaintance
	Black kills black, intimate, family
	White kills black, stranger
	White kills black, friend, acquaintance
Least serious	White kills black, intimate, family

Conclusions and Testable Hypotheses

Conclusion 1: Rates of criminal violence among American blacks, in comparison to other nonwhites and white ethnics, are attributable to their unique history of slavery and oppression.

Conclusion 2: The historical behavior of American law, especially in the South, created a hierarchy of the seriousness of criminal violence based primarily on the racial identity of and relationship between the victim and offender.

Conclusion 3: During slavery and in the immediate post-Reconstruction South, offenses committed by blacks against whites were seen as attacks on the racial social order.

Hypothesis 1: Past and present indices of official sanctioning of homicide offenders will reveal harshest penalties for offenses of blacks against whites who are in positions of authority and/or who are strangers to the offender. Least severely sanctioned will be offenses occurring among interracial acquaintances or family members where whites are offenders.

Hypothesis 2: Studies of black American public opinion will reveal blacks to believe that the behavior of the law protects the lives of whites more than the lives of blacks.

Proposition 2: Past And Present Racial And Social Class Differences In The Administration Of Justice Affect Black Criminal Violence

Even if it can be shown that the historical patterns described above are accurately depicted, one must still explain how such patterns affect rates of black homicide today. The conclusions reached thus far do not rule out the possibility of a slavery-produced subculture of violence among blacks.

However, as noted above, a simplistic proviolence values explanation may be inadequate for describing people's attitudes toward criminal violence. Violence, including homicidal aggression, is more acceptable under certain circumstances than it is under others. There are several plausible explanations of black criminal homicide that are not fully included in subculture of violence theory.

One such explanation is that blacks kill each other at higher rates because the legal system is seen as administering punishment unfairly. On the basis of the past behavior of the law, blacks may have come to believe that aggressive behavior of all types directed by blacks against each other will be tolerated and seldom severely punished. The only solution then becomes a kind of vigilantism for the handling of intraracial violence. Homicide becomes a form of conflict resolution (Levi, 1980).

This suggests that in addition to historical factors the present behavior of the law affects rates of black criminal violence. An assumption underlying any system of law enforcement is the idea that crime should not only be punished as a matter of just desserts but also that punishment serves to deter or prevent crime. Consequently, one plausible explanation for black homicide rates is that blacks kill blacks at a higher rate because there is less of a legal deterrent to such behavior among blacks than among whites. To the extent that homicide is a preventable or deterable crime, one must examine the role of law enforcement authorities in the genesis of black homicide, that is, the official responses to homicide and prehomicide behaviors. McNeeley and Pope (1981) provide recent analyses of black-white differences in the administration of justice.

Post-Homicide Punishment as a Deterrent

Though blacks have higher rates of interracial homicide than whites, Silberman (1978) and others have noted that given the extent of racial oppression in the United States it is surprising that there is not more black violence directed at whites. Some would suggest that the historical patterns of swift and often cruel punishment for blacks who have murdered whites have served to deter such behavior. On the other hand, leniency in the treatment of black interracial offenders may tend to encourage black-on-black aggression.

There is questionable empirical support for the deterrent effect on homicide of either a merely subjective perception of legal sanctions or of such perceptions with objective reinforcement, such as existence of a capital punishment statute as well as frequent use of the statute. Some studies have shown deterrent effects while others show none—for example, see Gibbs (1975), Erlich (1975), and Kleck (1979). Few, if any, studies have looked at differential deterrence effects based on victim characteristics, such as that proposed in this discussion.

Parker and Smith (1979) attempted to assess the effects of punishment on homicide deterrence while controlling for the victim-offender relationship. They classified homicides into "primary," family and acquaintance, and "nonprimary," felony-murder, stranger and nonintimate offenses. Certainty of punishment was found to affect significantly nonprimary homicide rates but not primary rates. Etiological variables, such as the level of poverty, were found to be better predictors of primary homicide rates. This finding supports the common speculation among law enforcement officials and criminologists that primary homicides are crimes of passion and are not deterred by perceptions of punishment.[8] What is needed, however, is classification of past punishment for homicide into race and relationship of offender-victim categories in order to test possible race-linked differences in deterrence.[9]

Even if it can be shown that patterns of punishment for homicide vary on the basis of racial characteristics and that punishment serves to deter homicide, one must still explain the large gap between black and white rates of intraracial offending. That is, why do blacks kill each other at much higher rates than whites kill whites? Why does expected punishment more effectively deter blacks from killing whites but not other blacks? Similarly, given the comparative leniency accorded white interracial offenders, why is this category of offending so small?

Some explanations may be offered. Most homicides involve family members or acquaintances and consequently are intraracial in a racially segregated society such as the United States. To the extent that there has been a devaluation of black life within a racially segregated society, such devaluation will result in homicide. Blacks will not murder whites both because white life is not similarly devalued and because of an absence of social interactions of the type that generally lead to homicide. On the other hand, despite the devaluation of black life, whites will seldom murder blacks because of limited interaction. All of these explanations, however, rely on social values and norms to explain the act of homicide. Below, I suggest that there are other factors to be considered.

Prehomicide Behaviors and the Lack of Deterrence

There is growing evidence that the way administration of justice agencies respond to various situational and circumstantial conditions factors preceding a homicide offense may profoundly affect the etiology of criminal violence. Much criminal homicide, for example, occurs among family members or acquaintances and is often preceded by somewhat predictable patterns of prehomicide behavior.[10] There is some evidence that the racial identity of the potential victim and offender may affect the way that the police, prosecutors, the courts, and other officials respond to prehomicide events.

Because a given homicidal act usually occurs within the context of a social relationship, homicide may often be anticipated. In many instances, these prehomicide events take the form of assault and may come to the attention of the public and/or law enforcement officials. Dunn (1976, p. 10) suggests that to the extent that assaults among family members are reported, these may represent "attempted homicides nipped in the bud." He notes, however, that this is an inference and is not based on definitive data. The same effects of the reporting of assaults and other prehomicide behaviors may also affect patterns of homicide outside the family. Studies of assaults have shown patterns similar to those observed for homicide (Pittman & Hardy, 1964; Pokorny, 1965b; Dunn, 1976). Assaults generally can be divided into primary and nonprimary categories, and are usually intraracial. Few, if any, studies have explored the link between a given homicide and assaults as a prehomicide occurrence prior to the commission of the act.

In a society characterized by racial stratification, race may be a crucial factor in determining whether acts of aggression lead to death, and the response of law enforcement officials may be of importance. Several studies have probed the behavior of police in minority communities. Many of their findings support the conclusion that majority and minority relations with the police differ in crucial ways—ways that might affect the etiology of crime, such as homicide.

Bayley and Mendelsohn (1969) and Bernard (1978) cite data which show that (1) blacks have more negative perceptions of police than do whites; (2) blacks have more contact with police than whites, but these experiences are less satisfactory than those reported by whites; and (3) in several large American cities minority groups filed by far the largest numbers of complaints about police misconduct. Bernard notes that factors other than racism may explain the findings; he also reports that the more violent the crime for which the person is suspected, the greater is the discrepancy between the treatment afforded white citizens and black citizens.[11]

A crucial question for the study of the etiology of homicide is whether black-white differences in perceptions and experiences with police lead to either a tendency for blacks to underreport prehomicide-type behavior or to differences in police response to black and white complainants. In a study of police service delivery in three cities, Ostrom (1978) reports that blacks do not differ from white respondents in their likelihood to report crimes, nor in their reasons for not reporting crimes. However, black respondents were more likely than whites to report slower police response times to victimization calls for service. There are some questions regarding the conclusiveness and generalizability of Ostrom's findings, but they do provide a stimulus for further research on this question.

The police are not the only agents of social control who may influence patterns of homicide. Prosecutors and the courts also play crucial roles. Swigert and Farrell (1977) have provided some empirical bases for speculation regarding racial differences in homicide prosecution. These researchers, using data from a sample of persons arrested for murder, found that a stereotype of the violent offender, the "normal primitive," affects legal decision making. Blacks and individuals of lower occupational status were assigned this label more often than were whites or higher status persons. The eventual result of such a label was more severe convictions by the court. Garfinkel (1949) suggests that a similar typing of black offenders may result in less severe punishment when blacks kill each other.

I suggest that the official view of violent behavior as normal among blacks, especially lower-class blacks, also affects the etiology of black homicide. This happens in several ways. First, prehomicide behavior among blacks will be treated more leniently by public law enforcement officials than similar behaviors among whites or behaviors directed by blacks against whites. That is, the hierarchy of values for homicide perceptions also affects prehomicide offenses. This means that police, prosecutors, and courts will be more likely to arrest, charge, and convict persons of interracial assaults or intraracial assaults among whites than those accused of black-on-black assaults.

Of course, many intraracial assaults mark domestic disputes. Such disputes account for 40% to 50% of all homicides in some studies. This poses many problems for both police and prosecutorial intervention in the prehomicide behavior of whites and blacks. Police are sometimes unable and/or reluctant to intervene in family matters. However, for black lower-class offenders who commit a disproportionate number of assaults and homicides, racial and class factors further reduce the probability of intervention. Such behavior may be seen as normal among such persons and is therefore unpreventable, or police may fear for their own safety when called to intervene in black lower-class neighborhoods, whether such intervention involves domestic or nondomestic disputes. On the other hand, fear of police brutality may cause blacks to underreport assaultive behavior. This mutual distrust and fear will often lead to ineffective intervention in instances that are known to present the potential for homicides.

We need, then, studies (so far largely lacking) of such precursors to homicide as repeated assaults, verbal threats, and so forth. Such a longitudinal view is missing in past studies of homicide etiology and homicide patterning. Further, I argue that the way in which police and other public officials respond to instances of reported assault tends to mirror the historical hierarchy noted for official response to homicide. That is, racial and social class variables affect official responses and these race or class based differences may affect rates of criminal homicide.

Of course, assaults are much more numerous than homicides and occur in various contexts. While not all assaults lead to homicide, many homicides are preceded by patterns of reported assault, especially aggravated assaults. Criminologists must examine more carefully the patterns such prehomicide offenses tend to take, and the link between them and acts of homicide.

There is also some evidence that other kinds of official response to aggressive behavior in minority communities may affect the etiology of homicide. For example, the extent to which emergency care is provided may mean the difference between an attempted murder or a murder statistic. The provision of emergency medical care, like medical care in general, may reflect patterns of racial and socioeconomic stratification. Thus, medical care must be seen as an important situational variable in the etiology of homicide.

In conclusion, I have suggested that official responses over time to situations of aggressive behavior in black lower-class communities may be a neglected variable in the study of causes of black homicide.

A homicide statistic must be seen as more than the result of a discrete, time-bound act on the part of a criminal offender. Rather, aspects of the social context, such as prehomicide behavior, police response to citizen complaints, perceptions of police, actions of prosecutors and courts, and medical service delivery may determine whether relatively common incidences of aggressive behavior lead to murder. Official responses to black potential homicide offenders are influenced by patterns of both social class stratification and race bias.

Conclusions and Testable Hypotheses

Conclusion 1: The response of police, prosecutors and courts to prehomicide type behaviors affects the rate of homicide.

Conclusion 2: Official response to prehomicide behaviors, such as assault, are affected by such factors as the race and social class of victims and offenders.

Conclusion 3: Like homicide itself, prehomicide behavior among the poor and blacks is likely to be perceived by law enforcement authorities as "normal" and inevitable.

Hypothesis 1: Intraracial, prehomicide violence among blacks will be less likely to be reported to police than such offenses will be among whites.

Hypothesis 2: Where reported, proportionately more of such encounters among blacks will eventually lead to homicide. This difference will be partly due to the failure of police to intervene at the same level for black-black and white-white aggression.

Hypothesis 3: Measures of response time and other indices of police availability and cooperativeness will show greater availability and cooperativeness for *inter*racial acts of criminal violence than for *intra*racial acts. Police will be less responsive to intraracial acts of violence among blacks than among whites; but social class variations will also be a factor. Greatest responsiveness will be to acts of violence among affluent whites and least responsiveness to lower-class blacks.

Hypothesis 4: Patterns of punishment for prehomicide-type behavior, such as aggravated assault, will mirror those for homicide. Most punishment will be given for black-on-white assaults involving a white authority person or stranger, and least punishment will be given for black-on-black assaults among family or intimate.

Proposition 3: Economic Deprivation Creates A Climate of Powerlessness In Which Individual Acts of Violence Are Likely To Take Place

While there may be some debate regarding the extent to which criminal statistics reflect the actual incidence of crime, there is agreement that persons arrested and charged with homicide are more likely to be not only a member of a minority group but also poor and undereducated. A recent survey conducted by the Law Enforcement Assistance Administration (LEAA) shows the extent of these trends for inmates sentenced and serving time in state prisons in 1974.[12]

The survey showed that of black inmates being held for all categories of crime, only 21% were high school graduates or higher. Of all black inmates with less than an eighth grade education, 24% were sentenced for murder and 10% were sentenced for manslaughter. Of all prisoners with less than an eighth grade education, 68% were charged with a violent crime.

Income and employment status data indicated similar disadvantage for black inmates in comparison to white inmates and to noninmate blacks. For blacks sentenced in all categories of crime, the median family income was $4,100. One third of the inmate families earned less than $3,000 in the year prior to their initial arrest; 64% earned less than $6,000. Only 9% of black inmates made more than $10,000. As expected, black inmates tended to come from lower status occupations and to have high rates of unemployment. Of the black inmates, 83% were employed as blue-collar or service workers just prior to arrest. This compared to 74% of the entire black male population being employed in these occupations. Finally, 39% of all black inmates were unemployed or working only part-time in the year prior to arrest. The study concluded that there was little relationship between income and type of crime for which an inmate had been sentenced. However, the low SES for all, whether imprisoned for property or violent offenses, was far below national norms, including the official poverty level.

Despite the perennial debate among criminologists regarding the extent to which prison populations are representative of all criminal offenders and the extent to which official statistics distort the criminality of the poor and minorities, several conclusions appear warranted. First, "street" crimes of the type most likely to be included in official crime statistics are more likely to be committed by blacks and lower-class persons than by other groupings. Second, the data above and those from numerous other studies of homicide provide reasonable support for the idea that poor and undereducated blacks are disproportionately represented among persons who have committed criminal violence, especially homicide.

If not subcultural factors (which I discuss later), what is the link between low SES and criminal violence among American blacks? Above, I argued that black poverty and crime must be seen in proper legal-historical perspective. However, historical data do not adequately explain why it is that present day criminal violence occurs more among lower-class than among middle-class blacks. Almost all American blacks are descended from families that were enslaved. Those who are not descendants of slaves have been nevertheless affected by the persisting patterns of prejudice and discrimination in the United States. The data on the SES of homicide offenders suggest that an adequate theory must explore the direct link between present-day black disadvantage and violent crime.

In the past, most often researchers have examined the relationship between economic condition and property crime. Blau and Blau (1982) have shown, however, that such factors also have an impact upon the murder rate within urban areas. They suggest that the traditional idea of relative deprivation might best account for such effects. A number of studies have shown that homicide offenders and victims, in comparison to suicide victims, have lower SES. Davis and Short (1978) have provided data and a theoretical model to examine black suicide in the United States. They note that integration into the community decreased the probability of suicide and that an increase in status was positively associated with increases in suicide. Social integration factors may also affect rates of homicide among blacks.

Rose (1978, 1981) has examined the relationship between aggregate measures of neighborhood stress and the black homicide rate. Although his approach is similar to that of earlier studies of ecological social disorganization, he provides new insight and data for understanding the wide variation in homicide within the black community. Since the work of Brearley (1932), it has been shown that the black homicide rate is much higher in some cities than in others. Rose shows that these rates are often correlated with various economic and related stress factors (overcrowding, health conditions, and so forth). These conditions resulted in what he called "the geography of despair."

Unlike subcultural theory, I suggest that the path between black socioeconomic disadvantage and crime is not mediated by the intervening variable—cultural values. Rather, such disadvantage generates sociopathological conditions in which violent crime among lower-class blacks represents a socially disapproved, but predictable, effort to achieve some measure of control in an environment characterized by social, political, and economic powerlessness. This type of psychologically oriented theory as an explanation for black criminal violence has been suggested by Fanon (1967, 1968), Grier and Cobbs (1968), and May (1972).

Fanon (1967, 1968) offered a psychoanalytic interpretation of the problems of blacks living under colonial rule. He suggested that intraracial violence represents a form of repressed aggression that will be reduced only when colonized peoples succeed in directing their aggression against the colonizer during acts of revolution. Grier and Cobbs (1968) described the almost constant state of rage found among blacks living in American society and noted the deleterious effects of such rage. May (1972) argues that powerlessness corrupts and that acts of violence under these conditions are merely pseudopower, an expression of impotence. A condition of relative powerlessness is precisely what characterizes the lives of blacks who are undereducated, unemployed, or working in menial, low-paying occupations.

Dennis (1977) has attributed the extraordinarily high rates of homicide among young black men to a variety of social stresses caused by rural-to-urban migration, changes in the family and age structure, denial of employment opportunities, and so forth. Valentine and Valentine (1972) have noted that advocates of black self-destruction theory believe many homicides among blacks are similar to suicides in that they are victim precipitated. They are responses to persisting patterns of oppression.[13]

These explanations for black aggression tend to suggest that a comprehensive theory of black criminal violence must consider the psychological dynamics at work under conditions of economic, political, and social powerlessness.[14] Many of the ideas proposed by Blauner (1972) to describe features of "internal colonialism" in the United States must be explored. Both Dennis (1977) and Valentine and Valentine (1972) have noted that patterns of black intragroup aggression, especially among young men, may be linked to increasing political awareness of oppression without concomitant means to affect social change or change in their own lives. The tendency of subcultural theory to focus on social values has led to an ignoring of such political concerns. The overemphasis on the causative role of attitudes toward violence has also led to an underemphasis on the more objective environmental conditions under which criminal violence is likely to occur.

These theories also suggest that the particularly lethal environment to be found among young, black males may be linked to age-related career and life-stage crises. The traditional subculture of youth explanations have most often concentrated on the antisocial values found among young adolescents. However, black criminal violence is also heavily concentrated in the young to middle-age adult, 25 to 44 age range. This suggests that a variety of economic factors such as underemployment must be considered as causal factors, including the notion of a more or less permanent, minority underclass living in urban areas—for example, see Glasgow (1980).[15] Urban areas are also more likely than nonurban areas to offer the kind of economic contrasts that may lead to "relative deprivation" and inequality as causal factors in homicide.

Conclusions and Testable Hypotheses

Conclusion 1: To the extent that criminal violence is caused by economic deprivation and powerlessness, homicide rates will occur at a higher rate among the black underclass than among the black middle class.

Hypothesis 1: Studies of attitudes toward violence will show no and middle-class blacks.

Hypothesis 2: Studies of psychological adaptation will show higher rates of personal stress, rage, and feelings of powerlessness among black lower-class males than among other comparable social groupings in American society.

Hypothesis 3: At the group level, improvements in the economic and social well-being of blacks will lead to reductions in acts of criminal violence.

Summary and Conclusions

Although subculture of violence theory is most often used to explain black–white differentials in homicide, it is inadequate in many respects. In this chapter, I have suggested a number of alternatives and supplements to this theory that have not been adequately explored in previous research. The long range utility of these alternatives will be measured by future studies that attempt to test the proposed hypotheses. The section on prehomicide behavior is likely to result in the most informative studies.

Though I have raised a number of theoretical and other issues in this chapter, its purpose has been rather limited. In no way have I attempted to propose a general theory of homicide causation, either among blacks or among the public at large. A fully adequate theory of this sort would have to address issues of age and sex differences in homicide rates, rural-urban differences, regional differences, and so forth. Rather, I have attempted to propose plausible theoretical direction for the analysis and understanding of the disproportionately high rates of homicide among American blacks. That is, why have American blacks consistently had higher rates of murder than other nonwhite and white Americans?

First, I offered a critique of subculture of violence theory and its sufficiency as an explanation for the consistently high rates of homicide among American blacks. Next, I suggested that etiological studies of criminal homicide must be broadened to include a variety of situational, structural, and institutional variables not usually considered in studies of crime causation. These include the historical behavior of the law and the operation of the criminal justice system. I suggest that these factors must be considered along with cultural values to explain why blacks commit a disproportionate share of homicides.

In contrast to much of previous criminological research, I suggest that the study of racial discrimination and bias in the administration of justice cannot be separated from the study of homicide causation among American blacks. The propositions presented are an attempt to address this important social problem by combining some of the tenets of subcultural theory with those found in the theory of conflict-oriented criminologists. The work of Quinney (1973, 1980), Turk (1969), and Taylor et al. (1974) must be seen as contributing not only to an understanding of the processing of criminals in society, but as contributing to the study of the cause of criminal behavior. The study of criminal homicide must include not only the actions of the criminal offender or victim, but also the actions of officials of the state.

Notes

1. While white American rates are generally lower than those of blacks, there is evidence that various white ethnic groups have differing rates and trends of rates over time. Rates of crime, including homicide, have tended to be higher for recent immigrants than for more settled groups. Jews have reportedly lower rates of all crime than do most other white ethnics. However, few studies have provided data comparing rates of homicide among whites. Among nonwhites, Asian Americans have tended to have low rates of homicide and American Indians have relatively high rates.
2. There is nothing intrinsic in conflict theory that makes it inapplicable to questions of crime etiology. However, conflict-oriented criminologists appear to have followed the lead of Karl Marx, who wrote little about crime causation. An exception is Bonger (1969). Many conflict criminologists do talk of the extent to which the ruling class overcriminalizes the behaviors of the lower classes, thus making them appear more criminal. However, the cause of such *mala in se* offenses as homicide is seldom probed from a conflict perspective.
3. The 1980 annual report on the nation's health status, *Health-United States: 1980*, by the Department of Health and Human Services gives causes of death among persons 15 to 24 years old. Among nonwhites, the homicide rate was 43 in every 100,000, compared to 25 for motor vehicle accidents and 22 for other accidents. Auto accidents was the leading cause of deaths for whites. Most homicide victims were black males.
4. For example, Shin et al. (1977), Dennis (1977, 1979), and Farley (1980) have all noted the extent to which homicide diminishes life expectancy probabilities for black males. A special issue of *Ebony* magazine, "Black on Black Crime" (August 1979), detailed the social, economic, and moral impact of black intraracial crime, especially homicide, on blacks.
5. FBI, *Uniform Crime Reports*, 1975, 210.
6. A number of recent studies of public perceptions of crime and official criminal justice responses suggests that actual or potential aggression by blacks against whites is thought to represent an attack on the social order. For example, research by Jacobs (1979), Jackson and Carrol (1980), Liska, Lawrence, and Benson (1981), and Loftin et al. (1981) report that the percentage nonwhite in American urban areas has an effect on police expenditures and strength. This is especially evident after the riots of the early 1960s.
7. The low incidence of reported white offender-black victim homicide in these studies is itself a manifestation of racism. Whites who kill blacks are also less likely to be prosecuted. The numerous lynchings of blacks from the 1890s through the 1960s are not reflected in official arrest statistics.

8. If expected punishment does prevent nonprimary (stranger) murders more than primary murders, the historical and current behavior of the law will have more impact on interracial offenses. That is, blacks will be more deterred from killing whites and whites will be more deterred from killing blacks than from killing members of their own race.
9. For example, will a jurisdiction with a reputation for being extremely lenient with black offender-black victim murderers, but severe with black offender-white victim murderers, show rates of these types of murders that are different from those found in jurisdictions with different punishment patterns?
10. By "prehomicide behavior," I mean something more than a *post facto* detailing of all events leading up to the murder. Something more systematic and predictable is proposed. For example, much police department folklore may be useful in identifying such behavior.
11. Black (1971) found no evidence that police arrest decisions are affected by the race of the offender. However, further studies are needed, particularly of the effects of victims' and offenders' race on arrest and on other aspects of police response to crime.
12. See *Profile of State Prison Inmates, 1974*, published by the U.S. Department of Justice (n.d.). SES data for all arrestees is not readily available.
13. The kind of "death wish" theory proposed by Valentine and Valentine (1972) suggests that a symbolic interactionist approach may be useful for describing aggressive encounters between blacks. Such a theoretical model for the study of violence has been proposed by Athens (1977).
14. Traditional psychiatric and psychoanalytic studies of homicide fail to consider the economic and social context within which most murders in the United States occur.
15. The ghettoization of various groups in America has, of course, included white ethnics as well as nonwhites. Many of these groups have resorted to crime as a means of responding to their deprivation and powerlessness. However, the ghettoization of blacks must be seen as occurring within the context of a slavery-influenced social system and persisting pattern of racial discrimination. To the extent that these historical-structural factors influence rates of homicide, blacks will have higher rates of homicide than oppressed whites.

References

Athens, L. H. 1977. Violent crime: A symbolic interactionist study. *Symbolic Interaction* 1: 56–70.

Bayley, D. and Mendelsohn, H. 1969. *Minorities and the police.* New York: Free Press.

Bernard, W. 1978. Unpublished manuscript. *Blacks and the police: A comparative study of police relations with black and white citizens.*.

Black, D. 1971. The social organization of arrest. *Stanford Law Review* 23: 1104–1109.

Black, D. *The behavior of the law.* 1976. New York: Academic Press.

Black, D. 1979. Common sense in the sociology of law. *American Sociological Review* 44: 18–27.

Blau, J. and Blau, P. M. 1982. Metropolitan structure and violent crime. *American Sociological Review* 47: 114–119.

Blauner, R. 1972. *Racial oppression in America.* New York: Harper & Row.

Block, R. 1975. Homicide in Chicago: A nine year study (1965–1973). *Journal of Criminal Law and Criminology* 66: 496–510.

Blumenthal, M. D., Kohn, R. L., Andrews, F., and Head, K. 1972. *Justifying violence.* Ann Arbor, MI: Institute for Social Research.

Bohannon, P. ed.. *African homicide and suicide.* Princeton, NJ: Princeton University Press.

Bonger, W. 1943. *Race and crime.* New York: Columbia University Press,

Bonger, W. 1969. *Criminality and economic conditions.* Bloomington: Indiana University Press,

Boudouris, J. *Trends in homicide, Detroit, 1926–68.* Unpublished doctoral dissertation, Wayne State University, 1970.

Brearley, H. C. 1932. *Homicide in the United States.* Chapel Hill: University of North Carolina Press.

Centerwall, B. S. *Race, socioeconomic status, and homicide: Atlanta, 1961–62, 1971–72.* Paper presented at the annual meeting of the Southern Sociological Society, Memphis, April 1982.

Curtis, L. A. 1974. *Criminal violence: National patterns of behaviors.* Lexington, MA: D. C. Heath.

———. 1975. *Violence, race and culture.* Lexington, MA: D. C. Heath.

David, P., Gutman, H. G., Sutch, R., Temin, P., and Wright, G. 1976. *Reckoning with slavery: A critical study in the quantitative history of American Negro slavery.* New York: Oxford University Press.

Davis, R. and Short, J. F. 1978. Dimensions of black suicide: A theoretical model. *Suicide and Life Threatening Behavior* 8: 161–173.

Dennis, R. E. 1977. Social stress and mortality among nonwhite males. *Phylon* 38: 315–328.

Dennis, R. E. 1979. The role of homicide in decreasing life expectancy. In H. M. Rose (Ed.), *Lethal aspects of urban violence.* Lexington, MA: D.C. Heath.

Doerner, W. G. 1975. A regional analysis of homicide rates in the United States. *Criminology* 13: 90–101.

Dunn, C. S. 1976. *The patterns and distribution of assault incident characteristics among social areas.* (Analytic Report 14.) Law Enforcement Assistance Administration, National Criminal Justice Information and Statistics Service, Washington, DC: U.S. Government Printing Office.

Ebony Magazine. 1979. Black on black crime: The causes; the consequences; the cure., Special issue, 34.

Erlanger, H. S. 1974. The empirical status of the subculture of violence thesis. *Social Problems* 22: 280–292.

Erlich, I. 1975. The deterrent effect of capital punishment: A question of life and death. *American Economic Review* 65: 397–417.

Fanon, F. 1967. *Black skin, white masks.* New York: Grove Press.

———. 1968. *The wretched of the earth.* New York: Grove Press.

Farley, R. 1980. Homicide trends in the United States. *Demography* 17: 177–188.
Farrell, R. A., & Swigert, V. L.1978. Legal disposition of inter-group and intra-group homicides. *Sociological Quarterly* 19: 565–576.
Federal Bureau of Investigation, United States Department of Justice. *Uniform Crime Reports for the United States, 1960–1979.* Washington, DC: U.S. Government Printing Office.
Fine, G. A. and Kleinman, S. 1979. Rethinking subculture: An interactionist analysis. *American Journal of Sociology* 85: 1–20.
Fogel, R. W. and Engerman, S. L. 1974. *Time on the cross: The economics of American Negro slavery.* Boston: Little, Brown..
Garfinkel, H. 1949. Research note on inter-and intra-racial homicides. *Social Forces* 27: 369–381.
Gastil, R. D. 1971. Homicide and a regional culture of violence. *American Sociological Review* 36: 412–427.
Gibbs, J. P. 1975. *Crime, punishment, and deterrence.* New York: Elsevier..
Glasgow, D. G. 1980. *The black underclass.* San Francisco: Jossey-Bass..
Gouldner, A. 1974. Foreword. In *The new criminology,* eds. Taylor et al. New York: Harper & Row,.
Green, E. 1964. Inter- and intra-racial crime relative to sentencing. *Journal of Criminal Law, Criminology and Police Science* 55: 348–358.
Grier, W. and Cobbs, P. M. 1968. *Black rage.* New York: Basic Books..
Hackney, S. 1969. Southern violence. In *The history of violence in America,* eds. H. D. Graham & T. R. Gurr. New York: Bantam.
Hagan, J. 1974. Extra-legal attributes and criminal sentencing: An assessment of a sociological viewpoint. *Law and Society Review* 8: 357–383.
Health-United States: 1980. (DHHS Publication No. (PHS)81-1232.) United States Department of Health and Human Services, Public Health Service, Office of Health Research, Statistics and Technology. National Center for Health Statistics. National Center for Health Services Research. Washington, DC: Government Printing Office, 1981.
Hindelang, M. J. 1969. Equality under the law. *Journal of Criminal Law, Criminology and Police Science* 60: 306–313.
Hindelang, M. J. 1981. Variations in sex-race-age-specific incidence rates of offending. *American Sociological Review* 46: 461–474.
Hindus, M. S. 1980. *Prison and plantation: Crime, justice and authority in Massachusetts and South Carolina, 1767–1878.* Chapel Hill: University of North Carolina Press.
Jackson, P. I. and Carrol, L. 1981. Race and the war on crime: The non-southern U.S. cities. *American Sociological Review* 46: 290–305.
Jacobs, D. 1979. Inequality and police strength: Conflict and coercive control in metropolitan areas. *American Sociological Review* 44: 913–925.
Johnson, G. B. 1941. The Negro and crime, *Annals of the American Academy of Political Social Science* 217: 93–104.
Kleck, G. 1979. Capital punishment, gun ownership, and homicide. *American Journal of Sociology* 84: 882–910.
Kleck, G. 1981. Racial discrimination in criminal sentencing. *American Sociological Review* 46: 783–805.
Levi, K. 1981. Homicide as conflict resolution. *Deviant Behavior* 1: 281–307.
Lewis, O. 1959. *Five families: Mexican case studies in the culture of poverty.* New York: Basic Books.
Liska, A. E., Lawrence, J. J., and Benson, M. 1981. Perspectives on the legal order: The capacity for social control. *American Journal of Sociology* 87: 413–426.
Loftin, C., Greenberg, D. F., and Kessler, R. C. *Income inequality, race, crime and crime control.* Paper presented at the annual meeting of the American Society of Criminology, Washington, DC, November 1981.
Lundsgaarde, H. P. 1977. *Murder in space city: A cultural analysis of Houston homicide patterns.* New York: University of Oxford Press.
McNeeley, R. L. and Pope, C. E. eds. 1981. *Race, crime and criminal justice.* Beverly Hills, CA: Sage.
Mangum, C. S., Jr. *The legal status of the Negro.* Chapel Hill: University of North Carolina Press.
May, R. 1972. *Power and innocence: A search for the source of violence.* New York: Norton.
Ostrom, E. *Race and equality of police service delivery in metropolitan areas: A preliminary sketch of an inquiry in process.* Paper presented at the meeting of the American Society of Public Administration, Phoenix, April 1978.
Parker, R. N. and Smith, M. D. 1979. Deterrence, poverty and type of homicide. *American Journal of Sociology* 67: 621–629.
Pettigrew, T. F. and Spier, R. B. 1962. The ecological structure of Negro homicide. *American Journal of Sociology* 67: 621–629.
Pittman, D. J. and Hardy, W. 1964. Patterns in criminal aggravated assault. *Journal of Criminal Law, Criminology and Police Science* 55: 462–470.
Pokorny, A. D. 1965a. A comparison of homicides in two cities. *Journal of Criminal Law, Criminology and Police Science* 56: 479–487.
———. 1965b. Human violence: A comparison of homicide, aggravated assault, suicide, and attempted suicide. *Journal of Criminal Law, Criminology and Police Science* 56: 488–497.
Quinney, R. 1973. *Critique of legal order: Crime control in a capitalist society.* Boston: Little, Brown.
———.1980. *Class; state, and crime* (2nd ed.). New York: Longman, 1980.
Radelet, M. 1981. Racial characteristics and the imposition of the death penalty. *American Sociological Review* 46: 918–927.
Reed, J. 1971. To live-and-die-in-Dixie: A contribution to the study of southern violence. *Political Science Quarterly* 86: 429–443.
Rose, H. M. 1978. The geography of despair. *Annals of the Association of American Geographers* 68: 453–464.
Rose, H. M. 1981 *Black homicide and the urban environment.* United States Department of Health and Human Services, National Institute of Mental Health. Washington, DC: U.S. Government Printing Office.

Ross, P. H., Bose, C. E. and Berk, R. E. 1974. The seriousness of crimes: Normative structure and individual difference. *American Sociological Review* 39: 224–237.

Shin, Y., Jedlicks, D. and Lee, E. S. 1977. Homicide among blacks. *Phylon* 38: 398–407.

Silberman, C. 1978 *Criminal violence—criminal justice: Criminals, police, courts, and prisons in America.* New York: Random House.

Smith, M. D. and Parker, R. N. 1980. Type of homicide and variation in regional rates. *Social Forces* 59: 136–147.

Swigert, V. L. and Farrell, R. A. 1977. Normal homicides and the law. *American Sociological Review* 42: 16–32.

Taylor, I., Walton, P., and Young, J. 1974. *The new criminology* (2nd ed.). New York: Harper & Row,

Taylor, I., Walton, P., and Young, J. 1975. *Critical criminology.* London: Routledge & Kegan Paul,

Turk, A. *Criminality and legal order.* Chicago: Rand McNally.

United States Department of Health and Human Services, Public Health Service, Office of Health Research, Statistics and Technology, National Center for Health Statistics. 1981. *Health-United States: 1980.* (DHHS Publication No. PHS 81-1232.) Washington, DC: U.S. Government Printing Office.

United States Department of Justice, Bureau of Justice Statistics. n.d. *Profile of state prison inmates: Sociodemographic findings from the 1974 survey of inmates of state correctional facilities.* Washington, DC: U.S. Government Printing Office.

Valentine, C. A. and Valentine, B. L. 1972. The man and the panthers. *Politics and Society*, 273–286.

Voss, H., & Hepburn, J. R. 1968. Patterns in criminal homicide in Chicago. *Journal of Criminal Law, Criminology and Police Science* 59: 499–508.

Wolfgang, M. E. 1958. *Patterns in criminal homicide.* New York: John Wiley.

Wolfgang, M. E. 1964. *Crime and race: Conceptions and misconceptions.* New York: Institute of Human Relations Press.

Wolfgang, M. E. and Ferracuti, F. 1967. *The subculture of violence: Towards an integrated theory in criminology.* London: Tavistock.

Wolfgang, M. E. and Reidel, M. 1975. Rape, race, and the death penalty in Georgia. *American Journal of Orthopsychiatry* 45: 658–668.

18

Revisiting the *Scarface* Legacy

The Victim/Offender Relationship and Mariel Homicides in Miami

Ramiro Martinez, Jr., Matthew T. Lee, and Amie L. Nielsen

By incorporating the direct impact of ethnicity and immigration on crime, this chapter is the first to use multivariate methods to compare and contrast Mariel to Afro-Caribbean, African, American, and non-Mariel Latino homicides in a predominately immigrant city. In the current study, Mariels were overinvolved in acquaintance homicides, but little evidence surfaced that they were disproportionately involved in stranger homicides or were unusually violent, both dominant themes in popular stereotypes. In fact, an analysis of homicide event narratives verified the mundane nature of Mariel homicides, implying that the legacy of *Scarface* is not the Mariel killer but the Mariel myth.

Portes and Stepick (1993, 18) write in the introductory paragraph on the Mariel exodus in *City on the Edge*, "If you were an old native, you probably still believed that nothing had really changed in Miami, that immigrants would eventually learn English and life would go on as usual." In fact, no one could foresee the processes at work in Cuba leading to the eventual release of 125,000 people over the summer of 1980. Few could anticipate the awkward federal government reception of the Mariel Cubans, vacillating between sympathy and rejection, over the span of several weeks. Even fewer could predict the local consequences of absorbing the newcomers, much less anticipate pate damaging stereotypes shaping the "Marielitos" public image almost as soon as they landed in Miami. In the end, the Mariel Cubans' arrival highlighted the most unique episode in American immigration history and completed Miami's transformation from a southern tourist destination to the capital of the Caribbean (Portes & Stepick, 1993, 21). For a host of reasons, 1980 was quite a year for all of Miami's residents.

This was especially true for the Marielitos. The popular media focused on the crime-prone element among the (Mariel) refugees and immediately portrayed the newcomers as steeped in the criminal cultural traditions of Cuba's prisons (Portes & Stepick, 1993). Cuban and U.S. officials contributed to these stereotypes.[2] Cuban researchers reported that "45.25 percent of all persons that abandoned Cuba through the port of Mariel had delinquent backgrounds" and the U.S. Immigration and Naturalization Service stated that 19% had been in Cuba's jails (see Martinez, 1997a; Pedraza, 1996; p. 270; Portes & Stepick, 1993, p. 20 for elaborations on these misleading figures). Moreover, the *Miami Herald* published a series of articles over the summer and fall of 1980 blaming the Mariels for a local youth crime wave, gang violence, and other random acts of street violence. The crime-prone Mariel image was soon entrenched in the public imagination (see Portes & Stepick, 1993).

Yet, little "research" assessed the adequacy of the notion that Mariel crime, or more specifically, homicide, was distinctive from that of other ethnic (immigrant) groups.[3] In fact, no one has systematically compared and contrasted the predictors of Mariel Cubans' criminal activities to those of other ethnic groups over a long time period. Moreover, previous studies of homicide rates support the contention that patterns of variation and influences accounting for the variation, including race and ethnicity, are different for different homicide types; intimates, family, acquaintance, and strangers. We anticipate that the less the intimacy in the victim/offender relationship, the greater will be the ethnic effect because Mariels were not welcomed with open arms, presumably had less time to form intimate relationships, had little power in the community, and were more isolated than more established Cubans. If the Mariel stereotype is correct, killings between and by strangers should be higher for Mariels than any other racial or ethnic group.

To examine these issues, we use several strategies to generate the most meaningful and valid results. First, the data were drawn from Miami, Florida, a city where most Mariels settled and a place with a multiethnic population, allowing us to capture the effects of each similarly situated ethnic group's local context on homicide. Second, because the interaction between victim and offender (e.g., acquaintance, family, intimate, and stranger) is an important unit of analysis, we explore these dimensions at the homicide event level (Messner & Tardiff, 1986). Third, because circumstances influencing homicide data set (African American, Afro-Caribbean, Anglo, Mariel Cuban, and non-Mariel Latinos) was collected directly from the city of Miami Homicide Investigations Unit. This strategy permits homicide incident linkage to situational circumstances data gathered for the period between 1980 and 1990, a time of intense local turmoil (see Portes & Stepick, 1993), and can reveal patterns that may be obscured in studies based on aggregated national data sets (Cohen, Cork, Engberg, & Tita, 1999). Finally, this study employs multinomial and logistic regression, the most appropriate statistical techniques (see DeMaris, 1995) for modeling these homicide events, thereby representing an advance over previous research, which has relied heavily on ordinary least squares regression models. Prior to exploring these relationships, we review the research setting and evaluate the contemporary literature.

The *Scarface* Legacy

Popular media accounts not only shaped the portrayal of the Mariel Cubans within the Miami metropolitan area but across the United States. The most prominent image appeared in the cinematic remake of the movie *Scarface*, previously about Al Capone but recast with a machine gun-toting drug lord Marielito wreaking havoc in the streets of Miami. Writers further fueled this image by proclaiming that Mariel-related crime was spreading across the United States without presenting *any* systematic evidence to support this notion (Tanton & Lutton, 1993). Nevertheless, the violent Mariel image flourished as politicians, pundits, and psuedoacademicians (cf. Lamm & Imhoff, 1985; Tanton & Lutton, 1993) continued to promote the notion of the crime-prone immigrant, a claim linked directly to the 1980 Mariel boatlift.

Public anxiety over the Mariel boat wave, in fact, resembles the popular discussion of the link between crime and turn-of-the-century immigration (Martinez & Lee, 2000a). Debate more than 100 years ago on the link between crime and European immigrants focused on several controversial issues. These included the criminal cultural traditions inherent in the newcomers' countries of origin, the crime-prone characteristics of immigrant areas, and the manner in which the lack of acculturation and assimilation into American society encouraged criminal involvement. These issues resurfaced in Miami and returned with a vengeance as public officials grappled with how to handle the Marielitos and the perceived Mariel crime wave (Martinez, 1997a).

In contrast to the conventional wisdom about the immigration/crime nexus, the small number of studies providing empirical evidence find that immigrants in the United States are generally less involved in crime than other ethnic groups. These findings are at odds with a wealth of prominent reasons why this should not be the case, such as settling in disorganized neighborhoods and acculturation difficulties (see Butcher & Piehl, 1998; Hagan & Palloni, 1999; Martinez & Lee, 2000a). Furthermore, immigrant experiences very greatly with local conditions and it is likely that these conditions shape criminal involvement to a larger degree than the cultural traditions of the groups themselves. For example, research on homicide in San Antonio over the period between 1940 and 1980 found that homicide rates among Mexican males fell between those of native Whites and Blacks, and that homicide remained concentrated in poor areas of the city, regardless of whether the residents were Black or Mexican (Bradshaw, Johnson, Cheatwood, & Blanchard, 1998). Another study found that immigration was not related to youth violence in California, whereas alcohol availability was an important influence on serious crime among young males in three cities with large Latino populations (Alaniz, Cartmill, & Parker, 1998). Finally, a study of Puerto Rican newcomers found that those living in New York City had high rates of homicide, whereas Puerto Ricans living elsewhere had rates comparable to native Whites (Rosenwaike & Hempstead, 1990).

A number of studies have examined homicide among several prominent ethnic groups in Miami, Florida. Although the media often portrayed Mariel refugees as crime prone, the empirical evidence demonstrated that they were rarely overrepresented as either homicide victims or offenders. In fact, after a short time period, they were much less likely to offend than Miami's established Cubans (Martinez, 1997a). In addition, despite a constant influx of Latino immigrants in the 1980s, Miami's homicide rates continued to decline (Martinez, 1997b). Finally, Martinez and Lee (1998) found that whereas African Americans were overrepresented in homicide incidents relative to group size, Miami's Haitians and Latinos were underrepresented, and in some cases the rate of homicide among the two immigrant groups was lower than that of non-Latino Whites (Anglos).

Consistent with earlier studies, the criminal involvement of immigrant groups varies considerably in different cities. A good example of this variation is provided in a study of Latino homicide among El Paso's Mexicans and Miami's Cubans (Lee, Martinez, & Rodriguez, 2000). Despite the two cities' similar structural characteristics (e.g., employment, poverty, etc.), Miami's Latino homicide rate was almost three times that of El Paso's. In addition to city-specific characteristics like Miami's greater income inequality (see Martinez, 1996, for a discussion of absolute versus relative deprivation among Latinos) and possibly greater availability of guns, other local conditions shaped the comparatively high Cuban homicide rate. For example, Cubans settled in a more violent area of the country (south Florida) than Latinos in El Paso, and regional contexts may shape each group's involvement in homicide. Wilbanks (1984; see also Epstein & Greene, 1993), demonstrated that Miami's homicide trends mirror those for south Florida generally, and that this area experienced a sharp rise in homicides prior to the arrival of thousands of Cuban refugees in the Mariel boatlift of 1980. Thus, Miami's Latinos lived in a location experiencing higher levels of violence than El Paso's Latinos.

Just as important differences were revealed by the experience of two groups of Latinos in the research described above, other studies have also examined within-group differences among ethnic groups (see Hawkins, 1999, for a similar strategy). Martinez and Lee (2000b) investigated Afro-Caribbean homicides in Miami and found that Mariel Cuban, Haitian, and Jamaican immigrants were generally less involved in homicide than natives. Comparing the early 1980s, when these groups first began arriving in Miami in large numbers, to the late 1990s, the authors discovered a strong pattern of declining violence, especially for Jamaicans and Mariels, whereas Haitians continuously maintained a low overall rate. As these immigrant groups grew in size, and had a lower proportion of young males, homicide rates rapidly declined. This finding suggests that rapid immigration may not create disorganized communities but may instead stabilize neighborhoods through the creation of new social and economic institutions (see also Portes & Stepick, 1993).

In sum, the present research examines ethnicity and the relationship between victims and perpetrators, net of other important explanatory and control variables. We extend previous research by examining whether there are differences in victim–offender relationship across racial/ethnic groups in Miami for the years 1980 through 1990. Past research has ignored both race/ethnic specific homicides and homicide types even though scholars have long demonstrated the need to disaggregate homicides into these categories. By examining, in a multivariate context, whether there are differences in homicide victim–violator relationships by ethnicity, net of other predictors, we can better determine whether Mariels are overrepresented in particular types of homicide. This enables a test of whether the perception of Mariels as disproportionately involved in crime and violence is in fact accurate or is a misleading stereotype. Furthermore, we not only examine homicide incidents involving family members, intimates, strangers, and acquaintances but also extend this relationship to include known versus unknown and gun related homicides. Offenders may use guns on more (or less) vulnerable targets, especially when victims are alone, male or immigrants adjusting to a new urban environment (Felson & Messner, 1996). The use of a weapon could play a mediating role in the victim–offender relationship as well as determine the likelihood of a lethal outcome.

Data and Method

Data

Our data collection was modeled on the work of Martinez (1997a) and updates that project. More than 1,600 homicide reports over the 1980 to 1990 time period were gathered from files in the Homicide Investigations Unit of the city of Miami Police Department (MPD) and the Miami-Dade Medical Examiner Office. Each individual homicide supplemental case was drawn from stored files, copied, read, and coded by the authors and trained research assistants. During their investigations, homicide detectives wrote detailed summaries of each homicide incident based on a variety of sources. Witnesses were asked for details about the circumstances leading up to the killing (in many cases suspects volunteer information during "interviews" with the investigators), and in some instances the victim provided information prior to succumbing to the fatal injury. These various sources were merged and summarized in each homicide report. Even though official police data portray a less than fully accurate image of all violent crime in the United States, homicide is the most reliably recorded index crime (Sampson, 1987).

Beginning in 1980, homicide detectives routinely coded ethnic/racial categories as "White," "Black," or "Latin." As the year progressed, and as the boatlift surged, MPD detectives noted if the victim/offender was a Mariel refugee.[4] Typically an Immigration and Naturalization Service (INS) Parole Identification card was found on the body, or during the course of the investigation, family members, acquaintances, or another party (e.g., neighbors, case workers, etc.) noted this identification. The *Mariel* designation was routinely used throughout most of the 1980s to distinguish the refugees from other Latinos. An exception, however, was in 1985 when the MPD homicide unit ceased to identify Mariels for that year. Confident that most of the Mariel homicide involvement had ended, the investigators ignored that category but subsequent homicides proved them incorrect. The category was therefore reinstated in 1986 and its use continued through the end of 1990.

Due to data concerns, attention is directed to individual-level victim data rather than offender data. For our purposes, victim data offer an advantage over offender data: The victim data are more complete. Although the police write a report for all homicides, and thus demographic information is available for all victims, offender information is not available for all homicides because some cases are not cleared by arrest and in some cases no suspect information is known. Because most homicides are intraracial and intraethnic, a more comprehensive picture of Mariel homicide can be obtained by concentrating on the more inclusive victim level. An emphasis on victims also yields more cases, in turn increasing our confidence in the statistical models (Martinez, 1997a).

We advance previous immigrant/crime research by categorizing killings into victim–offender relationships. The homicide detectives' case summaries describe whether an incident involved some type of prior contact between the killer and victim as well as the circumstances surrounding the killing. These relationships were categorized into four general types; *family* members or homicide between siblings, parents, children, and other relatives; *strangers*, or killings between persons with no known prior contact; *acquaintances*, or murders between persons who know each other but are not in an intimate relationship (this typically includes friends, neighbors, coworkers, or roommates); and killings between lovers, ex-lovers, or spouses are coded as *intimate* homicides.[5] Homicides involving unknown victim–offender relationships are examined separately. For comparison, gun-related homicides and those involving other weapons are also included to examine the array of homicide types.

Variables and Codings

Our intent is to explore the link between immigrants/ethnicity and types of criminal homicide in general, net of traditional determinants of homicide. To do so, three dependent variables related to the circumstances of the killings are examined. The first dependent variable is a polytomous measure that indicates the victim–offender relationship (for known cases). The victim–offender categories include acquaintance, family, intimate, and stranger homicides. The coding allows comparison, in the multinominal logit models, of the odds of being in each of the first three categories, respectively, relative to the victim and offender being strangers.[6] To further examine whether there are differences by victim ethnicity in the types of homicides, relationship status is also examined. "Unknown relationship" is coded 1 for cases in which the victim–offender relationship is unknown and is coded 0 for known relationships. The primary weapon used in the event is examined as both a dependent variable and as an independent variable (in the analyses involving the victim–offender relationship and unknown relationship outcomes). It is coded 1 for gun-related homicides and is coded 0 for other weapons.

Although homicide scholars are not in complete agreement on which set of predictors should be used in victim–offender relationship research, a number of commonly used measures are included as control variables (see Felson & Messner, 1996, for similar usage). Our rationale is that differences in the victim–offender relationship are influenced by a host of factors and ethnicity/immigrant status is but one aspect of a given homicide event. Thus, in addition to victims' ethnicity, a number of other predictors are included in the analyses.

With respect to victim ethnicity, three dummy variables were created. The "African American" category identifies native-born persons of Afro origin. Persons who are non-Mariel Latinos, that is "Latino," are almost exclusively older, more established Cubans. Persons of "Afro-Caribbean" origin are included to distinguish Jamaican and Haitian victims from African Americans. Each of these three variables is coded 1 for persons with that ethnic background and is coded 0 otherwise.

The victim ethnicity category of particular interest, Mariel Cubans, is the comparison category. By coding this group as the excluded category, direct examination of ethnic differences between African Americans, non-Mariel Latinos, persons of Afro-Caribbean origin, and Mariel Cubans on the victimization outcome measures are possible. The Mariel category identifies immigrant victims who arrived from the Mariel harbor in 1980. Mariel Cubans have many characteristics similar to coethnic Latinos, including language, settlement patterns, and a host of other factors. However, given the Mariels' economic characteristics, feelings of discrimination, potential adjustment problems, and media stereotypes (see Portes & Stepick, 1993), we compare and contrast the Marielitos to the three ethnic minority groups in the following sections. Because our focus is on similarly situated ethnic groups, non-Hispanic White victims are excluded.

Several measures linked to homicide incidents are used to predict type of killings. First, two age and two gender variables are used to control for the elements contributing to the segment of population most at risk for offending and victimization. "Offender age" and "victim age" are both coded 15 to 24 years = 1 and other age = 0. "Offender gender" and "victim gender" are also both dummy coded (males = 1, females = 0). A time dummy variable is included to account for the uncoded Mariel year (1985 = 1, other years = 0). The goal here is to discover whether the year with missing Mariel values is significantly different from years with Mariel coded. "Multiple offenders" indicates whether two or more perpetrators (coded 1) or a single perpetrator (coded 0) was involved in the homicide event.

Homicide characteristics reflect the situational context surrounding the event. Therefore, the weapon variable is dichotomous, with gun-related homicides = 1, other weapon = 0. Because private and public settings shape the likelihood of homicide types and the opportunities for crime in general (Parker & Rebhun, 1995), the homicide location is examined through two measures. "Indoor" killings (e.g., residence) and homicides occurring in or near an "alcohol location" (e.g., bar, liquor store) are each dummy coded, with events occurring in each type of location coded 1 and other locations coded 0. Outdoor locations are the excluded category.

Analyses

Two types of analyses are conducted in this study. First, multinomial logistic regression equations are estimated to examine whether victims' ethnicity and other predictors are significantly related to known victim–offender relationships among the Miami homicide victims. Multinominal logit entails the simultaneous estimation of logits for pairs of nonredundant categories of the dependent variable (DeMaris, 1992; Long, 1997). The simultaneous estimation of logits via multinominal logit is considered more efficient than estimating several logistic regression equations (Long, 1997) and may be preferable to other techniques (i.e., discriminant analysis) for polytomous dependent variables (DeMaris, 1992). For the victim–offender relationships, the models are estimated for acquaintances, family members, and intimates, with each category compared with stranger homicides. To further examine the relationship between victim ethnicity and homicide, the second analytic technique employed is logistic regression. In these analyses, the two dependent variables are dichotomous (unknown versus known victim–offender relationship and gun-related versus other weapon homicides).

For both the multinomial logit and logistic regression results, the odds ratios and the beta coefficients are presented, although the emphasis in discussing the results is on the odds ratios. The odds ratios are derived by exponentiating the beta coefficients; negative beta coefficients produce odds ration that are less than 1, whereas positive coefficients produce odds ratios that are greater than 1 (DeMaris, 1992). In the multinominal logit results, the presented odds ratios represent the change in the odds that the victim and offender were acquaintances, family members, or intimates, respectively, rather than strangers, associated with a 1-unit increase on each predictor net of the effects of the other independent variables in the model. For the logistic regression results, the odds ratios represent the change in the odds that the homicide involves an unknown relationship or was gun-related, respectively, associated with a 1-unit increase on each of the predictors (net of the effects of the other independent variables) (DeMaris, 1992).

Results

Table 18.1 presents frequency distributions for the variables used in the analyses, reflecting homicide incidents from 1980 through 1990. The distribution for the victim–offender relationship (in known cases) indicates that homicides involving acquaintances, killings initiated between people with some prior contact, comprised 55% of Miami homicides. On the other hand, just more than 5% of homicides involved nonintimate family members, whereas about 12% involved intimates. Furthermore, homicides committed between strangers comprise about one quarter (27.8%) of the homicides with known victim–offender relationships. The results also show that the relationship between victim and offender was unknown in just more than one fifth (20.5%) of all homicides examined. As with other accounts of violence during the 1980s, more than two thirds (69.8%) of all homicides involved use of a gun rather than other types of lethal weapons.

There is some ethnic variation in homicide victims. The two largest groups of victims are native-born African Americans (40.4%) and the older more established non-Mariel Latinos (37.7%, almost exclusively Cubans). Given the proportional similarities and dominance of the first two ethnic groups, the Mariel (15.8%) and Afro-Caribbean (6.1%) categories seem small in comparison but important ethnic differences may exist with respect to victim–offender relationships.

The frequencies of the other homicide characteristics also demonstrate the potential utility of examining these determinants of victim–offender relationships. First, the percentage of offenders (when known) in the age category of 15 to 24 years, the most at-risk age group, is similar to that of victims (29.1% and 36.7%, respectively). Second, males are overwhelmingly involved as homicide offenders and as victims (82.4% and 84.5%, respectively). Incident location also is dominated by one type: More than one-half (57.5%) of homicides occurred in an outdoor setting, such as the streets, street corner, a park, or other outdoor locations. Almost one-third (31.7%) of events occurred inside the victim or offender's home or other type of private setting. Finally, about 11% of homicides occurred in or around a bar or liquor store, places that attract people and activities, some of which are not directly associated with drinking, that increase the risk of violence (Alaniz et al., 1998; Parker & Rebhun, 1995).

To explore possible immigrant/ethnic differences in homicide types, we begin by examining the relationships between victim ethnicity and victim–offender relationships. Table 18.2 shows the multinomial logistic regression results for known victim–offender relationships, with odds ratios and betas presented. For the three categories of victim–offender relationships shown—acquaintance, family, intimate—the comparison group is strangers. For the ethnicity-of-victims variables, Mariel victims are the excluded group, allowing direct determination of ethnic differences (if any) in the types of homicides.

The results indicate that few ethnic differences are found for victim–offender relationships. Examining across the outcome categories for the African American victim, non-Mariel Latino victim, and Afro-Caribbean victim variables reveals that net of the effects of the other predictors, in only one category—acquaintances—are there ethnic differences in types of homicides. Specifically, members of the other groups were less likely than Mariel victims to be acquainted with their killers rather than be strangers: compared with Mariel victims, the odds of being killed by an acquaintance are only 0.49 times as high for African American victims, non-Mariel Latinos are 0.42 times as likely, and the odds of being killed by an acquaintance are 0.25 times as high for Afro-Caribbean victims as for Mariels. Victim ethnicity is not a significant predictor of either family or intimate homicides (relative to stranger killings), suggesting that Mariel Cubans and members of the other groups have similar odds of being represented as victims in those types of homicides net of the effects of the other predictors.[7]

Table 18.1 Frequency Distributions for Dependent and Independent Variables (N = 1,618)

Variable	Percentage
Victim–offender relationship (known only)	
Acquaintance	55.0
Family	5.5
Intimate	11.7
Stranger	27.8
Unknown relationship	
No (known relationship)	79.5
Yes (unknown relationship)	20.5
Weapon	
Non-gun	30.2
Gun	69.8
Victim ethnicity	
African American	40.4
Non-Mariel Latino	37.7
Afro-Caribbean	6.1
Mariel	15.8
Offender age	
Other age	70.9
15 to 24 years	29.1
Victim age	
Other age	63.3
15 to 24 years	36.7
Offender gender	
Female	17.6
Male	82.4
Victim gender	
Female	15.5
Male	84.5
Time dummy	
Other years	92.6
1985	7.4
Number of offenders	
One offender	85.2
Two or more	14.8
Location	
Outdoors	57.5
Indoors	31.7

Several of the other explanatory variables are associated with the victim–offender relationships. For acquaintance and intimate homicides, the offender's age is significant, with the perpetrator more likely to be between the ages of 15 to 24 years than other ages for these two homicide types. Gender, of both the offender and victim, are significant predictors. Males are more likely than females to be the perpetrators in homicides involving acquaintances, although males are less likely than females to be the offenders in killings involving family members and intimates (as opposed to strangers). Whereas gender of the victim is not associated with the victim–offender relationship for acquaintances, it is related to family and intimate homicides. In both cases, males are less likely than females to be victims in family and intimate killings, with the odds for males 0.2 times and 0.07 times as high, respectively, as those for females. These results are consistent with other findings concerning the greater involvement of females in family and intimate homicides as both perpetrators and victims compared with those involving acquaintances or strangers (e.g., Lee et al. 2000).

Other variables are also significant predictors. The dummy variable for time is significantly associated with acquaintance killings: In 1985 the estimated odds of the victim and offender being acquaintances is 3.13 times higher than for other years. The weapon used is significant only for homicides between family members, with a gun less likely than another weapon to have been used in such killings. The number of offenders is significant for all three outcome categories, with the odds of homicides between acquaintances 0.44 times as likely to involve multiple offenders rather than a single perpetrator, between family members 0.04 times as likely, and between intimates 0.09 times as likely to involve multiple perpetrators than a lone offender. The event location is also associated with victim–offender relationships. Specifically, the odds of family and intimate homicides are about three times higher in indoor locations than outdoor locations. That is, family and intimate homicides are more likely than homicides involving strangers to have occurred indoors rather than outdoors.

To further explore the relationship between victims' ethnicity and homicide, logistic regression is used to examine whether ethnicity and the other relevant predictors are associated with unknown victim–offender relationships and gun-related homicides. Particularly with regard to the victim–offender relationships, the lack of significant findings for victim ethnicity effects (except for homicides between acquaintances) in the multinomial logit results may be due to the relatively large (20.5%) percentage of cases where the nature of this relationship is unknown. If victims' ethnicity is associated with unknown-relationship homicides, this suggests that the lack of an association for known homicides is potentially attributable, at least in part, to the inability to classify the events. However, if victims' ethnicity is not a significant predictor of unknown relationship status, this

Table 18.2 Multinominal Logistic Regression for Homicide Victim–Offender Relationship (n = 1,286): Odds Ratios

Independent Variables	Dependent Variable Categories					
	Acquaintance Versus Stranger		Family Versus Stranger		Intimate Versus Stranger	
African American victim[a]	0.49***	(0.71)	0.89	(0.12)	0.78	(0.25)
Non-Mariel Latino victim[a]	0.42***	(0.87)	1.02	(0.02)	0.90	(0.10)
Afro-Caribbean victim[a]	0.25***	(1.39)	0.51	(0.68)	0.29	(1.23)
Young (15 to 24 years) killer	1.39*	(0.33)	1.56	(0.45)	1.63*	(0.49)
Young (15 to 24 years) victim	1.11	(0.10)	0.74	(0.30)	0.87	(0.14)
Male offender	1.78*	(0.58)	0.34**	(1.09)	0.19***	(1.65)
Male victim	1.15	(0.14)	0.20***	(1.61)	0.07***	(2.62)
1985 dummy	3.13***	(1.14)	1.32	(0.28)	1.99	(0.69)
Gun related	1.04	(0.04)	0.51*	(0.68)	0.71	(−0.35)
Multiple offenders	0.44***	(−0.83)	0.04**	(−3.19)	0.09***	(−2.41)
Indoor location[b]	0.87	(−0.14)	3.06***	(1.12)	2.84***	(1.04)
Alcohol location[b]	1.02	(0.02)	0.53	(−0.63)	0.14	(−1.97)
Model chi-square			494.11***			
df			36			

Note: Beta coefficients are in parentheses.
a. Comparison is Mariel victims.
b. Comparison is outdoor location.
* $p < .05$. ** $p < .01$. *** $p < .001$.

provides additional support for few differences by ethnicity in the nature of the victim–offender relationships. Similarly, if victim ethnicity is associated with gun-related homicides, this may suggest possible ethnic differences in access or willingness to use guns in violent situations (to the extent that homicides tend to be intraethnic).

The logistic regression results for unknown victim–offender relationship and gun-related homicides are shown in Table 18.3. For unknown relationship status, no offender variables are included (as few such offenders have been identified and have information available). The results show that only one predictor—weapon used—is associated with unknown status. In particular, the odds of unknown relationships are lower for events involving guns compared with those involving other weapons. The nonsignificant victim ethnicity variables indicate that the odds that type of relationship between the victim and offender is unknown are similar for Mariel Cuban victims and for victims from the other three ethnic groups. In other words, there are no significant ethnic differences for known and unknown relationships for Mariels and the other groups.

Table 3 also shows the results for gun-related homicides. Once again, victims' ethnicity is not associated with whether the homicide was committed with a gun (rather than with other weapons). Several other variables are significant predictors, however. The odds of perpetrating gun-related homicides are more than twice (2.17) as high for males as for females, and males are more likely than females to also be the victims in such killings. Furthermore, multiple offenders are more likely than single offenders to commit gun-related homicides. Finally, the odds of gun-related homicides are more than twice as high in or around alcohol outlets as they are outdoors. That is, alcohol locations are more likely than other settings to be the site of gun-related homicides.

More on Acquaintance Homicides

The stereotypes promoted by the media depicted Mariels as extremely violent and engaging in random acts of street crimes targeting strangers. In this context, the disproportionate involvement of Mariel

Table 18.3 Logistic Regression Results for Unknown Victim–Offender Relationship and Gun-Related Homicide (N = 1,618): Odds Ratios

Independent Variables	Dependent Variables: Unknown (1) Versus Known (0)		Gun Related (1) Versus Non-Gun (0)	
African American victim[a]	0.71	(–0.34)	0.74	(–0.30)
Non-Mariel Latino victim[a]	0.81	(–0.22)	0.81	(–0.21)
Afro-Caribbean victim[a]	1.11	(0.10)	0.92	(–0.08)
Young (15 to 24 years) killer	—		0.95	(–0.05)
Young (15 to 24 years) victim	0.86	(–0.15)	1.26	(0.23)
Male offender	—		2.17***	(0.78)
Male victim	1.35	(0.30)	1.80***	(0.59)
1985 dummy	1.52	(0.42)	1.07	(0.07)
Gun related	0.56***	(–0.58)	—	
Multiple offenders	—		1.41*	(0.34)
Indoor location[b]	0.76	(–0.27)	0.81	(–0.21)
Alcohol location[b]	0.80	(-0.23)	2.20***	(0.79)
Model chi-square	33.18***		103.28***	
df	9		11	

Note: Beta coefficients are in parentheses.
a. Comparison is Mariel victims.
b. Comparison is outdoor location.
* $p < .05$. ** $p < .01$. *** $p < .001$.

Cubans, compared with other ethnic groups, in acquaintance homicide rather than stranger homicide is somewhat puzzling. One possible explanation is that if other groups avoided Mariels (possibly due to negative publicity surrounding their alleged criminal inclinations), members of this group associated primarily with fellow newcomers. Thus, all types of interactions (including homicide) would involve coethnics and acquaintances, so our finding would be less surprising. This situation also contrasts with the findings of a classic study on immigration and homicide—the case of Polish peasants in the United States who were more likely than natives to react with violence against strangers as a result of the breakdown of community norms and institutions in areas in which the Polish settled (Thomas & Znaniecki, 1920). To uncover the reasons why the Mariel experience, as measured by the quantitative models, did not seem to fit the Polish case, we thought it worth the effort to undertake an extra step in examining this relationship. Therefore, we decided to qualitatively analyze the original supplemental reports in order to address this issue.

We discovered that Mariels were largely involved in mundane homicide events. The preponderance of garden-variety homicides between acquaintances described in the homicide detectives' accounts offer a stark contrast to the imagery of the *Scarface*-like killer. Several prominent themes emerged from a careful reading of these homicide narratives. Many of the killings were victim precipitated. In some cases, victims argued over pool games, politics, and female companionship (or the lack of it). Several were bar brawls, or arguments rising out of earlier bar fights that required retaliation. These incidents were fueled by alcohol, escalated into violence, and turned lethal. Other Mariel victims were killed while engaging in ordinary criminal activity, whereas some were innocent bystanders, and others were fatally injured while trying to prevent the escalation into violence of arguments between third parties.

Arguments were also exacerbated by crowded living conditions. Close quarters intensified quarrels between roommates, with the arguments turning violent and eventually lethal. Still others were over petty slights or imagined insults among friends. A few were retaliations over gambling debts, money owed from petty thefts, or proceeds from a car theft. Most homicides involved a combination of elements—victim precipitation, alcohol involvement, imagined or real slights, and available weapons (particularly guns)—that escalated into arguments that turned lethal between people who knew each other. The end result was not a function of the unique characteristics or culture of the Marielitos, but a deadly combination of American traditions that has historically shaped the violence of all ethnic groups in this country (see Parker & Rebhun, 1995).

Conclusions

By incorporating the direct impact of ethnicity and immigration on crime, this chapter is the first to use multivariate methods to compare and contrast Mariel with Afro-Caribbean, African American, and non-Mariel Latino homicides in a predominately immigrant city. Our primary purpose was to systematically compare and contrast Mariel Cubans with similarly situated ethnic groups in the major city where most Mariels settled (Portes, Clark, & Manning, 1985). Another was to examine these issues relative to distinct homicide types. Finally, our analysis covered an important decade in Miami's history.

Overall, this chapter demonstrates the utility of examining homicide and ethnicity at the individual level. The role of ethnicity vis-à-vis the Mariel Cubans and other ethnic groups revealed that there are differences only for acquaintance homicides but not for other homicide types. Mariels were overrepresented in acquaintance homicides but little evidence surfaced that they were disproportionately involved in stranger homicides, wreaking havoc in Miami, or engaged in high levels of drug-related violence. The legacy of *Scarface* is not the Mariel killer but the Mariel myth.

Several implications can be drawn from these findings. First, the impact of gender and place appears to transcend immigration and ethnicity. Our findings reveal that in most cases and across homicide types, lethal violence is strongly associated with gender, place, and other determinants. Recall that males are usually at greater risk as killers and victims, except as family members and intimates. Indoor/outdoor location, guns, and multiple offenders also played important albeit varying roles. It is worth noting that alcohol location was associated with gun-related homicides, a factor that could indirectly influence other homicide characteristics (e.g., gender, age, etc.).

Next, there is an important caveat. That is, rather than accounting for all aspects of homicide types, our goal was to determine whether ethnicity mattered. We found that it usually did not. Clearly, there are other distinct forces (e.g., employment status, type of work, family structure, etc.) shaping homicide, but those processes are beyond the scope of this chapter or official data collection. The results of this study demonstrate the utility of disaggregating by ethnicity and immigrant status, as well as homicide type, and will hopefully encourage others to undertake similar efforts in the future.

Finally, despite these findings and those of others (Hagan & Palloni, 1999; Martinez & Lee, 2000a) to the contrary, immigration and crime are consistently linked in the public imagination. The overwhelming number of Mariel Cubans in Miami never engaged in homicide or violent crime. Moreover, public discourse highlighting the *Scarface* Myth (little evidence of high crime), instead of the *Scarface* Legacy (high-crime killer), has been scarce as the media continue to focus on crime waves linked to Latinos and other immigrant groups across the United States. The popular notion of the criminal immigrant, which flourished more than 100 years ago and dominated policy debates during each wave of immigration (Butcher & Piehl, 1998; Hagan & Palloni, 1999; Martinez & Lee, 2000a), resurfaced once again in 1980 and continues to serve as a reminder that stereotypes often obscure the facts on the immigrant/crime linkage.

Acknowledgments

This chapter would not have been possible without the generous cooperation of several members of the Miami Police Department (MPD). We thank MPD Police Chief Raul Martinez, former Assistant Chief John Brooks, Lt. Bobbie Meeks, Lt. John Campbell, and past and present detectives in the MPD Homicide Investigation Unit. We also thank Janet Lauritsen and Steven Messner for comments on an earlier draft of this chapter. Funding was provided, in part, to the first author through the National Science Foundation (SBR-9515235), a Ford Foundation Postdoctoral Minority Fellowship, the Harry Frank Guggenheim Foundation, and the National Consortium on Violence Research (NCOVR). NCOVR is supported under grant number SBR-9513949 from the National Science Foundation. The conclusions presented in this chapter are ours alone and should not be taken as the view of any official agency. We are, of course, responsible for any errors, facts, or omissions.

Notes

1. The dramatic opening of the Mariel port to anyone wanting to leave Cuba was one of many episodes that year—the McDuffie riot, the growth of Haitian boat rafters, White-flight, and economic decline—that simultaneously coincided and sent the city reeling from one unexpected event to another one. For the purposes of this chapter, however, we focus on the consequence of the Mariel exodus.
2. In their polemic against immigration, former governor of Colorado Richard Lamm and his coauthor (Lamm & Imhoff, 1985, 57, 62) extensively quote a Pennsylvania police detective (described as "one of the foremost experts on Mariel criminals") who offered the following on the distinctiveness of the recent arrivals:

    > We wanted to educate not just the law-enforcement officials, but also the American public. We wanted them to know two things: these sons-of-bitches aren't Cubans like the old-school Cubans, first; and second, to be careful of them because they are violent and very, very dangerous.

3. In this chapter, we are interested in possible differences in types of homicide for different racial, ethnic, and immigrant groups. For the sake of brevity, however, we typically refer to such differences throughout as "ethnic" differences.
4. There were, of course, other categories noted. Data concerns prevented us from exploring these ethnic variations relative to the Mariels in the current chapter.
5. We direct attention to criminal homicides and restrict our analyses to these types of killings. Persons killed by police officers in the line of duty or excusable homicides (e.g., self-defense) are not covered in the following analysis.
6. The victim–offender variable is coded 1 = acquaintance, 2 = family, 3 = intimate, 4 = stranger.
7. To further explore this issue, in results not shown we examined all possible combinations of victim–offender relationship pairs; the only significant ethnic differences were found for acquaintances and strangers, as presented here.

References

Alaniz, M. L., Cartmill, R. S., and Parker, R. N. 1998. Immigrants and violence: The importance of neighborhood context. *Hispanic Journal of Behavioral Sciences* 20: 155–174.

Bradshaw, B., Johnson, D. R., Cheatwood, D., and Blanchard, S. 1998. A historical geographical study of lethal violence in San Antonio. *Social Science Quarterly, 79*, 863–878.

Butcher, K. F. and Piehl, A. M. 1998. Cross-city evidence on the relationship between immigration and crime. *Journal of Policy Analysis and Management* 17: 457–493.

Cohen, J., Cork, D., Engberg, J., and Tita, G. 1999. The role of drug markets and gangs in local homicide rates. *Homicide Studies* 2: 241–262.

DeMaris, A. 1992. *Logit modeling: Practical applications.* Sage University Paper series on Quantitative Applications in the Social Sciences, 07–086. Newbury Park, CA: Sage.

———. 1995. A tutorial in logistic regression. *Journal of Marriage and the Family* 57: 956–968.

Epstein, G. and Greene, R. Dade's crime rate is highest in U.S., Florida is first among states. *The Miami Herald,* October 3, 1993, 1A.

Felson, R. B. and Messner, S. 1996. To kill or not to kill? Lethal outcomes in injurious attacks. *Criminology* 34: 519–546.

Hagan, J. and Palloni, A. 1999. Sociological criminology and the mythology of Hispanic immigration and crime. *Social Problems* 46: 617–632.

Hawkins, D. F. 1999. What can we learn from data disaggregation? The case of homicide and African Americans. In *Homicide: A sourcebook of social research,* eds. M. D. Smith & M. A. Zahn, 195–210. Thousand Oaks, CA: Sage.

Lamm, R. D., & Imhoff, G. 1985. *The immigration time bomb: The fragmenting of America.* New York: Truman Talley.

Lee, M. T., Martinez, R., Jr., and Rodriguez, S. F. 2000. Contrasting Latino homicide: The victim and offender relationship in El Paso and Miami. *Social Science Quarterly* 8: 375–388.

Long, J. S. 1997. *Regression models for categorical and limited dependent variables.* Thousand Oaks, CA: Sage.

Martinez, R., Jr. 1996. Latinos and lethal violence: The impact of poverty and inequality. *Social Problems* 43: 131–146.

———. 1997a. Homicide among the 1980 Mariel refugees in Miami: Victims and offenders. *Hispanic Journal of Behavioral Sciences* 19: 107–122.

———. 1997b. Homicide among Miami's ethnic groups: Anglos, Blacks, and Latinos in the 1990s. *Homicide Studies* 1: 17–34.

Martinez, R., Jr., & Lee, M. T. 1998. Immigration and the ethnic distribution of homicide. *Homicide Studies* 2: 291–304.

———. 2000a. On immigration and crime. In *Criminal justice 2000: The changing nature of crime,* Vol. 1 eds. G. LaFree & R. J. Bursik, Jr., 485–524. Washington, DC. National Institute of Justice.

———. 2000b. Comparing the context of immigrant homicides in Miami: Haitians, Jamaicans, and Mariels. *International Migration Review 3*: 793–811.

Messner, S. F. andf Tardiff, K. 1986. Economic inequality and levels of homicide: An analysis of urban neighborhoods. *Criminology* 24: 297–317.

Ousey, G. 1999. Homicide, structural factors, and the racial invariance assumption. *Criminology* 37: 405–426.

Parker, R. N. and Rebhun, L. A. 1995. *Alcohol and homicide: A deadly combination of two American traditions.* Albany: State University of New York Press.

Pedraza, S. 1996. Cuba's refugees: Manifold migrations. In *Origins and destinies: Immigration, race, and ethnicity in America,* eds. S. Pedraza & R. G. Rumbaut, 263–279. Belmont, CA: Wadsworth.

Portes, A., Clark, J. M., and Manning, R. D. 1985. After Mariel: A survey of the resettlement experiences of 1980 Cuban refugees in Miami. *Cuban Studies* 15: 37–59.

Portes, A. and Stepick, A. 1993. *City on the edge: The transformation of Miami.* Berkeley: University of California Press.

Rosenwaike, I. and Hempstead, K. 1990. Mortality among three Puerto Rican populations: Residents of Puerto Rico and migrants in New York City and in the balance of the United States. *International Migration Review* 24: 684–702.

Sampson, R. J. 1987. Urban black violence: The effect of male joblessness and family disruption. *American Journal of Sociology* 93: 348–382.

Tanton, J. and Lutton, W. 1993. Immigration and criminality in the U.S.A. *Journal of Social, Political, and Economic Studies* 18: 217–234.

Thomas, W. I. and Znaniecki, F. 1920. *The Polish peasant in Europe and America: Volume IV, disorganization and reorganization in Poland.* Boston: Gorham Press.

Wilbanks, W. 1984. *Murder in Miami: An analysis of homicide patterns and trends in Dade country (Miami) Florida, 1917–1983.* Lanham, MD: University Press of America.

19

An Analysis of American Indian Homicide

A Test of Social Disorganization and Economic Deprivation at the Reservation County Level

Ronet Bachman

Although homicide rates among the American Indian population are documented to be double that of the White population, criminologists have devoted little attention to examining the etiology of American Indian homicide. This chapter presents a multivariate analysis of American Indian homicide at the reservation county level. The model tests indicators of social disorganization and economic deprivation while controlling for other demographic variables. Results indicate that both social disorganization and economic deprivation contribute to high levels of lethal violence in reservation communities.

Homicide rates among the American Indian population have been documented to be double those of the White population and among the highest of virtually all minority groups in the United States (Bachman forthcoming; Frederick 1973; Kraus and Buffler 1979; Westermeyer and Brantner 1972; Levy, Kunitz, and Everett 1969). When reservation county rates are examined, the severity of the problem is illuminated. Some counties have American Indian homicide rates near or over 100 per 100,000 population. For example, Marshal, South Dakota's rate is 97.5 per 100k; the Harney, Oregon statistic is 127.55 per 100k. This compares to 9.6 per 100,000 population for the U.S. American Indian total rate.

There is a proliferation of comparative research on some aspects of homicide, including those that have attempted to explain the homicide differentials that exist between the regions of our country (Wolfgang and Ferracuti 1967; Hackney 1969; Gastil 1971; Blau and Golden 1986; Blau and Blau 1982; Messner 1982, 1983a, 1983b, Williams 1984; Williams and Flewelling 1989; Loftin and Hill 1974; Loftin and Parker 1985) and those that have investigated the differences between Black and White rates (Sampson 1985; Huff-Corzine, Corzine, and Morre 1986). Yet there have been virtually no attempts to explore the etiology of American Indian homicide at the aggregate level.

Given the apparent seriousness of violent death among American Indians on reservations, coupled with the relative lack of research attention by criminologists, the need for a more detailed analysis of American Indian homicide is great. The theoretical model tested was guided by a model of American Indian homicide developed by Bachman (forthcoming). Based on an analysis of American Indian homicide offender interviews, she constructed a model of American Indian homicide that would more responsibly inform multivariate analysis. The model combines elements of social disorganization, economic deprivation, a subculture of violence, culture conflict, and an intervening variable of alcohol/drug abuse. This individual-level model has corresponding aggregate-level interpretations. Because of limited data availability, however, this article evaluated elements of this model at the reservation county level for which suitable indicators were available. Specifically, this research focused on two elements in the model: social disorganization and economic deprivation.

Theoretical Rationale

Social Disorganization

The foundation for the social disorganization perspective originates from one of Durkheim's arguments that rapid social change is associated with increases in crime due to the breakdown of social controls. It later emerged in the writings and research of sociologists at the University of Chicago (Park and Burgess 1921; Shaw and McKay 1931; Thomas and Znaniecki 1970).

While there is no single definition of social disorganization that all adhere to, the term is generally used to describe conditions that undermine the ability of traditional institutions to govern social behavior (Baron and Straus 1989; Skogan 1989). Skogan (1989) noted that while America's past is riddled with such things as illiteracy, cyclical unemployment, and low wages, crime rates remained low where the traditional agents of social control were strong (i.e. the family, schools, traditional values, and so on). He stated, "crime problems became worse when those agents lost their hold on the young" (p. 244).

Investigators in the comparative homicide tradition have also advanced social disorganization to explain partial variation in homicide differentials in this country (Blau and Blau 1982; Crutchfield, Geerken, and Gove 1982; Wilkinson 1984; Williams and Flewelling 1989). In reservation communities, this social disorganization is manifested in many forms, including the breakup of families and high rates of geographical mobility of reservation citizens between urban areas and the reservation and also between other reservations. This chapter empirically assessed the extent to which county-to-county differences in the level of social disorganization are associated with county-to-county differences in American Indian homicide.

Economic Deprivation

Economic deprivation can increase the likelihood of a number of pathologies, including lethal violence. The psychological consequences of being poor are many. It engenders hopelessness, apathy, and anger. One form of coping with the alienation and hostility that poverty may produce is through aggression. Williams and Flewelling (1989) maintained that conditions of extreme scarcity can create a host of manifestations such as "powerlessness and brutalization" which, in turn, can "provoke physical aggression in conflict situations" (p. 423). The evidence of American Indian poverty is so overwhelming that few observers would dispute the contention that some may respond aggressively.

Many reservations are plagued with high unemployment, high dropout rates, and a high percentage of families living below the poverty level. In addition, running water, central heating, indoor plumbing and electricity are not always present in reservation housing. After an analysis of American Indian homicide offender interviews, Bachman (forthcoming) concluded that poverty characterized virtually all of the offenders' lives prior to the act of killing. Only two had graduated from high school, and over 85% were unemployed at the time of the homicide. Further, each offender's annual income fell below the Social Security Administration's poverty level the year prior to the offense.

Although theoretical elaboration on economic sources of crime is somewhat limited, empirical evidence supporting the resource deprivation-homicide link is not (Loftin and Hill 1974; Loftin and

Parker 1985; Williams 1984; William and Flewelling 1989). For these reasons, it is assumed that at the reservation level of analysis, economic deprivation increases the likelihood of lethal violence.

This research sought to investigate the following hypotheses:

1. The higher the level of social disorganization within a reservation community, the higher the level of lethal violence.
2. The higher the level of economic deprivation in a reservation community, the higher the level of lethal violence.

Method

This analysis was performed on 114 counties that were all or partially located on reservation land. County-level independent variables were obtained from the 1980 U.S. Census Subject Reports of American Indians, Eskimos, and Aleuts on Identified Reservations and in the Historic Areas of Oklahoma. These were then matched to American Indian homicide rates which were calculated from county-level data obtained from the U.S. Department of Health and Human Services: Indian Health Service for the years 1980–1987.

Independent Variables

Social Disorganization

A two-indicator Social Disorganization Index was constructed to measure the degree of instability in reservation communities. The indicators are the percentage of female-headed American Indian families with no husband and where children under the age of 18 years are present and the percentage of American Indians who did not live on current reservations in 1979 or 1980, based on 1980 Census data. Both of these variables were selected because previous research provided empirical evidence and theoretical rationale for their contribution to the instability of American society.

Research suggests that "single mother families are less likely to become rooted in a stable residence and social networks and are more apt to find themselves overburdened with the competing demands of family and work" (Baron and Straus 1989, p. 135). Further evidence was offered by Skogan (1989), who noted that indicators of the extent of family disorganization, including female-headed households, are strongly related to neighborhood levels of crime. Based on this empirical support and on the assumption that inordinate strains on female-headed families might contribute to a climate of social instability, it is included in the Social Disorganization Index.

The mobility rate within a community has also been documented to be related to homicide and other criminal activity (Crutchfield et al. 1982, Stark 1983; Williams and Flewelling 1989; Baron and Straus 1989; Browne and Williams 1989). The theoretical rationale for including this indicator is that change in the residential population diminishes the sense of attachment to community norms and reduces the ability of established institutions to regulate social behavior.

Construction of this index was a simple additive procedure. The *z* scores of both indicators were added and then retransformed into a *z*-score index. This index was created to capture as many different spheres of social disorganization as was possible with data availability. The second column in Table 1 displays the ranking of counties on this index.

Economic Deprivation

An index to measure the extent of economic deprivation on reservation communities was constructed in the same manner already described. This index includes the percentage of American

Indian families below the Social Security Administration's defined poverty level, percentage of American Indians unemployed, and percentage of American Indians, aged 16 to 19 years, who are not enrolled in school and who are not high school graduates (i.e., dropout rate). The third column in Table 19.1 displays the rank ordering of counties on the Economic Deprivation Index.

Each of these indicators is believed to measure different spheres of economic deprivation. The number of families below the poverty level has been identified to contribute to high levels of homicide by other investigators (Williams, 1984; Williams and Flewelling 1989; Bachman, Linsky, and Straus 1988) as has the unemployment rate (Smith 1986; Bachman 1991). Although there is little direct evidence of a high school dropout rate and homicide relationship, Loftin and Hill (1974) included it in their Structural Poverty Index, where it proved significant when explaining variation in homicide rates.

Controls

The percentage of the American Indian population that is aged 18 to 24 years and percentage of the population that is American Indian were included in the analysis as demographic controls.

Dependent Variable

The homicide rate used in this analysis is presented in the first column of Table 1. The incidents of homicide used in rate calculations cover the entire 1980–1987 period, not individual years. This procedure was used to reduce the influence of random aberrations in year-to-year estimates, in addition to the possible unreliability of rates based on low frequencies. The total American Indian homicide rate at the country level was calculated by employing both denominators and numerators obtained from the Indian Health Service. The formula for rate calculation was as follows:

(Total AI Homicide Deaths 80–87/Total AI Population 82)/8) × 100,000

These rates were logarithmically transformed to base 10, as they were positively skewed.[1]

Although recent comparative homicide research has documented the fruitfulness of disaggregated homicide rate analysis (Williams and Flewelling 1989; Loftin and Parker 1985, Bachman et al. 1988), the low population of American Indians in this country coupled with the rarity of homicide as an event makes these disaggregated rates almost impossible to calculate at the county level.

Results

Table 19.2 displays the zero-order correlations of all variables included in the indexes with the total American Indian homicide rate. At this bivariate level, only percentage of high school dropouts retained a significant relationship with homicide.

Table 19.3 presents the results of a regression analysis of American Indian homicide. This model resulted in an R^2 of.41. Both the Social Disorganization Index and Economic Deprivation Index were significant predictors of American Indian homicide at the reservation county level. The demographic controls of American Indian population aged 18–24 and percentage of the population that is American Indian were not significantly related to Indian homicide. This might possibly be because there was relatively little variation in these variables at the reservation county level.

Thus support was provided for both hypotheses. High levels of social disorganization were significantly related to high levels of homicide in reservation communities as were high levels of economic deprivation.

Table 19.1 County-Level Rank Order Listings of the American Indian Homicide Rate, the Social Disorganization Index, and the Poverty Index (N = 114 reservation counties)

Rank	County	State	Homicide	County	State	Social Dis organ-ization	County	State	Poverty
1	Bingham	ID	6.41	Klickitat	WA	—	Klickitat	WA	—
2	Franklin	NY	6.74	Prince of Wales	AK	–2.16	Tuolurnne	CA	—
3	Prince of Wales	AK	8.21	Sonoma	CA	–1.91	Yellowstone	MT	—
4	Montezuma	CO	8.32	Pondera	MT	–1.71	Del Norte	CA	—
5	Cattaraugus	NY	8.43	Franklin	NY	–1.61	Day	SD	—
6	Dewey	SD	8.70	King	WA	–1.58	Kootnai	ID	—
7	Carson City	NV	9.36	San Juan	UT	–1.49	Wood	WI	—
8	Elko	NV	9.46	Jackson	NC	–1.23	Brown	KS	–2.27
9	Nez Perce	ID	9.82	Brown	WI	–1.23	Prince of Wales	AK	–1.87
10	Del Norte	CA	10.43	San Juan	NM	–1.23	Osage	OK	–1.52
11	Tulare	CA	10.92	Leake	MS	–1.20	Stevens	WA	–1.43
12	Taos	NM	11.13	Glacier	MT	–1.19	La Plata	CO	–1.37
13	Brown	WI	11.18	Navajo	AZ	–1.18	Ashland	WI	–1.35
14	Yavopai	AZ	11.27	Coconino	AZ	–1.14	Rio Ariba	NM	–1.35
15	Sonoma	CA	11.75	Valencia	NM	–1.11	Washoe	NV	–1.34
16	Grays Harbor	WA	11.89	Glades	FL	–1.10	Jackson	KS	–1.33
17	McKinley	NM	12.72	Mason	WA	–1.01	Elko	NV	–1.31
18	Ashland	WI	12.81	Otero	NM	–.94	NezPerce	ID	–1.28
19	Lake	MT	12.87	Elko	NV	–.94	Brouward	FL	–1.27
20	Washington	ME	13.14	McKinley	NM	–.93	Carson City	NV	–1.24
21	Snohomish	WA	13.17	Apache	AZ	–.92	Mohave	AZ	–1.23
22	Menominee	WI	13.58	Montezuma	CO	–.90	Ferry	WA	–1.13
23	Mahnomen	MN	13.59	Mohave	AZ	–.87	Outagamie	WI	–1.12
24	Ferry	WA	14.09	Ferry	WA	–.87	Taos	NM	–1.09
25	San Juan	NM	15.68	Bernalillo	NM	–.84	Inyo	CA	–1.05
26	Washoe	NV	15.77	Sauk	WI	–.81	Burnett	WI	–1.04
27	Charles Mix	SD	15.97	Bannock	ID	–.76	Leake	MS	–.94
28	Coconino	AZ	16.07	Marshall	SD	–.74	Nye	NV	–.93
29	Whatcom	WA	16.81	Swain	NC	–.72	Thurston	NB	–.92
30	San Juan	UT	17.01	Rio Ariba	NM	–.68	Umatilla	OR	–.90
31	Mendocino	CA	17.16	Taos	NM	–.68	Idaho	ID	–.86
32	Outagamie	WI	17.26	Polk	WI	–.68	Douglas	NV	–.70
33	Rolette	ND	17.27	Gila	AZ	–.66	Franklin	NY	–.66
34	Benson	ND	17.34	Mahnomen	MN	–.63	Neshoba	MS	–.64
35	Osage	OK	17.54	Big Horn	MT	–.61	Thurston	NB	–.64
36	Clark	NV	18.33	Tuolumne	CA	–.59	Brown	WI	–.63
37	Stevens	WA	18.39	Menominee	WI	–.59	Sonoma	CA	–.59
38	Mohave	AZ	18.59	Graham	AZ	–.56	Wasco	OR	–.57
39	Apache	AZ	19.04	Fremont	WY	–.52	Big Horn	MT	–.55
40	St. Louis	MN	19.40	Cattaraugus	NY	–.50	Knox	NB	–.52
41	Graham	AZ	20.23	Hendry	FL	–.50	Uintah	UT	–.50

(*Continued*)

Table 19.1 Continued

Rank	County	State	Homicide	County	State	Social Dis organ-ization	County	State	Poverty
42	Riverside	CA	21.06	Yuma	AZ	–.48	McLean	ND	–.45
43	Big Horn	MT	21.14	Neshoba	MS	–.48	Grays Harbor	WA	–.41
44	Okanogan	WA	21.21	Uintah	UT	–.45	Menominee	WI	–.40
45	Humboldt	NV	21.32	Whatcom	WA	–.44	Bernalillo	NM	–.38
46	Navajo	AZ	21.42	Pinal	AZ	–.42	Jefferson	OR	–.37
47	Brown	KS	21.84	Stevens	WA	–.41	San Juan	NM	–.35
48	Bannock	ID	22.37	Osage	OK	–.40	Humboldt	CA	–.35
49	Pierce	WA	22.84	Jefferson	OR	–.39	Snohomish	WA	–.33
50	Bernatillo	NM	22.92	Jackson	KS	–.33	Benewah	ID	–.32
51	Jackson	NC	22.93	Dewey	SD	–.31	Bingham	ID	–.31
52	Tuolumne	CA	23.38	Lake	MT	–.30	Bannock	ID	–.30
53	Hill	MT	23.43	Hill	MT	–.29	Lyman	SD	–.29
54	Becker	MN	23.59	Koochiching	MN	–.29	Fremont	WY	–.29
55	Pima	AZ	23.83	Blaine	MT	–.28	Lake	MT	–.26
56	Skagit	WA	24.44	Grays Harbor	WA	–.27	Sioux	ND	–.24
57	La Plata	CO	24.72	Missoula	MT	–.27	St. Louis	MN	–.22
58	Rio Ariba	NM	25.72	Rolette	ND	–.25	Rosebud	MT	–.21
59	Beltrami	MN	27.53	Becker	MN	–.20	Otero	NM	–.19
60	Jackson	KS	27.97	Shannon	SD	–.18	Harney	OR	–.17
61	Thurston	NB	28.23	Outagamie	WI	–.18	Okanogan	WA	–.17
62	Thurston	NB	28.23	Wasco	OR	–.11	Missoula	MT	–.17
63	Neshoba	MS	28.47	Rosebud	MT	–.08	Cattaraugus	NY	–.16
64	Klickitat	WA	28.98	Roosevelt	MT	–.04	Glades	FL	–.15
65	Humboldt	CA	29.14	Yakima	WA	–.04	Glacier	MT	–.12
66	Mountrail	ND	29.39	Pima	AZ	–.04	Whatcom	WA	–.10
67	Day	SD	29.52	Burnett	WI	–.01	Apache	AZ	–.09
68	Lyman	SD	29.67	Douglas	NV	.00	Swain	NC	–.09
69	Brouward	FL	30.01	La Plata	CO	.01	Lewis	ID	–.08
70	Yakima	WA	30.61	Idaho	ID	.02	McKinley	NM	–.05
71	Benewah	ID	30.72	McLean	ND	.03	Yakima	WA	–.02
72	King	WA	31.14	Beltrami	MN	.04	Mahnomen	MN	-.01
73	Valencia	NM	32.89	Maricopa	AZ	.14	Valencia	NM	–.01
74	Wood	WI	32.92	Washington	ME	.15	Jackson	NC	–.00
75	Hendry	FL	33.61	Lewis	ID	.18	Blaine	MT	.00
76	Jefferson	OR	33.90	Thurston	NB	.19	Hill	NT	.01
77	Burnett	WI	34.09	Nez Perce	ID	.19	Navajo	AZ	.09
78	Inyo	CA	34.26	Todd	SD	.26	Sawyer	WI	.17
79	Sioux	ND	34.80	Bingham	ID	.26	Imperial	CA	.21
80	Uintah	UT	34.95	Benson	ND	.27	Coconino	AZ	.26
81	Leake	MS	35.54	Yellowstone	MT	.29	Graham	AZ	.27

Table 19.1 Continued

Rank	County	State	Homicide	County	State	Social Dis organ-ization	County	State	Poverty
82	Yellowstone	MT	35.82	Washoe	NV	.32	Montezuma	CO	.29
83	Umatilla	OR	36.89	Carson City	NV	.33	Roosevelt	MT	.31
84	Koochiching	MN	38.71	Nye	NV	.33	Charles Mix	SD	.32
85	Nye	NV	38.82	Buffalo	SD	.35	Gila	AZ	.33
86	Maricopa	AZ	39.59	Sioux	ND	.36	Dewey	SD	.34
87	Fremont	WY	39.63	Snohomish	WA	.38	Pierce	WA	.39
88	Missoula	MT	39.82	Umatilla	OR	.41	Humboldt	NV	.43
89	Glacier	MT	40.17	Ashland	WI	.42	Newton	MS	.45
90	Modoc	CA	40.36	Del Norte	CA	.49	Mountrail	ND	.54
91	Sawyer	WI	40.38	Knox	NB	.52	Riverside	CA	.54
92	Mason	WA	40.47	Mendocino	CA	.56	San Juan	UT	.55
93	Fresno	CA	41.04	Yavopai	AZ	.66	Beltrami	MN	.56
94	Shannon	SD	41.28	Mountrail	ND	.68	Yavopai	AZ	.63
95	Yuma	AZ	42.20	Riverside	CA	.73	Pima	AZ	.75
96	Pondera	MT	42.39	Okanogan	WA	.73	King	WA	.81
97	Glades	FL	42.64	Benewah	ID	.73	Benson	ND	.82
98	Gila	AZ	42.74	Corson	SD	.83	Tulare	CA	.83
99	Blaine	MT	42.77	Skagit	WA	.84	Todd	SD	.86
100	Buffalo	SD	42.87	Harney	OR	.90	Clark	NV	.91
101	Wasco	OR	44.71	Tulare	CA	.98	Becker	MN	.92
102	Roberts	SD	44.84	Sawyer	WI	1.01	Yuma	AZ	.92
103	Pinal	AZ	45.28	Newton	MS	1.04	Skagit	WA	.97
104	Roosevelt	MT	48.98	Day	SD	1.08	Washington	ME	.97
105	McLean	ND	49.52	Fresno	CA	1.09	Mendocino	CA	1.00
106	Otero	NM	50.39	Clark	NV	1.11	Roberts	SD	1.01
107	Imperial	CA	50.41	Lyman	SD	1.12	Pinal	AZ	1.10
108	Swain	NC	54.80	Roberts	SD	1.12	Fresno	CA	1.13
109	Newton	MS	54.95	Brown	KS	1.30	Buffalo	SD	1.13
110	Kootnai	ID	59.15	Imperial	CA	1.35	Rolette	ND	1.15
111	Knox	NB	60.28	Charles Mix	SD	1.39	Marshall	SD	1.18
112	Todd	SD	61.98	Kootnai	ID	1.47	Shannon	SD	1.26
113	Polk	WI	63.21	Thurston	NB	1.55	Corson	SD	1.49
114	Lewis	ID	64.94	Modoc	CA	1.66	Hendry	FL	1.51
115	Rosebud	MT	71.93	Humboidt	CA	1.92	Koochiching	MN	1.57
116	Corson	SD	72.18	Inyo	CA	1.97	Maricopa	AZ	1.60
117	Sauk	WI	73.26	Humboldt	NV	2.00	Pondera	MT	1.84
118	Marshall	SD	97.51	St. Louis	MN	2.01	Modoc	CA	1.93
119	Douglas	NV	103.52	Brouward	FL	2.35	Mason	WA	2.05
120	Harney	OR	127.55	Pierce	WA	2.89	Sauk	WI	2.83
121	Idaho	ID	140.06	Wood	WI	3.46	Polk	WI	4.10

Note: Dash denotes data is missing.

Table 19.2 Correlation of All American Indian–Specific Variables Included in the Indexes with Each Other and with the Total American Indian Homicide Rate

	1	2	3	4	5	6	7	8
1. Homicide	—							
2. Movers	.08	—						
3. Female house	.16	.16	—					
4. Poor	.18	–.18	.13	—				
5. Unemployed	.14	–.03	.05	.01	—			
6. Dropouts	.31*	–.03	.12	.36**	.19	—		
7. 18–24	–.18	–.03	.03	.05	–.13	.17	—	
8. American Indian	.07	–.39**	.09	.38	.04	.02	.05	—

Note: % Female house = percentage of American Indian families who are female headed with no husband and have children under the age of 18; % Movers = percentage of American Indians who did not live on this reservation in 1979 or 1980, % Poor = percentage of American Indian families below the poverty level; % Unemployed = percentage of American Indians unemployed; % Dropouts = percentage of American Indians, aged 16–19 years, who are not enrolled in school and who are not high school graduates; % 18–24 = percentage of the American Indian population that is aged 18–24 years; % American Indian = percentage of the population that is American Indian. *$p < .05$; **$p < .01$.

Discussion

This article presented a multivariate analysis of American Indian homicide at the reservation county level. Regression results indicate that both social disorganization and poverty contribute to high levels of lethal violence in reservation communities.

Although this research tested only two elements of a model proposed by Bachman (forthcoming), it has added insight into what is known about the etiology of American Indian homicide at the aggregate level. Future research must investigate other possible sources of lethal violence among the American Indian population such as culture conflict, a subculture of violence, and alcoholism. To enable this investigation at an aggregate level, attention must focus on developing indicators for these variables. Other variables such as medical resource availability and discriminatory imposition of the law may also contribute to high levels of lethal violence among the American Indian population and must also be explored in future empirical work.

In addition, attention must be focused on American Indian homicide in urban settings. At this time, we are investigating this phenomenon by conducting a contextual analysis of American Indian homicide in standard metropolitan areas.

The results of this research have implications for policy reform regarding the American Indian population. Economic opportunities must be given those who choose to remain on the reservation.

Table 19.3 Regression Analysis of American Indian Homicide Rates on Four American Indian–Specific Independent Variables, 1980–1987 (N = 114 reservation counties)

	B	SE B	Beta	p
Social disorganization	.04	.02	.16	.02
Poverty	.08	.02	.31	.00
Percentage American Indians	.02	.04	.04	.60
Percentage aged 18–24 years	–.01	.05	–.20	–.07

Note: Social disorganization = percentage of American Indian families who are female headed with no husband and have children under the age of 18 + percentage of American Indians who did not live on this reservation in 1979, Poverty = percentage of American Indian families below the poverty level + percentage of American Indians unemployed + percentage of American Indians, aged 16–19, who are not enrolled in school and who are not high school graduates; percentage American Indian = percentage of the population that is American Indian; Percentage aged 18–24 years = percentage of the American Indian population that is aged 18–24.

Unemployment is a serious problem on reservations, averaging 45% to 55% on most reservations. Economic opportunities will allow reservations to become economically viable as well as help reduce the amount of migration that goes on in between urban and reservation areas. As Frederick (1973) stated, "The Indian is forced to leave the reservation to search for a job or to accept low-paying jobs at home. By remaining on the reservation, he is likely to become trapped in an insidious net of dependency which denies him the pride and satisfaction of self-reliance" (p. 8). If the decision is made to leave the reservation, the security of known surroundings and family are given up for an unfamiliar world for which he or she is totally unprepared.

Similar to Wilson's (1987) proposal for programs based on the principle of equality of life chances, systematic long-term planning must be undertaken by policymakers to promote both economic growth and sustained full employment. For as Wilson stated, "Most current planning, whether undertaken by the executive branch, by Congress, or by the Federal Reserve looks no further than the next election" (p. 211).

What is meant by this economic development is certainly not coercive assimilation but, rather, culturally sensitive economic opportunities. While low labor costs and an abundance of natural resources on some reservations are incentives to industrial development, efforts must be made to decrease the factors which limit such development, such as providing new transportation facilities.

If a community is given little hope for the future and no opportunity for self-reliance, high rates of family disruption, migration, and high school dropout are a logical consequence. The cycle of dependence and poverty must be broken. If reservations are allowed economic opportunity, both levels of economic deprivation and social disorganization as well as rates of lethal violence may decrease.

Acknowledgments

An earlier version of this chapter was presented at the annual meeting of the American Society of Criminology in Reno, Nevada, November 1989. This research was supported by a grant from the Family Research Laboratory, University of New Hampshire under National Institute of Mental Health grant #MH15161-13. I would like to thank the anonymous reviewers for their insightful suggestions. I would also like to thank Kirk Williams and Murray Straus for their inexhaustible support of my work and Kimberly Keezel for her meticulous and tireless assistance in the preparation of the data.

Note

1. Several tests were performed to check for problems of multicollinearity and heteroskedasticity. Multicollinearity exists when "one or more of the explanatory variables included in the model are highly correlated in a sample of data" (Hanushek and Jackson 1977, p. 86). When regressing each independent variable in the equation on all other independent variables, the highest R^2 obtained was .38. This indicates that it is safe to assume that multicollinearity is not severe enough to warrant concern. "Heteroskedasticity indicates that the variances of the error terms are not equal for each observation" (Hanushek and Jackson 1977, p. 142). For example, instead of being constant across values of an independent variable, the variance gets larger as the independent variable increases. This would indicate that the variance of the error term is positively correlated with the independent variable. Residual plots were examined, and all produced random scatters. Heteroskedasticity was, therefore, not a problem in this analysis.

References

Bachman, Ronet. Forthcoming. *Death and Violence on the Reservation: Homicide, Suicide and Family Violence in American Indian Populations.* Dover, MA: Auburn House.

Bachman, Ronet, Arnold S. Linsky, and Murray A. Straus. 1988. "Homicide of Family Members, Acquaintances, and Strangers, and State-to-state Differences in Social Stress, Social Control and Social Norms." Paper presented at the annual meeting of the American Sociological Association, Atlanta, GA, August.

Baron, Larry and Murray Straus. 1989. *American Society: A State Level Analysis.* New Haven, CT: Yale University Press.

Blau, Judith R. and Peter M. Blau. 1982. "The Cost of Inequality: Metropolitan Structure and Violent Crime." *American Sociological Review* 7: 114–29.

Blau, Peter M. and Reid M. Golden. 1986. "Metropolitan Structure and Criminal Violence." *Sociological Quarterly* 27: 15–26.

Broudy, D. W. and P. A. May. 1983. "Demographic and Epidemiologic Transition Among the Navajo Indians." *Social Biology* 30: 1–16.

Browne, Angela and Kirk R. Williams, 1989. "Exploring the Effect of Resource Availability and the Likelihood of Female-Perpetrated Homicides." *Law and Society Review* 23(1): 75–94.

Crutchfield, Robert D., Michael D. Geerken, and Walter R. Gove. 1982. "Crime Rate and Social Integration." *Criminology* 20: 467–78.

Frederick, Calvin J. 1973. *Suicide, Homicide, and Alcoholism Among American Indians: Guidelines for Help*. Rockville, MD: National Institute of Mental Health.

Gastil, Raymond P. 1971. "Homicide and Regional Culture of Violence." *American Sociological Review* 36: 412–27.

Hackney, Sheldon. 1969. Southern Violence. In *Violence in America*, eds.. Hugh David Graham and Ted Robert Gurr, 479–500. New York: Signet.

Hanushek, Eric A., and John E. Jackson. 1977. *Statistical Methods for Social Scientists*. New York: Academic Press.

Huff-Corzine, Lin, Jay Corzine, and David C. Morre. 1986. Southern Exposure: Deciphering the South's Influence on Homicide Rates. *Social Forces* 64: 906–24.

Krauss, Robert F. and Patricia A. Buffler. 1979. Sociocultural Stress and the American Native in Alaska: An Analysis of Changing Patterns of Psychiatric Illness and Alcohol Abuse Among Alaska Natives. *Culture, Medicine and Psychiatry* 3: 111–59.

Levy, Jerrold E., Stephen J. Kunitz, and Michael Everett. 1969. Navajo Criminal Homicide. *Southwestern Journal of Anthropology* 25: 124–52.

Loftin, Colin and Robert H. Hill. 1974. Regional Subculture and Homicide. *American Sociological Review* 39: 714–24.

Loftin, Colin and Robert Parker. 1985. An Errors-In-Model of the Effect of Poverty on Urban Homicide Rates. *Criminology* 23: 269–79.

Messner, Steven F. 1982. Poverty, Inequality, and the Urban Homicide Rate. *Criminology* 20: 103–14.

———. 1983a. Regional and Racial Effects on the Urban Homicide Rate: The Subculture of Violence Revisited. *American Journal of Sociology* 88: 997–1007.

———. 1983b. Regional Differences in the Economic Correlates of Urban Homicide Rates. *Criminology* 21: 477–88.

Park, Robert and Ernest W. Burgess. 1921. *Introduction to the Science of Sociology*. Chicago: University of Chicago Press.

Sampson, Robert J. 1985. Race and Criminal Violence: A Demographically Disaggregated Analysis of Urban Homicide. *Crime & Delinquency* 31: 47–82.

Shaw, Clifford and Henry D. McKay. 1931. *Report on the Causes of Crime*. Vol. 12, No. 13. Washington, DC: National Commission on Law Observance and Enforcement.

Skogan, Wesley G. 1989. Social Change and the Future of Violent Crime. In *Violence in America: The History of Crime*, ed. Ted Robert Gurr, 235–50. Newbury Park, CA: Sage.

Smith, M. Dwayne. 1986. The Era of Increased Violence in the United States: Age, Period, or Cohort Effect? *Sociological Quarterly* 27: 239–51.

Stark, Rodney, 1983. Crime and Delinquency in the Roaring Twenties. *Journal of Research in Crime and Delinquency* 19: 4–24.

Westermeyer, Joseph and John Brantner. 1972. Violent Death and Alcohol Use Among the Chippewa in Minnesota. *Minnesota Medicine* 55: 749–52.

Williams, Kirk R. 1984. Economic Sources of Homicide: Reestimating the Effects of Poverty and Inequality. *American Sociological Review* 49: 283–89.

Williams, Kirk and Robert L. Flewelling. 1989. The Social Production of Criminal Homicide: A Comparative Study of Disaggregated Rates in American Cities. *American Sociological Review* 53: 421–31.

Wilkinson, Kenneth P. 1984. A Research Note on Homicide and Rurality. *Social Forces* 63: 445–52.

Wilson, William Julius. 1989. *The Truly Disadvantaged: The Inner City, the Underclass, and Public Policy*. Chicago: University of Chicago Press.

Wolfgang, Marvin E. and Franco Ferracuti. 1967. *The Subculture of Violence*. Beverly Hills, CA: Sage.

20

Attitudes toward Marital Violence

An Examination of Four Asian Communities

Marianne R. Yoshioka, Jennifer DiNoia, and Komal Ullah

Domestic violence has become a prominent issue in Asian American communities. Although national survey findings reveal that Asian American women are significantly less likely to report incidents of rape and physical assault than women of other racial and ethnic backgrounds (Tjaden & Thoennes, 1998), anecdotal evidence suggests that partner violence is a major concern among these women (Ho, 1990; Huisman, 1996; Song, 1996; Tang, 1994). Asian cultural themes and family values have been implicated as reasons why many of these women fail to disclose abuse to authorities and to seek help when abuse occurs (Abraham, 1995; Frye, 1995; Ho, 1990; Patel, 1992; West, 1998). Although interethnic differences in cultural themes and family values have received attention in the scholarly literature (B. C. Kim, 1996; Lee, 1996; Leung & Boehnlein, 1996; McKenzie-Pollock, 1996; Rhee, 1997; Song, 1996; West, 1998), there has been a paucity of research examining interethnic differences in attitudes toward domestic violence that presumably spring from these themes and values.

This study is intended to bridge this gap. Using data from 507 Chinese, Korean, Vietnamese, and Cambodian adults residing in the northeastern United States, interethnic differences in approval of violence, endorsement of male privilege, and perceived alternatives for addressing abuse are examined. The association between selected demographic characteristics and childhood exposure to violence in predicting each of these attitudinal dimensions is explored.

Cultural Themes

Although there are commonalties among Asian American groups, any generalizations must be tempered by knowledge of important variables such as gender, socioeconomic status, immigration status, degree of acculturation, education, and strength of religious beliefs (Wong, 1985). For purposes of this discussion, traditional values and themes will be discussed with the assumption that the extent to which these describe any particular individual will vary.

Asian societies are often described in terms of their collectivist orientation and respect for authority, Influenced by the teachings of Confucianism and Buddhism, which emphasize harmonious interpersonal relationships and interdependence, the interests of the family take precedence over those of the individual (Hsu, 1970; Kitano & Kikumura, 1976; Lee, 1996; Root, Ho, & Sue, 1986). Because the maintenance of harmonious relationships is stressed, there is an implicit value placed on the avoidance of conflict that may disrupt group relations or bring guilt and shame to the family (Ho, 1990; Hu & Chen, 1999; McLaughlin & Braun, 1998).

Asian cultures are also described as power distance societies in which large power differences between individuals and groups are accepted, and this is viewed as a natural and correct state (Hofstede, 1984; Kirkbride, Tang, & Westwood, 1991). Individuals are expected to conform to their predefined roles both inside and outside of the family, based on age, gender, and social class (Lee, 1996). Among some Asian groups, language reinforces these power differentials: The Korean language, for example, contains more than three classes of nouns and verbs that signify the rank ordering of relationships (Kim, 1996).

Divorce is not a common practice in Asian cultures (Lee, 1996). Emphasis is placed on settling disputes within the family, often with the help of older family members who serve as mediators. When marital problems do occur, outside intervention is strongly discouraged for fear that this will bring shame and dishonor to the family. In many Asian cultures, suffering and perseverance are valued virtues (Ho, 1990). Women are given recognition for enduring hardship and are discouraged from discussing family problems when they do occur.

Shaped by these cultural forces, Asian families tend to be patriarchal and hierarchical, giving husbands great authority over wives and children. In this cultural context, where respect, hierarchy, and interdependence among family members are highly valued, the use of violence is often viewed as a husband's prerogative. Feelings of shame and perceptions of the withdrawal of support from kin may pose significant barriers for women to disclose marital difficulties and seek outside assistance when problems occur (Catolico, 1997; Ho, 1990; Patel, 1992).

Attitudes toward Marital Violence

Despite these shared values and beliefs, a limited number of studies have identified interethnic differences in attitudes toward domestic violence among Asian subgroups. Using focus group data obtained from Chinese, Vietnamese, Cambodian (Khmer), and Laotian respondents, Ho (1990) found that of these four groups, Chinese men and women were the least tolerant of the use of physical force as a means of resolving marital disputes. Although Chinese women were the only group who felt it was appropriate for a woman to temporarily leave the home, they emphasized the importance of not seeking outside intervention for fear that this would bring shame and dishonor to the family. These findings suggest that despite overall disapproval of domestic violence within Chinese American communities, outside help seeking is unlikely and the privacy of the event is maintained.

Yick and Agbayani-Siewert (1997) reported similar findings on the basis of interviews with 31 Chinese households. Respondents as a group disapproved of violence overall. However, approximately half felt that violence was justified in certain situations. These included learning of a wife's extramarital affair, a wife losing emotional control, or gender role violations such as a wife making a financial decision without her husband's approval. Yick and Agbayani-Siewert found that age and gender influenced attitudes toward domestic violence with older respondents and males reporting greater tolerance of the use of force as a means of resolving interpersonal conflict. The authors suggested that older cohorts may still adhere to traditional beliefs about family and gender roles and that differences in attitudes between male and female respondents are likely the result of cultural notions of male privilege and authority.

Kulig's (1994) study of Cambodian women revealed similar themes. Findings underscored the strong emphasis placed on proper behavior for Cambodian women; wives were expected to obey and respect their husbands and to accept the problems of the marriage. Great importance was placed on controlling a woman's sexuality because her behavior reflected on the family. As such, women were more likely to be held responsible for marital problems (Caplan, 1987). According to Legerwood (1990), Cambodian women who were physically abused were viewed as having deserved punishment.

Frye and D'Avanzo (1994) identified two common responses to family violence among Cambodian women: nonconfrontation and withdrawal. When asked what they would do if a family member became violent, "talk softly" and "do nothing" were the most frequent solutions offered. This is not surprising given the emphasis in Cambodian society on harmony and balance; conflict is to be avoided at all costs (Ebihara, 1968). Although these authors did not inquire directly about spouse abuse, they reported that there were indicators that it is not uncommon. According to one of their informants, "Most Khmer men, they hit their wives but the women don't know who can help" (Frye & D'Avanzo, 1994, p. 72).

Very few studies have examined attitudes toward domestic violence among other Southeast Asian American groups (e.g., Laotian and Vietnamese). Although commonalties across groups are often emphasized in the literature (e.g., as compared with other Asian American groups, Southeast Asians have substantially lower educational attainment, and a large percentage live below the poverty line) (Lee, 1996; Leung & Boehnlein, 1996; McKenzie-Pollock, 1996), intergroup differences have also been noted. Whereas Cambodian families tend to be nuclear and bilateral in nature, the patriarchal extended-family model is characteristic of traditional Vietnamese families (Frye, 1995; Nguyen, 1999). In addition, although women hold favorable economic positions within both Vietnamese and Cambodian families, decision making is relegated to men in Vietnamese families, whereas it is more egalitarian in Cambodian families (Frye, 1995).

Bui and Morash (1999) compared the responses of 10 Vietnamese women in physically abusive relationships with an equal number of nonabused women to determine factors associated with wife abuse. Variables correlated with physical and emotional abuse included male domination in family decision making, family conflicts arising over changing family norms and values, husbands' lack of educational attainment, and patriarchal beliefs. Findings confirmed women's economic contributions to the family as reported in the literature, although their favorable economic condition did not reduce or influence the dominant position of their husbands within the family.

Despite the absence of published studies concerning Korean American attitudes toward domestic violence, prominent cultural themes and family values that may influence these attitudes have been noted in the literature. According to Rhee (1997), "Korean society has a long history of male domination in which women are taught to obey their husbands and accept their submissive roles" (p. 70). However, as immigrant Korean women increasingly enter the paid labor force, traditional gender roles have started to break down. Korean women are considered to be at increased risk for partner violence, despite these changes, due to Korean husbands' still strongly adhering to traditional attitudes favoring dominant and subordinate relations between husbands and wives. Korean women must still conform to their prescribed roles within the family and outside of it, and their achievements continue to be measured on the basis of their husbands' status and the achievements of their children (Min, 1998).

The limited research available suggests that there is a complex interweaving of cultural, environmental, and interpersonal factors that may place Asian American women at increased risk for violence. Although the influence of Asian cultural themes and family values has been emphasized in the domestic violence literature, few studies have examined their influence in shaping interethnic attitudinal differences. This study is intended to bridge this gap by examining interethnic differences in approval of violence, endorsement of male privilege, and perceived alternatives to abuse among four Asian American subgroups. The contributions of selected demographic characteristics and childhood exposure to violence in predicting proviolence attitudes are also examined. The following questions are addressed: Are there interethnic differences in approval of violence, in endorsement of male privilege, and in perceived alternatives for addressing abuse among Chinese, Korean, Vietnamese, and Cambodian adults? What are the salient predictors of differences in attitudes?

Method

Sample

Short, self-administered questionnaires were distributed at five ethnic community fairs held in a northeastern urban area during the spring and summer of 1999. These fairs provided opportunities for community gatherings and were typically organized around days of ethnic celebration. A convenience sample was used because of the difficulty and expense of recruiting a random sample of immigrant participants who may have legal status difficulties. Elsewhere in the literature, the absence of immigrant respondents in studies of domestic violence has been noted due to a variety of factors, which include language barriers, fear of officials, fear of deportation, and fear that applications for relatives may be affected (National Research Council, 1996).

Given the paucity of data currently available on the attitudinal preferences of differing Asian subgroups, an overarching goal of this exploratory study was to capture as diverse a cross section of Asian respondents as possible. The ethnic community fairs provided access to large numbers of individuals of diverse Asian heritage (Chinese, Cambodian, Vietnamese, Korean, South Asian, and mixed Asian heritage). Specific groups were not targeted on an *a priori* basis. Instead, post hoc analyses were used to determine groups for which there were sufficient numbers of responses available to permit subgroup analyses. Approximately 900 questionnaires were distributed at these fairs. Of this total, sufficient numbers of questionnaires (a minimum of 70 in each case) completed by respondents of Chinese, Vietnamese, Cambodian, and Korean heritage were available. Data from these four ethnic groups were used in this research.

Procedure

Questionnaires were available in English, Mandarin, Korean, Vietnamese, or Khmer, depending on the targeted community of the celebration. To ensure the quality of the translation, items were translated into each of these languages and then back translated into English. This process has been strongly recommended to ensure that translated items are understandable and meaningful in the new language (Brislin, 1986). Each translated version of the measure was pilot tested with groups of Chinese, Cambodian, Vietnamese, and Korean adults who volunteered at a local, Asian, domestic violence agency. This procedure provided a high degree of assurance that the integrity of each question was preserved following translation.

The questionnaire had five sections: demographics, attitudes toward domestic violence, exposure to violence as a child, subjective explanations for wife abuse, and where one would most likely turn for help if violence were occurring. Respondents were verbally assured of anonymity and confidentiality. No names were written on the questionnaires, making it impossible to link a response to a specific individual. Data from the demographic, attitudinal, and exposure to violence sections of the questionnaire were used for the present investigation.

Measures

Dependent Variable: Attitudes toward Domestic Violence

The Revised Attitudes toward Wife Abuse Scale (RAWA) (Yoshioka & DiNoia, 2001) was used to measure attitudes toward wife abuse. Items were measured on 4- or 6-point Likert-type scales, ranging from strongly disagree to strongly agree. Eight of the items were derived from the Attitudes toward Wife Abuse Scale (Briere, 1987). One of the shortcomings of the Attitudes toward Wife Abuse Scale is that it does not reflect specific conditions under which a person may feel that a man is justified in hitting his wife. An individual may not endorse proviolence attitudes generally but may feel there are situations in which the use of violence is justified. To overcome this limitation, six items that assess the degree to which respondents feel that the use of violence is warranted in specific situations were added to the Attitudes toward Wife Abuse Scale. Five of these items were taken from the Likelihood of Battering Scale (Briere, 1987).

In developing the Likelihood of Battering Scale, Briere (1987) drew on his clinical experience to identify situations commonly associated with abuse. In the original form of the Likelihood of Battering Scale, male respondents considered the likelihood that they would hit their wives in each of the situations listed (if she had sex with another man, refused to cook and keep the house clean, refused to have sex with him, made fun of him at a party, or told friends he was sexually pathetic). Because the focus of the present study was on attitudes toward wife abuse, the wording of these five items was revised to elicit to what extent the respondent believed that a husband "has the right" to hit his wife under the same five conditions (e.g., a husband has the right to hit his wife if she had sex with another man). Staff at an Asian domestic violence agency reviewed this set of items for completeness. Following this consultation, a sixth item (nags him too much) was added. The staff reported that Asian women commonly identified nagging as accounting for the abusive behavior of their husbands.

The RAWA was developed and tested with a sample of 335 Chinese and Cambodian respondents. Principal components analysis was performed on the 14 items that composed this measure, yielding a three-factor solution. The five Likelihood of Battering Scale items plus the additional item generated by domestic violence service providers composed the Situation-Specific Approval of Violence subscale (SSA). Four items were combined to form the Male Privilege subscale (MP): a husband should have the right to discipline his wife, a man is the ruler of his home, a husband is entitled to have sex with his wife whenever he wants it, and some wives seem to ask for beatings from their husbands. The final subscale, Perceived Alternatives for Confronting Abuse (PA), was composed of four items: a wife should move out of the house if her husband hits her, a husband is never justified in hitting his wife, a husband should be arrested if he hits his wife, and wife beating is grounds for divorce. Alpha coefficients of reliability for each of these subscales were .89, .66, and .68, respectively. For the present study sample, corresponding coefficients were .88, .68, and .64, respectively.

Each of the RAWA items was scored such that higher scores denoted stronger endorsement of proviolence attitudes. Higher scores on the PA subscale, for example, indicated that respondents did not agree that divorce or moving out of the home was an option for a woman being abused or that being arrested was an alternative for the batterer. Scores for the MP and PA subscales ranged from 4 to 24. Scores for the SSA subscale ranged from 6 to 24.

Independent Variables

Two categories of variables, hypothesized to influence attitudes toward wife abuse, were assessed: sociodemographic variables and childhood exposure to violence. Sociodemographic variables included gender, age, educational level, and ethnicity.

Childhood-exposure-to-violence variables included being physically hit by one or both parents and witnessing domestic violence between one's parents. Respondents were asked to rate the frequency of occurrence of each using a 5-point Likert-type scale where 1 = never and 5 = always. A substantial body of research supports the relationship between childhood exposure to violence (witnessing of or experiencing abuse firsthand) and the use of violence toward an intimate partner as an adult (Garden, 1994).

Results

Description of the Sample

In total, 507 adults participated in this research. The sample was disproportionately female (59%) and younger than age 40. The Asian population living in the United States as a whole tends to be a young population with a median age that is below the national median of 33 years (U.S. Bureau of the Census, 1993). Subgroup comparisons revealed, however, that Vietnamese respondents tended to be older than the Vietnamese population as a whole residing in the United States. The Vietnamese population in the United States tends to be younger with a median age of 25 years (U.S. Bureau of the Census, 1993).

Respondents were a relatively educated group with 58% having had some college or technical school education. These figures are lower than those reported for the total Asian population in the United States; three-fourths of which had high school or higher level completion rates in 1990 (U.S. Bureau of the Census, 1993). Subgroup comparisons revealed that Korean respondents had the highest levels of educational attainment followed next by Cambodian respondents. For the United States as a whole, 89% of Korean males and 74% of Korean females had high school or higher level completion rates (U.S. Bureau of the Census, 1993).

The corresponding figures for Cambodian males and females are 46.2% and 25.3%, respectively (U.S. Bureau of the Census, 1993). Nearly two-thirds of Cambodians in the study sample completed high school, revealing that these respondents tended to have considerably higher attainments than those reported for Cambodians in the nation as a whole.

Three quarters of the sample were foreign born and had been living in the United States for an average of 14 years. in response to questions about their exposure to domestic violence as children, 27% reported having witnessed one of their parents hit the other at least once while growing up, and approximately 10% witnessed marital violence between their parents on a regular basis.

As Table 20.1 shows, there were notable differences between ethnic groups. Analyses indicated that the overall test statistic was statistically significant in the group comparisons of all the demographic variables: gender (x^sup 2^ = 38.71, $df = 3$, $p < .001$); age, $F(3, 472) = 10.83$, $p < .001$; education (x^sup 2^ = 124.17, $df = 6$, $p < .000$); immigration status (x^sup 2^ = 105.05, $df = 9$, $p < .001$); and length of time in the United States, $F(3, 283) = 9.01$, $p < .001$. Examination of follow-up tests showed that in terms of each of the demographic variables, the Vietnamese were clearly distinct from the remaining three groups.

Although the overall sample was composed of more women than men (59% vs. 41%), the opposite was true for the Vietnamese group. This group was predominantly male (67%) (x^sup 2^ = 24.72, $df = 1$, $p < .001$). The Vietnamese had the oldest average age (in contrast to each of the other groups, Tukey's HSD, $p = .000$), followed by the Chinese. The Chinese were found to be significantly older than both the Korean and Cambodian groups (Tukey's HSD, $p = .005$ and $p = .009$, respectively). There was no difference in the average age between these latter two groups.

The Vietnamese also had less education on average in contrast to the other groups (x^sup 2^ = 90.99, $df = 2$, $p < .001$). A greater proportion of the Vietnamese respondents were immigrants compared with the other groups, and among those who immigrated, they had been in the United States for a shorter period of time (for all tests, Tukey's HSD, $p = .000$ to $p = .001$).

Interethnic differences were detected in terms of ever witnessing domestic violence as a child (x^sup 2^ = 9.4, $df = 3$, $p < .05$), of witnessing domestic violence regularly (x^sup 2^ = 11.66, $df = 3$, $p < .01$), and of ever being hit as a child (x^sup 2^ = 12.89, $df = 3$, $p = .01$). Overall, fewer Chinese adults reported childhood exposure to violence. In terms of witnessing domestic violence, follow-up tests showed that there was a statistically significant difference in the proportions of Cambodian

Table 20.1 Sociodemographic Characteristics of the Study Sample

Characteristic	Chinese (n = 255)	Korean (n = 103)	Cambodian (n = 73)	Vietnamese (n = 76)	Total (N = 507)
Gender*** (%)					
Male	30.6	38.8	54.8	67.1	41.2
Female	69.4	61.2	45.2	32.9	58.8
Age*** (%)					
Younger than 20	17.5	10.0	15.2	13.2	14.9
20 to 29	20.1	44.0	36.4	21.1	27.5
30 to 39	28.2	28.0	27.3	19.7	26.7
40 to 49	14.1	12.0	15.2	6.6	12.6
50 to 59	6.0	5.0	6.1	13.2	6.9
60 to 69	8.1	1.0	0.0	18.4	7.1
70 and older	6.0	0.0	0.0	7.9	4.2
Education*** (%)					
Less than high school	12.3	0.0	15.5	4.0	7.6
Some high school	33.0	12.5	21.1	81.3	34.8
Some college	54.7	87.5	63.4	14.7	57.6
Immigration status*** (%)					
Born in the United States	26.7	13.9	9.1	2.7	18.1
Immigrated	71.0	59.4	87.9	95.9	74.6
Visa	1.6	24.8	1.5	1.4	6.3
Visiting the United States	0.8	2.0	1.5	0.0	1.0
Mean years in the United States[a]***	14.6	16.1	15.2	9.8	13.8
SD	8.9	7.8	5.3	6.8	8.0
Year immigrated[a]*** (%)					
Prior to 1980	22.6	30.0	8.2	5.6	17.4
1980 to 1984	20.8	21.7	63.3	12.5	26.1
1985 to 1989	25.5	31.7	14.3	20.8	23.7
1990 to 1994	22.6	11.7	8.2	44.4	23.3
1995 to 1999	8.5	5.0	6.1	16.7	9.4
Childhood exposure to domestic violence					
Ever witnessed domestic violence*	21.4	33.7	35.6	28.6	26.9
W itnessed regularly**	6.5	8.7	19.2	13.0	9.7
Ever hit as a child**	61.1	80.4	70.1	72.0	67.9
Hit regularly	32.0	33.0	37.3	48.0	35.4

[a] Chinese, n = 181; Korean, n = 60; Cambodian, n = 58; and Vietnamese, n = 72.
* $p < .05$.
** $p < .01$.
*** $p < .001$.

and Chinese adults who were child witnesses. Specifically, a greater proportion of Cambodian adults had ever witnessed domestic violence (x^sup 2^ = 6.27, *df*= 1, *p*< .05) or had witnessed it regularly (x^sup 2^ = 10.95, *df*= 1, *p*< .01).

In terms of the variable of ever being hit as a child by a parent, an overall group difference was found (x^sup 2^ = 12.89, *df*= 3, *p*< .01). Follow-up tests showed that the difference lay between the Chinese and Korean groups. A greater proportion of Korean adults reported being hit by a parent while growing up (x^sup 2^ = 11.63, *df* = 1, *p* < .001). No differences were found between the groups for the variable of being hit as a child on a regular basis by a parent.

Attitudes toward Wife Abuse

Table 20.2 presents the RAWA data in terms of the percentage agreement with the RAWA items by ethnicity. Items were recoded to reflect basic agreement or disagreement with statements regardless of the strength of endorsement. To help keep the presentation of data consistent, the percentages listed for items in the PA subscale reflected the proportion of individuals that disagreed with the statement. For example, for the item, wife beating is grounds for divorce, 11.1% of the Chinese respondents disagreed with this statement.

Pronounced interethnic differences were evident in the percentage of respondents who endorsed statements supporting wife abuse. For example, 60% of the Vietnamese group agreed with the item "a man is the ruler of his home" in contrast with only 14% of the Chinese group who agreed. On the item "a husband is entitled to sex with his wife whenever he wants it," the Southeast Asian groups were quite distinct from the East Asian groups. Approximately one-quarter of the Cambodians and Vietnamese endorsed this item in comparison with 10% and 3% of the Chinese and Korean groups, respectively.

The Vietnamese group was distinguished from the remaining groups on the MP subscale with a relatively high proportion of respondents endorsing three of the items (54% to 60%). A much lower proportion (23%) endorsed the sexual entitlement item. Consistently, 22% to 28% of the Cambodian group endorsed all four items. There was more variation within the Chinese and Korean groups with regard to their endorsements of the items of this subscale. For example, although one fifth of

Table 20.2 Proportion of Respondents Who Endorsed the Revised Attitudes toward Wife Abuse Scale (RAWA) Items by Ethnicity

RAWA Item	Chinese (*n* = 251)	Korean (*n* = 101)	Cambodian (*n* = 67)	Vietnamese (*n* = 72)	Total (*N* = 491)
Endorsement of male privilege[a]					
A husband should have the right to discipline his wife	14.3	22.8	22.4	54.2	23.0
A man is the ruler of his home	14.3	21.8	27.3	60.0	24.2
A husband is entitled to have sex with his wife whenever he wants it	9.9	2.9	27.7	22.5	12.7
Some wives seem to ask for beatings from their husbands	22.9	5.8	25.0	56.5	24.4
Situation-specific approval of violence[a]					
Had sex with another man	35.7	24.2	35.5	54.4	36.2
Refused to cook and keep the house clean	25.7	4.3	43.5	29.9	24.5
Refused to have sex with him	33.6	5.4	32.8	17.9	25.4
Made fun of him at a party	29.6	7.6	37.7	45.3	28.4
Told friends that he was sexually pathetic	28.9	12.0	38.3	32.3	27.2
Nagged him too much	34.5	7.8	34.4	46.2	30.8
Perceived lack of alternatives[b]					
A wife should move out of the house if husband hits her	18.2	10.0	21.7	20.9	17.4
A husband is never justified in hitting his wife	7.3	5.8	34.9	5.6	10.3
A husband should be arrested if he hits his wife	14.0	34.0	33.3	17.6	21.8
Wife beating is grounds for divorce	11.1	13.6	42.0	43.1	20.7

[a] Data reflect the percentage of agreement.

[b] Data reflect the percentage of disagreement.

the Korean group agreed that a husband should have the right to discipline his wife, only 3% felt he was entitled to have sex with this wife whenever he wished. Finally, among the Chinese respondents, relatively lower proportions endorsed these items, although more than one-fifth agreed that some wives seem to ask for beatings.

In contrast, consistently one-quarter to one-third of the Chinese respondents felt that the use of violence by a husband against a wife was justified in specific situations. Similarly, consistently one third to two fifths of the Cambodian respondents likewise endorsed these items. Within the Vietnamese group, there was more variation in proportions of individuals who agreed with the statements. However, these proportions were notably high on three of the items (45% to 54%). In contrast, only 18% agreed that refusing to have sex justified the use of violence. Finally, relatively low proportions of the Korean group endorsed these items. Almost one quarter agreed that if a wife had sex with another man, violence would be justified. However, on the remaining items, only 4% to 12% agreed that violence would be understandable.

On the items of the PA subscale, the Cambodian group was distinguished by the relatively higher proportion that disagreed with these statements: 22% to 42% of Cambodians disagreed with these items. Much higher proportions of both Cambodians and Vietnamese did not believe that divorce was an option for battered women in comparison with the East Asian groups, and slightly higher proportions disagreed that a wife should move out of the home. Relatively higher proportions of both Cambodian and Korean adults disagreed that a husband should be arrested for hitting his wife. Finally, relatively consistent and low proportions of the Chinese group (7% to 18%) disagreed that there were alternatives for battered women.

Table 20.3 presents the subscale and item scores for the RAWA by ethnicity. What is apparent is that respondents did not generally endorse proviolence attitudes. On a scale from 4 to 24, the average scores on the MP and PA subscales were 8.6 (SD = 4.4) and 8.8 (SD = 4.4), respectively. For the SSA subscale, which ranges from 6 to 24, the average scale score was 8.8 (SD = 4.0).

An examination of interethnic comparisons revealed statistically significant differences in terms of each of the subscale scores. Post hoc tests showed that on the MP subscale, Vietnamese respondents had a higher average score when compared with each of the other groups (for all tests, Tukey's HSD, $p = .000$). On the SSA subscale, the Korean group was distinct from all of the other groups by their lower average score (for all tests, Tukey's HSD, $p = .000$). Finally, on the PA subscale, the Cambodian and Vietnamese groups did not score differently from each other, but both scored higher than the Chinese and Korean groups (for all tests, Tukey's HSD, $p = .000$). There was no difference in scores between the Chinese and Korean groups. In terms of the individual items, statistically significant interethnic differences were found on all items ($p < .01$). In almost all cases, the Southeast Asian groups scored higher than the East Asian groups.

Predicting Attitudinal Scores

To test for the effects of the sociodemographic variables and childhood exposure to domestic violence in predicting attitudes sanctioning wife abuse, multiple regression analyses were performed using the forced block entry method with each of the attitudinal measures entered as a separate outcome. The intercorrelations among all of the predictors were examined to ensure that regression assumptions regarding collinearity were not violated. According to Lewis-Beck (1980), coefficients of .8 are an indication that multicollinearity is present. Correlations ranged from .19 to .58, revealing that multicollinearity was not a problem. Because a focus of this investigation was on the identification of interethnic variation, ethnicity was entered into the regression model separate from the other demographic variables with Vietnamese identified as the reference group. We had planned to enter immigration status (i.e., immigrant vs. nonimmigrant) in the model. However, this was not possible

Table 20.3 The Revised Attitudes toward Wife Abuse (RAWA) Subscale and Item Scores by Ethnicity

RAWA Item	Chinese ($n = 251$)	Korean ($n = 101$)	Cambodian ($n = 67$)	Vietnamese ($n = 72$)	Total ($N = 491$)
Endorsement of male privilege**	7.8 (3.9)	8.1 (3.6)	9.1 (4.5)	12.0 (5.6)	8.6 (4.4)
A husband should have the right to discipline his wife	1.9 (1.5)	2.3 (1.4)	2.1 (1.6)	3.3 (2.1)	2.2 (1.6)
A man is the ruler of his home	1.9 (1.4)	2.4 (1.5)	2.3 (1.6)	3.8 (2.2)	2.3 (1.7)
A husband is entitled to have sex with his wife whenever he wants it	1.7 (1.2)	1.6 (.96)	2.3 (1.8)	1.9 (1.7)	1.8 (1.4)
Some wives seem to ask for beatings from their husbands	2.3 (1.5)	1.7 (1.1)	2.3 (1.6)	3.3 (1.9)	2.3 (1.6)
Situation-specific approval of violence**	9.0 (4.0)	6.9 (2.1)	9.8 (4.7)	10.3 (4.6)	8.8 (4.0)
Had sex with another man	1.7 (1.0)	1.4 (0.76)	1.7 (1.1)	2.2 (1.2)	1.7 (1.0)
Refused to cook and keep the house clean	1.4 (0.72)	1.0 (0.21)	1.7 (0.97)	1.6 (0.94)	1.4 (0.73)
Refused to have sex with him	1.5 (0.83)	1.1 (0.29)	1.5 (0.87)	1.4 (0.87)	1.4 (0.77)
Made fun of him at a party	1.5 (0.85)	1.1 (0.40)	1.7 (0.96)	1.9 (1.1)	1.5 (0.84)
Told friends that he was sexually pathetic	1.6 (0.88)	1.2 (0.62)	1.6 (0.88)	1.6 (0.98)	1.4 (0.82)
Nagged him too much	1.5 (0.84)	1.1 (0.41)	1.5 (0.79)	1.8 (1.0)	1.5 (0.80)
Perceived lack of alternatives[a]**	7.9 (3.8)	8.0 (3.7)	11.6 (5.5)	10.7 (4.7)	8.8 (4.4)
A wife should move out of the house if husband hits her	2.2 (1.5)	2.0 (1.3)	2.4 (1.8)	2.9 (1.8)	2.3 (1.6)
A husband is never justified in hitting his wife	1.7 (1.2)	1.5 (1.1)	3.2 (1.9)	1.7 (1.3)	1.8 (1.4)
A husband should be arrested if he hits his wife	2.1 (1.4)	2.6 (1.6)	2.8 (2.0)	2.4 (1.8)	2.4 (1.6)
Wife beating is grounds for divorce	2.0 (1.4)	2.0 (1.5)	3.2 (1.9)	3.7 (2.1)	2.4 (1.7)

[a] Higher scores denote greater disagreement.
** $p < .01$.

because virtually all of the Vietnamese and a disproportionate number of Cambodians were foreign born. Because of this confound between ethnicity and immigration, immigration status was not entered as a separate variable. In an effort to examine the relationship between immigration status and attitude scores, separate ANOVA and correlation tests were computed.

Tables 20.4 through 20.6 present the results of the regressions. In terms of the MP score, gender and educational level were strong predictors. MP scores fell with education, and women scored on the order of.4 points lower than men. The demographic variables accounted for 21% of variation in male privilege scores. Controlling for ethnicity, only gender remained a significant predicator. In terms of ethnicity, each of the groups scored lower than the Vietnamese. The Chinese scored an average of .31 points lower ($p < .001$). This figure for the Koreans and Cambodians is .298 ($p < .001$) and .232 ($p < .05$), respectively. The addition of ethnicity into the model increased the proportion of variance explained by 4%. With regard to the childhood exposure variables, only witnessing domestic violence as a child emerged as a strong predictor ($p < .001$). The inclusion of this variable explained an additional 2.5% of the variation in these scores. Each of the models tested were significant, accounting for a total of 28% (adjusted R^sup 2^ = .258) of the variation in MP scores, F(8, 303) = 14.17, $p < .001$.

In terms of SSA scores, education was the only significant demographic predictor ($p < .05$). The Chinese respondents, as a group, scored .20 points lower than the Vietnamese ($p < .05$), and the Korean respondents scored on average .267 points lower ($p < .01$). In terms of the childhood exposure variables, witnessing domestic violence as a child emerged as a significant predictor. Those who

Table 20.4 Beta Regression of the Revised Attitudes toward Wife Abuse Male Privilege Scores on Demographics, Ethnicity, and Childhood Exposure Variables

Predictor	Model 1	Model 2	Model 3	Model 4
Gender	−.386***	−.360***	−.344***	−.350***
Age	.051	−.039	−.023	−.038
Education	−.187**	−.080	−.072	−.062
Chinese		−.311***	−.302***	−.308***
Korean		−.283***	−.294***	−.302***
Cambodian		−.213**	−.226***	−.236***
Witnessed domestic violence			.162***	.168***
Hit as child				−.053
F	25.87***	16.47***	16.04***	14.16***
R^2	.206	.250	.275	.278
Adjusted R^2	.198	.235	.258	.258
ΔR^2	.206***	.044***	.025***	.002

Note: The following is the dummy coding for gender: 0 = male; 1 = female. The following is the dummy coding for education: 0 = less than college; 1 = more than college. For ethnicity variables, Vietnamese are the reference group.
** $p \leq .01$.
*** $p \leq .001$.

witnessed violence as a child had slightly higher levels of approval of violence in specific situations. In total, the demographic variables accounted for 10% (adjusted RZ = .092) of the variance. Including the ethnicity variables increased the variance explained by 6%. The addition of the child-witnessing variable increased it by 1.6%. The full model was statistically significant, F(8, 289) = 7.61, $p < .001$, accounting for 18% of the variance in SSA scores (adjusted R^sup 2^ = .155).

Finally, in terms of PA scores, the three demographic variables (i.e., gender, age, and education) were significant predictors, accounting for only 8% of the variance in these scores. Older individuals tended to perceive fewer options for battered women as did men. As educational level fell, so did one's endorsement of options for women living with violence. In the full model, only age remained significant ($p < .05$). In terms of ethnicity, Koreans scored lower than Vietnamese on the order of.18 points, and Cambodians scored higher on the order of .16 points. In the final model, the scores of the Korean group remained significantly different from those of the Vietnamese ($p < .05$). The inclusion of the ethnicity variables increased the variance explained by almost 8%. Finally, none of the childhood exposure variables were a significant predictor. Those individuals who were never hit as a child perceived fewer options for battered women. In total, the full model was statistically significant, F(8, 296) = 7.47, $p < .001$, accounting for 17% of the variance explained (adjusted R^sup 2^ = .15).

Immigration Variables and RAWA Scores

In an effort to examine the influence that immigration status and acculturation may have on the strength of one's attitudes, two additional analyses were conducted. In the first, subscale scores were compared between foreign born and U.S. born respondents. In the second, among the foreign born respondents, age at the time of immigration was correlated with subscale scores.

The results showed that the foreign born respondents as a group scored significantly higher on each of the MP, F(1, 454) = 6.42, $p < .05$; SSA, F(1, 431) = 14.33, $p < .000$; and PA, F(1, 441) = 6.01, $p < .05$ subscales. When these differences in subscale scores were examined by ethnicity, it was found that this difference did not hold across all the ethnic groups. There was a significant difference in SSA scores between Chinese respondents who immigrated to the United States and those who did

Table 20.5 Beta Regression of the Revised Attitudes toward Wife Abuse Scale Situation-Specific Approval of Violence Scores on Demographics, Ethnicity, and Childhood Exposure Variables

Predictor	Model 1	Model 2	Model 3	Model 4
Gender	–.158**	–.115*	–.103	–.100
Age	.094	.052	.016	.073
Education	–.241***	–.157*	–.152*	–.160*
Chinese		–.214*	–.209*	–.203*
Korean		–.266**	–.273**	–.267***
Cambodian		.020	.012	.019
Witnessed domestic violence			.128*	.123*
Hit as child				.036
F	10.77***	9.04***	8.67***	7.61***
R^2	.102	.161	.177	.178
Adjusted R^2	.092	.143	.156	.155
ΔR^2	.102***	.059***	.016*	.001

Note: The following is the dummy coding for gender: 0 = male; 1 = female. The following is the dummy coding for education: 0 = less than college; 1 = more than college. For ethnicity variables, Vietnamese are the reference group.
* $p \leq .05$.
** $p \leq .01$.
*** $p \leq .001$.

not, F(1, 225) = 14.71, $p < .001$. Chinese immigrant adults scored an average of 2 points higher on the SSA scale than did Chinese nonimmigrants. However, in terms of MP and PA subscale scores, there were no significant differences between foreign born and U.S. born respondents in the Chinese, Korean, or Cambodian groups. Subscale scores were contrasted between the foreign born ($n = 71$) and U.S. born ($n = 6$) Vietnamese adults. The foreign born respondents scored an average of 5 points greater on the MP, 2 points greater on the PA, and less than 1 point greater on the SSA scale than their U.S. born counterparts. Thus, the results suggested that Chinese immigrant adults more

Table 20.6 Beta Regression of the Revised Attitudes toward Wife Abuse Perceived Lack of Alternatives for Battered Women Scores on Demographics, Ethnicity, and Childhood Exposure Variables

Predictor	Model 1	Model 2	Model 3	Model 4
Gender	–.149**	–.104	–.094	–.099
Age	.167**	.153***	.160**	.146*
Education	–.152**	–.107	–.103	–.091
Chinese		–.123	–.122	–.126
Korean		–.171*	–.179*	–.186*
Cambodian		.163*	.159*	.149
Witnessed domestic violence			.098	.104
Hit as child				–.059
F	8.72***	8.89***	3.26	1.12
R^2	.082	.159	.169	.172
Adjusted R^2	.073	.142	.149	.149
ΔR^2	.082***	.077***	.009	.003

Note: The following is the dummy coding for gender: 0 = male; 1 = female. The following is the dummy coding for education: 0 = less than college; 1 = more than college. For ethnicity variables, Vietnamese are the reference group.
* $p \leq .05$.
** $p \leq .01$.
*** $p \leq .001$.

highly endorsed the use of violence against wives in specific situations in contrast to Chinese adults who were born in the United States. Vietnamese immigrant adults more highly endorsed attitudes of male entitlement and did not support alternatives to violence for battered women than did Vietnamese adults who were born in the United States. Due to the small number of U.S. born Vietnamese respondents, this latter finding could not be tested.

Finally, Pearson bivariate correlation coefficients were computed to assess the strength of association among one's age at immigration, the number of years one had spent in the United States, and attitudes toward marital violence. These analyses were necessarily restricted to only those respondents who immigrated to the United States. The results found that age at immigration was significantly and positively associated with only SSA scores ($r = .272$, $p < .001$). This indicated that the older one was at the time of immigration, the greater one's endorsement of the use of violence against wives in specific situations. However, length of time spent in the United States was not correlated with any of the other subscale scores.

Discussion

This study sought to identify to what extent there are differences among Asian communities in terms of their attitudes toward wife abuse. Very often, the single, monolithic term Asian is used to capture the experiences of a wide range of diverse communities. These communities differ not only in their cultural aspects, such as language and religion, but also in terms of their immigration patterns and, as found here, their attitudes regarding wife abuse.

The results of this study are in keeping with those of the few other attitude studies conducted with Asian ethnic groups. However, this study extends previous research by including immigration status and childhood exposure in the examination of interethnic attitudinal differences. One of the noteworthy findings was the relatively high proportion of Asian adults who reported witnessing domestic violence and being hit as a child. An average of 27% of all adults had witnessed parental marital violence at least once as a child. These figures ranged across the communities from 21% for the Chinese to 35% for the Cambodians. Greater proportions of the Southeast Asian adults reported witnessing marital violence on a regular basis in comparison with their East Asian counterparts. Similarly, upward of one third of the adults within these Asian communities reported being hit regularly by at least one of their parents. Estimates based on the U.S. population reveal that approximately 3.3 million children between the ages of 3 and 17 witness parental abuse annually (Campbell & Lewandowski, 1997), and 11 out of every 100 are severely assaulted by a parent each year (Straus & Gelles, 1990). The absence of data obtained from a probability sample of Asian adults tempers any generalizations that can be made concerning these findings; however, they add to the growing body of literature that suggests that family violence is a serious problem within Asian communities. More research is needed to determine the extent to which Asian American communities are affected by abuse. The use of random probability samples and interview strategies designed to overcome problems associated with underreporting of violence among Asian groups (e.g., matching of interviewer and interviewee on the basis of gender and ethnicity, conducting interviews in respondent's native language) are needed.

Overall, the two Southeast Asian groups more strongly endorsed male privilege, were more likely to see violence as justified in certain situations, and were less likely to endorse alternatives to living with violence such as moving away from or divorcing a batterer. Likewise, there was similarity between the Chinese and Koreans in terms of the strength of their beliefs in male privilege and their perceptions of alternatives. The Koreans were the least likely to view violence as justified in specific situations, a finding that contradicts what has been suggested by the literature. As noted previously, Korean families have well-defined marital roles in which women assume submissive and subordinate roles relative to their spouses. After coming to the United States, however, Korean immigrant families have undergone rapid changes in their family role structures (Min, 1998). Despite these changes, Rhee (1997) argued that there is no indication that Korean husbands change their traditional beliefs, thereby increasing the likelihood for violence to occur within these families. Our finding may be an artifact of sampling. Our sample included Asian immigrants and Asian Americans residing in the northeastern United States. The literature to date on rates of violence among Korean immigrant groups has been based largely on samples from the West Coast (Rhee, 1997). Regional differences in rates of physical assault have been identified elsewhere in the literature (Jaffee & Straus, 1987). This finding may also have to do with the younger overall age of Korean respondents as compared with their Chinese counterparts. Although average lengths of stay in the United States are similar for both groups, Korean respondents immigrated at younger ages. The results here suggest that age at the time of immigration is positively associated with the strength of attitude toward marital violence.

Another factor that may have influenced these interethnic differences in responding pertains to differences across groups in patterns of immigration. Many adults from Vietnam and Cambodia immigrated to the United States to escape oppressive social conditions including political turmoil and war. In contrast, many Korean and Chinese adults immigrated to the United States to improve their economic stability. In the past 35 years, immigrants from Korea have been largely well-educated adults who are looking for better career opportunities (B. C. Kim, 1996). During this same time period, Chinese immigration was boosted by the reestablishment of diplomatic relations between the United States and China allowing individuals to enter the country to work and/or study (Lee, 1996).

Conceivably, the marital violence attitudes that these adults bring with them to the United States were shaped in part by the socioeconomic differences in their countries of origin. However, how and to what extent across the countries of origin these differences influence marital violence attitudes is unknown and was not tested in this study. Although each of these countries is patriarchal in terms of family values, Korea is the most affluent. Research has shown both that the status of women is tied to a nation's socioeconomic development and urbanization (H. C. Kim, 1990) and that violence toward women is linked to larger systemic issues of gender equality (Yllo & Straus, 1990). Levinson's (1989) cross-cultural anthropological study demonstrated that marital violence tends to be less common when women have independent social and economic resources. This discussion is speculative, however, and is raised only to suggest the possibility that there are important and influential contextual variables that may be at play.

Interethnic differences in attitudes may also be a by-product of the differing levels of educational attainment among the four groups. Smith's (1990) findings provide empirical support for the inverse relationship between educational attainment and adherence to an ideology of familial patriarchy. Findings reported here provide additional support for this finding given the lower attitudinal endorsements found among groups with higher levels of educational attainment.

Similar to the findings of Yick and Agbayani-Siewert (1997), this sample overall did not strongly endorse attitudes supportive of wife abuse. However, a sizable percentage of the Chinese, Vietnamese, and Cambodian adults evidenced proviolence attitudes. Situations such as a wife's sexual infidelity, her nagging or making fun of her partner, or her refusal to cook or keep the house clean most commonly justified the use of violence. Korean respondents were unique in that they were the least likely to approve of the use of violence under such circumstances.

Multiple regression analyses were performed to determine predictors of each attitudinal dimension. Gender was predicative of attitudes of male privilege. Educational level was predictive of one's endorsement of the use of violence in specific situations, and age was predictive of one's perception that battered women had some alternatives available to them. Witnessing domestic violence as a child predicated both MP scores and PA scores. These findings are consistent with intergenerational approaches to the study of family violence, which emphasize the link between witnessing interparental violence and being violent toward an intimate partner as an adult (Barnett & Hamburger, 1992; Hotaling & Sugarman, 1986). From an intergenerational transmission perspective, witnessing interparental violence that is culturally sanctioned as normative conveys a powerful message about prescribed male-female roles and behaviors.

There were several limitations of this research that should be noted. First, there were pronounced demographic differences across the four community samples. these differences likely stemmed from differences in immigration patterns, and they may bias the findings. Unfortunately, important variables, such as marital status and victimization status, were not collected precluding the opportunity to assess their relative importance. Also, the study used a voluntary, nonrandom sample of individuals attending ethnic community fairs. Results may therefore be subject to self-selection biases. Finally, although findings reported here help to delineate interethnic differences in attitudes toward violence, the inclusion of other non-Asian groups would have contributed immensely to an understanding of the continuum of culturally unique differences in attitudinal responding. Future research in this area would be greatly enhanced through the inclusion of reference group that would enable attitudinal differences within and across differing ethnic groups to be studied.

Despite these limitations, findings reported here add to the limited body of research examining interethnic differences in attitudes toward marital violence. The differences that were found among the communities highlight the importance of understanding the unique immigration history and culture of Asian ethnic communities and of moving away from the depiction of a single, monolithic group. Findings suggest the need to educate the general public and members of the helping professions about these unique differences. In the case of Asian immigrant women, vulnerability to violence may be heightened due to their relative isolation and lack of social and financial resources. This coupled with cultural themes and family values that discourage seeking outside intervention suggest the need for increased outreach efforts. Innovative strategies are needed that involve members of differing Asian communities to help educate others about the cultural dynamics of abuse and to encourage help seeking when abuse is occurring.

Acknowledgments

This research was supported by funds provided by the Center for the Study of Social Work Practice, by the Columbia University School of Social Work, and by the Asian Task Force against Domestic Violence in Boston, Massachusetts. We would like to thank the tireless advocates of the task force for their help and support.

References

Abraham, M. 1995. Ethnicity, gender and marital violence: South Asian women's organizations in the United States. *Gender & Society* 9: 450–468.

Barnett, O. W. and Hamburger, L. K. 1992. The assessment of maritally violent men on the California Personality Inventory. *Violence and Victims* 7: 15–28.

Briere, J. 1987. Predicting self-reported likelihood of battering: Attitudes and childhood experiences. *Journal of Research in Personality* 21: 61–69.

Brislin, R. W. 1986. The wording and translation of research instruments. In Field methods in cross-cultural research, eds. W. J. Lonner & J. W. Berry, 137–164). Beverly Hills, CA: Sage.

Bui, H. N. and Morash, M. 1999. Domestic violence in the Vietnamese immigrant community: An exploratory study. *Violence Against Women* 5: 769–795.

Campbell, J. C. and Lewandowski, L. A. (1997). Mental and physical health effects of intimate partner violence on women and children. *Psychiatric Clinics of North America* 20: 353–374.

Caplan, P. 1987. *The myth of women's masochism.* New York Signet

Carden, A. D. 1994. Wife abuse and the wife abuser: Review and recommendations. *The Counseling Psychologist* 22: 539–582.

Catolico, O. 1997. Psychological well-being of Cambodian women in resettlement. *Advances in Nursing Science* 19: 75–84.

Ebihara, M. 1968. The Khmer village in Cambodia. Dissertation Abstracts International. Ann Arbor, MI: University Microfilms.

Frye, B. A. 1995. Use of cultural themes in promoting health among Southeast Asian refugees. *American Journal of Health Promotion* 9: 269–280.
Frye, B. A. and D'Avanzo, C. D. 1994. Cultural themes in family stress and violence among Cambodian refugee women in the inner city. *Advances in Nursing Science* 16: 64–77.
Ho, C. K. 1990. An analysis of domestic violence in Asian American communities: A multicultural approach to counseling. *Women & Therapy* 9: 129–150.
Hofstede, G. 1984. The cultural relativity of the quality of life concept. *Academy of Management Review* 9: 389–398.
Hotaling, G. T. and Sugarman, D. B. 1986. An analysis of risk markers in husband to wife violence: The current state of knowledge. *Violence and Victims* 1: 101–124.
Hsu, E. L. K. 1970. *Americans and Chinese.* Garden City, NY: Doubleday
Hu, X. and Chen, G. 1999. Understanding cultural values in counseling Asian families (Eds.), In *Counseling Asian families from a systems perspective. The family psychology and counseling series*, eds. . K. S. Ng et al., 27–37. Alexandria, VA: American Counseling Association.
Huisman, K. A. 1996. Wife battering in Asian American communities. *Violence Against Women* 2: 260–283.
Jaffee, D. and Straus, M. A. 1987. Sexual climate and reported rape: A state-level analysis. *Archives of Sexual Behavior* 16: 107–123.
Kim, B. C. 1996. Korean families. In *Ethnicity and family therapy*,eds. M. McGoldrick, G. Giordao, & J. K. Pierce, 281–294. New York: Guilford.
Kim, H. C. 1990. The changing status of women 1965–1980: A cross-national analysis. *Sociological Abstracts*, 038(03).
Kirkbride, P S., Tang, S. E, & Westwood, R. I. 1991. Chinese conflict preferences and nego tiating behavior. Cultural and psychological influences. *Organization Studies* 12: 365–386.
Kitano, H. and Kikumura, A. 1976. The Japanese American family. In *Ethnic families in America*, eds. C. H. Mindel & R. W. Havenstein. New York: Elsevier North-Holland.
Kulig, J. C. 1994. Those with unheard voices: The plight of a Cambodian refugee woman. *Journal of Community Health Nursing* 11:99–107.
Lee, E. 1996. Asian American families: An overview. In *Ethnicity and family therapy*,eds. M. McGoldrick, G. Giordao, & J. K. Pierce, 227–247. New York: Guilford.
Legerwood, J. 1990. Changing Khmer conception of gender: Women, stories, and the social order. Dissertation Abstracts International. Ann Arbor, MI: University Microfilms.
Leung, P K. and Boehnlein, J. 1996. Vietnamese families. In *Ethnicity and family therapy*,eds. M. McGoldrick, G. Giordao, & J. K. Pierce, 295–305. New York: Guilford.
Levinson, D. 1989. *Family violence in cross-cultural perspective.* Newbury Park, CA: Sage.
Lewis-Beck, M. S. 1980. *Applied regression: An introduction.* Beverly Hills, CA: Sage.
McKenzie-Pollock, L. 1996. Cambodian families. In *Ethnicity and family therapy*,eds. M. McGoldrick, G. Giordao, & J. K. Pierce, 307–315. New York: Guilford.
McLaughlin, L. A. and Braun, K. L. 1998. Asian and Pacific Islander cultural values: Considerations for health care decision making. *Health & Social Work* 23: 116–126.
Min, P. G. 1998. *Changes and conflicts: Korean immigrant families in New York.* Boston: Allyn & Bacon.
National Research Council. 1996. *Understanding violence against women.* Washington, DC: National Academy Press.
Nguyen, W. 1999. Using the task-centered approach with Vietnamese Families. In *Counseling Asian families from a systems perspective*, eds. J. K. S. Ng et al., 55–62). Alexandria, VA: American Counseling Association.
Patel, N. 1992. Psychological disturbance, social support and stressors: A community survey of immigrant Asian women and the indigenous population. *Counseling Psychology Quarterly* 5: 263–276.
Rhee, S. 1997. Domestic violence in the Korean immigrant family. *Journal of Sociology and Social Welfare* 24: 63–77.
Root, M., Ho, C. H., and Sue, S. 1986. Issues in the training of counselors for Asian Americans. In *Cross-cultural training for mental health professionals*, eds. H. Petley & P. B. Pedersen, 199–209. Springfield, IL: Charles C. Thomas.
Smith, M. D. 1990. Patriarchal ideology and wife beating: A test of a feminist hypothesis. *Violence and Victims* 5: 257–273.
Song, Y. 1996. *Battered women in Korean immigrant families: The silent scream.* New York: Garland.
Straus, M. A. and Gelles, R. J. 1990. How violent are American families? Estimates from the National Family Violence Survey and other studies. In *Physical violence in American families: Risk factors and adaptations to violence in 8,145 families*, eds. M. A. Straus & R. J. Gelles, 95–112. New Brunswick, NJ: Transaction Publishing.
Tang, C. S. 1994. Prevalence of spouse aggression in Hong Kong. *Journal of Family Violence*, cl.a7-CSC,
Tjaden, P. and Thoennes, N. 1998. *Prevalence, incidence, and consequences of violence against women: Findings from the National Violence Against Women Survey.* Washington, DC: U.S. Department of Justice.
U.S. Bureau of the Census. 1993. *We the Americans: Asians.* Washington, DC: Author.
West, C. M. 1998. Lifting the political gag order: Breaking the silence around partner violence in ethnic minority families. In *Partner violence: A comprehensive review of 20 years of research*, eds. J. L. Jasinski & L. M. Williams, 184–209. Thousand Oaks, CA: Sage.
Wong, A. T. 1985. Effects of client socioeconomic status, race, and acculturation on the treatment plans and expectations of Asian American therapists. *Asian American Psychological Association Journal* 10: 30–39.
Yick, A. G. and Agbayani-Siewert, P. 1997. Perception of domestic violence in a Chinese American community. *Journal of Interpersonal Violence* 12: 832–846.
Yllo, K. A. and Straus, M. 1990. Patriarchy and violence against wives: The impact of structural and normative factors. In *Physical violence in American families*, eds. M. A. Straus & R. J. Gelles, 383–389. New Brunswick, NJ: Transaction Publishing.
Yoshioka, M. R. and DiNoia, J. 2001. The revised attitudes Toward wife abuse scale: A study of Asian immigrant and Asian American adults. Unpublished manuscript.

Race, Crime, and Punishment

Punishment is the final phase of the criminal justice system. After a person has been convicted of a crime, a penalty is imposed. At a sentencing hearing, a judge either may impose a fine, probation, imprisonment, or death. While most persons who are found guilty of a crime are placed on probation, most sentencing research focuses on incarceration or confinement in prison. When penal institutions first opened in the United States they were conceived as a more humane alternative to capital and corporal punishment. These early penitentiaries were designed as places where offenders could undergo a transformation by considering their misdeeds, and performing labor, while removed from the bad influences of society and each other (Clear and Cole 1990). By the nineteenth century the penitence goal of prisons was replaced with the goal of punishment. Between the time that the first penitentiaries and prisons were opened and the turn of the twentieth century, these institutions became disproportionately black. Although blacks did not comprise the majority of offenders in prisons in the late 1800s, their numbers had increased dramatically during the post-Reconstruction period. A century later, in 2002, blacks and Hispanics comprised 63.2% of prisoners under state and federal jurisdiction (Harrison and Beck 2003).

As discussed in previous sections, there is an ongoing debate about whether or not discrimination or criminality is the best explanation for the overrepresentation of minorities in the criminal justice system. Clearly both are factors. Unfortunately, research on the effect of race on sentencing is still conflicting. Everyone agrees that persons who violate the law should be sanctioned and that incarceration is appropriate for the most serious offenders, regardless of race. Until we understand that race was used in a discriminatory manner to criminalize minorities, and the effect that and other structural and cultural factors has had on minorities who commit crimes, we will continue to overlook the dimensions of the problem of race in America.

The chapters in this section address the issue of race and punishment. The first chapter by Marjorie Zatz analyzes four waves of research on sentencing disparities. At the beginning of the chapter, Zatz explains the concept of discrimination and how it has been examined in sentencing research from the 1930s through the 1980s. In addition to providing an overview of the research, Zatz critiques the methodologies and potential for biases in the legal system. While emphasizing that race/ethnicity is not the only determinant of sanctioning, and that there is less bias in the later waves than in the early ones, Zatz maintains that discrimination has simply changed to a more subtle form.

Native Americans have received limited attention in sentencing research. This is due, at least in part, to the complexities of the administration of justice for Native Americans who fall under federal, state, and tribal authority. Additionally, statistics on Native Americans who are under correctional authority are not readily available since they are included in the "other" category in prison statistics. In 1997, Native Americans comprised about 1%, or 62,600 persons under correctional supervision according to a study entitled, *American Indians and Crime* (Greenfield and Smith 1999). The second chapter by Alvarez and Bachman examines sentencing disparity among American Indians in the state of Arizona. The authors describe factors that might contribute to discrimination against this group including oppression, stereotyping, and marginalization. A comparative analysis of American Indian and Caucasian sentences revealed several interesting patterns. The authors conclude with a discussion of explanations of their anomalous findings.

The third chapter, by Loïc Wacquant, provides a historical context for understanding the role of prisons in American society. He traces the role of several "peculiar institutions" in maintaining social control including chattel slavery, the Jim Crow system, the ghetto, and the prison. Wacquant presents a thought provoking analysis of how prisons have become judicial ghettos comprised of young black men. As economic conditions and attitudes toward prison labor change, this chapter challenges us to consider their implications for "prisoner workfare," or the neo-convict-lease system that might emerge in what some refer to as the prison industrial complex.

The last chapter in this section, by Kautt and Spohn, tackles the difficult issue of understanding how race and type of drug interact. For example, do blacks receive harsher sentences for crack cocaine offenses than whites do for powder cocaine offenses? This issue has sparked considerable debate during the past decade. During the 1990s the United States Congress enacted two sentencing strategies, sentencing guidelines and mandatory minimums. The goal of sentencing guidelines was to promote "equality and proportionality in sentencing," while mandatory minimums were designed to emphasize the seriousness of the crime. After presenting several perspectives on sentencing disparities and discussing federal sentencing policies, Kautt and Spohn test several hypotheses to explore the role of race in sentencing federal drug offenders between 1997–1998. While acknowledging the complexities of their research, the authors did find support for the interaction effects of race and sentencing strategy. However, they did not find support for the detrimental effect of drug factors on blacks. The authors correctly conclude that their study produced more questions than answers.

References

Clear, T. R. and Cole, G. F. 1990. *American corrections.* Belmont, CA: Wadsworth.
Greenfeld, L. A., and Smith, S. K. 1999. *American Indians and crime.* Washington, DC: US Department of Justice.
Harrison, P. M., and Beck, A. J. 2003. *Prisoners in 2002.* Washington, DC: US Department of Justice.

21

The Changing Forms of Racial/Ethnic Biases in Sentencing

Marjorie S. Zatz

Racial/ethnic discrimination in criminal justice processing has been the subject of heated debate for several decades. This chapter traces findings from four historical waves of research on sentencing disparities. Particular attention is given to changes in research methodologies and data sources, the social contexts within which research has been conducted, and the various forms that bias can manifest. It explores the change from findings of overt racial/ethnic disparities to more subtle, but still systematic, institutionalized biases. In so doing, the movement toward determinate sentencing is discussed, and the biases identified are partially explained by the need for the system to maintain legitimacy in the face of social change.

The question of whether or not the legal system discriminates on the basis of racial/ethnic group membership has sparked considerable controversy and heated debate. Indeed, it may well have been the major research inquiry for studies of sentencing in the 1970s and early 1980s (see Hagan, 1974; Kleck, 1981; Garber, Klepper, and Nagin, 1983; Hagan and Bumiller, 1983; Klepper, Nagin, and Tierney, 1983, for comprehensive reviews and assessments of the literature). Not surprisingly, this controversy is rooted in ideological, theoretical, and methodological conflicts that encompass the meaning and pervasiveness of "discrimination" and the appropriate methods for assessing its existence, strength, and form.

Across what I shall term four *waves* of research on sentencing disparities, conflicting conclusions have been drawn. Research conducted through the mid-1960s (Wave I) indicated some overt discrimination against minority defendants. Reanalyses of these studies during the late 1960s and 1970s (Wave II) concluded that, with the exception of use of the death penalty in the South, findings of discrimination were an artifact of poor research designs and analyses. Original research conducted in this period suggested that minorities were overrepresented in prison because of their proportionately greater involvement in crime, rather than as a consequence of judicial bias. A third wave of research was published in the late 1970s and 1980s, using data from the late 1960s and 1970s. These studies benefited from advances in research design and analytic techniques, and indicated that both overt and more subtle forms of bias against minority defendants *did* occur, at least in some social contexts. Finally, we are in the midst of the fourth wave of studies, begun in the early 1980s and relying on data from states following determinate sentencing guidelines. These studies show subtle, if no longer overt, bias against minority defendants.

A key element in this controversy is the scope of the concept *discrimination*. In part, this scope consideration asks whether discrimination is restricted to the behavior of individuals or whether it also includes administrative processes that serve to institutionalize biases against minorities. Some researchers limit discrimination to main effects of race/ethnicity on sentence severity after other factors have been statistically held constant. Such disparities reflect *overt* discrimination. Other researchers conceptualize discrimination more broadly to include indirect and interaction effects of race/ethnicity, operating through other variables. These disparities reflect more *subtle* institutionalized biases, but still fall within the purview of discrimination if they systematically favor one group over another.

Proponents of this second position argue that although policy changes such as the new determinate sentencing statutes sweeping across the country could reduce inequities in sanctioning, the inevitable outcomes of formal rationality in a capitalist society favor capital and maintain class and racial/ethnic disparities (see Greenberg and Humphries, 1980; Irwin, 1980; Michalowski, 1985). Also, the increased bureaucratization and formal rationalization, which accrue from implementing the rules of determinate sentencing, enhance the legitimacy of the legal system. Accordingly, claims by Hindelang (1978) and others that the poor and minorities are not being discriminated against, but rather that the system is simply responding to their high levels of street crime, are also legitimized without calling attention to the harmful acts of the wealthy or to biased administrative processes and policies.

This chapter reviews the controversy over racial/ethnic bias in sentencing. It proceeds in three stages. First, findings from four waves of research on sentencing disparities are traced. The studies discussed are representative of research in different time periods and social contexts, and using different methodologies. They do not represent a comprehensive overview of all relevant research; rather they are used for illustrative purposes. Studies in the first two waves are deemphasized since others (e.g., Hagen, 1974; Kleck, 1981) have dealt with them adequately. For each wave, the major findings and their implications are discussed and a methodological critique offered. Then, potential biases in data collection and analysis are explored, along with bias that is institutionalized in the workings of the legal system. Finally, the biases identified are partially explained by the need for the system to maintain legitimacy in the face of social change.

Throughout the discussion that follows, the broader term *race/ethnicity* is used rather than *race*. Although somewhat cumbersome, race/ethnicity more accurately reflects the overlap between color and culture that may disadvantage minorities, particularly those from Latin America. For example, while one Puerto Rican may appear white and another black, and thus only the latter would suffer from *racial* discrimination, both may be the victims of cultural and linguistic barriers and prejudices.

Prior Research on Race/Ethnicity and Sentencing

Wave I (1930s—mid-1960s)

A number of studies conducted from the 1930s through the mid-1960s showed clear and consistent bias against nonwhites in sentencing (e.g., Sellin, 1935; Lemert and Rosberg, 1948; Johnson, 1957; Bullock, 1961; Wolfgang, Kelly, and Nolde, 1962; Bedau, 1964). This period preceded the major gains of the civil rights movement and included the early race riots beginning with the 1943 Zoot Suit Riot between sailors and Chicano youths in California and continuing through the 1960s.

These early scholars emphasized the social prejudice against blacks and foreign-born persons, a prejudice shared by the American judiciary:

> Laws are made by dominant interest groups in society, who believe in protection for the social values which they conceive to be important. These laws are, furthermore, administered by men imbued with the ideas and concepts of the social environment which has molded their personalities. The judge is no exception to the rule. . . . When the judge dons his robes of office he is unable to divest himself of his social beliefs and prejudices [Sellin, 1935, p. 212].

Thus Sellin and others working at this time concluded that "equality before the law is a social fiction" (p. 217). A chilling example of the level that racist sentiment could reach is evident in a statement by Judge Chargin of Santa Clara, California, in 1969, during juvenile court proceedings against a Chicano boy:[1]

> We ought to send you back to Mexico. You belong in prison for the rest of your life for doing things of this kind. You ought to commit suicide. That's what I think of people of this kind. You are lower than animals and haven't the right to live in organized society—just miserable, lousy, rotten people. . . . Maybe Hitler was right [in Hernandez, Haug, and Wagner, 1976, pp. 62–63].

While Judge Chargin was censured by his colleagues and forced to retract this statement and publicly apologize, he was reelected in 1972, receiving twice as many votes as his closest opponent. This may, and probably does, reflect an extreme position, but it is significant nonetheless because a high level of generalized racist sentiment is suggested when a judicial official feels comfortable making such a statement publicly and the statement apparently does not offend voters.

As was pointed out in the U.S. Commission on Civil Rights report on *Mexican Americans and the Administration of Justice in the Southwest* (1970), differences at early stages of decision making (e.g., bail) can accumulate and be compounded further in the system. This notion of "cumulative disadvantage" became important in later studies, but the earliest researchers somewhat naively failed to recognize or appreciate the possibility that bias could accumulate in this fashion. As later critics noted, these studies were flawed by a number of serious methodological problems. The most damning flaw was the lack of controls for legally relevant factors, especially prior record. In addition, the models used were somewhat simplistic, and the analytic techniques (mostly cross tabular, with few controls) relatively unsophisticated, in part due to the limited data sources and analytic techniques available. Yet some of the differentials observed by these earlier researchers were quite large, suggesting that even with better controls they might still show evidence of discrimination.[2]

Wave II (late 1960s–1970s)

Following in the wake of the civil rights movement, research findings showing no discrimination emerged. Increased fears of urban street crime and high rates of unemployment caused by an economic recession turned attention away from eliminating the sources and consequences of racial/ethnic discrimination and repression, and toward more extensive social control (see Greenberg and Humphries, 1980). Nevertheless, the obvious manifestations of discrimination were no longer socially acceptable, at least in public forums. The courthouse was one such public forum, and was also an extremely visible symbol of equality and justice for all. As such, it served a very important legitimating function for the state.

With major advances in quantitative data analytic techniques, sentencing researchers began to question whether or not some of the disparities noted earlier might have been mistaken. Using data from the early 1970s, researchers such as Hindelang (1978) and Cohen and Kluegel (1978) argued that minorities were overrepresented in the criminal justice system and prisons because of their greater proportional involvement in crime, and not because of any bias in the system. Others, such as Pruitt and Wilson (1983), examined data drawn from several points in time, and concluded that sentencing was discriminatory in the late 1960s, but changes in the composition and bureaucratization of the judiciary did away with this bias by the 1970s.

Reanalyses of earlier studies were conducted, with results typically interpreted to mean that discrimination was no longer an issue. Critics such as Hagan (1974) and Kleck (1981) argued that the effect of race was in part a proxy for prior record and, once this was controlled for, the direct effect of race would be greatly diminished. These reanalyses often concluded with two very important but unheeded caveats. The first was that race might have a cumulative effect by operating *indirectly* through other variables to the disadvantage of minority group members. The second was that race and other extralegal attributes of the offender could *interact* with other factors to influence decision making (see, for example, Hagan 1974, pp. 379–380). These caveats were usually lost on readers who later placed such studies squarely in the "no discrimination found" side of the debate.

Wave III (data from late 1960s–1970s, conducted in 1970s and 1980s)

Paradoxically, the lessons learned in the third wave of research suggest that a countervailing bias might call into question these "no discrimination" findings. Recent studies using data from the period of Wave II research, but employing new techniques to mitigate or avoid earlier problems, are particularly enlightening. Ironically, some of these more recent studies were conducted by the same researchers whose earlier work constituted the bulwark of the "no discrimination" group. For example, one of the most frequently cited studies from Wave II was Hagan's reanalysis of twenty studies, published in 1974. Yet his later analyses of the sentencing of white and black drug offenders in New York from 1963 to 1976 (Peterson and Hagan, 1984) and of white and black draft dodgers for the same years (Hagan and Bernstein, 1979) showed that changing conceptions of race in this controversial time led to racial disparities in sanctioning. Depending on the degree of victimization and the relative social harm perceived, minority members were treated more harshly in some situations and whites in others. Thus a sense was beginning to emerge among researchers that examination of main effects was not sufficient if we were to explicate fully the impact of minority status on sentencing.

Advances in data sources and analytic techniques during the late 1970s and early 1980s paved the way for a new approach to the study of bias in decision making. These improvements substantially altered the ways in which research was conducted and the conclusions drawn from them. Because the justice system itself started using computers, data collection was made easier and more systematic. Rather than digging through dusty piles of court records to unearth what happened to a given defendant, researchers gained access to data tapes such as the Offender-Based Transaction Statistics (OBTS) and the Prosecutor's Management Information System (PROMIS). While there are some serious biases and methodological problems inherent in these data sets (discussed below), the longitudinal databases created by such systems allowed researchers to trace repeated processings of the same individuals from arrest to sentencing. Alongside these improvements in the data came increases in methodological sophistication, again due in part to the decreased cost and increased ease of use of statistical computing packages.

Two major methodological problems, and their solutions, came to light during the late 1970s and early 1980s: selection bias and specification error. *Selection bias* refers to the selection of the sample to be analyzed. When persons who were filtered out of the system at earlier decision points are excluded from a sample, variation in sentencing outcomes due to race/ethnicity, as well as social class and gender, may be inappropriately removed. It was first thought that this bias primarily limited the generalizability of the findings. Now, however, the problem is recognized as a more serious one. Bias in the sample selection process can invalidate our estimates; a typical consequence being a statistical masking of discrimination (see Berk, 1983; Klepper, Nagin, and Tierney, 1983; Zatz and Hagan, 1985).

Specification error means that the model to be analyzed was not drawn correctly. Since at least Wave II research, it has been recognized that models are misspecified when relevant variables are omitted. In addition, we now know that erroneous results will be obtained if the ways in which variables influence outcomes are not properly identified.[3] In particular, recent work has shown that beyond any main, or direct, effect on sentencing, race/ethnicity can operate *indirectly* through its effect on other factors. It can also *interact* with other factors to affect sentencing. That is, the impact of other variables (e.g., prior record, type of offense) could differ, depending on the defendant's race/ethnicity. If indirect and interaction effects in fact exist, but are not included in the equations, then the models are misspecified and the results inaccurate. Fortunately, methods of mitigating selection biases and of properly specifying our models have been developed, and were used starting with Wave III research.

Indirect effects refer to the situation in which a variable operates *through* some other factor, rather than directly. For example, using 1971 data from Chicago, Lizotte (1978) found that the defendant's race and occupation indirectly influenced sentencing through their effects on bail status. That is, blacks and persons in lower occupational strata were more likely than whites and persons in higher prestige occupations to be detained pending trial, and detention increased the length of the prison sentence. Similarly, LaFree (1985) examined 1976–1977 court processing data for whites, blacks, and Hispanics in Tucson and El Paso. He did not find evidence of discrimination in Tucson, but in El Paso, ethnicity had an indirect effect operating through bail status. Also, being Hispanic was the single best predictor of guilty verdicts in El Paso. While Lizotte and LaFree were unable to control for income (since court records rarely include economic data), they argued that economic status may help explain why minority defendants and laborers received less favorable pretrial release outcomes.

Another type of indirect effect is what has come to be called *cumulative disadvantage*. This refers to a situation in which race/ethnicity has small, and often statistically nonsignificant, effects on decision making at various stages of the process (e.g., arrest, prosecution, conviction, sentencing, and parole). But, as the person moves through the system, these add up to substantial, and often statistically significant, disparities in processing and outcomes for different social groups.

For example, based on data from the period 1970–1976 and supplemented with findings reported by Hall and Simkus (1975), Bynum (1981) showed that Native Americans were sent to prison for offenses for which whites received non-prison sanctions. When whites were sent to prison, their court-imposed sentences were longer than those for Native Americans. But, parole boards compensated by releasing whites when they had served shorter parts of their sentences than Native Americans. Thus the discrimination was double edged, and the disparity accumulated. Similarly, Spohn, Gruhl, and Welch (1981) found, for the period 1968–1979, that race operated indirectly through case processing variables to influence both the decision to incarcerate and the length of the prison sentence. Their work suggests that in borderline cases where either a long term of probation or short prison sentence is appropriate, judges accord whites the greater leniency, granting them probation while blacks go to prison (1981, p. 85).

Race/ethnicity has also been shown to *interact* with other factors to influence sentencing jointly. This means that while "main" effects may not be found, the effects of other factors vary systematically, depending on the defendant's race/ethnicity. Interaction effects can be assessed in either of two ways. First, a new variable can be created by multiplying together the values for the original variables suspected of interacting. This new variable is then added to the equation and its effect estimated. Second, separate models can be estimated for each group (e.g., for blacks and whites, or males and females) to determine whether the decision-making process varies in fundamental ways for members of different social groups. The latter procedure allows the effects of all variables in the equation to differ for the two groups, and the differences can be tested for statistical significance. The choice of technique depends upon whether just one or a few factors are hypothesized to interact, or whether the entire process is thought to operate differently for members of various social groups. Both types of interactions are evident in the following illustrative examples.

Using 1974 data from Washington, D.C., Albonetti (1985) found that blacks received longer sentences than did whites. In addition, she observed that race interacted with bail status to affect sentencing, further disadvantaging blacks. These findings closely resemble Lizotte's (1978) study discussed above, in which race and occupation influenced sentencing indirectly through bail status. Paralleling these findings, Burke and Turk (1975) found that sentencing in Indianapolis in 1964 was influenced by interactions among race, occupational status, and type of offense, and among race, age, and prior incarceration, leading them to conclude that "the race effect may be masked by its complex relations with other factors" (1975, p. 328). Spohn, Welch, and Gruhl (1985) further suggest that failure to examine the interaction of gender and race can result in misleading findings. They note that sentencing for black women resembled that for white men in a northeastern city between 1968 and 1979, and interpret this to mean that not all women are treated equally paternalistically, and that black men receive the brunt of racial discrimination. Finally, Farnworth and Horan (1980) found interaction effects that also suggest cumulative disadvantage. They observed that separate equations for blacks and whites were required to specify properly the processes by which decisions surrounding bail, conviction, type of sentence, and sentence length were reached for felony cases in North Carolina between 1967 and 1969.

While these findings present a somewhat disjointed picture of when and how differential treatment occurs, one pattern that has become accepted even by many in the "no discrimination" camp (e.g., Kleck, 1981) is devaluation of nonwhite victims. That is, injury to a white victim is dealt with considerably more harshly than injury to a minority victim. For example, using 1974–1976 data, Myers (1979) demonstrated the indirect influence of the racial composition of the victim–offender dyad on sentencing. This effect was mediated by the probation officers' recommendations, with blacks who victimized other blacks treated most leniently. Typically, however, the greatest harshness occurs when the offender is black and the victim white. For instance, LaFree (1980a) found a direct effect of the victim–offender dyad in his 1970–1975 data from a Midwestern city, with black men who raped white women sanctioned most harshly at every stage of court processing. He interpreted this as a consequence of sexual stratification by race, where violation of women who were the "property" of white men was treated quite severely, and this severity was further aggravated when the offense crossed racial lines.

Studies that found indirect, interaction, and/or cumulative effects of race/ethnicity on sentencing were based on data from a time during which popular and judicial conceptions of race and ethnicity were undergoing marked changes. Also, the research designs and analytic techniques used by Wave III researchers reflected major improvements in social science research. These factors might explain some of the diverse findings. In a few cases (e.g., Albonetti, 1985; LaFree, 1985), main or direct effects of race/ethnicity were found. Such effects are indicative of *overt* discrimination. Other studies did not find main effects, but report interaction or indirect effects of race/ethnicity with other variables. Such forms of disparity still reflect a bias, but it is a more *subtle*, rather than overt, form of discrimination. As Feyerherm concluded from his research on juveniles, "while there is not evidence of blatant discrimination in these data, there is a suggestion of accumulations of discrimination which collectively may have the same results" (1981, pp. 142–143).

Thus the weight of the evidence on the key question of whether the overrepresentation of minorities in prison was due to their greater proportional involvement in crime or to biases in their administrative processing began to shift toward the latter interpretation. Nevertheless, the data sources, and thus the analyses that could be conducted, were limited because the decision to record data on certain factors and not others was made by the judiciary, rather than by the researchers themselves. This potential source of bias became even more salient during Wave IV, the era of determinate sentencing.

Wave IV (data from late 1970s–1980s, conducted in 1980s)

We are still in the midst of the fourth period of research to be discussed, and research findings are just beginning to emerge. While analytic techniques continued to improve and data collection became increasingly systematic, no major methodological breakthroughs signaled the transition to this fourth wave. Rather, it was the initiation of a policy change to determinate sentencing that distinguishes research during this period from its predecessors. The first states enacted determinate sentencing statutes in the mid-1970s, and additional states are still passing them.

The determinate sentencing debate is widespread and complex. From the various discussions, a picture emerges in which the call for fixed sentencing was initiated by a liberal and radical reform agenda charging that the rhetoric of rehabilitation hid repressive social control. Reformers sought to advance the interests of prisoners through short, fixed, sentences and reform of substantive law. These reforms were co-opted by conservatives in the early 1970s when the liberal and radical coalitions, and the social movements that supported them (e.g., the civil rights and anti-Vietnam War movements), faltered in the face of a deteriorating economy, unemployment, prison riots, and reported increases in urban street crime (see Greenberg and Humphries, 1980; Irwin, 1980; Greenberg, 1983; Humphries, 1984; Reiman and Headlee, 1981; Von Hirsch, 1976). The conservatives, like the liberals and radicals, indicated the rehabilitation model and the widespread discretion it engendered. Unlike the liberals (who saw its arbitrariness as an abridgement of rights) and radicals (who viewed it as a repressive expansion of social control), conservatives viewed rehabilitation as too lenient. At the same time that rehabilitation was losing its intellectual legitimacy, it also lost its popular support. Legislators were confronted with a system that simply did not seem to work, and were charged by their constituents and law enforcement lobbies with the task of quickly reducing urban street crime.

Under the new determinate sentencing statutes that arose, legislatures retained a portion of what had been judicial discretion. In addition to mandating presumptive sentences and any enhancements, they set guidelines and criteria stipulating how other actors in the system should use their discretion. These guidelines severely constrained the discretion of judges and parole boards, though judges were still relatively free to decide when to grant or withhold probation, hand out concurrent or consecutive sentences, and use the aggravating and mitigating circumstances loophole to alter the presumptive sentence.[4]

Nevertheless, most of the discretion shifted further behind the scenes to the prosecutor. Since the sentence was prescribed for each offense, the only way to substantially alter the sanction was to change the charge. Plea bargaining thus became exceedingly important. However, LaFree (1980b), Petersilia (1983), and Zatz and Lizotte (1985) have shown that cases involving black offenders are less likely to be resolved through guilty pleas than are cases involving white offenders, with the latter two studies conducted in a determinate sentencing state. Whether the racial disparities found are the result of defendant preferences or bias on the part of prosecutors is still unclear, and raises questions about the quality of the deals being offered to white and minority defendants. In addition, language barriers place Hispanics (and others for whom English is not the primary language) at a disadvantage if the benefits and implications of pleading guilty rather than going to trial are communicated in subtle ways requiring knowledge of the multiple meanings and intricacies of the English language.

One of the most comprehensive studies during this period was Petersilia's (1983) analysis of sentencing for whites, blacks, and Hispanics. Using the 1978 Rand Inmate Survey for California,

Michigan, and Texas to supplement 1980 OBTS data for California, she examined disparities in the decision to proceed with felony prosecution, the type of sentence, the length of court-imposed sentence, and the length of sentence actually served. Some differences arose across states in the effects of race/ethnicity on these various outcomes, but generally Petersilia found that nonwhites convicted of felonies were more likely than whites to receive prison sentences, and these sentences were longer than those handed down to whites.

In my earlier research using California OBTS data for felony arrests in the years immediately preceding Petersilia (1977–1979), I found that the factors that can legally enhance or mitigate sentence lengths (e.g., prior record) were invoked differentially, depending upon whether the defendant was white, black, or Chicano (Zatz, 1984, 1985). Race/ethnicity also interacted with the size of the jurisdiction in influencing police and prosecutorial decision making (Hagan and Zatz, 1985). In comparison with whites, we found that blacks and Chicanos (but especially blacks) in small cities were *repeatedly* arrested and then quickly released by the police in the three-year period studied. When the police did not release minority suspects, the prosecutor often denied the case due to insufficient evidence. Since the police did not have sufficiently strong cases to hold the suspects, but then soon after release would re-arrest them, this pattern can be interpreted as harassment of minorities.[5] This pattern is particularly interesting because the existence of a lengthy prior record can be legally invoked to increase sentence lengths, but at least in California, it has been used primarily against Chicanos.

Finally, Miethe and Moore (1985) analyzed sentencing and presentence decisions in Minnesota before (1978) and after (1980–1981) implementation of Sentencing Commission Guidelines to assess whether or not the determinants of these outcomes changed over time. They found little change overall in the importance of socioeconomic characteristics on decision making over time, suggesting that neutrality in sentencing has not been displaced to non-regulated sentencing decisions (e.g., charge bargaining). However, they found indirect effects of race on sentencing decisions, operating through prior criminal history and use of a weapon, leading them to conclude that under determinate sentencing social and economic biases in decision making "are slightly more subtle, but no less real" (1985, p. 358).

It is difficult to critique research during this fourth wave midstream, but a few gaps in the literature are beginning to emerge. First, although investigations by Bynum (1981) and Spohn, Gruhl, and Welch (1981) suggest that social groups differ in their likelihood of receiving sentences to probation, the question of who gets probation and who gets prison has not yet been explored adequately.[6] Second, researchers are only now starting to return to questions raised fifteen years ago by Quinney (1970), Chambliss and Seidman (1971), and others who argued that cases enter the system in a biased fashion. While some of their assertions about the gatekeeping of the criminal justice system appear conspiratorial and instrumentalist, the still unresolved question of institutionalized bias has since been reframed in more structural terms (e.g., Greenberg,1977; Burns, 1982; Chambliss and Seidman, 1982; Michalowski, 1985). It is to the various sources of bias that we now turn.

Sources of Bias

A clearer understanding of racial/ethnic bias in sentencing requires that we step back from the research findings for a moment and address two questions: (1) Are our research designs inadvertently biased against findings of discrimination? and (2) Are court processing and decision making systematically biased due to institutionalized discrimination?

Bias in Research Methodology

Coincident with widespread determinate sentencing reforms, the increased use of computers has made longitudinal tracking systems (e.g., OBTS, PROMIS) more common. Whether the computer revolution stimulated development of tracking systems or simply facilitated their implementation, a computerized database that tracks defendants as they repeatedly traverse the system is useful, perhaps even necessary, for implementation and evaluation of determinate sentencing. These systems necessitate collection of certain data for each defendant processed. But, some interesting variables are frequently omitted, leading radical criminologists to question data collection and coding decisions. For example, the defendant's income is typically not recorded, and so is unavailable to researchers. Similarly, California stopped recording information on the type of attorney in 1978, shortly after its new determinate sentencing statute came into effect (July 1977). Failure of courts to collect and record such information means that researchers cannot test for class-based disparities in case processing and sentencing. Additional variables that are often not recorded but that would be useful for research purposes include the defendant's occupation and education and the victim's race/ethnicity, gender, and social class.

Coding decisions can also be problematic. For example, the coding of race/ethnicity is often unclear and inconsistent. Typically, it is coded as white versus nonwhite (with all nonwhites arbitrarily lumped together) or white versus black (with all others excluded from analyses). As Gruhl, Welch, and Spohn (1984), Zatz (1984, 1985), and LaFree (1985) have shown, blacks and Hispanics are processed in different ways, and these differences will be obscured if all nonwhites are collapsed into one category. When race is broken down beyond white–nonwhite, the nonwhite codes are not systematic; sometimes the defendant is asked his or her ethnicity, other times the determination is made by court officials based on primary language, surname, or physical appearance. Since sentencing researchers rely almost exclusively on court data, data collection and coding decisions will inevitably shape research findings by determining the range of questions that can be addressed.

In a rather provocative paper, Myers (1984, p. 5) claims that sentencing research has "failed to tackle squarely" the problems of the measurement of discrimination. His assessment of the weaknesses of traditional analytic techniques is correct, but his framing of the problem leads us astray, particularly where he asks whether racially biased punishment is "efficient" for reducing recidivism. Essentially, he argues for use of a methodology in which "residual discrimination" is measured, based on average differences between racial groups. This methodology, which is borrowed from labor economics, certainly improves upon simple regression estimates of main effects, but it ignores the problems of selection bias and specification error. Moreover, it represents an attempt to measure the exact amount of discrimination, without ever considering its various manifestations and forms.

It may well be the case that research has become bogged down by efforts to distinguish between discrimination, differential treatment, and disparity. Where findings of differences in the processing and outcomes to which members of different racial/ethnic groups are subjected are substantial, significant, and repeatable, however, distinctions of this sort may be unnecessary.[7] A more useful approach might be to focus on whether overt, subtle, or no racial/ethnic biases exist, and why. By *overt*, I refer to main or direct effects of race/ethnicity (or gender or class) on court processing and sanctioning. *Subtle* forms of bias exist where membership in a particular social group influences decision making indirectly or in interaction with other factors, with the outcome favoring one group over another. Such biases are no less systematic or harmful than overt bias; they simply differ in form. They have become institutionalized, and thus are less glaring and harder to find. As a consequence, research that tests only for main effects (i.e., overt bias) and does not investigate all of the possible manifestations of discrimination may erroneously conclude that discrimination does not exist when, in fact, it does.

Other Sources of Bias in Court Processing and Decision Making

Our stereotypic perceptions of who and what is threatening rest on the fear of immediate, visible danger. Yet the visibility of danger is to some extent socially conditioned. That is, we learn to fear, and to actively guard against, certain threats (e.g., street crime) and not others (e.g., offenses occurring in the privacy of one's home or office). In addition to learning what and where to fear, we also learn who to fear. As Lemert and Rosberg (1948), Swigert and Farrell (1977), Poole and Regoli (1980), and Balbus (1973) have shown, minority members are stereotypically perceived as more threatening to society than are whites.

Determinate sentencing provides a set of rules for calculating the appropriate sanction for a given offense, as well as aggravating and mitigating circumstances and the range within which they can lengthen or shorten the sentence; all presumably independent of stereotypic images of who constitutes a threat. The indicators of "aggravating circumstances" and the factors invoking sentence enhancements, however, are based on our socially learned fears of persons using guns, inflicting great bodily injury, or who are "habitual" criminals.[8] These fears do not typically extend to such harmful acts as corporate crime or violence against women behind the gates of middle- or upper-class homes. Such acts may be injurious and even fatal to thousands of people and may occur habitually, but, if defined as crimes and prosecuted, they are not accorded harsh statutory sentences. On the contrary, persons convicted of such acts may benefit from the "mitigating circumstances" clause that, although formally applicable across all crimes and all offenders, by its very nature tends to favor the middle-class offender.

Social groups differ in their abilities not only to shape and define deviance, but also to mobilize resources once involved in the legal system as defendants (Chambliss and Seidman, 1971; Troyer and Markle, 1982). The more favorable outcomes tend to go to those who have the greatest social, political, and economic resources, while the lack of resources needed to combat the legal system from a truly adversarial position disadvantages the poor and minorities. For example, decisions to release defendants on their own recognizance or on unsecured bonds are based primarily on the strength of community ties, determined largely by steady employment and home ownership. Such indicators tend to favor middle-class whites over poorer whites and minorities. Also, financial resources become important where attempts at acquittals or dismissals require delaying case processing until the evidence stales or public interest in the case dissipates (see, for example, Nardulli, 1978). Finally, the wealthy executive who is "an upstanding pillar of the community" may be viewed as having "suffered enough" if conviction results in loss of position, wealth, or reputation, but these same losses are apparently not sufficient for the poor and minorities who fill our prisons. Thus the factors that serve to differentiate those receiving lenient treatment from those given the full measure of the legal system's available sanctions are not class or race-neutral.

Legitimacy, Formal Rationality, and Institutionalized Bias

The increased watchdogging of the courts under determinate sentencing makes overt discrimination unlikely. This does *not*, however, necessarily imply that discrimination no longer occurs. While that is one possibility, the evidence presented here suggests that racial/ethnic bias has become institutionalized in more subtle ways, and occurs earlier in the system, so that it is no longer caught by the guardian of determinate sentencing.

The legal system is a bureaucracy that increasingly is becoming what Weber (1968) has called "formal rational." Following Weber, the formalization of the legal system along rational lines does not occur in a social, political, or economic vacuum:

> Formal justice guarantees the maximum freedom for the interested parties to represent their formal legal interests. But *because of the unequal distribution of economic power, which the system of formal justice legalizes*, this very freedom must time and again produce consequences which are contrary to the substantive postulates of religious ethics or of political expediency [Weber, 1968, p. 812, my emphasis].

Also:

> It is precisely this abstract character which constitutes the decisive merit of formal justice to those who wield the economic power at any given time and who are therefore interested in its unhampered operation. . . . Among those groups who favor formal justice we must include all those political and economic interest groups to whom the stability and predictability of legal procedure are of very great importance. . . . Above all, those in possession of economic power look upon a formal rational administration of justice as a guarantee of "freedom" [Weber, 1968, p. 813].

More concretely, the legal system receives greater legitimacy through formal rationality and the bureaucratization that goes with it. It is seen as meeting out justice fairly and blindly. Yet as Marxist scholars have long argued and the evidence presented here indicates, the factors that go into the decision-rules may themselves be biased, and, in following the rules, this bias necessarily continues into the final sanctioning decisions.

When fixed sentencing reforms were initially suggested, law makers and law enforcers were faced with an increasingly vocal and organized minority community inside and outside of prison that accused the police and courts of discrimination. Liberal whites concerned about what they perceived to be injustices perpetrated against minorities joined in, lending their political support and intellectual credibility to the movement. Before this movement became effectual, however, the political climate grew increasingly conservative, and the proposed fixed sentencing reforms were co-opted by conservative proponents of the "justice model" (Greenberg and Humphries, 1980; see also Greenberg, 1983 and Humphries, 1984). As a consequence of, and in response to, these political shifts, the legislature and the judiciary had to adapt new strategies if they were to maintain a semblance of legitimacy. One such strategy was determinate sentencing; a practice that, at first glance, appears fair and equitable. As Balbus concluded from his analysis of the legal system's response to the major ghetto riots of the 1960s:

> Although court authorities in the liberal state may temporarily disregard the constraints of formal rationality and organizational maintenance, they may not ignore them for very long or without suffering serious consequences [Balbus, 1973, p. 240].

Conclusions

Court officials and researchers of the courts have expressed long-term concern over the possible existence of discriminatory sanctioning on the basis of race/ethnicity, class, and gender. A plethora of research has been published, without arriving at any definitive answers. Findings over the years have been contradictory, and the quest for answers seen as elusive. With each wave of research, methodological flaws in its predecessors have been discovered. Overall, however, research has consistently unearthed subtle, if not overt, bias.

Contrary to the dictates of the positivist approach to scientific inquiry, our data often determine our methods of analysis, and our choice of methodology often constrains, and perhaps even determines, our theories and research questions. One consequence of this is that our data and methodologies will be biased toward findings of no discrimination if, as the research discussed here suggests, the legal system and the bases for legal decision making are themselves biased. In part, this bias results from socially conditioned fears and prejudices that have become institutionalized in the very nature of who and what are defined as harmful; definitions that arise within a social context in which resources are unequally distributed across social groups.

A few caveats are in order. First, this is not a comprehensive review of all studies of race/ethnicity and sentencing. As was noted earlier, several such reviews already exist (e.g., Hagan, 1974; Kleck,

1981; Hagan and Bumiller, 1983; Klepper, Nagin, and Terney, 1983). Instead, the studies reviewed were chosen for illustrative purposes, and as representative of research conducted during each of the four periods. Second, it would be misleading to suggest that race/ethnicity is *the* major determinant of sanctioning. Other factors (e.g., type of offense, number of prior arrests and convictions, plea bargaining, pretrial detention) typically explain larger amounts of variation in sentencing. But, race/ethnicity is *a* determinant of sanctioning, and a potent one at that. Third, gender has not been discussed except as it interacts with race/ethnicity, and age is noticeably absent from this review. While one's race/ethnicity, gender, and usually class are constant throughout an individuals' lifetime, age is always changing, making it a qualitatively different type of social attribute. Also, the juvenile court traditionally has followed substantive rational rather than formal rational justice. Nevertheless, the same trend toward finding subtle interaction effects of race is suggested by recent studies of juvenile court processing (e.g., Feyerherm, 1981; Dannefer and Schutt, 1982; Thornberry and Christenson, 1984; Bortner and Reed, 1985). Finally, this chapter does not even begin to develop a theory of social harm, nor does it undertake the task of defining "justice." These are necessary tasks at this juncture, and must be informed by the biases documented here.

In response to the varied pressures facing them, the "state managers" of justice have established mechanisms for controlling "problematic" populations. The currently used mechanisms (e.g., determinate sentencing) are less blatantly biased than were their predecessors, and are cloaked with the legitimacy accruing from formalized rules. This does not mean, however, that the end result has been a change in our prison population. Minority and lower-class males still overwhelmingly constitute the bulk of the prison population. It is just the path by which they are sent to prison that has changed, not the end result. The road to this end is more subtle now. Differential processing and treatment is now veiled by legitimacy, but it is a legitimacy in which certain biases have become rationalized and institutionalized. Stereotypes of who is threatening, and disparities in available resources with which to combat the legal system from a truly adversarial stance, have not dissipated.

Consequently, discrimination has not gone away. It has simply changed its form to become more acceptable. Increased formal rationality of the legal process has caused discrimination to undergo cosmetic surgery, with its new face deemed more appealing. The result is bias in a different form than it showed in the past. It is now subtle rather than overt. But, to borrow and twist an expression from Weber (1958), the "iron cage" still locks primarily minorities and lower-class whites behind its bars.

Notes

1. Although Judge Chargin's statement was made in 1969 (thus falling into the time frame covered by the second wave), it more appropriately reflects the sentiment at the end of Wave 1.
2. This is, of course, an empirical question. It would be interesting to see whether similar analyses (i.e., cross tabular, lacking control variables) using contemporary data would show similar results. If there has been a real change in discrimination, then results from contemporary data should yield fewer differences between groups than in the past. This would, however, only constitute a partial test of discrimination; differences could still exist in the processing of various groups, but they might only be visible in interaction with "legally relevant" variables.
3. Sample selection bias can also be viewed as falling under the general rubric of specification error. They are treated as separate issues here for conceptual convenience.
4. Under determinate sentencing, legislatures generally set three sentences: the presumptive sentence, a shorter term for mitigating circumstances, and a longer term for aggravating circumstances. Judges must typically set down in writing their reasons for invoking the mitigating or aggravating clauses. However, as research on mandatory sentence enhancements for gun offenses has shown (e.g., Heumann and Loftin, 1979; Loftin, Heumann, and McDowall, 1983; Lizotte and Zatz, 1986), legislative mandates are not necessarily followed by court officials.
5. Longitudinal data aid in exploration of racial/ethnic biases. Since discrimination can accumulate both over time and across stages of the system, cross-sectional data can create a censoring problem by unrealistically carving a slice out of time, thus potentially distorting findings. For example, if we had looked only at one incident, our findings might suggest bias against whites. But, examination of a series of arrests showed a recurring pattern over time, with the same minority persons repeatedly arrested and released. This suggests that whites were not arrested unless there was a strong case against them, while the same consideration was not extended to minorities. Findings by Hepburn (1978), Petersilia (1983), and others lend further credence to this interpretation.

6. A recent study by Myers and Talarico (1986) examined both the likelihood of receiving a prison sentence and the length of a prison sentence for blacks and whites in Georgia, using data for the period 1976–1982. Using sophisticated analytic techniques to control for selection bias, they found both main and interaction effects of race, some of which disadvantage blacks, others whites. Their findings suggest that where relatively recent data from a *non*determinate sentencing state are used, the racial composition of the county and the type of offense are the most important determinants of racial disparities in sentencing.
7. An analogy can be made to employment litigation. Although this appears to be changing under the Reagan administration, for many years "disparate impact" of a policy was actionable. That is, if a hiring or promotion policy negatively affected some protected group, it was seen as deserving redress.
8. The Minnesota and Pennsylvania Sentencing Commission guidelines include certain white-collar offenses in their lists of potentially aggravating circumstances, presumably to address the problem of inordinate leniency for middle- and upper-class offenders. Nevertheless, "aggravating circumstances" still consist primarily of factors related to street-crime, and the presumptive sentences tend to be longer for crimes involving personal injury (e.g., robbery with injury, aggravated assault with serious injury) than for general theft offenses. Since the former category of offenses are more likely to involve lower-class and minority offenders than are the latter, the result may be, as Irwin (1980, p. 226) suggests, "sentences equally as disparate and discriminatory, but even longer."

References

Albonetti, C. 1985. Sentencing: The effects of uncertainty. Presented at the Law and Society Association meetings, San Diego, CA.

Balbus, I. D. 1973. *The dialectics of legal repression: Black rebels before the American criminal courts.* New York: Russell Sage.

Bedau, H. A. 1964. Death sentences in New Jersey. *Rutgers Law Review* 19: 1–2.

Berk, R. A. 1983. Anntroduction to sample selection bias in sociological data. *American Sociological Review* 48: 386–398.

Bortner, M. A. and W. L. Reed. 1985. The preeminence of process: An example of refocused justice research. *Social Science Quarterly* 66: 413–425.

Bullock, H. 1961. Significance of the racial factor in the length of prison sentences. *Journal of Criminal Law, Criminology, and Police Science* 52: 411–417.

Burke, P. J. and A. T. Turk. 1975. Factors affecting postarrest dispositions: A model for analysis. *Social Problems* 22: 313–332.

Burns, W. H. 1982. Law and Race in America. In *The politics of law: A progressive critique*, ed. D. Kairys. New York: Pantheon.

Bynum, T. 1981. Parole decision making and Native Americans. In *Race, crime, and criminal justice*, eds. R. L. McNeely and C. E. Pope. Newbury Park, CA: Sage.

Chambliss, W. J. and R. B. Seidman. 1971. *Law, order, and power.* Reading, MA: Addison-Wesley.

——— 1982. *Law, order, and power*, second ed. Reading, MA: Addison-Wesley.

Cohen, L., and J. R. Kluegel. 1978. Determinants of juvenile court dispositions: Ascriptive and achieved factors in two metropolitan courts. *American Sociological Review* 43: 162–176.

Dannefer, D. and R. K. Schutt. 1982. Race and juvenile justice processing in court and police agencies. *American Journal of Sociology* 87: 1113–1132.

Farnworth, M. and P. M. Horan. 1980. Separate justice: An analysis of race differences in court processes. *Social Science Research* 9: 381–399.

Feyerherm, W. 1981. Juvenile court dispositions of status offenders: An analysis of case decisions. In *Race, crime and criminal justice*, ed. R. L. McNeely and C. E. Pope. Newbury Park, CA: Sage.

Garber, S., S. Klepper, and D. Nagin. 1983. The role of extralegal factors in determining criminal case disposition. In *Research in sentencing: The search for reform, Vol. II*, ed. Blumstein et al. Washington, DC: National Academy Press.

Greenberg, D. F. 1977. Socioeconomic status and criminal sentences: Is There an Association?" *American Sociological Review* 42: 174–176.

——— 1983. Reflections on the justice model debate. *Contemporary Crises* 7:313–327.

——— and D. Humphries. 1980. The co-optation of fixed sentencing reform. *Crime & Delinquency* 26: 206–225.

Gruhl, J., S. Welch, and C. Spohn. 1984. Women as criminal defendants: A test for paternalism. *Western Political Quarterly* 37: 456–467.

Hagan, J. 1974. Extra-legal attributes and criminal sentencing: An assessment of a sociological viewpoint. *Law and Society Review* 8: 357–383.

Hagan, J. and I. N. Bernstein. 1979. Conflict in context: The sanctioning of draft resisters, 1963–76. *Social Problems* 27: 109–122.

Hagan, J. and K. Bumiller. 1983. Making sense of sentencing: A review and critique of sentencing research. In *Research in sentencing: The search for reform, Vol. II.*, eds. Blumstein et al. Washington, DC: National Academy Press.

Hagan, J. and M. S. Zatz. 1985. The social organization of criminal justice processing activities. *Social Science Research* 14: 103–125.

Hall, E. L., and A. A. Simkus. 1975. Inequality in the types of sentences received by Native Americans and Whites. *Criminology* 13: 199–222.

Hepburn, J. R. 1978. Race and the decision to arrest: An analysis of warrants issued. *Journal of Research in Crime and Delinquency* 15: 54–73.

Hernandez, C. A., M. J. Haug, and N. N. Wagner. 1976. *Chicanos: Social and psychological perspectives.* St. Louis: C. V. Mosby.

Heumann, M., and C. Loftin. 1979. Mandatory sentencing and the abolition of plea bargaining: The Michigan felony firearm statute. *Law and Society Review* 13: 401–407.
Hindelang, M. 1978. Race and involvement in common law personal crimes. *American Sociological Review* 43: 93–109.
Humphries, D. 1984. Reconsidering the justice model. *Contemporary Crises* 8: 167–173.
Irwin, J. 1980. *Prisons in turmoil.* Boston: Little, Brown.
Johnson, E. H. 1957. Selective factors in capital punishment. *Social Forces* 36: 165–169.
Kleck, G. 1981. Racial discrimination in criminal sentencing: A critical evaluation of the evidence with additional evidence on the death penalty. *American Sociological Review* 46: 783–805.
Klepper, S., D. Nagin, and L. Tierney. 1983. Discrimination in the criminal justice system: A critical appraisal of the literature. In *Research in sentencing: The search for reform, Volume II.*, eds. A. Blumstein et al. Washington, DC: National Academy Press.
LaFree, G. D. 1980a. The effect of sexual stratification by race on official reactions to rape. *American Sociological Review* 45: 842–854.
——— 1980b. Variables affecting guilty pleas and convictions in rape cases: Toward a social theory of rape processing. *Social Forces* 58: 833–850.
——— 1985. Official reactions to Hispanic defendants in the southwest. *Journal of Research in Crime and Delinquency* 22: 213–237.
Lemert, E. M. and J. Rosberg. 1948. The administration of justice to minority groups in L. A. county. *University of California Publications in Culture and Society 1–27.*
Lizotte, A. J. 1978. Extra-legal factors in Chicago's criminal courts: Testing the conflict model of criminal justice. *Social Problems* 25: 564–580.
Lizotte, A. J. and M. S. Zatz. 1986. The use and abuse of sentence enhancement for firearms offenses in California. *Law and Contemporary Problems* 49: 199–221.
Loftin, C., M. Heumann, and D. McDowall. 1983. Mandatory sentencing and firearms violence: Evaluating an alternative to gun control. *Law and Society Review* 17: 287–318.
Michalowski, R. J. 1985. *Order, law, and crime: An introduction to criminology.* New York: Random House.
Miethe, T. D. and C. A. Moore. 1985. Socioeconomic disparities under determinate sentencing systems: A comparison of preguideline and postguideline practices in Minnesota. *Criminology* 23: 337–363.
Myers, M. A. 1979. Offended parties and official reactions: Victims and the sentencing of criminal defendants. *Sociological Quarterly 20: 529–540.*
Myers, M. A. and S. M. Talarico. 1986. The social contexts of racial discrimination in sentencing. *Social Problems* 33: 236–251.
Myers, S. L. Jr. 1984. Statistical tests of discrimination in punishment. Presented at the Law and Society Association meetings, Boston.
Nardulli, P. 1978. *The courtroom elite: An organizational perspective on criminal justice.* Cambridge, MA: Ballinger.
Petersilia, J. 1983. *Racial disparities in the criminal justice system.* Santa Monica, CA: Rand.
Peterson, R. D. and J. Hagan. 1984. Changing conceptions of race: Towards an account of anomalous findings of sentencing research. *American Sociological Review* 49: 56–70.
Poole, E. D. and R. M. Regoli. 1980. Race, institutional rule-breaking, and disciplinary response: A study of discretionary decision making in prison. *Law and Society Review* 14: 931–946.
Pruitt, C. R. and J. Q. Wilson. 1983. A longitudinal study of the effect of race on sentencing. *Law and Society Review* 7: 613–635.
Quinney, R. 1970. *The social reality of crime.* Boston: Little, Brown.
Reiman, J. H. and S. Headlee. 1981. Marxism and criminal justice policy. *Crime & Delinquency* 27: 24–47.
Sellin, T. 1935. Race prejudice in the administration of justice. *American Journal of Sociology* 41: 212–217.
Spohn, C., J. Gruhl, and S. Welch. 1981. The effect of race on sentencing: A re-examination of an unsettled question. *Law and Society Review* 16: 71–88.
Spohn, C., S. Welch, and J. Gruhl. 1985. Women defendants in court: The interaction between sex and race in convicting and sentencing." *Social Quarterly* 66: 178–185.
Swigert, V. L. and R. A. Farrell. 1977. Normal homicides and the law. *American Sociological Review* 42: 16–32.
Thornberry, T. P. and R. L. Christenson. 1984. Juvenile justice decision-making as a longitudinal process. *Social Forces* 63: 433–444.
Troyer, R. J. and G. E. Markle. 1982. Creating deviance rules: A macroscopic model. *Sociological Quarterly* 23: 157–169.
U.S. Commission on Civil Rights. 1970. *Mexican Americans and the administration of justice in the southwest.* Washington, DC: Government Printing Office.
Von Hirsch, A. 1987. *Doing justice: The choice of punishments.* New York: Hill & Wang.
Weber, M. 1958. *The protestant ethic and the spirit of captalism.* New York: Charles Scribner's Sons.
——1968. *Economy and society.* New York: Bedminster.
Wolfgang, M. E., A. Kelly, and H. C. Nolde. 1962. Comparisons of the executed and the communted among admissions to death row. *Journal of Criminal Law, Criminology Law, Criminology and Police Science* 53: 301–311.
Zatz, M. S. 1984. Race, ethnicity, and determinate sentencing: A new dimension to an old controversy. *Criminology* 22: 147–171.
—— 1985. Pleas, priors and prison: Racial/ethnic differences in sentencing. *Social Science Research* 14: 169–193.
Zatz, M. S. and J. Hagan. 1985. Crime, time, and punishment: An exploration of selection bias in sentencing research. *Journal of Quantitative Criminology* 1: 103–126.
Zatz, M. S. and A. J. Lizotte. 1985. The timing of court processing: Towards linking theory and method. *Criminology* 23: 313–335.

22

American Indians and Sentencing Disparity

An Arizona Test

Alexander Alvarez and Ronet D. Bachman

Introduction

In a society in which the symbol of justice is blindfolded to indicate that all are equal before the law, the discriminatory imposition of the law is an issue that strikes at the heart of assumptions concerning the nature of justice. Shaped by Jeffersonian notions of natural and inalienable rights, definitions of justice are founded upon ideals of parity, fairness, and impartiality. The actions of the criminal justice system, however, do not always live up to these ideals. Justice, it seems, is not always blind. This is especially true where minority groups are concerned. Spurred in large part by the extreme overrepresentation of minority groups in prison (see Blumstein, 1982; Langan, 1985; Tonry, 1994, 1995), there has been a long history of research investigating the possible discriminatory applications of the law. The phrase *discriminatory application of the law* refers to the differential treatment of individuals by official agents of justice based on legally irrelevant or extra-legal characteristics such as race, socio-economic status, and gender. Of these extra-legal factors, race has emerged in the literature as one of the most important factors that influence how the law is applied. For example, there is evidence that, in different jurisdictions and at different stages, African Americans are more likely to be detained, arrested, tried, found guilty, sentenced to longer terms, sentenced to death, and serve more of their sentences than Caucasians (for reviews, see Conley, 1994; D'Allessio and Stolzenberg, 1993; Kleck, 1981; Mann, 1993; Petersillia, 1983; Pope and Feyerheim, 1990a, 1990b).

Although there is a sizable body of research that examines African Americans and the discriminatory application of the law, comparatively little research has examined the issue of discrimination in relation to other minority groups. As Leiber (1994) points out, most studies looking at race and discrimination in the administration of justice focus either exclusively on African Americans and ignore other minority groups, or alternatively, group all minority groups together. More specific to the concerns of this chapter, after conducting an extensive literature search, [Green (1991) could only find twenty examples of research investigating American Indian criminality and criminal justice processing.] This omission in the literature coupled with the fact that research has found American Indians also to be disproportionately represented in arrest, court, and prison statistics (see Lynch and Patterson, 1991; Mann, 1993), clearly highlights the need to pursue investigations of this nature as they relate to American Indian populations. Thus, the purpose of this chapter is to investigate the extent to which the discriminatory application of the law may impact American Indians.

In addition to the paucity of research in this area, there are several other reasons for examining potential discriminatory applications of law toward American Indians. First, in many locations, rates of American Indian victimization and criminality have been shown to be higher than most other minority groups, including African Americans (Bachman, 1992; Levy, Kunitz, and Everett, 1969; Peak and Spencer, 1987). Second, American Indians have also been found to be overrepresented in several adjudication statistics such as arrest, conviction, and incarceration statistics both in the United States (Bachman, 1992; Feimer, Pommersheim, and Wise, 1990; Flowers, 1990; French, 1982; Stewart, 1964), and Canada (Bonta, 1989; Griffiths and Yerbury, 1984; LaPrairie, 1984). In addition, American Indians are one of the most oppressed minority groups in U.S. society and are the recipients of some of the most negative and degrading stereotypes (Bachman, 1992; Bynum and Paternoster, 1984; Flowers, 1990; Levy, Kunitz, and Everett, 1969; Stratton, 1973). While many have noted that stereotyping in general often contributes to the discriminatory application of law (Miethe, 1987; Miethe and Moore, 1986; Swigert and Farrell, 1977), others have more specifically contended that the impact of stereotypical imagery regarding American Indians not only perpetuates, but encourages, discriminatory application of the law against American Indians (Zatz, Lujan, and Snyder-Joy, 1991). In fact, it could be argued that by failing to investigate the application of the law as it affects American Indians, the scholarly community has contributed to these stereotypes. As Young (1990,112) asserts:

> For the most part criminal justice scholars have ignored issues relating to Native Americans. This tendency probably reflects the marginal social, political, and economic status of Native Americans. Unfortunately, this lack of scholarly research means that Native Americans commonly are viewed in terms of narrow, ethnocentric stereotypes (e.g., drunken savages).

Additionally, the conflict model, which has most often been used as the conceptual framework within which to examine the discriminatory application of law to African Americans, would suggest that other similarly disadvantaged and powerless groups, including American Indians, would also fare badly relative to Caucasians.

Each of these issues is suggestive of the possible role that discrimination may play in producing the arrest and prison population disparities that have been found between American Indians and Caucasians in the United States. The primary purpose of this chapter is to explore this question and thereby extend the understanding of the discriminatory application of the law as it affects a minority group that has remained among the least examined and understood in the criminological literature. Specifically, this chapter examines the extent to which American Indian defendants in the state of Arizona receive different sentences compared to their Caucasian counterparts. In order to maintain a sharp empirical and theoretical focus on the treatment of American Indians relative to Caucasians, other racial/ethnic groups including African Americans and Latinos were not included in the analyses. Studies including multiple minority groups are important, however, the exclusive focus on American Indians allows for more specific analyses and discussion of this neglected group, and will therefore highlight the importance of investigating the treatment of American Indians in research examining the differential application of the law.

Theoretical Framework

Relying largely upon a conflict paradigm, a large body of theoretical writing contends that the imposition of the law is a selective process that discriminates against certain groups. From this point of view, the differential application of the law is not an aberration, but more often the norm. Discriminatory patterns evident in the application and administration of justice are indicative therefore, not of "a few bad apples," but rather of systematic and widespread biases, stereotyping, and prejudices on the part of legal officials who either consciously or unconsciously apply and enforce the law preferentially in order to maintain class, gender, and/or race based power differentials. Although the conflict perspective has been subdivided into various subcategories, it can generally be asserted that conflict theorists argue that the application of law varies depending upon power differentials (Chambliss and Seidman, 1971; Hills, 1971; Quinney, 1970; Turk, 1969). Many argue that those groups with the least economic, political, and social power will be sanctioned the most severely. This position was well articulated by Chambliss and Seidman (1971, 475) who asserted:

> In complex societies, political power is closely tied to social position. Therefore, those laws which prohibit certain types of behavior popular among lower-class persons are more likely to be enforced, while laws restricting the behavior of middle or upper-class persons are not likely to be enforced. Where laws are so stated that people of all classes are equally likely to violate them, the lower the social position of an offender, the greater is the likelihood that sanctions will be imposed on him. When sanctions are imposed, the most severe sanctions will be imposed on persons in the lowest social class.

Some conflict theorists have specifically argued that powerless groups in society are more likely to have their actions defined as criminal when those actions are defined as a threat to the existing power structure (Gordon, 1973; Quinney 1970, 1979; Spitzer, 1975). Turk (1969), on the other hand, has suggested that discrimination occurs because the powerless are politically, economically, and socially less able to resist the application of law at all stages of the legal process. Chambliss (1993a, 1993b) has more recently argued that it is not the application of the law that is of primary importance, rather it is the creation of law that illustrates power differentials. Of key importance to each of these conflict arguments, however, is the power differential between those who create and apply the law and those to whom it is applied.

Previous Research

As noted earlier, research analyzing the discriminatory treatment of minorities in the legal system has focused predominantly on differences between African Americans and Caucasians. Relatively little research attention has been directed at exploring these issues as they relate to the American Indian population (Bachman, 1992; Bachman, Alvarez, and Perkins, 1996; Bynum, 1981; Bynum and Paternoster, 1984; Feimer, Pommersheim, and Wise, 1990; Hall and Simkus, 1975; Leiber, 1994; Pommersheim and Wise, 1989; Swift and Bickel, 1974; Williams, 1979), and only some of these studies have employed multivariate models to control for the effects of other important predictors of sentencing outcomes (Bynum, 1981; Bynum and Paternoster, 1984; Feimer, Pommersheim, and Wise, 1990; Hall and Simkus, 1975; Leiber, 1994; Pommersheim and Wise, 1989; Swift and Bickel, 1974; Williams, 1979).

Unfortunately, the results of the extant research examining sentencing disparities between American Indians and Caucasians remains inconclusive. Although a few investigators have found no evidence of discrimination against American Indians in the adjudication process (Feimer, Pommersheim, and Wise, 1990; Pommersheim and Wise, 1989), several studies have found that American Indians do receive harsher treatment by the criminal justice system compared to Caucasians (Hall and Simkus, 1975; Williams, 1979), or that differential treatment exists between American Indian and Caucasian defendants for particular types of crimes only (Bachman, Alvarez, and Perkins, 1996; Flowers, 1990; Leiber, 1994; Swift and Bickel, 1974). Some of the earliest research to examine sentencing disparities between American Indians and Caucasians was performed by Swift and Bickel (1974) who found that American Indians received longer sentences than Caucasians in Federal courts even after controlling for other important predictors of sentence length. Other early work was conducted by Hall and Simkus (1975) who compared the sentence lengths received by Caucasians and American Indians in a "western" state. After controlling for several important factors, including the number of prior felonies and prior juvenile offenses, as well as the average degree of harshness of the sentencing judge, their analysis indicated that American Indians still received harsher sentences than Caucasians.

Other research has found that the differential treatment of American Indians goes beyond sentencing decisions. For example, Bynum and Paternoster (1984) discovered that American Indians served significantly more of their prison sentence before parole or release than did Caucasians within a "midwestern" state's correctional population. Similarly, Bachman, Alvarez, and Perkins (1996) found that within five state jurisdictions analyzed, and for virtually every type of crime, American Indians served significantly more of their sentences before receiving parole compared to Caucasians. Bynum (1981) and Swift and Bickel (1974) found similar differentials between American Indian and Caucasian convicted felons in the amount of time served.

It is clear that there is a gap in the understanding of the discriminatory imposition of the law as it affects American Indians in society today. The goal of this chapter is to advance understanding about the role, if any, that discrimination plays in producing differential sentence outcomes for American Indian and Caucasian convicted felony offenders. Specifically, using OLS regression analysis to control for other important factors such as a defendant's prior record and type of offense, sentence length differentials that exist between American Indian and Caucasian inmates serving time in Arizona state correctional facilities in 1990 will be examined. It will be seen that conducting multivariate analyses within a crime-specific context such as this can serve to clarify some of the inconsistencies evident in the extant research investigating the adjudication outcomes of American Indian and Caucasian defendants.

Methods

Arizona Data

Data for the state of Arizona were obtained directly from the Arizona Department of Corrections.[2] This state was selected in part because it was one of the only states with a large enough American Indian population represented within the correctional system to examine this issue. Arizona was also selected because conflict theory would suggest that "the minority threat to the hegemony of whites is likely to be greatest where the minority population is large . . . Thus nonwhites will also experience especially high rates of imprisonment in areas where the percentage of minorities is highest" (Bridges, Crutchfield, and Simpson, 1987, 347). Because Arizona has the third largest American Indian population (following Oklahoma and California), it certainly fits this description (Reddy, 1993). Numbering over 203,000 individuals, American Indians in Arizona comprised 5.6 percent of the population in 1990, over one-half of whom live off the reservations (Reddy, 1993). Evidence of powerlessness is also apparent. American Indians in Arizona have one of the lowest life expectancy rates in the state, high unemployment rates ranging from 23.4 percent to 35.3 percent depending on the particular county, and a high percentage of families living below the poverty line, actually approaching 50 percent in one county (Reddy, 1993). Extrapolating from conflict theory, then, American Indians in Arizona have very little power, are unable to resist application of the law, and can be defined as a threat simply because of their relatively large numbers in the population. Theoretically, they represent a clearly identifiable and visible minority group, and consequently are more likely to be discriminated against in the Arizona legal system. Additionally, this state level of analysis was utilized because aggregating states tends to mask individual state level variance (Crutchfield, Bridges, and Pitchford, 1994).

Specifically, the data used for this chapter were obtained by extracting a file that reflects a snapshot of the active inmate population detained in state correctional facilities on an average day in May of 1990. These data are assumed to be representative of the average Arizona state correctional population for the entire 1990 year. This data source was utilized because it not only provided the dependent variable of interest, sentence received, but also other important variables such as prior felony convictions, level of educational attainment, age, and gender. With this information, appropriate multivariate models were constructed to predict the extent to which American Indians received longer sentences for a given offense compared to Caucasians, while controlling for the other factors which may also have affected an offender's sentencing outcome.

Data Limitations

While these data provide an excellent opportunity to explore sentencing disparities between American Indians and Caucasians, it is important to underscore the limitations of these data as well. The first limitation has to do with the level of analysis itself and the complicated nature of the relationship between jurisdiction and American Indians status. As Zatz, Lujan, and Snyder-Joy (1991) point out, jurisdiction regarding American Indians is, to say the least, a complicated issue. American Indians are, in fact, subject to three distinct jurisdictional levels: tribal, state, and federal, depending on the location and type of offense, as well as the ethnic identity of the involved parties (Utter, 1993). Since tribal courts deal almost exclusively with American Indians, however, this is not a productive venue for analysis of sentencing patterns between American Indians and Caucasians. Additionally, tribal courts usually deal exclusively with misdemeanors or offenses against tribal laws. When American Indians commit felonies on the reservation, federal court has jurisdictional privilege, and felonies committed by American Indians off the reservation are disposed of at the state level. Because there is no readily available data set at the federal level that contains the appropriate control variables (e.g., prior record, etc.), these state level data were selected.

The second limitation of this analysis is that information on earlier decision-making stages in the legal process were unavailable, thus necessitating exclusive reliance on sentencing outcomes. Many have recently pointed out the weaknesses of single-stage analyses, regardless of the utilized stage (Dannefer and Schutt, 1982; Crutchfield, Bridges, and Pitchford, 1994; Bortner and Reed, 1985; Bridges and Crutchfield, 1988; Bishop and Frazier, 1988; Frazier, Bishop, and Henretta, 1992). These criticisms usually center around the fact that discrimination may exist sporadically at different decision points along the way from arrest to disposition. As Crutchfield, Bridges, and Pitchford (1994, 169) write, "Within any single jurisdiction, racial differences in treatment may be pronounced at one stage (e.g., filing of charges or pretrial diversion) and small at another (e.g., conviction and sentencing)." Thus when analyzing sentencing outcomes, the irregular patterns of discrimination may bias the sample utilized, as those who are actually sentenced represent only a small proportion of those who were initially subject to legal sanction. Clearly, the preferred method would involve analysis of multiple stages in the justice process.

In the absence of multi-stage data, however, single-stage analysis can still be meaningfully conducted. The primary deficiency of such data is that any single-stage analysis may find no evidence of discrimination, when in fact, discrimination might exist at a different stage. Herein lies the importance of the Crutchfield, Bridges, and Pitchford (1994,169) cautionary note that, "studies focusing solely on single points of decision making in criminal justice, or those that overlook the sample selection problem in studying sentencing, should not be generalized beyond those points in the system to jurisdictions dissimilar from those studied." The results of the present analysis, therefore, while limited in their generalizability to other stages of the criminal justice process, can offer useful insights into the application of the law to American Indians at the sentencing stage. Although this limitation is regrettable, it does not affect the validity of the findings regarding sentencing disparities that are presented in this chapter.

Another limitation of the data is that they do not contain information on the race of the victim. As suggested by Hawkins (1987) and Black (1976, 1989), the race of the victim in relation to the race of the offender is an important element in determining the way in which the law is applied. Previous research has supported this contention (Bachman, in press; Baldus, Pulaski, and Woodworth, 1983; Bowers and Pierce, 1980; Gross and Mauro, 1984; LaFree, 1980; Myers, 1979; Paternoster, 1983; Radelet, 1981; Thomson and Zingraff, 1981; Wolfgang and Reidel, 1973; Zimring, Eigen, and O'Malley, 1976). Although information on the race of victims was not available, data on the specific context of the crime were. Evidence suggests that, given the absence of information on race of the victim, crime-specific analyses can be conducted that in some ways approximate the victim effects noted above (Bachman, Alvarez, and Perkins, 1996; Kelly, 1976; Thompson and Zingraff, 1981). For example, it has long been noted that criminality tends to follow crime-specific patterns in terms of the race of the victim and offender (see Peterson and Hagan, 1984, for discussion). Data from the National Crime Victimization Survey indicate that violent crime is predominantly intraracial, while a higher proportion of property crime is interracial. In 1991, for example, Caucasians victimized other Caucasians in violent crimes 71.5 percent of the time while African Americans victimized other African Americans in violent crimes 83.8 percent of the time (U.S. Department of Justice, 1992). When looking at discrimination in the application of the law, patterns may become evident based upon this crime-specific context. Kelly (1976), for example, found that American Indians and Mexican Americans received more lenient sentences for homicide than did Caucasians, while African Americans received more harsh treatment for burglary. In addition, Thomson and Zingraff (1981) found that Caucasians received more lenient sentences for robbery than did African Americans. These authors argued that this was, in part, brought about by racial discrimination because robbery is a crime that is largely interracial. Although not ideal, crime-specific analyses, such as those presented in this chapter, can provide an acceptable substitute in the absence of victim/perpetrator race-specific data. With the exception of Bachman, Alvarez, and Perkins (in press), none of the studies examining discriminatory application of the law for American Indians have utilized crime-specific analysis.

Dependent Variable

Sentence length in years was used as the dependent variable for this study. Life and death sentences were recoded to reflect fifteen and twenty years above the longest sentence received, respectively. Thus, a life sentence was recoded to reflect a 505-year sentence (530 Caucasians and twenty American Indians received life sentences) and death sentences were recoded to reflect a 510-year sentence[3] (fifty-three Caucasians and two American Indians received death sentences).

Independent Variable

Previous Record

Because research has found that a defendant's previous criminal history is one of the most consistent predictors of sentence length (Adams and Cutshall, 1987; Chiricos and Waldo, 1975; D'Allessio and Stolzenberg, 1993; Spohn and Welch, 1987; Welch, Gruhl, and Spohn, 1984; Welch and Spohn, 1986), a defendant's prior criminal record was included in the regression models for this research. A dichotomous variable was created to reflect the presence or absence of any prior felony convictions for each inmate's record. If inmates had been convicted of a felony prior to the offense they were now serving time for, "Prior Record" was coded 1. If there were no prior felony convictions on an offender's record, "Prior Record" was coded 0.

Demographic Controls

The variable denoting an inmate's racial/ethnic status was also dichotomous and was coded 1 for American Indians and 0 for Caucasian inmates. This classification relied exclusively on existing records and was based primarily on a defendant's self-classification.[4] These self-identification records included a mutually exclusive code not only for American Indians, but also for those who classified themselves as Caucasians, African Americans, and Latinos as well. As was noted earlier, those who classified themselves as something other than Caucasian or American Indian were excluded from the analyses.

In addition, several other demographic variables were included in regression models. Age represented a continuous variable ranging from sixteen to seventy-two. All those cases that fell below the age of sixteen and above the age of seventy-two were deleted from the analysis because the integrity of these values could not be verified. A dichotomous variable was included in the analysis to represent each inmate's gender: females were coded 0 and males were coded 1. Inmate's educational attainment was also included in models used to predict sentences received. This variable was continuous in nature and represented the number of school years an inmate reported he/she had completed.

Results

Before presenting the results of the multivariate regression analysis, it is first useful to examine the univariate distribution of the sentences received by both American Indians and Caucasians. Table 22.1 displays the mean sentence length in years received by American Indian and Caucasian defendants who were incarcerated in Arizona state correctional facilities in 1990 by type of crime.

A review of Table 22.1 reveals a differential pattern of sentencing across offenses for American Indians and Caucasians. For example, in cases of homicide, sexual assault, and assault, Caucasians, on average, received longer sentences compared to American Indians. In cases of robbery and burglary, however, American Indians received longer mean sentences than Caucasians. This initial evidence

Table 22.1 Mean Sentence Length by Type of Crime for Caucasians and American Indians, Arizona State Correctional Facilities, 1990

Offense Categories	Caucasians	American Indians
Assault		
Mean sentence (years)	14	8
Number of cases	2062	330
Sexual assault		
Mean sentence (years)	26	19
Number of cases	2094	110
Homicide[a]		
Mean sentence (years)	175	74
Number of cases	1238	94
Larceny		
Mean sentence (years)	4	4
Number of cases	4752	236
Burglary		
Mean sentence (years)	6	8
Number of cases	2480	893

[a] Means include death and life sentences. These sentences were recorded to maintain distinctions between sentences.

suggests the possibility of a systematic pattern of bias in how Caucasians and American Indians are sentenced based on the type of crime committed. For American Indians, property crimes are the ones that draw the harsher sentences, while for Caucasians, it is violent crimes. Other factors may, of course, be responsible for these sentencing differences other than a defendant's race. To examine the simultaneous influences of all independent variables, OLS regression analyses predicting sentence length within each type of crime were next conducted.

Table 22.2 presents the results of OLS regression analyses predicting the sentence length received for American Indian and Caucasian defendants by type of crime while controlling for the offender's age, gender, education, and prior felony convictions. Analyses were performed separately for each type of crime. Recall that the variable indicating racial status was coded 1 for American Indians, and 0 for Caucasians. Thus, a positive coefficient for this variable indicates that American Indians received longer sentences for the crime of interest than their Caucasian counterparts, net of the other variables; a negative coefficient indicates that Caucasian defendants received longer sentences.

Table 22.2 Results of Regression Analysis Predicting Sentence Length Received by Crime, 1990

Offense Categories	B	SE(B)	T	R^2
Assault				
Age	2.8	1.49	1.4	.15
Gender	3.9	6.22	.9	
American Indian	-5.8	4.74	−1.2	
Prior record	6.2	3.12	3.2**	
Education	−4.1	3.22	−1.5	
Sexual Assault				
Age	1.9	1.39	1.4	.19
Gender	6.4	3.92	3.2**	
American Indian	−8.2	7.56	−1.7	
Prior record	8.5	2.12	3.1**	
Education	−2.7	2.39	−1.1	
Homicide				
Age	2.4	1.29	2.2*	.18
Gender	5.5	7.5	2.0*	
American Indian	−7.8	8.34	−2.3*	
Prior record	9.8	3.42	3.4**	
Education	3.4	2.73	−1.2	
Larceny				
Age	2.9	1.76	2.1*	.21
Gender	6.9	8.32	1.2	
American Indian	4.0	4.99	.5	
Prior record	5.5	3.41	4.1**	
Education	−3.3	2.36	−1.1	
Burglary				
Age	3.1	1.89	2.0*	.21
Gender	4.6	7.32	.8	
American Indian	4.9	5.84	1.9*	
Prior record	5.9	2.88	3.9**	
Education	−4.9	2.92	−1.3	

** Indicates coefficient significant at the $p < .05$ level.
** Indicates coefficient significant at the $p < .01$ level.

For the crime of homicide, Caucasian defendants received significantly longer sentences than American Indians, even after controlling for the other variables. Age, gender, and prior record also affected the sentence length received by defendants. Older defendants received longer sentences than younger defendants, and males received longer sentences than females. Defendants who had previously been convicted of other felonies received longer sentences than those with no prior record.

In contrast, American Indian defendants received significantly longer sentences than Caucasians for both theft related crimes of robbery and burglary. Age and prior record also explained a significant amount of the variation in sentence length for these theft related crimes.

The only variable that predicted sentence length in a consistent manner across all types of crime was prior criminal record. Regardless of crime type and racial status, if a defendant had any prior felony convictions, he/she received a significantly longer sentence than those without a prior felony conviction. It should be noted, however, that prior record itself may be based upon differential and raced-based treatment. In other words, for certain crimes and for certain individuals, there may be a greater likelihood of official treatment and prosecution. Thus, it may be that minority offenders have a greater chance of receiving a prior record while Caucasians may be more likely to escape this labeling process.

Discussion

In this chapter, disparities in sentence length were examined between American Indian and Caucasian inmates incarcerated in Arizona while simultaneously controlling for prior felony record, age, gender, and educational level. When prior felony record and other demographic variables were controlled in multivariate models predicting sentence length, the crimes of robbery and burglary were the only crimes for which American Indians received longer sentences than Caucasians convicted of the same offense. Caucasian defendants received significantly longer sentences than American Indians for cases of homicide. A defendant's prior felony record was the only variable that consistently increased the length of sentence received by defendants across all types of crime. These findings are consistent with research that has found other minorities to be treated more severely for property offenses, while Caucasians were treated more severely for violent offenses (Bachman, Alvarez, and Perkins, 1996; Kelly, 1976; Thomson and Zingraff, 1981).

It is useful to draw upon Hawkins' (1986, 1987) work to aid in interpretation of these findings. Recognizing the limitations of traditional theoretical formulations regarding the relationship between race and social control, Hawkins (1987) contends that harsh sanctions will be given for offenses perpetrated by African Americans against Caucasians who are in positions of authority and/or who are strangers to the offender, while offenses by Caucasians against African Americans would be less severely punished. Based on the empirical evidence in the empirical evidence in the literature (Baldus, Pulaski, and Woodworth, 1983; Bowers and Pierce, 1980; Johnson, 1941; LaFree, 1980; Myers, 1979; Paternoster, 1983; Radelet, 1981), Hawkins (1987) suggests a "hierarchy of seriousness" of crime based not only on the race of the offender, but also on the race of the victim. In addition to the empirical patterns he discusses, these hypotheses were also predicated on two justifications. The first is the notion that offenses in which African Americans victimize Caucasians would be the most harshly punished because such acts represent the greatest threat to the Caucasian structure of authority. That is, unlike other racial combinations, African American offenses against Caucasians represent both symbolic and instrumental attacks on the existing state authority which, Hawkins (1987) contends, is stratified by race. The second explanation centers exclusively around the race of the victim, not on the dyadic relationship between victim and offender. Based on the unique history of African Americans in the United States, particularly the slavery era, this explanation posits that African American lives have a devalued status in this country compared to Caucasians. Therefore, offenses against Caucasians in general will be more severely punished than those against African

Americans regardless of the race of the offender. For Hawkins, the fact that empirical studies sometimes find minorities are treated more harshly than Caucasians, and other times more leniently, is potentially consistent with his theoretical propositions. This argument can also be extended to the sentencing disparities found here between American Indians and Caucasians.

The work of Donald Black (1976, 1989) is also of special interest here as he suggests an alternative argument to the issue of the discriminatory application of law that in many ways augments the work of conflict theorists such as Hawkins (1986, 1987). While conflict theorists usually rely on macro-structural analysis, Black (1976, 1989) had relied more on a micro-interactional analysis to study the application of law. Utilizing a Weberian approach, some of his central assertions and conclusions augment and support those of conflict theory. Black's (1976, 1989) analysis suggests that the law is applied differentially based on the relative social distance between a complex network of social groupings. To illustrate this argument, Black (1989, 9–10) writes:

> We must consider simultaneously each adversary's social status in relation to the other's. This will show that any advantage associated with high status arises primarily when it entails social superiority over an opposing party, while any disadvantage of low status arises primarily when it entails inferiority. In fact, a high-status defendant accused of an offense against an equally high-status victim is likely to be handled more severely than a low-status defendant accused of an offense against an equally low-status victim. . . . all known legal systems tend to be relatively lenient when people of low status victimize their peers. . . . But when people offend a social superior or inferior, another pattern becomes evident.

Black (1976, 1989) also argues that, in some cases, because the criminality may not be viewed as seriously, minority defendants will be treated more leniently when their victim is also a member of a minority group. Black (1989, 10) notes in reference to the death penalty:

> In modern America, for example, a white convicted of killing a white is more likely to receive a capital punishment than a black convicted of killing a black. During a five-year period in the 1970's—in Florida, Georgia, Texas, and Ohio—Caucasians convicted of killing a white were about five times more likely to be sentenced to death than blacks convicted of killing a black. Blacks convicted of killing a black were sentenced to death in fewer than one percent of the cases.

In essence then, Black (1976, 1989) proposes an argument similar to conflict based theories; the law is applied differently depending on the social relationship between the actors involved in the justice drama. This differential application depends upon the hierarchical positioning of the actors vis-à-vis each other. Crimes between social "inferiors" are defined and treated more leniently than are crimes in which the victim is a social "superior" to the perpetrator.

These theoretical arguments are particularly relevant to the findings of this chapter. The disregard for African American life during the slavery era was comparable to the contempt experienced by the American Indians during the European colonization and subsequent expansion westward. The historical literature is replete with examples documenting the attitudes and actions that ultimately led to the widespread destruction of American Indian culture and life (Bachman, 1992; Stannard, 1992; Steele, 1994; Thornton, 1987). Fostered by prevalent racist beliefs, and aided by dehumanizing definitions and perceptions, the settlers, soldiers, traders, and politicians pursued policies that directly and indirectly degraded and destroyed American Indian culture and life. These stereotypic beliefs are not historic relics of a bygone age, safely relegated to the dead past. Contemporary research suggests that these stereotypical attitudes are alive and well among the general population today, particularly among those who live on or near American Indian populations (Bachman, 1992; Reddy,

1993; Zatz, Lujan, and Snyder-Joy, 1991). It is not unreasonable to suggest, then, that the status of American Indians may be deemed inferior to the status of being Caucasian in many regions of the United States.

With this assumption made, the theoretical arguments, as outlined by Hawkins (1986, 1987) and Black (1976, 1989), provide possible interpretations for the results of this present analysis. Because violent crime is primarily *intra*racial, it can be assumed that when American Indians assault and murder, they usually victimize other American Indians. Because the lives of American Indian victims may not be especially valued by U.S. society and the justice system, these American Indian defendants may receive more lenient sentences for their crime. In contrast, when a Caucasian assaults or kills, the victim is also usually Caucasian. This scenario, in contrast, would result in a sentence that is correspondingly more severe because Caucasian life, according to Hawkins (1987), is more highly valued. It should be noted that this also corresponds to the arguments proposed by Black (1976, 1989). As Black (1989, 10) asserts, "A high-status defendant accused of an offense against an equally high-status victim is likely to be handled more severely than a low-status defendant accused of an offense against an equally low-status victim." This argument can also be used to explain the fact that American Indians were sentenced more severely for property offenses than were Caucasians. Because property crime is more often *inter*racial, American Indians are more likely to have victimized higher-status Caucasians when they commit crimes such as robbery and burglary and, thus, would theoretically be more likely to receive harsher sentences. In the absence of information on the race of the victim, however, these interpretations are speculative at best.

What is clear from this research is the need for more crime-specific analyses to investigate discriminatory practices in processing and sentencing minority group members, especially American Indians who have been particularly underrepresented in the scholarly literature. Although this chapter has suggested some possible interpretations of the sentencing disparities observed between American Indians and Caucasians in the state of Arizona, more definitive and conclusive insights and understanding cannot be achieved without more complete information on the race of the victims and how American Indians are treated at different stages of the justice process. Additionally, this chapter has suggested possible theoretical interpretations to help explain the anomalous results found in this analysis as well as past research. It is hoped that this work will provide an impetus to further research investigating the discriminatory application of the law as it impacts American Indians.

Notes

1. The term *American Indian* is utilized in this chapter for a number of reasons. Although the preferred method would be to refer to American Indians by their affiliations, this is not possible in this study since Arizona contains numerous tribes and these data do not identify the offenders's tribal affiliation. In the absence of this alternative, *American Indian* and *Native American* remain as the most acceptable alternatives. Among scholars, non-Indians and Indians alike, there is no clear agreement as to which term is preferable. The reader is referred to Axtell (1988), Deloria (1974), Giago (1991), Mann (1993), and Utter (1993) for a thorough review of this issue. One shortcoming of the term *Native American* is that it can refer to anyone born in America. Additionally, *Native American* is a broadly-defined term that typically includes Hawaiian Islanders, Aleuts, and Inuits, and the term *American Indian* typically refers only to indigenous peoples from the contiguous forty-eight states. For these reasons, the term *American Indian* is utilized throughout this chapter.
2. For a detailed accounting of the state correctional facility population in Arizona for 1990, see *Arizona Department of Corrections: 1990 Annual Report*, published by the Planning Bureau of the Arizona Department of Corrections.
3. This recoding was carried out in order to maintain a distinction between regular sentence lengths, life sentences, and sentences of death.
4. It is very difficult to operationally define American Indians as a racial/ethnic group because not everyone agrees on just *who* an American Indian is. For example, according to the federal government's Bureau of Indian Affairs (BIA), an American Indian is legally defined as a person who is an enrolled or registered member of a tribe or whose blood quantum is one-fourth or more genealogically derived. This level varies, however, with some tribe setting their blood quantum requirements much lower and some setting them much higher.

   It would be an almost impossible task to operationally define what is meant by *American Indian* here as there were numerous points in the adjudication process at which an individual may have been labeled "American Indian." It is assumed, however, that a defendant (ultimately inmate) self-classified him/herself as American Indian during the intake process. This is similar to the manner in which the U.S. Bureau of the Census estimates the American Indian population in the United States. For purposes of this study, then, American Indians are assumed to represent all those who self-classified themselves as such.

References

Adams, K. C. and Cutshall, C. R. 1987. Refusing to prosecute minor offenses: The relative influence of legal and extralegal factors. *Justice Quarterly* 4: 595–630.

Axtell, J. 1988. *After Columbus: Essays in ethnohistory of colonial North America.* New York: Oxford University Press.

Bachman, R. 1992. *Death and violence on the reservation.* New York: Auburn House.

Bachman, R. (in press). Victim's perceptions of initial police responses to robbery and aggravated assault: Does race matter? *Journal of Quantitative Criminology.*

Bachman, R., Alvarez, A., and Perkins, C. 1996. The discriminatory imposition of the law: Does it affect sentencing outcomes for American Indians? In *Native Americans, crime and justice*, eds. M. Nielsen and R. Silverman. Boulder, CO: Westview Press.

Baldus, D. C., Pulaski, C., and Woodworth, G. 1983. Comparative review of death sentences. *Journal of Criminal Law and Criminology* 74: 661–753.

Bishop, D. M. and Frazier, C. E. 1988. The influence of race in juvenile justice processing *Journal of Research in Crime and Delinquency* 25: 242–63.

Black, D. 1976. *The behavior of law.* New York: Academic Press.

———. 1989. *Sociological justice.* New York: Oxford University Press.

Blumstein, A. 1982. On the racial disproportionality of United States' prison populations. *Journal of Criminal Law and Criminology* 73: 1259–81.

Bonta, J. 1989. Native inmates: Institutional response, risk, and needs. *Canadian Journal of Criminology* 29: 49–62.

Bortner, M. and Reed, W. 1985. The preeminence of process: An example of refocused justice research. *Social Science Quarterly* 25: 413–25.

Bowers, W. J. and Pierce, G. L. 1980. Arbitrariness and discrimination under post-Furman capital statutes. *Crime and Delinquency* 26:563–635.

Bridges, G. S. and Crutchfield, R. D. 1988. Law, social standing, and racial disparities in imprisonment. *Social Forces* 66: 699–724.

Bridges, G. S., Crutchfield, R. D., and Simpson, E. E. 1987. Crime, social structure, and criminal punishment: White and nonwhite rates of imprisonment. *Social Problems* 34:345–60.

Bynum, T. 1981. Parole decision making and Native Americans. In *Race, crime, and criminal justice*, eds. R. L. McNeely and C. E. Pope. Beverly Hills, CA: Sage.

Bynum, T. and Paternoster, R. 1984. Discrimination revisited: An exploration of frontstage and backstage criminal justice decision making. *Sociology and Social Research* 69: 90–108.

Chambliss, W. J. 1993a. On lawmaking. In *Making law: The state, the law, and structural contradictions*, eds. W. J. Chambliss and M. S. Zatz. Bloomington: Indiana University Press.

———. 1993b. The creation of criminal law and crime control in Britain and America. In *Making law: The state, the law, and structural contradictions*, eds. W. J. Chambliss and M. S. Zatz. Bloomington: Indiana University Press.

Chambliss, W. J. and Seidman, R. D. 1971. *Law, order, and power.* Reading, MA: Adison-Wesley Publishing Co.

Chiricos, T. G. and Waldo, G. P. 1975. Socioeconomic status and criminal sentencing: An empirical assessment of a conflict proposition. *American Sociological Review* 40: 753–72.

Conley, D. J. 1994. Adding color to a Black and White picture: Using qualitative data to explain racial disproportionality in the juvenile justice system. *Journal of Research in Crime and Delinquency* 31: 135–48.

Crutchfield, R. D., Bridges, G. S., and Pitchford, S. R. 1994. Analytical and aggregation biases in analyses of imprisonment: Reconciling discrepancies in studies of racial disparity. *Journal of Research in Crime and Delinquency* 31: 166–82.

Dannefer, D., and Schutt, R. 1982. Race and juvenile justice processing in court and police agencies. *American Journal of Sociology* 87:113–32.

D'Allessio, S. J. and Stolzenberg, L. 1993. Socioeconomic status and the sentencing of the traditional offender. *Journal of Criminal Justice* 21: 61–77.

Deloria, V. Jr. 1974. *The Indian affair.* New York: Friendship Press.

Feimer, S., Pommersheim, F., and Wise, S. 1990. Marking time: Does race make a difference? A study of disparate sentencing in South Dakota. *Journal of Crime and Justice* 13: 86–102.

Flowers, R. B. 1990. *Minorities and criminality.* New York: Praeger.

Frazier, C. E., Bishop, D. M., and Henretta. J. C. 1992. The social context of race differentials in juvenile justice dispositions. *The Sociological Quarterly* 33: 447–58.

French, L. ed. 1982. *Indians and criminal justice.* Allanheld: Osmun Publishers.

Giago, T. 1991. What do you call an Indian? *Lakota Times*, December 14.

Gordon, D. M. 1973. Capitalism, class, and crime in America. *Crime and Delinquency* 19: 163–86.

Green, D. E. 1991. American Indian criminality: What do we really know? In *American Indians: Social justice and public policy*, eds. D. E. Green and T. V. Tonnessen. Madison, WI: University of Wisconsin System Institute on Race and Ethnicity.

Griffiths, C. T. and Yerbury, J. C. 1984. Natives and criminal justice policy: The case of native policing. *Canadian Journal of Criminology* 26: 147–60.

Gross, S. R. and Mauro, R. 1984. Patterns of death: An analysis of racial disparities in capital sentencing and homicide victimization. *Stanford Law Review* 37: 27–153.

Hall, E. and Simkus, A. A. 1975. Inequality in the types of sentences received by Native Americans and Whites. *Criminology* 13: 199–222.

Hawkins, D. F. 1986. Devalued lives and racial stereotypes: Ideological barriers to the prevention of family violence among Blacks. In *Violence in the Black family*, ed. R. L. Hampton. Lexington, MA: Lexington Books.

Hawkins, D. F. 1987. Beyond anomalies: Rethinking the conflict perspective on race and criminal punishment. *Social Forces* 65: 719–45.

Hills, S. 1971. *Crime, power, and morality*. Scranton, PA: Chandler.

Johnson, G. B. 1941. The Negro and crime. *The Annals of the American Academy of Political and Social Sciences* 217: 93–104.

Kelly, H. E. 1976. A comparison of defense strategy and race as influences in differential sentencing. *Criminology* 14: 241–49.

Kleck, G. 1981. Racial discrimination in criminal sentencing: A critical evaluation of the evidence with additional evidence on the death penalty. *American Sociological Review* 46:783–95.

LaFree. G. D. 1980. The effect of sexual stratification by race on official reactions to rape. *American Sociological Review* 45: 842–54.

Langan, P. A. 1985. Racism on trial: New evidence to explain the racial composition of prisons in the United States. *The Journal of Criminal Law and Criminology* 76: 666–83.

LaPrairie, C. P. 1984. Selected criminal justice and sociodemogaphic data on native women. *Canadian Journal of Criminology* 26: 161–70.

Leiber, M. J. 1994. A comparison of juvenile court outcomes for Native Americans, African Americans, and Whites. *Justice Quarterly* 11: 257–79.

Levy, J. E., Kunitz, S. J., and Everett, M. 1969. Navajo criminal homicide. *Southwestern Journal of Anthropology* 25: 124–52.

Lynch, M. J. and Patterson, E. B. eds.. 1991. *Race and criminal justice*. New York: Harrow and Heston.

Mann, C. R. 1993. *Unequal justice: A question of color*. Bloomington: Indiana University Press.

Miethe, T. D. 1987. Stereotypical conceptions and criminal processing: The case of the victim-offender relationship. *Justice Quarterly* 4: 571–93.

Miethe, T. D. and Moore. C. A. 1986. Racial differences in criminal processing: The consequences of model selection on conclusion about differential treatment. *Sociological Quarterly* 27: 217–37.

Myers, M. A. 1979. Offended parties and official reactions: Victims and the sentencing of criminal defendants. *Sociological Quarterly* 20: 529–40.

Paternoster, R. 1983. Race of victim and location of crime: The decision to seek the death penalty in South Carolina. *Journal of Criminal Law and Criminology* 74: 754–85.

Peak. K. and Spencer, J. 1987. Crime in Indian country: another "trail of tears." *Journal of Criminal Justice* 15: 485–94.

Petersilia, J. 1983. *Racial disparities in the criminal justice system*. Santa Monica. CA: Rand.

Peterson, R. D. and Hagan, J. 1984. Changing conceptions of race: Towards an account of anomalous findings of sentencing research. *American Sociological Review* 49: 56–70.

Pommersheim, F. and Wise, S. 1989. Going to the penitentiary: A study of disparate sentencing in South Dakota. *Criminal Justice and Behavior* 16: 155–65.

Pope, C. and Feyerheim. W. 1990a. Minority status and juvenile justice processing: An assessment of the research literature. *Criminal Justice Abstracts* June: 327–35.

———. 1990b. Minority status and juvenile justice processing: An assessment of the research literature. *Criminal Justice Abstracts* September: 527–42.

Quinney, R. 1970. *The social reality of crime*. Boston: Little, Brown.

———. 1979. *Criminology* (2nd ed.). Boston: Little, Brown.

Radelet, M. L. 1981. Racial characteristics and the imposition of the death penalty. *American Sociological Review* 46: 918–27.

Reddy, M. A. 1993. *Statistical record of native North Americans*. Detroit, MI: Gale Research Inc.

Spitzer, S. 1975. Toward a Marxian theory of deviance. *Social Problems* 22: 638–51.

Spohn, C. and Welch, S. 1987. The effect of prior record in sentencing research: An examination of the assumption that any measure is adequate. *Justice Quarterly* 4: 287–307.

Stannard, D. E. 1992. *American holocaust*. New York: Oxford University Press.

Steele, I. K. 1994. *Warpaths: Invasions of North America*. New York: Oxford University Press.

Stewart, O. 1964. Questions regarding American Indian criminality. *Human Organization* 23: 61–66.

Stratton, J. 1973. Cops and drunks: Police attitudes and actions in dealing with Indian drunks. *International Journal of Addictions* 8: 613–21.

Swift, B. and Bickel, G. 1974. *Comparative parole treatment of American Indians and non-Indians at U.S. federal prisons*. Washington, DC: Bureau of Social Science Research.

Swigert, V. L. and Farrell, R. A. 1977. Normal homicides and the law. *American Sociological Review* 42: 16–32.

Thomson, R. J. and Zingraff, M. J. 1981. Detecting sentencing disparity: Some problems and evidence. *American Journal of Sociology* 86:869–80.

Thornton, R. 1987. *American Indian holocaust and survival*. Norman: University of Oklahoma Press.

Tonry, M. 1994. Racial disproportion in US prisons. *British Journal of Criminology* 34: 97–115.

———. 1995. *Malign neglect: Race, crime, and punishment in America*. New York: Oxford University Press.

Turk, A. T. 1969. *Criminality and the legal order*. New York: Rand McNally.

Utter, J. 1993. *American Indians: Answers to today's questions*. Lake Ann, MI: National Woodlands Publishing Company.

U.S. Department of Justice. 1992) *Uniform crime reports for the United States: Crime in the United States*. Washington, DC: U.S. Government Printing Office.

Welch, S., Gruhl, J., and Spohn, C. 1984. Sentencing: The influence of alternative measures of prior record. *Criminology* 22: 215–22.

Welch, S. and Spohn, C. 1986. Evaluating the impact of prior record on judges' sentencing decisions: A seven-city comparison. *Justice Quarterly* 3: 389–407.

Williams, L. E. 1979. *Antecedents of urban Indian crime*. Unpublished doctoral dissertation, Brigham Young University, Provo, UT.

Wolfgang, M. E. and Reidel, M. 1973. Race, judicial discretion, and the death penalty. *The Annals of the American Academy of Political and Social Science* 407: 119–33.

Young, T. J. 1990. Native American crime and criminal justice require criminologists' attention, *Journal of Criminal Justice Education* 1: 111–16.

Zatz, M. S., Lujan, C. C., and Snyder-Joy, Z. K. 1991. American Indians and criminal justice: Some conceptual and metholodological considerations. In *Race and criminal justice*, eds. M. J. Lynch and E. B. Patterson. New York: Harrow and Heston.

Zimring, F. E., Eigen, J., and O'Malley, S. 1976. Punishing homicide in Philadelphia: Perspectives on the death penalty. *University of Chicago Law Review* 43: 227–52.

23

The New "Peculiar Institution"

On the Prison as Surrogate Ghetto

Loïc Wacquant

Vehicles for Labor Extraction and Caste Division

America's first three "peculiar institutions," slavery, Jim Crow, and the ghetto, have this in common that they were all instruments for the conjoint *extraction of labor* and *social ostracization* of an outcast group deemed unassimilable by virtue of the indelible threefold stigma it carries. African-Americans arrived under bondage in the land of freedom. They were accordingly deprived of the right to vote in the self-appointed cradle of democracy (until 1965 for residents of the southern states). And, for lack of a recognizable national affiliation, they were shorn of ethnic honor, which implies that, rather than simply standing at the bottom of the rank ordering of group prestige in American society, they were barred from it *ab initio.*[1]

Slavery is a highly malleable and versatile institution that can be harnessed to a variety of purposes (Drescher and Engerman, 1998) but in the Americas property-in-person was geared primarily toward the provision and control of labor. Its introduction in the Chesapeake, Middle Atlantic, and Low Country regions of the United States in the seventeenth century served to recruit and regulate the unfree workforce forcibly imported from Africa and the West Indies to cater to their tobacco, rice, and mixed-farming economy. (Indentured laborers from Europe and native Indians were not enslaved because of their greater capacity to resist and because their servitude would have impeded future immigration as well as rapidly exhausted a limited supply of labor.) By the close of the eighteenth century, slavery had become self-reproducing and had expanded to the fertile crescent of the southern interior, running from South Carolina to Louisiana, where it supplied a highly profitable organization of labor for cotton production and the basis for a plantation society distinctive for its feudal-like culture, politics, and psychology (Wright, 1978; Kolchin, 1993).

An *unforeseen by-product* of the systematic enslavement and dehumanization of Africans and their descendants on North American soil was the creation of a racial caste line separating what would later become labeled "blacks" and "whites." As Barbara Fields (1990) has shown, the American ideology of "race," as putative biological division anchored by the inflexible application of the "one-drop rule" together with the principle of hypodescent, crystallized to resolve the blatant contradiction between human bondage and democracy. The religious and pseudo-scientific belief in racial difference reconciled the brute fact of unfree labor with the doctrine of liberty premised on natural rights by reducing the slave to live property—three-fifths of a man according to the sacred scriptures of the Constitution.

Racial division was a consequence, not a precondition, of U.S. slavery, but once it was instituted it became detached from its initial function and acquired a social potency of its own. Emancipation thus created a double dilemma for southern white society: how to secure anew the labor of former slaves, without whom the region's economy would collapse, and how to sustain the cardinal status distinction between whites and "persons of color," i.e., the social and symbolic distance needed to prevent the odium of "amalgamation" with a group considered inferior, rootless, and vile. After a protracted interregnum lasting into the 1890s, during which early white hysteria gave way to partial if inconsistent relaxation of ethnoracial strictures, when blacks were allowed to vote, to hold public office, and even to mix with whites to a degree in keeping with the intergroup intimacy fostered by slavery, the solution came in the form of the "Jim Crow" regime.[2] It consisted of an ensemble of social and legal codes that prescribed the complete separation of the "races" and sharply circumscribed the life chances of African-Americans (Woodward, 1957) while binding them to whites in a relation of suffusive submission backed by legal coercion and terroristic violence.

Imported from the North where it had been experimented in cities, this regime stipulated that blacks travel in separate trains, streetcars, and waiting rooms; that they reside in the "darktown" slums and be educated in separate schools (if at all); that they patronize separate service establishments and use their own bathrooms and water fountains; that they pray in separate churches, entertain themselves in separate clubs and sit in separate "nigger galleries" in theaters; that they receive medical care in separate hospitals and exclusively from "colored" staff; and that they be incarcerated in separate cells and buried in separate cemeteries. Most crucial of all, laws joined mores in condemning the "unspeakable crime" of interracial marriage, cohabitation, or mere sexual congress so as to uphold the "supreme law of self-preservation" of the races and the myth of innate white superiority. Through continued white ownership of the land and the generalization of sharecropping and debt peonage, the plantation system remained virtually untouched as former slaves became a "dependent, property less peasantry, nominally free, but ensnared by poverty, ignorance, and the new servitude of tenantry" (McMillen, 1990: 126). While sharecropping tied African-American labor to the farm, a rigid etiquette ensured that whites and blacks never interacted on a plane of equality, not even on the track field or in a boxing ring—a Birmingham ordinance of 1930 made it unlawful for them to play at checkers and dominoes with one another.[3] Whenever the "color line" was breached or even brushed, a torrent of violence was unleashed in the form of periodic pogroms, Ku Klux Klan and vigilante raids, public floggings, mob killings and lynchings, this ritual caste murder designed to keep "uppity niggers" in their appointed place. All this was made possible by the swift and near-complete disenfranchisement of blacks as well as by the enforcement of "Negro law" by courts which granted the latter fewer effective legal safeguards than slaves had enjoyed earlier by dint of being both property and persons.

The sheer brutality of caste oppression in the South, the decline of cotton agriculture due to floods and the boll weevil, and the pressing shortage of labor in northern factories caused by the outbreak of the First World War created the impetus for African-Americans to emigrate en masse to the booming industrial centers of the Midwest and Northeast (over 1.5 million left in 1910–30, followed by another 3 million in 1940–1960). But as migrants from Mississippi to the Carolinas flocked to the northern metropolis, what they discovered there was not the "promised land" of equality and full citizenship but another system of racial enclosure, the ghetto, which, though it was less rigid and fearsome than the one they had fled, was no less encompassing and constricting. To be sure, greater freedom to come and go in public places and to consume in regular commercial establishments, the disappearance of the humiliating signs pointing to "Colored" here and "White" there, renewed access to the ballot box and protection from the courts, the possibility of limited economic advancement, release from personal subservience and from the dread of omnipresent white violence, all made life in the urban North incomparably preferable to continued peonage in the rural South: it was "better to be a lamppost in Chicago than President of Dixie," as migrants famously put it to Richard Wright. But restrictive covenants forced African-Americans to congregate in a "Black Belt" which quickly became overcrowded, underserved, and blighted by crime, disease, and dilapidation, while the "job ceiling" restricted them to the most hazardous, menial, and underpaid occupations in both industry and personal services. As for "social equality," understood as the possibility of "becoming members of white cliques, churches, and voluntary associations, or marrying into their families," it was firmly and definitively denied (Drake and Cayton, 1962 [1945], vol. 1: 112–28).

Blacks had entered the Fordist industrial economy, to which they contributed a vital source of abundant and cheap labor willing to ride along its cycles of boom and bust. Yet they remained locked in a precarious position of structural economic marginality and consigned to a secluded and dependent microcosm, complete with its own internal division of labor, social stratification, and agencies of collective voice and symbolic representation: a "city within the city" moored in a complexus of black churches and press, businesses and professional practices, fraternal lodges and communal associations that provided both a "milieu for Negro Americans in which they [could] imbue their lives with meaning" and a bulwark "to 'protect' white America from 'social contact' with Negroes" (Drake and Cayton, 1962 [1945], vol. 2: xiv). Continued caste hostility from without and renewed ethnic affinity from within converged to create the ghetto as the third vehicle to extract black labor while keeping black bodies at a safe distance, to the material and symbolic benefit of white society.

The era of the ghetto as paramount mechanism of ethnoracial domination had opened with the urban riots of 1917–1919 (in East St. Louis, Chicago, Longview, Houston, etc.). It closed with a wave of clashes, looting, and burning that rocked hundreds of American cities from coast to coast, from the Watts uprising of 1965 to the riots of rage and grief triggered by the assassination of Martin Luther King in the summer of 1968 (Kerner Commission, 1988). Indeed, by the end of the 1960s, the ghetto was well on its way to becoming functionally obsolete or, to be more precise, increasingly *unsuited* to accomplishing the twofold task historically entrusted to America's "peculiar institutions." On the side of *labor extraction*, the shift from an urban industrial economy to a suburban service economy and the accompanying dualization of the occupational structure, along with the upsurge of working-class immigration from Mexico, the Caribbean and Asia, meant that large segments of the workforce contained in the "Black Belts" of the northern metropolis were simply no longer needed. On the side of *ethnoracial closure*, the decades-long mobilization of African-Americans against caste rule finally succeeded, in the propitious political conjuncture of crisis stemming from the Vietnam war and assorted social unrest, in forcing the federal state to dismantle the legal machinery of caste exclusion. Having secured voting and civil rights, blacks were at long last full citizens who would no longer brook being shunted off into the separate and inferior world of the ghetto.[4]

But, while whites begrudgingly accepted "integration" in principle, in practice they strove to maintain an unbridgeable social and symbolic gulf with their compatriots of African descent. They abandoned public schools, shunned public space, and fled to the suburbs in the millions to avoid mixing and ward off the specter of "social equality" in the city. They then turned against the welfare state and those social programs upon which the collective advancement of blacks was most dependent. *A contrario*, they extended enthusiastic support for the "law-and-order" policies that vowed to firmly repress urban disorders connately perceived as racial threats (Edsall and Edsall, 1991; Quadagno, 1994; Beckett and Sasson, 2000: 49–74). Such policies pointed to yet another special institution capable of confining and controlling, if not the entire African-American community, at least its most disruptive, disreputable and dangerous members: the prison.

The Ghetto as Ethnoracial Prison, the Prison as Judicial Ghetto

To grasp the deep kinship between ghetto and prison, which helps explain how the structural decline and functional redundancy of the one led to the unexpected ascent and astonishing growth of the other during the last quarter-century,[5] it is necessary first to characterize accurately the ghetto. But here we come upon the troublesome fact that the social sciences have failed to develop a robust *analytic concept* of the ghetto; instead they have been content to borrow the *folk concept* current in political and popular discourse at each epoch. This has caused a good deal of confusion, as the ghetto has been successively conflated with—and mistaken for—a segregated district, an ethnic neighborhood, a territory of intense poverty or housing blight and even, with the rise of the policy myth of the "underclass" in the more recent period, a mere accumulation of urban pathologies and antisocial behaviors.[6]

A comparative and historical sociology of the reserved Jewish quarters in the cities of Renaissance Europe and of America's "Bronzeville" in the Fordist metropolis of the twentieth century reveals that a ghetto is essentially a sociospatial device that enables a dominant status group in an urban setting simultaneously to *ostracize and exploit* a subordinate group endowed with *negative symbolic capital*, that is, an incarnate property perceived to make its contact degrading by virtue of what Max Weber calls "negative social estimation of honor." Put differently, it is a *relation* of ethnoracial control and closure built out of four elements:

1. stigma;
2. constraint;
3. territorial confinement; and
4. institutional encasement.

The resulting formation is a distinct *space*, containing an ethnically homogeneous *population*, which finds itself forced to develop within it a set of interlinked *institutions* that duplicates the organizational framework of the broader society from which that group is banished and supplies the scaffolding for the construction of its specific "style of life" and social strategies. This parallel institutional nexus affords the subordinate group a measure of protection, autonomy, and dignity, but at the cost of locking it in a relationship of structural subordination and dependency.

The ghetto, in short, operates as an *ethnoracial prison*: it encages a dishonored category and severely curtails the life chances of its members in support of the "monopolization of ideal and material goods or opportunities" by the dominant status group (Weber, 1978: 935) dwelling on its outskirts. Recall that the ghettos of early modern Europe were typically delimited by high walls with one or more gates which were locked at night and within which Jews had to return before sunset on pain of severe punishment (Wirth, 1928: 32), and that their perimeter was subjected to continuous monitoring by external authorities. Note next the structural and functional homologies with the prison conceptualized as a *judicial ghetto*: a jail or penitentiary is in effect a reserved *space* which serves to forcibly confine a legally denigrated *population* and wherein this latter evolves its distinctive *institutions*, culture, and sullied identity. It is thus formed of the same four fundamental constituents, stigma, coercion, physical enclosure and organizational parallelism and insulation, that make up a ghetto, and for similar purposes.

Much as the ghetto protects the city's residents from the pollution of intercourse with the tainted but necessary bodies of an outcast group in the manner of an "urban condom," as Richard Sennett (1994: 237) vividly put it in his depiction of the "fear of touching" in sixteenth-century Venice, the prison cleanses the social body from the temporary blemish of those of its members who have committed crimes, that is, following Durkheim, individuals who have violated the socio-moral integrity of the collectivity by infringing on "definite and strong states of the collective conscience."

Students of the "inmate society" from Donald Clemmer and Gresham Sykes to James Jacobs and John Irwin have noted time and again how the incarcerated develop their own argot roles, exchange systems, and normative standards, whether as an adaptive response to the "pains of imprisonment" or through selective importation of criminal and lower-class values from the outside, much like residents of the ghetto have elaborated or intensified a "separate sub-culture" to counter their sociosymbolic immurement (Drake and Cayton, 1962 [1945], vol. 2: xiii). As for the secondary aim of the ghetto, to facilitate exploitation of the interned category, it was central to the "house of correction" which is the direct historical predecessor of the modern prison and it has periodically played a major role in the evolution and operation of the latter (Spierenburg, 1991).[7] Finally, both prison and ghetto are authority structures saddled with inherently dubious or problematic legitimacy whose maintenance is ensured by intermittent recourse to external force.

By the end of the 1970s, then, as the racial and class backlash against the democratic advances won by the social movements of the preceding decade got into full swing, the prison abruptly returned to the forefront of American society and offered itself as the universal and simplex solution to all manners of social problems. Chief among these problems was the "breakdown" of social order in the "inner city," which is scholarly and policy euphemism for the patent incapacity of the dark ghetto to contain a dishonored and supernumerary population henceforth viewed not only as deviant and devious but as downright dangerous in light of the violent urban upheavals of the mid-1960s. As the walls of the ghetto shook and threatened to crumble, the walls of the prison were correspondingly extended, enlarged, and fortified, and "confinement of differentiation," aimed at keeping a group apart (the etymological meaning of *segregare*), gained primacy over "confinement of safety" and "confinement of authority"—to use the distinction proposed by French sociologist Claude Faugeron (1995). Soon the black ghetto, converted into an instrument of naked exclusion by the concurrent retrenchment of wage labor and social protection, and further destabilized by the increasing penetration of the penal arm of the state, became bound to the jail and prison system by a triple relationship of functional equivalency, structural homology, and cultural syncretism, such that they now constitute a single *carceral continuum* which entraps a redundant population of younger black men (and increasingly women) who circulate in closed circuit between its two poles in a self-perpetuating cycle of social and legal marginality with devastating personal and social consequences.[8]

Now, the carceral system had already functioned as an *ancillary* institution for caste preservation and labor control in America during one previous transition between regimes of racial domination, that between slavery and Jim Crow in the South. On the morrow of Emancipation, southern prisons turned black overnight as "thousands of ex-slaves were being arrested, tried, and convicted for acts that in the past had been dealt with by the master alone" (Oshinsky, 1996: 32) and for refusing to behave as menials and follow the demeaning rules of racial etiquette. Soon thereafter, the former confederate states innovated "convict leasing" as a response to the moral panic of "Negro crime" that presented the double advantage of generating prodigious funds for the state coffers and furnishing abundant bound labor to till the fields, build the levees, lay down the railroads, clean the swamps, and dig the mines of the region under murderous conditions.[9] Indeed, penal labor, in the form of the convict-lease and its heir, the chain gang, played a major role in the economic advancement of the New South during the Progressive era, as it "reconciled modernization with the continuation of racial domination" (Lichtenstein, 1999: 195).

What makes the racial intercession of the carceral system different today is that, unlike slavery, Jim Crow and the ghetto of the midcentury, it does not carry out a positive economic mission of recruitment and disciplining of the workforce: it serves only to warehouse the precarious and deproletarianized fractions of the black working class, be it that they cannot find employment owing to a combination of skills deficit, employer discrimination and competition from immigrants, or that they refuse to submit to the indignity of substandard work in the peripheral sectors of the service economy—what ghetto residents commonly label "slave jobs." But there is presently mounting financial and ideological pressure, as well as renewed political interest, to relax restrictions on penal labor so as to (re)introduce mass unskilled work in private enterprises inside American prisons (Wacquant, 1999: 82–3): putting most inmates to work would help lower the country's "carceral bill" as well as effectively extend to the inmate poor the workfare requirements now imposed upon the free poor as a requirement of citizenship.[10] The next decade will tell whether the prison remains an appendage to the dark ghetto or supersedes it to go it alone and become America's fourth "peculiar institution."

Notes

1. Among the groups commonly considered unassimilable, the Negro people is by far the largest. The Negroes do not, like the Japanese and the Chinese, have a politically organized nation and an accepted culture of their own outside of America to fall back upon. Unlike the Oriental, there attaches to the Negro an historical memory of slavery and inferiority. It is more difficult for them to answer prejudice with prejudice and, as the Orientals may do, to consider themselves and their history superior to the white Americans and their recent cultural achievements. The Negroes do not have these fortifications of self-respect. They are more helplessly *imprisoned* as a subordinate caste, a caste of people deemed to be lacking a cultural past and assumed to be incapable of a cultural future. (Myrdal, 1944: 54, emphasis added)
2. The term "Jim Crow" comes from a song and dance by that title first performed in 1828 by Thomas Dartmouth Rice (1808–1860), a popular traveling actor considered the father of the minstrel show, in which a blackfaced white minstrel caricatured the singing and dancing of African-American slaves. Such shows enjoyed great popularity in the United States as well as England, peaking in the decade leading to abolition.
3. The legislature of Mississippi went so far as to outlaw the advocacy of social equality between blacks and whites in a law of 1920 that subjected anyone "found guilty of printing, publishing or circulating printed, type-written or written matter urging or presenting for public acceptation or general information, arguments or suggestions in favor of social equality or of intermarriage" (cited in McMillen, 1990: 8–9) to a fine of $500 and six months' imprisonment.
4. This was the meaning of Martin Luther King's "Freedom Campaign" in the summer of 1966 in Chicago: it sought to apply to the ghetto the techniques of collective mobilization and civil disobedience used with success in the attack on Jim Crow in the South to reveal and protest "the slow, stifling death of a kind of concentration camp life" to which blacks were condemned in the northern metropolis (M. L. King, cited by Oates, 1982: 373). The campaign to "make Chicago an open city" was swiftly crushed by a formidable combination of state repression (spearheaded by 4,000 National Guard troops), white mob violence, vitriolic media campaigns of denunciation by the *Chicago Tribune* and *Chicago Sun Times*, furious resistance from City Hall, the real estate industry, and the courts, all with the knowing acquiescence of the White House and Congress.
5. It must be recalled that, as of the mid-1970s, the carceral population of the U.S. had been steadily declining for nearly two decades to reach a low of 380,000 inmates in 1975. The leading analysts of the penal question, from David Rothman to Michael Foucault to Alfred Blumstein, were then unanimous in predicting the imminent marginalization of the prison as an institution of social control or, in the worst-case scenario, the long-term stability of penal confinement at a historically moderate level. No one foresaw the impending quadrupling of America's incarcerated population over the ensuing 20 years, via runaway growth that has catapulted that figure past the 2-million mark in 2000 even as crime levels remained stagnant over that period.
6. See Wacquant (2000a) for a historical recapitulation of the meanings of "ghetto" in American society and social science, leading to a diagnosis of the curious expurgation of race from a concept expressly forged to denote a mechanism of ethnoracial domination, which ties it to the changing concerns of state elites over the nexus of poverty and ethnicity in the metropolis.
7. Describing the London Bridewell, the *Zuchthaus* of Amsterdam, and Paris's *Hôpital Général*, Rusche and Kirschheimer (1939: 42) write: "The essence of the house of correction was that it combined the principles of the poorhouse, workhouse and penal institution." Its main aim was "to make the labor power of the unwilling people socially useful" by forcing them to work under close supervision in the hope that, once released, "they would voluntarily swell the labor market."
8. A fuller discussion of this "deadly symbiosis" between ghetto and prison in the post-Civil Rights era is provided elsewhere (Wacquant, 2000b).
9. This is not a figure of speech: the annual mortality rate for convicts reached 16 percent in Mississippi in the 1880s, where "not a single leased convict ever lived long enough to serve a sentence of ten years or more" (Oshinsky, 1996: 46). Hundreds of black children, many as young as 6 years old, were leased by the state to the benefit of planters, businessmen and financiers, to toil in conditions that even some patrician southerners found shameful and "a stain upon our manhood."
10. Expert testimony presented to the Committees on the Judiciary and Crime of the U.S. House of Representatives during discussion of the "Prison Industries Reform Act of 1998" (still under deliberation at this writing) explicitly links welfare reform and the need to expand private prison labor.

References

Beckett, Katherine and Theodore Sasson. 2000. *The politics of injustice.* Thousand Oaks, CA: Pine Forge Press.

Berlin, Ira. 1998. *Many thousands gone: The first two centuries of slavery in north America.* Cambridge: Harvard University Press.

Drake, St. Clair and Horace Cayton. 1962 [1945]. *Black metropolis: A study of negro life in a northern city.* New York: Harper & Row.

Drescher, Seymour and Stanley L. Engerman. 1998. *A historical guide to world slavery.* New York: Oxford University Press.

Edsall, Thomas Byrne and Mary D. Edsall. 1991. *Chain reaction: The impact of race, rights, and taxes on American politics.* New York: W.W. Norton.

Faugeron, Claude. 1995. La dérive pénale. *Esprit* 215 (October): 132–44.

Fields, Barbara Jeanne. 1990. Slavery, race, and ideology in the United States of America, *New Left Review* 181 (May-June): 95–118.

Kerner Commission. 1988 [1968]. *The Kerner Report: The 1968 report of the national advisory commission on civil disorders.* New York: Pantheon.

Kolchin, Peter. 1993. *American slavery: 1619–1877.* New York: Hill & Wang.

Lichtenstein, Alex. 1999. *Twice the work of free labor: The oolitical economy of convict labor in the new south.* New York: Verso.

Litwack, Leon F. 1998. *Trouble in mind: Black southerners in the age of Jim Crow.* New York: Knopf.

McMillen, Neil R. 1990. *Dark journey: Black mississippians in the age of Jim Crow.* Urbana: University of Illinois Press.

Myrdal, Gunnar. 1944. *An American dilemma: The negro problem and modern democracy.* New York: Harper Torchbook.

Oates, Stephen B. 1982. *Let the trumpet sound: The life of Martin Luther King.* New York: New American Library.

Oshinsky, David M. 1996. *Worse than slavery: Parchman farm and the ordeal of Jim Crow justice.* New York: Free Press.

Quadagno, Jill. 1994 *The color of welfare: How racism undermined the war on poverty.* Oxford: Oxford University Press.

Rusche, Georg and Otto Kirschheimer. 1939. *Punishment and social structure.* New York: Columbia University Press.

Sennett, Richard. 1994. *Flesh and stone: The body and the city in western civilization.* New York: W.W. Norton.

Spear, Allan H. 1968. *Black Chicago: The making of a negro ghetto, 1890–1920.* Chicago: The University of Chicago Press.

Spierenburg, Pieter. 1991. *The prison experience: Disciplinary institutions and their inmates in early modern europe.* New Brunswick, NJ: Rutgers University Press.

Stampp, Kenneth M. 1956.*The peculiar institution: Slavery in the ante-bellum south.* New York: Vintage Books.

Tonry, Michael. 1995. *Malign neglect: Race, cClass, and punishment in America.* New York: Oxford University Press.

Wacquant, Loïc. 1998. Crime et châtiment en Amérique de Nixon à Clinton. *Archives de Politique Criminelle* 20 (Spring): 123–38.

Wacquant, Loïc. 1999. *Les prisons de la misère.* Paris: Editions Raisons d'Agir.

Wacquant, Loïc. 2000a. Gutting the ghetto: Political censorship and conceptual retrenchment in the American debate on urban destitution. In *Globalisation and the new city,* eds. Malcolm Cross and Robert Moore. Basingstoke: Macmillan.

Wacquant, Loïc. 2000b. Deadly symbiosis: When ghetto and prison meet and merge. Paper presented at the Conference "The Causes and Consequences of Mass Imprisonment in the USA," New York University School of Law, 26 February.

Weber, Max. 1978. *Economy and society,* eds Guenter Roth and Claus Wittich. Berkeley, CA: University of California Press.

Wirth, Louis. 1928. *The ghetto,* Chicago: The University of Chicago Press.

Woodward, C. Vann. 1957. *The strange career of Jim Crow,* 3rd rev. ed. New York: Oxford University Press.

Wright, Gavin. 1978. *The political economy of the cotton south.* New York: W.W. Norton.

24

Crack-ing Down on Black Drug Offenders?

*Testing for Interactions among Offenders' Race, Drug Type, and Sentencing Strategy in Federal Drug Sentences**

Paula Kautt and Cassia Spohn

Although charges of racial discrimination have been leveled at all stages of the criminal justice process, much of the harshest criticism has focused on judges' sentencing decisions. Critics of the sentencing process contend that crimes by racial minorities are punished more harshly than are similar crimes by equally culpable whites. Other scholars have challenged this assertion, contending that the harsher sentences imposed on racial minorities reflect the seriousness of their crimes and prior criminal records, as well as other legally relevant factors that judges consider in determining the appropriate sentence. The findings of over 40 years of research on the effect of race on sentencing have not resolved this debate (for reviews, see Chiricos & Crawford, 1995; Spohn, 2000; Zatz, 1987).

Partially as a result of such mixed findings, the past few decades have witnessed a virtual revolution in sentencing policies and practices. At both the state and federal levels, legislators have adopted sentencing reforms designed to curb judicial discretion and reduce the extra-legal disparity in sentences—particularly by defendants' race. As part of this mission, Congress passed the Sentencing Reform Act of 1984 (SRA), which established a guideline-based determinate sentencing system. During the same period, a "tough on crime" stance ruled many criminal justice organizations and issues. In accordance with this orientation, Congress also passed a series of mandatory penalty statutes for criminal behavior that it deemed particularly egregious. As a result of these congressional initiatives, federal criminal sentencing is currently ruled by two coexisting determinate sentencing strategies: the federal sentencing guidelines (hereafter guidelines) and federal mandatory minimums statutes (hereafter mandatory minimums). Although both are presumptive, the guidelines are based on past sentencing practices, while the mandatory minimums are meant to reflect the gravity of particular offenses. Both initiatives were intended to reduce the disparity in sentencing—particularly by extra-legal factors such as race (Myers, 1989)—by curtailing the allegedly exorbitant judicial discretion in sentencing that was thought to exist under the previous indeterminate system.

Although these interventions have been successful in some respects, the racial disparity in sentences for drug offenses has increased dramatically since they were introduced (Beck & Mumola, 1999;

*The views expressed in this research are solely those of the authors and do not necessarily reflect those of the Drug Enforcement Administration or the federal government.

Bonczar & Beck, 1997; Bureau of Justice Statistics, 1999; Tonry, 1995; Tonry & Hatlestad, 1997). Moreover, federal drug laws disproportionately affect racial minorities (United States Sentencing Commission, USSC, 1995) and research has uncovered racial variation in federal sentencing outcomes for drug offenses that legally relevant factors do not explain (Albonetti, 1997; General Accounting Office, GAO, 1992; Heaney, 1991; McDonald & Carlson, 1993; Meierhoefer, 1992; Schulhofer, 1992; Steffensmeier & Demuth, 2000; USSC, 1991a, 1991b). Thus, despite the racially neutral, legally relevant factors employed by both interventions, racial inequality persists in federal drug sentences.

However, before this disparity can be remedied, one must first identify its cause. The aforementioned research findings suggest a possible three-way interaction between a defendant's race, drugs, and sentencing strategy. Thus, our research tested this proposition under the assumption that racial discrimination in sentencing has changed forms—from overt to covert (Zatz, 1987)—with the most disguised forms the most prevalent and the most blatant forms a rarity in federal sentencing outcomes. This expectation specifically arises from the discretion limiting nature and intent of the guidelines and the mandatory minimums. In addition, we believe that each strategy interacts uniquely with legal (such as drug type) and extra-legal factors (like defendant's race) to produce persistent, albeit different, racial disparity in federal drug cases. We examined this possibility by assessing whether predictors of sentencing outcomes for 1997–1998 drug offenses varied between the two main racial groups (blacks and whites) under these different strategies.

Race, Drugs, and Sentencing Strategy: Fitting the Pieces Together

A number of explanations for racial variation in sentencing have been put forth. One widely cited individual-level perspective, "focal concerns theory" (Steffensmeier, Ulmer, & Kramer, 1998), contends that judges' sentencing decisions reflect their assessment of the culpability of the offender, their desire to protect the community, and their concerns about the social costs of sentencing decisions. Because judges rarely have enough information to determine accurately an offender's culpability or dangerousness, they develop a "perceptual shorthand" (Hawkins, 1981, p. 280; Steffensmeier et al., 1998, p. 767) on the basis of stereotypes and attributions that are themselves linked to offender characteristics such as race, gender, and age. Thus, "race, age, and gender will interact to influence sentencing because of images or attributions relating these statuses to membership in social groups thought to be dangerous and crime prone" (Steffensmeier et al., 1998, p. 768). This perspective is similar to Albonetti's (1991, 1997) assertions regarding "bounded rationality." Like Steffensmeier et al. Albonetti attributed the harsher sentences imposed on racial minorities to officials' tendency to stereotype racial minorities as more dangerous, threatening, and likely to recidivate. Addressing the issue from an organizational perspective, Dixon (1995) took a somewhat different approach, arguing that racial disparity may result from indirect institutionalized processes. That is, under the guise of organizational maintenance, the courts and their actors encourage white offenders to plead guilty, thereby reducing their sentences, but process racial minorities in ways that prohibit such sentence reductions. Thus, organizational expediency and political motives combine to produce racial disparity in sentencing (Dixon, 1995). However, the perception of defendants' characteristics remains a key factor in determining the organizational and political goals that are served.

Although each of these perspectives is unique, they all assert that the influence of race is fluid rather than static, its impact changing over time, place, and circumstance. For example, under focal concerns and bounded rationality, a judge's assessment of any given offender changes by the defendant's characteristics (such as race), as well as the facts of the case. Likewise, according to Dixon's (1995) perspective, the organizational goals served—and therefore the impact of case and personal characteristics—vary from jurisdiction to jurisdiction. Thus, for each of the aforementioned theories, the effect of any influential factor varies by the race of the offender. As a result, the particular sentencing context—such as the type, seriousness, and location of the offense—would have a different impact on the sentencing outcomes of black and white defendants. Hence, from the joint consideration of these theories, we derived the following hypothesis:

> Hypothesis 1: The predictors of the length of a sentence will operate differently for white and black drug offenders.

Unfortunately, although useful in explaining aspects of racial disparity in sentencing, these same theories do not provide a complete picture of sentencing outcomes at the federal level, where sanctions are supposedly determined by factors deemed relevant under the mandatory minimums or the guidelines, rather than by unfettered judicial discretion. However, when considered under the rubric of our expectation that influential factors will operate differently for blacks and whites, each provides a means for predicting *how* these guidelines and mandatory minimums-specific factors will differ between blacks and whites. For example, we expect race-linked attributions of dangerousness and threat to affect a prosecutor's charging decisions and use of substantial assistance motions, as well as various court actors' determination of the final criminal-history category and offense-seriousness scores.[1] The institutional perspective, on the other hand, could be manifest in differential requests for and awards of acceptance-of-responsibility departures, as well as in variation in the effect of going to trial by race. In alignment with the foregoing perspectives, we expect racial differences in the magnitude of influence for each factor such that the effect of mitigating factors is enhanced for blacks. From this expectation, we also derived the following two hypotheses (for more details, see Table 24.2):

> Hypothesis 2: The magnitudes of the effects of aggravating factors will be greater for black defendants than for white defendants. Specifically, the aggravating effect of conviction for a crack offense will be greatest for blacks. In addition, measures of the degree of harm produced by the offense at hand (offense seriousness) and threat posed by the defendant (criminal-history category) will have a greater positive effect on the length of sentences for black than white for defendants.

> Hypothesis 3: The magnitudes of the effects of mitigating factors will be greater for white defendants than for black defendants. Specifically, the mitigating effect of conviction for a marijuana offense will be greatest for whites. Likewise, the impact of mitigating factors, such as the awarding of a substantial assistance departure, will be greater for whites than for blacks.

But how will these expected results vary by the context of the sentencing strategy? At the federal level, several explanations exist. A number of scholars squarely place the blame for increased racial disparity on the mandatory minimums (Nagel & Schulhofer, 1992; Schulhofer, 1992; Tonry, 1993; USSC, 1991a). These critics cite the mandatory minimums' "Draconian" penalties as a primary avenue for racially disparate treatment and argue that such statutes are disproportionately invoked for racial minorities. Evaluations of mandatory minimums sentencing at the state (Crawford, 2000; Crawford, Chiricos, & Kleck, 1998) and federal (Albonetti, 1997; Meierhoefer, 1992; USSC, 1991b)[2] levels provide support for both assertions. These findings, coupled with the fact that the most heavily used mandatory minimums are for drug offenses (Meierhoefer, 1992), provide circumstantial evidence for condemning mandatory minimums as the primary source of disparity in federal sentencing. However, the guidelines are not entirely blameless. Although early evaluations of guidelines sentencing indicated that they reduced the disparity in sentencing, subsequent findings revealed a steady return of direct, indirect, and interactive racial effects (GAO, 1992; Heaney, 1991; Karle & Sager, 1991; McDonald & Carlson, 1993; Nagel & Schulhofer, 1992; Schulhofer, 1992; Steffensmeier & Demuth, 2000; USSC, 1991a). Thus, research has failed to support a theoretical expectation that either intervention is solely responsible for the disparity in sentences by race. Clearly, additional factors must be considered.

One such factor quickly emerges from federal sentencing literature: the different federal punishment scales for crack and powder cocaine. Federal penalties demand the same sentence for offenses involving one gram of crack cocaine as for those involving one hundred grams of powder cocaine (USSC, 1997). Pointing to this reality, some have suggested that this difference, either purposefully (Chambliss, 1995; LaFree, 1995; Tonry, 1995; Tonry & Hatlestad, 1997) or unintentionally (McDonald & Carlson, 1993), vilified and targeted the black population—particularly young men. Specifically, they argued that the importance of factors correlated with race under the guidelines causes the disparity (McDonald & Carlson, 1993). By providing harsher penalties for criminal behavior in which blacks are primarily involved—such as crack offenses—compared to those in which whites are primarily involved—such as powder cocaine offenses—some have argued that the guidelines actually *produce* racially disparate sentencing outcomes. Supporting this contention, previous research indicated that if these amount penalties were equalized, the racial disparity in federal drug sentences would not only disappear but would reverse slightly (McDonald & Carlson, 1993). Yet, other studies found that the crack and black disparities in federal sentencing outcomes are not directly related (Kautt, 2000; Kautt & DeLone, 2000)—suggesting that the cause of the persisting racial disparity is not as simple as this "targeting" explanation proposes.

Combining the sentencing strategy and the differential penalty explanations produces an interactive theoretical approach (Tonry, 1995) based on both research findings and federal sentencing provisions. For example, research has indicated that if the guidelines were changed so that the mandatory minimums were the exception, instead of the rule, the existing racial disparity would decrease substantially (McDonald & Carlson, 1993). This reality, coupled with the guidelines' provisions regarding "relevant conduct" and "substantial assistance" (Stith & Cabranes, 1998), are thought to exacerbate further the potential for racially disparate sentences when crack cocaine is involved (GAO, 1992; Nagel & Schulhofer, 1992; Schulhofer, 1992; Tonry, 1996). Moreover, since the guidelines for drug crimes are quantity driven and dominated by the mandatory minimums, the quantity and type of drugs are thought to be, by default, the *only* factors used in federal drug sentencing (Schulhofer, 1992). Finally, the imbalance between the available upward and downward offense level and the guidelines' range adjustments interacts with the mandatory minimums for drug offenses to produce an enormous potential for aggravated sentences but little comparable opportunity for mitigated sentences (Schulhofer, 1992). All these factors, it is argued, combine to produce the racially disparate outcomes that are currently seen in federal drug sentences—forming an explanation of sentence disparity that incorporates the nuances of both the applicable determinate sentencing strategy and the drug type involved.

Yet, while this latter explanation has convincing elements, it still operates from the perspective that the factors that influence sentencing outcomes operate identically for white and black drug offenders. To address this limitation, we integrated the previously discussed racial and sentencing theories into this combined approach. Such an incorporation led us to the supposition that the effect of sentence determinants in federal drug cases will vary by a defendant's race, sentencing intervention, *and* drug type, thereby providing an explanatory mechanism for the continued presence of racial disparity in federal drug sentences. However, the question remains: Precisely how do the sentencing strategies interact with a defendant's race?

To answer this question, we developed two sets of potential, albeit conflicting, expectations regarding the impact of sentencing strategy. The first rests on the degree of discretion allowed under each intervention. Under the SRA, Congress appointed the USSC to develop and implement the guidelines (GAO, 1992). This group of nationally recognized sentencing practitioners and experts designed the guidelines to incorporate a wide variety of legally relevant factors that were considered important under prior federal sentencing (Doob, 1995). In addition, they attempted to address specific problems that were previously encountered under structured sentencing (such as the disparity in charges), as well as to allow judicial consideration of individual factors (such as family ties or community involvement) as justification for mitigating sentence departures (USSC, 1991b). Conversely, Congress created and enacted the mandatory minimums (USSC, 1997), intended to demonstrate the particular heinousness of certain offenses (Parent, Dunworth, McDonald, & Rhodes, 1997), without the benefit of such expert input. As a result, offense factors alone dictate the sentence received under the mandatory minimums. Because of these differences in design and origin, the guidelines permit consideration of a varied array of aggravating and mitigating factors, while the mandatory minimums purportedly rely solely on the characteristics of the offense. Thus, sentencing under the guidelines involves multiple decision points and looser control over discretion than does sentencing under the mandatory minimums. Given that greater discretion can lead to more opportunities for consideration of extralegal factors, one may expect a greater disparity in sentencing under the guidelines than under the mandatory minimums. Simply, the more mechanical and less discretionary nature of the mandatory minimums would short-circuit decision makers' use of race-linked perceptual shorthands, whereas the guidelines would provide avenues through which these attributions would affect sentencing outcomes. As a result, in light of our previous hypotheses, we could expect that greater mitigating effects for whites and aggravating effects for blacks would be more prevalent under the guidelines than the mandatory minimums.

The second set of expectations posits a more complex relationship. As we noted previously, the mandatory minimums were enacted to demonstrate the egregiousness of particular offenses (Parent et al., 1997) while the guidelines were intended to promote equality and proportionality in sentencing (GAO, 1992; McDonald & Carlson, 1993). This difference in intent suggests that personal assessments of what constitutes "egregiousness" entered into the construction of the mandatory minimums but not that of the guidelines. Supporting this supposition, congressional records clearly indicate that causal attribution and perceptual shorthand played key roles in determining which offenses and types of drugs garnered specific mandatory minimums penalties.[3] It would not be surprising if the same influences were manifest in sentencing outcomes. Thus, along these lines and merging the focal concerns perspective with a villain-victim perspective (Myers, 1989), one may also expect that differences in application by defendants' characteristics would be more prevalent under mandatory minimums than under guidelines for drug offenses. In other words, officials' beliefs about the relative dangerousness of black and white offenders would interact with the "villainous" or "egregious" behavior involved under the mandatory minimums to enhance and exacerbate any racial disparity present under the guidelines. Therefore, under this perspective, greater aggravating effects for blacks and mitigating effects for whites would be more prevalent under the mandatory minimums than under the guidelines. This viewpoint is supported by the findings of Kautt and DeLone (2000) and comports with popularized conceptualizations of the mandatory minimums.

We believe that this latter, more complex perspective better captures the dynamics of federal sentencing under the guidelines and the mandatory minimums, since it incorporates and accounts for the aforementioned theories and findings concerning race, drugs, and sentencing strategy. Thus, this perspective guided our research and shaped the following hypothesis:

> Hypothesis 4: The racial variations in the effects of the predictors of the length of sentences will differ for mandatory minimums drug crimes compared to guidelines drug crimes. Specifically, we expect greater variation in the effects of the predictors of sentence outcomes by race under mandatory minimums drug offenses than under simple guidelines drug offenses.

Unfortunately, capturing the impact of federal sentencing strategies on sentencing outcomes cannot end here. Adding to the theoretical complexity, categorizing federal drug cases into one of the two sentencing strategies can quickly become conceptually murky—as is the case when a mandatory minimums statute covers the criminal activity, but the offense behavior itself does not meet the criteria needed to garner the minimums sentence.[4] Although these are technically guidelines cases (since the guidelines alone are used to determine the sentences), such instances actually represent the intersection of the two strategies because they involve areas in which the existing mandatory minimums specifically shaped and drove the guidelines penalty ranges (Doob, 1995; Tonry, 1996). Thus, in such cases, *both* strategies affect the sentencing outcome—making their categorization as either purely mandatory minimums or purely guidelines conceptually problematic. This issue is particularly salient to drug cases because such cases are where the bulk of mandatory minimums occur (USSC, 1991b) and the quantity-driven nature of the drug-related mandatory minimums produces a greater overlap in strategies for drug offenses than for other offenses (Tonry, 1996). As a result, when assessing the impact of structured sentencing on federal drug offenses, these "intersection" cases must be directly addressed to provide a realistic picture of either intervention's impact.

To accomplish this task, we created a third theoretical "category"—the *hybrid* case—to represent such instances. This addition enabled us to assess separately the coinciding impact of the mandatory minimums and guidelines from the influence of either the guidelines or the mandatory minimums alone. Conceptually, we expected that such hybrid cases represent a "middle ground" between the two formal strategies, with differences in effect by race greater than under the guidelines but less than under the mandatory minimums. Unfortunately, while there is ample supposition (see, e.g., Doob, 1995; Tonry, 1995, 1996), there has been little empirical research on sentencing outcomes for cases falling in between two different sentencing strategies to guide our expectations (but see Kautt & DeLone's, 2000, research). Therefore, we did not attempt to speculate about variable-specific differential effects by race under this category. However, we did develop one related hypothesis that was based on our expectation of greater racial variation under the mandatory minimums than under the guidelines, as well as our view of hybrid cases as representing the intersection of the guidelines and mandatory minimums:

> Hypothesis 5: The racial variations in the effects of the predictors of the length of sentences will differ for mandatory minimums drug cases as compared to hybrid drug cases. Specifically, we expect greater variation in the effects of predictors of sentence outcomes by race under mandatory minimums cases than under hybrid cases.

Methods and Data

To test our hypotheses, we used a two-stage partitioning strategy. As we noted earlier, we categorized federal drug-offense sentences into three groups: offenses that carry a mandatory minimums and receive a minimum sentence, offenses that fall under a mandatory minimums statute but do not receive a minimum sentence (hybrid offenses), and offenses that are simple guidelines drug cases. We used the following procedures to separate the data into these three groups (see Kautt & DeLone, 2000, for a more detailed description of this process). Using the title of the major offense for each case, we first identified the cases involving drug offenses. Next, we used the first and second statutes referenced in the first count of conviction, in combination with the indicator of the minimum length of a sentence for a drug offense, to identify the drug cases in which a mandatory minimums statute was involved and a minimum sentence was applied, to separate these cases from all others. Following this step, we identified and separated hybrid cases and simple guidelines cases. The result was three separate data sets—each capturing one of our three sentencing contexts. Finally, we further subdivided these data sets into black and white subsets and analyzed each separately—a process similar to Albonetti's (1997) and Steffensmeier and Demuth's (2000). This last step enabled us to assess the degree of variation in the predictive factors between the two racial groups for each of the three different sentencing contexts. While many studies have used dummy variables to estimate racial effects, we contend that the data-partitioning strategy, which allows researchers to test for differences between groups on all theoretically relevant factors, is a better approach. In fact, if one hypothesizes that the impact of the predictors varies by the test factor, data partitioning is the only way to test this proposition adequately. To do otherwise oversimplifies the actual relationship between both the sentencing outcome and the attribute of interest and between that attribute and other potentially influential factors (Myers, 1985; Wooldredge, 1998).

To test our hypotheses, we used USSC data for defendants who were sentenced in 1997–98 (ICPSR 9317).[5] Table 24.1 presents the frequencies or means of the variables included in our analyses. The dependent variable,[6] sentence duration, is continuous, captured at the interval level, and operationalized as sentence length in months[7] imposed for the main title offense. Basic *t*-tests for independent samples indicated that black defendants' mean length of sentence is significantly longer than white offenders' under each sentencing context—thereby justifying our racial partitioning strategy.

Because we partitioned by both sentencing strategy and defendant's race, our remaining test factors, related to the drugs involved in the offense, are represented as independent variables in our models. We used two measures: type and amount of drugs involved. We tested our premise that these drug indicators would interact with both race and sentencing-strategy category by running models that included only the type and amount of drugs for each strategy and racial partition. The results indicated a differential impact of the type and amount of drugs across both races and all three sentencing strategies—thereby supporting our expectation that drug type should exhibit differential effects by both race and sentencing-strategy category.

As control variables, our analyses also included legally relevant factors identified by the USSC in formulating the guidelines as indicative of the degree of harm done to the society by the current offense or the threat posed to the society by the current offender. The included indicators of these concepts were drug offense conduct, the number of counts of conviction, the final offense level as determined by the court, acceptance of responsibility, the weapons adjustment, and the final criminal-history category. In addition, process-related factors, such as the application of career criminal status and the presence of a downward departure, substantial assistance departure, or safety valve adjustment, were included because their presence or absence legitimately affects Federal sentencing outcomes. Thus, each of the aforementioned factors is legally relevant to sentence determinations under the guidelines.[8]

Extra-legal factors were also included as control variables. We controlled for the offender's gender, age, ethnicity, citizenship status, education, and number of dependent children, as well as for the mode of disposition in the case (trials versus guilty pleas) and for the circuit in which the case was adjudicated. Table 24.2 lists both the expected effects and the expected difference in effects between the racial groups for many of these variables.

As a result of our continuous, interval–level dependent variable, ordinary least squares (OLS) regression is the appropriate statistical tool to model the length of sentences. Diagnostics for multicollinearity were conducted for all models, and correctional procedures applied when necessary. In addition, varied specifications of the functional form[9] of sentence length were tested in preliminary analyses.[10] The results of these procedures were inconclusive; therefore, we used a simple linear additive model for the length of sentences. Since our analytical strategy entailed data partitioning,

Table 24.1 Means and Frequencies for Variables

	Mandatory Minimums		Hybrid Drug Offenses		Guideline Drug Offenses	
	Whites	Blacks	Whites	Blacks	Whites	Blacks
Incarcerated?						
Yes	6,666	5,047	4,157	1,180	535	422
No	215	74	678	182	90	41
Length of Sentence (in months)	82.03	135.62	22.25	45.66	52.35	81.64
Drug Type Dummies						
Crack	391	3,433	114	525	42	180
Powder cocaine[a]	2,065	1,189	520	294	166	192
Heroin	796	259	286	171	79	47
Marijuana	1,907	193	3,343	277	139	25
Methamphetamine	1,601	31	255	5	116	0
Other drugs	123	35	238	19	63	5
Drug Amount in Grams						
Cocaine	156.94	172.51	25.30	79.48	167.68	247.48
Crack	12.00	178.69	.51	34.23	3.58	41.95
Heroin	57.20	16.71	18.68	22.92	63.18	33.52
Methamphetamine	113.68	1.49	5.39	1.58	72.49	0
Marijuana	377.85	95.34	70.84	30.26	502.39	26.86
Other drugs	25.98	2.84	48.24	1.89	98.70	95.47
Offense Code Dummies						
Distribution	19	58	2	2	0	2
Import/export[a]	608	192	1,412	128	129	97
Communication facility	0	2	4	3	214	156
Possession	5	21	335	127	3	2
Manufacture	6,269	4,859	3,114	1,112	157	166
Final Criminal-History Category						
1	4,298	1,877	3,122	532	409	237
2	811	666	519	181	58	51
3	790	976	597	233	50	47
4	323	496	195	119	26	32
5	111	240	90	55	14	18
6	300	654	192	184	36	51
Presence of Criminal History						
Yes	4,622	4,460	3,013	1,119	381	314
No[a]	2,269	687	1,760	227	232	145
Statutory Minimum Sentence (in months)	94.07	112.43	1.44	4.28	33.24	46.08
Number Conviction Counts	1.42	1.56	1.18	1.28	1.81	1.75
Downward Departure						
Yes	712	245	1,197	152	77	68
No[a]	6,030	4,739	3,570	1,178	528	376
Substantial Assistance Departure						
Yes	2,379	1,856	878	270	141	107
No[a]	4,363	3,128	3,889	1,060	464	337

Table 24.1 Continued

	Mandatory Minimums		Hybrid Drug Offenses		Guideline Drug Offenses	
	Whites	Blacks	Whites	Blacks	Whites	Blacks
Safety-Valve Departure						
Yes	2,862	1,027	266	109	130	91
No[a]	4,061	4,127	4,609	1,264	496	372
Career Criminal Status						
Yes	188	426	99	112	21	24
No[a]	6,703	4,719	4,671	1,233	593	435
Acceptance of Responsibility						
Yes	6,155	4,162	4,482	1,179	550	401
No[a]	740	985	293	167	64	58
Weapon Enhancement						
Yes	708	837	204	104	51	51
No[a]	6,215	4,317	4,671	1,269	575	412
Final Offense-Seriousness Score	26.83	29.93	15.60	18.41	23.18	25.01
Gender						
Female	878	469	820	218	126	109
Male[a]	6,045	4,685	4,055	1,155	500	354
Age	34.62	30.49	32.20	31.55	36.69	32.26
Number of dependents	1.62	1.79	1.48	1.57	1.38	1.65
U.S. Citizen						
Yes	4,112	4,565	2,907	1,206	414	379
No[a]	2,811	589	1,968	167	212	84
Defendant's Ethnicity						
Hispanic	4,181	303	2,942	53	291	34
Non-Hispanic[a]	2,742	4,849	1,932	1,319	335	428
Educational Level	10.18	10.96	10.06	10.85	11.04	11.17
Trial						
Yes	536	709	133	64	41	33
No[a]	6,376	4,432	4,728	1,304	584	428
Circuit Dummies						
1st Circuit	235	97	94	24	24	22
2nd Circuit	492	280	338	231	71	61
3rd Circuit	365	243	96	58	33	28
4th Circuit	390	1,154	268	255	28	47
5th Circuit[a]	1,335	663	1,561	235	77	61
6th Circuit	400	588	247	126	53	64
7th Circuit	252	308	72	79	5	16
8th Circuit	558	346	182	61	25	14
9th Circuit	1323	172	1534	60	118	45
10th Circuit	419	139	246	34	61	17
11th Circuit	1,143	1,067	233	180	129	74
D.C. Circuit	11	97	4	30	2	14
N	6,923	5,154	4,875	1,373	626	463
N Valid	5,283	3,758	3773	1009	427	321

[a] = reference category.

Table 24.2 Expected Differences in Effect by Defendant's Race

	Expected Effect	Difference in Effect by Race
Crack	Presence increases sentence length	Greater aggravating black
Heroin	Presence increases sentence length	Greater aggravating black
Marijuana	Presence decreases sentence length	Greater mitigating white
Methamphetamine	Presence increases sentence length	Greater aggravating black
Crack amount	The larger the amount, the longer the sentence	Greater aggravating black
Heroin amount	The larger the amount, the longer the sentence	Greater aggravating black
Methamphetamine amount	The larger the amount, the longer the sentence	Greater aggravating black
Distribution	Longer sentence than import/export	Greater aggravating black
Possession	Shorter sentence than import/export	Greater mitigating white
Manufacture	Longer sentence than import/export	Greater aggravating black
Final criminal history category	The higher the category, the longer the sentence	Greater aggravating black
Presence of criminal history	Presence increases sentence length	Greater aggravating black
PSR recommended minimum sentence	The higher the recommendation, the longer the sentence	Greater aggravating black
Number of conviction counts	The more counts, the longer the sentence	Greater aggravating black
Downward departure	Presence decreases sentence length	Greater mitigating white
Substantial assistance	Presence decreases sentence length	Greater mitigating white
Safety valve	Presence decreases sentence length	Greater mitigating white
Career criminal	Presence increases sentence length	Greater aggravating black
Acceptance of responsibility	Presence decreases sentence length	Greater mitigating white
Weapon enhancement	Presence increases sentence length	Greater aggravating black
Final offense-seriousness score	The higher the score, the longer the sentence	Greater aggravating black
Gender	Women receive shorter sentences than men	Greater mitigating for whites
Age	Sentence length increases with age for whites but decreases with age for blacks	Greater aggravating blacks, greater mitigating whites
Number of dependents	The more dependents, the shorter the sentence	Greater mitigating for whites
Educational level	The higher the level of education, the shorter the sentence	Greater mitigating effect whites
Trial	Going to trial increases sentence length	Greater aggravating for blacks

our analyses addressed potential interactions between the focus factors (sentencing strategy and race) and all the included independent variables. Recall that these were expected to have different effects across the different specific contexts—being significant influences in some and not others. Although some of the control variables may interact with one another, all were expected to have significant direct *effects*. To identify any differences in the amount of variance explained, we calculated the Z test for the equality of coefficients across the models (Clogg, Petkova, & Haritou, 1995).

Results

As indicated in Table 24.1, there are racial and contextual differences in the frequencies of several theoretically relevant factors. For example, black defendants, regardless of context, are rarely convicted of drug crimes involving methamphetamine and "other" drugs, while whites are infrequently convicted of those involving crack cocaine. Likewise, across racial groups, there are few distribution offenses among guidelines and hybrid drug offenses. As a result of these and other differences, a few variables that were included in some models were omitted in others. For example, the differences in the incidence of the offense behaviors dictates that indicators for both drug possession and drug distribution be omitted for the guidelines drug-offense models, that possession be included only in the hybrid models, and that distribution be included only in the mandatory minimums models. Likewise, since few white defendants were sentenced in the D.C. circuit, that indicator was omitted for the white defendant models.

Table 24.3 displays the results for the length of sentences for black and white drug offenders convicted of a mandatory minimums offense. Whites who were convicted of marijuana offenses receive longer sentences than do those convicted of powder cocaine offenses. In addition, the amount of crack cocaine involved has a positive relationship with the duration of sentences for whites. A surprising finding is that white defendants who are convicted of drug manufacturing receive shorter sentences than do those who are convicted of drug importing or exporting. However, as expected, the final criminal-history category, probation officers' minimum sentence recommendation, number of conviction counts, and final offense-seriousness score all have a positive relationship with the length of sentences. In addition, the application of career criminal status or presence of a weapon enhancement increases the length of sentences, while the presence of a downward or substantial assistance departure or acceptance of responsibility decreases it. For extra-legal factors, white women receive shorter sentences than do white men, while going to trial results in longer sentences than does pleading guilty. Finally, the defendant's number of dependents positively affects the length of the sentence.

Cases involving black defendants who are convicted of mandatory minimum offenses exhibit a similar pattern. With only a few exceptions, the independent variables exhibit the same effects for black defendants as for white defendants. The exceptions are that for black defendants, the presence of a safety-valve adjustment lengthens sentences by 18 months on average, while conviction for a marijuana offense, the defendant's gender, and the number of dependents does not affect the sentence imposed. These differences are further sharpened by the *Z* test comparisons of the individual coefficients (see Table 24.6). The mitigating effects of a conviction for manufacturing drugs or receiving a downward or substantial assistance departure are larger for blacks than for whites. However, the aggravating effects of criminal history, the probation officer's recommended minimum sentence, the number of conviction counts, the presence of a safety-valve adjustment, a weapon enhancement, the final offense level, and going to trial are greater for blacks than for whites. Conversely, the aggravating effects of the application of career criminal status are greater for whites than for blacks.

Table 24.4 presents the results of the hybrid offense analyses. For white defendants, conviction of an offense involving an "other" drug results in longer sentences than does conviction of a comparable offense involving powder cocaine. In addition, the amount of crack and methamphetamine involved has a positive effect on the length of sentences. A surprising finding is that drug possession results in longer sentences than does importing or exporting drugs, whereas drug manufacturing garners shorter sentences. As expected, the final criminal-history category, probation officer's recommended minimum sentence, number of conviction counts, application of career criminal status, and final offense-seriousness score all demonstrate a positive effect on the duration of sentences. Similarly, the presence of a downward, substantial assistance or safety-valve adjustment, as well as

Table 24.3 Estimated Length of Sentences: Mandatory Minimum Drug Offenses

Offenses	Whites			Blacks		
	b	*SE*	β	*b*	*SE*	β
Crack cocaine	3.14	3.62	0	–1.98	3.69	0
Heroin	–0.78	3.16	–0	–1.88	9.06	0
Marijuana	9.79**	2.23	0.05	–0.26	7.78	0
Methamphetamine	2.38	2.50	0.01	—	—	—
Other drugs	0.73	6.00	0	—	—	—
Amount of powder cocaine	0	0	0	0	0	0
Amount of crack	0.005*	0	0.01	0.006**	0	0.04
Amount of heroin	0	0	0	0	0	0
Amount of methamphetamine	0	0	0.01	0	0.04	0
Amount of other drugs	0	0	0	0.07	0.07	0
Amount of marijuana	0	0	0	0	0	0
Manufacture	–6.33*	2.72	–0.02	–19.13**	5.86	–0.03
Final criminal-history category	13.60**	0.77	0.20	16.80**	1.02	0.20
Presence of criminal history	1.57	1.87	0	1.39	4.55	0
Minimum sentence by PSR	0.40**	0.01	0.24	0.58**	0.01	0.40
Number of conviction counts	3.27**	0.43	0.06	5.88**	0.75	0.07
Downward departure	–29.27**	2.70	–0.10	–56.93**	6.10	–0.08
Substantial assistance departure	–52.57**	1.76	–0.28	–76.65**	3.05	–0.25
Safety-valve departure	–1.17	2.07	0	18.38**	4.16	0.05
Career criminal status	25.69**	4.14	0.06	14.25**	4.33	0.03
Acceptance of responsibility	–31.57**	3.80	–0.11	–32.70**	5.68	–0.09
Weapon enhancement	8.06**	2.62	0.02	22.28**	3.78	0.05
Final offense-seriousness score	6.35**	0.20	0.40	8.28**	0.32	0.33
Gender	–4.96*	2.31	–0.01	1.79	4.71	0
Age	–0.09	0.07	–0.01	–0.26	0.16	–0.01
Number of dependents	1.15*	0.46	0.02	1.18	0.72	0.01
U.S. citizen	–2.21	2.05	–0.01	–0.27	5.13	0
Hispanic	–3.11	2.25	–0.01	–3.10	6.57	0
Educational level	0.12	0.25	0	–0.45	0.63	0
Trial	16.58**	4.25	0.05	36.54**	6.31	0.09
1st Circuit	–7.39	4.59	–0.01	–15.25	10.41	–0.01
2nd Circuit	–7.33	3.81	–0.01	–15.69	6.95	–0.02
3rd Circuit	0.09	3.88	0	–18.67	7.06	–0.02
4th Circuit	–4.79	4.09	–0.01	0.68	4.51	0
6th Circuit	6.94	3.73	0.01	–1.12	5.35	0
7th Circuit	2.02	4.38	0	–3.88	6.43	0
8th Circuit	–6.25	3.47	–0.01	-8.83	6.00	–0.01
9th Circuit	–3.78	2.50	–0.01	–6.78	7.90	0
10th Circuit	3.22	3.33	0	–13.42	8.314	–0.01
11th Circuit	–3.08	2.46	–0.01	–3.38	4.274	–0.01
D.C. Circuit	—***	—	—	–27.47	9.789	–0.02
(Constant)	–100.76	8.66		–157.69	15.72	
R^2/Adjusted R^2	.62	.62		.69	.68	

* $p < .05$, ** $p < .01$, ***insufficient cases for inclusion.

Table 24.4 Estimated Length of Sentences: Hybrid Drug Offenses

	Whites			Blacks		
	b	*SE*	β	*b*	*SE*	β
Crack cocaine	2.84	1.71	0.01	−2.16	2.42	−0.01
Heroin	1.72	1.40	0.01	−6.95*	3.46	−0.03
Marijuana	−0.34	0.88	0	−2.00	2.82	−0.01
Methamphetamine	1.33	1.38	0.01	—***	—	—
Other drugs	4.78**	1.49	0.03	—***	—	—
Amount of powder cocaine	0	0	0	0	0	0
Amount of crack	0.16**	0.01	0.11	−0.003**	0	−0.04
Amount of heroin	0	0	0.01	0	0	0.01
Amount of methamphetamine	0.01**	0	0.05	0.01	0.01	0.01
Amount of other drugs	0	0	0	−0.03	0.04	−0.01
Amount of marijuana	0	0	0	0	0	0
Possession	15.75**	1.57	0.10	19.87**	5.87	0.06
Manufacture	−1.17*	0.59	−0.02	6.07	3.75	0.03
Final criminal-history category	5.88**	0.21	0.27	6.52**	0.63	0.19
Presence of criminal history	−0.71	0.56	−0.01	−4.12	2.75	−0.02
Minimum sentence by PSR	0.18**	0.01	0.13	0.71**	0.02	0.46
Number of conviction counts	4.96**	0.42	0.10	−1.29	1.03	−0.01
Downward departure	−10.86**	0.71	−0.17	−17.83**	3.13	−0.09
Substantial assistance departure	−16.99**	0.67	−0.23	−30.48**	2.19	−0.20
Safety-valve departure	−7.95**	1.15	−0.06	−3.19	3.61	−0.01
Career criminal status	13.05**	1.22	0.09	19.79**	4.00	0.09
Acceptance of responsibility	-4.83**	1.22	−0.04	−11.84**	3.10	−0.06
Weapon enhancement	0.94	1.17	0	−2.92	3.05	−0.01
Final offense-seriousness score	3.37**	0.06	0.64	4.69**	0.16	0.55
Gender	−1.98**	0.64	−0.02	1.53	2.39	0
Age	0	0.02	0	−0.04	0.08	0
Number of dependents	−0.03	0.14	0	0.99*	0.45	0.03
U.S. citizen	−1.18	0.64	−0.02	−3.44	3.57	−0.01
Hispanic	−1.13	0.69	−0.02	−7.63	4.68	−0.02
Educational level	−0.06	0.08	0	−0.07	0.37	0
Trial	3.24	1.71	0.01	6.01	4.91	0.02
1st Circuit	1.25	1.90	0	1.01	7.05	0
2nd Circuit	−3.19*	1.39	−0.02	−3.43	3.45	−0.02
3rd Circuit	0.88	2.07	0	7.56	5.06	0.02
4th Circuit	−0.19	1.33	0	3.08	2.82	0.01
6th Circuit	1.11	1.28	0	2.06	3.51	0
7th Circuit	6.82**	2.07	0.02	9.09**	3.77	0.03
8th Circuit	1.35	1.29	0.01	3.98	4.14	0.01
9th Circuit	−1.71*	0.72	−0.02	2.69	4.96	0.00
10th Circuit	−2.57*	1.06	−0.02	−0.68	5.24	0
11th Circuit	2.27	1.19	0.01	−2.32	2.99	−0.01
D.C. Circuit	—***	—	—	−22.00**	5.24	−0.06
(Constant)	−33.81	2.48		−40.51	8.50	
R^2/Adjusted R^2	.74	.73		.82	.82	

* $p < .05$, ** $p < .01$, ***insufficient cases for inclusion.

acceptance of responsibility, shorten sentences. Extra-legal factors also affect the length of sentences for white offenders who are convicted of hybrid offenses. Women receive shorter sentences than do comparable men, and those who go to trial receive longer sentences than do those who plead guilty.

The predictors of the length of sentences for black defendants who are convicted of hybrid offenses are somewhat different. Conviction of a heroin offense results in shorter sentences than does conviction of a powder cocaine offense. Moreover, the amount of crack cocaine involved in the conviction offense shortens the duration of sentences—an effect opposite to that uncovered for comparable white defendants. In addition, for black defendants, the number of dependents has a positive effect on the length of sentences but has no effect on the severity of sentences for whites. Yet, the other significant factors influenced the length of sentences as expected and in a manner similar to that for whites. Still, the *Z* test coefficient comparisons between the two groups (see Table 24.6) demonstrate differences in the magnitudes of effects for several factors. The aggravating impact of the amount of crack involved and the number of conviction counts is greater for whites, while the aggravating effect of the probation officer's recommended minimum sentence, the final offense-seriousness score, and the number of dependents is greater for blacks. Conversely, the mitigating effect of being convicted of a heroin offense, a downward or substantial assistance departure, and acceptance of responsibility is greater for blacks, while the mitigating effect of conviction for a manufacturing offense is greater for whites.

Table 24.5 lists the results of the guidelines drug-offense models. White defendants who are convicted of drug manufacturing receive shorter sentences than do those who are convicted of importing or exporting drugs. In addition, the probation officer's recommended minimum sentence, the number of conviction counts, the application of career criminal status, going to trial, and the final offense-seriousness score increase the length of sentences, while the presence of a downward or substantial assistance departure decreases it. For black defendants, the probation officer's recommended minimum sentence, the number of conviction counts, and the final offense-seriousness score demonstrate a positive relationship with the length of sentences; conviction of a crack offense, the presence of a substantial assistance departure, or acceptance of responsibility shortens it. A comparison of the coefficients using the *Z* test reveals that the aggravating effects of the probation officer's recommended sentence and the number of conviction counts are greater for blacks than for whites, while the aggravating influence of the application of career criminal status is greater for whites than for blacks. In addition, the mitigating effect of conviction of a crack offense, a substantial assistance departure, or acceptance of responsibility is greater for blacks than for whites (see Table 24.6).

Discussion

Our findings clearly demonstrate that the effects of several independent variables vary by both the defendant's race and sentencing-strategy context. Specifically, they reveal that federal determinate sentencing has been unable to curtail the conditioning effects of race, particularly for legally relevant factors. These results support Hypothesis 1 and bolster the findings of previous research (Kautt & DeLone, 2000) that demonstrated a conditioning effect of sentencing strategy on sentencing outcome. However, as summarized in Tables 24.7 and 24.8, several factors did not behave as predicted, and the differences in effect between the two racial groups did not always comport with expectation—producing mixed results for Hypotheses 2 and 3.

As a primary example of these unexpected outcomes, the variables for the type and amount of drugs have surprisingly little influence in the saturated model. For instance, conviction of a crack offense has no effect in five of the six models tested. In fact, it directly affects only black guidelines drug offenders—mitigating their sentences compared to those of whites. The same pattern appears for heroin—whose presence mitigates the sentences of blacks who are convicted of hybrid offenses.

Table 24.5 Estimated Length of Sentences: Guideline Drug Offenses

	Whites			Blacks		
	b	*SE*	β	*b*	*SE*	β
Crack cocaine	7.40	11.07	0.02	−27.68*	10.77	−0.09
Heroin	0.62	9.46	0	−9.70	21.45	−0.02
Marijuana	4.00	6.81	0.02	−8.17	22.21	−0.01
Methamphetamine	7.75	7.71	0.04	—***	—	—
Other drugs	2.14	13.56	0	—***	—	—
Amount of powder cocaine	0	0	0.01	0	0	0
Amount of crack	0.01	0.05	0	0.01	0.02	0.02
Amount of heroin	0	0	−0.03	0	0.02	0.01
Amount of methamphetamine	0	0	0.02	—***	—	—
Amount of other drugs	0	0	−0.02	—***	—	—
Amount of marijuana	0	0	0	−0.01	0.01	−0.02
Communication facility	−9.29	6.09	−0.05	1.64	12.70	0
Manufacture	−25.43**	6.24	−0.13	−11.91	12.26	−0.04
Final criminal-history category	1.97	2.08	0.03	4.39	3.39	0.05
Presence of criminal history	9.13	5.31	0.05	2.91	11.66	0
Minimum sentence by PSR	0.53**	0.05	0.40	0.68**	0.03	0.62
Number of conviction counts	7.46**	1.31	0.16	12.44**	1.44	0.26
Downward departure	−17.32*	7.32	−0.07	−21.70	13.90	−0.05
Substantial assistance departure	−33.61**	5.37	−0.17	−53.21**	10.35	−0.16
Safety -valve departure	−11.29	6.28	−0.06	−8.80	12.89	−0.02
Career criminal status	104.40**	13.86	0.25	14.75	19.96	0.02
Acceptance of responsibility	2.22	10.76	0	−54.82**	13.51	−0.12
Presence of weapon	14.23	8.19	0.05	25.94	13.25	0.06
Final offense-seriousness score	3.04**	0.36	0.30	3.36**	0.69	0.18
Gender	2.09	5.72	0.01	−10.58	10.66	−0.03
Age	0.22	0.20	0.03	−0.51	0.43	−0.03
Number of dependents	−0.09	1.36	0	−0.10	2.31	−0.00
U.S. citizen	−4.27	6.28	−0.02	10.01	14.92	0.02
Hispanic	−0.08	6.00	0	−3.01	17.28	−0
Educational level	0.49	0.69	0.02	−1.84	1.51	−0.03
Trial	47.98**	13.28	0.15	—***	—	—
1st Circuit	−3.12	12.09	0	—***	—	—
2nd Circuit	7.69	10.06	0.02	26.54	16.83	0.05
3rd Circuit	−1.11	11.37	0	12.40	16.91	0.02
4th Circuit	24.17	12.44	0.05	40.86**	18.13	0.07
6th Circuit	9.17	10.79	0.02	20.86	15.80	0.05
7th Circuit	—***	—	—	23.55	27.06	0.02
8th Circuit	39.51**	12.25	0.09	34.28	22.02	0.04
9th Circuit	−1.68	7.40	0	11.72	16.12	0.02
10th Circuit	1.81	8.35	0	26.95	21.65	0.03
11th Circuit	−4.06	7.89	−0.02	9.19	13.22	0.02
D.C. Circuit	—***	—	—	−0.88	32.55	0
(Constant)	−59.13	20.48		19.93	37.50	
R^2/Adjusted R^2	.76	.73		.79	.76	

* $p < .05$, ** $p < .01$, ***insufficient cases for inclusion.

Table 24.6 Z Test Comparison of Coefficients for the Length of Sentences for Blacks and Whites

	Mandatory Minimums	Hybrid	Guideline
Crack cocaine offense			2.271*
Heroin offense		2.320*	
Amount of crack cocaine		12.870**	
Manufacturing drugs	1.979*	–1.907*	
Defendant's criminal-history category	–2.487**		
Minimum sentence by PSR	–8.299**	–20.787**	–2.332**
Number of conviction counts	–3.004**	5.594**	–2.548**
There was a downward departure	4.145**	2.170*	
There was a substantial assistance departure	6.830**	5.876**	1.679*
There was a safety-valve departure	–4.202**		
Career criminal status applied	1.908*		3.688**
Acceptance of responsibility		2.099**	3.301**
Weapon enhancement	–3.086**		
Final offense level	–5.094**	–7.491**	
Number of dependents		–2.138*	
Defendant went to trial	–2.622**		

Note: The *Z* test is calculated via the equation:

$$z = b_{1a} - b_{1b}/\text{Sort}\ (SE_{1a}^{\ 2} + SE_{1b}^{\ 2}),$$

where b_{1a} is the unstandardized coefficient of a given variable for white model and b_{1b} is the unstandardized coefficient of the same variable for the black model. Likewise, SE_{1a} is the standard error of the variable in the first model, while SE_{1b} is the standard error of the same variable in the second model (Clogg, Petkova, & Haritou, 1995).

* $p < .05$,

** $p < .01$.

Like drug type, drug amount has little impact on the length of sentences. Only the amount of crack cocaine demonstrates significant differences in effect between the two racial groups—being mitigating for blacks but aggravating for whites in hybrid cases. Clearly, neither the type nor the amount of drugs operates as predicted—in terms of direction or magnitude of effect. Instead, crack and heroin and the amount of crack cocaine mitigate the length of sentences to the benefit of black defendants. Thus, these findings support Hypothesis 1, which posited that there would be differences in effect across the racial models, but refute Hypotheses 2 and 3, which assert that any differences between those models would be detrimental to blacks and beneficial for whites.

These findings indicate that drug factors play a much smaller direct role than expected and that their effect varies little between blacks and whites. Moreover, the racial differences favor black, rather than white, defendants. Clearly, these results do not reinforce the findings and speculations of previous research concerning the relationship between the defendant's race and crack cocaine (Doob, 1995; McDonald & Carlson, 1993; Tonry, 1993, 1995, 1996). Simply, our analyses indicate that there is no direct relationship between the differential punishment scales for crack and powder cocaine and racial disparity adverse to black defendants in federal sentencing outcomes for 1997–1998. In other words, the defendant's race and crack cocaine—either the mere presence or the amount—do not interact to produce harsher sentences for black federal drug defendants. Rather, they interact to produce *less severe* sentences for black defendants than for comparable whites in two of the three sentencing contexts.

One explanation for these surprising findings arises from the possibility of indirect effects. As we mentioned previously, given that the type and amount of drugs are each components of the final offense-seriousness score, it is possible that drug attributes operate indirectly through that score to

Table 24.7 Expected and Observed Effect on the Length of Sentences

		Observed					
	Expected	Mandatory Minimums		Hybrid		Guidelines	
		W	B	W	B	W	B
Crack	Positive						–
Heroin	Positive				–		
Marijuana	Negative	+					
Amount of crack	Positive	+	+	+	–		
Amount of methamphetamine	Positive			+			
Possession	Negative			+	+		
Manufacture	Positive	–	–	–		–	
Final criminal-history category	Positive	+	+	+	+		
PSR recommended minimum sentence	Positive	+	+	+	+	+	+
Number of conviction counts	Positive	+	+	+		+	+
Downward departure	Negative	–	–	–	–	–	
Substantial assistance	Negative	–	–	–	–	–	–
Safety valve	Negative		+	–			
Career criminal	Positive	+	+	+	+	+	
Acceptance of responsibility	Negative	–	–	–	–		–
Weapon enhancement	Positive	+	+				
Final offense-seriousness score	Positive	+	+	+	+	+	+
Gender	Negative	–		–			
Number of dependents	Negative	+			+		
Trial	Positive	+	+			+	NA

Note: Omitted variables were nonsignificant in any model or had no predicted direction of effect. Blank cells indicate that the variable did not have a significant influence for that specific model.

affect the length of sentences. In other words, the effect of the drug factors (and therefore any racial differences produced by them) may be washed out with the inclusion of the final offense-seriousness score—a proposition that is circumstantially supported by that score's differential aggravating effects for blacks and whites in the hybrid and mandatory minimums models. We tested this possibility by running each of the saturated models without the offense-seriousness score. The results indicate that certain types and amounts of drugs became significant in some racial and strategy models but not in others.[11] In other words, for each strategy and race model, the drug indicators that affected the length of sentences changed when the seriousness of the offense was removed. However, this process produced no additional racial differences for either guidelines or mandatory minimums cases. The outcome was different for the hybrid models. There, the effects of marijuana and amount of heroin became greater for blacks while that of the amount of cocaine was greater for whites. Yet, these results, like the original findings, are opposite of what we predicted. Thus, although they validate our suspicions concerning the indirect influences of drug indicators, these results do nothing to explain our surprising original findings about the interaction among race, sentencing strategy, and type of drug.

Alternately and geared specifically to our findings on original crack cocaine, another possible explanation is that federal judges and other court actors have responded to the publicity and criticism regarding the alleged disparity in the sentencing of blacks for crack cocaine offenses and have used any discretion at their disposal (greater judicial latitude under hybrid and guidelines cases and prosecutorial discretion under mandatory minimums cases) to intentionally and deliberately mitigate

Table 24.8 Expected and Observed Differences in Effect by Race

		Observed		
	Expected	**Mandatory Minimums**	**Hybrid**	**Guidelines**
Crack	Greater aggravating black			Greater mitigating B
Heroin	Greater aggravating black		Greater mitigating B	
Marijuana	Greater mitigating white	No difference		
Amount of crack	Greater aggravating black	No difference	Greater aggravating W	
Amount of methamphetamine	Greater aggravating black		No difference	
Possession	Greater mitigating white		No difference	
Manufacture	Greater aggravating black	Greater mitigating B	Greater mitigating W	No difference
Final criminal-history category	Greater aggravating black	Greater aggravating B	No difference	
PSR recommended minimum sentence	Greater aggravating black	Greater aggravating B	Greater aggravating B	Greater aggravating B
Number of conviction counts	Greater aggravating black	Greater aggravating B	Greater aggravating W	Greater aggravating B
Downward departure	Greater mitigating white	Greater mitigating B	Greater mitigating B	No difference
Substantial assistance	Greater mitigating white	Greater mitigating B	Greater mitigating B	Greater mitigating B
Safety valve	Greater mitigating white	Greater aggravating B	No difference	
Career criminal	Greater aggravating black	Greater aggravating W	No difference	Greater aggravating W
Acceptance of responsibility	Greater mitigating white	No difference	Greater mitigating B	Greater mitigating B
Weapon enhancement	Greater aggravating black	Greater aggravating B		
Final offense-seriousness score	Greater aggravating black	Greater aggravating B	Greater aggravating B	No difference
Gender	Greater mitigating whites	No difference	No difference	
Number of dependents	Greater mitigating whites	No difference	Greater aggravating B	
Trial	Greater aggravating blacks	Greater aggravating B		

Note: Omitted variables were nonsignificant in any model or had no predicted differences. Blank cells indicate that the variable was not significant in either the black or the white model.

the impact of crack on the length of sentences for black drug offenders. This "deliberate mitigation" would be the product of organizational and/or individual reactions to external or environmental forces and pressures, such as the USSC, the news media, public interest groups, and civil liberty watchdog organizations. If this explanation is valid, one would expect that the crack cocaine effects uncovered here would not be uncovered in data from years prior to or coinciding with the most ardent criticism and publicity surrounding the purported black-crack disparity. It may also be the case that the alleged aggravating direct effects for black crack cocaine offenders did exist in previous years but disappeared as such effects became highly publicized. Yet, it is impossible to test this proposition with the current data alone. Rather, such investigation would require multilevel data, analysis by sentencing district, and analysis of data from years before the wide dissemination of the evident black-crack disparity in sentences.

Were our discussion to end with the drug-related predictors, we would conclude that Hypotheses 2 and 3, which outline our expectations concerning the types of racial differences, had been soundly refuted. However, the impact of other legally relevant factors indicates that such a conclusion would be premature. One such example is the varied effects uncovered for offense behavior. Contrary to expectation, conviction of drug possession has an equivalent aggravating effect for black and white hybrid defendants. Another unexpected finding is that conviction of drug manufacturing mitigated sentences across all three sentencing strategies. This latter effect was greater for blacks than for whites in mandatory minimums cases—providing further support for our earlier "deliberate mitigation" argument but refuting Hypothesis 2. Yet, this factor influenced sentences for whites but not for blacks under hybrid or Guidelines cases. This difference in effect by defendant's race, significant only for hybrid cases, suggests that white defendants who are convicted of manufacturing drugs under this strategy are given the benefit of the doubt *not* provided to blacks—a finding that supports Hypothesis 3. Such results reveal an odd juxtaposition of the racially conditioned effects of drug manufacturing. This "switching" of the race "benefiting" from the manufacture-mitigation effect between hybrid and mandatory minimums cases is unexpected. As one possible explanation, hybrid cases, having characteristics of both the guidelines and the mandatory minimums, may permit the increased discretion of the guidelines in conjunction with the perceived egregiousness of offense behavior under the mandatory minimums to yield an effect that benefits white over black defendants. In other words, for such cases, causal attribution produces outcomes more favorable to whites. At the same time, judicial discretion in cases falling under the mandatory minimums could indeed be constrained, allowing the discretion of other court actors, such as the prosecutor and probation officer, to fill the void and deliberately mitigate the sentences of black defendants. Unfortunately, there are no direct measures of either discretion or relevant conduct in these data to test such possibilities.[12]

Turning to guidelines-specific factors, the final criminal-history score behaves as expected only for the mandatory minimums and hybrid models—having an aggravating effect greater for blacks than for whites in mandatory minimums cases.[13] Like criminal history, the final offense-seriousness score lengthens sentences and, for both hybrid and mandatory minimums cases, this aggravating effect is greater for blacks than for whites.[14] In a similar vein, the Pre-Sentence Investigation Reports' recommended minimums sentence, the number of conviction counts, and the presence of a weapon enhancement all have an aggravating effect that is almost uniformly greater for blacks than for whites. Each of these findings suggests that whites are given the benefit of the doubt in terms of these factors while blacks are not—supporting Hypothesis 2 and seeming to demonstrate that causal attribution is present in the use of legally relevant factors regardless of sentencing strategy. Given the rationale behind federal structured sentencing, it is doubtful that the framers of modern federal determinate sentencing intended such variation in the primary factors that were designed to determine sentences and produce equitable outcomes.[15]

Turning to the expected mitigating influences, the presence of a downward departure, a substantial assistance departure, or acceptance of responsibility all shorten the length of sentences and have greater impact for blacks than for whites. These findings support our previously articulated "deliberate mitigation" proposition but also refute Hypothesis 3. Conversely, while supporting Hypothesis 2, the effect of the safety-valve adjustment exhibits an aggravating racial effect for blacks sentenced in mandatory minimums cases. In other words, blacks who are given a safety-valve adjustment receive longer sentences than do comparable whites. This finding could indicate that black mandatory minimums defendants receive a safety-valve adjustment only for the most serious offenses and suggests an interaction between the offense-seriousness score and the presence of a safety-valve adjustment for black mandatory minimums defendants.[16] Alternately, perhaps whites are given safety-valve adjustments more frequently and/or under different circumstances than are blacks—thereby reducing the impact of this factor for whites.[17] Both suggest a complex relationship between offense seriousness and use of the safety valve adjustment under different contexts. Regardless, these findings imply that safety-valve adjustments are not being used as intended—particularly for black mandatory minimums defendants.

Moving to extra-legal influences, we found no gender differences by race. Yet, the number of dependents unexpectedly has an aggravating effect for blacks compared to whites in hybrid cases. Likewise, going to trial has an aggravating effect that is greater for blacks than for whites under the mandatory minimums, indicating that black defendants pay a larger jury tax for being convicted at trials in such cases. These findings partially confirm Hypothesis 2—that any aggravating effects will be greater for blacks than for whites. Moreover, they indicate that extra-legal factors retain significant direct effects over structured federal sentencing—regardless of intervention—that vary by race.

Backing away from the specific influential predictors to discuss the broader picture addressed by Hypotheses 4 and 5, our findings reveal distinct racial patterns for each of the three sentencing contexts. Twelve factors—the bulk of which were legally relevant—demonstrate racial conditioning under the mandatory minimums. A disturbing finding is that nearly all these factors exhibit a greater effect for blacks than for whites. Although this greater effect benefits black defendants in terms of the three mitigating factors, it is a decided liability in terms of the seven aggravating factors, suggesting that causal attribution affects mandatory minimums sentencing to intensify the influence of such factors for blacks. Clearly, a defendant's race retains a strong influence over sentencing outcomes under the mandatory minimums.[18]

Revealing a completely different pattern, hybrid offenses yielded a mixed bag of differential effects by race. Here, 10 factors interact with race. Although more of these factors exhibited a greater impact for blacks than for whites, the split between those factors in terms of being aggravating (3) and mitigating (4) was nearly even. Moreover, two factors that had a greater influence for whites than for blacks were aggravating, and only one was mitigating. Thus, while a defendant's race retains influence in hybrid cases, its effect is not as clear cut as the effect for mandatory minimums cases. Being black does not intensify the influence of the bulk of the factors as it did for the mandatory minimums cases. Likewise, the hybrid effects are not as generally detrimental to black defendants as they are for mandatory minimums cases. These patterns support both the middle-of-the road approach we took regarding outcomes under hybrid cases and Hypothesis 5, since there were fewer differences by race for hybrid than for mandatory minimums cases.

Unfortunately, this pattern was not continued for guidelines cases, which yielded outcomes surprisingly similar to those of the mandatory minimums. Here, almost all the factors that demonstrate racial effects have a greater impact for blacks than for whites. Thus, it seems that being black intensifies the impact of the predictors of sentence length under the guidelines just as it does under the mandatory minimums. However, the number of racial differences in the effects of predictors is decidedly smaller for guidelines cases (6) than for mandatory minimums cases (11)—showing clear support for Hypothesis 4. It is also interesting to note that the guidelines cases were the only cases for which there were no interactions between race and offender-based extra-legal factors. Thus, it would appear that the guidelines have been successful in minimizing both the direct influence of defendant-based extra-legal factors and any interaction between those factors and defendant's race, while the other sentencing contexts have not.

Throughout this discussion, we have mentioned various issues that have limited our ability to investigate further our theoretical interpretations of the findings. Apart from those limitations, our research had additional restrictions. For example, the identity of the sentencing judges is not available for the cases, thereby precluding control for the influence of such individual-level factors over the sentencing outcome. Moreover, because this research focused only on sentencing outcomes, it could not address potential bias or manipulation by the police and other criminal justice decision makers, or the data-submission practices of the various federal districts. Also, because we use a single level of data, we could not examine the extent to which the differences uncovered between the models are a product of interaction between different interventions and race versus specific differences in the organization or location-based contexts. In addition, our use of a single year of data precluded our controlling for year-to-year variation. Finally, because the research was restricted to a secondary analysis, it could not qualitatively evaluate the policies, politics, and practices of each circuit and district court. Clearly, future research should endeavor to gather data on these various issues and include them in any analysis of federal sentencing outcomes.

Another issue to be considered is the problem of "cumulative disadvantage" (Zatz, 1987). Every step in the criminal justice process, from the enactment of specific statutes to the arrest decision or prosecutorial charging practices to the charging of relevant conduct should be explored as influential in federal sentencing outcomes. Future research should further investigate how the disparity produced at one stage of the federal sentencing process exacerbates the disparity present at later stages. Previous research on federal sentencing found disparities in substantial assistance (Maxfield & Kramer, 1998) and acceptance of responsibility (Everett & Nienstedt, 1999) departures. Other findings have suggested that the "driving while black" phenomenon may affect sentencing outcomes for black offenders via the criminal-history score (Blackwell, 1999). These findings, when coupled with the variety of indirect effects that were uncovered, demonstrate a clear need to examine federal sentencing through a multistage lens.

As a final note, using the final offense-seriousness score and criminal-history category as the only legally relevant factors included in models of the length of sentences would have masked the differences we uncovered in the impact of the legally relevant factors that constitute offense seriousness. Future research should bear these findings in mind when constructing research strategies and statistical models that are designed to investigate the factors predicting federal sentencing outcomes. Analytical tools, such as structural equation modeling, may be used to identify the model that captures the truest picture of federal sentencing outcomes. Furthermore, given the previous discussion, other avenues for future research should include multilevel analysis, time-series analysis, and multistage analysis of federal sentencing outcomes. Moreover, our discovery of indirect extra-legal effects operating through the offense-seriousness score suggests that future research should incorporate the possibility of such effects into both the theoretical framework and the overall design.

Conclusions

The results of this study indicate that the predictors of the length of sentences operate differently for white and black defendants and for guidelines, mandatory minimums, and hybrid drug cases. There are more racial differences in the effects of the predictors for mandatory minimums cases than for hybrid or, especially, guidelines cases. On the basis of these findings, it would appear that our more complex theoretical framework for explaining the persistence of racial disparity in federal sentencing (i.e., the villain-victim thesis combined with causal attribution) better captures the process of federal sentencing than does the simpler discretion-control thesis.

Nevertheless, our findings uncovered racial differences in predictor effects across all three sentencing contexts. Such a discovery effectively demonstrates that defendant's race retains an influence over federal determinate sentencing outcomes—despite the intentions and efforts of the framers of modern federal structured sentencing. Moreover, an inspection of the specific individual factors reveals unexpected results. Our expectation of larger aggravating effects for blacks and greater mitigating effects for whites was not supported. Rather than uncovering a host of greater aggravating effects for black defendants, we instead found several effects that were more beneficial to black defendants than to white defendants. Moreover, at least one aggravating factor consistently had a greater effect on the sentences of white defendants than black defendants. Although some of these findings do not comport with the traditional reading of conflict theory, alternate specifications of it, such as the devaluing of minority communities through the lenient treatment of minority drug offenders (Hawkins, 1987; Tonry, 1995), were supported. At the same time, other theoretical frameworks were supported. The most obvious example arose from our examination of the type and amount of drugs, which found that these drug indicators do not interact with a defendant's race and sentencing strategy to have an adverse effect on the length of sentences for black federal drug offenders. Rather, our results indicate that when the type or amount of drugs has a direct effect, it serves to mitigate the sentences of black drug defendants. As an explanation of these surprising results, we posited that federal court actors may be deliberately mitigating the impact of the type and amount of drugs—specifically crack—in response to the publicity concerning the purported "black-crack" disparity throughout the early and mid-1990s. However, our analyses also suggest that these factors operate indirectly through the offense- seriousness score and other legally relevant factors to produce the racial disparity that is present in federal drug sentences.

Our findings clearly suggest that federal determinate sentencing produces outcomes that are much more complex than simply castigating black drug defendants while protecting comparable white defendants. Moreover, the relationship between a defendant's race and sentencing outcome appears to be more complicated than either causal attribution or "deliberate mitigation" alone. Instead, both seem jointly to explain federal sentencing outcomes, with the precise mixture of the explanatory value of each perspective varying by the sentencing strategy invoked. Causal attribution appears to play a larger role in mandatory minimums sentencing while "deliberate mitigation" seems to be more prominent in guidelines sentencing. A further examination of other potential interactive and indirect effects would serve to clarify the degree to which each perspective explains federal sentencing outcomes. Regardless, the primary implication of these findings is that the predictors of federal determinate sentencing outcomes are not as uniform as the framers of either the guidelines or the mandatory minimums intended them to be.

Clearly, this study produced more questions than it answered. Therefore, it falls to future research to untangle this complex web of indirect, direct, and varied effects. However, our investigation began to excavate the true nature of the relationship between race and the modern federal determinate sentencing interventions. Although the study merely scratched the surface, we hope that it is just the first step in many such endeavors to capture the true impact of the current federal sentencing strategies on drug defendants of both races.

Notes

1. As one anonymous reviewer pointed out, the probation officer is not the only participant who will calculate the offense-seriousness and criminal-history scores. Rather, the defense attorney, prosecutor, and the judge also often independently calculate these scores for use during the case.
2. Although Albonetti (1997) purported to study the impact of the guidelines, her choice to analyze cases falling under two mandatory minimums drug statutes makes her research an evaluation of the mandatory minimums.
3. The auctioneer approach they used to devise the sanction scales for crack cocaine (Tonry, 1995) succinctly illustrates this fact.
4. For example, possession of 5 grams of crack cocaine falls under the mandatory minimum Statute 21 USC § 844 and invokes a minimum sentence of five years. Yet, possession of 4.9 grams of crack cocaine is offense behavior that falls under the same mandatory minimums statute but does not invoke the five-year sentence (USSC, 1995). However, at the same time, the guidelines' punishment scale that would be used in the latter case was shaped and driven by the existing mandatory minimums penalties to prevent "sentencing cliffs" between cases, such as those listed earlier, where there are only small differences in the actual offense behavior (Doob, 1995; Tonry, 1995; USSC, 1991a). As a result sentencing outcomes for cases such as our latter example simultaneously reflect the influence of both guidelines and mandatory minimums.
5. As with many studies using secondary data, missing data were a problem. Slightly more than 10 percent of the cases had no data on the final criminal-history category or the final assigned offense level. Unfortunately, elimination of these factors was not feasible, since they were designed to be the two primary factors determining sentence under the guidelines and therefore were expected to wield significant and substantial influence over the length of sentences. Thus, those cases with missing data on these factors were simply excluded from the analyses.
6. Initially we intended to include models for the incarceration decision. However, since few drug offenders were not imprisoned, modeling incarceration—especially to make racial comparisons—was problematic. As a result, incarceration models were dropped from the current investigation.

7. Some have argued that because of the positively skewed nature of this variable, the correct specification of the model would be semilogged in *Y*. We used the P_c test (Davidson & MacKinnon, 1981; Greene, 2000; MacKinon, White, & Davidson, 1983) to determine whether this or a nonlogged in *Y* model is the correct specification. The results, however, were inconclusive. Thus, these analyses default to the linear additive model.
8. Some argue that including certain legally relevant factors in the same model as the final offense-seriousness score results in a "double counting" of their effects (because they are included in the computation of the offense-seriousness score). However, we see several factors affecting the offense-seriousness score (such as the type of offense, amount and type of drugs involved, number of conviction counts, acceptance of responsibility, and presence of career criminal status) as important enough to have their potential direct effects individually taken into account. Relying on the aggregate measure of the final offense-seriousness score to reflect the impact of these factors oversimplifies their influence and masks any variation in sentencing outcomes by and/or the direct effects of such factors. This would be akin to taking factors, such as age, gender, race, and socioeconomic status; merging them into a single score; and then drawing conclusions about their impact. While this reality seems to suggest that these individual factors, rather than the final offense-seriousness score would result in *severe* model misspecification. One solution would be to determine whether the correlation between the independently included offense-seriousness factors and the final offense-seriousness score is sufficient to preclude their joint presence. If double counting was occurring, one would expect either a significant correlation between these factors and the final offense-seriousness score or for regression diagnostics to indicate collinearity between these variables. However, our correlation matrix indicates a minimal overlap between the final offense-seriousness score and any one of these factors. Moreover, neither the Variance Inflation Factor nor the Condition Index test revealed collinearity among these (or any other) variables. Thus, it appears that concern over double counting by including both sets of factors is unfounded.
9. These specifications were a parabolic relationship between age and sentence length, a semilogged in *X* (offense seriousness and number of conviction counts) model, and a semilogged in *Y* model.
10. These analyses were the *J* test and P_E tests (Davidson & MacKinnon, 1981; MacKinon et al., 1983; Smith & Maddala, 1983).
11. These analyses also showed that several factors either operate exclusively through the offense-seriousness score (becoming significant only when that factor is omitted), have their direct effects on the length of sentences conditioned by offense seriousness (the direction of the effect changes with the inclusion of that factor), or operate completely independent of offense seriousness (no change in significance or direction of effect with the omission of offense seriousness). The additional factors that indicate indirect effects are offense behavior, presence of a safety-valve departure, gender, age, number of dependents, and various circuits. Conversely, the number of conviction counts, acceptance of responsibility, and career criminal status exhibit direct effects that are independent of the seriousness of the offense. The pattern of effect also varies both by sentencing strategy and defendant's race. These results are available, on request, from the first author.
12. Also related to the offense-behavior findings, the victim-villain thesis (Myers, 1989) suggests that conviction of drug possession should produce shorter sentences than conviction of drug importing or exporting drugs, while conviction of drug manufacturing should produce longer sentences because the former offense may be the result of addiction—and therefore diminished responsibility—while the latter produces a greater level of harm to the society. Our findings refute this thesis, suggesting instead that drug possession is deemed more egregious than drug manufacturing in federal court practice. In explanation of these findings, it is possible that only the most severe possession cases are brought to the federal, rather than the state or local, courts. At the same time, most drug-manufacturing cases could be waived to federal jurisdiction. In this scenario, the entire spectrum of drug-manufacturing cases—both the large and small-level cases—would be brought to federal court. As a result, a number of the manufacturing cases would receive relatively light sentences. Yet, because only the most serious possession cases would be brought to the federal venue, one would expect all such cases to receive comparatively harsher sentences. However, it is not possible to test this proposition using the current data alone, since such an investigation would require the examination of both federal- and state-level drug cases and sentencing outcomes.
13. It is unclear why the final criminal history score, designed to be so integral to guidelines sentencing, should have no effect for simple guidelines cases. Perhaps this lack of effect is related to the various downward departures available under that strategy—particularly the substantial assistance departure. Alternately, this factor may operate through career criminal status for guidelines offenses so that inclusion of career criminal status reduces the effect of the final criminal-history score to insignificant levels. Removing the indicator of career criminal status from both the black and white guidelines models bears this latter proposition out—suggesting that the influence of both career criminal status and the final criminal-history score varies by the specific sentencing context under which a case falls.
14. From the previous diagnostics indicating that multiple legal and extra-legal factors operate indirectly through the final offense-seriousness score, we discovered that both the type and amount of drugs, as well as a defendant's age, gender, number of dependents, weapons adjustment, safety-valve departures, circuit, and offense behavior all operate through the offense-seriousness score. These effects undoubtedly function to explain this difference. Moreover, the presence of such indirect extra-legal effects through offense seriousness suggest that judges may attempt to mitigate the aggravating influence of the probation officer's predetermined offense-seriousness score in certain cases—notably black drug defendants.
15. However, not all the included legally relevant factors follow this racial pattern. Unexpectedly, career criminal status has an aggravating effect greater for whites than for blacks. These differences may reflect the courts punishing whites for not adhering to the "norms" of "race-appropriate" behavior (Hawkins, 1987). Under such a thesis, the impact would be less for blacks because by attaining career criminal status, they conform to the expectations of causal attribution. In contrast, white career criminals are seen as more insidious because such behavior is not in alignment with

the causal attributions made concerning whites and the "threat" they pose to the society. Unlike the previous findings, these results support Hypothesis 1 but refute Hypotheses 2 and 3.

16. Subsequent analyses of black mandatory minimums cases including such an interaction term support this proposition—with both the interaction term and the two independent factors all demonstrating significant individual influence over the length of sentences. Unfortunately, these results are nondefinitive because they also exhibited severe collinearity between the individual factors and the interaction term. The previous diagnostics also indicate that safety valve operates indirectly through the seriousness of offenses.
17. This proposition is bolstered by the frequencies of this factor for blacks and whites, as well as significant results of *t*-tests and analyses of variance indicating differences for these data in the awarding of substantial assistance departures by race. Moreover, it is also supported by the findings of previous empirical research (Maxfield & Kramer, 1998). An OLS regression model for white mandatory minimums defendants including an interaction term between the presence of a safety-valve departure and the final offense-seriousness score, however, refutes this proposition. Yet, serious collinearity exists between these factors, calling these results into question.
18. At this point, it is crucial to note that this evidence cannot conclusively support the proposition that racial causal attribution operates in mandatory minimums drug sentencing. Using a Marxian perspective, it is possible that the lower socioeconomic status of the average black defendant actually explains these differential effects rather than race itself (Title, 1994). Unfortunately, a major data limitation is that socioeconomic indicators either are not available (defendant's income) or have too many missing cases (type of defense attorney) to be included in our analyses. As a result, we cannot rule out the Marxian explanation in favor of racial causal attribution with these data. However, on the basis of the evidence that we do have, it seems overwhelmingly clear that there are a large number of differences in the impact of legally relevant factors on the basis of a defendant's race for cases falling under the mandatory minimums.

References

Albonetti, C. A. 1991. An integration of theories to explain judicial discretion. *Social Problems* 38: 247–266.

———. 1997. Sentencing under the federal sentencing guidelines: Effects of defendant characteristics, guilty pleas, and departures on sentence outcomes for drug offenses. *Law and Society Review* 31: 789–822.

Beck, A. J. and Mumola, C. J. 1999. *Prisoners in 1998* (NCJ 175687). Washington, DC: Bureau of Justice Statistics.

Blackwell, K. 1999 (November). *Race and traffic stops: Its effect on criminal history.* Paper presented at the American Society of Criminology, Toronto, Canada.

Bonezar, T. P. and Beck, A. J. 1997. *Lifetime likelihood of going to state or federal prison.* Washington, DC: Bureau of Justice Statistics.

Bureau of Justice Statistics. 1999. *Compendium of federal justice statistics* (NCJ172849). Washington, DC: Bureau of Justice Statistics.

Chambliss, W. J. 1995. Crime control and ethnic minorities: Legitimizing racial oppression by creating moral panics. In *Ethnicity, race, and crime: Perspectives across time and spac,* ed. D. Hawkins 235–258. Albany: State University of New York Press.

Chiricos, T. G. and Crawford, C. 1995. Race and imprisonment: A contextual assessment of the evidence. In *Ethnicity, race, and crime: Perspectives across time and space,* ed. D. F. Hawkins, 281–309. Albany: State University of New York Press.

Clogg, C. C., Petkova, E., and Haritou, A. (1995). Statistical methods for comparing regression coefficients between models. *American Journal of Sociology* 100: 1261–1293.

Crawford, C. 2000. Gender, race, and habitual offender sentencing in Florida. *Criminology* 38: 263–279.

Crawford, C., Chiricos, T., and Kleck, G. 1998. Race, racial threat, and sentencing of habitual offenders. *Criminology* 36: 481–512.

Davidson, R. and MacKinnon, J. G. 1981. Several tests for model specification in the presence of alternative hypotheses. *Econometrica* 49: 781–793.

Dixon, J. 1995. The organizational context of criminal court sentencing. *American Journal of Sociology* 100: 1157–1198.

Doob, A. N. 1995. The United States Sentencing Commission guidelines: If you don't know where you are going, you might not get there. In *The politics of sentencing reform,* eds. C. Clarkson & R. Morgan . Oxford, England: Clarendon Press.

Everett, R. S. and Nienstedt, B. C. 1999. Race, remorse, and sentence reduction: Is saying you're sorry enough? *Justice Quarterly* 26: 99–122.

General Accounting Office. 1992. *Sentencing guidelines: Central questions remain unanswered* (GAO/GDD 92–93). Washington, DC: Author.

Greene, W. H. 2000. *Econometric analysis* (4th ed.). Upper Saddle River, NJ: Prentice Hall.

Hawkins, D. F. 1981. Causal attribution and punishment for crime. *Deviant Behavior* 2: 207–230.

Hawkins, D. F. 1987. Beyond anomalies: Rethinking the conflict perspective on race and capital punishment. *Social Forces* 65: 719–743.

Heaney, G. W. 1991. The reality of guidelines sentencing: No end to disparity. *American Criminal Law Review* 28: 161–233.

Karle, T. W. and Sager, T. 1991. Are the federal sentencing guidelines meeting congressional goals? An empirical and case law analysis. *Emory Law Journal 40*: 393–444.

Kautt, P. 2000. *Separating and estimating the effects of the federal sentencing guidelines and the federal mandatory minimums: Isolating the sources of racial disparity.* Unpublished doctoral dissertation, University of Nebraska at Omaha.

Kautt, P. and DeLone, M. 2000. *Federal sentencing outcomes under sentencing guidelines and mandatory minimum statutes: Untying the Gordian knot.* Paper presented at the meeting of the Academy of Criminal Justice Sciences, New Orleans, March 22.

LaFree, G. 1995. Race and crime trends in the United States: 1946–1990. In *Ethnicity, race, and crime: Perspectives across time and space,* ed. D. Hawkins, 169–193. Albany: State University of New York Press.

MacKinon, J., White, H., and Davidson, R. 1983. Tests for model specification in the presence of alternative hypotheses: Some further results. *Journal of Econometrics* 21: 53–70.

Maxfield, L. D. and Kramer, J. H. 1998. *Substantial assistance: An empirical yardstick gauging equity in current federal policy and practice.* Washington, DC: United States Sentencing Commission.

McDonald, D. C. and Carlson, K. E. 1993. *Sentencing in the federal courts: Does race matter? The transition to sentencing guidelines,* 1986–90 (NCJ-145332). Washington, DC: Bureau of Justice Statistics.

Meierhoefer, B. S. 1992. *The general effect of mandatory minimum prison terms: A longitudinal study of federal sentences imposed.* Washington, DC: Federal Judicial Center.

Myers, M. A. 1989. Symbolic policy and the sentencing of drug offenders. *Law and Society Review* 23: 295–313.

Myers, S. L. 1985. Statistical tests of discrimination in punishment. *Journal of Quantitative Criminology* 1: 191–218.

Nagel, I. H. and Schulhofer, S. J. 1992. A tale of three cities: An empirical study of charging and bargaining practices under the federal sentencing guidelines. *Southern California Law Review* 66: 501–566.

Parent, D., Dunworth, T., McDonald, D., and Rhodes, W. 1997. *Key legislative issues in criminal justice: Mandatory sentencing: Research in action.* Washington, DC: National Institute of Justice.

Schulhofer, S. J. 1992. Assessing the federal sentencing process: The problem is uniformity not disparity. *American Criminal Law Review 28*(833), 833–873.

Smith, M. A. and Maddala, G. S. 1983. Multiple model testing for non-nested heteroskedastic censored regression models. *Journal of Econometric,* 21: 71–81.

Spohn, C. (2000). Thirty years of sentencing reform: The quest for a racially neutral sentencing process. In *Policies, processes, and decisions of the criminal justice system,* ed. J. Horney (vol. 3), 427–501. Washington, DC: National Institute of Justice.

Steffensmeier, D. and Demuth, S. 2000. Ethnicity and sentencing outcomes in U.S. federal courts: Who is punished more harshly? *American Sociological Review* 65: 705–729.

Steffensmeier, D., Ulmer, J., and Kramer, J. (1998). The interaction of race, gender, and age in criminal sentencing: The punishment cost of being young, black, and male. *Criminology* 36: 763–798.

Stith, K. and Cabranes, J. A. 1998. *Fear of judging: Sentencing guidelines in the federal courts.* Chicago: University of Chicago Press.

Tittle, C. R. 1994. The theoretical bases for inequality in formal social control. In *Inequality, crime and social control,* eds. G. Bridges & M. Myers, 21–51. Boulder, CO: Westview Press.

Tonry, M. 1993. The failure of the U.S. Sentencing Commission's guidelines. In *Courts and justice: A reader,* eds. G. L. Mays & P. R. Gregware, 449–467. Prospect Heights, IL: Waveland Press.

Tonry, M. 1995. *Malign neglect.* New York: Oxford University Press.

———. *Sentencing matters.* New York: Oxford University Press.

Tonry, M. and Hatlestad, K. eds. 1997. *Sentencing reform in overcrowded times: A Comparative perspective.* New York: Oxford University Press.

United States Sentencing Commission. 1991a. *The federal sentencing guidelines: A Report on the operation of the guidelines system and short-term impacts on disparity in sentencing, use of incarceration, and prosecutorial discretion and plea bargaining.* Washington, DC. Author.

United States Sentencing Commission. 1991b. *Special report to Congress: Mandatory minimum penalties in the federal criminal justice system.* Washington, DC: Author.

United States Sentencing Commission. 1995. *Special report to Congress: Cocaine and federal sentencing policy.* Washington, DC: Author.

United States Sentencing Commission. 1997. *Special report to Congress: Cocaine and federal sentencing policy.* Washington, DC: Author.

Wooldredge, J. D. 1998. Analytical rigor in studies of disparities in criminal case processing. *Journal of Quantitative Criminology* 14: 155–179.

Zatz, M. S. 1987. The changing forms of racial/ethnic bias in sentencing. *Journal of Research in Crime and Delinquency* 24: 69–92.

Permissions

Chapter 1 W. E. B. Du Bois (1901) "The Spawn of Slavery: The Convict-Lease System in the South" *Missionary Review of the World* 14: 737–745.

Chapter 2 Norman S. Hayner (1938) "Social Factors in Oriental Crime" *American Journal of Sociology*" 43(6): 908–919.

Chapter 3 Norman S. Hayner (1942) "Variability in the Criminal Behavior of American Indians" *American Journal of Sociology* 47(4): 602–613.

Chapter 4 Oliver C. Cox (1945) "Lynching and the Status Quo" *Journal of Negro Education* 14: 576–588.

Chapter 5 Alfred Blumstein (1982) "On Racial Disproportionality of United States' Prison Populations" *Journal of Criminal Law and Criminology* 73: 1259–1281.

Chapter 6 Ruth D. Peterson and John Hagan (1984) "Changing Conceptions of Race: Toward an Account of Anomalous Findings of Sentencing Research" *American Sociological Review* 49: 56–70.

Chapter 7 John J. DiLulio, Jr. (1996) "My Black Crime Problem, and Ours" *City Journal* 6(2): 14–28.

Chapter 8 Matt DeLisi and Robert Regoli (1999) "Race, Conventional Crime, and Criminal Justice: The Declining Importance of Skin Color" *Journal of Criminal Justice* 27(6): 549–557.

Chapter 9 Hans von Hentig (1942) "The Criminality of the Colored Woman" University of Colorado Study Series 1 No. 3 (pp. 231–260)

Chapter 10 Jacklyn Huey and Michael J. Lynch (1996) "The Image of Black Women in Criminology: Historical Stereotypes as Theoretical Foundation" Excerpt from *Justice With Prejudice.* Albany, NY: Harrow and Heston.

Chapter 11 Jody Miller (1998) "Up It Up: Gender and the Accomplishment of Street Robbery" *Criminology* 36: 37–65.

Chapter 12 Carolyn M. West, Glenda Kaufman Kantor, and Jana L. Jasinski (1998) 'Sociodemographic Predictors and Cultural Barriers to Help-Seeking Behavior by Latina and Anglo American Battered Women" *Violence and Victims* 13(4): 361–375.

Chapter 13 Robert J. Sampson and William Julius Wilson (1995) "Toward a Theory of Race, Crime, and Urban Inequality" (pp. 37–54) chapter from *Crime and Inequality* (edited by J. Hagan and Peterson). Palo Alto, CA: Stanford University Press.

Chapter 14 Albert J. Meehan and Michael C. Ponder (2002) "Race and Place: The Ecology of Racial Profiling African American Motorists" *Justice Quarterly* 19(3): 399–430.

Chapter 15 Jared Taylor and Glayde Whitney (2002) "Crime and Racial Profiling by U.S. Police: Is There an Empirical Basis?" *Mankind Quarterly* 42(3): 285–312.

Chapter 16 Barbara Perry (2002) "Defending the Color Line: Racially and Ethnically Motivated Hate Crime" *The American Behavioral Scientist* 46(1): 72–92.

Chapter 17 Darnell F. Hawkins (1984) "Black and White Homicide Differentials: Alternatives to an Inadequate Theory" *Criminal Justice and Behavior* 10(4): 407–440.

Chapter 18 Ramiro Martinez, Jr., Matthew T. Lee, and Amie L. Nielson (2001) "Revisiting the *Scarface* Legacy: The Victim/Offender Relationship and Mariel Homicides in Miami" *Hispanic Journal of Behavioral Sciences* 23(1): 37–56.

Chapter 19 Ronet Bachman (1991) "An Analysis of American Indian Homicide: A Test of Social Disorganization and Economic Deprivation at the Reservation County Level" *Journal of Research in Crime and Delinquency* 28(4): 456–471.

Chapter 20 Marianne R. Yoshioka, Jennifer DiNoia, and Komal Ullah (2001) "Attitudes toward Marital Violence: An Examination of Four Asian Communities" *Violence Against Women* 7(8): 900–926.

Chapter 21 Marjorie S. Zatz (1987) "The Changing Forms of Racial/Ethnic Biases in Sentencing." *Journal of Research in Crime and Delinquency* 24(1): 69–92.

Chapter 22 Alexander Alvarez and Ronet D. Bachman (1996) "American Indians and Sentencing Disparity: An Arizona Test" *Journal of Criminal Justice* 24(6): 549–561.

Chapter 23 Loïc Wacquant (2000) "The New 'Peculiar Institution': On the Prison as Surrogate Ghetto" *Theoretical Criminology* 4(3): 377–389.

Chapter 24 Paula Kautt and Cassia Spohn (2002) "Crack-ing Down on Black Drug Offenders? Testing for Interactions among Offenders' Race, Drug Type, and Sentencing Strategy in Federal Drug Sentences" *Justice Quarterly* 19(1): 1–36.

Index

Page numbers in italics refer to tables or figures

T

U